Lecture Notes in Computer Science 4989

Commenced Publication in 1973
Founding and Former Series Editors:
Gerhard Goos, Juris Hartmanis, and Jan van Leeuwen

Jacques Garrigue   Manuel Hermenegildo (Eds.)

Functional and Logic Programming

9th International Symposium, FLOPS 2008
Ise, Japan, April 14-16, 2008
Proceedings

 Springer

Volume Editors

Jacques Garrigue
Nagoya University
Graduate School of Mathematics
Chikusa-ku, Nagoya 464-8602, Japan
E-mail: garrigue@math.nagoya-u.ac.jp

Manuel Hermenegildo
U. Politecnica de Madrid
IMDEA-Software Facultad de Informatica
28660 Boadilla del Monte, Madrid, Spain
E-mail: herme@acm.org

Library of Congress Control Number: 2008923757

CR Subject Classification (1998): D.1.6, D.1, D.3, F.3, I.2.3

LNCS Sublibrary: SL 2 – Programming and Software Engineering

ISSN	0302-9743
ISBN-10	3-540-78968-5 Springer Berlin Heidelberg New York
ISBN-13	978-3-540-78968-0 Springer Berlin Heidelberg New York

Springer is a part of Springer Science+Business Media

springer.com

© Springer-Verlag Berlin Heidelberg 2008
Printed in Germany

Typesetting: Camera-ready by author, data conversion by Scientific Publishing Services, Chennai, India
Printed on acid-free paper   SPIN: 12251537   06/3180   5 4 3 2 1 0

Preface

This volume contains the proceedings of the 9th International Symposium on Functional and Logic Programming (FLOPS 2008), held in Ise, Japan, April 14–16, 2008 at the Ise City Plaza.

FLOPS is a forum for research on all issues concerning functional programming and logic programming. In particular it aims to stimulate the cross-fertilization as well as integration of the two paradigms. The previous FLOPS meetings took place in Fuji-Susono (1995), Shonan (1996), Kyoto (1998), Tsukuba (1999), Tokyo (2001), Aizu (2002), Nara (2004), and again Fuji-Susono (2006). Since its 1999 edition, FLOPS proceedings have been published by Springer in its *Lecture Notes in Computer Science* series, as volumes 1722, 2024, 2441, 2998 and 3945, respectively.

In response to the call for papers, 59 papers were submitted. Each paper was reviewed by at least three Program Committee members, with the help of expert external reviewers. The Program Committee meeting was conducted electronically, for a period of two weeks in December 2007. After careful and thorough discussion, the Program Committee selected 20 papers (33%) for presentation at the conference. In addition to the 20 contributed papers, the symposium included talks by three invited speakers: Peter Dybjer (Chalmers University of Technology), Naoki Kobayashi (Tohoku University) and Torsten Schaub (University of Potsdam).

On behalf of the Program Committee, we would like to thank the invited speakers, who agreed to give talks and contribute papers, and all those who submitted papers to FLOPS 2008. As Program Chairs, we would like to sincerely thank all the members of the FLOPS 2008 Program Committee for their excellent job, and all the external reviewers for their invaluable contribution. We are also grateful to Andrei Voronkov for making EasyChair available to us. The support of our sponsors is acknowledged. We are indebted to the Japan Society for Software Science and Technology (JSSST) SIG-PPL, the Association for Logic Programming (ALP), the Asian Association for Foundation of Software (AAFS), the Association for Computing Machinery (ACM) SIGPLAN and the International Information Science Foundation. Finally, we would like to thank members of the Local Arrangements Committee for their invaluable support throughout the preparation and organization of the symposium.

Ferbruary 2008   Jacques Garrigue
                                                                     Manuel Hermenegildo

Symposium Organization

Program Chairs

Jacques Garrigue   Nagoya, Japan
Manuel Hermenegildo   New Mexico, USA and Madrid, Spain

Program Committee

Marìa Alpuente   Valencia, Spain
Sergio Antoy   Portland, OR, USA
Matthias Blume   TTI, Chicago, USA
Tyng-Ruey Chuang   Academia Sinica, Taiwan
Zhenjiang Hu   Tokyo, Japan
Oleg Kiselyov   FNMOC, Monterey, USA
Herbert Kuchen   Münster, Germany
Dale Miller   INRIA, Palaiseau, France
Atsushi Ohori   Tohoku, Japan
Enrico Pontelli   New Mexico, USA
Kristoffer Rose   IBM T.J. Watson Research Center, USA
Kazunori Ueda   Waseda, Japan
Peter Van Roy   Louvain-la-Neuve, Belgium
Benjamin Werner   INRIA, Palaiseau, France

Local Arrangements Chair

Shoji Yuen   Nagoya, Japan

External Reviewers

Zena Ariola
Christian Arndt
David Baelde
Demis Ballis
Sylvie Boldo
Bernd Braßel
Sebastien Briais
Daniel Brown
Chin-Lung Chang
Kung Chen
Olaf Chitil

Marco Comini
Mario Coppo
Alessandro Dal Palu
Olivier Danvy
Mariangiola Dezani
Agostino Dovier
Derek Dreyer
Kento Emoto
Santiago Escobar
Moreno Falaschi
Jean-Christophe Filliâtre

Robby Findler
Sebastian Fischer
Matthew Fluet
Gopal Gupta
Susumu Hayashi
Makoto Hamana
John Harrison
Hugo Herbelin
Christian Hermanns
Jose Hernandez-Orallo
Petra Hofstedt
Jose Iborra
Yves Jaradin
Christophe Joubert
Yukiyoshi Kameyama
Herbert Kuchen
Andres Löh
Roman Leshchinskiy
Dongxi Liu
Rita Loogen
Salvador Lucas
Sunita Marathe
Kazutaka Matsuda
Kiminori Matsuzaki
Boris Mejias
Greg Michaelson
Akimasa Morihata
Shin-Cheng Mu

Chet Murthy
Keisuke Nakano
Russell O'Connor
John O'Donnell
James Ortiz
Sungwoo Park
Frances Perry
David Pichardie
Inna Pivkina
Maurizio Proietti
Frank Raiser
Maria José Ramirez
Isao Sasano
Max Schaefer
Peter Schneider-Kamp
Chung-chieh Shan
Zhong Shao
Matthieu Sozeau
Lutz Strassburger
Doaitse Swierstra
Ashish Tiwari
Andrew Tolmach
Lorenzo Tortora de Falco
Son Tran
Helmut Veith
Alicia Villanueva
Fei Xie
Na Xu

Table of Contents

Rewriting

Program Transformation

Logic and Lambda-Calculus

Types

Constraints II

Debugging

Model-Based Knowledge Representation and Reasoning Via Answer Set Programming

Torsten Schaub*

Universität Potsdam, Institut für Informatik,
August-Bebel-Str. 89, D-14482 Potsdam, Germany
torsten@cs.uni-potsdam.de

Abstract. The field of knowledge representation and reasoning has been going through a methodological shift during recent years. While the past was dominated by query-oriented reasoning, model-based techniques become more and more popular nowadays. This development was primarily driven by the availability of highly efficient Boolean constraint solvers, like satisfiability and answer set solvers. The general idea is to translate an application problem into a logical specification. This specification is in turn passed to a solver, which outputs models representing solutions to the initial application problem.

The talk will provide an introduction to answer set programming (ASP), its proof-theoretic foundations, methodology, implementation techniques along with a glimpse of an exemplary application. Besides knowledge representation and reasoning, ASP has its roots in deductive databases, nonmonotonic reasoning, and logic programming. Applications are specified in ASP in terms of sets of logical rules. Modern ASP solvers rely on high-performance Boolean constraint solving techniques, which allow them to tackle application domains consisting of millions of variables. Meanwhile, this approach proved to be an effective tool in a range of applications, like planning, model checking, and bio-informatics.

References

1. Gelfond, M., Lifschitz, V.: The stable model semantics for logic programming. In: Kowalski, R., Bowen, K. (eds.) Proceedings of the Fifth International Conference and Symposium of Logic Programming (ICLP 1988), pp. 1070–1080. MIT Press, Cambridge (1988)
2. Niemelä, I.: Logic programs with stable model semantics as a constraint programming paradigm. Annals of Mathematics and Artificial Intelligence 25(3-4), 241–273 (1999)
3. Marek, V., Truszczyński, M.: Stable models and an alternative logic programming paradigm. In: Apt, K., Marek, W., Truszczyński, M., Warren, D. (eds.) The Logic Programming Paradigm: A 25-Year Perspective, pp. 375–398. Springer, Heidelberg (1999)

---

* Affiliated with the School of Computing Science at Simon Fraser University, Burnaby, Canada, and the Institute for Integrated and Intelligent Systems at Griffith University, Brisbane, Australia.

J. Garrigue and M. Hermenegildo (Eds.): FLOPS 2008, LNCS 4989, pp. 1–2, 2008.
© Springer-Verlag Berlin Heidelberg 2008

4. Baral, C.: Knowledge Representation, Reasoning and Declarative Problem Solving. Cambridge University Press, Cambridge (2003)
5. Anger, C., Konczak, K., Linke, T., Schaub, T.: A glimpse of answer set programming. Künstliche Intelligenz 19(1), 12–17 (2005)
6. Ferraris, P., Lifschitz, V.: Mathematical foundations of answer set programming. In: Artëmov, S., Barringer, H., d'Avila Garcez, A., Lamb, L., Woods, J. (eds.) We Will Show Them! Essays in Honour of Dov Gabbay, vol. 1, pp. 615–664. College Publications (2005)
7. Gebser, M., Liu, L., Namasivayam, G., Neumann, A., Schaub, T., Truszczyński, M.: The first answer set programming system competition. In: Baral, C., Brewka, G., Schlipf, J. (eds.) LPNMR 2007. LNCS (LNAI), vol. 4483, pp. 3–17. Springer, Heidelberg (2007)
8. Gelfond, M.: Answer sets. In: Handbook of Knowledge Representation, Elsevier, Amsterdam (2008)

On the Algebraic Foundation
of Proof Assistants
for Intuitionistic Type Theory

Andreas Abel[1], Thierry Coquand[2], and Peter Dybjer[2]

[1] Institut für Informatik, Ludwig-Maximilians-Universität
Oettingenstr. 67, D-80538 München
[2] Department of Computer Science, Chalmers University of Technology
Rännvägen 6, S-41296 Göteborg

Abstract. An algebraic presentation of Martin-Löf's intuitionistic type theory is given which is based on the notion of a category with families with extra structure. We then present a type-checking algorithm for the normal forms of this theory, and sketch how it gives rise to an initial category with families with extra structure. In this way we obtain a purely algebraic formulation of the correctness of the type-checking algorithm which provides the core of proof assistants for intuitionistic type theory.

1 Introduction

The type-checking algorithm [6] is the core of proof assistants for intensional dependent type theories such as Coq [3], Agda [13], and Epigram [5]. Such a proof assistant is essentially a tool for checking whether a given term a has a given type A relative to a context Γ:

$$\Gamma \vdash a : A$$

The user writes a type A representing a proposition to be proved, and the proof assistant aids her in constructing a proof a which witnesses the truth of A.

We shall here assume that Γ, A, and a are all in normal form with respect to the reduction rules, although this restriction may not be strictly imposed in proof assistants.

In this note we shall present a new algebraic approach to the correctness of the type-checking algorithms. Such correctness is not only important for the trust in the proof assistants, it is also philosophically significant. The decidability of typing is one of the main reasons for preferring intensional [10,12] to extensional type theory [9]. According to a certain point of view in constructivism it should be mechanically decidable whether a certain construction a is a witness to the truth of a given proposition A.

We will here consider a core dependent type theory: Martin-Löf's intuitionistic type theory where the only type formers are dependent function types and a universe of small types. This is essentially Martin-Löf's *logical framework* [10,12],

J. Garrigue and M. Hermenegildo (Eds.): FLOPS 2008, LNCS 4989, pp. 3–13, 2008.

except that we here consider β-conversion only and do not have the η-rule. Moreover, we use the same normal terms for codes for small types and for the small types themselves. In this sense our universe of small type is formulated à la Russell, in spite of the fact that our algebraic framework inevitably uses universes à la Tarski.

We expect our approach to extend smoothly if we add more type formers such as $\Sigma, +, \mathrm{N}, \mathrm{N}_n$ to our theory. We also expect that our approach can be extended to deal with η-conversion [1,2].

Martin-Löf type theory is usually expressed as a system of axioms and inference rules with four forms of judgements

$$\Gamma \vdash a : A$$
$$\Gamma \vdash A \; type$$
$$\Gamma \vdash a = a' : A$$
$$\Gamma \vdash A = A'$$

Implicitly, there is also a judgement expressing the correctness of contexts:

$$\Gamma \vdash$$

In this inference rule presentation it is not assumed that contexts, types, and terms are normal. However, we expect that whenever Γ, A, and a are normal (with respect to the reduction rules of the theory) then the type-checking algorithm will accept $\Gamma \vdash a : A$ whenever it is a provable from the axioms and inference rules of Martin-Löf type theory.

The situation is analogous for the judgements $\Gamma \vdash A \; type$, and $\Gamma \vdash$, although the proof assistant may not give the user access to them.

As regards the equality judgements, we have that if Γ, A, a, and a' are normal, then $\Gamma \vdash a = a' : A$ is derivable by the axioms and inference rules iff a and a' are identical (up to α-congruence), and similarly for $\Gamma \vdash A = A'$.

However, in spite of many years of research into type-checking dependent types a completely satisfactory state of affairs has not yet been reached. On the one hand it has shown difficult to use traditional methods to obtain a clear proof of some essentially lemmas, such as the fact that the dependent function space former Π is one-to-one. On the other hand there are many different syntactic formulations of dependent type theory, and it is not clear which is the canonical one. There are different treatments of variables. Should we use explicit or implicit substitutions? Is the inference rule for substitution primitive? Should we use Curry or Church-style lambda terms? Etc.

In this note we present an algebraic formulation of Martin-Löf's intensional intuitionistic type theory which is based on the notion of a *category with families (cwfs)* [7]. In this way we hope to achieve a more satisfactory basis for developing the metatheory of type theory.

There are several reasons for preferring an algebraic formulation to the usual formulations based on the lambda calculus:

- It can be argued that it is more "canonical". There is less freedom of choice of syntactic detail.
- The presentation becomes cleaner since we do not first need to prove a number of meta-theorems of syntax.
- You get a clearer notion of model which is easier to work with.

We shall here present a type-checking algorithm inspired by the notion of categories with families. We have here also benefited from our recent work on *normalization by evaluation (nbe)* [1,2]. In these papers decidability of equality is proved for some fairly standard lambda-calculus based formulations of Martin-Löf type theory. We propose to extend this work and also formulate nbe for categories with families (with extra structure).

The rest of the note is organized as follows. We first recall the notion of a category with families. Then we extend this notion with extra structure for interpreting dependent function types and universes. Finally, we outline how to construct the cwf of type-checked normal forms.

2   Categories with Families

Categories with families (cwfs) [7,8] is a categorical notion of model of the most basic rules of dependent type theory; those which deal with context formation, variables, and substitution. Categories with families are equivalent to Cartmell's categories with attributes, but the reformulation makes it possible to obtain a straightforward correspondence to the inference rules of dependent type theory, especially when formulated as a calculus of explicit substitutions, see Martin-Löf [11].

A category with families consists of a category C and a family-valued functor $T : C^{op} \to \mathbf{Fam}$, where C has a terminal object. Moreover, there is an operation of *context comprehension* closely related to Lawvere's notion of comprehension for hyperdoctrines.

Here $\mathbf{Fam}$ is the category of families of sets, where an *object* is a family of sets $(B(x))_{x \in A}$ and a *morphism* with source $(B(x))_{x \in A}$ and target $(B'(x'))_{x' \in A'}$ is a pair consisting of a function $f : A \to A'$ and a family of functions $g(x) : B(x) \to B'(f(x))$ indexed by $x \in A$.

C is the category of contexts and substitutions. If $\Gamma \in |C|$ is a context, then $T(\Gamma)$ is the family of terms of a type A in Γ which is indexed by the well-formed types A in Γ. The arrow part of the functor T represents substitution in types and terms. The terminal object of C represents the empty context and the terminal arrow represents the empty substitution. The context comprehension operation provides representations for context extension, substitution extension, assumption, and a weakening substitution. The reader is referred to Dybjer [7] and Hofmann [8] for details.

The category $\mathbf{Cwf}$ is obtained by defining the notion of cwf-morphism as follows. Let (C, T) denote a cwf with base category C and functor T. A *morphism of cwfs* with source (C, T) and target (C', T') is a pair (F, σ), where $F : C \to C'$

is a functor and $\sigma : T \to T'F$ is a natural transformation, such that terminal object and context comprehension are preserved on the nose.

The notion of a category with families can be formalized as a *generalized algebraic theory* in the sense of Cartmell [4]. Generalized algebraic theories generalize many-sorted algebraic theories, by using dependent types. They consist of *sort symbols, operator symbols,* and *equations* between well-formed *sort expressions.* Here we present the generalized algebraic theory of categories with families using inference rule notation, to highlight the fact that it provides a variable-free substitution calculus for dependent types. To improve readability we use "polymorphic" notation. For example, we write $\delta \circ \gamma$ instead of the proper $\delta \circ_{\Theta, \Delta, \Gamma} \gamma$, etc.

Rules for the category C

$$\text{Ctxt sort}$$

$$\frac{\Delta, \Gamma : \text{Ctxt}}{\Delta \to \Gamma \text{ sort}}$$

$$\frac{\Theta, \Delta, \Gamma : \text{Ctxt} \qquad \gamma : \Delta \to \Gamma \qquad \delta : \Theta \to \Delta}{\gamma \circ \delta : \Theta \to \Gamma}$$

$$\frac{\Gamma : \text{Ctxt}}{\text{id}_\Gamma : \Gamma \to \Gamma}$$

$$(\gamma \circ \delta) \circ \theta = \gamma \circ (\delta \circ \theta)$$
$$\text{id}_\Gamma \circ \gamma = \gamma$$
$$\gamma \circ \text{id}_\Gamma = \gamma$$

Rules for the functor T

$$\frac{\Gamma : \text{Ctxt}}{\text{Ty}(\Gamma) \text{ sort}}$$

$$\frac{\Gamma : \text{Ctxt} \qquad A : \text{Ty}(\Gamma)}{\Gamma \vdash A \text{ sort}}$$

$$\frac{\Delta, \Gamma : \text{Ctxt} \qquad A : \text{Ty}(\Gamma) \qquad \gamma : \Delta \to \Gamma}{A[\gamma] : \text{Ty}(\Delta)}$$

$$\frac{\Delta, \Gamma : \text{Ctxt} \quad A : \text{Ty}(\Gamma) \quad a : \Gamma \vdash A \quad \gamma : \Delta \to \Gamma}{a[\gamma] : \Delta \vdash A[\gamma]}$$

$$A[\gamma \circ \delta] = A[\gamma][\delta]$$
$$A[\text{id}_\Gamma] = A$$
$$a[\gamma \circ \delta] = a[\gamma][\delta]$$
$$a[\text{id}_\Gamma] = a$$

Rules for the terminal object

$$[\,] : \mathrm{Ctxt}$$

$$\frac{\Gamma : \mathrm{Ctxt}}{\langle\rangle_\Gamma : \Gamma \to [\,]}$$

$$\langle\rangle_\Gamma \circ \gamma = \langle\rangle_\Gamma$$
$$\mathrm{id}_{[\,]} = \langle\rangle_{[\,]}$$

Rules for context comprehension

$$\frac{\Gamma : \mathrm{Ctxt} \qquad A : \mathrm{Ty}(\Gamma)}{\Gamma; A : \mathrm{Ctxt}}$$

$$\frac{\Delta, \Gamma : \mathrm{Ctxt} \quad A : \mathrm{Ty}(\Gamma) \quad \gamma : \Delta \to \Gamma \quad a : \Delta \vdash A[\gamma]}{\langle\gamma, a\rangle : \Delta \to \Gamma; A}$$

$$\frac{\Gamma : \mathrm{Ctxt} \qquad A : \mathrm{Ty}(\Gamma)}{\mathrm{p}_{\Gamma,A} : \Gamma; A \to \Gamma}$$

$$\frac{\Gamma : \mathrm{Ctxt} \qquad A : \mathrm{Ty}(\Gamma)}{\mathrm{q}_{\Gamma,A} : \Gamma; A \vdash A[\mathrm{p}_{\Gamma,A}]}$$

$$\mathrm{p}_{\Gamma,A} \circ \langle\gamma, a\rangle = \gamma$$
$$\mathrm{q}_{\Gamma,A}[\langle\gamma, a\rangle] = a$$
$$\langle\delta, a\rangle \circ \gamma = \langle\delta \circ \gamma, a[\gamma]\rangle$$
$$\mathrm{id}_{\Gamma;A} = \langle\mathrm{p}_{\Gamma,A}, \mathrm{q}_{\Gamma,A}\rangle$$

3   Adding Dependent Function Types and a Universe of Small Types

Categories with families only provide the most basic structure for interpreting dependent type theories, and provide no structure for interpreting any type formers at all. In these notes we consider a type theory with dependent function types and one universe. To interpret these we need some extra structure. We present this structure by adding new operators corresponding to the formation, introduction, and elimination rules for the new type constructor, and to add new equations corresponding to the equality rules. This is done by translating the usual inference rules of type theory into the variable free language of categories with families.

Rules for dependent function types

$$\frac{\Gamma : \text{Ctxt} \qquad A : \text{Ty}(\Gamma) \qquad B : \text{Ty}(\Gamma; A)}{\Pi(A, B) : \text{Ty}(\Gamma)}$$

$$\frac{\Gamma : \text{Ctxt} \quad A : \text{Ty}(\Gamma) \quad B : \text{Ty}(\Gamma; A) \quad b : \Gamma; A \vdash B}{\lambda(b) : \Gamma \vdash \Pi(A, B)}$$

$$\frac{\Gamma : \text{Ctxt} \quad A : \text{Ty}(\Gamma) \quad B : \text{Ty}(\Gamma; A) \quad c : \Gamma \vdash \Pi(A, B) \quad a : \Gamma \vdash A}{\text{ap}(c, a) : \Gamma \vdash B[\langle \text{id}_\Gamma, a \rangle]}$$

$$\Pi(A, B)[\gamma] = \Pi(A[\gamma], B[\langle \gamma \circ p_{\Gamma, A}, q_{\Gamma, A} \rangle])$$
$$\lambda(b)[\gamma] = \lambda(b[\langle \gamma \circ p_{\Gamma, A}, q_{\Gamma, A} \rangle])$$
$$\text{ap}(c, a)[\gamma] = \text{ap}(c[\gamma], a[\gamma])$$
$$\text{ap}(\lambda(b), a) = b[\langle \text{id}_\Gamma, a \rangle]$$

The three first of the five equations represent the laws for substitution under Π, λ, and ap. The fourth represents β-conversion.

Rules for a universe of small types

$$\frac{\Gamma : \text{Ctxt}}{\text{U} : \text{Ty}(\Gamma)}$$

$$\frac{\Gamma : \text{Ctxt} \qquad a : \Gamma \vdash \text{U}}{\text{T}(a) : \text{Ty}(\Gamma)}$$

$$\frac{\Gamma : \text{Ctxt} \qquad a : \Gamma \vdash \text{U} \qquad b : \Gamma; \text{T}(a) \vdash \text{U}}{\hat{\Pi}(a, b) : \text{U}}$$

$$\text{U}[\gamma] = \text{U}$$
$$\text{T}(a)[\gamma] = \text{T}(a[\gamma])$$
$$\hat{\Pi}(a, b)[\gamma] = \hat{\Pi}(a[\gamma], b[\langle \gamma \circ p_{\Gamma, A}, q_{\Gamma, A} \rangle])$$
$$\text{T}(\hat{\Pi}(a, b)) = \Pi(\text{T}(a), \text{T}(b))$$

This is a universe of small types which is closed under dependent function types. This formulation is inevitably à la Tarski rather than à la Russell.

A cwf with extra structure for dependent function types and a universe will be called a ΠU-cwf . We can extend the notion of cwf-morphism to a notion of morphism of ΠU-cwfs by requiring that all extra structure is preserved on the nose. Let **Cwf$_{\Pi U}$** be the category of ΠU-cwfs and ΠU-cwf -morphisms. Since ΠU-cwfs can be described as a generalized algebraic theory, it follows from a general result by Cartmell that **Cwf$_{\Pi U}$** has an initial object, given syntactically by derivations in a certain formal system for generalized algebraic theories. This initial object is the "syntax-free" representation of a version of Martin-Löf type theory.

4   A ΠU-cwf of Normal Forms

We shall now suggest how to build the ΠU-cwf $\mathcal{N}$ of type-checked normal forms. We write some Haskell code and explain how to define $\mathcal{N}$ in terms of it. We would like to emphasize that the content of this section is preliminary. We have not yet proved our type-checking algorithm correct.

First, we introduce raw syntax for normal terms t (including normal types). They are generated together with the auxiliary subclass of neutral terms s:

$$t ::= s \mid \lambda(a) \mid \Pi(a,a) \mid \text{U}$$
$$s ::= i \mid \text{ap}(s,t)$$

where i is a natural number (a de Bruijn index). Raw normal contexts and raw normal substitutions are represented as lists of normal terms.

Note that these raw normal terms are not type-decorated! This is unlike the notation for cwfs, where contexts and type-arguments are part of the official notation but were sometimes surpressed to improve readability.

The category $\mathcal{N}$ will be built up by type-checked normal forms. We could write the type-checking algorithm in Haskell by introducing the data types of normal and neutral expressions defined as follows:

```
data No = Ne Ne | Lam No | Pi No No | U
data Ne = Var Int | App Ne No
```

However, for simplicity we will define the type-checking algorithm on the type of all (raw) expressions

```
data Exp = Var Int | App Exp Exp | Lam Exp | Pi Exp Exp | U
```

although it is intended to be applied only to those expressions in `Exp` which are normal.

To this end we define four functions; `isCo`, `isSu`, `isTy`, and `isTm` which will check the correctness of contexts, substitutions, types, and terms, respectively. Here a type is represented by a raw expression, and substitutions and contexts by lists of raw expressions:

```
type Ty    = Exp
type Subst = [Exp]
type Cxt   = [Ty]
```

Checking contexts

```
isCo :: Cxt -> Bool
isCo []       = True
isCo (a:cxt) = isCo cxt && isTy cxt a
```

checks whether a list of expressions represents a correct context. Such lists of expressions will be the objects in the category of contexts of $\mathcal{N}$.

Checking substitutions

```
isSu :: Cxt -> Cxt -> Subst -> Bool
isSu cxt []      []     = True
isSu cxt (b:bs) (t:ts) = isSu cxt bs ts &&
                          isTm cxt (subst b cxt) t
```

checks whether a list of expressions (the third argument) is a correct substitution with respect to a source and a target context (the first and second argument). Such substitutions wil be the arrows in the category of contexts of $\mathcal{N}$.

Checking types

```
isTy :: Cxt -> Ty -> Bool
isTy cxt (Pi a b) = isTy cxt a && isTy (a:cxt) b
isTy cxt U        = True
isTy cxt a        = isTm cxt U a
```

checks whether an expression is a correct type with respect to a context. Such types will be the "types" of $\mathcal{N}$.

Checking terms

```
isTm :: Cxt -> Ty -> Exp -> Bool
isTm cxt (Pi a b) (Lam t)  = isTm (a:cxt) b t
isTm cxt a        (Lam t)  = False
isTm cxt U        (Pi a b) = isTm cxt U a && isTm (a:cxt) U b
isTm cxt a        (Pi a b) = False
isTM cxt a        U        = False
isTm cxt a        s        = case inferTy cxt s of
                               Just a' -> a == a'
                               Nothing -> False
```

checks whether an expression has a type with respect to a context. Such terms will be the "terms" of $\mathcal{N}$.

Infering the type of a neutral term. The type-checking algorithm is as usual bidirectional: to check whether an application has a given type we try to infer the type of the function and then check whether it matches the type of the argument.

```
inferTy :: Cxt -> Exp -> Maybe Ty
inferTy cxt (Var i)   = Just (shift (cxt !! i) (i+1))
inferTy cxt (App s t) = case inferTy cxt s of
   Just (Pi a b) -> if isTm cxt a t
                    then Just (subst b (t : ide))
                    else Nothing
         otherwise    -> Nothing
```

This function expects a neutral expression as input and tries to infer its type. It calls an auxiliary function

```
shift :: Exp -> Int -> Exp
shift t i = subst t (map Var [i ..])
```

so that `shift e n` increases all free variables in `e` by `n`.

Implementing the operations of ΠU-cwfs. To perform type inference we also call the "hereditary" substitution function `subst`. This is one of the cwf-combinators. We will now implement them in the order they appear in the above definition of cwf. Note that many of the equations for the cwf-combinators reappear in the programs below, a fact which will facilitate the checking that $\mathcal{N}$ is a cwf.

The empty context is just the empty list and context extension is implemented by the `Cons`-operation on lists. The composition ∘ and the identity id combinators are implemented by

```
comp :: Subst -> Subst -> Subst
comp []     ts' = []
comp (t:ts) ts' = (subst t ts'):(comp ts ts')

ide :: Subst
ide = map Var [0 .. ]
```

The length of the identity substitution id$_\Gamma$ depends on the context Γ, but here we use a lazy infinite list for simplicity. Note that when we check that `ide` is a correct substitution with respect to a context of length n we only check the n first elements of the list `ide`.

Substitution $-[-]$ in types and terms is the same function:

```
subst :: Exp -> Subst -> Exp
subst (Var i)   ts = ts !! i
subst (App s t) ts = app (subst s ts) (subst t ts)
subst (Lam t)   ts = Lam (subst t (lift ts))
subst (Pi a b)  ts = Pi (subst a ts) (subst b (lift ts))
subst U         ts = U
```

where we use the lifting function

```
lift :: Subst -> Subst
lift ts = q : comp ts p
```

which is just an abbreviation of a cwf combinator expression.

The terminal arrow is just the empty list, and substitution extension is just the `Cons` operation on lists. The projections p and q are

```
p :: Subst
p = map Var [1 .. ]

q :: Exp
q = Var 0
```

Like in the case of the identity the length of the substitution $p_{\Gamma,A}$ depends on the context Γ and for simplicity we implement it by an infinite list.

The type constructor Π and the term constructor λ are implemented by the constructors Pi and Lam. Application is

```
app :: Exp -> Exp -> Exp
app (Lam t) s = subst t (s:ide)
app r s       = App r s
```

The type constructor U and the term constructor $\hat{\Pi}$ are implemented by the constructors U and Pi. The decoding function T is implemented by the identity function on expressions. We have a universe à la Russell.

We can now formulate the correctness of our type-checking algorithm as follows: $\mathcal{N}$ is an initial object in $\mathbf{Cwf_{\Pi U}}$. This states in particular that $\mathcal{N}$ is categorically equivalent to any other initial ΠU-cwf, such as the variable-free substitution calculus obtained by using Cartmell's method for constructing initial objects from generalized algebraic theories, or any traditional presentation of Martin-Löf type theory which we can organize as an ΠU-cwf and prove initial in $\mathbf{Cwf_{\Pi U}}$. See Hofmann [8] for a description of the correspondence between cwfs and lambda calculus presentations of type theory.

References

1. Abel, A., Aehlig, K., Dybjer, P.: Normalization by evaluation for Martin-Löf type theory with one universe. Electr. Notes Theor. Comput. Sci. 173, 17–39 (2007)
2. Abel, A., Coquand, T., Dybjer, P.: Normalization by evaluation for Martin-Löf type theory with typed equality judgements. In: LICS, pp. 3–12 (2007)
3. Bertot, Y., Castéran, P.: Interactive Theorem Proving and Program Development Coq'Art: The Calculus of Inductive Constructions. Texts in Theoretical Computer Science. An EATCS Series (2004)
4. Cartmell, J.: Generalised algebraic theories and contextual categories. Annals of Pure and Applied Logic 32, 209–243 (1986)
5. Chapman, J., Altenkirch, T., McBride, C.: Epigram reloaded: A standalone type-checker for ETT. In: Proceedings of TFP (July, 2005)
6. Coquand, T.: An algorithm for type-checking dependent types. Sci. Comput. Program. 26(1-3), 167–177 (1996)
7. Dybjer, P.: Internal type theory. In: Berardi, S., Coppo, M. (eds.) TYPES 1995. LNCS, vol. 1158, pp. 120–134. Springer, Heidelberg (1996)
8. Hofmann, M.: Syntax and semantics of dependent types. In: Pitts, A., Dybjer, P. (eds.) Semantics and Logics of Computation, Cambridge University Press, Cambridge (1996)
9. Martin-Löf, P.: Constructive mathematics and computer programming. In: Logic, Methodology and Philosophy of Science, 1979, vol. VI, pp. 153–175. North-Holland, Amsterdam (1982)
10. Martin-Löf, P.: Amendment to intuitionistic type theory. Notes from a lecture given in Göteborg (March, 1986)

11. Martin-Löf, P.: Substitution calculus. Unpublished notes from a lecture in Göteborg (November, 1992)
12. Nordström, B., Petersson, K., Smith, J.: Programming in Martin-Löf's Type Theory: An Introduction. Oxford University Press, Oxford (1990)
13. Norell, U.: Towards a practical programming language based on dependent type theory. PhD thesis, Department of Computer Science and Engineering, Chalmers University of Technology, SE-412 96 Göteborg, Sweden (September, 2007)

Substructural Type Systems
for Program Analysis

Naoki Kobayashi

Graduate School of Information Sciences, Tohoku University
koba@kb.ecei.tohoku.ac.jp

Since linear logic was proposed by Girard, a number of type systems inspired by linear logic (or substructural logics in general) have been proposed. Examples include linear type systems, where the weakening and contraction rules are restricted, and ordered type systems, where the exchange rule is also restricted. Those type systems turned out to be very useful for reasoning about temporal properties of programs, like a memory cell is deallocated only once, or a memory cell is never read or written after it is deallocated. In this talk, I will focus on substructural type systems for program analysis, and review their principles and applications [1,2,3,4,5]. I will also discuss some emerging techniques and future directions of substructural-type-based program analysis.

References

1. Igarashi, A., Kobayashi, N.: Resource usage analysis. ACM Transactions on Programming Languages and Systems 27(2), 264–313 (2005)
2. Kobayashi, N.: Quasi-linear types. In: Proceedings of ACM SIGPLAN/SIGACT Symposium on Principles of Programming Languages, pp. 29–42 (1999)
3. Kobayashi, N., Pierce, B.C., Turner, D.N.: Linearity and the pi-calculus. ACM Transactions on Programming Languages and Systems 21(5), 914–947 (1999)
4. Kodama, K., Suenaga, K., Kobayashi, N.: Translation of tree-processing programs into stream-processing programs based on ordered linear type. Journal of Functional Programming (to appear). A preliminary summary appeared in: Chin, W.-N. (ed.) APLAS 2004. LNCS, vol. 3302, pp. 41–56. Springer, Heidelberg (2004)
5. Turner, D.N., Wadler, P., Mossin, C.: Once upon a type. In: Proceedings of Functional Programming Languages and Computer Architecture, San Diego, California, pp. 1–11 (1995)

J. Garrigue and M. Hermenegildo (Eds.): FLOPS 2008, LNCS 4989, p. 14, 2008.

Integrating Answer Set Reasoning with Constraint Solving Techniques

Veena S. Mellarkod and Michael Gelfond

Texas Tech University
{veena.s.mellarkod,michael.gelfond}@ttu.edu

Abstract. The paper introduces a collection of knowledge representation languages, $\mathcal{V}(\mathcal{C})$, parametrised over a class $\mathcal{C}$ of constraints. $\mathcal{V}(\mathcal{C})$ is an extension of both CR-Prolog and CASP allowing the separation of a program into two parts: a regular program of CR-Prolog and a collection of denials[1] whose bodies contain constraints from $\mathcal{C}$ with variables ranging over large domains. We study an instance $\mathcal{AC}_0$ from this family where $\mathcal{C}$ is a collection of constraints of the form $X - Y > K$. We give brief implementation details of an algorithm computing the answer sets of programs of $\mathcal{AC}_0$ which does not ground constraint variables and tightly couples the "classical" ASP algorithm with an algorithm checking consistency of difference constraints. We present several examples to show the methodology of representing knowledge in $\mathcal{AC}_0$. The work makes it possible to solve problems which could not be solved by pure ASP or constraint solvers.

1 Introduction

Language CR-Prolog has been shown to be a useful tool for knowledge representation and reasoning [6]. The language is expressive, and has a well understood methodology inherited from Answer Set Prolog (ASP)[9], for representing defaults, causal properties of actions and fluents, various types of incompleteness, etc. In addition it allows reasoning with complex exceptions to defaults and hence avoids the occasional inconsistencies of ASP. CR-Prolog allows natural encoding of "rare events". These events are normally ignored by a reasoner associated with the program and only used to restore consistency of the reasoner's beliefs. For instance a program

$\neg p(X) \leftarrow not\ p(X).$
$q(a) \leftarrow \neg p(a).$
$[r(X)]\ :\ p(X) \overset{+}{\leftarrow}.$

consists of two regular rules of Answer Set Prolog and the consistency restoring rule, $[r(X)]$, which says that in some rare cases, $p(X)$ may be true. The rule is ignored in the construction of the answer set $\{\neg p(a), q(a)\}$ of this program. If however the program is expanded by $\neg q(a)$ the rule $r(a)$ will be used to avoid inconsistency. The answer set of the new program will be $\{p(a), \neg q(a)\}$.

---

[1] By a denial we mean a logic programming rule with an empty head.

J. Garrigue and M. Hermenegildo (Eds.): FLOPS 2008, LNCS 4989, pp. 15–31, 2008.

CR-Prolog solvers built on top of the ASP solvers: Smodels [11] and Surya [10], proved to be sufficiently efficient for building industrial size applications related to intelligent planning and diagnostics [6]. Neither ASP nor CR-Prolog however, can deal with applications which require a combination of, say, planning and scheduling. This happens because scheduling normally requires programs which include variables with rather large numerical domains. ASP and CR-Prolog solvers compute answer sets of a ground instance of the input program. If a program contains variables with large domains such an instance can be too large, which renders the program unmanageable for the solver, despite the use of multiple optimization procedures.

A step toward resolving this problem was made in [7], where the authors introduced a language $CASP$. The algorithm for computing answer sets of $CASP$ programs only performs a partial grounding of variables and computes answer sets of the resulting, partially ground program by combining the classical ASP algorithm and a constrained solver for the constraints of $\mathcal{C}$. The CASP solver built loosely couples off-the-shelf ASP solver Smodels [11] and constraint solver GNU-Prolog [2].

In this paper we expand the idea to CR-Prolog. In particular, we introduce a collection, $\mathcal{V}(\mathcal{C})$, of languages parametrised over a class $\mathcal{C}$ of constraints. $\mathcal{V}(\mathcal{C})$ is an extension of both, CR-Prolog and CASP. We study an instance $\mathcal{AC}_0$ of the resulting language where $\mathcal{C}$ is a collection of constraints of the form $X - Y > K$. We design and implement an algorithm computing the answer sets of programs of $\mathcal{AC}_0$ which does not ground constraint variables and tightly couples the classical ASP algorithm with constraint solving mechanisms. To our knowledge the solver built is the first tightly coupled solver integrating ASP reasoning mechanisms and constraint solving techniques to compute answer sets from partially ground programs. This makes it possible to declaratively solve problems which could not be solved by pure ASP or by pure constraint solvers. The use of the language and the efficiency of its implementation is demonstrated by a number of examples. The paper is organized as follows: In section 2 we define the syntax and semantics of $\mathcal{V}(\mathcal{C})$ and $\mathcal{AC}_0$. Section 3 contains a brief description of the algorithm for computing answer sets of programs in $\mathcal{AC}_0$. Section 4 gives examples of knowledge representation and reasoning in $\mathcal{AC}_0$ and gives experimental results of on the use of $\mathcal{AC}_0$ for solving a sizable planning and scheduling problem related to the decision support system for the space shuttle controllers.

2   Syntax and Semantics of $\mathcal{V}(\mathcal{C})$

2.1   Syntax

The language $\mathcal{V}(\mathcal{C})$ contains a sorted signature Σ, with sorts partitioned into two classes: *regular*, s_r, and *constraint*, s_c. Intuitively, the former are comparatively small but the latter are too large for the ASP grounders. Functions defined on regular (constraint) classes are called r-functions (c-functions). Terms are built as in first-order languages. Predicate symbols are divided into three disjoint sets called *regular*, *constrained* and *mixed* and denoted by P_r, P_c and P_m respectively.

Constraint predicate symbols are determined by $\mathcal{C}$. Parameters of regular and constraint predicates are of sorts s_r and s_c respectively. Mixed predicates have parameters from both classes. Atoms are defined as usual. A literal is an atom a or its negation $\neg a$. An extended literal is a literal l or $not\ l$, where not stands for *default negation*. Atoms formed from regular, constraint, and mixed predicates are called r-atoms, c-atoms and m-atoms respectively. Similarly for literals. We assume that predicates of P_c have a predefined interpretation, represented by the set M_c of all true ground c-atoms. For instance, if $'>' \in P_c$, and ranges over integers, M_c consists of $\{...0 > -1, 1 > 0, 2 > 0, ..., 2 > 1, 3 > 1, ...\}$. The c-literals allowed in $\mathcal{V}(\mathcal{C})$ depend on the class $\mathcal{C}$. The $\mathcal{V}(\mathcal{C})$ rules over Σ are defined as follows.

Definition 1 [rules]

1. *A regular rule (r-rule) ρ is a statement of the form:*

$$h_1\ or\ \cdots or\ h_k \leftarrow l_1,\ \cdots, l_m,\ not\ l_{m+1}, \cdots, not\ l_n$$

   where $k >= 0$; h_i's and l_i's are r-literals.
2. *A constraint rule (c-rule) is a statement of the form:*

$$\leftarrow l_1,\ \cdots, l_m,\ not\ l_{m+1}, \cdots, not\ l_n$$

   where at least one l_i is non-regular.
3. *A consistency restoring rule (cr-rule) is a statement of the form:*

$$r:\ h_1\ or\ \cdots or\ h_k \overset{+}{\leftarrow} l_1,\ \cdots, l_m,\ not\ l_{m+1}, \cdots, not\ l_n$$

   where $k > 0$, r is a term which uniquely denotes the name of the rule and h_i's and l_i's are r-literals.

$head(r) = h_0\ or\ \cdots or\ h_k$; $body(r) = \{l_1,\ \cdots, l_m,\ not\ l_{m+1}, \cdots, not\ l_n\}$; and $pos(r)$, $neg(r)$ denote, respectively, $\{l_1, \cdots, l_m\}$ and $\{l_{m+1}, \cdots, l_n\}$.

A regular rule and constraint rule have the same intuitive reading as standard rules of ASP. The intuitive reading of a cr-rule is: *if one believes in $l_1, \ldots l_m$ and have no reason to believe $l_{m+1}, \ldots, l_n$, then one may possibly believe one of $h_1, \ldots, h_k$.* The implicit assumption is that this possibility is used as little as possible, and only to restore consistency of the agent's beliefs.

Definition 2 [program]. *A $\mathcal{V}(\mathcal{C})$ program is a pair $\langle \Sigma, \Pi \rangle$, where Σ is a sorted signature and Π is a set of $\mathcal{V}(\mathcal{C})$ rules over Σ.*

Example 1. To represent conditions: "John goes to work either by car which takes 30 to 40 minutes, or by bus which takes at least 60 minutes", we start by defining the signature $\Sigma = \{C_r = \{start, end\}, P_r = \{by\_car, by\_bus\}, C_c = \{D_c = [0..1439], R_c = [-1439..1439]\}, V_c = \{T_s, T_e\}, F_c = \{-\}, P_c = \{>\}, P_m = \{at\}\}$. The sets C_r and P_r contain regular constants and predicates; elements of C_c, V_c, F_c, and P_c are constrained constants, variables, functions and predicate symbols. P_m is the set of mixed predicates. Values in D_c represent time in minutes. Consider one whole day from 12:00am to 11:59pm mapped to 0 to 1439 minutes. Regular atom "*by_car*" says that "John travels by car"; mixed atom $at(start, T)$ says that "John starts from home at time T". Similarly for "*by_bus*" and "$at(end, T)$". Function "$-$" has the domain D_c and range R_c; T_s, T_e are variables for D_c. The rules below represent the information from the story.

% 'John travels either by car or bus' is represented by an r-rule
r_a : *by_car or by_bus*.
% Travelling by car takes between 30 to 40 minutes. This information is encoded by two c-rules
r_b : $\leftarrow by\_car, \ at(start, T_s), \ at(end, T_e), T_e - T_s > 40.$
r_c : $\leftarrow by\_car, \ at(start, T_s), \ at(end, T_e), \ T_s - T_e > -30.$
% Travelling by bus takes at least 60 minutes
r_d : $\leftarrow by\_bus, \ at(start, T_s), \ at(end, T_e), \ T_s - T_e > -60.$

Example 2. Let us expand the story from example 1 by new information: '*John prefers to come to work before 9am*'. We add new constant $'time0'$ to C_r of Σ which denotes the start time of the day, regular atom 'late' which is true when John is late and constrained variable T_t for D_c. Time 9am in our representation is mapped to 540th minute. We expand example 1 by the following rules:

% Unless John is late, he comes to work before 9am
r_e : $\leftarrow at(time0, T_t), \ at(end, T_e), \ \neg late, \ T_e - T_t > 540$
% Normally, John is not late
r_f : $\neg late \leftarrow not \ late$
% On some rare occasions he might be late, which is encoded by a cr-rule
r_g : $late \overset{+}{\leftarrow}$

In this paper, we study an instance $\mathcal{AC}_0$ of $\mathcal{V(C)}$, where $\mathcal{C}$ consists of constraints of type $X - Y > K$, where X, Y are variables and K is a number. Examples 1 and 2 are examples of $\mathcal{AC}_0$ programs.

2.2 Semantics

We denote the sets of r-rules, cr-rules and c-rules in Π by Π^r, Π^{cr} and Π^c respectively. A rule r of $\langle \Pi, \Sigma \rangle$ will be called *r-ground* if regular terms in r are ground. A program is called *r-ground* if all its rules are r-ground. A rule r^g is called a *ground instance* of a rule r if it is obtained from r by: (1). replacing variables by ground terms of respective sorts; (2). replacing the remaining terms by their values. For example, 3+4 will be replaced by 7. The program $ground(\Pi)$ with all ground instances of all rules in Π is called the *ground instance* of Π. Obviously $ground(\Pi)$ is an r-ground program.

  We first define semantics for programs without cr-rules. For the definition, we use the term *asp answer set* to refer to the definition of answer sets in answer set prolog [9].

Definition 3 [answer set 1]. *Given a program* (Σ, Π)*, where* Π *contains no cr-rules, let* X *be a set of ground m-atoms such that for every predicate* $p \in P_m$ *and every ground r-term* t_r*, there is exactly one c-term* t_c *such that* $p(\bar{t}_r, \bar{t}_c) \in X$*. A set* S *of ground atoms over* Σ *is an answer set of* Π *if* S *is an asp answer set of* $ground(\Pi) \cup X \cup M_c$*.*

Example 3. Consider Example 1 and let $X = \{at(start, 430), at(end, 465)\}$. The set $S = \{by\_car, at(start, 430), at(end, 465)\} \cup M_c$ is an asp answer set of *ground* $(\Pi) \cup X \cup M_c$ and therefore is an answer set of Π. According to S, John starts to travel by car at 7:10am and reaches work at 7:45am. Of course there are other answer sets where John travels by car and his start and end times differ but satisfy given constraints. There are also answer sets where John travels by bus.

Now we give the semantics for programs with cr-rules. By $\alpha(r)$, we denote a regular rule obtained from a cr-rule r by replacing $\xleftarrow{+}$ by $\leftarrow$; α is expanded in a standard way to a set R of cr-rules. Recall that according to [6], a minimal (with respect to set theoretic inclusion) collection R of cr-rules of Π such that $\Pi^r \cup \Pi^c \cup \alpha(R)$ is consistent (i.e. has an answer set) is called an *abductive support* of Π.

Definition 4 [answer set 2]. *A set* S *is called an answer set of* Π *if it is an asp answer set of program* $\Pi^r \cup \Pi^c \cup \alpha(R)$ *for some abductive support* R *of* Π*.*

Example 4. Consider Example 2 and let $X = \{at(start, 430), at(end, 465)\}$. The set $S = \{by\_car, \neg late, at(time0, 0), at(start, 430), at(end, 465)\} \cup M_c$ is an answer set of $ground(\Pi) \cup X \cup M_c$ and therefore is an answer set of Π. According to S, John starts by car at 7:10am and reaches work at 7:45am and is not late. The cr-rule was not applied and $\alpha(\emptyset) = \emptyset$.

3 $\mathcal{AD}solver$

In this section we describe the algorithm which takes a program $\langle \Sigma, \Pi \rangle$ of $\mathcal{AC}_0$ as input and returns a simplified answer set $A \cup X$ (regular and mixed atoms) such that $M = A \cup X \cup M_c$ is an answer set of Π where M_c is the intended interpretation of c-predicates. The algorithm works for a class of $\mathcal{AC}_0$ programs satisfying the following syntax restrictions:

- *There are no disjunctions in the head of rules.*
- *Every c-rule of the program contains exactly one c-literal in the body.*

$\mathcal{AD}solver$ consists of a partial grounder $\mathcal{P}ground_d$ and an inference engine $\mathcal{AD}engine$. Given a $\mathcal{AC}_0$ program Π, $\mathcal{AD}solver$ first calls $\mathcal{P}ground_d$ to ground r-terms of Π, to get an r-ground program, $\mathcal{P}_d(\Pi)$. The $\mathcal{AD}engine$ combines constraint solving techniques with answer set reasoning and abduction techniques to compute simplified answer sets of $\mathcal{P}_d(\Pi)$.

3.1 $\mathcal{P}ground_d$

Given a $\mathcal{AC}_0$ program Π, $\mathcal{P}ground_d$ grounds the r-variables in Π and outputs a r-ground program $\mathcal{P}_d(\Pi)$. The implementation of $\mathcal{P}ground_d$ uses intelligent grounder *lparse* [16]. To allow for partial grounding by *lparse*, we need intermediate transformations before and after grounding by *lparse*. The transformations ensure that c-variables are not ground and rules containing m-atoms are not removed by *lparse*. The transformations remove and store c-variables, m-atoms and c-atoms from Π before grounding and then restore them back after grounding.

Example 5. Let $a1$ and $a2$ be two actions. For representing the condition "a1 should occur 30 minutes before a2", we begin by defining a signature. $\Sigma = \{C_r = \{\{a1, a2\}, \{1, 2\}\}, V_r = \{S\}, P_r = \{o\}, P_m = \{at\}, C_c = \{D_c = \{0..1440\}, R_c = \{-1440..1440\}\}, V_c = \{T_1, T_2\}, F_c = \{-\}, P_c = \{>\}\}$ and Π be the following rules:

```
step(1..2).
% only one action can occur at each step
o(a1, S) :- step(S), not o(a2, S).
o(a2, S) :- step(S), not o(a1, S).
% an action can occur at most once
:- step(S1), step(S2), o(a1, S1), o(a1, S2), S1 != S2.
:- step(S1), step(S2), o(a2, S1), o(a2, S2), S1 != S2.
% define 'time' as a csort, and 'at' as a mixed predicate
#csort time(0..1440).
#mixed at(step,time).
% time should be increasingly assigned to steps
:- step(S1), step(S2), at(S1,T1), at(S2,T2), S1<S2, T1-T2 > 0.
% a1 should occur 30 minutes before a2
:- step(S1), step(S2), o(a1, S1), o(a2, S2),
   at(S1, T1), at(S2, T2), T1 - T2 > -30.
```

We get $\mathcal{P}_d(\Pi)$ as follows:

```
step(1).                        step(2).
o(a1, 1) :- not o(a2, 1).       o(a1, 2) :- not o(a2, 2).
o(a2, 1) :- not o(a1, 1).       o(a2, 2) :- not o(a1, 2).
:-  o(a1, 1), o(a1, 2).         :-  o(a2, 1), o(a2, 2).
#csort time(0..1440).
:- at(1, V1), at(2, V2), V1 - V2 > 0.
:- o(a1, 1), o(a2, 2), at(1, V1), at(2, V2), V1 - V2 > -30.
:- o(a1, 2), o(a2, 1), at(2, V2), at(1, V1), V2 - V1 > -30.
```

Note that $V1$ and $V2$ are constraint variables with domain $[0..1440]$.

3.2 $\mathcal{AD}engine$

The $\mathcal{AD}engine$ integrates a standard CR-Prolog solver and a difference constraint solver. CR-Prolog solver consists of a meta layer and computes answer sets by using an underlying ASP inference engine. For $\mathcal{AD}engine$, we use $Surya$ [10] as the underlying inference engine.

Suppose there are no c-rules in a program Π, then Π is a CR-Prolog program. Typical CR-Prolog solvers available now, compute answer sets of Π as follows:

1. a meta-layer selects a minimal set R of cr-rules of Π called a candidate abductive support of Π;
2. an ASP inference engine is used to check program $\Pi^r \cup \alpha(R)$ for consistency and compute an answer set.
3. if an answer set is found at step (2) then R is an abductive support with respect to Π and the answer set computed is an answer set of Π and is returned[2]; otherwise the solver loops back to step(1) to find another minimal set R not tried so far.

To compute answer sets of $\mathcal{AC}_0$ programs, we modify the solver to accept c-rules; and then change step(2) of the algorithm. Given a $\mathcal{AC}_0$ program Π, we modify the underlying inference engine Surya to compute answer sets of $\Pi^r \cup \Pi^c \cup \alpha(R)$. Note that the program $\Pi^r \cup \Pi^c \cup \alpha(R)$ does not contain cr-rules but only r-rules and c-rules.

$\mathcal{AD}engine$ integrates a form of abductive reasoning using the meta-layer with answer set reasoning and constraint solving of the underlying inference engine. Surya has been modified to tightly couple with a difference constraint solver (for constraint solving). The algorithm presented in [7] uses constraint solving techniques for checking consistency of constraints with respect to a partial model computed. Our algorithm uses constraint solving techniques for checking consistency and for computing consequences with respect to a given program and a partial model computed. The solver implemented for constraint solving is an incremental difference constraint solver that computes solutions of a set of constraints (constraint store) using a previous solution and changes to the constraint store. This method is more efficient than computing solutions from scratch.

To our knowledge this is the first tightly coupled solver for integrating answer set reasoning and constraint solving to compute answer sets from partially ground programs. In the next section, we show that the solver can efficiently compute answer sets for a large complex system and it makes it possible to solve problems which could not be solved by pure ASP, CR-Prolog or constraint solvers. $\mathcal{AD}solver$ is available at [1].

4   Representing Knowledge in $\mathcal{AC}_0$

Normally, a variable with a large domain is viewed as a constraint variable. Those with small domains are regular variables. We select mixed predicates as those which contain both these variables. A limitation to select mixed predicates is to note that these predicates can be used only in body of denials. With respect to $\mathcal{AC}_0$, constraints of the form $X - Y > K$ are only allowed. Therefore

---

[2] This algorithm is a simplification of the actual algorithm [5], which requires additional checking due to dynamic and special preference rules allowed in the language.

knowledge represented by constraint variables in mixed predicates are limited to these constraints. Interestingly, these constraints are used widely in constraint programming [13,12,14].

$\mathcal{AC}_0$ is good for representing planning and scheduling problems. Given a task of executing n actions and time restrictions on their executions, a scheduling problem consists of finding times $T_1, \ldots, T_n$ such that action 'a_i occurs at time T_i' and satisfies all the time restrictions. The timing restrictions can be temporal distance constraints between any two actions. Such constraints can be represented in $\mathcal{AC}_0$ as follows. Let $a_1, \ldots, a_n$ be n actions and $S_1, \ldots, S_n$ be variables in domain $[1..n]$. The r-atom $occurs(a_i, S_i)$ is read as, "action a_i occurs at step S_i". The step S_i is a number and denotes a time point T_i and is represented by an m-atom $at(S_i, T_i)$. Atom $at(S, T)$ is read as 'step S occurs at time T'. The domain of a step S (r-variable) is comparatively smaller to domain of a time variable T (c-variable).

When actions have durations, the scheduling problem finds the start and end time points of actions such that all timing restrictions are satisfied. One method of representing constraints on action durations in $\mathcal{AC}_0$ is as follows. Let $a_1, \ldots, a_n$ be actions and $S_1, \ldots, S_n$ be variables from the domain $[1..n]$. The r-atom $occurs(a_i, S_i)$ is read as, "action a_i occurs at step S_i". The variable S_i is a number which denotes a time interval $[T_{si}, T_{ei}]$. The time interval of step S_i is represented by two m-atoms $at(S_i, start, T_{si})$ and $at(S_i, end, T_{ei})$. Atom $at(S, start, T)$ is read as 'step S starts at T'. We can write temporal constraints using the c-variables T_{si} and T_{ei}.

Example 6 [14 **Breakfast problem***]*. We have a scheduling problem, "Prepare coffee and toast. Have them ready within 2 minutes of each other. Brew coffee for 3-5 minutes; toast bread for 2-4 minutes." We start by defining signature, $\Sigma = \{C_r = \{ start, end, brew, toast, S_c = [1..2] \}, P_r = \{step, occurs\}, C_c = \{D_c = [0..1439], R_c = [-1439..1439]\}, V_c = \{T_1, T_2\}, F_c = \{-\}, P_c = \{>\}, P_m = \{at\}\}$. Constants "$brew, toast$" represents actions 'brewing coffee' and 'toasting bread'. To solve this, we first represent constraints and then we have a small planning module to represent action a_i occurs at some time step S_i. The constraints are as follows.

% Brew coffee for 3 to 5 minutes is represented using two c-rules
    $\leftarrow occurs(brew, S), at(S, start, T_1), at(S, end, T_2), T_2 - T_1 > 5.$
    $\leftarrow occurs(brew, S), at(S, start, T_1), at(S, end, T_2), T_1 - T_2 > -3.$
% Toast bread for 2 to 4 minutes is represented by two c-rules
    $\leftarrow occurs(toast, S), at(S, start, T_1), at(S, end, T_2), T_2 - T_1 > 4.$
    $\leftarrow occurs(toast, S), at(S, start, T_1), at(S, end, T_2), T_1 - T_2 > -2.$
% Coffee and bread should be ready between 2 minutes of each other
    $\leftarrow occurs(brew, S_1), occurs(toast, S_2), at(S_1, end, T_1),$
      $at(S_2, end, T_2), T_2 - T_1 > 2.$
    $\leftarrow occurs(brew, S_1), occurs(toast, S_2), at(S_1, end, T_1),$
      $at(S_2, end, T_2), T_1 - T_2 > -2.$
% Start time of step 1 is before step 2
    $\leftarrow at(S_1, start, T_1), at(S_2, start, T_2), S_1 < S_2, T_1 - T_2 > -1.$

% A simple planning module to represent occurrence of actions:
$step(1..2)$.
$occurs(brew, S)$ or $occurs(toast, S) \leftarrow step(S)$.
$\leftarrow action(A), occurs(A, S_1), occurs(A, S_2), S_1 \neq S_2$.

The first c-rule is read as: 'If brewing coffee occurs at step S, then duration between start and end of S cannot be more than 5 minutes'. The second c-rule says that 'start and end times for S cannot be less than 3 minutes. The c-atom is written as $T_1 - T_2 > -3$ instead of $T_2 - T_1 < 3$ as the implementation allows only constraints of the form $X - Y > K$. The disjunctions in the head of the rules of the above program can be eliminated using non-disjunctive rules. A solution to the above breakfast scheduling problem can be found by computing answer sets of the program using $\mathcal{AD}solver$. A solution would be to start brewing coffee at 0th minute and end at 3rd minute; start toasting bread at 2nd minute and end at 4th minute. This solution can be extracted from an answer set $\{occurs(brew, 1), occurs(toast, 2), at(1, start, 0), at(1, end, 3), at(2, start, 2), at(2, end, 4)\} \cup M_c$.

Suppose we would like to schedule an action a such that it occurs either between 3am and 5am or between 7am and 8am. To represent this restriction, we would require a constraint of the form, *if action 'a' occurs at step S and step S occurs at time T, then T cannot be outside intervals [3-5] or [7-8]*. We cannot represent this directly in $\mathcal{AC}_0$. Instead we introduce two r-atoms int_1 and int_2 to represent intervals [3-5] and [7-8] respectively. The r-atom int_1 denotes that action a occurs in interval [3-5]. We write a disjunction on int_i to choose the interval and then use int_i to write the constraints. The following example shows the representation of the constraint.

Example 7. "Action a should be performed in between intervals [3-5] am or [7-8] am". Let r-atoms int_1 and int_2 represent intervals [3-5] and [7-8] respectively and int_i is true when action a occurs in interval int_i. To keep it simple, let us suppose that action a occurs at some step say 1. We need to assign time for this step. Atom $at(0, T)$ denotes time of step 0 and represents start time for our problem 12 am.

   $occurs(a, 1)$.
% action 'a' occurs in interval int_1 or int_2
   int_1 or int_2.
% 'If a occurs at step S and int_1 is true, then S should be between [3-5]', is encoded using two c-rules
   $\leftarrow int_1, occurs(a, S), at(0, T_1), at(S, T_2), T_1 - T_2 > -3$
   $\leftarrow int_1, occurs(a, S), at(0, T_1), at(S, T_2), T_2 - T_1 > 5$
% 'If a occurs at step S and int_2 is true, then S should be between [7-8]', is encoded using two c-rules
   $\leftarrow int_2, occurs(a, S), at(0, T_1), at(S, T_2), T_1 - T_2 > -7$
   $\leftarrow int_2, occurs(a, S), at(0, T_1), at(S, T_2), T_2 - T_1 > 8$

An answer set for this program would be $\{occurs(a, 1), int_2, at(0, 0), at(1, 7)\} \cup M_c$, where a occurs at 7 am. The following example is from [8], we show that we can represent the problem and answer some of the questions asked in the example. Though, syntax of $\mathcal{AC}_0$ does not allow choice rules and cardinality constraints [11], $\mathcal{AD}solver$ built on top of *lparse* and *Surya* allows these type of rules in its input language. We use choice rules in the following example.

Example 8 [8] **Carpool**/. John goes to work either by car (30-40 mins), or by bus (at least 60 mins). Fred goes to work either by car (20-30 mins), or in a car pool (40-50 mins). Today John left home between 7:10 and 7:20, and Fred arrived between 8:00 and 8:10. We also know that John arrived at work about 10-20 mins after Fred left home. We wish to answer queries such as: "Is the information in the story consistent?", "Is it possible that John took the bus, and Fred used the carpool?", "What are the possible times at which Fred left home?".

```
%% John goes to work either by car or by bus. (a choice rule)
1{ j_by_car, j_by_bus }1.
%% Fred goes to work either in car or by car pool
1{ f_by_car, f_by_cpool }1.

%% define 'time' as csort and 'at' as a mixed predicate
#csort time(0..1440).
timepoint(start_time; start_john; end_john; start_fred; end_fred).
#mixed at(timepoint, time).

%% "It takes John 30 to 40 minutes by car"
:- j_by_car, at(start_john,T1), at(end_john,T2), T2 - T1 > 40.
:- j_by_car, at(start_john,T1), at(end_john,T2), T1 - T2 >-30.

%% "It takes John atleast 60 minutes by bus"
:- j_by_bus, at(start_john,T1), at(end_john,T2), T1 - T2 >-60.

%% We view the start time as 7am, that is 0 minutes = 7am
%% Today John left home between 7:10 and 7:20
:- at(start_john,T), at(start_time,T0), T0 - T > -10.
:- at(start_john,T), at(start_time,T0), T - T0 > 20.
```

The other informations in the example are represented by similar c-rules. Now let us look at answering each of the questions in the problem.

```
Question (1) Is the information in story consistent?
To answer this question, we find answer sets of the program.
Answer Set: j_by_car f_by_cpool at(start_fred,20) at(end_fred,60)
            at(start_time,0) at(start_john,10) at(end_john,40)
```

The above answer set corresponds to John using the car and Fred using the car pool. John starts at 7:10 am and reaches at 7:40 am. Fred starts at 7:20 am and reaches at 8:00 am. The information is consistent since the program has an answer set. The time taken by $\mathcal{AD}solver$ to find an answer set was 0.065 secs of which 0.018 secs was used by $\mathcal{P}ground_d$.

```
Question(2) Is it possible that John took the bus and Fred
used carpool? To answer this question, we add the following
knowledge to our program and compute answer sets.
j_by_bus.
f_by_cpool.
There are no answer sets for this new program.
```

Therefore, according to the story, it is not possible for John to take a bus and Fred to use a carpool and have the story consistent. The time taken by $\mathcal{AD}solver$ was 0.029 secs of which $\mathcal{P}ground_d$ took 0.018 secs.

```
Question (3) What are the possible times that Fred left home?
To answer this question, we need to find the interval of time
when Fred can leave home and still have the story consistent.
```

This answer cannot be found using $\mathcal{AD}solver$, as the underlying constraint solver built cannot answer these type of interval questions.

The temporal constraints from the above problems are examples of simple and disjunctive temporal constraints [8]. Using cr-rules in $\mathcal{AC}_0$ we can represent important information like, "an event e may happen but it is very rare". Such information is very useful in default reasoning. Combining such information together with c-rules allows us to represent qualitative soft constraints [15] like, "an event e may happen but it is very rare; if event e happens then ignore constraint c". The following example is an extension of Example 8 and shows the representation of qualitative soft temporal constraints.

Example 9. Consider example 8, we remove information that "John arrived at work about 10-20 mins after Fred left home" and extend the story as follows: It is desirable for Fred to arrive atleast 20 mins before John.

```
%% Fred desires to arrive atleast 20 mins before John.
:- at(end_fred,T1), at(end_john,T2), not is_late, T1-T2 >-20.
%% CR-rule r1: We may possibly believe that Fred is late
r1: is_late +-.
```

For the newly added information, we get two models where Fred arrives before John in each of them.

```
Answer set(1):j_by_bus f_by_car at(end_john,100) at(end_fred,60)
            at(start_time,0) at(start_john,20) at(start_fred,30)
Answer set(2):j_by_bus f_by_cpool at(end_john,80) at(end_fred,60)
            at(start_time,0) at(start_john,20) at(start_fred,20)
```

To compute the two models, $\mathcal{AD}solver$ took 0.064 seconds of which 0.019 seconds were used for grounding and loading. Now we would like to expand our story, "We come to know that Fred's car is broken and therefore, he cannot use it". We add the following rule to the program.

```
:- f_by_car.
```

For the new program, we get one model where John travels by bus and Fred uses the carpool and still reaches before John.

```
Answer set:j_by_bus f_by_cpool at(end_john,80) at(end_fred,60)
         at(start_time,0) at(start_john,20) at(start_fred,20)
```

$\mathcal{AD}solver$ took 0.053 seconds to compute the model. Suppose we know that John used his car today. Will Fred arrive atleast 20 mins before John as desired? For this, we add the following rule to the program.

```
j_by_car.
```

There is no model where Fred arrives 20 minutes before John and the cr-rule was fired to give the following answer set.

```
Answer set: j_by_car f_by_cpool is_late at(start_fred,20)
at(end_fred,60) at(start_time,0) at(start_john,20) at(end_john,60)
```

Fred is late and cannot arrive 20 minutes before John as desired. $\mathcal{AD}solver$ took 0.052 seconds to compute the model.

The examples show that $\mathcal{AC}_0$ allows a natural representation of simple temporal constraints, disjunctive temporal constraints and qualitative soft constraints. The implemented solver is faster than a standard ASP solver when domains of constraint variables are large. The language of CR-Prolog also allows preferences on the cr-rules [4]. Given two cr-rules r_1 and r_2, the statement $prefer(r_1, r_2)$ allows preference to cr-rule r_1 when compared to cr-rule r_2. CR-Prolog allows static and dynamic preferences. The language $\mathcal{AC}_0$ does not allow preferences but $\mathcal{AC}_0$ syntax can be easily extended to allow CR-Prolog style preferences and the semantics would be a natural extension of CR-Prolog. Though language $\mathcal{AC}_0$ does not allow preferences, the solver $\mathcal{AD}solver$ which is built using the meta layer of CR-Prolog solver, allows preferences. So, we can express soft qualitative temporal constraints with preferences which is used in constraint programming [15].

Example 10. This example shows the representation of qualitative soft temporal constraints with preferences. Let us use example 9. We remove information that "John arrived at work about 10-20 mins after Fred left home and Fred arrived between 8:00 and 8:10" and extend the story as follows: It is desirable for Fred to arrive atleast 20 mins before John. If possible, Fred desires to start from home after 7:30am. We also know that Fred's car is broken and John used his car today.

```
%% If possible, Fred desires to leave after 7:30am
:- at(start_time,T1), at(start_fred,T2), not start_early,
   T1 - T2 > -30.
%% CR-rule r2: sometimes, Fred may need to start early.
r2: start_early +-.
```

The above rules along with other rules from examples 9 and 8 represent the information in the story. We get two answer sets where cr-rules were used in both.

```
Answer set (1):    j_by_car f_by_cpool is_late
           at(start_john,20) at(start_fred,30)
           at(end_john,60) at(end_fred,70) at(start_time,0)
Answer set (2): j_by_car f_by_cpool start_early
           at(start_john,20) at(start_fred,0)
           at(end_john,60) at(end_fred,40) at(start_time,0)
```

Now we add new preference information that "Fred prefers coming before John than starting late from home". we represent the preference as follows:

```
% Prefer starting early to reaching late
prefer(r2,r1).
```

Now, we get only one model:

```
Answer set: j_by_car f_by_cpool start_early
           at(start_john,20) at(end_john,60)
           at(start_fred,0) at(end_fred,40) at(start_time,0)
```

The other model is not preferred when compared to this one and therefore is not returned. $\mathcal{AD}solver$ computed the answer set in 0.13 seconds.

The above example clearly shows the use of preferences from CR-Prolog along with c-rules gives a natural representation of qualitative soft constraints with preferences. Similarly, we can use cr-rules, cr-preferences and c-rules together to represent disjunctive soft temporal constraints and disjunctive soft temporal constraints with preferences which are also useful for scheduling problems.

Another investigation we are concerned with is whether $\mathcal{AC}_0$ can be used for complex planning and scheduling problems. Also, whether we can use $\mathcal{AD}solver$ to compute answer sets in realistic time for these problems. To test this, we have used the system USA-Advisor[6] , a decision support system for the Reaction Control System (RCS) of the Space Shuttle.

The RCS has primary responsibility for maneuvering the aircraft while it is in space. It consists of fuel and oxidizer tanks, valves and other plumbing needed to provide propellant to the maneuvering jets of the shuttle. It also includes electronic circuitry: both to control the valves in the fuel lines and to prepare the jets to receive firing commands. Overall the system is rather complex, on that it includes 12 tanks, 44 jets, 66 valves, 33 switches, and around 160 computer commands (computer-generated signals). The RCS can be viewed, in a simplified form, as a directed graph whose nodes are tanks, jets and pipe junctions, and whose arcs are labeled by valves. For a jet to be ready to fire, oxidizer and fuel propellants need to flow through the nodes (tanks, junctions) and valves which are open and reach the jet. A node is pressurized when fuel or oxidizer reaches the node.

The system can be used for checking plans, planning and diagnosis. To test our solver, we have expanded the system to allow explicit representation of time to perform some scheduling. We use it to solve planning and scheduling tasks. We will illustrate our extension by the following example.

Example 11 [**Planning and scheduling in USA-Advisor**]. Assume that after a node N gets pressurized it takes around 5 seconds for the oxidizer propellant to get stabilized at N and 10 seconds for fuel propellant to get stabilized. Further, we cannot open a valve V which links N1 to N2, (link(N1,N2,V)), until N1 has been stabilized. We would like to assign real times to the time steps given in the program such that this constraint is satisfied. Also, can we answer questions like: can the whole manuver take less than 30 secs?

$\Sigma = \Sigma_{old} \cup \{P_r = \{otank, ftank, got\_opened, got\_pressurized\}, P_m = \{at\}, C_c = \{D_c = [0..400], R_c = [-400..400]\}, F_c = \{-\}, P_c = \{>\}\}$. Atoms $otank(X)$ and $ftank(X)$ denote that X is a oxidizer tank and fuel tank respectively. Fluent $got\_opened(V, S)$ is true when valve V was closed at step $S-1$ and got opened at step S. Fluent $got\_pressurized(N, X, S)$ is true when node N is not pressurized at step $S - 1$ and is pressurized at step S by tank X. Atom $at(S, T)$ is read as 'step S is performed at time T', where S is a regular variable with domain 0 to plan length; T is a constraint variable with domain $[0..400]$ seconds. The new program contains all rules from original advisor, and new rules describing the scheduling constraints. The first rule is from USA-Advisor, followed by some new rules. The second rule shows the connection between original program and new one.

% Tank node N_1 is pressurized by tank X if it is connected by an open valve to a node which is pressurized by tank X of sub-system R

$h(pressurized\_by(N_1, X), S) \leftarrow step(S), tank\_of(N_1, R),$
$\qquad\qquad\qquad\qquad h(in\_state(V, open), S), \ link(N_2, N_1, V),$
$\qquad\qquad\qquad\qquad tank\_of(X, R), \ h(pressurized\_by(N_2, X), S).$

% node gets pressurized when it was not pressurized at S and pressurized at S+1.

$got\_pressurized(N, X, S + 1) \leftarrow link(N_1, N, V), \ tank\_of(X, R),$
$\qquad\qquad\qquad\qquad not \ h(pressurized\_by(N, X), S),$
$\qquad\qquad\qquad\qquad h(pressurized\_by(N, X), S + 1).$

% A valve V linking N_1 to N_2 cannot be opened unless N_1 is stabilized.
% If N_1 is pressurized by oxidizer tank, N_1 takes 5 seconds to stabilize.

$\leftarrow link(N_1, N_2, V), got\_pressurized(N_1, X, S_1), S_1 < S_2, otank(X),$
$\qquad got\_opened(V, S_2), at(S_1, T_1), at(S_2, T_2), T_1 - T_2 > -5$

% If N_1 is pressurized by fuel tank, N_1 takes 10 seconds to stabilize.

$\leftarrow link(N_1, N_2, V), got\_pressurized(N_1, X, S_1), S_1 < S_2, ftank(X),$
$\qquad got\_opened(V, S_2), at(S_1, T_1), at(S_2, T_2), T_1 - T_2 > -5$

% time should be increasingly assigned to steps

$\leftarrow S_1 < S_2, at(S_1, T_1), at(S_2, T_2), T_1 - T_2 > -1$

% The jets of a system should be ready to fire by 30 seconds

$\leftarrow system(R), goal(S, R), at(0, T_1), at(S, T_2), T_2 - T_1 > 30$

$\mathcal{AD}solver$ was tested using USA-Advisor extension example 11. We tested the solver on 450 auto-generated instances. The files used were "rcs1, plan, heuristics, problem-base" [3], an instance file and scheduling constraints file (see example 11). The files and instances can be found at [3]. Due to space limitations, timing results of only 300 instances are shown in Figure 1. The instances of the left

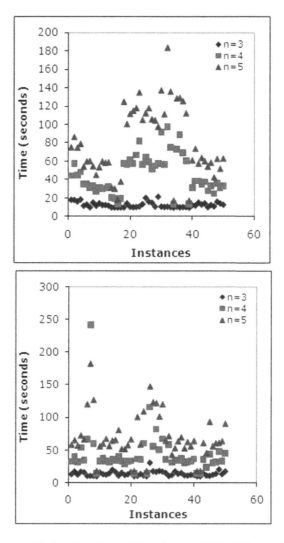

Fig. 1. $\mathcal{AD}$*solver* Timing Results on Planning and Scheduling in USA-Advisor

(right) figure are the first 50 instances from folder 'instances/instances-auto /ins' (instances/instances-auto /ins-4). Each instance is run to compute answer sets to find plans of length n=3, n=4 and n=5. The timing results shown is the time taken for $\mathcal{AD}$*solver* to compute a single answer set or return *false* to denote no plan for the specified plan length (n) exists.

The results show that $\mathcal{AD}$*solver* could compute answer sets for most of the instances tried in less than two minutes. There was one instance not shown in the figure (from ins-4, n=4) that took around 3359 seconds to find that there was no plan, this was the only instance that took so long. The number of rules (partially ground) for instances with n=3 was approximately 95,000 rules. The domain of time variables was 0..400 seconds. The USA-Advisor example 11 can be transformed to a regular ASP program. ASP solvers [10,11,6] were not able to compute answer sets, the grounder *lparse* they use returned a malloc error because of huge memory requirements.

5   Conclusions

This paper introduces a collection $\mathcal{V}(\mathcal{C})$ of languages parameterized over a class $\mathcal{C}$ of constraints. We study an instance $\mathcal{AC}_0$ of the resulting language where $\mathcal{C}$ is a collection of constraints of the form $X - Y > k$. We design and implement an algorithm for computing the answer sets of a class of $\mathcal{AC}_0$ programs. The algorithm computes answer sets from partial ground programs and tightly couples answer set reasoning mechanisms with constraint solving techniques. This makes it possible to declaratively solve problems which could not be solved by pure ASP or by pure constraint solvers. The use of the language and efficiency of the solver is demonstrated.

Acknowledgments

This work was partially supported by ARDA grant ASU06C-0143 and NASA grant NASA-NNG05GP48G. The authors wish to thank Marcello Balduccini, and Yuan-Lin Zhang for useful discussions on this subject.

References

1. Adsolver, http://www.cs.ttu.edu/~mellarko/adsolver.html
2. GNU Prolog, http://www.gprolog.org
3. Rcs, http://www.krlab.cs.ttu.edu/Software/Download/rcs/
4. Balduccini, M.: Answer Set Based Design of Highly Autonomous, Rational Agents. PhD thesis, Texas Tech University (December, 2005)
5. Balduccini, M.: CR-models: An inference engine for CR-prolog. In: Logic Programming and Nonmonotonic Reasoning (May, 2007)
6. Balduccini, M., Gelfond, M., Nogueira, M.: Answer set based design of knowledge systems. Annals of Mathematics and Artificial Intelligence (2006)
7. Baselice, S., Bonatti, P.A., Gelfond, M.: Towards an integration of answer set and constraint solving. In: Gabbrielli, M., Gupta, G. (eds.) ICLP 2005. LNCS, vol. 3668, pp. 52–66. Springer, Heidelberg (2005)
8. Dechter, R., Meiri, I., Pearl, J.: Temporal constraint networks. Artificial Intelligence 49, 61–95 (1991)
9. Gelfond, M., Lifschitz, V.: The stable model semantics for logic programming. In: Proceedings of ICLP-1988, pp. 1070–1080 (1988)
10. Veena, S.: Mellarkod. Optimizing the computation of stable models using merged rules. Master's thesis, Texas Tech University (May, 2002)
11. Niemela, I., Simons, P.: Extending the Smodels System with Cardinality and Weight Constraints. In: Logic-Based Artificial Intelligence, pp. 491–521. Kluwer Academic Publishers, Dordrecht (2000)

12. Pollack, M.E., et al.: Pearl: A mobile robotic assistant for the elderly. In: AAAI Workshop on Automation as Eldercare (August, 2002)
13. Pollack, M.E., et al.: Autominder: An intelligent cognitive orthotic system for people with memory impairment. Robotics and Autonomous Systems 44(3-4), 273–282 (2003)
14. Pollack, M.E., Muscettola, N.: Temporal and resource reasoning for planning, scheduling and execution. In: Tutorial Forum Notes, AAAI 2006 (July, 2006)
15. Rossi, F., Sperduti, A., Venable, K., Khatib, L., Morris, P., Morris, R.: Learning and solving soft temporal constraints: An experimental study (2002)
16. Syrjanen, T.: Implementation of logical grounding for logic programs with stable model semantics. Technical Report 18, Digital Systems Laboratory, Helsinki University of Technology (1998)

Optimizing Compilation of CHR
with Rule Priorities

Leslie De Koninck[1,*], Peter J. Stuckey[2], and Gregory J. Duck[2]

[1] Department of Computer Science, K.U.Leuven, Belgium
Leslie.DeKoninck@cs.kuleuven.be
[2] NICTA Victoria Laboratory
University of Melbourne, 3010, Australia
{pjs,gjd}@cs.mu.oz.au

Abstract. Constraint Handling Rules were recently extended with user-definable rule priorities. This paper shows how this extended language can be efficiently compiled into the underlying host language. It extends previous work by supporting rules with dynamic priorities and by introducing various optimizations. The effects of the optimizations are empirically evaluated and the new compiler is compared with the state-of-the-art K.U.Leuven CHR system.

1 Introduction

Constraint Handling Rules (CHR) [7] is a rule based language, originally designed for the implementation of constraint programming systems, but also increasingly used as a general purpose programming language [11,15]. CHR is very flexible with respect to the specification of program logic, but it lacks high-level facilities for execution control. In particular, the control flow is most often fixed by the call-stack based refined operational semantics of CHR [5]. In [2], CHR is extended with user-definable rule priorities. This extended language, called CHR[rp], supports more high-level and flexible execution control than previously available while retaining the expressive power needed for the implementation of general purpose algorithms. An example of CHR with rule priorities is:

Example 1 (Less-or-Equal). The less-or-equal (`leq`) program is a classic CHR example. It implements a less-than-or-equal constraint by eventually translating it into equality constraints. Below is a CHR[rp] version of the `leq` program.

```
1 :: reflexivity  @ leq(X,X) <=> true.
1 :: antisymmetry @ leq(X,Y), leq(Y,X) <=> X = Y.
1 :: idempotence  @ leq(X,Y) \ leq(X,Y) <=> true.
2 :: transitivity @ leq(X,Y), leq(Y,Z) ==> leq(X,Z).
```

* Research funded by a Ph.D. grant of the Institute for the Promotion of Innovation through Science and Technology in Flanders (IWT-Vlaanderen).

J. Garrigue and M. Hermenegildo (Eds.): FLOPS 2008, LNCS 4989, pp. 32–47, 2008.

The first rule has priority 1 (before ::) and name `reflexivity` (before @). It is a simplification rule that states that any constraint of the form leq(a,a) should be "simplified" to (i.e. replaced by) *true*. The second rule `antisymmetry` states that two constraints leq(a,b) and leq(b,a) should be replaced with $a = b$, constraining the arguments to be equal. The third rule is a simpagation rule that says that given two constraints of the form leq(a,b) we should replace the second one (after the \) by *true*. The fourth rule is a propagation rule, which says given constraints leq(a,b) and leq(b,c) we should add a new constraint leq(a,c) without deleting anything. We have given the transitivity rule a lower priority (2), because we should only apply it if other rules do not apply.   □

Dynamic rule priorities allow the priority of a rule to depend on the variables occurring on the left hand side of the rule.

Example 2 (Dijkstra's Shortest Path). Dijkstra's single source shortest path algorithm can be implemented in CHR^{rp} as follows:

```
1 :: source(V) ==> dist(V,0).
1 :: dist(V,D₁) \ dist(V,D₂) <=> D₁ =< D₂ | true.
D+2 :: dist(V,D), edge(V,C,U) ==> dist(U,D+C).
```

The input consists of a set of directed weighted edges, represented as `edge`/3 constraints where the first and last arguments respectively denote the begin and end nodes, and the middle argument represents the weight. The source node is given by the `source`/1 constraint. The first rule initiates the algorithm by creating the distance to the source node. The second rule introduces a guard D1 =< D2 which must hold before the rule can fire. It ensures only the shortest path to node V is kept in the store. The last rule has a dynamic priority that orders the updates of distances as required by Dijkstra's algorithm.   □

In the paper defining CHR^{rp} [2], its theoretical operational semantics as well as an implementation based on a source-to-source transformation were presented. In this paper, we show how CHR^{rp} programs can be efficiently compiled into the host language. We present the compilation process based on a refined version of the CHR^{rp} operational semantics, which is similar in concept to the refined operational semantics of CHR [5]. This semantics requires that every active constraint determines the priorities of all the rules in which it may participate. The compilation of rules with a dynamic priority is therefore handled by first applying a pseudo code source-to-source transformation which ensures that this condition holds. Next, it is shown how the generated code can be made more efficient by introducing optimizations that prevent unnecessary indexing and operations on the schedule. These optimizations are evaluated on benchmarks and the optimized system's performance is compared (with respect to equivalent programs in regular CHR) with the state-of-the-art K.U.Leuven CHR system [13] as well as with the result of the source-to-source transformation presented in [2].

This paper presents the *first* implementation of CHR^{rp} with *dynamic* priorities. It is about an order of magnitude faster than the one of [2] which is limited to programs with static priorities only, and is already almost as fast as the highly optimized K.U.Leuven CHR system while offering a much more high level form of execution control.[1] The rest of this paper is organized as follows. Section 2 reviews the syntax and semantics of CHR^{rp}. A basic compilation schema is presented in Section 3 and optimizations for this schema are given in Section 4. The resulting system is evaluated in Section 5. We conclude in Section 6.

2   Preliminaries

This section reviews the syntax and semantics of Constraint Handling Rules with Rule Priorities (CHR^{rp}). For a more thorough introduction into CHR, see [7] or [12]. See [2] for more information about CHR^{rp}.

Syntax. A constraint $c(t_1, \ldots, t_n)$ is an atom of predicate c/n with t_i a host language value (e.g., a Herbrand term in Prolog) for $1 \leq i \leq n$. There are two types of constraints: built-in constraints and CHR constraints (also called user-defined constraints). The CHR constraints are solved by the CHR program whereas the built-in constraints are solved by an underlying constraint solver (e.g., the Prolog unification algorithm).

There are three types of Constraint Handling Rules: *simplification rules*, *propagation rules* and *simpagation rules*. They have the following form:

$$\begin{array}{llll}
\textbf{Simplification} & p :: r \ @ & H^r & \Longleftrightarrow \ g \mid B \\
\textbf{Propagation} & p :: r \ @ \ H^k & & \Longrightarrow \ g \mid B \\
\textbf{Simpagation} & p :: r \ @ \ H^k \setminus H^r & \Longleftrightarrow \ g \mid B
\end{array}$$

where p is the rule priority, r is the rule *name*, H^k and H^r are non-empty sequences of CHR constraints and are called the *heads* of the rule. The rule *guard* g is a sequence of built-in constraints and the rule *body* B is a sequence of both CHR and built-in constraints. The rule priority is either a number in which case the rule is called a *static* priority rule, or an arithmetic expression whose variables appear in the heads H^k and/or H^r in which case the rule is called a *dynamic* priority rule. We say that priority p is higher than priority p' if $p < p'$. For simplicity, we sometimes assume priorities are integers and the highest priority is 1. Finally, a program P is a set of CHR rules.

Operational Semantics. Operationally, CHR constraints have a multi-set semantics. To distinguish between different occurrences of syntactically equal constraints, CHR constraints are extended with a unique identifier. An identified CHR constraint is denoted by $c\#i$ with c a CHR constraint and i the identifier. We write $\mathsf{chr}(c\#i) = c$ and $\mathsf{id}(c\#i) = i$. We extend these to map sequences in the obvious manner. We use $+\!\!+$ for sequence concatenation.

The operational semantics of CHR^{rp}, called the priority semantics and denoted by ω_p, is given in [2] as a state transition system, similar to the approach of [5] for the theoretical and refined operational semantics of CHR. A CHR execution state σ is represented as a tuple $\langle G, S, B, T \rangle_n$ where G is the goal, a

---

[1] When benchmarked on operationally equivalent programs.

Table 1. Transitions of ω_p

---

1. Solve $\langle\{c\} \uplus G, S, B, T\rangle_n \overset{\omega_p}{\rightarrowtail}_P \langle G, S, c \wedge B, T\rangle_n$ where c is a built-in constraint.

---

2. Introduce $\langle\{c\} \uplus G, S, B, T\rangle_n \overset{\omega_p}{\rightarrowtail}_P \langle G, \{c\#n\} \cup S, B, T\rangle_{n+1}$ where c is a CHR constraint.

3. Apply $\langle\emptyset, H_1 \cup H_2 \cup S, B, T\rangle_n \overset{\omega_p}{\rightarrowtail}_P \langle C, H_1 \cup S, \theta \wedge B, T \cup \{t\}\rangle_n$ where P contains a rule of priority p of the form

$$p :: r @ H_1'\backslash H_2' \iff g \mid C$$

and a matching substitution θ such that $\mathsf{chr}(H_1) = \theta(H_1')$, $\mathsf{chr}(H_2) = \theta(H_2')$, $\mathcal{D} \models B \rightarrow \bar{\exists}_B(\theta \wedge g)$, $\theta(p)$ is a ground arithmetic expression and $t = \mathsf{id}(H_1) \mathbin{+\!\!+} \mathsf{id}(H_2) \mathbin{+\!\!+} [r] \notin T$. Furthermore, no rule of priority p' and substitution θ' exists with $\theta'(p') < \theta(p)$ for which the above conditions hold.

---

multi-set of constraints to be solved; S is the CHR constraint store, a set of identified CHR constraints; B is the built-in store, a conjunction of built-in constraints; T is the propagation history, a set of tuples denoting the rule instances that have already fired; and n is the next free identifier, used to identify new CHR constraints. The transitions of ω_p are shown in Table 1. They are exhaustively applied starting from the state $\langle G, \emptyset, true, \emptyset\rangle_1$ with G the initial goal.

Example 3. And example derivation for the `leq` program given in Example 1 and initial goal $G = \{leq(A, B), leq(B, C), leq(B, A)\}$ is shown below:

$$\langle\{leq(A, B), leq(B, C), leq(B, A)\}, \emptyset, true, \emptyset\rangle_1$$

Introduce $\overset{\omega_p}{\rightarrowtail}_P \langle\{leq(B, C), leq(B, A)\}, \{leq(A, B)\#1\}, true, \emptyset\rangle_2$

Introduce $\overset{\omega_p}{\rightarrowtail}_P \langle\{leq(B, A)\}, \{leq(A, B)\#1, leq(B, C)\#2\}, true, \emptyset\rangle_3$

Introduce $\overset{\omega_p}{\rightarrowtail}_P \langle\emptyset, \{leq(A, B)\#1, leq(B, C)\#2, leq(B, A)\#3\}, true, \emptyset\rangle_4$

Apply `antisymmetry` $\theta = \{X/A, Y/B\} \overset{\omega_p}{\rightarrowtail}_P \langle\{A = B\}, \{leq(B, C)\#2\}, true, \emptyset\rangle_4$

Solve $\overset{\omega_p}{\rightarrowtail}_P \langle\emptyset, \{leq(B, C)\#2\}, A = B, \emptyset\rangle_4$

For termination, the antisymmetry rule must fire before the transitivity rule. □

3   Basic Compilation Schema

This section gives an overview of the basic compilation schema for CHR^{rp} programs. First, in Section 3.1, we present a refinement of the ω_p semantics that follows the actual implementation more closely. This refinement, called the refined priority semantics and denoted by ω_{rp}, is based on the refined operational semantics ω_r of (regular) CHR and is thus also based on lazy matching and the concept of active constraints. The ω_{rp} semantics requires that each active constraint determines the actual (ground) priorities of all rules in which they may

Table 2. Transitions of ω_{rp}

---

1. **Solve** $\langle[c|A], Q, S_0 \cup S_1, B, T\rangle_n \xrightarrow{\omega_{rp}}_P \langle A, Q', S_0 \cup S_1, c \wedge B, T\rangle_n$ where c is a built-in constraint, $vars(S_0) \subseteq fixed(B)$ is the set of variables fixed by B, and $Q' = Q \cup \{c\#i @ p \mid c\#i \in S_1 \wedge c$ has an occurrence in a priority p rule$\}$. This reschedules constraints whose matches might be affected by c.

2. **Schedule** $\langle[c|A], Q, S, B, T\rangle_n \xrightarrow{\omega_{rp}}_P \langle A, Q', \{c\#n\} \cup S, B, T\rangle_{n+1}$ with c a CHR constraint and $Q' = Q \cup \{c\#n @ p \mid c$ has an occurrence in a priority p rule$\}$.

3. **Activate** $\langle A, Q, S, B, T\rangle_n \xrightarrow{\omega_{rp}}_P \langle[c\#i : 1 @ p|A], Q \setminus \{c\#i @ p\}, S, B, T\rangle_n$ where $c\#i @ p = \mathsf{find\_min}(Q)$, and $A = [c'\#i' : j' @ p'|A']$ with $p < p'$ or $A = \epsilon$.

4. **Drop** $\langle[c\#i : j @ p|A], Q, S, B, T\rangle_n \xrightarrow{\omega_{rp}}_P \langle A, Q, S, B, T\rangle_n$ if there is no j^{th} priority p occurrence of c in P.

5. **Simplify** $\langle[c\#i : j @ p|A], Q, \{c\#i\} \cup H_1 \cup H_2 \cup H_3 \cup S, B, T\rangle_n \xrightarrow{\omega_{rp}}_P \langle C \mathbin{+\!\!+} A, Q, H_1 \cup S, \theta \wedge B, T\rangle_n$ where the jth priority p occurrence of c is d_j in rule

$$p' :: r @ H_1' \setminus H_2', d_j, H_3' \iff g \mid C$$

and there exists a matching substitution θ such that $c = \theta(d_j)$, $p = \theta(p')$, $\mathsf{chr}(H_1) = \theta(H_1')$, $\mathsf{chr}(H_2) = \theta(H_2')$, $\mathsf{chr}(H_3) = \theta(H_3')$ and $\mathcal{D} \models B \to \bar{\exists}_B(\theta \wedge g)$. This transition only applies if the **Activate** transition does not.

6. **Propagate** $\langle[c\#i : j @ p|A], Q, \{c\#i\} \cup H_1 \cup H_2 \cup H_3 \cup S, B, T\rangle_n \xrightarrow{\omega_{rp}}_P \langle C \mathbin{+\!\!+} [c\#i : j @ p \mid A], Q, H_1 \cup S, \theta \wedge B, T \cup \{t\}\rangle_n$ where the jth priority p occurrence of c is d_j in

$$p' :: r @ H_1', d_j, H_2' \setminus H_3' \iff g \mid C$$

and there exists a matching substitution θ such that $c = \theta(d_j)$, $p = \theta(p')$, $\mathsf{chr}(H_1) = \theta(H_1')$, $\mathsf{chr}(H_2) = \theta(H_2')$, $\mathsf{chr}(H_3) = \theta(H_3')$, $\mathcal{D} \models B \to \bar{\exists}_B(\theta \wedge g)$, and $t = \mathsf{id}(H_1) \mathbin{+\!\!+} [i] \mathbin{+\!\!+} \mathsf{id}(H_2) \mathbin{+\!\!+} [r] \notin T$. This transition only applies if the **Activate** transition does not.

7. **Default** $\langle[c\#i : j @ p|A], Q, S, B, T\rangle_n \xrightarrow{\omega_{rp}}_P \langle[c\#i : j + 1 @ p|A], Q, S, B, T\rangle_n$ if the current state cannot fire any other transition.

---

participate. In Section 3.2, we show how dynamic priority rules can be transformed so that this property holds for all active constraints. Finally, Section 3.3 gives an abstract version of the code generated for each of the ω_{rp} transitions.

3.1   The Refined Priority Semantics ω_{rp}

The refined priority semantics ω_{rp} is given as a state transition system. Its states are represented by tuples of the form $\langle A, Q, S, B, T\rangle_n$, where S, B, T and n are as in the ω_p semantics, A is a sequence of constraints, called the activation stack, and Q is a priority queue. In the ω_{rp} semantics, constraints are scheduled for activation at a given priority. By $c\#i : j @ p$ we denote the identified constraint $c\#i$ being tried at its jth occurrence of fixed priority p. In what follows, the priority queue is considered a set supporting the operation $\mathsf{find\_min}$ which returns one of its highest priority elements.

The transitions of the ω_{rp} semantics are shown in Table 2. The main differences compared to the ω_r semantics are the following. Instead of adding new or reactivated constraints to the activation stack, the **Solve** and **Schedule**[2] transitions schedule them for activation, once for each priority at which they have occurrences. The **Activate** transition activates the highest priority scheduled constraint if it has a higher priority than the current active constraint (if any). This transition only applies if the **Solve** and **Schedule** transitions are not applicable, i.e., after processing the initial goal or a rule body. Noteworthy is that once a constraint is active at a given priority, it remains so at least until a rule fires or it is made passive by the **Drop** transition. Hence we should only check the priority queue for a higher priority scheduled constraint at these program points. Again, the transitions are exhaustively applied starting from an initial state $\langle G, \emptyset, \emptyset, true, \emptyset \rangle_1$ with G the goal, given as a sequence.

Example 4. The ω_{rp} state corresponding to the ω_p state after the 3 **Introduce** transitions in Example 3 is:[3]

$$\langle [], \{leq(A,B)\#1@\{1,2\}, leq(B,C)\#2@\{1,2\}, leq(B,A)\#3@\{1,2\}\},$$
$$\{leq(A,B)\#1, leq(B,C)\#2, leq(B,A)\#3\}, true, \emptyset \rangle_4$$

If $leq(B,C)\#2@1$ is activated first then it finds no matching partners and is eventually dropped. If $leq(A,B)\#1@1$ is activated next, then we have

$$\langle [leq(A,B)\#1 : 1@1], \{leq(A,B)\#1@2, leq(B,C)\#2@2, leq(B,A)\#3@\{1,2\}\},$$
$$\{leq(A,B)\#1, leq(B,C)\#2, leq(B,A)\#3\}, true, \emptyset \rangle_4 \stackrel{\omega_{rp}}{\rightarrowtail}_P (\textbf{Default})$$
$$\langle [leq(A,B)\#1 : 2@1], \{leq(A,B)\#1@2, leq(B,C)\#2@2, leq(B,A)\#3@\{1,2\}\},$$
$$\{leq(A,B)\#1, leq(B,C)\#2, leq(B,A)\#3\}, true, \emptyset \rangle_4 \stackrel{\omega_{rp}}{\rightarrowtail}_P (\textbf{Simplify})$$
$$\langle [A = B], \{leq(A,B)\#1@2, leq(B,C)\#2@2, leq(B,A)\#3@\{1,2\}\},$$
$$\{leq(B,C)\#2\}, true, \emptyset \rangle_4 \stackrel{\omega_{rp}}{\rightarrowtail}_P (\textbf{Solve})$$
$$\langle [], \{leq(A,B)\#1@2, leq(B,C)\#2@\{1,2\}, leq(B,A)\#3@\{1,2\}\},$$
$$\{leq(B,C)\#2\}, A = B, \emptyset \rangle_4$$

This last transition reschedules the $leq(B,C)\#2$ constraint at priorities 1 and 2. None of the remaining constraints in the schedule lead to a rule firing.   □

3.2   Transforming Dynamic Priority Rules

In the description of the ω_{rp} semantics, we have assumed that every constraint knows the priorities of all rules in which it may participate. For rules with a dynamic priority, this is obviously not always the case.

Example 5. Consider the rule

```
X+Y :: r @ a(X,Z) \ b(Y,Z), c(X,Y) <=> d(X).
```

---

[2] The **Schedule** transition corresponds to the **Activate** transition in ω_r.
[3] We use the notation $c\#i @ \{p_1, \ldots, p_n\}$ to denote $\{c\#i @ p_1, \ldots, c\#i @ p_n\}$.

In this rule the c/2 constraint with ground arguments X and Y knows the priority of the rule, but neither the a/2 nor the b/2 constraints do. Given the a/2 constraint, we need to combine (join) it with either the b/2 or c/2 constraint to determine the actual priority.   □

In this section, we present a pseudo code source-to-source transformation to transform a program such that this property is satisfied. In what follows, we refer to the *join order* for a given constraint occurrence, which is the order in which the partner constraints for this occurrence are retrieved (by nested loops). We consider a join order Θ to be a permutation of $\{1, \ldots, n\}$ where n is the number of heads of the rule. Now, consider a dynamic priority rule

$$p :: r \ @ \ C_1, \ldots, C_i \backslash C_{i+1}, \ldots, C_n \iff g \mid B$$

an active head C_j, a join order Θ with $\Theta(1) = j$ and a number k, $1 \leq k \leq n$ such that the first k heads, starting with C_j and following join order Θ, determine the rule priority. We rewrite rule r as follows (for every j, $1 \leq j \leq n$):

$$1 :: r_j \ @ \ C_{\Theta(1)} \# Id_1, \ldots, C_{\Theta(k)} \# Id_k \implies$$
$$r\text{-match}_j(Id_1, \ldots, Id_k, \mathit{Vars}) \text{ pragma passive}(Id_2), \ldots, \text{passive}(Id_k)$$
$$1 :: r'_j \ @ \ r\text{-match}_j(Id_1, \ldots, Id_k, \mathit{Vars}) \iff$$
$$\text{ground}(p) \mid r\text{-match}'_j(Id_1, \ldots, Id_k, \mathit{Vars})$$
$$p :: r''_j \ @ \ r\text{-match}'_j(Id_1, \ldots, Id_k, \mathit{Vars}), C_{\Theta(k+1)} \# Id_{k+1}, \ldots, C_{\Theta(n)} \# Id_n \implies$$
$$\text{alive}(Id_1), \ldots, \text{alive}(Id_k), g \mid \text{kill}(Id_{\Theta^{-1}(i+1)}), \ldots, \text{kill}(Id_{\Theta^{-1}(n)}), B$$
$$\text{pragma passive}(Id_{k+1}), \ldots, \text{passive}(Id_n),$$
$$\text{history}([Id_{\Theta^{-1}(1)}, \ldots, Id_{\Theta^{-1}(n)}, r])$$

where Vars are the variables shared by the first k heads on the one hand, and the remaining heads, the guard, the body and the priority expression on the other, i.e., $\mathit{Vars} = \left(\cup_{i=1}^{k} \mathit{vars}(C_{\Theta(i)})\right) \cap \left(\left(\cup_{i=k+1}^{n} \mathit{vars}(C_{\Theta(i)})\right) \cup \mathit{vars}(g \wedge B \wedge p)\right)$. The first rule generates a partial match that knows its priority once the necessary arguments are ground (fixed). It runs at the highest possible value of the dynamic priority expression.[4] The second rule ensures that the priority expression is ground before the partial match is scheduled at its dynamic priority. The rule runs at the same priority as the first one. Finally, the third rule extends the partial match (with ground priority) into a full match. There we check whether all constraints in the partial match are still alive (calls to `alive/1`), and delete the removed heads (calls to `kill/1`). The *pragma*[5] `passive/1` denotes that a given head is passive, i.e., no occurrence code is generated for it (see further in Section 3.3). The pragma `history/1` states the tuple layout for the propagation history. All rule copies share the same history which ensures that each instance of the original rule can fire only once.

Example 6. Given the rule r of Example 5 and join orders $\Theta_1 = [1, 2, 3]$, $\Theta_2 = [2, 3, 1]$ and $\Theta_3 = [3, 2, 1]$.[6] Furthermore assuming we schedule at a dynamic priority as soon as we know it, we generate the following rules:

---

[4] We assume 1 is an upperbound. A tighter one can be used instead if such is known.

[5] Most CHR systems support compiler directives by using the keyword **pragma**.

[6] By slight abuse of syntax, we denote $\Theta(1) = \theta_1, \ldots, \Theta(n) = \theta_n$ by $\Theta = [\theta_1, \ldots, \theta_n]$.

```
  1 :: r₁ @ a(X,Z) #Id₁, b(Y,Z) #Id₂ ==>
        r-match₁(Id₁,Id₂,X,Y) pragma passive(Id₂).
  1 :: r₁' @ r-match₁(Id₁,Id₂,X,Y) <=>
        ground(X+Y) | r-match₁'(Id₁,Id₂,X,Y).
X+Y :: r₁'' @ r-match₁'(Id₁,Id₂,X,Y), c(X,Y) #Id₃ ==>
        alive(Id₁), alive(Id₂) | kill(Id₂), kill(Id₃), d(X)
        pragma passive(Id₃), history([Id₁,Id₂,Id₃],r).

  1 :: r₂ @ b(Y,Z) #Id₁, c(X,Y) #Id₂ ==>
        r-match₂(Id₁,Id₂,X,Y,Z) pragma passive(Id₂).
  1 :: r₂' @ r-match₂(Id₁,Id₂,X,Y,Z) <=>
        ground(X+Y) | r-match₂'(Id₁,Id₂,X,Y,Z).
X+Y :: r₂'' @ r-match₂'(Id₁,Id₂,X,Y,Z), a(X,Z) #Id₃ ==>
        alive(Id₁), alive(Id₂) | kill(Id₁), kill(Id₂), d(X)
        pragma passive(Id₃), history([Id₃,Id₁,Id₂,r]).

  1 :: r₃ @ c(X,Y) #Id₁ ==> r-match₃(Id₁,X,Y).
  1 :: r₃' @ r-match₃(Id₁,X,Y) <=> ground(X+Y) | r-match₃'(Id₁,X,Y).
X+Y :: r₃'' @ r-match₃'(Id₁,X,Y), b(Y,Z) #Id₂, a(X,Z) #Id₃ ==> alive(Id₁) |
        kill(Id₁), kill(Id₂), d(X) pragma history([Id₃,Id₂,Id₁,r]).
```

Note that since this is a simpagation rule, a propagation history is not necessary. We only show it for illustrative purposes.   □

The proposed translation schema implements a form of eager matching: all r-$match_j$ constraints are generated eagerly at the highest priority before one is fired. This approach resembles the TREAT matching algorithm [10]. Also similar to the TREAT algorithm and unlike the RETE algorithm [6], we allow different join orders for each active head.

3.3   Compilation

Now that we have shown how a program can be transformed such that each constraint knows the priorities of all rules in which it may participate, we are ready to present the compilation schema. The generated code follows the ω_{rp} semantics closely. In what follows, we assume the host language is Prolog, although the compilation process easily translates to other host languages as well. We note that the generated code presented in this section, closely resembles that of regular CHR under the refined operational semantics, as described in for example [12]. The differences correspond to those between ω_r and ω_{rp} as given in Section 3.1.

CHR Constraints. Whenever a new CHR constraint is asserted, it is scheduled at all priorities at which it may fire (**Schedule** transition). Furthermore, it is attached to its variables for the purpose of facilitating the **Solve** transition. In Prolog this is done using attributed variables. The idea is similar to that of subscribing to event notifiers. Finally, the constraint is inserted into all indexes on its arguments. Schematically, the generated code looks as follows:

```
c(X₁,...,Xₙ) :- GenerateSuspension, S = Suspension,
                schedule(p₁,c/n_prio_p₁_occ_1_1(S)),
                ...
                schedule(pₘ,c/n_prio_pₘ_occ_1_1(S)),
                AttachToVariables, InsertIntoIndexes.
```

The *GenerateSuspension* code creates a data structure (called the *suspension term* in CHR terminology) for representing the constraint in the constraint store. It has amongst others fields for the constraint identifier, its state (dead or alive), its propagation history,[7] its arguments, and pointers for index management. The scheduling code consists of insertions of calls to the code for the first occurrence of each priority p_i $(1 \leq i \leq m)$ into the priority queue. With respect to the usual code for CHR constraints under the ω_r semantics, we have added the schedule/2 calls and removed the call to the code of the first occurrence of the constraint.

Built-in Constraints. Built-in constraints are dealt with by the underlying constraint solver, in this case the Prolog Herbrand solver. Whenever this solver binds a variable to another variable or a term (during unification), a so-called *unification hook* is called. In this hook, the CHR part of the **Solve** transition is implemented. It consists of reattaching the affected constraints, updating the indexes, and scheduling the affected constraints again at each priority for which they have occurrences.

Occurrence Code. For each constraint occurrence, a separate predicate is generated, implementing the **Simplify** and **Propagate** transitions. Its clauses are shown below. The approach is very similar to how occurrences are compiled under the refined operational semantics of CHR. The differences are that only the occurrences of the same priority are linked, where occurrences with a dynamic priority are assumed to run at different priorities, and the priority queue is checked (check_activation/1) after each rule firing. The code below is for the jth priority p occurrence of the c/n constraint which is in an m-headed rule. The indices $r(1),...,r(i)$ refer to the removed heads.

```
c/n_prio_p_occ_j_1(S₁) :-
        (   alive(S₁), HeadMatch, LookupNext(S̄₂)
        ->  c/n_prio_p_occ_j_2(S̄₂,S₁).
        ;   c/n_prio_p_occ_j+1_1(S₁)
        ).

c/n_prio_p_occ_j_2([S₂|S̄₂],S₁) :-
        (   alive(S₂), S₂ \= S₁, HeadMatch, LookupNext(S̄₃)
        ->  c/n_prio_p_occ_j_3(S̄₃,S₂,S̄₂,S₁)
```

---

[7] We use a distributed propagation history, like in the K.U.Leuven CHR system [12].

```
      ;   c/n_prio_p_occ_j_2(S̄₂,S₁)
      ).
c/n_prio_p_occ_j_2([],S₁) :- c/n_prio_p_occ_j + 1_1(S₁).

...


c/n_prio_p_occ_j_m([Sₘ|S̄ₘ],Sₘ₋₁,...,S₁) :-
    (   alive(Sₘ), Sₘ \= S₁, ..., Sₘ \= Sₘ₋₁,
        HeadMatch, RemainingGuard, HistoryCheck
    -> AddToHistory, kill(Sᵣ₍₁₎), ..., kill(Sᵣ₍ᵢ₎),
        Body, check_activation(p),
        (   alive(S₁)
        -> (   ...
        ... (   alive(Sₘ₋₁)
             -> c/n_prio_p_occ_j_m(S̄ₘ,...,S₁)
             ;  c/n_prio_p_occ_j_m - 1(S̄ₘ₋₁,...,S₁)
             )
             ...
        ;   true
        )
    ;   c/n_prio_p_occ_j_m(S̄ₘ,Sₘ₋₁,...,S₁)
    ).
c/n_prio_p_occ_j_m([],_,S̄ₘ₋₁,...,S₁) :-
        c/n_prio_p_occ_j_m - 1(S̄ₘ₋₁,...,S₁).
```

The *HeadMatch* call checks whether the newly looked up head matches with the rule and with the previous heads. A list of all candidates for the next head is returned by *LookupNext*/1. *RemainingGuard* is the part of the guard that has not already been tested by the *HeadMatch* calls. Propagation history checking and extending is handled by respectively *HistoryCheck* and *AddToHistory*. After having gone through all rule instances for the given occurrence, the next occurrence is tried (**Default**) or the activation call returns (**Drop**). The check_activation/1 call in the occurrence code checks whether a constraint occurrence is scheduled at a higher priority than the current one. It implements the **Activate** transition.

4 Optimization

We now present the main optimizations implemented in the CHR^{rp} compiler. The proposed optimizations mainly improve constant factors, but might cause complexity improvements for some programs as well. We start with optimizations that reduce the number of priority queue operations. We note that such operations may have a higher than constant cost.

4.1 Reducing Priority Queue Operations

A first optimization consists of only scheduling the highest priority occurrence of every new constraint. Only when the constraint has been activated at this priority and has gone through all of its occurrences without being deleted, it is scheduled for the next priority. This is a simple extension of the continuation based approach we already applied for constraint occurrences at equal priority.

In the basic compilation scheme, it is checked whether a higher priority scheduled constraint exists after each rule firing. In a number of cases, this is not needed. If the active constraint is removed, it is popped from the top of the activation stack and the activation check that caused it to be activated in the first place, checks again to see if other constraints are ready for activation. So, since a priority queue check will take place anyway, there is no need to do this twice. If the body of a rule does not contain CHR constraints with a priority higher than the current one, nor built-in constraints that can trigger any CHR constraints to be scheduled at a higher priority, then after processing the rule body, the active constraint remains active and we do not need to check the priority queue. We denote the above optimizations by *reduced activation checking*.

Building further on this idea, we note that by analyzing the body, we can sometimes determine which constraint will be activated next. Instead of scheduling it first and then checking the priority queue, we can activate it directly at its highest priority. We call this *inline activation*. Inline activation is not limited to one constraint: we can directly activate all constraints that have the same highest priority. Indeed, when the first of these constraints returns from activation, the priority queue cannot contain any constraint scheduled at a higher priority, because such a constraint would have been activated before returning.

Example 7. We illustrate the applicability of the proposed optimizations on the leq program given in Example 1. The leq/2 constraint has 5 occurrences at priority 1 and 2 at priority 2. New leq/2 constraints are only scheduled at priority 1. Only if an activated constraint has passed the 5th priority 1 occurrence, it is scheduled at priority 2. For the first three priority 1 occurrences, as well as for the removed occurrence in the idempotence rule, the active constraint is removed and so there is no need to check the priority queue after firing the rule body. Since the body of the remaining priority 1 occurrence equals true, no higher priority constraint is scheduled and so we do not need to check the queue here either. Finally, for the transitivity rule we have that the only constraint in the body has a higher priority occurrence than the current active occurrence, and so we can apply inline activation there.   □

4.2   Late Indexing

Similar to an optimization from regular CHR, we can often postpone storage of constraints, reducing cost if the constraint is removed before these operations are be applied. We extend the late storage concept of [9] to late indexing, where we split up the task of storing a constraint into the subtasks of inserting it into different indexes. The main idea is that an active constraint can only lose activation to another constraint in rules of a higher priority. This implies that when a constraint is active at a given current priority, it should only be stored in those indexes that are used by higher priority rules.

Example 8. In the `leq` program (Example 1), the `leq/2` constraints are indexed

- on the combination of both arguments (`antisymmetry` and `idempotence`);
- on the first argument and on the second argument (`transitivity`);
- on the constraint symbol for the purpose of showing the constraint store.

By using late indexing, new `leq/2` constraints are not indexed at the moment they are asserted, but only scheduled (only at priority 1). When an active `leq/2` constraint 'survives' the 5th priority 1 occurrence, it is indexed on the combination of both arguments and rescheduled at priority 2. We can postpone the indexing this long because only one constraint can be on the execution stack for each priority and hence all partner constraints have either been indexed already, or still need to be activated. Only after a reactivated `leq/2` constraint has passed the second priority 2 occurrence, it is stored in the remaining indexes. Note that our approach potentially changes the execution order of the program, which can sometimes contribute to changes in the running time (in either direction).   □

4.3   Passive Occurrences

In [4] we give a criterion to decide whether a given constraint occurrence can be made passive. Passive occurrences allow us to avoid the overhead of looking up partner constraints, and sometimes also the overhead related to scheduling and indexing. Due to space considerations, we do not go into detail here.

5   Evaluation

Less-or-Equal. The `leq` benchmark uses the program of Example 1 and for given n, the initial goal $G = G_1 \cup G_2$ with

$$G_1 = \{\text{leq}(X_1, X_2), \ldots, \text{leq}(X_{n-1},\ X_n)\} \wedge G_2 = \{\text{leq}(X_n, X_1)\}$$

From the goal G, a final state is derived in which $X_1 = X_2 = \ldots = X_{n-1} = X_n$.

In [2], it was shown that the benchmark scales better using priorities and batch processing of the goal, because of the order in which constraints are activated (i.e., more recently added constraints are preferred). Using this order, the `leq`(X_1, X_n) constraint that causes the loop to be detected, is asserted after a linear number of firings of the transitivity rule. Interestingly, by using the late indexing optimization, we get a higher complexity because the necessary partner constraints for the optimal firing order are not yet stored. However, when we first assert subgoal G_1, wait for a fixpoint, and then assert G_2, then both the versions with and without late indexing behave the same.

Optimizations. Table 3 shows benchmark results for various programs where the effect on the runtime of each of the optimizations is measured. The runtimes are given as percentages of the runtime of the unoptimized version for each program. For the unoptimized and fully optimized versions, we also give times in

Table 3. Benchmark results

LI	IA	RAC	loop	leq	dijkstra	union-find	sudoku
			24.54s	15.80s	40.43s	15.24s	13.44s
		√	88%	99%	98%	93%	98%
	√		73%	97%	97%	82%	99%
√		√	46%	63%	97%	40%	112%
√	√	√	8%	56%	92%	17%	109%
√	√	√	2.03s	8.86s	37.14s	2.54s	14.63s

seconds. We used a Pentium IV, 2.8GHz running SWI-Prolog version 5.6.28. The results do not include garbage collection times. The `loop` benchmark consists of the following two rules (and does not rely on priorities):

```
1 :: a(X) <=> X > 0 | a(X-1).        1 :: a(0) <=> true.
```

and initial goal $\{a(2^{20})\}$; the `leq` benchmark is the same as in the previous subsection, with $n = 80$; the `dijkstra` benchmark uses the program of Example 2 with a graph of 2^{15} nodes and $3 \cdot 2^{15}$ edges; the `union-find` benchmark is based on the naive union-find program given in [15] and uses 2^{12} random `union/2` constraints over an equal number of elements (see also [4]). Finally, the `sudoku` benchmark uses an adapted version of the Sudoku solver from the CHR website [14] (see also [2]) and solves a puzzle in which initially 16 cells have a value. The benchmarks are executed with the late indexing (LI), inline activation (IA) and reduced activation checking (RAC) optimizations switched on and off.

The inline activation analysis assumes that dynamic priority rules run at the highest possible value of the priority expression. It currently assumes this value is 1, but a bounds analysis or a user declaration can give a tighter upperbound. In the `dijkstra` and `sudoku` benchmarks, we have used a tight upperbound of 2 for the dynamic priority rules. The passive analysis applied to the `union-find` benchmark cuts off another 2% and reduces the runtime with full optimization to about 15% of the runtime without optimization. The late indexing optimization can change the execution order. We have already shown how this affects the `leq` benchmark. Similarly, it also affects the `sudoku` benchmark which has (amongst others) 11% more rule firings, hence the increase in runtime. Moreover, late indexing only reduces the amount of index insertions by 3% in this benchmark.

We also compare CHR^{rp} against the K.U.Leuven CHR system under the ω_r semantics. For `leq`, `loop` and `union-find`, we execute the same code ignoring priorities (though sometimes relying on rule order). For `dijkstra` and `sudoku` the K.U.Leuven CHR code encodes equivalent behavior obtained using priorities by other methods. Hence the rules are more involved. The `leq` benchmark takes about 4% less using CHR^{rp} and the `union-find` benchmark takes 53% more time. The `loop` benchmark takes about 5.3 times longer in our system compared to the code generated by the K.U.Leuven CHR system, which corresponds to a pure Prolog loop. The main remaining overhead is the generation and destruction of internal data structures, which is avoided in K.U.Leuven CHR. Comparison for the sudoku benchmark is difficult because the search trees are different. In this particular case, K.U.Leuven CHR is about 10% faster than our CHR^{rp} system (without late indexing), but also has 5% less rule firings.

For the dijkstra benchmark, we compared with the CHR program given in [16].[8] Our implementation runs about 2.4 times slower than the (regular) CHR implementation, but it is also arguably more high level. Noteworthy is the following optimization, implemented in [16] and reformulated here in terms of our CHR^{rp} implementation. The rule

```
1 :: dist(V,D₁) \ dist(V,D₂) <=> D₁ =< D₂ | true.
```

removes the dist(V,D$_2$) constraint which might still be scheduled at priority $D_2 + 2$. After firing the rule, the dist(V,D$_1$) constraint is scheduled at priority $D_1 + 2$. Instead of first (lazily) deleting a scheduled item, and then inserting a new one, the cheaper decrease_key operation can be used instead (because $D_1 \leq D_2$). Compared to an altered version of the original CHR implementation in which this optimization is turned off, our code remains (only) 13% slower. The results are for the described problem instances and vary somewhat over different problem sizes. Nonetheless, the asymptotic time complexities are the same in both CHR and CHR^{rp} versions and so the results are sufficiently generalizable.

Finally, we compare to the source-to-source transformation given in [2]: the leq benchmark runs about 4.7 times faster on our system; the loop benchmark about 39 times, and the union-find benchmark about 19 times. The remaining benchmarks could not run because they contain rules with a dynamic priority which are not supported by the source-to-source transformation.

6   Concluding Remarks

This paper presents a compilation schema for CHR^{rp}: CHR with rule priorities. We have shown the feasibility of implementing rules with both static and dynamic rule priorities using a lazy matching approach, in contrast with the eager matching as implemented by the RETE algorithm and derivatives. We have proposed various ways to optimize the generated code and shown their effectiveness on benchmarks. Our benchmark results furthermore indicate that our implementation already comes close to the state-of-the-art K.U.Leuven CHR system (and sometimes even surpasses it), while offering a much more high level form of execution control. Compared to the implementation given in [2], our system is about an order of magnitude faster on the benchmarks. This work extends [2] by introducing the refined priority semantics, offering support for dynamic priority rules, presenting the first *compiler* for CHR^{rp}, and by proposing several optimizations for the generated code. The optimizations consist of both completely new optimizations (those related to reducing priority queue operations), as well as refinements of previously known optimizations for (regular) CHR (i.e., late indexing and the passive analysis).

---

[8] For a fair comparison, we use a combination of Fibonacci heaps for the dynamic priorities, and an array for static priorities 1 and 2, as priority queue.

Related Work. Rule priorities (sometimes called *salience*) are found in many rule based languages, including production rule systems and active database systems. Priority based execution control is also found in many Constraint (Logic) Programming systems. We refer to [2] for a deeper discussion. The implementation presented here is based on lazy matching and hence has the advantage of low memory requirements compared to RETE style eager matching. In [8], a rule based language with prioritized rules is presented, and an implementation based on a form of eager matching is proposed. [1] shows this language easily translates into CHR^{rp}. CHR^{rp} goes beyond earlier priority based rewriting systems by interacting with an underlying solver and supporting propagation rules.

Future Work. The late indexing and passive occurrence optimizations were inspired by similar optimizations in the K.U.Leuven CHR system (and earlier systems). Some other optimizations could easily be transferred to the CHR^{rp} compiler. The analyses implemented so far are very ad hoc and a more general approach based on abstract interpretation could be worthwhile. Finally, we have not taken advantage of some of the nondeterminism introduced by the ω_p semantics. In particular this concerns reordering or merging rules with equal priority. An extension of the join ordering cost model of [3] could help us choose a more optimal rule order within the boundaries imposed by the priorities.

References

1. De Koninck, L., Schrijvers, T., Demoen, B.: The correspondence between the Logical Algorithms language and CHR. In: Dahl, V., Niemelä, I. (eds.) ICLP 2007. LNCS, vol. 4670, pp. 209–223. Springer, Heidelberg (2007)
2. De Koninck, L., Schrijvers, T., Demoen, B.: User-definable rule priorities for CHR. In: 9th ACM SIGPLAN Symp. on Principles and Practice of Declarative Programming, pp. 25–36 (2007)
3. De Koninck, L., Sneyers, J.: Join ordering for Constraint Handling Rules. In: 4th Workshop on Constraint Handling Rules, pp. 107–121 (2007)
4. De Koninck, L., Stuckey, P.J., Duck, G.J.: Optimized compilation of CHR^{rp}. Technical Report CW 499, K.U.Leuven, Belgium (2007)
5. Duck, G.J., Stuckey, P.J., García de la Banda, M., Holzbaur, C.: The refined operational semantics of Constraint Handling Rules. In: Demoen, B., Lifschitz, V. (eds.) ICLP 2004. LNCS, vol. 3132, pp. 90–104. Springer, Heidelberg (2004)
6. Forgy, C.L.: Rete: A fast algorithm for the many pattern/many object pattern match problem. Artif. Intell. 19(1), 17–37 (1982)
7. Frühwirth, T.: Theory and practice of Constraint Handling Rules. J. Log. Program. 37(1-3), 95–138 (1998)
8. Ganzinger, H., McAllester, D.A.: Logical algorithms. In: Stuckey, P.J. (ed.) ICLP 2002. LNCS, vol. 2401, pp. 209–223. Springer, Heidelberg (2002)
9. Holzbaur, C., García de la Banda, M., Stuckey, P.J., Duck, G.J.: Optimizing compilation of Constraint Handling Rules in HAL. Theory and Practice of Logic Programming: Special Issue on Constraint Handling Rules 5(4 & 5), 503–531 (2005)
10. Miranker, D.P.: TREAT: A better match algorithm for AI production system matching. In: 6th National Conf. on Artificial Intelligence, pp. 42–47. AAAI Press, Menlo Park (1987)

11. Morawietz, F.: Chart parsing and constraint programming. In: 18th Intl. Conf. Computational Linguistics, pp. 551–557. Morgan Kaufmann, San Francisco (2000)
12. Schrijvers, T.: Analyses, Optimizations and Extensions of Constraint Handling Rules. PhD thesis, K.U.Leuven, Leuven, Belgium (2005)
13. Schrijvers, T., Demoen, B.: The K.U.Leuven CHR system: Implementation and application. In: 1st Workshop on CHR, Selected Contributions, Ulmer Informatik-Berichte 2004-01, pp. 1–5. Universität Ulm, Germany (2004)
14. Schrijvers, T., et al.: The Constraint Handling Rules home page (2007),
    `http://www.cs.kuleuven.be/~dtai/projects/CHR/`
15. Schrijvers, T., Frühwirth, T.: Optimal union-find in Constraint Handling Rules. Theory and Practice of Logic Programming 6(1&2) (2006)
16. Sneyers, J., Schrijvers, T., Demoen, B.: Dijkstra's algorithm with Fibonacci heaps: An executable description in CHR. In: 20th Workshop on Logic Programming, INFSYS Research Report 1843-06-02, pp. 182–191. TU Wien (2006)

Certified Exact Real Arithmetic Using Co-induction in Arbitrary Integer Base

Nicolas Julien

INRIA Sophia Antipolis

Abstract. In this paper we describe some certified algorithms for exact real arithmetic based on co-recursion. Our work is based on previous experiences using redundant digits of base 2 but generalizes them using arbitrary integer bases. The goal is to take benefit of fast native integer computation. We extend a technique to compute converging series. We use this technique to compute the product and the inverse. We describe how we implement and certify our algorithms in the proof system Coq and evaluate the efficiency of the library inside the prover.

1 Introduction

We built a library to describe computations on real numbers in a certified way. This library can be used inside a theorem prover and it relies on a particular form of recursive programming known as co-recursion. The data manipulated in this library are streams of signed digits, in other words infinite sequences. The central concept is the computation of series, which was already studied in [2]. We suggest a few improvements on the known results and we implement division, a function that had not been considered yet in this particular framework. One of the original characteristics of our work is that our library is parametrized by the base used to interpret the digit streams.

First we will see why we represent real numbers as streams of signed digits of an arbitrary positive integer base. Then we will describe how the formalization of the base influences the complexity of the operations and what are the solutions we provide to adapt the algorithms to this new framework. We will also see how we improve the technique to compute converging series. Finally after giving an idea of the formalization in Coq [3,5], we will illustrate the benefits in efficiency of using large bases with some benchmarks.

2 Representation of Real Numbers

It is well known that datatypes containing only finite objects are not suitable for representing real numbers. Real numbers are commonly described in computer programs as floating point numbers. This representation actually describes a finite subset of rational numbers. When accumulating computations on such approximations one has to handle round-off problems in order to avoid erroneous results [9].

J. Garrigue and M. Hermenegildo (Eds.): FLOPS 2008, LNCS 4989, pp. 48–63, 2008.

A common approach used in every day life is to view real numbers as fractional numbers with a possibly infinite fractional part. More formally these representations are sequences of digits i.e. function from positive integers to integers so that the sequence $0.x_1 \ldots x_n \ldots$ actually has the value $\sum_{i=1}^{\infty} \frac{x_i}{\beta^i}$. In such a representation, every day practice relies on the x_i being between 0 and $\beta - 1$, but a more efficient approach is to take x_i between $-\beta + 1$ and $\beta - 1$. This extension with signed digits adds redundancy but this redundancy supports more efficient algorithms and is some time essential to ensure that some computations terminate. Some other models of exact real arithmetic have been implemented using infinite datatypes. For instance with continued fractions [14], regular functions of rationals [12] or streams of linear fractional transformations [6].

Describing the sequences of digits as simple functions from positive integers to integers seems appropriate to work in a higher order setting but this technique has flaws when you compute the function for a given n and then you want to compute for a higher integer. The second time you need to recompute all that was already computed for n.

With co-inductive types we can represent a real number in a more natural way i.e. as the infinite stream of its digits. Co-inductive objects are lazily evaluated, thus the first n digits of a stream will be reused when computing the following digits and then avoid re-computation. These objects are defined by co-recursive functions and properties over these functions can be proved by co-induction.

Since co-induction [7] in Coq provides such a framework to reason on infinite datatypes, several certified implementations of exact real arithmetic arose using streams of a set of three redundant digits [2,4] or streams of linear fractional transformations [11].

We chose to represent real numbers as streams of signed digits of an arbitrary integer base. The set of signed digits of a base β is $\{-\beta+1, \ldots, \beta-1\}$. The negative digits will be written with a bar: $\bar{1} = -1$. This representation is redundant in the sense that a number will have several representations. For instance the streams $3::3::3::3::3\ldots$ and $4::\bar{7}::3::3::3\ldots$ are suitable representations of the number $\frac{1}{3} = 0.33333\ldots$ in base ten.

Often, we will not make any difference between a stream and the real value it represents. The stream beginning by the digit k and followed by the stream s is denoted by $k::s$ and its value is $\frac{k+s}{\beta}$, since $\sum_{i=1}^{\infty} \frac{d_i}{\beta^i} = \frac{d_1 + \sum_{i=1}^{\infty} \frac{d_{i+1}}{\beta^i}}{\beta}$.

The interval of numbers that can be represented by a stream beginning with a digit k is $[\frac{k-1}{\beta}, \frac{k+1}{\beta}]$. Indeed the value of a stream $k::s$ is $\frac{k+s}{\beta}$ and a stream s represents a value of $[-1, 1]$. The redundancy comes from the fact that two consecutive intervals of this kind overlap: $[\frac{k-1}{\beta}, \frac{k+1}{\beta}] \cap [\frac{(k+1)-1}{\beta}, \frac{(k+1)+1}{\beta}] = [\frac{k}{\beta}, \frac{k+1}{\beta}]$. The benefit of the redundancy can be understood noticing that the magnitude of overlaps of intervals of consecutive digits is a constant equal to $\frac{1}{\beta}$. Thus knowing an interval of this magnitude containing a real is always enough to decide the first digit for one of its representations.

Since we have a way to describe all the real numbers in $[-1, 1]$ we can use a couple (mantissa, exponent) to represent all the real numbers. So when describing an algorithm, we first describe the part on the mantissa and then we extend it to the full representation. Since the second part is standard however the mantissa is represented, we will focus on the first part.

To compute the mantissa of a real number we try to obtain an interval which contains the number such that we can decide the first digit of the number. Thus the operations on mantissa are described by co-recursion as functions that produce the first digit and are called recursively to produce the following digits.

We work with bases greater than 4 since it is required by some algorithms. Because our goal is to use larger bases, this should not be a real restriction.

3   Computing Addition

The problem with addition is that the result of adding two numbers of $[-1, 1]$ is not in $[-1, 1]$ but in $[-2, 2]$ and so it could not be represented only with a stream. Bertot proposes to avoid this by first defining the "half-sum" $x, y \mapsto \frac{x+y}{2}$. Then he defines the function that multiplies a number by 2 if it's in $[0, \frac{1}{2}]$, $x \mapsto \begin{cases} 2x \text{ if } & x \leq \frac{1}{2} \\ 1 \text{ otherwise} \end{cases}$. Finally he obtains some kind of addition by composing the two functions.

As we work with an arbitrary integer base we have adapted this idea replacing 2 by the base in the division and the multiplication. Thus we first describe a function that given a base, two streams and a integer remainder computes a stream of the sum of the streams and the remainder, all divided by the base:

$$\text{sum\_div\_base}_\beta \begin{cases} [-1, 1]^2 \times [-\beta + 2, \beta - 2] \mapsto [-1, 1] \\ x, y, r \mapsto \frac{x+y+r}{\beta} \end{cases}$$

This operation is stable in $[-1, 1]$ and we provide an algorithm to compute it:

- We read the first digit of x and y. We now have k_1, k_2, x' and y' such that $x = k_1 :: x', y = k_2 :: y'$. Thus we have:

$$\text{sum\_div\_base}_\beta(x, y, r) = \frac{r + \frac{x'+y'+k_1+k_2}{\beta}}{\beta}.$$

Since k_1 and k_2 are signed digits of the base, $-2\beta + 2 \leq k_1 + k_2 \leq 2\beta - 2$. Thus r seems to be a good candidate for a first digit of the result and $k_1 + k_2$ for the next remainder.
- If $\beta - 1 \leq k_1 + k_2$ then $k_1 + k_2$ is too big to be a suitable remainder, but $k_1 + k_2 - \beta$ is acceptable. Hence the first digit can be $r + 1$ which is in the set of signed digits of the base because r is the previous remainder $-\beta + 2 \leq r \leq \beta - 2$.

$$\text{sum\_div\_base}_\beta(x, y, r) = \frac{r + 1 + \frac{x'+y'+k_1+k_2-\beta}{\beta}}{\beta}$$
$$= (r + 1) :: \text{sum\_div\_base}_\beta(x', y', k_1 + k_2 - \beta).$$

- If $k_1 + k_2 \leq -\beta + 1$ then $k_1 + k_2$ is too small to be a suitable remainder, but $k_1 + k_2 + \beta$ is acceptable. Hence the first digit can be $r - 1$ which is in the set of signed digits of the base because r is the previous remainder $-\beta + 2 \leq r \leq \beta - 2$.

$$\texttt{sum\_div\_base}_\beta(x, y, r) = \frac{r - 1 + \frac{x' + y' + k_1 + k_2 + \beta}{\beta}}{\beta}$$

$$= (r - 1) :: \texttt{sum\_div\_base}_\beta(x', y', k_1 + k_2 + \beta).$$

- Otherwise $k_1 + k_2$ is a suitable value for the remainder and r can be the first digit.

$$\texttt{sum\_div\_base}_\beta(x, y, r) = \frac{r + \frac{x' + y' + k_1 + k_2}{\beta}}{\beta}$$

$$= r :: \texttt{sum\_div\_base}_\beta(x', y', k_1 + k_2).$$

By initializing r with 0 and increasing the exponent of the result by 1 we obtain an exact addition. But we also need an addition on streams. We now have to define the function that multiplies a stream by the base when the result can be represented by a stream or gives a dummy result otherwise.

$$\texttt{mult\_base} : \begin{cases} \mathbb{Z} \times [-1, \ 1] \mapsto [-1, \ 1] \\ \beta, x \qquad \mapsto \begin{cases} -1 & \text{if } x \leq \frac{-1}{\beta} \\ 1 & \text{if } x \geq \frac{1}{\beta} \\ x \times \beta \ \text{otherwise} \end{cases} \end{cases} .$$

We first have to notice that the real numbers -1 and 1 obviously have only one representation since they are the edges of the representable values. The only way to represent 1 (resp. -1) is the sequence where only the maximal (resp. minimal) digit $\beta - 1$ (resp. $-\beta + 1$) occurs. This is justified by the following equality.

$$\sum_{i=1}^{\infty} \frac{\beta - 1}{\beta^i} = \frac{\beta - 1}{\beta} \sum_{i=0}^{\infty} \frac{1}{\beta^i} = \frac{\beta - 1}{\beta} \frac{1}{1 - \frac{1}{\beta}} = 1$$

Now we can describe the algorithm of the function $\texttt{mult\_base}$:

- We read the first digit of x: $x = k_1 :: x'$
- If $k_1 = 0$ then the result is x': $\beta \frac{0 + x'}{\beta} = x'$
- If $k_1 \leq -2$, then we can deduce that $x \leq \frac{-1}{\beta}$ hence the result must be the constant -1.
- If $k_1 \geq 2$, then we can deduce that $x \geq \frac{1}{\beta}$ hence the result must be the constant 1.
- If $k_1 = 1$ we need to look at one more digit of x: $x = 1 :: k_2 :: x''$
  - If $k_2 < 0$, then we use the redundancy of the representation to reduce the problem to a previous case $x = 1 :: k_2 :: x'' = 0 :: (k_2 + \beta) :: x''$, hence the result is $(k_2 + \beta) :: x''$.

- If $k_2 > 0$, we also come to a previous case $x = 1::k_2::x'' = 2::(k_2 - \beta)::x''$, hence the result is 1.
- If $k_2 = 0$ then we need a recursive call:

$$\mathtt{mult\_base}(\beta, 1::0::x'') = \beta \times \frac{1 + \frac{0 + x''}{\beta}}{\beta}$$

$$= \frac{\beta - 1 + \beta \times \frac{1 + x''}{\beta}}{\beta}$$

$$= \beta - 1::\mathtt{mult\_base}(\beta, 1::x'').$$

In this case we can't know if our parameter x is lesser or equal to $\frac{1}{\beta}$. And maybe it won't be possible even if we read an arbitrary large finite number of more digits of x. Nevertheless, if it was lesser or equal, we would know that it would be close enough to $\frac{1}{\beta}$ to be sure that the result could begin with the digit $\beta - 1$. And if it was greater, then the result should be the constant 1 that begins with the same digit $\beta - 1$. So it's correct to produce the digit and to let the recursive call try to decide later or construct the constant 1 step by step.

– If $k_1 = -1$ we have a symmetrical reasoning as the previous case $k_1 = 1$.

By composing our two functions, we finally get a function over two mantissas which computes their sum when this is in $[-1, \ 1]$.

$$\mathtt{add}(\beta, x, y) = \mathtt{mult\_base}(\beta, \mathtt{sum\_div\_base}_\beta(x, y, 0))$$

$$\mathtt{add} : \begin{cases} \mathbb{Z} \times [-1, \ 1] \times [-1, \ 1] \mapsto [-1, \ 1] \\ \beta, x, y \qquad\qquad\qquad \mapsto \begin{cases} -1 & \text{if } x + y \leq -1 \\ 1 & \text{if } x + y \geq 1 \\ x + y \ \text{otherwise} \end{cases} \end{cases}$$

4   The Function `make_digit`

We have described an algorithm for addition which computes the first digit of their sum from the first two digits of the parameters and so on recursively. Another method is possible when we know that one argument is close enough to zero. In this case computing a prefix of the other parameter is enough to compute the first digit of their sum.

Indeed, suppose that we want to add x and y and we know $|y| \leq \frac{\beta - 2}{2\beta^2}$. If we compute the first two digits of $x = d_1::d_2::x''$ then we know a frame of x of magnitude $\frac{2}{\beta^2}$. Thus we know a frame of their sum of magnitude $\frac{1}{\beta}$ which is enough to compute the first digit of the sum.

We propose here to define a function `make_digit` which from the stream x representing a real number, gives another stream $k::x'$ representing the same number but such that k could be the possible first when adding a number close enough to zero.

Let y be a number "close enough of 0":

$$x + \frac{-\beta + 2}{2\beta^2} \leq \texttt{make\_digit}(\beta, x) + y \leq x + \frac{\beta - 2}{2\beta^2}.$$

We describe the algorithm of $\texttt{make\_digit}$ as follow:

– We first look at the first two digits of $x = k_1 :: k_2 :: x''$. So we have

$$\frac{k_1 + \frac{k_2 + x''}{\beta}}{\beta} + \frac{-\beta + 2}{2\beta^2} \leq \texttt{make\_digit}(\beta, x) + y \leq \frac{k_1 + \frac{k_2 + x''}{\beta}}{\beta} + \frac{\beta - 2}{2\beta^2}$$

$$\frac{k_1 + \frac{2k_2 + 2x'' - \beta + 2}{2\beta}}{\beta} \leq \texttt{make\_digit}(\beta, x) + y \leq \frac{k_1 + \frac{2k_2 + 2x'' + \beta - 2}{2\beta}}{\beta}$$

Since $x'' \in [-1, \ 1]$ we also have

$$\frac{k_1 + \frac{2k_2 - \beta}{2\beta}}{\beta} \leq \texttt{make\_digit}(\beta, x) + y \leq \frac{k_1 + \frac{2k_2 + \beta}{2\beta}}{\beta}$$

– If $-\beta \leq 2k_2 \leq \beta$, then we have

$$\frac{k_1 - 1}{\beta} \leq \texttt{make\_digit}(\beta, x) + y \leq \frac{k_1 + 1}{\beta}$$

Thus the result can start with the digit k_1 and the remaining stream is $k_2 :: x''$:

$$\texttt{make\_digit}(\beta, x) = k_1 :: k_2 :: x'' = x.$$

– Otherwise, if $\beta < 2k_2$

  • If $k_1 \neq \beta - 1$, then we use the redundancy of the representation $k_1 :: k_2 :: x''$ $= k_1 + 1 :: k_2 - \beta :: x''$, we can then show that

$$\frac{(k_1 + 1) - 1}{\beta} \leq \texttt{make\_digit}(\beta, x) + y \leq \frac{(k_1 + 1) + 1}{\beta}$$

  The result can be:

$$\texttt{make\_digit}(\beta, x) = k_1 + 1 :: k_2 - \beta :: x''.$$

  • Otherwise $k_1 + 1 = \beta$, it is not in the set of digits, but since we suppose the result is in $[-1, \ 1]$, we have

$$\frac{(\beta - 1) - 1}{\beta} \leq \texttt{make\_digit}(\beta, x) + y \leq 1 = \frac{(\beta - 1) + 1}{\beta}$$

  The result can be:

$$\texttt{make\_digit}(\beta, x) + y = \beta - 1 :: k_2 :: x''.$$

– Otherwise $2k_2 < -\beta$ and we have a similar reasoning.

5   Computing Series

In his work Bertot describes how to compute converging series using the technique described in the function make_digit. Indeed a converging series can be split into a finite part and an infinite part as close to zero as needed. We have adapted this technique for an arbitrary integer base and improved its description by defining the function make_digit.

To compute the stream of a series $\sum_{i=0}^{\infty} a_i$ which converges in $[-1,\ 1]$, we start with defining a more general function

$$f(\beta, j, n, r) = \beta^j \times \sum_{i=n}^{\infty} a_i + r.$$

Then we should compute the series as a particular case: $f(\beta, 0, 0, 0) = \sum_{i=0}^{\infty} a_i$.

We first have to find a $p \geq n$ such that $|\beta^j \times \sum_{i=p}^{\infty} a_i| \leq \frac{\beta-2}{2\beta^2}$. Because the series is converging we know that such a p exists.

$$f(\beta, j, n, r) = (\beta^j \times \sum_{i=n}^{p-1} a_i + r) + \beta^j \times \sum_{i=p}^{\infty} a_i$$

We are in the situation that make_digit was designed for. We can compute a digit k and a stream r' such that $k::r' = \beta^j \times \sum_{i=n}^{p-1} a_i + r$ with k a possible first digit of the result of $f(\beta, j, n, r)$. Then we can produce this k as the first digit and continue computing the series with a recursive call:

$$
\begin{aligned}
f(\beta, j, n, r) &= (\beta^j \times \sum_{i=n}^{p-1} a_i + r) + \beta^j \times \sum_{i=p}^{\infty} a_i \\
&= \frac{k + r'}{\beta} + \beta^j \times \sum_{i=p}^{\infty} a_i \\
&= \frac{k + \beta \times \beta^j \sum_{i=p}^{\infty} a_i + r'}{\beta} \\
&= k :: f(\beta, j+1, p, r')
\end{aligned}
$$

Thus the schema to define a co-recursive function that computes a series is:

- To find the p that split the series such that the infinite part is close enough to 0. This is often done with a recursive function.
- To compute a possible first digit using make_digit and produce it.
- To define the stream of the following digits with a co-recursive call.

The part of the function that uses make_digit to produce the first digit and perform the recursive call does not depend on the series and can be formalized once and for all. The parameter r of f could be understood as the difference between the series and its approximation given by its first digit. In general, the parameters of the function f will not exactly be the ones we used to describe the technique. Sometimes a parameter is simplified or hidden in another parameter. And often we will use extra parameters to describe intermediate computations. For instance to avoid re-computing a $n!$ that appears in a series.

The number $\beta^j \times \sum_{i=n}^{p-1} a_i + r$ we give to `make_digit` is not necessarily in $[-1, 1]$. But the result of adding the stream representing $\beta^j \times \sum_{i=n}^{p-1} a_i$ and the stream r is guaranteed only if it is in $[-1, 1]$. To ensure the correctness of our computations we previously relied on tricks, like grouping terms of the series to have only positive terms.

We recently found a better solution. It consists in guaranteeing that the parameter r is always inside the interval $[-\frac{\beta+2}{2\beta}, \frac{\beta+2}{2\beta}]$. This parameter is either the initial value 0 or computed by `make_digit` at a previous step. The function `make_digit` is trying to produce r as close to 0 as possible, thanks to redundancy. We can see in its algorithm that r is not in this interval only if the input is too close to the bounds of $[-1, 1]$ where redundancy cannot be used i.e. outside $[-\frac{2\beta^2-\beta-2}{2\beta^2}, \frac{2\beta^2-\beta-2}{2\beta^2}]$. But when computing series, the input of `make_digit` is the sum of a previous r and the finite part of the series: $\beta^j \times \sum_{i=n}^{p-1} a_i$. Our solution is to consider series converging inside $[-\frac{\beta-4}{2\beta}, \frac{\beta-4}{2\beta}]$. Then splitting the series in order to ensure its infinite part is in $[-\frac{\beta-2}{2\beta^2}, \frac{\beta-2}{2\beta^2}]$ forces its finite part in $[-\frac{\beta^2-3\beta-2}{2\beta^2}, \frac{\beta^2-3\beta-2}{2\beta^2}]$. Thus the sum of the finite part of the series and a number in $[-\frac{\beta+2}{2\beta}, \frac{\beta+2}{2\beta}]$ is a suitable input for `make_digit` to produce a stream that is still in $[-\frac{\beta+2}{2\beta}, \frac{\beta+2}{2\beta}]$ an so on.

A simple way to compute series converging in $[-1, 1]$ but outside $[-\frac{\beta-4}{2\beta}, \frac{\beta-4}{2\beta}]$ is to divide its terms by the base β by adding a zero in front of the stream of each finite part of the series. Thus the series will converge in the right interval if $\beta \geq 6$ and finally we multiply it by the base to compute the initial series.

6   Computing Multiplication

Multiplication can be defined as a series and we can use the previous technique to define it.

$$u \times v = \sum_{i=1}^{\infty} \frac{u_i}{\beta^i} \times v$$

Bertot shows that in the multiplication, the parameter y that appears in the technique we described, is useless. Indeed at each step it is multiplied by β but then it is used in a computation where it is divided by β. The parameter n is also useless because $\sum_{i=n}^{\infty} \frac{u_i}{\beta^i}$ is the original stream u without its first n digits. The general function we have to defined is $f(\beta, u, v, r) = u \times v + r$. To do this, we first have to read the first digit of $u = k::u'$, then:

$$f(\beta, u, v, r) = \frac{k + u'}{\beta} \times v + r = \frac{k \times v}{\beta} + r + \frac{u' \times v}{\beta}$$

Then we use `make_digit` to find the first digit of the result.
If $d::r' = \mathtt{make\_digit}(\frac{k\times v}{\beta} + r)$ and $|\frac{u'\times v}{\beta}| \leq \frac{\beta-2}{2\beta^2}$ then

$$f(\beta, u, v, r) = d::f(\beta, u', v, r')$$

As we said before, we can see here the division of $u' \times v$ by the base which is canceled by the multiplication that appears in the recursive call. We need that the inequality $|\frac{u'\times v}{\beta}| \leq \frac{\beta-2}{2\beta^2}$ holds to make this definition valid. A simple way to ensure it is to divide the parameter v by the base, adding the digit 0 in the head of the stream, and multiply the result by the base:

$$\beta \times f(\beta, u, 0::v, r) = \beta \times u \times \frac{v}{\beta} + r = u \times v + r$$

Then it becomes trivial that for all streams u' and v representing numbers in $[-1, 1]$, $|\frac{u'\times \frac{v}{\beta}}{\beta}| \leq \frac{\beta-2}{2\beta^2}$ holds.

Another problem we have to deal with is to ensure that the parameter we give to `make_digit` can be computed i.e. $\frac{k\times v}{\beta} + r \in [-1, 1]$. Our first approach was to modify the algorithm, reading one more digit of u. In this way, thanks to redundancy, we could easily modify the argument given to `make_digit` in order to be in $[-1, 1]$. But seven different cases had to be considered so it became much more difficult to understand the algorithm and especially proof. When we improved our specification of `make_digit` we decided to use it to simplify our multiplication. We just have to ensure that $|\frac{k\times v}{\beta}| \leq \frac{\beta-3\beta-2}{2\beta}$. Here adding a zero in front of v is almost enough. Adding a second one makes the needed inequality holds.

So we now compute the multiplication in this way:

$$\beta \times \beta \times f(\beta, u, 0::0::v, 0) = \beta \times \beta \times u \times \frac{\frac{v}{\beta}}{\beta} + 0 = u \times v$$

The last requirement we need is a way to compute the multiplication of a stream by a digit as $\frac{k\times v}{\beta}$ occurs in the parameter of `make_digit`.

First we defined it as a series similarly as the multiplication of streams. Among the requirements for this series, we need to compute the representation of rational numbers. This easy operation was already done in the first basic functions we defined.

Unfortunately this computation of multiplication was less efficient than the definition of Bertot for the base two. Indeed when using arbitrary integers base the multiplication of a stream by a digit becomes a problem. In base 2 it was just a multiplication by 0 or by 1 or a division by the base i.e. direct operations but now we compute it as a series.

We found inspiration in Avizienis' work [1] to improve our multiplication of a stream by a digit. The idea is that with the set of digits we use, we have enough redundancy to produce at the same time the digits of the addition of $\lceil\frac{\beta}{2}\rceil$ numbers. This addition can be defined in the same schema we used for the addition of two streams.

$$Add_{\beta,n} \begin{cases} [-1, \ 1]^n \times [-\beta+n, \beta-n] \mapsto [-1, \ 1] \\ x_1, \ldots, x_n, r \mapsto \frac{x_1+\ldots+x_n+r}{\beta} \end{cases}$$

Since r is a remainder of a division by β, the thinnest set of values it needs is $[-\lfloor\frac{\beta}{2}\rfloor, \lfloor\frac{\beta}{2}\rfloor]$. And thus the maximal number of streams we can add is $\lceil\frac{\beta}{2}\rceil$.

Actually, using this idea, we defined a particular case of this addition where all inputs are the same stream. This define the multiplication of a stream by a digit of $[0, \lceil\frac{\beta}{2}\rceil]$. To compute multiplication by a digit larger than $\lceil\frac{\beta}{2}\rceil$, we use this multiplication and an extra addition: $\frac{k \times x}{\beta} = \frac{(k-\beta) \times x}{\beta} + x$. If the digit is negative, then we proceed as described with the positive value and then we compute the opposite.

7 Computing Inverse

The inverse function does not fit well with the tradition of theorem provers to only support total functions. Moreover the inverse function cannot be extended easily into a total function because it is undecidable to know whether a given stream represents 0. A second problem is that the inverse of a number in $[-1, 1]$ normally is outside this interval.

A way to avoid this problem is to define a function that is only guaranteed to coincide with $x \mapsto \frac{1}{\beta^n x}$ when the input is outside $[-\frac{1}{\beta^n}, \frac{1}{\beta^n}]$ and may return a value that cannot be trusted otherwise.

The algorithm we propose is the following.

- If $n = 0$ the result should be x itself. Indeed the result we produce has to be correct only if $1 = \beta^0 \le |x|$. Then x should be equal to -1 or 1 because it is in $[-1, 1]$. In both cases we have $\frac{1}{x} = x$.
- Otherwise $1 \le n$ and we have to read the first digit of $x = k_1 :: x'$.
  - If $2 \le |k_1|$, we can turn the function into a converging series:

$$\frac{1}{\beta^n \times \frac{k_1 + x'}{\beta}} = \frac{1}{\beta^{n-1}}\frac{1}{k_1}\frac{1}{1 - \frac{-x'}{k_1}} = \frac{1}{\beta^{n-1}}\frac{1}{k_1}\sum_{i=0}^{\infty}\left(\frac{-x'}{k_1}\right)^i$$

As $2 \le |k_1|$, $|\frac{-x}{k_1}| \le \frac{1}{2}$ so it is straightforward that the series $\sum_{i=0}^{\infty}\left(\frac{-x}{k_1}\right)^i$ converges in $[-2, 2]$. The division by k_1 makes the series converging in $[-1, 1]$. Therefore a representation of the result could be the stream of this series where $n - 1$ zeros were added in front of it to compute the remaining division by β^{n-1}.
  - If $k_1 = 0$ then $\frac{1}{\beta^n \times \frac{0 + x'}{\beta}} = \frac{1}{\beta^{n-1} \times x'}$. This yields a recursive call on $n - 1$ and x'.
  - If $k_1 = 1$ then we need to read a second digit of $x = k_1 :: k_2 :: x''$.
    * If $k_2 < 0$ then $k_2 + \beta$ is in the set of signed digits of β and the prefixes $1 :: k_2$ and $0 :: (k_2 + \beta)$ are equivalent i.e. $\frac{1}{\beta} + \frac{k_2}{\beta^2} = \frac{0}{\beta} + \frac{k_1 + \beta}{\beta^2}$. Therefore we can proceed as in a previous case.
    * If $k_2 > 0$ then $k_2 - \beta$ is in the set of digits and the prefixes $1 :: k_2$ and $2 :: (k_2 - \beta)$ are equivalent. Therefore we can proceed as in a previous case.

* Otherwise $k_2 = 0$ then we cannot choose another representation of x but we can use again a series to compute the inverse:

$$\frac{1}{\beta^n \times (1::0::x'')} = \frac{1}{\beta^n \frac{1+\frac{0+x''}{\beta}}{\beta}} = \frac{1}{\beta^{n-1}} \frac{1}{1 - \frac{-x''}{\beta}} = \frac{1}{\beta^{n-1}} \sum_{i=0}^{\infty} \left(\frac{-x''}{\beta}\right)^i$$

Here again we rely on a converging series. But it is converging in $[-\frac{\beta}{\beta-1}, \frac{\beta}{\beta-1}]$ which is larger than $[-1, 1]$.

We can then distinguish two cases.

* If $2 \le n$ then we can write

$$\frac{1}{\beta^{n-1}} \sum_{i=0}^{\infty} \left(\frac{-x''}{\beta}\right)^i = \frac{1}{\beta^{n-2}} \frac{1}{\beta} \sum_{i=0}^{\infty} \left(\frac{-x''}{\beta}\right)^i$$

Thanks to the division by the base we can make the series converge inside $[-\frac{1}{\beta-1}, \frac{1}{\beta-1}]$ which is inside $[-1, 1]$. Thus the inverse will be the stream beginning by $n - 2$ zeros followed by the stream of the series.

* Otherwise $n = 1$ then we can compute

$$\frac{1}{\beta^0} \sum_{i=0}^{\infty} \left(\frac{-x''}{\beta}\right)^i = \beta \frac{1}{\beta} \sum_{i=0}^{\infty} \left(\frac{-x''}{\beta}\right)^i$$

In this case we can also compute the stream of the series divided by the base. And if the x satisfies $\frac{1}{\beta^n} \le |x|$ then this stream should be in $[-\frac{1}{\beta}, \frac{1}{\beta}]$. Therefore the result of the multiplication by the base will be guaranteed and we obtain the inverse.

• If $k_1 = -1$ then we can proceed symmetrically as $k_1 = 1$

In three cases this first step requires to describe how to compute a converging series

$$\frac{1}{k} \sum_{i=0}^{\infty} x^i \quad \text{with} \quad 2 \le |k| \le \beta \quad \text{and} \quad |x| \le \frac{1}{k}.$$

So we first should define the function $f(x, j, n, r) = r + \beta^j \sum_{i=n}^{\infty} x^i$. As we saw, to compute this series we need to find a $p \ge n$ such that $|\beta^j \sum_{i=p}^{\infty} x^i| \le \frac{\beta-2}{2\beta^2}$. So our first intuition was that finding a suitable p and computing $r + \beta^j \sum_{i=n}^{p-1} x^i$ iteratively should be too expensive. So we tied to find a different way to compute the series that need less computation for each step.

We noticed that for each $l \ge 1$,

$$\frac{1}{k} \sum_{i=0}^{\infty} x^i = \frac{1}{k}(1 + \ldots + x^{l-1} + x^l(1 + \ldots + x^{l-1}) + \ldots)$$

$$= \frac{1}{k} \sum_{i=0}^{l-1} x^i \sum_{i=0}^{\infty} (x^l)^i.$$

In this way we can find a l such that the computation of the series could be simplified. If we choose it even, then the terms of the series $\sum_{i=0}^{\infty}(x^l)^i$ will be all positive and if we choose it larger than $\log_k \beta$ then we will have $|x^l| \leq \frac{1}{\beta}$, since $|x| \leq \frac{1}{k}$.

It will be now easy to define the function that for $0 \leq x \leq \frac{1}{\beta}$ and y in $[-1, 1]$, computes:

$$f(\beta, n, x, y, r) = r + \beta^n \times y \sum_{i=n}^{\infty} x^i$$

$$= r + \beta^n \times y \times x^n + \beta^n \times y \sum_{i=n+1}^{\infty} x^i.$$

As we described in the technique, to split the series in $n + 1$ we need:

$$|\beta^n \times y \sum_{i=n+1}^{\infty} x^i| \leq \frac{\beta - 2}{2\beta^2}$$

$$\beta^n \times |y| \times |\frac{x^{n+2}}{1 - x}| \leq \frac{\beta - 2}{2\beta^2}$$

$$\beta^n \frac{x^{n+2}}{1 - x} \leq \frac{\beta - 2}{2\beta^2}$$

$$\frac{x}{\beta(1 - x)} \leq \frac{\beta - 2}{2\beta^2}$$

$$2x\beta^2 \leq \beta(1 - x)(\beta - 2)$$

$$2\beta \leq (\beta - 1)(\beta - 2)$$

$$4 < \beta$$

So at each step we can split the series in this way if we work with a base greater than 4. We use extra parameters to keep the precomputed value $\beta^n \times y \times x^n$. In this way, our implementation requires one multiplication and one addition for each step. The initialization requires to compute x^l and $\sum_{i=0}^{l-1} x^i$ such that l is even and $|x^l| \leq \frac{1}{\beta}$. And by composing all this functions, we define the inverse $x, n \mapsto \frac{1}{\beta^n \times x}$ when x is outside $[-\frac{1}{\beta^n}, \frac{1}{\beta^n}]$.

8   Formalization and Proofs of Correctness

We give here a brief an idea of how to use co-induction to implement and certify these algorithms in Coq. Co-induction [7] in Coq provides a way to define types of potentially infinite objects. It allows us to implement this representation of real numbers and our algorithms as we described them. The type of infinite sequences of objects of any type A could be define as follow.

```
CoInductive stream (A:Set): Set :=
  | Cons : A → stream A → stream A.
```

Cons should not be understood as a way to construct an infinite stream from another since we cannot give an initial infinite stream, but as a way to decompose an infinite stream into a finite part and an infinite part that could be described again with Cons and so on. A co-inductive object is lazily evaluated each time one asks for a better description. The only way to force a step of evaluation of such an object in Coq is using pattern matching.

We can then define streams using co-recursive functions, for instance the stream of 0 which obviously represents the real number 0.

```
Cofix zero : stream ℤ :=
  Cons 0 one.
```

Coq prevents the users from defining non terminating functions. The way to certify that recursive functions always terminate in Coq is to only provide structural recursion on inductive types. For co-recursive functions it means that one can expect the evaluation of any finite part of the object described by the function to terminate. This is guaranteed if co-recursive calls are done after producing a part of the result i.e. inside a constructor of the co-inductive type. Coq automatically rejects co-recursive definitions that do not satisfy this *guarded condition*.

Co-inductive predicates can be defined to describe an infinite behavior of such an object. We defined in this way a relation between a stream and the number it represents using the fact we explained before: $k::s = \frac{k+s}{\beta}$.

```
CoInductive represents (β : ℤ): stream ℤ → ℝ → Prop :=
  | rep : ∀ s r k, −β < k < β →  −1 ≤ r ≤ 1 →
    represents β s r → represents β (Cons k s) (k+r)/β .
```

It means that if k is in the set of signed digits of base β and s is the representation in this base of a number $r \in [-1, 1]$, then $\frac{k+r}{\beta}$ is the value represented by Cons k s in base β.

Then to show that an algorithm we define on our representation is computing a mathematics function, we prove that the predicate **represents** is some kind of a morphism between the algorithm and the function. For instance, the theorem that the stream **zero** represents the real value 0 is

```
Theorem zero_correct :
  ∀ β, represents β zero 0.
```

Proving a co-inductive predicate in Coq means constructing a co-recursive function whose type is the predicate. The tactic cofix helps to construct interactively such functions. It simply adds the goal to the hypothesis. But one has to prove a finite and non-empty part of the theorem before applying this hypothesis since it corresponds to describe a co-recursive call. When the user has finished the proof he asks Coq to validate it. The system Coq will perform the verification that the guarded condition holds and accept the proof only if it is successful.

All the algorithms presented here are implemented and certified in Coq. We provide additional certified algorithms:

- absolute value
- minimum and maximum
- injection from rational numbers to our representation
- constant π
- a comparison test: $\texttt{compare}(x, y, n) = true$ if $x + \frac{1}{\beta^n} \leq y$

The development and some additional information can be found in $\texttt{http://}$ $\texttt{www-sop.inria.fr/marelle/Nicolas.Julien/exactreals.html}$.

9 Benchmarks

The goal of formalizing the base in this library was to use fast operations on integers. We present here some benches inside the proof system Coq. The digits are implemented with the library $\texttt{BigZ}$ [8] which provides fast operations on non-bounded integers using an implementation of native integers [13] in Coq.

We compared the time of computation of the same number in different bases. We also compared with previous work on base 2 (LCR) [2]. For each base we computed the number of digit needed for the same precision: n digits in base β give a precision of the number of $\frac{1}{\beta^n}$. For instance knowing 10 digits in base 2^{10} is equivalent to knowing 1 digit in base 2^{100}. These computations were made on a computer with two processors P4 3.40GHz and 1GB of memory.

- Computation of $\frac{3}{7} + \frac{5}{9}$

Used Base	LCR (2)	2^{31}	2^{62}	2^{124}	2^{248}	2^{496}
Number of digit	248000	16000	8000	4000	2000	1000
Time (s)	Computation failure	3.600	1.896	1.036	0.584	0.348

- Computation of $\frac{3}{7} \times \frac{5}{9}$

Used Base	LCR (2)	2^{31}	2^{62}	2^{124}	2^{248}	2^{496}
Number of digit	7440	240	120	60	30	15
Time (s)	77	7.032	2.364	0.852	0.384	0.220

It is clear here that the use of big bases improves computations. The reason is that since the complexity of operation we use should not be affected when the size of the base is increasing, reducing the number of digit reduces the number of recursive steps.

– Computation of $\frac{\pi}{4}$

Used Base	LCR (2)	2^{31}	2^{62}	2^{124}	2^{248}	2^{496}
Number of digit	3472	112	56	28	14	7
Time (s)	Computation failure	14.6	5.57	3.49	4.03	6.93

Here $\frac{\pi}{4}$ is computed with more than one thousand of decimals : $\frac{1}{2^{3472}} = \frac{1}{4\times(2^{10})^{347}} \leq \frac{1}{10^{1041}}$. We can see here that even if the efficiency is firstly growing with the base, with very large bases it is decreasing. A reason could be that since we need to compute only a few digits with big bases, the efficiency of computation on integers starts to matter. Indeed for the test on adding or multiplying all computed integers were lower than the square of the base. Here as contrary we used integers for intermediate computation that can be much larger.

– Computation of $\frac{1}{\beta^1\times\left(\frac{3}{7}+\frac{5}{9}\right)}$

Used Base	2^{31}	2^{62}	2^{124}	2^{248}	2^{496}
Number of digit	16	8	4	2	1
Time (s)	0.056	0.196	0.740	3.176	15.3

Surprisingly we can observe an inverse behavior here. A possible explanation is that in the trick we use, we split the series in finite sums of $2 \times \log_k \beta$ terms to compute each digit. It's more than needed. And the bigger the base, the larger the difference between what we compute and what we need. Redesigning the inverse with the new technique we described may be a way to improve its efficiency.

10   Conclusion and Future Work

Our work contributes mainly to the problem of computing converging series. Previous work only gave insights for the computation of series with all positive terms, but we identified the problems that may be encountered when terms may have different signs. We propose a new approach to decompose each step of the computation, embodied in our function make_digit and we show that series that are proved to converge in a shorter interval than [-1,1] are easier to handle and we propose a technique to map all cases to the easy ones. Properties and tactics are also described to simplify the certification of implementation of new series.

An important point is that this library is compatible with the reduction mechanism of Coq. It means that all operations we provide can be evaluated inside the proof assistant and computation on real numbers can be used as genuine proofs. This could be helpful for theorems relying on computations [10]. Moreover by formalizing the base, the operations are much more efficient than previous work on base two.

We are now working on improving the efficiency of the inverse thanks to our better description of the computation of series. We also would like to define analytic functions using their taylor series. Better understanding the issues of computing converging power series would be helpful.

References

1. Avizienis, A.A.: Signed-digit number representations for fast parallel arithmetic. IRE Transactions on Electronic Computers 10, 389–400 (1961)
2. Bertot, Y.: Affine functions and series with co-inductive real numbers. Mathematical Structure in Computer Sciences 17(1) (2007)
3. Bertot, Y., Castéran, P.: Interactive Theorem Proving and Program Development. In: Coq'Art:the Calculus of Inductive Constructions, Springer, Heidelberg (2004)
4. Ciaffaglione, A., Di Gianantonio, P.: A coinductive approach to real numbers. In: Coquand, T., Nordström, B., Dybjer, P., Smith, J. (eds.) TYPES 1999. LNCS, vol. 1956, pp. 114–130. Springer, Heidelberg (2000)
5. Coq development team. The Coq Proof Assistant Reference Manual, version 8.0 (2004)
6. Edalat, A., Heckmann, R.: Computing with Real Numbers. In: Barthe, G., Dybjer, P., Pinto, L., Saraiva, J. (eds.) APPSEM 2000. LNCS, vol. 2395, pp. 193–267. Springer, Heidelberg (2000)
7. Giménez, E.: Codifying guarded definitions with recursive schemes. In: Smith, J., Dybjer, P., Nordström, B. (eds.) TYPES 1994. LNCS, vol. 996, pp. 39–59. Springer, Heidelberg (1995)
8. Grégoire, B., Théry, L.: A Purely Functional Library for Modular Arithmetic and Its Application to Certifying Large Prime Numbers. In: Furbach, U., Shankar, N. (eds.) IJCAR 2006. LNCS (LNAI), vol. 4130, pp. 423–437. Springer, Heidelberg (2006)
9. Muller, J.-M.: Elementary Functions, Algorithms and implementation. Birkhäuser, Basel (1997)
10. Nipkow, T., Bauer, G., Schultz, P.: Flyspeck I: Tame Graphs. In: Furbach, U., Shankar, N. (eds.) IJCAR 2006. LNCS (LNAI), vol. 4130, pp. 21–35. Springer, Heidelberg (2006)
11. Niqui, M.: Coinductive Correctness of Homographic and Quadratic Algorithms for Exact Real Numbers. In: Altenkirch, T., McBride, C. (eds.) TYPES 2006. LNCS, vol. 4502, pp. 203–220. Springer, Heidelberg (2007)
12. O'Connor, R.: A monadic, functional implementation of real numbers. Mathematical Structures in Computer Science 17, 129–159 (2007)
13. Spiwack, A.: Ajouter des entiers machine coq (2006), http://arnaud.spiwack.free.fr/papers/nativint.pdf
14. Vuillemin, J.E.: Exact real computer arithmetic with continued fractions. IEEE Transactions on Computers 39(8), 1087–1105 (1990)

Pure, Declarative, and Constructive Arithmetic Relations (Declarative Pearl)[*]

Oleg Kiselyov[1], William E. Byrd[2], Daniel P. Friedman[2], and Chung-chieh Shan[3]

[1] FNMOC
oleg@pobox.com
[2] Indiana University
{webyrd,dfried}@cs.indiana.edu
[3] Rutgers University
ccshan@cs.rutgers.edu

Abstract. We present *decidable* logic programs for addition, multiplication, division with remainder, exponentiation, and logarithm with remainder over the *unbounded* domain of natural numbers. Our predicates represent *relations* without mode restrictions or annotations. They are fully decidable under the common, DFS-like, SLD resolution strategy of Prolog or under an interleaving refinement of DFS. We prove that the evaluation of our arithmetic goals always terminates, given arguments that share no logic variables. Further, the (possibly infinite) set of solutions for a goal denotes exactly the corresponding mathematical relation. (For SLD without interleaving, and for some infinite solution sets, only half of the relation's domain may be covered.) We define predicates to handle unary (for illustration) and binary representations of natural numbers, and prove termination and completeness of these predicates. Our predicates are written in pure Prolog, without cut (!), var/1, or other nonlogical operators. The purity and minimalism of our approach allows us to declare arithmetic in other logic systems, such as Haskell type classes.

1 Introduction

Logic programming is said to be programming with relations, but arithmetic is often dealt with in a non-relational, restricted way. For example, Prolog's built-in is/2 predicate for evaluating arithmetic expressions does not allow free (unbound) logic variables in the expressions. Whereas the goal Z is 6*7 succeeds, binding 42 to Z, the related goal 42 is X*Y is considered erroneous because its multiplicands 'are not sufficiently instantiated.' Multiplication is not treated as a ternary relation between multiplicands and the product because of mode restrictions on the first two arguments. Constraint logic programming (CLP) overcomes this drawback to some extent [1]; for example, disjunctive Datalog [2] treats arithmetic relationally. Indeed, relational handling of arithmetic was one of

---

[*] We thank Ronald Garcia and the anonymous reviewers for many helpful comments.

J. Garrigue and M. Hermenegildo (Eds.): FLOPS 2008, LNCS 4989, pp. 64–80, 2008.
© Springer-Verlag Berlin Heidelberg 2008

the motivations for CLP. Unfortunately, this flexibility has a price: CLP restricts the arithmetic domain to be finite and changes the evaluation mode of the logic programming system away from Kowalski's 'predicate as function' model [3].

We present fully relational arithmetic on the *unbounded* domain of binary natural numbers for conventional (SLD [4], or SLD with interleaving [5]) logic programming systems. We define predicates for addition, multiplication, division with remainder, and logarithm with remainder. These predicates express the remaining arithmetic operations, including subtraction and exponentiation. These so-called base predicates have *no* mode restrictions or annotations on their arguments, and are implemented in a *pure* logic system without cut (!), the var/1 predicate, or negation. Furthermore, each base predicate terminates under SLD evaluation (and re-evaluation, upon backtracking), provided that the predicate's arguments share no logic variables. The stream of answers produced by (re-)evaluating each arithmetic predicate under SLD with interleaving [5] covers exactly the corresponding mathematical relation; under SLD resolution and some infinite domains, only half of the relation is covered.

In particular, we define the following decidable predicates:

add/3 such that add(X, Y, Z) can be used to add two numbers X and Y to get Z, to subtract X or Y from Z, to decompose Z into summands, or to compare two naturals. For example, we can determine that the triple $(1, 2, 3)$ is in the ternary addition relation[1] by evaluating either the goal add($\mathbf{1, 2, 3}$)[2] or the goal add(X, Y, Z), $X = \mathbf{1}, Y = \mathbf{2}, Z = \mathbf{3}$. By evaluating add($X, \mathbf{3}, \mathbf{2}$) we determine, also in finite time, that the addition relation does *not* include *any* triple $(n, 3, 2)$.

mul/3 such that mul(X, Y, Z) can be used, inter alia, to multiply X and Y, to factor Z, or to generate a stream of triples related by multiplication.

div/4 such that div(N, M, Q, R) succeeds if and only if $N = M \cdot Q + R < M \cdot (Q + 1)$.[3] For instance, the goal div(1,0,_,_) to relate the divisor zero to a non-zero dividend fails instantly, without trying to enumerate all natural numbers. The goal div($5, M, \mathbf{1}, \_$) finds all numbers M that divide 5, perhaps unevenly, with a quotient of 1. The answers are 5, 4, and 3. Finally, div(5,M,7,_) fails in finite time rather than diverging.

log/4 such that log(N, B, Q, R) succeeds if and only if $N = B^Q + R < B^{Q+1}$. We can use log/4 to perform exponentiation, find logarithms, and find n-th roots.

We prove that these base predicates are decidable and that the arithmetic relations over natural numbers form their universal model (see the *faithfulness* property introduced in §2).

---

[1] We mean a relation that relates triples of numbers (x, y, z) so that $x + y = z$.

[2] $\mathbf{3}$ means the representation of the binary numeral 3, which in Prolog is encoded as [1,1] (§3).

[3] This equation implies that div/4 fails when M is $\mathbf{0}$. Hence mul/3 is not reducible to div/4. Besides, the former is simpler and is part of the implementation of the latter.

1.1 Challenges

We require the predicates to be both effective and efficient. First, the evaluation of base arithmetic goals must terminate. Put differently, it must be effectively computable whether a tuple of naturals is included in or *excluded* from a base arithmetic relation (addition, multiplication, division with remainder, and logarithm with remainder). Further, these computations must finish without taking an exponential amount of time or space with respect to the 'search depth' (corresponding, in the case of binary numbers, to the logarithm of the largest number appearing in the computation). In other words, we wish to maintain the efficiency of depth-first search (DFS) (or DFS with interleaving [5, 6]) of the and-or tree expressing the solution space of our base goals.

The main challenge in defining our predicates is that the domains of natural numbers, and of arithmetic relations in general, are infinite—enumerating them is not an option. The incompleteness of DFS (used in SLD resolution) immediately presents a problem. For example, assuming that `gen/1` is a predicate that generates all (ground) natural numbers in sequence, one may be tempted to implement `mul/3` (separating the generation and testing for clarity) as

```
mul(X,Y,Z) :- gen(A), X=A, gen(B), Y=B, gen(C), Z=C, C is A*B.
```

In addition to its obvious inefficiency, this implementation[4] often diverges under DFS. For example, evaluating $mul(X, Y, 1)$ instantiates A and B to 0 and C to 1, causing the goal `C is A*B` to fail; after backtracking into `gen(B)`, `mul/3` keeps forever instantiating B to larger and larger positive numbers, each time resulting in failure of the goal `1 is 0*B`.

One may attempt to fix this problem by using a complete search strategy, such as breadth-first search (BFS) or iteratively-deepening DFS. Even ignoring efficiency concerns, this implementation of `mul/3` is still unacceptable: a complete search strategy will find a solution *if it exists*, but if no solution exists the search will continue forever. For example, although BFS finds the instantiation of Y that satisfies $mul(1, Y, 2)$, the goal $mul(2, Y, 1)$ still diverges. Thus we must devise a termination criterion for `mul/3`.

Devising a termination criterion may seem easy. For example, when searching for X and Y that satisfy the goal $mul(X, Y, 5)$, we only need to examine X and Y values up to 5—since the search space is finite, the evaluation of the goal certainly terminates. The problem arises when determining whether the third argument in a specific use of `mul/3` is instantiated to a ground numeral. This task is trivial if we use the 'impure' non-logical features provided by Prolog's reflection facilities, such as the infamous `var/1` predicate. Even if `var/1` were absent from Prolog, it could be emulated using cuts and negation. We disavow such tools—we aim to implement our predicates in a pure subset of Prolog, without cuts, reflection, or any way to distinguish a logic variable. This aim for purity is a challenge that in return makes our approach most elucidating and extensible.

---

[4] Braßel, Fischer, and Huch [7] describe the drawbacks of this residuation-based approach in functional logic programming.

The final challenge is that the binary representation of a number may not be structurally part of that of its successor. For example, the binary numeral 111 (in decimal, 7) is not structurally part of its successor 1000. This lack of structural inclusion prevents straightforward structural recursion.

1.2 Termination and Solvability

These challenges make the arithmetic predicates tricky to code. It is not obvious that the resulting predicates have the claimed properties, in particular, that they terminate in all modes. We therefore devote much of the paper to proofs. A typical termination theorem we prove assures that evaluating or re-evaluating add(X, Y, Z) terminates, provided that the terms initially associated with X, Y, and Z share no logic variables. Successive re-evaluations of this goal recursively enumerate the stream of unique triples (X, Y, Z) of potentially non-ground terms whose denotation (§2.2) is the domain $\{ (u, v, w) \in X \times Y \times Z : u+v = w \}$. Thus, membership and non-membership are computable for base arithmetic relations.

We guarantee termination only for stand-alone base arithmetic goals but not their conjunctions (see §2.1). This non-compositionality is expected, since conjunctions of arithmetic goals can express Diophantine equations; were such conjunctions guaranteed to terminate, we would be able to solve Hilbert's 10th problem, which is undecidable [8]. We also do not guarantee termination if the goal's arguments share variables. Such a goal can be expressed by conjoining a sharing-free base goal and equalities.

We proceed as follows. In §2 we define addition and multiplication predicates for a *unary* representation of natural numbers. We introduce solution sets, §2.1, to carefully establish termination for these predicates, laying a foundation for our analysis of binary predicates. In §3 we introduce our representation of binary numerals, and in §4 and §5 we define predicates for binary addition and subtraction, and multiplication, respectively. In §6 we briefly describe our predicates for binary division, exponentiation, and logarithm. For lack of space, we relegate our pure Prolog implementation of exponentiation, logarithm, and non-interleaving binary multiplication to the accompanying source code,[5] along with additional proofs, tests, examples, and discussion. We review related work in §7, and conclude in §8. The full version of this paper[6] includes appendices outlining proofs of the properties of solution sets. We have also implemented declarative arithmetic as Haskell type-level relations (type classes) [9].

2 Predicates for Unary Arithmetic

We begin with unary numerals. Unary is simpler than binary, since every unary numeral is structurally part of its successor, so we may use structural recursion. However, membership and non-membership still need to be decidable for the base arithmetic predicates, whose domains are infinite however they are represented.

---

[5] http://okmij.org/ftp/Prolog/Arithm/
[6] http://okmij.org/ftp/Prolog/Arithm/arithm.pdf

Hence, the unary case already presents our main challenges. The unary case also lets us introduce and illustrate most of our terminology in this section.

We represent unary numerals as lists of atoms u: [] denotes zero, [u] denotes one, [u,u] denotes two, etc.[7] Throughout this section we use the shorthand **n** to indicate our representation of the number n—that is, the list of u's of length n.

Although Prolog is not statically typed, we assume an implicit type of 'unary numerals' and an implicit typing of logic variables. For example, the implicit type of the term $[u, u \mid X]$ is 'unary numeral'; the logic variable X has the same type. The type predicate for unary numerals can be expressed as a generator:

```
genu([]).
genu([u|X]) :- genu(X).
```

A term t has the type of 'unary numeral' if the goal genu(t) succeeds. When providing denotations for terms and goals we use the implicit type of a logic variable to characterize the variable's domain.

We can add unary numerals with a special case of the append/3 predicate.

```
add([],X,X).
add([u|X],Y,[u|Z]) :- add(X,Y,Z).
```

We can use add/3 to add numerals: the goal add($1, 2, X$) unifies X with **3**. We can also use add/3 for subtraction: both add($X, 1, 3$) and add($1, X, 3$) unify X with **2**, and the evaluation of add($X, 3, 1$) fails finitely. We can further use add/3 to decompose a number into its summands: for example, add($X, Y, 3$) has four solutions, in which X and Y are unified in turn with **0** and **3**, **1** and **2**, **2** and **1**, and **3** and **0**. Finally, passing three distinct uninstantiated logic variables to add/3 lets us enumerate the domain of addition over the natural numbers. The evaluation of the query add(X, Y, Z) in Prolog yields an infinite set of solutions:

```
X = []        Y = _G188   Z = _G188 ;
X = [u]       Y = _G188   Z = [u|_G188] ;
X = [u, u]    Y = _G188   Z = [u, u|_G188] ;
```

and so forth. This stream of solutions represents the infinite addition relation *in two different ways*. First, the goal produces an infinite number of solutions; we can always re-evaluate the goal to get another solution. Second, each solution represents infinitely many triples, all members of the addition relation. For example, the second solution compactly represents the infinitely many triples of naturals (x, y, z) for which x is one and z is the successor of y. Each instantiation of the free logic variable _G188 to a member of its domain (corresponding to its implicit type) yields a new triple of naturals that is a member of the addition relation. We will make extensive use of this compact representation of infinite domains when proving termination properties of our predicates.

---

[7] We could just as easily use a more common representation z, $s(z)$, $s(s(z))$, etc. We chose lists for consistency with our binary representation.

2.1   Solution Sets

To formulate propositions about `add/3` and other predicates, we introduce the notion of *solution sets*, which accounts for the search strategy used to run a logic program (unlike other procedural notions of solutions). We use Prolog syntax [4]. We identify a bound logic variable with the term it is bound to, so all variables are free for us, as for Lloyd [4]. Our goals are all pure (contain no `var/1`, negation, or cuts).

We assume an *idempotent* notion of substitution [10]: a substitution θ is a finite map $\{ X_i = t_i \}$ from logic variables X_i to terms t_i such that no t_j contains any X_i. We write the application of the substitution θ to a term t as $t\theta$; this application easily extends to tuples of terms and sets of tuples.

Definition 1 (Conjunction of substitutions). *We define the* conjunction $\theta\xi$ *of two substitutions θ and ξ by treating them as sets of equations $\{ X_i = t_i \}$: we combine both sets (the result may contain two equations for the same X_i) and use unification to solve the resulting equations [10, §2.2.3]. Our conjunction of substitutions is thus commutative and associative. Because of the unification our conjunction is partial: if unification fails we call the original substitutions* contradictory.

We can interpret a goal g as a function from a substitution to a (finite or infinite) stream of substitutions. Both SLD and SLD-interleaving [5] interpret (right-associative and non-commutative) disjunction and conjunction by

$$(g_1; g_2)(\theta) = g_1(\theta) \oplus g_2(\theta),$$
$$(g_1, g_2)(\theta) = g_1(\theta) \star g_2$$

where the *bind* operation $\star$ is defined recursively by

$$[] \star f = [],$$
$$[\theta \mid \vec{\theta}] \star f = (f\theta) \oplus (\vec{\theta} \star f).$$

The difference between SLD and SLD-interleaving is that $\oplus$ above is defined as stream concatenation in SLD but stream interleaving in SLD-interleaving.

Definition 2 (Solution sequence and set). *Given a predicate g/n and n terms $t_1, \ldots, t_n$ that may contain logic variables, a solution of a goal $g(t_1, \ldots, t_n)$ is an n-tuple $(t'_1, \ldots, t'_n)$ where each t'_i instantiates t_i after the evaluation of the goal succeeds using SLD or SLD-interleaving strategy. A solution can be represented as $(t_1, \ldots, t_n)\theta$ for some substitution θ. A solution sequence is a sequence of solutions obtained by evaluating and successively re-evaluating a goal. The sequence is a* solution set *if no two of its members unify with each other.*

A goal that fails has the empty solution set. A goal whose evaluation or re-evaluation does not terminate does not have a solution sequence. In contrast, the goal $\mathbf{genu}(X)$ does have a solution sequence (which can be infinite) because its evaluation and re-evaluation always terminates. We assume SLD as the default solution strategy. If we add the clause add(X,[],X). as a well-meaning optimization $(X + 0 = X)$ after the first clause of add/3 above, the solution sequence may not necessarily be a solution set: for example, the goal $\text{add}(X, Y, \mathbf{0})$ will have $(\mathbf{0}, \mathbf{0}, \mathbf{0})$ in duplicate.

The notion of solution sequence is constructive, 'proof-theoretic,' to be distinguished from a model of a logic program: each solution has been actually *derived*, in finite time, from the facts and rules at hand using the given solution strategy. A term in a solution may contain free logic variables. We can prove the following properties of solution sets (see Appendix A of our full paper).

Proposition 1. *If a goal $g(t_1, \ldots, t_n)$ has a (finite or infinite) solution set $\{ (t_1, \ldots, t_n)\theta_i \}$ and ξ is a substitution that contradicts only finitely many θ_i, then the goal $g(t_1\xi, \ldots, t_n\xi)$ has a solution set $\{ (t_1, \ldots, t_n)(\theta_i\xi) \}$, omitting the elements where θ_i and ξ are contradictory.*

The solution set of a conjunction of goals $g_1(t_{11}, \ldots, t_{1n})$ and $g_2(t_{21}, \ldots, t_{2n})$ is (as in a natural database join) the set of tuples $\{ (t_{11}, \ldots, t_{1n}, t_{21}, \ldots, t_{2n}) \}$ after the evaluation of the conjunction has succeeded.

Proposition 2. *If the goals g_1 and g_2 have a finite solution set, then the conjunction g_1, g_2 has a finite solution set.*

This proposition is a corollary of the previous proposition. It does not generally hold if the solution set of one of the conjuncts is infinite. For example,

```
mf([],[u|Y]) :- genu(Y).
mf([u|X],Y)  :- mf([u|X],Y).
```

The goal $\text{mf}(X, Y)$, with the variables X and Y free, has the infinite solution set $\{ (\mathbf{0}, \mathbf{i}) : i \in \mathbb{N}^+ \}$. However, the (left or right) conjunction of this goal with $X = \mathbf{1}$ diverges and has no solution set. Similarly, the conjunction of $\text{mf}(X, Y)$ with $X = Y$ has no solution set either. Prop. 1 applies to neither conjunction because the substitutions $\{X = \mathbf{1}\}$ and $\{X = Y\}$ both contradict infinitely many solution-set substitutions (in fact, all of them). The latter conjunction is equivalent to the goal $\text{mf}(X, X)$; such sharing of variables among the arguments of a goal is lethal to the termination guarantees below (such as Prop. 9).

Proposition 3. *If a goal $g_1(t_1, \ldots, t_n)$ has a finite solution set $\{ (t_1, \ldots, t_n)\theta_i \}$ and the goal $g_2(t'_1\theta_1, \ldots, t'_m\theta_1)$ has an infinite solution set $\{ (t'_1\theta_1, \ldots, t'_m\theta_1)\xi_j \}$, then the conjunction g_1, g_2 has the infinite solution set $\{ (t_1, \ldots, t_n, t'_1, \ldots, t'_m)(\theta_1\xi_j) \}$.*

This proposition describes the incompleteness of SLD: its underlying depth-first search becomes trapped exploring the leftmost infinite branch of the search tree. However, using the SLD-interleaving strategy, we can strengthen the proposition:

Proposition 4. *If a goal $g_1(t_1, \ldots, t_n)$ has a (finite or infinite) solution set $\{ (t_1, \ldots, t_n)\theta_i \}$ and the goal $g_2(t'_1\theta_i, \ldots, t'_m\theta_i)$ has a non-empty (finite or infinite) solution set $\{ (t'_1\theta_i, \ldots, t'_m\theta_i)\xi_{ij} \}$ for each i, then the conjunction g_1, g_2 has the solution set $\{ (t_1, \ldots, t_n, t'_1, \ldots, t'_m)(\theta_i\xi_{ij}) \}$.*

The proof is based on the laws of fair conjunction and disjunction in [5]; details are given in Appendix B of our full paper. We use analogous properties for disjunctions of goals.

2.2 Properties of Addition: Solution Sets of Addition

If t is a term and n is a natural number, then we write $[\mathsf{u}^n \,|\, t]$ to mean $[\mathsf{u}, \ldots, \mathsf{u} \,|\, t]$ where $\mathsf{u}, \ldots, \mathsf{u}$ consists of n occurrences of u.

One can easily prove the following propositions:

Proposition 5. *The goal* $\mathtt{add}(X, Y, Z)$, *where* X *and* Y *are instantiated to ground numerals and* Z *is free, has a singleton solution set unifying* Z *with the numeral that is the sum of those corresponding to* X *and* Y.

That is, if the first two arguments of $\mathtt{add/3}$ are instantiated to numerals, the goal is decidable and has one solution.

Proposition 6. *The goal* $\mathtt{add}(X, Y, Z)$ *where* Z *is instantiated to a ground numeral has a finite solution set.*

The proof is an easy induction on the third argument.

Proposition 7. *The goal* $\mathtt{add}(X, Y, Z)$, *where* X *is a ground numeral* n *and* Y *and* Z *are free, has the singleton solution set* $\{\,(\mathsf{n}, G, [\mathsf{u}^n \,|\, G])\,\}$ *where* G *is a free logic variable.*

The proof is by induction on X. The proposition easily extends to the case where Y and Z are arbitrary terms, using Prop. 1.

Proposition 8. *The goal* $\mathtt{add}(X, Y, Z)$, *where the arguments are distinct free logic variables, has an infinite solution set* $\{\,(\mathsf{n}, G, [\mathsf{u}^n \,|\, G]) : n \in \mathbb{N}\,\}$ *where* G *is a free logic variable. In each solution,* X *is unified to a ground numeral.*

The proof is by induction on X and soundness of SLD resolution.

Definition 3 (Denotation of arithmetic solutions). *The* denotation $\llbracket \cdot \rrbracket$ *of an arithmetic term or solution set is defined as follows.*

$$\llbracket \mathsf{n} \rrbracket = \{n\}$$
$$\llbracket t \rrbracket = \{\, n \in \mathbb{N} : n \geq m \,\}$$
where t is the non-ground term $[\mathsf{u}^m \,|\, X]$
where X is a free logic variable of the type of unary numerals
$$\llbracket (t_1, \ldots, t_n) \rrbracket = \llbracket t_1 \rrbracket \times \cdots \times \llbracket t_n \rrbracket$$
$$\llbracket S \rrbracket = \cup_{s \in S} \llbracket s \rrbracket \quad \text{*for a solution set S (whose elements are all disjoint)*}$$

The previous propositions along with Prop. 1 let us prove:

Proposition 9. *The goal* $\mathtt{add}(X, Y, Z)$ *where the arguments have no shared logic variables has a solution set with* X *always unified to a ground numeral. The denotation of the solution set is* $\{\,(u, v, w) \in \llbracket X \rrbracket \times \llbracket Y \rrbracket \times \llbracket Z \rrbracket : u + v = w\,\}$.

The proof simply invokes Prop. 6 or Prop. 7 if Z or X is ground. If neither Z nor X is ground, then the arguments of the goal, since they share no logic variables, contradict only finitely many solutions in the set of Prop. 8, so we invoke Prop. 1.

The proposition states that the predicate add/3 is fully decidable: for any arguments sharing no free variables, the predicate decides if the denotation of these arguments is in the domain of addition *or not*. Furthermore, for any subset of the domain of addition of the form $\{\,(u, v, w) \in [\![X]\!] \times [\![Y]\!] \times [\![Z]\!] : u + v = w\,\}$, there is a goal with exactly this denotation. We call such a predicate *faithful*.

2.3   Multiplication

Multiplication of unary numbers may seem as trivial as addition. (We will be developing several versions of multiplication, so we label the mul predicates with a numeric version suffix to distinguish them.)

```
mul1([],_,[]).
mul1([u|X],Y,Z) :- mul1(X,Y,Z1), add(Z1,Y,Z).
```

This predicate directly encodes the inductive definition of multiplication: $0 \cdot x = 0$, $(x+1) \cdot y = x \cdot y + y$. Indeed, the goal $\text{mul1}(\mathbf{3}, \mathbf{2}, X)$ has the singleton solution set with X unified with $\mathbf{6}$. However, the goal $\text{mul1}(X, \mathbf{2}, \mathbf{6})$ diverges after producing the first solution, the goal $\text{mul1}(X, \mathbf{2}, \mathbf{5})$ diverges without producing anything, and $\text{mul1}(X, Y, \mathbf{6})$ overflows the stack after producing three solutions.

The problem is left-recursion in the second clause: the goal $\text{mul1}(X, \mathbf{2}, Z)$ with free X and Z requires evaluating $\text{mul1}(X', \mathbf{2}, Z')$ again with free X' and Z'. Reordering goals in the body of the second clause eliminates left-recursion:

```
mul2([],_,[]).
mul2([u|X],Y,Z) :- add(Z1,Y,Z), mul2(X,Y,Z1).
```

Now $\text{mul2}(X, \mathbf{2}, \mathbf{6})$ has a singleton solution set and $\text{mul2}(X, \mathbf{2}, \mathbf{5})$ fails finitely. However, whereas before $\text{mul1}(\mathbf{3}, \mathbf{2}, X)$ had a singleton solution set (with $X = \mathbf{6}$), this version mul2 diverges after the first solution, so the goal has no solution set.

Interestingly, simply swapping the arguments to add/3 fixes the problems.

```
mul3([],_,[]).
mul3([u|X],Y,Z) :- add(Y,Z1,Z), mul3(X,Y,Z1).
```

Now $\text{mul3}(X, \mathbf{2}, \mathbf{6})$ and $\text{mul3}(\mathbf{3}, \mathbf{2}, X)$ both have singleton solution sets, and $\text{mul3}(X, \mathbf{2}, \mathbf{5})$ fails finitely. The reason is important. Evaluating $\text{mul2}(\mathbf{3}, \mathbf{2}, Z)$ requires evaluating $\text{add}(Z_1, \mathbf{2}, Z)$ whereas evaluating $\text{mul3}(\mathbf{3}, \mathbf{2}, Z)$ requires evaluating $\text{add}(\mathbf{2}, Z_1, Z)$. Although both addition goals denote the same relation, the former has the infinite solution set $\{\,(\mathbf{0}, \mathbf{2}, \mathbf{2}), (\mathbf{1}, \mathbf{2}, \mathbf{3}), (\mathbf{2}, \mathbf{2}, \mathbf{4}), \ldots\,\}$ whereas the latter has the singleton solution set $\{(\mathbf{2}, G, [\mathbf{u}, \mathbf{u} \mid G])\}$ (Prop. 7). That makes all the difference, as we prove below.

However, mul3 is not perfect. Evaluating $\text{mul3}(X, Y, \mathbf{6})$ overflows the stack, because it requires evaluating $\text{add}(Y, Z_1, \mathbf{6})$, which gives $Z_1 = \mathbf{6}, Y = \mathbf{0}$ as one solution. This solution causes a recursive call $\text{mul3}(X', Y, \mathbf{6})$, same as the original call. Thus we must treat zero multiplicands separately, taking care to avoid overlapping solutions so that the solution sequence remains a solution set.

```
mul([],_,[]).
mul([u|_],[],[]).
mul([u|X],[u|Y],Z) :- add([u|Y],Z1,Z), mul(X,[u|Y],Z1).
```

This pattern of fixing one problem only to see another problem emerge is quite common, which is why we need proofs.

Proposition 10. *The goal* $\mathtt{mul}(X, Y, Z)$*, where X and Y are instantiated to ground numerals and Z is free, has the singleton solution set that unifies Z with the numeral that is the product of the numerals for X and Y.*

The proof is an induction on X using Prop. 2 and Prop. 7.

Proposition 11. *The goal* $\mathtt{mul}(X, Y, Z)$*, where Z is instantiated to a ground numeral, has a finite solution set.*

The proof depends on Prop. 2 and Prop. 6: each solution of $\mathtt{add}([\mathtt{u}\,|\,Y], Z_1, Z))$ instantiates Z_1 to a ground numeral smaller than the numeral for Z.

Proposition 12. *The goal* $\mathtt{mul}(X, Y, Z)$*, where Y is instantiated to a positive ground numeral* $\mathbf{n}$ *and X and Z are free, has the solution set* $\{\,(\mathbf{i}, \mathbf{n}, \mathbf{i}\cdot\mathbf{n}) : i \in \mathbb{N}\,\}$*. If Y is* $\mathbf{0}$*, the solution set is finite:* $\{\,(\mathbf{0}, \mathbf{0}, \mathbf{0}), ([\mathtt{u}\,|\,X], \mathbf{0}, \mathbf{0})\,\}$*.*

The proof is by induction on Y and Prop. 7.

Proposition 13. *Under the SLD-interleaving strategy, the goal* $\mathtt{mul}(X, Y, Z)$*, where the arguments share no logic variables, has a solution set that denotes* $\{\,(u, v, w) \in [\![X]\!] \times [\![Y]\!] \times [\![Z]\!] : u \cdot v = w\,\}$*.*

The proof depends on Props. 9, 12 and 4. Thus under SLD with interleaving, our $\mathtt{mul/3}$ predicate is faithful to the multiplication relation on naturals.

Without interleaving, the goal $\mathtt{mul}(X, Y, Z)$ has the solution set $\{(\mathbf{0}, G, \mathbf{0}),$ $([\mathtt{u}\,|\,G'], \mathbf{0}, \mathbf{0}), (\mathbf{1}, \mathbf{1}, \mathbf{1}), (\mathbf{2}, \mathbf{1}, \mathbf{2}), (\mathbf{3}, \mathbf{1}, \mathbf{3}), \ldots\}$. The denotation of this solution set obviously does not cover the entire multiplication relation: the second argument gets 'stuck' on 1. Under SLD, then, our predicate $\mathtt{mul}$ covers only an infinitesimal part of the domain of multiplication. We can do better: we define a predicate $\mathtt{semimul}$ that has the *same* termination properties as $\mathtt{mul}$ but covers *half* of the domain of multiplication, namely $Y \leq X$, whichever arguments are instantiated.

We first define the predicate $\mathtt{less/2}$, corresponding to the less-than relation.

```
less([],[_|_]).
less([u|X],[u|Y]) :- less(X,Y).
```

The $\mathtt{semimul/3}$ predicate is then as follows.

```
semimul([],_,[]).
semimul([u|_],[],[]).
semimul([u|X],[u|Y],Z) :- less(X,Z), less(Y,[u|X]),
                          mul([u|X],[u|Y],Z).
```

Proposition 14. *The goal* semimul(X, Y, Z), *where the arguments are free logic variables, has a solution set that denotes* $\{ (u, v, w) \in \mathbb{N}^3 : v \leq u, \, u \cdot v = w \}$.

The proof depends on the goal less(X, Z), which asserts the trivial inequality $x < (x+1) \cdot (y+1)$ for all $x, y \in \mathbb{N}$. With free X and Z, the goal less(X, Z) has an infinite solution set whose solutions each instantiate X to a ground numeral. The goal less$(Y, [\mathsf{u} \mid X])$ then has a *finite* solution set that grounds Y as well. The last goal has thus a singleton solution set, by Prop. 10.

These attempts to define decidable multiplication even for the seemingly trivial unary case show the difficulties that become more pronounced as we move to binary arithmetic. We rely on a finite representation of infinite domains, precise instantiatedness analysis, and reasoning about SLD using search trees.

3   Binary Numerals

We represent numerals as lists of binary digits in little-endian order (least significant bit first), with zero represented as the empty list. A zero bit is denoted by o (lower-case 'oh') and a one bit is denoted by 1 (lower-case 'el')—to distinguish a number from its representation. For example, the terms [], [1], [o,1], [1,1], [o,o,1] represent 0 through 4. The last bit of a positive numeral *must* be 1. Our code below takes special care to maintain this well-formedness condition. It is trivial to convert between this and Prolog's native representations of integers.

We often use the auxiliary one-clause predicates zero/1, pos/1, and gtl/1:

```
zero([]).
pos([_|_]).
gtl([_,_|_]).
```

The goal zero(N) succeeds if N is zero. The goal pos(N) succeeds if N is positive. The goal gtl(N) succeeds if N is at least two.

The predicate genb/1 below expresses the implicit type of binary numerals.

```
genb([]).
genb([1|X]) :- genb(X).
genb([o|X]) :- pos(X), genb(X).
```

The presence of pos(X) in the last clause ensures that the last bit of a positive numeral is 1. The code below contains similar guarding occurrences of pos/1.

Recall that one challenge of binary arithmetic is that a numeral is not structurally part of its successor. However, such a notion of inclusion exists (with the attendant induction principle) if we consider the 'length' of a binary number, i.e., the number of bits in its binary representation. More precisely, the length $\|n\|$ of a numeral n is $\lfloor \log_2 n \rfloor + 1$ if $n > 0$, and 0 if $n = 0$. We define lessl/2 by

```
lessl([],[_|_]).
lessl([_|X],[_|Y]) :- lessl(X,Y).
```

It has the meaning and form of the unary less in §2.3—and the same termination properties—but compares the length of binary numbers rather their magnitude.

4   Addition and Subtraction

Our treatment of addition is inspired by hardware full-adders and multi-bit adders, as found in a digital computer's arithmetic logic unit [11]. A one-bit full-adder `full1_adder`$(C_{in}, A, B, S, C_{out})$ relates two input bits A, B and the incoming carry bit C_{in} with the sum bit S and the outgoing carry bit C_{out}, according to the equation $C_{in}+A+B = S+2C_{out}$. In Prolog, we define `full1_adder/5` by enumerating eight facts: `full1_adder(o,o,o,o,o).`, `full1_adder(o,1,o,1,o).`, etc. The multi-bit adder `fulln_adder`(C_{in}, A, B, S) relates the incoming carry bit C_{in} (either o or 1), two binary numbers A, B, and their sum S, according to the equation $C_{in} + A + B = S$. It is defined by recursively combining one-bit adders as in a ripple-carry adder of digital logic, only in our case, the summands' bitwidths need not be the same or limited.

```
fulln_adder(o,A,[],A).
fulln_adder(o,[],B,B) :- pos(B).
fulln_adder(1,A,[],R) :- fulln_adder(o,A,[1],R).
fulln_adder(1,[],B,R) :- pos(B), fulln_adder(o,[1],B,R).

fulln_adder(Cin,[1],[1],R) :- R = [R1,R2],
    full1_adder(Cin,1,1,R1,R2).
fulln_adder(Cin,[1],[BB|BR],[RB|RR]) :- pos(BR), pos(RR),
    full1_adder(Cin,1,BB,RB,Cout),
    fulln_adder(Cout,[],BR,RR).
fulln_adder(Cin,A,[1],R) :- gt1(A), gt1(R),
    fulln_adder(Cin,[1],A,R).

fulln_adder(Cin,[AB|AR],[BB|BR],[RB|RR]) :-
    pos(AR), pos(BR), pos(RR),
    full1_adder(Cin,AB,BB,RB,Cout),
    fulln_adder(Cout,AR,BR,RR).
```

The first four clauses above deal with the cases of a summand being zero. The next three clauses handle the cases of a summand being one. The last clause adds numbers at least two bits wide. We take care to keep clauses from overlapping, so the solution sequence of a `fulln_adder` goal is a solution set. The splitting of the cases and the many occurrences of `pos/1` are necessary to keep all numerals in a solution 'well-typed': If logic variables in a solution are instantiated according to their implicit types, we never see a list whose last element unifies with o.

This multi-bit adder expresses binary addition, subtraction, and ordering:

```
add(A,B,C)  :- fulln_adder(o,A,B,C).
sub(A,B,C)  :- add(B,C,A).
less(A,B)   :- pos(X), add(A,X,B).
```

Our predicate `add/3` for binary numerals satisfies Prop. 5 (by induction on $4C_{in} + 3A + B$) and Prop. 6. However, due to carry propagation (clauses 4 and 6 of `fulln_adder`), Prop. 7 and Prop. 8 no longer accurately describe the solution sets of binary add: the goal $\mathrm{add}(X, Y, Z)$, with either X or Y ground and the other arguments being distinct free variables, has an infinite solution set.

Prop. 9 holds (without X being always ground) only in the case of SLD with interleaving; for SLD, we can develop a binary addition predicate that covers half of the domain of addition, as in §2.3. The proofs begin by unrolling the recursion in clauses 3, 4, and 7 of `fulln_adder` (splitting cases for clauses 3 and 4), so that `fulln_adder` invokes itself recursively only for shorter arguments.

5   Multiplication

Binary multiplication may seem an obvious generalization of unary multiplication. The most complex case is to multiply an odd number by a positive one, $(2N+1)M = 2(NM) + M$, because it involves addition. One may think that the approach in `mul` in §2.3 will work here. Alas, binary addition does not satisfy Prop. 7, so we must turn to a much less obvious solution.

```
mul([],M,[]).
mul(N,[],[]) :- pos(N).
mul([1],M,M) :- pos(M).
mul([o|NR],M,[o|PR]) :- pos(M), pos(NR), pos(PR), mul(NR,M,PR).
mul([1|NR],M,P) :- pos(M), pos(NR), gtl(P),
    less13(P1,P,[1|NR],M),
    mul(NR,M,P1), add([o|P1],M,P).
```

This solution relies on a seemingly contrived predicate `less13`:

```
less13([],[_|_],_,_).
less13([_|P1R],[_|PR],[],[_|MR]) :- less13(P1R,PR,[],MR).
less13([_|P1R],[_|PR],[_|NR],M)  :- less13(P1R,PR,NR,M).
```

The goal `less13`(P_1, P, N, M) relates four numerals such that $\|P_1\| < \min(\|P\|, \|N\| + \|M\| + 1)$. As long as the arguments of the goal, *however instantiated*, share no logic variables, the goal has a solution set. In any solution, P_1 is a numeral whose bits may be free but whose length is fixed. We call such numerals *L-instantiated*. Moreover, whenever P_1, P, or both N and M are L-instantiated, the solution set is finite.

In the code for binary `mul` above, `less13` occurs in a clause that is selected when multiplying an odd number $2N+1$ (where $N > 0$) by a positive number M to yield P. Under these conditions, clearly $\lfloor \log_2 NM \rfloor$ is less than both $\lfloor \log_2 P \rfloor$ and $\lfloor \log_2(2N+1) \rfloor + \lfloor \log_2 M \rfloor + 2$, so the constraint imposed by `less13` does not affect the declarative meaning of `mul`. The guarantee of `less13` mentioned above lets us prove Prop. 10 and Prop. 11 for binary multiplication. For Prop. 11, `less13` ensures that P_1 is L-instantiated, so we can use induction to prove that `mul`(N, M, P) with an L-instantiated P has a finite solution set.

The important role of `less13` can be informally explained as follows. Given the goal `mul`(X, Y, Z), when X and Y are instantiated but Z is free, or when Z is instantiated but X and Y are free, the search space is finite even though the free variables can be instantiated an infinite number of ways: the length of the product limits the lengths of the multiplicands, and vice versa. The predicate `less13` enforces these limits, even though our code cannot distinguish these two cases by determining which arguments are instantiated.

The `mul` predicate also satisfies Prop. 13 (the proof again relies on the properties of `less13`). As in the unary case, using SLD without interleaving, we cannot cover the whole domain of natural multiplication—but we can cover half of it. The technique is essentially the same as explained for unary multiplication.

6   Division, Exponentiation, and Logarithm

Our predicate for division with remainder $\mathtt{div}(N, M, Q, R)$ relates four natural numbers such that $N = M \cdot Q + R < M \cdot (Q + 1)$. The implementation is quite complex so as to finitely fail as often as possible: for example, not only when the divisor M is zero, but also in the case $\mathtt{div}([\mathtt{o} \,|\, X], [\mathtt{o}, \mathtt{1}], Q, [\mathtt{1}])$ with *free* X and Q, as no even number divided by 2 gives the remainder 1. Our algorithm is akin to long division as taught in elementary school, only done right-to-left. At each step, we determine at least one bit of the quotient in finite time.

First, we handle the easy case when the divisor M is bigger than the dividend N, so $Q = 0$ and $N = R$.

```
div(N,M,[],R) :- N = R, less(N,M).
```

Otherwise, Q must be positive. The second easy case is when N is at least M and has the same length as M.

```
div(N,M,[1],R) :- samel(N,M), add(R,M,N), less(R,M).
```

This code relies on the auxiliary predicate `samel`, which holds if its two arguments are binary numerals with the same number of digits.

```
samel([],[]).    samel([_|X],[_|Y]) :- samel(X,Y).
```

The main case of division is when N has more digits than M. The key is to represent $N = M \cdot Q + R < M \cdot (Q + 1)$ as the conjunction of the two relations

$$2^{l+1} R_1 = M Q_2 + R - N_2 \qquad \text{and} \qquad N_1 = M Q_1 + R_1$$

where

$$N = 2^{l+1} N_1 + N_2, \qquad Q = 2^{l+1} Q_1 + Q_2, \qquad l = \|R\|,$$

and N_2 and Q_2 are at most $l + 1$ long. Given l, then, we can decide the first relation. Because $0 \leq R_1 < M$, we can invoke $\mathtt{div}(N_1, M, Q_1, R_1)$ recursively to decide the second relation. That gives us a convenient induction principle: either N_1 is zero and so Q_1 and $M Q_2 + R - N_2$ are both zero, or N_1 is positive and shorter than N. These two cases correspond to the disjunction below.

```
div(N,M,Q,R) :- lessl(M,N), less(R,M), pos(Q),
                split(N,R,N1,N2), split(Q,R,Q1,Q2),
                (
                    N1 = [],
                    Q1 = [],
                    sub(N2,R,Q2M),
                    mul(Q2,M,Q2M)
                ;
                    pos(N1),
                    mul(Q2,M,Q2M),
                    add(Q2M,R,Q2MR),
                    sub(Q2MR,N2,RR),
                    split(RR,R,R1,[]),
                    div(N1,M,Q1,R1)
                ).
```

The calls to lessl/2 and less/2 at the beginning of this code ensure that M and then R are both L-instantiated. The code also relies on the predicate split/4 to 'split' a binary numeral at a given length: The goal $split(N, R, N_1, N_2)$ holds if $N = 2^{l+1}N_1 + N_2$ where $l = \|R\|$ and $N_2 < 2^{l+1}$. The goal should be invoked only when R is L-instantiated, which is the case in the div code above. The goal has a finite solution set, in which N_2 is L-instantiated in every solution.

```
split([],       _, [],    []).
split([o,B|N], [], [B|N], []).
split([1|N],    [], N,     [1]).

split([o,B|N], [_|R], N1, [])     :- split([B|N],R,N1,[]).
split([1|N],   [_|R], N1, [1])    :- split(N,R,N1,[]).
split([B|N],   [_|R], N1, [B|N2]) :- pos(N2), split(N,R,N1,N2).
```

Our predicate $\log(N, B, Q, R)$ relates four numbers such that $N = B^Q + R < B^{Q+1}$, so it implements exponentiation, logarithm, and n-th root. Our implementation uses an upper bound on R, namely $RB < N(B-1)$, and upper and lower bounds on Q, namely $(\|B\| - 1)Q < \|N\|$ and $\|N\| - 1 < \|B\|(Q+1)$. These bounds constrain the search just as lessl3 does for binary multiplication in §5. Because the base-2 case is so simple, we treat it separately.

7   Related Work

We first presented arithmetic predicates over binary natural numbers (including division and logarithm) in a book [12]. The book used miniKanren [13], which like its big sister Kanren [6] is an embedding of logic programming in Scheme. That presentation had no detailed explanations, proofs, or formal analysis, which is the focus of this paper.

Braßel, Fischer, and Huch's paper [7] appears to be the only previous description of declarative arithmetic. It is a practical paper couched in the programming language Curry. It argues for declaring numbers and their operations in the language itself, rather than using external numeric data types and operations. It also uses a little-endian binary encoding of natural numbers (later extended to signed integers). Our encodings differ, however, in that our representation of natural numbers includes zero.

Whereas our implementation of arithmetic uses a pure logic programming language, Braßel, Fischer, and Huch use a non-strict functional-logic programming language. Therefore, our implementations use wildly different strategies and are not directly comparable. Also, we implement the logarithm relation.

Braßel, Fischer, and Huch leave it to future work to prove termination of their predicates. In contrast, the thrust of this paper is to formulate and prove decidability of our predicates under DFS or DFS with interleaving. To ensure decidability and completeness under generally incomplete strategies like DFS, our implementation is much more complex.

We present no benchmarks, but we are encouraged by Braßel, Fischer, and Huch's conclusion that declarative arithmetic is practical—and, in fact, has been used satisfactorily as part of a Haskell-based Curry system.

Our notion of solution sets can be defined in terms of Lloyd's SLD-trees [4]. Unlike Lloyd, we use solution sets not to show SLD incomplete. Rather, we use them to characterize the solutions generated by programs using SLD. Our solution sets are coarser, and thus easier to reason with, than the *partial trace semantics* often used to study termination of constraint logic programs [14].

Our approach is minimalist and pure; therefore, its methodology can be used in other logic systems, specifically, Haskell type classes. Hallgren [15] first implemented (unary) arithmetic in such a system, but with restricted modes. Kiselyov [16, §6] treats decimal addition more relationally. Kiselyov and Shan [9] first demonstrated all-mode arithmetic relations for arbitrary binary numerals, so to represent numerical equality and inequality constraints in the type system. Their type-level declarative arithmetic library enabled resource-aware programming in Haskell with expressive static guarantees.

8 Conclusions

In a pure logic programming system, we have declared decidable arithmetic of unrestricted unary and binary natural numbers: addition, multiplication, division with remainder, exponentiation, and logarithm with remainder. The declared relations have unlimited domain and are free from any mode restrictions or annotations. We have proven that our arithmetic predicates are fully decidable and faithfully represent the corresponding arithmetic relations. Our technique can be easily extended to full integers (i.e., a tuple of the sign and a natural number).

The gist of our approach is to limit the search space by a balancing act of computing *bidirectional* bounds from arguments of unknown instantiatedness. For example, the key to decidable multiplication is to limit the search using bounds that the inputs place on each other, without testing whether any input is instantiated. We also rely on the ability to finitely represent infinite domains using logic variables, so that goals with infinite denotations may have only a finite solution set. Our notion of solution sets and the associated proof techniques are not specific to arithmetic and SLD; rather, they appear applicable to logic programming in other domains using a variety of search strategies.

References

[1] Apt, K.R.: Principles of Constraint Programming. Cambridge University Press, Cambridge (2003)
[2] Eiter, T., Gottlob, G., Mannila, H.: Disjunctive Datalog. ACM Transactions on Database Systems 22(3), 364–418 (1997)
[3] Kowalski, R.: Predicate logic as programming language. In: Rosenfeld, J.L. (ed.) Information Processing, pp. 569–574. North-Holland, Amsterdam (1974)
[4] Lloyd, J.W.: Foundations of Logic Programming. Springer, Heidelberg (1987)
[5] Kiselyov, O., Shan, C.c., Friedman, D.P., Sabry, A.: Backtracking, interleaving, and terminating monad transformers. In: Proceedings of the International Conference on Functional Programming, pp. 192–203 (2005)
[6] Friedman, D.P., Kiselyov, O.: A declarative applicative logic programming system (2005), http://kanren.sourceforge.net/
[7] Braßel, B., Fischer, S., Huch, F.: Declaring numbers. In: Workshop on Functional and (Constraint) Logic Programming, pp. 23–36 (2007)
[8] Matiyasevich, Y.V.: Hilbert's Tenth Problem. MIT Press, Cambridge (1993)
[9] Kiselyov, O., Shan, C.c.: Lightweight static resources: Sexy types for embedded and systems programming. In: Draft Proceedings of Trends in Functional Programming, Seton Hall University (2007), TR-SHU-CS-2007-04-1
[10] Baader, F., Snyder, W.: Unification theory. In: Robinson, A., Voronkov, A. (eds.) Handbook of Automated Reasoning, pp. 445–532. Elsevier, Amsterdam (2001)
[11] Hennessy, J.L., Patterson, D.A.: Computer Architecture: A Quantitative Approach, 3rd edn. Morgan Kaufmann, San Francisco (2002)
[12] Friedman, D.P., Byrd, W.E., Kiselyov, O.: The Reasoned Schemer. MIT Press, Cambridge (2005)
[13] Byrd, W.E., Friedman, D.P.: From variadic functions to variadic relations: A miniKanren perspective. In: 7th Scheme and Functional Programming Workshop, University of Chicago, pp. 105–117 (2006), TR-2006-06
[14] Colussi, L., Marchiori, E., Marchiori, M.: On termination of constraint logic programs. In: Montanari, U., Rossi, F. (eds.) CP 1995. LNCS, vol. 976, pp. 431–448. Springer, Heidelberg (1995)
[15] Hallgren, T.: Fun with functional dependencies.
http://www.cs.chalmers.se/~hallgren/Papers/wm01.html (2001)
[16] Kiselyov, O.: Number-parameterized types. The Monad.Reader 5 (2005)

On-Demand Refinement of Dependent Types

Hiroshi Unno[1] and Naoki Kobayashi[2]

[1] University of Tokyo
uhiro@yl.is.s.u-tokyo.ac.jp
[2] Tohoku University
koba@ecei.tohoku.ac.jp

Abstract. Dependent types are useful for statically checking detailed specifications of programs and detecting pattern match or array bounds errors. We propose a novel approach to applications of dependent types to practical programming languages: Instead of requiring programmers' declaration of dependent function types (as in Dependent ML) or trying to infer them from function *definitions* only (as in size inference), we *mine* the output specification of a dependent function from the function's *call sites*, and then propagate that specification *backward* to infer the input specification. We have implemented a prototype type inference system which supports higher-order functions, parametric polymorphism, and algebraic data types based on our approach, and obtained promising experimental results.

1 Introduction

Dependent types are useful for statically verifying that programs satisfy detailed specifications and for detecting data-dependent errors such as pattern match or array bounds errors. For example, the function $\lambda x.x + 1$ is given a type $\texttt{int} \rightarrow \texttt{int}$ in the simple type system, but with dependent types, it is given a type $\Pi x : \texttt{int}.\{y : \texttt{int} \mid y = x + 1\}$, so that we can conclude that the array access $a[(\lambda x.x + 1)\ 0]$ is safe (if the size of array a is more than 1).

There are several approaches to introducing dependent types into programming languages. Size inference [1,2,3] fixes the shape of dependent types *a priori* (e.g., a list type is of the form $\tau\ \texttt{list}^n$ where n is the length of a list), and tries to infer a dependent type of a function automatically from the function's definition. Shortcomings of that approach are inflexibility and inefficiency; for example, it would be hard to infer that a sorting function indeed returns a sorted list. Dependent ML (DML) [4,5] lets users declare the dependent type of each function manually, and checks whether the declaration is correct. A shortcoming of that approach is that it is often cumbersome for users to declare types for *all* functions. For example, consider the following function `isort` for insertion sort, and suppose that one wants to verify that `isort` returns a sorted list.

```
fun insert (x, xs) = match xs with
    Nil _ -> Cons(x, Nil ())
  | Cons(y, ys) -> if x <= y then Cons(x, xs) else Cons(y, insert (x, ys))
```

J. Garrigue and M. Hermenegildo (Eds.): FLOPS 2008, LNCS 4989, pp. 81–96, 2008.

```
fun isort xs = match xs with
   Nil _ -> Nil ()
 | Cons(x, xs') -> insert (x, isort xs')
```

It would be fine to declare that `isort` returns a sorted list (because that is indeed the property to be verified). It is, however, cumbersome to declare a dependent type of the auxiliary function `insert` as well. Knowles and Flanagan [6] propose a complete type reconstruction algorithm for a certain dependent type system, but the inferred types include fixed-point operators on predicates, so that the inferred types alone cannot be used for actual verification or bug finding (without a reasonable algorithm for computing fixed-points).

We propose an alternative, complementary approach to the previous approaches discussed above. Instead of requiring programmers' declaration of dependent function types or trying to infer them from function *definitions* only, we infer a function's type using information about not only the function's definition but also the function's *call sites*. Another related, distinguishing feature of our approach is that types are refined *on-demand*; we start with the simplest type for each function, and refine the type gradually, when it turns out that more precise type information is required by a call site of the function. For example, the function $f \stackrel{\triangle}{=} \lambda x.x + 1$ is first given a type $\texttt{int} \to \texttt{int}$, but if a calling context $a[f\ y]$ is encountered, the type is refined to $\Pi x : \texttt{int}.\{y : \texttt{int} \mid y = x + 1\}$ (since from the calling context, we know that the actual return value of f is important for the whole program to be typed). For another example, consider the sorting function `isort` above. The auxiliary function `insert` is first given a type $\texttt{int list} \to \texttt{int list}$. If the type of `isort` is declared as $\texttt{int list} \to \texttt{ordlist}$ (where `ordlist` denotes the type of sorted lists), however, we can find from the call site `insert` $(x, \texttt{isort}\ xs')$ that the type of the output of `insert` should be `ordlist`. We can then propagate that information backward to infer the type of an argument of `insert` (see Section 5 for a more detailed description of this refinement step). In this manner, we expect that our approach can deal with more flexible dependent types (without losing efficiency) than the size inference. Indeed, we have already implemented the prototype inference system and succeeded in verifying the sorting function above.

The idea of on-demand type refinement mentioned above, so called *type-error-guided type refinement*, has been inspired from that of counter-example-guided abstraction refinement (CEGAR) in abstract model checking [7]. In CEGAR, the coarsest abstraction is first used for model checking; the predicates used for abstraction are gradually refined when a false counter-example is encountered. In our approach, simple types are first used for type-checking. If the type-checking fails, types are gradually refined by inspecting a fragment of the program which causes the failure (until no further refinement is possible, when a type error is reported).

To formalize the idea mentioned above, Section 2 introduces a simple first-order functional language with assert expressions and a dependent type system for it. The assert expressions are used to model array bound checks and user-supplied specifications. Section 3 formalizes our type inference algorithm, and proves its soundness. In Section 4, we briefly discuss extension of the type inference algorithm to deal with higher-order functions, parametric polymorphism, and algebraic data types. Section 5 reports on a prototype implementation of our algorithm (for the full language, including higher-order functions, parametric polymorphism, and algebraic data types) and experiments. Section 6 discusses related work and Section 7 concludes.

2   Language and Dependent Type System

We use a call-by-value, first-order functional language to present our type inference algorithm. We extend the language with higher-order functions in Section 4. The language is essentially an "implicitly-typed" version of a subset of DML [4,5] extended with assert expressions.

The syntax of the language is defined as follows:

$$\text{(expressions) } e ::= x \mid n \mid (e_1, e_2) \mid \textbf{fun } f\ x = e_1 \textbf{ in } e_2 \mid f\ e$$
$$\mid\ \textbf{let } x = e_1 \textbf{ in } e_2 \mid \textbf{let } (x_1, x_2) = e_1 \textbf{ in } e_2$$
$$\mid\ \textbf{if } e_1 \textbf{ then } e_2 \textbf{ else } e_3 \mid \textbf{assert } e_1 \textbf{ in } e_2$$
$$\text{(values) } v ::= n \mid (v_1, v_2) \mid \textbf{fun } f\ x = e$$

Here, x, n, and f are meta-variables ranging over a set of variables, integer constants, and function names respectively. We write $\text{FV}(e)$ for the set of free variables in e. We assume given primitive operators such as $+$, $\times$, $=$ and $\leq$ on integers, and $\neg$, $\wedge$, and $\Rightarrow$ on booleans. Actually, booleans are represented by integers (the truth $\top$ by a non-zero integer, and the false $\bot$ by zero). Thus, $e_1 \leq e_2$ returns 1 if the value of e_1 is less than or equal to that of e_2, and returns 0 otherwise. In the function definition $\textbf{fun } f\ x = e_1 \textbf{ in } e_2$, f may appear in e_1 for recursive calls. However, we do not allow mutually recursive functions in the language for the sake of simplicity. Our framework can be easily extended to deal with mutually recursive functions. An assertion $\textbf{assert } e_1 \textbf{ in } e_2$ evaluates to e_2 only if the conditional e_1 holds. Otherwise, it gets stuck. Assertions are used for modeling array bounds errors and user-supplied specifications. For example, the array access $a[x]$ is modeled as $\textbf{assert } 0 \leq x < h \textbf{ in } \cdots$, where h is the size of a. See the full paper [8] for the operational semantics.

We introduce a dependent type system, which ensures that well-typed programs never get stuck. In particular, an assertion $\textbf{assert } e_1 \textbf{ in } e_2$ is accepted only if e_1 is statically guaranteed to be non-zero. The type system is used to state properties of our type inference algorithm in Section 3. The type system is undecidable, since the constraint language includes integer addition and multiplication.

The syntax of types is defined as follows:

$$\text{(base types) } t ::= \texttt{int}^\rho \mid t_1 \times t_2 \quad \text{(function types) } \sigma ::= \forall \widetilde{\rho}.\langle \phi \mid t \to \tau \rangle$$
$$\text{(expression types) } \tau ::= \{t \mid \phi\} \quad \text{(constraints) } \phi ::= \rho \mid n \mid \textbf{op}(\widetilde{\phi}) \mid \forall \rho.\phi \mid \exists \rho.\phi$$
$$\text{(type environments) } \Gamma ::= \emptyset \mid \Gamma, x : t \mid \Gamma, f : \sigma$$

A constraint, denoted by ϕ, is an *index variable* ρ, a constant n, an operator expression $\mathsf{op}(\widetilde{\phi})$, or a quantifier expression. $\widetilde{o}$ signifies a list of objects $o_1, \ldots, o_m$ for some $m \geq 0$. We often write $\top$ for 1 and $\bot$ for 0. Note that the set of operators contains standard logical operators like $\wedge$ and $\neg$.

The base type $\mathtt{int}^\rho$ is the type of an integer whose value is denoted by ρ. The base type $t_1 \times t_2$ is the type of pairs consisting of values with the types t_1 and t_2. The expression type $\{t \mid \phi\}$ is a subtype of t whose index variables are constrained by ϕ. For example, $\{\mathtt{int}^{\rho_1} \times \mathtt{int}^{\rho_2} \mid \rho_1 > \rho_2\}$ is the type of integer pairs whose first element is greater than the second element. The index variables in t are bound in $\{t \mid \phi\}$. The function type $\forall \widetilde{\rho}.\langle \phi \mid t \to \tau \rangle$ is the type of functions that take an argument of the type $\{t \mid \phi\}$ and return a value of the type τ. For example, $\langle \rho_1 > 0 \wedge \rho_2 > 0 \mid \mathtt{int}^{\rho_1} \times \mathtt{int}^{\rho_2} \to \{\mathtt{int}^{\rho_3} \mid \rho_3 = \rho_1 + \rho_2\}\rangle$ is the type of functions that take a pair of positive integers as an argument, and return the sum of the integers. The index variables in t and $\widetilde{\rho}$ are bound in $\forall \widetilde{\rho}.\langle \phi \mid t \to \tau \rangle$. We often abbreviate $\forall \widetilde{\rho}.\langle \phi \mid t \to \tau \rangle$ as $\forall \widetilde{\rho}.\{t \mid \phi\} \to \tau$ if the index variables in t do not occur in τ and as $\forall \widetilde{\rho}.t \to \tau$ if $\phi \equiv \top$. We assume that α-conversion is implicitly performed so that bound variables are different from each other and free variables.

A typing judgment is of the form $\phi; \Gamma \vdash e : \tau$. It reads that on the assumption that index variables satisfy ϕ, the expression has the type τ under the type environment Γ. For example, $\rho > 0; x : \mathtt{int}^\rho \vdash x + 1 : \{\mathtt{int}^{\rho'} \mid \rho' > 1\}$.

$$\frac{\begin{array}{c} x : t \in \Gamma \quad \widetilde{\rho}' = \mathrm{FIV}(t) \\ \widetilde{\rho} \cap \mathrm{FIV}(\phi, \Gamma) = \emptyset \end{array}}{\phi; \Gamma \vdash x : \{[\widetilde{\rho}/\widetilde{\rho}']t \mid \widetilde{\rho} = \widetilde{\rho}'\}} \ (\text{T-Var})$$

$$\frac{}{\phi; \Gamma \vdash n : \{\mathtt{int}^\rho \mid \rho = n\}} \ (\text{T-Int})$$

$$\frac{\begin{array}{c} \phi; \Gamma \vdash e_1 : \{t_1 \mid \phi_1\} \\ \phi; \Gamma \vdash e_2 : \{t_2 \mid \phi_2\} \end{array}}{\phi; \Gamma \vdash (e_1, e_2) : \{t_1 \times t_2 \mid \phi_1 \wedge \phi_2\}} \ (\text{T-Pair})$$

$$\frac{\begin{array}{c} \phi \wedge \phi_1; \Gamma, f : \sigma, x : t_1 \vdash e_1 : \tau_1 \\ \widetilde{\rho} \cap \mathrm{FIV}(\Gamma, \phi) = \emptyset \\ \sigma = \forall \widetilde{\rho}.\langle \phi_1 \mid t_1 \to \tau_1 \rangle \\ \phi; \Gamma, f : \sigma \vdash e_2 : \tau_2 \end{array}}{\phi; \Gamma \vdash \mathbf{fun}\ f\ x = e_1\ \mathbf{in}\ e_2 : \tau_2} \ (\text{T-Let-Fun})$$

$$\frac{\begin{array}{c} f : \sigma \in \Gamma \quad \phi \vdash \sigma \leqslant \tau_1 \to \tau_2 \\ \phi; \Gamma \vdash e : \tau_1 \end{array}}{\phi; \Gamma \vdash f\ e : \tau_2} \ (\text{T-App})$$

$$\frac{\begin{array}{c} \phi; \Gamma \vdash e_1 : \{t \mid \phi'\} \\ \phi \wedge \phi'; \Gamma, x : t \vdash e_2 : \tau \\ \mathrm{FIV}(t) \cap \mathrm{FIV}(\tau) = \emptyset \end{array}}{\phi; \Gamma \vdash \mathbf{let}\ x = e_1\ \mathbf{in}\ e_2 : \tau} \ (\text{T-Let})$$

$$\frac{\begin{array}{c} \phi; \Gamma \vdash e_1 : \{t_1 \times t_2 \mid \phi'\} \\ \phi \wedge \phi'; \Gamma, x_1 : t_1, x_2 : t_2 \vdash e_2 : \tau \\ \mathrm{FIV}(t_1, t_2) \cap \mathrm{FIV}(\tau) = \emptyset \end{array}}{\phi; \Gamma \vdash \mathbf{let}\ (x_1, x_2) = e_1\ \mathbf{in}\ e_2 : \tau} \ (\text{T-Let-Pair})$$

$$\frac{\begin{array}{c} \phi; \Gamma \vdash e_1 : \{\mathtt{int}^\rho \mid \phi'\} \\ \phi \wedge \exists \rho.(\phi' \wedge \rho \neq 0); \Gamma \vdash e_2 : \tau \\ \phi \wedge \exists \rho.(\phi' \wedge \rho = 0); \Gamma \vdash e_3 : \tau \end{array}}{\phi; \Gamma \vdash \mathbf{if}\ e_1\ \mathbf{then}\ e_2\ \mathbf{else}\ e_3 : \tau} \ (\text{T-If})$$

$$\frac{\begin{array}{c} \phi; \Gamma \vdash e_1 : \{\mathtt{int}^\rho \mid \rho \neq 0\} \\ \phi; \Gamma \vdash e_2 : \tau \end{array}}{\phi; \Gamma \vdash \mathbf{assert}\ e_1\ \mathbf{in}\ e_2 : \tau} \ (\text{T-Assert})$$

$$\frac{\begin{array}{c} \phi_1'; \Gamma \vdash e : \{t \mid \phi_2'\} \\ \models \phi_1 \Rightarrow (\phi_1' \wedge (\phi_2' \Rightarrow \phi_2)) \end{array}}{\phi_1; \Gamma \vdash e : \{t \mid \phi_2\}} \ (\text{T-Sub})$$

Fig. 1. Typing Rules

The typing rules are given in Figure 1. In the figure, $\text{FIV}(o)$ is the set of free index variables in some object o. The relation $\eta \models \phi$ means that an index environment η (a function from index variables to integers) satisfies a constraint ϕ. We write $\models \phi$ if $\emptyset \models \forall \widetilde{\rho}.\phi$, where $\{\widetilde{\rho}\} = \text{FIV}(\phi)$.

The subtyping relation $\phi \vdash \sigma \leqslant \sigma'$ on function types is defined by:

$$\frac{\models \phi \Rightarrow \forall \widetilde{\rho}', \text{FIV}(t_1).(\phi_1' \Rightarrow \exists \widetilde{\rho}.(\phi_1 \wedge \forall \text{FIV}(t_2).(\phi_2 \Rightarrow \phi_2')))}{\phi \vdash \forall \widetilde{\rho}.\langle \phi_1 \mid t_1 \rightarrow \{t_2 \mid \phi_2\}\rangle \leqslant \forall \widetilde{\rho}'.\langle \phi_1' \mid t_1 \rightarrow \{t_2 \mid \phi_2'\}\rangle}$$

The type system ensures that evaluation of a well-typed, closed expression (i.e., an expression e such that $\top; \Gamma_0 \vdash e : \tau$, where Γ_0 is the type environment for primitive operators) never gets stuck: See [8] for a formal discussion.

3   Type Inference Algorithm

This section formalizes our type inference algorithm and proves its soundness. First, we extend the syntax of constraints with predicate variables to denote unknown predicates. We also introduce *extended type environments* to model an intermediate state for on-demand type refinement.

$$\begin{aligned}
\text{(constraints) } \phi &::= \cdots \mid P(\widetilde{\phi}) \\
\text{(constraint substitutions) } S &::= \emptyset \mid S, P \mapsto \lambda\widetilde{\rho}.\phi \\
\text{(extended function types) } T &::= (\sigma; \phi; \widetilde{S}) \\
\text{(extended type environments) } \Delta &::= \emptyset \mid \Delta, x : t \mid \Delta, f : T
\end{aligned}$$

Here, P is a meta-variable ranging over the set of predicate variables, which are used to express unknown specifications of functions. We write $\text{FPV}(o)$ for the set of free predicate variables in some object o. Constraint substitutions map predicate variables to predicates (i.e., functions from index variables to constraints). An extended type environment Δ maps a function name f to an extended function type which is a triple of the form $(\sigma; \phi; \widetilde{S})$. Here, σ is a *template* for the type of f, which may contain predicate variables. For example, a template for a function from integers to integers is $\forall \widetilde{\rho}.\langle P(\widetilde{\rho}, \rho_x) \mid \text{int}^{\rho_x} \rightarrow \{\text{int}^{\rho_y} \mid Q(\widetilde{\rho}, \rho_x, \rho_y)\}\rangle$, where $\widetilde{\rho}$ denotes a sequence of index variables (whose length is unknown). The second element ϕ is a constraint that records a sufficient condition on predicate variables for the definition of f to be well-typed; this is used to avoid re-checking the function's definition when the function's type needs to be refined. The third element $\widetilde{S}$ records solutions for ϕ (which are substitutions for predicate variables) found so far.

The type inference algorithm is specified as inference rules for the 5-tuple relation $\Delta \rhd e : \tau \dashv \phi; \Delta'$. Here, Δ, e, and τ should be regarded as inputs of the algorithm, and ϕ and Δ' as outputs of the algorithm. Intuitively, ϕ is a sufficient condition for e to have type τ, and Δ' describes types refined during the inference. For example, let e, τ, and Δ be $f(z)$, $\{\text{int}^\rho \mid \rho > 1\}$, and $z : \text{int}^{\rho_z}$,

$f : (\sigma; \phi_1; \{S\})$, where $\sigma = \forall \widetilde{\rho}.\langle P(\widetilde{\rho}, \rho_x) \mid \mathtt{int}^{\rho_x} \to \{\mathtt{int}^{\rho_y} \mid Q(\widetilde{\rho}, \rho_x, \rho_y)\}\rangle$, $\phi_1 = \forall \widetilde{\rho}, \rho_x.P(\widetilde{\rho}, \rho_x) \Rightarrow \forall \rho_y.(\rho_y = \rho_x + 1 \Rightarrow Q(\widetilde{\rho}, \rho_x, \rho_y))$, and $S = \{P \mapsto \lambda \rho_x.\top, Q \mapsto \lambda(\rho_x, \rho_y).\top\}$. Then, ϕ and Δ' would be $\rho_z > 0$ and $z : \mathtt{int}^{\rho_z}, f : (\sigma; \phi_1; \{S, S'\})$, where S' is $\{P \mapsto \lambda \rho_x.\rho_x > 0, Q \mapsto \lambda(\rho_x, \rho_y).\rho_y > 1\}$.

The inference rules for the relation $\Delta \rhd e : \tau \dashv \phi; \Delta'$ (which are a declarative description of our type inference algorithm) are given in Figures 2 and 3. Figure 3 shows the rules for function definitions and applications, and Figure 2 shows the rules for other expressions. The sub-algorithm $\sigma \leqslant \sigma' \dashv \phi$ for computing a sufficient condition ϕ for σ to be a subtype of σ' is also defined in Figure 3. In the figures, $\mathrm{TypeOf}(\Delta, o)$ is a *template* for the type of some object o, obtained from the simple type of o by decorating it with fresh index variables and predicate variables. For example, if the simple type of o is $\mathtt{int}$, then $\mathrm{TypeOf}(\Delta, o)$ returns $\mathtt{int}^\rho$; if the simple type of o is $\mathtt{int} \to \mathtt{int}$, $\mathrm{TypeOf}(\Delta, o)$ returns $\forall \widetilde{\rho}.\langle P(\widetilde{\rho}, \rho_x) \mid \mathtt{int}^{\rho_x} \to \{\mathtt{int}^{\rho_y} \mid Q(\widetilde{\rho}, \rho_x, \rho_y)\}\rangle$.

In the rules in Figure 2, type inference proceeds in a backward manner: For example, in B-VAR, given the required type $\{t \mid \phi\}$ of the variable x, if $x : t' \in \Delta$, we check whether $|t| = |t'|$ (where $|t|$ is the simple type obtained from t by removing index variables). If the check succeeds, we produce the constraint $[t'/t]\phi$, which is the constraint obtained from ϕ by replacing each occurrence of an index variable of t with the corresponding index variable of t'.

In B-PAIR, given the required type $\{t_1 \times t_2 \mid \phi\}$ of the pair (e_1, e_2), we compute the constraint ϕ_2 which is sufficient for e_2 to have $\{t_2 \mid \phi\}$. Then, we compute the constraint ϕ_1 which is sufficient for e_1 to have $\{t_1 \mid \phi_2\}$. The remaining rules in Figure 2 can be read in a similar manner.

We now explain the rules for functions in Figure 3. In B-LET-FUN, a template for the function's type is first prepared (see the first line). We then check the function's definition, and compute a sufficient condition ψ on predicate variables for the definition to be well-typed (see the second line). Then, we find a solution S for ψ (i.e., a substitution such that $\models S(\psi)$) by using an auxiliary algorithm $\mathrm{Solve}(\mathrm{FPV}(\sigma); \psi)$, which is explained later. As a result, we obtain the input specification of f which is sufficient for no assertion violation to occur in f. At this stage, there is no requirement for the output of f, so that the inferred return type of f is of the form $\{t \mid \top\}$. Finally, we check e_2 and produce ϕ_2 and Δ'. Note that f's type may be refined during the type inference for e_2.

B-APP is the rule for applications. From the type τ of $f\,e$ and the simple type of e, we prepare a template of f's type: $\{t \mid P(\widetilde{\rho})\} \to \tau$. The value of the predicate variable P is computed by a sub-algorithm, expressed by using the relation $\Delta \rhd f : \sigma \dashv_{\{P\}} S; \Delta'$ (which is defined using B-REUSE and B-REFINE: see below). Finally, we check that the function's argument e has the required type $\{t \mid S(P(\widetilde{\rho}))\}$.

We have two rules B-REUSE and B-REFINE for the auxiliary judgment $\Delta \rhd f : \sigma \dashv_{\widetilde{\rho}} S; \Delta'$. The rule B-REUSE supports the case where the type of f in Δ is precise enough to be a subtype of σ, while B-REFINE supports the case where the type of f needs to be refined. The rules are non-deterministic, in the sense that both rules may be applied. In the actual implementation, B-REUSE is given a higher priority, so that B-REFINE is used only when applications of B-REUSE fail. For recursive calls and primitive operators, B-REFINE is not used.

In B-REUSE, we pick up an already inferred type $S_k(\sigma')$, and match it with the required type σ. (Since the argument type of σ is a predicate variable, we actually match the return types of σ and σ' here.) The constraint ψ, computed by using B-SUB, is a sufficient condition for $S_k(\sigma')$ to be a subtype of σ. We then solve ψ by using Solve.

In B-REFINE, we match the template σ' of the function's type with the required type σ, and compute a sufficient condition ψ for σ' to be a subtype of σ. We then compute a solution for $\psi \wedge \phi$ by using Solve. The key point here is that both information about the function's definition (expressed by ϕ) and that about the call site (expressed by ψ) are used to compute the function's type. Solve can use predicates occurring in ψ as hints for computing a solution of $\psi \wedge \phi$.

$$\frac{x : t' \in \Delta \qquad |t| = |t'|}{\Delta \rhd x : \{t \mid \phi\} \dashv [t'/t]\phi; \Delta} \text{ (B-VAR)}$$

$$\frac{}{\Delta \rhd n : \{\mathtt{int}^\rho \mid \phi\} \dashv [n/\rho]\phi; \Delta} \text{ (B-INT)}$$

$$\frac{\Delta \rhd e_2 : \{t_2 \mid \phi\} \dashv \phi_2; \Delta_2 \qquad \Delta_2 \rhd e_1 : \{t_1 \mid \phi_2\} \dashv \phi_1; \Delta_1}{\Delta \rhd (e_1, e_2) : \{t_1 \times t_2 \mid \phi\} \dashv \phi_1; \Delta_1} \text{ (B-PAIR)}$$

$$\frac{t = \text{TypeOf}(\Delta, e_1) \qquad \Delta, x : t \rhd e_2 : \tau \dashv \phi_2; \Delta_2 \qquad \Delta_2 \setminus x \rhd e_1 : \{t \mid \phi_2\} \dashv \phi_1; \Delta_1}{\Delta \rhd \mathtt{let}\ x = e_1\ \mathtt{in}\ e_2 : \tau \dashv \phi_1; \Delta_1} \text{ (B-LET)}$$

$$\frac{t_1 \times t_2 = \text{TypeOf}(\Delta, e_1) \qquad \Delta, x_1 : t_1, x_2 : t_2 \rhd e_2 : \tau \dashv \phi_2; \Delta_2 \qquad \Delta_2 \setminus \{x_1, x_2\} \rhd e_1 : \{t_1 \times t_2 \mid \phi_2\} \dashv \phi_1; \Delta_1}{\Delta \rhd \mathtt{let}\ (x_1, x_2) = e_1\ \mathtt{in}\ e_2 : \tau \dashv \phi_1; \Delta_1} \text{ (B-LET-PAIR)}$$

$$\frac{\Delta \rhd e_2 : \tau \dashv \phi_2; \Delta_2 \qquad \Delta_2 \rhd e_3 : \tau \dashv \phi_3; \Delta_3 \qquad \rho : \text{fresh} \qquad \phi = (\rho \neq 0 \wedge \phi_2) \vee (\rho = 0 \wedge \phi_3) \qquad \Delta_3 \rhd e_1 : \{\mathtt{int}^\rho \mid \phi\} \dashv \phi_1; \Delta_1}{\Delta \rhd \mathtt{if}\ e_1\ \mathtt{then}\ e_2\ \mathtt{else}\ e_3 : \tau \dashv \phi_1; \Delta_1} \text{ (B-IF)}$$

$$\frac{\rho : \text{fresh} \qquad \Delta \rhd e_1 : \{\mathtt{int}^\rho \mid \rho \neq 0\} \dashv \phi_1; \Delta_1 \qquad \Delta_1 \rhd e_2 : \tau \dashv \phi_2; \Delta_2}{\Delta \rhd \mathtt{assert}\ e_1\ \mathtt{in}\ e_2 : \tau \dashv \phi_1 \wedge \phi_2; \Delta_2} \text{ (B-ASSERT)}$$

Fig. 2. Type inference rules (for basic expressions)

Constraint Solving. We now describe a heuristic algorithm Solve($\widetilde{P}; \varphi$) to obtain a solution for φ (i.e., a substitution for the predicate variables $\widetilde{P}$ that satisfy φ).

If φ contains a subformula of the form $\forall \widetilde{\rho}.(P(\widetilde{\rho}) \Rightarrow \psi(\widetilde{\rho}, P))$, and $\psi(\widetilde{\rho}, P)$ does not contain negative occurrences of P, then the algorithm tries to compute the greatest fixed-point of $F = \lambda P.\lambda \widetilde{\rho}.\psi(\widetilde{\rho}, P)$ by iterations from $\lambda \widetilde{\rho}.\top$ (i.e., by computing $F^n(\lambda \widetilde{\rho}.\top)$ for $n = 1, 2, \ldots$). (As a special case, if $\psi(\widetilde{\rho}, P)$ does not contain P, then the iteration immediately converges with the solution $P = \lambda \widetilde{\rho}.\psi(\widetilde{\rho}, P)$.) The algorithm also uses widening [9] to accelerate convergence.

If the above iteration does not converge, the algorithm chooses a new starting point of iterations by extracting a sub-formula of $\psi(\widetilde{\rho}, P)$ which does not contain P and generalizing its constants. This phase roughly corresponds to predicate

$$\frac{\begin{array}{c} \sigma = \forall \widetilde{\rho}.\langle \phi \mid t \to \tau_1 \rangle = \mathrm{TypeOf}(\Delta, \mathtt{fun}\ f\ x = e_1) \\ \Delta, f : \sigma, x : t \rhd e_1 : \tau_1 \dashv \phi_1; \Delta_1, f : \sigma, x : t \qquad \psi = \forall \widetilde{\rho}, \mathrm{FIV}(t).(\phi \Rightarrow \phi_1) \\ S = \mathrm{Solve}(\mathrm{FPV}(\sigma); \psi) \qquad \Delta_1, f : (\sigma; \psi; \{S\}) \rhd e_2 : \tau \dashv \phi_2; \Delta_2 \end{array}}{\Delta \rhd \mathtt{fun}\ f\ x = e_1\ \mathtt{in}\ e_2 : \tau \dashv \phi_2; \Delta_2 \setminus f} \ (\text{B-Let-Fun})$$

$$\frac{\begin{array}{c} t = \mathrm{TypeOf}(\Delta, e) \qquad \widetilde{\rho} = \mathrm{FIV}(t) \qquad P : \mathrm{fresh} \\ \Delta \rhd f : \{t \mid P(\widetilde{\rho})\} \to \tau \dashv_{\{P\}} S; \Delta_1 \qquad \Delta_1 \rhd e : \{t \mid S(P(\widetilde{\rho}))\} \dashv \phi_2; \Delta_2 \end{array}}{\Delta \rhd f\ e : \tau \dashv \phi_2; \Delta_2} \ (\text{B-App})$$

$$\frac{f : (\sigma'; \phi; \{S_j\}_{j=1}^m) \in \Delta \qquad 1 \le k \le m \qquad S_k(\sigma') \le \sigma \dashv \psi \qquad S = \mathrm{Solve}(\widetilde{P}; \psi)}{\Delta \rhd f : \sigma \dashv_{\widetilde{P}} S; \Delta} \ (\text{B-Reuse})$$

$$\frac{\begin{array}{c} \Delta = \Delta_b, f : (\sigma'; \phi; \{S_j\}_{j=1}^m), \Delta_a \qquad \sigma' \le \sigma \dashv \psi \\ \mathrm{dom}(S) = \widetilde{P} \qquad \mathrm{dom}(S_{m+1}) = \mathrm{FPV}(\sigma') \qquad S, S_{m+1} = \mathrm{Solve}(\widetilde{P} \cup \mathrm{FPV}(\sigma'); \psi \wedge \phi) \end{array}}{\Delta \rhd f : \sigma \dashv_{\widetilde{P}} S; \Delta_b, f : (\sigma'; \phi; \{S_j\}_{j=1}^{m+1}), \Delta_a} \ (\text{B-Refine})$$

$$\frac{\phi = \forall \widetilde{\rho'}, \mathrm{FIV}(t_1).(\phi_1' \Rightarrow \exists \widetilde{\rho}.(\phi_1 \wedge \forall \mathrm{FIV}(t_2).(\phi_2 \Rightarrow \phi_2')))}{\forall \widetilde{\rho}.\langle \phi_1 \mid t_1 \to \{t_2 \mid \phi_2\}\rangle \le \forall \widetilde{\rho'}.\langle \phi_1' \mid t_1 \to \{t_2 \mid \phi_2'\}\rangle \dashv \phi} \ (\text{B-Sub})$$

Fig. 3. Type inference rules (for functions)

discovery in abstract model checking. Unlike model checking, however, we do not repeat the whole verification process; we just redo the fixed-point computation.

We use the following examples to illustrate how type inference works.

Example 1. `fun pred` $x = $ `assert` $x > 0$ `in` $x - 1$ `in assert` $e_1 = $ `pred` e_2 `in ()`
By B-Let-Fun, we first check the definition of `pred`. We prepare the template $\sigma = \forall \widetilde{\rho}.\langle P(\widetilde{\rho}, \rho_x) \mid \mathtt{int}^{\rho_x} \to \{\mathtt{int}^{\rho_y} \mid Q(\widetilde{\rho}, \rho_x, \rho_y)\}\rangle$ for the type of `pred`. Then we check $\Delta \rhd$ `assert` $x > 0$ `in` $x - 1 : \{\mathtt{int}^{\rho_y} \mid Q(\widetilde{\rho}, \rho_x, \rho_y)\} \dashv \phi'; \Delta'$ for $\Delta = \Delta_0, \mathtt{pred}{:}\sigma, x{:}\mathtt{int}^{\rho_x}$, and obtain $\phi' = \rho_x > 0 \wedge Q(\widetilde{\rho}, \rho_x, \rho_x - 1)$. Here, $\Delta_0 = +{:}\langle \top \mid \mathtt{int}^{\rho_1} \times \mathtt{int}^{\rho_2} \to \{\mathtt{int}^{\rho_3} \mid \rho_3 = \rho_1 + \rho_2\}\rangle, \ldots, \le{:}\langle \top \mid \mathtt{int}^{\rho_1} \times \mathtt{int}^{\rho_2} \to \{\mathtt{int}^{\rho_3} \mid \rho_3 = \rho_1 \le \rho_2\}\rangle, \ldots$ is the extended type environment for primitive operators. Thus, we obtain the constraint $\phi = \forall \widetilde{\rho}, \rho_x.P(\widetilde{\rho}, \rho_x) \Rightarrow \phi'$ on P and Q. We then check `assert` $e_1 = $ `pred` e_2 `in ()` under $\Delta_1 = \Delta_0, \mathtt{pred} : (\sigma; \phi; \{P \mapsto \lambda\rho_x.\rho_x > 0, Q \mapsto \lambda(\rho_x, \rho_y).\top\})$. To check `pred` e_2 against the type $\{\mathtt{int}^{\rho_y} \mid \rho = \rho_y\}$, the rule B-Refine is used. From $\sigma \le \{\mathtt{int}^{\rho_x} \mid R(\rho_x)\} \to \{\mathtt{int}^{\rho_y} \mid \rho = \rho_y\} \dashv \psi$, we get $\psi = \forall \rho_x.R(\rho_x) \Rightarrow \exists \widetilde{\rho}.(P(\widetilde{\rho}, \rho_x) \wedge \forall \rho_y.(Q(\widetilde{\rho}, \rho_x, \rho_y) \Rightarrow \rho = \rho_y))$. Then, $\psi \wedge \phi$ is passed to Solve as an input. From the subformula $Q(\widetilde{\rho}, \rho_x, \rho_y) \Rightarrow \rho = \rho_y$, Solve infers that $Q(\rho, \rho_x, \rho_y) \equiv \rho = \rho_y$. From the subformula ϕ, $P(\rho, \rho_x)$ is inferred to be $\rho_x > 0 \wedge \rho = \rho_x - 1$. Thus, we obtain the refined type $\forall \rho.\langle \rho_x > 0 \wedge \rho = \rho_x - 1 \mid \mathtt{int}^{\rho_x} \to \{\mathtt{int}^{\rho_y} \mid \rho = \rho_y\}\rangle$ of `pred`.

Example 2

`fun` $fact\ x = $ `if` $x \le 0$ `then` 1 `else` $x * fact\ (x - 1)$ `in assert` $fact\ e > 0$ `in ()`

By B-LET-FUN, we first check the definition of `fact`. We prepare the template $\sigma = \forall \widetilde{\rho}.\langle P(\widetilde{\rho}, \rho_x) \mid \mathtt{int}^{\rho_x} \to \{\mathtt{int}^{\rho_y} \mid Q(\widetilde{\rho}, \rho_x, \rho_y)\}\rangle$ for the type of `fact`. Then we check $\Delta \rhd$ `if` $x \leq 0$ `then` 1 `else` $x * fact$ $(x - 1) : \{\mathtt{int}^{\rho_y} \mid Q(\widetilde{\rho}, \rho_x, \rho_y)\} \dashv \phi'; \Delta'$ for $\Delta = \Delta_0, \mathtt{fact} : \sigma, x : \mathtt{int}^{\rho_x}$, and obtain $\phi' = (\rho_x \leq 0 \wedge \phi_1) \vee (\rho_x > 0 \wedge \phi_2)$. Here, $\phi_1 = Q(\widetilde{\rho}, \rho_x, 1)$ and $\phi_2 = \exists \widetilde{\rho}'.(P(\widetilde{\rho}', \rho_x - 1) \wedge \forall \rho_y.(Q(\widetilde{\rho}', \rho_x - 1, \rho_y) \Rightarrow Q(\widetilde{\rho}, \rho_x, \rho_x * \rho_y)))$ are respectively obtained from the then- and else- branches. Thus, we obtain the constraint $\phi = \forall \widetilde{\rho}, \rho_x.P(\widetilde{\rho}, \rho_x) \Rightarrow \phi'$ on P and Q. We then check `assert fact` $e > 0$ `in ()` under $\Delta_1 = \Delta_0, \mathtt{fact} : (\sigma; \phi; \{P \mapsto \lambda \rho_x.\top, Q \mapsto \lambda(\rho_x, \rho_y).\top\})$. To check `fact` e against the type $\{\mathtt{int}^{\rho_y} \mid \rho_y > 0\}$, the rule B-REFINE is used. From $\sigma \leqslant \{\mathtt{int}^{\rho_x} \mid R(\rho_x)\} \to \{\mathtt{int}^{\rho_y} \mid \rho_y > 0\} \dashv \psi$, we get $\psi = \forall \rho_x.R(\rho_x) \Rightarrow \exists \widetilde{\rho}.(P(\widetilde{\rho}, \rho_x) \wedge \forall \rho_y.(Q(\widetilde{\rho}, \rho_x, \rho_y) \Rightarrow \rho_y > 0))$. Then, $\psi \wedge \phi$ is passed to Solve as an input. From the subformula $Q(\widetilde{\rho}, \rho_x, \rho_y) \Rightarrow \rho_y > 0$, Solve infers that $Q(\rho_x, \rho_y) \equiv \rho_y > 0$. From the subformula ϕ, $P(\rho_x)$ is inferred to be $\top$ as the result of the greatest fixed-point computation of the function $F = \lambda P.\lambda \rho_x.(\rho_x \leq 0 \wedge 1 > 0) \vee (\rho_x > 0 \wedge P(\rho_x - 1) \wedge \forall \rho_y.(\rho_y > 0 \Rightarrow \rho_x * \rho_y > 0)) \equiv \lambda P.\lambda \rho_x.\rho_x \leq 0 \vee (\rho_x > 0 \wedge P(\rho_x - 1))$ by iterations from $\lambda \rho_x.\top$, which converge immediately since $F(\lambda \rho_x.\top) \equiv \lambda \rho_x.\rho_x \leq 0 \vee \rho_x > 0 \equiv \lambda \rho_x.\top$. Thus, we obtain the refined type $\langle \top \mid \mathtt{int}^{\rho_x} \to \{\mathtt{int}^{\rho_y} \mid \rho_y > 0\}\rangle$ of `fact`.

3.1 Soundness

We say that Δ is valid if and only if for any $f : (\sigma; \phi; \{S_j\}_{j=1}^{m}) \in \Delta$, $\models S_k(\phi)$ holds for any $k \in \{1, \ldots, m\}$.

Let us define the function $(\![\Delta]\!)$, which maps an extended type environment Δ to an ordinary type environment, as follows:

$$(\![\emptyset]\!) = \emptyset \qquad (\![\Delta, x : t]\!) = (\![\Delta]\!), x : t$$
$$(\![\Delta, f : (\sigma; \phi; \{S_j\}_{j=1}^{m})]\!) = (\![\Delta]\!), f : \mathrm{merge}(\{S_j(\sigma)\}_{j=1}^{m}).$$

Here, $\mathrm{merge}(\{\sigma_j\}_{j=1}^{m}) = \langle \phi_1 \vee \cdots \vee \phi_m \mid t \to \{t' \mid (\phi_1 \Rightarrow \phi_1') \wedge \cdots \wedge (\phi_m \Rightarrow \phi_m')\}\rangle$ if $\sigma_j = \langle \phi_j \mid t \to \{t' \mid \phi_j'\}\rangle$ for any $j \in \{1, \ldots, m\}$. The following theorem states that the type inference algorithm is sound with respect to the dependent type system presented in Section 2. (We assume the soundness of Solve here; see the full paper [8] for the proof).

Theorem 1 (Soundness). *If* $\Delta \rhd e : \tau \dashv \phi$; Δ' *is derivable and* Δ *is valid then,* Δ' *is valid,* $\vdash (\![\Delta']\!) \leqslant (\![\Delta]\!)$, *and* $\phi; (\![\Delta']\!) \vdash e : \tau$ *is derivable.*

Note that the type inference algorithm is *not* complete with respect to the type system because of the incompleteness of Solve.

4 Extensions

In this section, we briefly discuss how to extend our type inference algorithm formalized in Section 3 with higher-order functions, parametric polymorphism, and algebraic data types. Interested readers are referred to the full paper [8] for the formalization of the extended algorithm.

Higher-Order Functions. A main new issue in handling higher-order functions is what kind of template is prepared for higher-order functions. For example, for a function of type $(\texttt{int} \rightarrow \texttt{int}) \rightarrow \texttt{int}$, one may be tempted to consider a template of the form: $\langle R_1(P_1, Q_1) \mid \langle P_1(\rho_1) \mid \texttt{int}^{\rho_1} \rightarrow \{\texttt{int}^{\rho_2} \mid Q_1(\rho_1, \rho_2)\}\rangle \rightarrow \{\texttt{int}^{\rho_3} \mid R_2(P_1, Q_1, \rho_3)\}\rangle$, which is the type of a function that takes a function whose precondition P_1 and postcondition Q_1 satisfy $R_1(P_1, Q_1)$, and returns an integer that satisfies $R_2(P_1, Q_1, \rho_3)$. This allows us to express a higher-order function that is polymorphic on the property of a function argument, but requires a significant extension of the constraint solving algorithm due to the presence of higher-order predicates.

Instead, we consider only first-order predicate variables, and use a template $\langle P_1(\rho_1) \mid \texttt{int}^{\rho_1} \rightarrow \{\texttt{int}^{\rho_2} \mid Q_1(\rho_1, \rho_2)\}\rangle \rightarrow \{\texttt{int}^{\rho_3} \mid Q_2(\rho_3)\}$ for $(\texttt{int} \rightarrow \texttt{int}) \rightarrow \texttt{int}$. This allows us to extend the algorithm in Section 3 in a fairly straightforward manner. A shortcoming of the approach is that a higher-order function is monomorphic on the property of function arguments; we use parametric polymorphism to overcome that disadvantage to some extent.

Parametric Polymorphism. The above treatment of higher-order functions sometimes results in too specific types. For example, the following type of `map` would be inferred from the calling context $(\texttt{map } (\lambda x.x + 1) \; l) : \{\texttt{int}^w \; \texttt{list} \mid w \geq 0\}$:

$$(\{\texttt{int}^x \mid x \geq -1\} \rightarrow \{\texttt{int}^y \mid y \geq 0\}) \rightarrow \{\texttt{int}^z \; \texttt{list} \mid z \geq -1\} \rightarrow \{\texttt{int}^w \; \texttt{list} \mid w \geq 0\}.$$

This is too specific to be used in other calling contexts of `map`. To remedy the problem, we use parametric polymorphism. In the case of `map` function, the polymorphic type $\forall \alpha, \beta.(\alpha \rightarrow \beta) \rightarrow \alpha \; \texttt{list} \rightarrow \beta \; \texttt{list}$ is assigned to `map`, which can be instantiated to $(\{\texttt{int}^x \mid P(x)\} \rightarrow \{\texttt{int}^y \mid Q(y)\}) \rightarrow \{\texttt{int}^z \; \texttt{list} \mid P(z)\} \rightarrow \{\texttt{int}^w \; \texttt{list} \mid Q(w)\}$ for any P and Q.

Algebraic Data Types. We require users to declare data type invariants and dependent types for constructors of each user-defined algebraic data type as in DML. Then, our algorithm infers dependent types of functions automatically unlike in DML. We allow users to declare *multiple* types for each data constructor; for example, for lists, users may declare `Nil` as $\forall \alpha.\texttt{unit} \rightarrow \{\alpha \; \texttt{list}^\rho \mid \rho = 0\}$ and $\forall \rho.\texttt{unit} \rightarrow \{\texttt{ordlist}^{\rho_1} \mid \rho_1 = \rho\}$ (see Section 5.1). This allows users to specify multiple properties like the list length and sortedness.

The main new difficulty in type inference is how to handle multiple types declared for each constructor as mentioned above. An extended type environment Δ now maps each function name to *a set of* extended function types, instead of a single extended function type. For example, a list function may have the following four templates: $\{ \langle P_1(\rho_x) \mid \texttt{int} \; \texttt{list}^{\rho_x} \rightarrow \{\texttt{int} \; \texttt{list}^{\rho_y} \mid Q_1(\rho_x, \rho_y)\}\rangle,$ $\langle P_2(\rho_x) \mid \texttt{int} \; \texttt{list}^{\rho_x} \rightarrow \{\texttt{ordlist}^{\rho_y} \mid Q_2(\rho_x, \rho_y)\}\rangle, \langle P_3(\rho_x) \mid \texttt{ordlist}^{\rho_x} \rightarrow \{\texttt{int} \; \texttt{list}^{\rho_y} \mid Q_3(\rho_x, \rho_y)\}\rangle, \langle P_4(\rho_x) \mid \texttt{ordlist}^{\rho_x} \rightarrow \{\texttt{ordlist}^{\rho_y} \mid Q_4(\rho_x, \rho_y)\}\rangle\},$ which are generated on-demand (based on calling contexts), in order to avoid a combinatorial explosion of the number of templates. Once an appropriate template is chosen, the rest of the algorithm is basically the same as the one described in Section 3: constraints on predicate variables are generated and solved.

5 Implementation and Experiments

We have implemented a prototype type inference system (available from http://web.yl.is.s.u-tokyo.ac.jp/~uhiro/depinf/) according to the formalization in Section 3. It supports higher-order functions, parametric polymorphism, and algebraic data types as described in Section 4. We adopted Cooper's algorithm for checking satisfiability of integer constraints. We report two kinds of experiments to show the effectiveness of our approach. All the experiments were performed on Intel Xeon CPU 3GHz with 3GB RAM.

5.1 Verification of Sorting Algorithms

This experiment shows an application of our system to infer the specifications for auxiliary functions from the specification of the top-level function. The programs used in the experiment are the insertion sort defined in Section 1, and a merge sort. We discuss below the experiment for the insertion sort. The experiment for the merge sort is similar: The merge sort program consists of a main function `msort` and two auxiliary functions `merge` and `msplit`. The types of `merge` and `msplit` have been automatically inferred from the type specification that `msort` should return a sorted list only.

In the experiment, `Nil` is defined as a constructor having two types: $\forall \alpha.\text{unit} \rightarrow \{\alpha \text{ list}^\rho \mid \rho = 0\}$ and $\forall \rho.\text{unit} \rightarrow \{\text{ordlist}^{\rho_1} \mid \rho_1 = \rho\}$. `Cons` is defined as a constructor having two types: $\forall \alpha.\alpha \times \alpha \text{ list}^{\rho_1} \rightarrow \{\alpha \text{ list}^{\rho_2} \mid \rho_2 = \rho_1 + 1\}$ and $\langle \rho_1 \leq \rho_2 \mid \text{int}^{\rho_1} \times \text{ordlist}^{\rho_2} \rightarrow \{\text{ordlist}^{\rho_3} \mid \rho_3 = \rho_1\}\rangle$. Here, $\alpha \text{ list}^\rho$ is the type of lists of length ρ, whose elements have the type α. ordlist^ρ is the type of ordered lists, whose elements are integers greater than or equal to ρ. As in this example, multiple types can be declared for each constructor in our system, and an appropriate type is chosen depending on each context. We also added a type declaration that `isort` should return a value of type $\{\text{ordlist}^\rho \mid \top\}$. The full paper [8] shows the whole code used in the experiment.

Our system succeeded in verifying the program, and inferred the following types in 0.912 seconds:

$$\text{insert} : \forall \rho.\langle \rho \leq \rho_1 \wedge \rho \leq \rho_2 \mid \text{int}^{\rho_1} \times \text{ordlist}^{\rho_2} \rightarrow \{\text{ordlist}^{\rho_3} \mid \rho \leq \rho_3\}\rangle,$$
$$\text{isort} : \text{int list} \rightarrow \text{ordlist}.$$

The type of `insert` means that `insert` returns a sorted list whose head is greater than or equal to the first argument or the head of the second argument if a sorted list is given as the second argument.

We describe below how the type of the auxiliary function `insert` is refined. From the definition of `insert`, the initial type assigned to `insert` is int × int list → int list. When the call site insert $(x, \text{isort } xs')$ (on the last line of the definition of `isort`) is checked (with the required output specification $\{\text{ordlist}^\rho \mid \top\}$), the following new template for the type of `insert` is prepared:

$$\forall \tilde{\rho}.\langle P(\tilde{\rho}, \rho_1, \rho_2) \mid \text{int}^{\rho_1} \times \text{ordlist}^{\rho_2} \rightarrow \{\text{ordlist}^{\rho_3} \mid Q(\tilde{\rho}, \rho_1, \rho_2, \rho_3)\}\rangle,$$

Since the required type for insert $(x, \text{isort } xs')$ is $\{\text{ordlist}^\rho \mid \top\}$, the system first infers that $Q(\rho_1, \rho_2, \rho_3) \equiv \top$, and checks the constraint extracted from the definition of isort. That type is, however, not precise enough to check the recursive call $\text{insert}(x, ys)$ (on the last line of the definition of insert), which requires that $\forall \rho_{ret}.Q(\tilde{\rho}', \rho_x, \rho_{ys}, \rho_{ret}) \Rightarrow \rho_y \leq \rho_{ret}$ holds. Thus, $Q(\rho, \rho_1, \rho_2, \rho_3)$ is strengthened to $\rho \leq \rho_3$. Then, the system successfully infers the input specification $P(\rho, \rho_1, \rho_2) \equiv \rho \leq \rho_1 \wedge \rho \leq \rho_2$ by propagating the output specification.

5.2 Experiment with Functions from the OCaml List Module

In this experiment, we demonstrate an application of our system to learn specifications of library functions. We use the list module of the OCaml programming language (http://caml.inria.fr/) as the target of the experiment.

The experiment proceeded as follows.

1. We manually translated the source code of the list module into our language. We have also added the definition of list constructors Nil : $\forall \alpha.\text{unit} \rightarrow \{\alpha \text{ list}^\rho \mid \rho = 0\}$ and Cons : $\forall \alpha.\alpha \times \alpha \text{ list}^{\rho_1} \rightarrow \{\alpha \text{ list}^{\rho_2} \mid \rho_2 = \rho_1 + 1\}$.
2. We executed our system for the translated code above. No call site information was used in this phase (except for the calls inside libraries).
3. Let f be a function whose argument type constraint inferred in the previous step is not $\top$. (For example, the argument type of combine was inferred to be $\{\alpha \text{ list}^{\rho_1} \times \beta \text{ list}^{\rho_2} \mid \rho_1 = \rho_2\}$ in Step 2.) Let g be another library function. Then, we searched for code fragments of the form $f (\ldots g (\ldots) \ldots)$ from various application programs. (Here, we have used Google Code Search, http://www.google.com/codesearch/.)
4. We executed our system on the code fragments collected in the above step, to refine the types of library functions.

The first and third steps of the experiment have been conducted manually, but automation of those steps would not be difficult.

The result of the experiment is summarized in Table 1. Table 2 shows some of the call sites used in the final step. The filed "time" indicates the time spent in the second and fourth steps.

For most of the library functions, the inferred types are the same as the expected types (modulo simplification of some constraints). For some functions, the inferred types were less precise than expected: For example, the type of rev_map2 in Table 1 does not capture the property that the length of the returned list is the same as that of the second argument. We expect that those types can be refined by using more appropriate call sites.

As for the efficiency, our system was slow for length, map2, and combine. We think that this is due to the present naive implementation of the fixed-point computation algorithm, and that we can remedy the problem by using convex-hull or selective hull operator [10] to keep the size of the constraints small.

As already mentioned, we have collected the call sites manually in step 3. To confirm that our choice of call sites did not much affect the quality of the inferred types, we have tested our system also with call sites other than those shown in Table 2, and confirmed that similar types are inferred from them.

Table 1. The specifications of the library functions from the OCaml list module. Our system automatically inferred them from the call sites of the functions in Table 2.

function name	inferred specification	time (sec.)
length	$\forall \alpha. \forall \rho, \rho'. \{\alpha \; \texttt{list}^{\rho_1} \mid \rho \geq \rho_1 \geq \rho'\} \rightarrow \{\texttt{int}^{\rho_2} \mid \rho \geq \rho_2 \geq \rho'\}$	27.773
hd	$\forall \alpha. \{\alpha \; \texttt{list}^{\rho} \mid \rho > 0\} \rightarrow \alpha$	0.004
tl	$\forall \alpha. \forall \rho. \{\alpha \; \texttt{list}^{\rho_1} \mid \rho_1 > 0 \wedge \rho_1 = \rho + 1\} \rightarrow \{\alpha \; \texttt{list}^{\rho_2} \mid \rho_2 = \rho\}$	0.064
nth	$\forall \alpha. \{\alpha \; \texttt{list}^{\rho_1} \times \texttt{int}^{\rho_2} \mid \rho_1 > \rho_2 \geq 0\} \rightarrow \alpha$	0.268
rev	$\forall \alpha. \forall \rho. \{\alpha \; \texttt{list}^{\rho_1} \mid \rho_1 = \rho\} \rightarrow \{\alpha \; \texttt{list}^{\rho_2} \mid \rho_2 = \rho\}$	0.540
append	$\forall \alpha. \forall \rho. \{\alpha \; \texttt{list}^{\rho_1} \times \alpha \; \texttt{list}^{\rho_2} \mid \rho_1 + \rho_2 = \rho\} \rightarrow$ $\{\alpha \; \texttt{list}^{\rho_3} \mid \rho_3 = \rho\}$	2.892
map	$\forall \alpha, \beta. (\alpha \rightarrow \beta) \rightarrow \forall \rho. \{\alpha \; \texttt{list}^{\rho_1} \mid \rho_1 = \rho\} \rightarrow \{\beta \; \texttt{list}^{\rho_2} \mid \rho_2 = \rho\}$	0.292
iter2	$\forall \alpha, \beta. (\alpha \times \beta \rightarrow \texttt{unit}) \rightarrow$ $\{\alpha \; \texttt{list}^{\rho_1} \times \beta \; \texttt{list}^{\rho_2} \mid \rho_1 = \rho_2\} \rightarrow \texttt{unit}$	0.276
map2	$\forall \alpha, \beta, \gamma. (\alpha \times \beta \rightarrow \gamma) \rightarrow$ $\forall \rho. \{\alpha \; \texttt{list}^{\rho_1} \times \beta \; \texttt{list}^{\rho_2} \mid \rho_1 = \rho_2 = \rho\} \rightarrow \{\gamma \; \texttt{list}^{\rho_3} \mid \rho_3 = \rho\}$	14.236
rev_map2	$\forall \alpha, \beta, \gamma. (\alpha \times \beta \rightarrow \gamma) \rightarrow$ $\{\alpha \; \texttt{list}^{\rho_1} \times \beta \; \texttt{list}^{\rho_2} \mid \rho_1 = \rho_2\} \rightarrow \gamma \; \texttt{list}$	0.448
fold_left2	$\forall \alpha, \beta, \gamma. (\alpha \times \beta \times \gamma \rightarrow \alpha) \rightarrow$ $\{\alpha \times (\beta \; \texttt{list}^{\rho_1} \times \gamma \; \texttt{list}^{\rho_2}) \mid \rho_1 = \rho_2\} \rightarrow \alpha$	0.276
fold_right2	$\forall \alpha, \beta, \gamma. (\alpha \times \beta \times \gamma \rightarrow \gamma) \rightarrow$ $\{(\alpha \; \texttt{list}^{\rho_1} \times \beta \; \texttt{list}^{\rho_2}) \times \gamma \mid \rho_1 = \rho_2\} \rightarrow \gamma$	0.276
for_all2	$\forall \alpha, \beta. (\alpha \times \beta \rightarrow \texttt{bool}) \rightarrow$ $\{\alpha \; \texttt{list}^{\rho_1} \times \beta \; \texttt{list}^{\rho_2} \mid \rho_1 = \rho_2\} \rightarrow \texttt{bool}$	0.276
exists2	$\forall \alpha, \beta. (\alpha \times \beta \rightarrow \texttt{bool}) \rightarrow$ $\{\alpha \; \texttt{list}^{\rho_1} \times \beta \; \texttt{list}^{\rho_2} \mid \rho_1 = \rho_2\} \rightarrow \texttt{bool}$	0.276
split	$\forall \alpha, \beta. \forall \rho. \{(\alpha \times \beta) \; \texttt{list}^{\rho_1} \mid \rho_1 = \rho\} \rightarrow$ $\{\alpha \; \texttt{list}^{\rho_2} \times \beta \; \texttt{list}^{\rho_3} \mid \rho_2 = \rho_3 = \rho\}$	0.340
combine	$\forall \alpha, \beta. \forall \rho. \{\alpha \; \texttt{list}^{\rho_1} \times \beta \; \texttt{list}^{\rho_2} \mid \rho_1 = \rho_2 = \rho\} \rightarrow$ $\{(\alpha \times \beta) \; \texttt{list}^{\rho_3} \mid \rho_3 = \rho\}$	15.576

Table 2. The call sites used to infer the specifications of the functions in Table 1. We collected them from existing programs written in OCaml.

file name	call site	refined functions
predabst.ml	combine (a1, (tl a2))	tl
completion.ml	nth (a3, (length a3 - 1))	length
xdr.ml	let (a4, a5) = split a6 in combine (a4, map f1 a5)	split, map
pmlize.ml	combine (rev a7, a8)	rev
ass.ml	combine (append (fst (split a9), fst (split a10)), append (snd (split a9), snd (split a10)))	append, split
printtyp.ml	map2 f2 (a11, map2 f3 (a12, a13))	map2
ctype.ml	fold_left2 f4 (a14, a15, combine (a16, a17))	combine

6   Related Work

As already mentioned in Section 1, closely related to ours is the work on DML [4,5] and size inference [1,2,3].

DML [4,5] is an extension of ML with a restricted form of dependent types. DML requires users to declare function types, and then automatically performs implicit argument inference and type checking. An advantage of our approach is that users need not always declare function types, as demonstrated in the verification of sorting functions.

Size inference can automatically infer size relations between arguments and return values of functions [1,2,3]. A main difference is that the size inference tries to infer as precise specification as possible from the definition of a function, while our algorithm starts with simple types, and gradually refines the types based on information about functions' call sites. A main advantage of our approach is that we can allow more flexible dependent types based on the user's demand (as demonstrated in the verification of sorting functions, where two kinds of list types were declared). Another possible advantage of our approach (that has yet to be confirmed by more experiments) is that the on-demand inference can be more efficient, especially when precise specification is not required for most functions. On the other hand, an advantage of size inference is that it can find more precise specification than ours, and that it needs to infer the specification of a function just once.

Rich type systems which include dependent types with datasort and index refinements [11,12], and generalized algebraic data types [13,14,15] have been introduced to practical programming languages so that non-trivial program invariants can be expressed as types [16,17]. *Partial* type inference in the spirit of local type inference [18] is employed in those type systems, to reduce type annotations. Type information can, however, be propagated locally, so that the types of recursive functions cannot be inferred automatically.

Flanagan proposed hybrid type checking which allows users to refine data types with arbitrary program terms [19]. A type reconstruction algorithm for that type system has been proposed by Knowles and Flanagan [6]. The result of their type inference algorithm, however contains fixed-point operators on predicates, so that their algorithm alone can neither statically detect errors, nor produce useful documentations for the program. Their algorithm does not support compound data structures and parametric polymorphism.

Theorem provers such as Coq [20] can also be used for writing dependently typed programs [21,22]. Epigram [23] and Cayenne [24] support interactive development of dependently typed programs: a program template and sub-goals are automatically generated from a type. These systems greatly reduce users' burden of writing programs and types. However, these systems currently seem to be difficult to master for ordinary programmers without a knowledge of formal logic.

As mentioned in Section 1, the idea of our approach has been inspired by automatic predicate discovery and loop invariant inference in other verification techniques, such as predicate abstraction [25,26,7,27], the induction-iteration method [28], on-demand loop invariant refinement by Leino [29], and constraint-based invariant generation which solves unknown parameters in invariant templates [30,31]. Our main contribution in this respect is to bring those techniques into the context of dependently-typed functional languages; The advantage of using the type-based setting is that the verification technique can be smoothly extended to support algebraic data types, higher-order functions, etc.

7   Conclusion

We have proposed a novel approach to applying dependent types to practical programming languages: Our type inference system first assigns simple types to functions, and refines them *on demand*, using information about both the functions' definitions and call sites. A prototype type inference system has been already implemented and tested for non-trivial programs.

Future work includes an extension of our system for producing better error messages. With the current system, when type inference fails, it is difficult for the user to judge whether the failure is due to a bug of the program, or the incompleteness of our type inference algorithm. Finding minimal unsatisfiable constraints as in [16] would be useful for producing better error messages.

Our type inference algorithm presented in this paper assumes that all the function definitions are available. To support separate type inference for each module, we have to let users declare module interface (i.e., dependent types of the exported functions). Some module interface may be, however, automatically generated as shown in the experiments in Section 5.2.

Acknowledgments

We thank anonymous reviewers for their comments.

References

1. Hughes, J., Pareto, L., Sabry, A.: Proving the correctness of reactive systems using sized types. In: POPL 1996, pp. 410–423. ACM Press, New York (1996)
2. Chin, W.N., Khoo, S.C.: Calculating sized types. In: PEPM 2000, pp. 62–72. ACM Press, New York (1999)
3. Chin, W.N., Khoo, S.C., Xu, D.N.: Extending sized type with collection analysis. In: PEPM 2003, pp. 75–84. ACM Press, New York (2003)
4. Xi, H., Pfenning, F.: Eliminating array bound checking through dependent types. In: PLDI 1998, pp. 249–257. ACM Press, New York (1998)
5. Xi, H., Pfenning, F.: Dependent types in practical programming. In: POPL 1999, pp. 214–227. ACM Press, New York (1999)
6. Knowles, K., Flanagan, C.: Type Reconstruction for General Refinement Types. In: De Nicola, R. (ed.) ESOP 2007. LNCS, vol. 4421, pp. 505–519. Springer, Heidelberg (2007)
7. Ball, T., Majumdar, R., Millstein, T., Rajamani, S.K.: Automatic predicate abstraction of C programs. In: PLDI 2001, pp. 203–213. ACM Press, New York (2001)

8. Unno, H., Kobayashi, N.: On-demand refinement of dependent types (Full version) (January, 2008), http://web.yl.is.s.u-tokyo.ac.jp/~uhiro/
9. Cousot, P., Halbwachs, N.: Automatic discovery of linear restraints among variables of a program. In: POPL 1978, pp. 84–96. ACM Press, New York (1978)
10. Popeea, C., Chin, W.N.: Inferring disjunctive postconditions. In: Okada, M., Satoh, I. (eds.) ASIAN 2006. LNCS, vol. 4435, Springer, Heidelberg (2008)
11. Dunfield, J.: Combining two forms of type refinements. Technical Report CMU-CS-02-182, Carnegie Mellon University (September, 2002)
12. Dunfield, J., Pfenning, F.: Tridirectional typechecking. In: POPL 2004, pp. 281–292. ACM Press, New York (2004)
13. Xi, H., Chen, C., Chen, G.: Guarded recursive datatype constructors. In: POPL 2003, pp. 224–235. ACM Press, New York (2003)
14. Pottier, F., Régis-Gianas, Y.: Stratified type inference for generalized algebraic data types. In: POPL 2006, pp. 232–244. ACM Press, New York (2006)
15. Peyton Jones, S., Vytiniotis, D., Weirich, S., Washburn, G.: Simple unification-based type inference for GADTs. In: ICFP 2006, pp. 50–61. ACM Press, New York (2006)
16. Sulzmann, M., Voicu, R.: Language-based program verification via expressive types. Electronic Notes in Theoretical Computer Science 174(7), 129–147 (2007)
17. Kiselyov, O., Shan, C.c.: Lightweight static capabilities. Electronic Notes in Theoretical Computer Science 174(7), 79–104 (2007)
18. Pierce, B.C., Turner, D.N.: Local type inference. In: POPL 1998, pp. 252–265. ACM Press, New York (1998)
19. Flanagan, C.: Hybrid type checking. In: POPL 2006, pp. 245–256. ACM Press, New York (2006)
20. Bertot, Y., Casteran, P.: Interactive Theorem Proving and Program Development. Springer, Heidelberg (2004)
21. Leroy, X.: Formal certification of a compiler back-end or: programming a compiler with a proof assistant. In: POPL 2006, pp. 42–54. ACM Press, New York (2006)
22. Chlipala, A.: Modular development of certified program verifiers with a proof assistant. In: ICFP 2006, pp. 160–171. ACM Press, New York (2006)
23. Altenkirch, T., McBride, C., McKinna, J.: Why dependent types matter. Manuscript (April, 2005)
24. Augustsson, L.: Cayenne – a language with dependent types. In: ICFP 1998: Proceedings of the third ACM SIGPLAN international conference on Functional programming, pp. 239–250. ACM Press, New York (1998)
25. Graf, S., Saïdi, H.: Construction of abstract state graphs with PVS. In: Grumberg, O. (ed.) CAV 1997. LNCS, vol. 1254, pp. 72–83. Springer, Heidelberg (1997)
26. Flanagan, C., Qadeer, S.: Predicate abstraction for software verification. In: POPL 2002, pp. 191–202. ACM Press, New York (2002)
27. Henzinger, T.A., Jhala, R., Majumdar, R., Sutre, G.: Lazy abstraction. In: POPL 2002, pp. 58–70. ACM Press, New York (2002)
28. Suzuki, N., Ishihata, K.: Implementation of an array bound checker. In: POPL 1977, pp. 132–143. ACM Press, New York (1977)
29. Leino, K.R.M., Logozzo, F.: Loop invariants on demand. In: Yi, K. (ed.) APLAS 2005. LNCS, vol. 3780, pp. 119–134. Springer, Heidelberg (2005)
30. Sankaranarayanan, S., Sipma, H.B., Manna, Z.: Constraint-based linear-relations analysis. In: Giacobazzi, R. (ed.) SAS 2004. LNCS, vol. 3148, pp. 53–68. Springer, Heidelberg (2004)
31. Beyer, D., Henzinger, T.A., Majumdar, R., Rybalchenko, A.: Path invariants. In: PLDI 2007, pp. 300–309. ACM Press, New York (2007)

Proving Properties about Lists Using Containers

Rawle Prince[1], Neil Ghani[1], and Conor McBride[2]

[1] School of Computer Science,
Jubilee Campus,
University of Nottingham,
Nottingham, NG8 1BB,
England
{rcp,nxg}@cs.nott.ac.uk
[2] Alta Systems (Northern Ireland) Ltd.,
Unit A, 2 Derryvolgie Avenue,
Belfast, BT9 6FL,
Northern Ireland
conor@strictlypositive.org

Abstract. Bundy and Richardson [7] presented a technique for reasoning about lists using ellipsis (the dots in $1 + 2 + \ldots + 10$), where a polymorphic function, denoted by $\square$, is used to encapsulate recursive definitions of list functions and a portrayal system using ellipsis gives an informal proof. We highlight certain limitations of this technique and address these limitations using the recently developed theory of containers which capture the idea that many important datatypes consist of templates where data is stored. We implement our ideas in Coq and demonstrate how they can be used to prove theorems that eluded Bundy and Richardson in [7].

1 Introduction

Foremost among the characteristics of inductive datatypes is the relationship between definitions by recursion and proofs by induction. This relationship is rather intimate, as we define a function by recursion then prove properties of the function by induction. However, some inductive proofs turn out to be more difficult than first anticipated. For example, consider the function $rev : List(\tau) \to List(\tau)$, where

$$rev([]) \mapsto [] \tag{1}$$
$$rev(x :: xs) \mapsto rev(xs) +\!\!+ [x].$$

If we want to prove the property

$$\forall l : List(\tau).\, rev(rev(l)) = l, \tag{2}$$

we may proceed by induction on l but get stuck at:

$$rev(rev(x :: xs)) = rev(rev(xs) +\!\!+ [x]).$$

J. Garrigue and M. Hermenegildo (Eds.): FLOPS 2008, LNCS 4989, pp. 97–112, 2008.

At this point we may introduce an intermediate lemma to make further progress; in this case, a distributive lemma of reverse over append:

$$\forall x\,y : List(\tau), rev(x +\!\!+ y) = rev(y) +\!\!+ rev(x),$$

then the proof can be completed.

Sometimes the lemmas required to complete a proof are not so easily deducible, and such lemmas need to be conjectured and proved. This is an instance of the search control problems raised by inductive theorem proving [4], which have been well studied: specialised heuristics exist for addressing these problems (for instance recursion analysis and rippling [5]), but none is complete.

In [7] Bundy and Richardson explored a novel way of proving properties of lists by giving a formal basis for proofs using ellipsis. At the core of their technique is the representation of $List(\tau)$ as pairs $(n, f : \mathbb{N} \to \tau)$, via a polymorphic function

$$\square : \mathbb{N} \times (\mathbb{N} \to \tau) \to List(\tau),$$

where $n : \mathbb{N}$ represents the length of the list, and $f(i)$ is the element stored at the ith position in the list, i.e. $\square(n, f) = [f(1), \ldots, f(n)]$. Notice on the right of the equation we have an informal representation of a list using ellipsis, while on the left we have a formal representation of it. Similarly, reverse can be represented informally as mapping the list $[f(1), \ldots, f(n)]$ to $[f(n), \ldots, f(1)]$ or formally as mapping $\square(n, f)$ to the list $\square(n, \lambda i.f(n - i - 1))$. We call this the ellipis technique.

The advantage of the ellipsis technique is that once can reason formally with expressions involving $\square$ and then obtain a clear, concise, correct and informal proof using ellipsis. As was demonstrated in [7], there are a number of proofs for which an inductive approach flounders, but which can be straightforwardly established using the ellipis technique.

Apart from addressing the limitations of inductive inference, the ellipsis technique also endorses definitions and proofs which, by using ellipsis, are intuitive and concise. Such *schematic* definitions and proofs are usually thought to be easier to understand than their regular counterparts (see [6]). The success of this technique was reasonable: 50% of properties tested were proved [7].

This success, however, could not be repeated for properties of append $+\!\!+ : List(\tau) \times List(\tau) \to List(\tau)$, where

$$[\,] +\!\!+ ys \mapsto ys \tag{3}$$
$$(x :: xs) +\!\!+ ys \mapsto x :: (xs +\!\!+ ys).$$

More fundamentally, lists cannot be uniquely represented with the ellipsis technique: the domain of the function f in $(n, f : \mathbb{N} \to \tau)$ is too large and, consequently, $\square$ is not injective. Further, there is no explanation as to which programs can be represented in this way and which cannot. Additionally, the ellipsis technique does not generalise to other datatypes, including nested lists. This limitation was recognized in [7] and properties of the function $flatten : List(List(\tau)) \to List(\tau)$, where

$$flatten([\,]) \mapsto [\,] \tag{4}$$
$$flatten(x :: xs) \mapsto x +\!\!+ flatten(xs)$$

were not considered.

The theory of containers [2,1] admits a refinement of the theory of ellipsis, which solves all of the problems mentioned above. Containers capture the idea that concrete datatypes consists of memory locations where data can be stored. For example, an element of the type $List(\tau)$ can be uniquely written as a natural number n — its *shape*, given by its length — and a function $f : \{0,\dots,n-1\} \to \tau$, which labels each position in the list with some data. This guarantees a unique representation, as the domain of f is now correct. Further, containers not only model lists, but also all *strictly positive* datatypes. [1] Additionally, all polymorphic functions between strictly positive types can be captured as *container morphisms* [2,1]. Containers thus seem to be an ideal foundation for reasoning about such datatypes.

This paper explores containers as a basis for reasoning about lists. We show how containers subsume the ellipsis technique and demonstrate how we can reason with containers. We then discuss our formalisation and compare our results to [7].

In summary, this paper makes the following contributions:

1. We introduce containers to the theorem proving community and show that containers subsume the ellipsis technique. Consequently, we present containers as an alternative representation from which schematic proofs can be derived.
2. We extend the work in [7] to show how containers can be used to reason about lists. In particular, we demonstrate how some properties which eluded Bundy and Richardson can be resolved via containers.
3. We present an implementation of the core theory of containers in Coq, as well as a formalisation of lists as container types. We also discuss a number of challenges that arose during this implementation and how we address them.

The example theorems in this paper all have well-known inductive proofs, straighforward to execute once the appropriate generalizations have been made. Our purpose in this paper, like that of Bundy and Richardson, is to capture these properties more systematically and schematically, reducing carefully crafted inductions to essentially unremarkable arithmetic facts.

Section 2 gives a brief introduction to containers and details the constructions and results required in our system. In section 3 we describe key aspects of such a reasoning system and demonstrate how proofs are resolved. Section 4 discusses issues raised in the implementation, while the sections following offer some discussions and comments on related work and possible future work.

In what follows, we provide the Coq definitions and lemmas so one can relate the article to the formalisation.[2]

2   Introduction to Containers

Containers capture the idea that concrete datatypes consists of memory locations where data can be stored. For instance, any element of type $List(\tau)$ can be uniquely written as a natural number n given by the length of the list, together with a function

---

[1] Strictly positive types are those formed using 0, 1, $+$, $\times$, $\to$, μ, ν with the restriction that types on the left side of the arrow are closed with respect to types variables [8]. For instance, in initial algebra semantics, $list(X) = \mu Y. 1 + X \times Y$ so the type list is a strictly posistive type.

[2] The formal development is available on the web at http://www.cs.nott.ac.uk/~rcp/work.html.

$\{0, \ldots, n-1\} \to \tau$ which labels each position within the list with an element from τ. Thus we may write:

$$List\,(\tau) \triangleq \sum n : \mathbb{N}.\,Fin\,n \to \tau.$$

Fin n can be thought of as the type containing n memory locations, while the function $f : Fin\,n \to \tau$ attaches to these locations the data stored there. We call $n : \mathbb{N}$ the *shape* of the list and $Fin\,n$ the type of *positions* in a list with shape n. Similarly, any binary tree tree can be described by its underlying shape which is obtained by deleting the data stored at the leaves and a function mapping the positions in this shape to the data, thus:

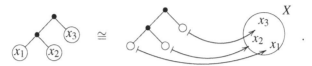

In general, we can consider datatypes which are given by a type of shapes S and, for each $s : S$, a type of positions Ps which we may think of as locations in memory where data can be stored.

Definition 2.1. *Container.* *A container* $(S \triangleleft P)$ *consists of a type* S *and, for each shape* $s : S$, *a type of positions* $P\,s$.

Notice that the type P is a dependent type. We may equivalently write $(S \triangleleft P)$ in *pointwise* notation $(s : S \triangleleft P(s))$, especially if we need to be explicit about the patterns which shapes can match.

Coq's record type provides a shorthand notation for an inductive type with one constructor: every field in a record type can depend on values in the preceding field and field names can act as projection functions. We thus define a container in Coq as:

```
Record Fam (X:Type)   : Type := ucont {s:Set; p: s -> X}.
Definition Ucontainer : Type := Fam Set.
```

As suggested above, lists can be presented as the container $(\mathbb{N} \triangleleft Fin)$. In Coq, we can leave the shape set to be inferred:

```
Definition Lst := ucont Fin.
```

where nat and Fin — the set $\{0, \ldots, n-1\}$ — are as follows,

```
Inductive nat : Set :=
  | O : nat
  | S : nat -> nat.

Inductive Fin : nat -> Set :=
  |fz : forall n, Fin (S n)
  |fs : forall n, Fin n -> Fin (S n).
```

The datatype represented by a container has as values, a shape and a function assigning to each position of that shape, a piece of data. This is called the extension of a container.

Definition 2.2. *Extension of a Container. Let* $(S \triangleleft P)$ *be a container. Its extension is the functor* $T_{(S \triangleleft P)} : \mathbf{Set} \rightarrow \mathbf{Set}$ *defined by:*

$$T_{(S \triangleleft P)} \tau \triangleq \sum s : S . P(s) \rightarrow \tau,$$

which we formalise as:

```
Record Ext (S:Ucontainer )(X:Set):Set :=
   uext {u: s S; f: p S u -> X }.
```

An element of $T_{(S \triangleleft P)} \tau$ is thus a pair (u, f) where $u : S$ is the shape and $f : P s \rightarrow \tau$ labels positions over s with elements from τ.

2.1 Container Morphisms

Consider reverse on a list (n, f). Assume that $rev(n, f) = (n', f')$. Since *rev* does not change the shape of the list, $n = n'$. For the positions, we observe that the data stored at the ith position of the output is the data stored at the $(n - i - 1)^{th}$ position from the input. More generally, a polymorphic function between containers consists of a covariant map between shapes and a contravariant mapping between positions.

Definition 2.3. *Container Morphism. Given* $(S \triangleleft P)$ *and* $(S' \triangleleft P')$, *the morphism* $(S \triangleleft P) \rightarrow (S' \triangleleft P')$ *consists of a pair* (u, f), *where* $u : S \rightarrow S'$ *and* $f : \prod s : S . P'(u s) \rightarrow P s . \prod s : S . P'(u s) \rightarrow P s.$

We formalise this as:

```
Record cmr (C D:Container):Type :=
    ucmr {u: s C -> s D;
          f: forall a: s C, p D (u a) -> p C a}.
```

Example 2.4. $idm : (S \triangleleft P) \rightarrow (S \triangleleft P)$ is the identity morphism which is defined by $(\lambda s. s, \lambda s. \lambda p. p)$.

Example 2.5. $crev : (n : \mathbb{N} \triangleleft Fin n) \rightarrow (n : \mathbb{N} \triangleleft Fin n)$ is the representation of reverse ((1) on p.97) as a container morphism. It is given by the identity on shapes and the map rv on positions: in effect, $rv_n(i) = n - i - 1$. We define it as follows:

$$rv : \forall n. Fin\, n \rightarrow Fin\, n$$
$$rv_{(Sn)} fz \mapsto top_n \tag{5}$$
$$rv_{(Sn)} (fs\, i) \mapsto emb\, (rv_n\, i),$$

where top_n returns the largest element of $Fin\, n$ (corresponding to $n - 1$), and emb_n embeds the elements of $Fin\, n$ into $Fin\, (Sn)$ preserving their numerical value.

$$
\begin{array}{ll}
top : \forall n. Fin\, (Sn) & emb : \forall n. Fin\, n \rightarrow Fin\, (Sn) \\
top_O \mapsto fz & emb\, fz_n \mapsto fz_{(Sn)} \\
top_{(Sn)} \mapsto fs\, (top_n) & emb\, (fs\, i) \mapsto fs\, (emb\, i)
\end{array}
\tag{6}
$$

Observe that *top* and *emb* partition $Fin\, (Sn)$:

$$\forall i : Fin\, (Sn) . i = top_n \vee \exists i' : Fin\, n . i = emb\, i'. \tag{7}$$

We formalise *crev* as :

```
Definition crev : cmr Lst Lst :=
  ucmr (id (s Lst)) (fun n: s Lst => fun fn: Fin n => rv fn).
```

The contravariance of the function on position may seem surprising. But it can be intuitively understood by considering that we can always show where a datum in the output comes from but not where a datum from the input goes to, since it may be copied or disappear.

Example 2.6. The tail function is given by the container morphism

$$(u, f) : (\mathbb{N} \triangleleft Fin) \rightarrow (1 + \mathbb{N} \triangleleft \{inl(*) \mapsto 0 \mid inr(n) \mapsto Fin\,n\})$$

defined by

$$u(0) = inl(*) \quad u(1 + n) = inr(n)$$

and with $f_0 = !$ and $f_{n+1} : Fin\,n \rightarrow Fin\,(n+1)$ defined by $f_{n+1}i = 1 + i$ This can be visualised as

2.2 Constructions on Containers

Containers are closed under various type forming operations such as sums, products, constants, fixed exponentiation, (nested) least fixed point, and (nested) greatest fised points [2,1]. Thus they encapsulate a large number of types. In what follows, we detail the constructions which are pertinent to this presentation: products, sums and compositions.

Definition 2.7. Products. $(S \triangleleft P) \times (S' \triangleleft P')$ *is the container* $(A \triangleleft B)$, *where* $A = S \times S'$ *and for each* $s : S$ *and* $s' : S'$, $B : S \times S' \rightarrow \mathbf{Set}$ *is defined as* $B(s, s') = Ps + P's'$.

```
Definition cont_prod (C D: Ucontainer) :=
  ucont (fun q : (s C) * (s D) =>
    sum (p C (fst q)) (p D (snd q))).
```

For the sum $(S \triangleleft P) + (S' \triangleleft P')$, the shapes are given by $S + S'$. For the positions: if our shape is of the form $inl(s)$ then it is given by Ps and, alternatively, if it is of the form $inr(s')$ then it is given by $P's'$.

Definition 2.8. Sums. $(S \triangleleft P) + (S' \triangleleft P')$ *is the container* $(A \triangleleft B)$, *where* $A = S + S'$ *and for* $s : S$ *and* $s' : S'$, $B(inl(s)) = Ps$ *and* $B(inr(s')) = P's'$.

In Coq syntax we write;

```
Definition sum (f : S1 -> Set)
               (g : S2 -> Set) (H: S1 + S2):=
        match H with
        | inl a => f a
        | inr b => g b
        end.
Definition cont_sum (C D: Ucontainer) := ucont (sum (p C) (p D)).
```

When we come to reason about $List(List(\tau))$, we will need to represent this datatype as a container. The *principled* way to do this is to observe that $List(List(\tau))$ is the composite $(List \circ List)\tau$; this composition of functors can be reflected via composition of containers.

Definition 2.9. *Composing Containers.* Let $(S \triangleleft P)$ and $(S' \triangleleft P')$ be containers, the composition $(S \triangleleft P) \circ (S' \triangleleft P')$ is the container $\left((s, f) : T_{(S \triangleleft P)} S' \triangleleft \Sigma i : P s. P'(f i)\right)$.

We formalise this as:

```
Record CPos (C D : Ucontainer)  (a : Ext C (s D) )  : Set :=
   cpos {cs : p C (u a); cp :  p D ((f a) cs)}.
Definition cComp (C D : Ucontainer) : Ucontainer :=
   ucont (fun a : Ext C (s D)  => CPos D a).
```

The shape of the composition must determine the outer shape together with the inner shape for each outer position. We can therefore take it to be a $(S \triangleleft P)$ structure holding S' elements. A composite position first locates an inner $(S' \triangleleft P')$ structure at an outer position, then an individual element within it.

Example 2.10. Nested lists $List(List\ X)$ can be represented by the composite of the container $(\mathbb{N} \triangleleft Fin)$ with itself. It's shape is given by

$$List\ (\mathbb{N}) = T_{(\mathbb{N} \triangleleft Fin)} \mathbb{N} \triangleq \Sigma n : \mathbb{N}.\ Fin\ n \to \mathbb{N},$$

and it's positions by $P : List\ (\mathbb{N}) \to \mathbf{Set}$ which is defined by

$$P\ (n, f) = \Sigma i : Fin\ n.\ Fin\ (f\ i).$$

In general, all constructions on containers extend to container morphisms. Additionally, we can represent the composition of functions by constructing the composite of container morphisms.

Definition 2.11. *Composing Container Morphisms.* If $(u_1, f_1) : (S \triangleleft P) \to (S' \triangleleft P')$ and $(u_2, f_2) : (S' \triangleleft P') \to (S'' \triangleleft P'')$ are container morphisms, their composite is the container morphism $(u, f) : (S \triangleleft P) \to (S'' \triangleleft P'')$ defined by $u\ s = u_s \circ (u_1\ s)$ and $f\ s\ p = f_1\ s\ (f_2\ (u_1\ s)\ p)$.

This is implemented as:

```
Definition m_comp (cd : cmr C D) (de : cmr D E)  : cmr C E:=
  match cd with
  | ucmr v0 g0 =>
    match de with
    | ucmr v1 g1 =>
      ucmr (comp v0 v1)
      (fun (sc : s C) (pe : p E (comp v0 v1 sc)) =>
             comp (g1 (v0 sc)) (g0 sc) pe)
      end
    end.
```

3   Reasoning with Containers

Given a container morphism $(u, f) : (S \triangleleft P) \to (S' \triangleleft P')$, does (u, f) really define a polymorphic function $T_{(S \triangleleft P)} \to T_{(S' \triangleleft P')}$? If so, are all polymorphic function uniquely defined in this manner? The central result in the theory of containers addresses these questions.

Theorem 3.1. *The functor* $T : \mathscr{C}_I \to [\mathbb{C}^I, \mathbb{C}]$ *is full and faithful.*

In other words, container morphisms $(S \triangleleft P) \to (S \triangleleft P)$ are in bijection with natural transformations $T_{(S \triangleleft P)} \to T_{(S' \triangleleft P')}$. For a proof, the interested reader may consult [2,1,8]. This addresses the flaw in [7] as it ensures us that by reasoning about container morphisms, we reason about polymorphic functions. In particular, we can prove two polymorphic functions are equal (i.e. have the same computational result) by proving that their representations as container morphisms are equal - i.e. both their maps on shapes and positions have the same computational result. Further, we ensure we reason about lists by giving a natural isomorphism from lists to extensions: $T_{(\mathbb{N} \triangleleft Fin)} \tau \leftrightarrows List(\tau)$. So by reasoning about container morphisms, we reason about lists and vice versa. Our approach can be visualized as shown:

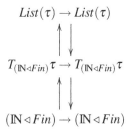

3.1   Equality of Container Morphisms

Given two container morphisms $(u, f), (u', f') : (S \triangleleft P) \to (S' \triangleleft P')$, we want to consider when their action on shapes and positions correspond. Recall that container morphisms $(S \triangleleft P) \to (S' \triangleleft P')$ are *dependent* pairs: they inhabit the type

$$\sum \alpha : S \to S'. \prod s : S. P'(\alpha s) \to P s.$$

To state their equality, we need to cope with two issues: *heterogeneity* and *extensionality*. The first of these arises when we try to consider the components of container morphisms separately. Their types are as follows:

$$u, u' : S \to S'$$
$$f : \prod s : S. P'(u s) \to P s$$
$$f' : \prod s : S. P'(u' s) \to P s$$

The conventional Martin-Löf definition of equality *within a given type* allows us to express that $u = u'$, but prevents us from asserting that $f = f'$ because their types are considered distinct. Such *heterogeneous* equations occur naturally whenever not only our propositions but even our data structures are expressed as dependent types. In [10,11], McBride proposed a convenient way to treat them: the 'John Major' equality predicate, written as $=_{jm}$, admits comparison of objects of any type, but they can be only treated as equal (*i.e.* substituted) if they are of the same type. If we can identify u with u' by substitution, say, then the types of f and f' become the same and the resulting homogeneous equation can be exploited.

The formation, introduction and elimination rules, respectively are as follows:

$$\frac{a : A \quad b : B}{a =_{jm} b : Prop} \qquad \frac{a : A}{refl : a =_{jm} a} \qquad \frac{\begin{array}{c} a : A \\ \Phi : \forall a' : A.\, a =_{jm} a' \to Type \\ \phi : \Phi\, a\, (refl\, a) \end{array}}{\forall a' : A.\, \forall q : a =_{jm} a'.\, \Phi\, a'\, q}$$

Thus $=_{jm}$ can compare anything to a, even if its type is different from A. However, the introduction and elimination rules follow the conventional *homogeneous* definition: only objects of the same type can really be equal or treated as such.

The second issue is that types such as $u = u'$ are only inhabited if u and u' have the same implementation, but we need to consider functions *extensionally*. We therefore define equality for container morphisms such that each component takes equal inputs to equal outputs. Since the position components are dependent functions, $=_{jm}$ again provides the flexibility required:

Definition 3.2. *Equality of Container Morphisms.* Let $(u, f), (u', f') : (S \triangleleft P) \to (S' \triangleleft P')$.

$$\frac{\begin{array}{c} \forall s : S.\, u\,s = u'\,s \\ \forall s : S.\, \forall p : P(u\,s).\, \forall p' : P(u'\,s).\, p =_{jm} p' \to f\,s\,p =_{jm} f'\,s\,p' \end{array}}{(u, f) =_{mor} (u', f')}$$

The $=_{jm}$ relation is predefined in the Coq library and we use it in our formalisation:

```
Inductive Eqmor (i j : cmr C D) : Prop :=
 morq : (forall a : s C,  u i a  = u j a )->
   (forall (a : s C)(p0 : p D (u i a))(p1 : p D (u j a)),
     JMeq p0 p1 -> f i a p0 = f j a p1) -> Eqmor i j.
```

As suggested before, if $(u, f), (u', f') : (\mathbb{N} \triangleleft Fin) \to (\mathbb{N} \triangleleft Fin)$, then proving $(u, f) =_{mor} (u', f')$ reduces to arithmetical proofs about $\mathbb{N}$ and $Fin\, n$. Now, armed with theorem 3.1 and the elimination rule given by definition 3.2, we can safely proceed to give container based proofs of list-theoretic results. For instance, we may specify (2) on p.97 as:

```
Theorem crev_crev_sm : Eqmor (m_comp crev crev) (idm Lst).
```

Unpacking the definitions, our proofs obligations are to show:

1. $\forall n : \mathbb{N}.\, n = n$ for shapes and,
2. $\forall n : \mathbb{N}.\, \forall i : Fin\, n.\, rv\,(rv\,i) = i$ for positions—in effect, $n - (n - i - 1) - 1$

The latter requires a proof that reversing the finite type $Fin\, n$ is also self inverse.

In this way, properties of list manipulators are transformed into arithmetic assertions. Ultimately, these too require inductive proofs, but it seems reasonable to hope that container-based reasoning might benefit from tactics and libraries designed to support arithmetic.

4   Analysing Finite Types

If we are to define and reason about our container morphisms for list manipulation, we will need some tools for working with the *Fin* family. Here, we can borrow some useful techniques from programming in Epigram [12,3], in particular the use of *views*— alternative methods of data decomposition, presented via inductive relations.

4.1   Appending Lists

Let us define (3) on p.98 as a container morphism:

$$cappend : ((n,m) : \mathbb{N} \times \mathbb{N} \triangleleft Fin\,n + Fin\,m) \rightarrow (\mathbb{N} \triangleleft Fin)$$

The length of the output should be the sum of the lengths of the inputs, so it is clear what to do for shapes:

$$u : \mathbb{N} \times \mathbb{N} \rightarrow \mathbb{N}$$
$$u_{cappend}\,(n,m) \mapsto n+m.$$

Now we need to map output positions in $Fin\,(n+m)$ to input positions in $Fin\,n + Fin\,m$, reflecting the sum structure of finite types. It's easy to build injections which map the other way. In our formalisation, we write

```
Fixpoint finl (n m : nat ) (i : Fin n) {struct i} : Fin (n + m):=
  match i  in Fin n return Fin (n + m) with
  | fz _  => fz
  | fs x k => fs (finl x m k)
  end.
```

```
Fixpoint finr (n m : nat) (i:Fin m) {struct n}: Fin (n + m):=
   match n return Fin (n + m) with
   | 0 => i
   | S n' => fs (finr n' m i)
   end.
```

If we knew that *finl* and *finr* covered $Fin\,(n+m)$, we could write

$$f_{cappend} : \forall (n,m) : \mathbb{N}.\,Fin\,(n+m) \rightarrow Fin\,n + Fin\,m$$
$$f_{cappend}\,((n,m),finl\,n\,m\,i) \mapsto inl\,i$$
$$f_{cappend}\,((n,m),finr\,n\,m\,j) \mapsto inr\,j$$

Correspondingly, we may define a relation which expresses what it means to be covered by *finl* and *finr*, then show that this relation always holds:

```
Inductive FinSum (n m : nat) : Fin (n + m) -> Set :=
 | is_inl : forall i: Fin n, FinSum (finl n m i)
 | is_inr : forall j: Fin m, FinSum (finr n m j).
```

```
Definition finSum (n m: nat) (k : Fin (n + m)): FinSum n m k.
```

The definition of *finSum* is straightforward. Case analysis on the output of *finSum n m k* will deliver exactly the decomposition of k as *finl n m i* or *finr n m j* required to give $f_{cappend}$ as specified above. The very same view is exactly what we need in order to reason about *cappend*.

4.2 Flattening Lists of Lists

Where (3) concatenates two lists, *flatten* (see (4) on p.98) takes a list of lists, represented by a container composition

$$cflatt : (((n, l) : T_{(\mathbb{N} \triangleleft Fin)} \mathbb{N}) \triangleleft \Sigma i : Fin\, n.\, Fin\, (l\, i)) \to (\mathbb{N} \triangleleft Fin).$$

For shapes, we must add the lengths of all n input lists, each given by the l function:

$$u_{cflatt} : T_{(\mathbb{N} \triangleleft Fin)} \mathbb{N} \to \mathbb{N}$$
$$u_{cflatt} (0, l) \mapsto 0$$
$$u_{cflatt} (S\, n, l) \mapsto l\, fz + u_{cflatt} (n, l \circ fs).$$

That is, $u_{cflatt} (n, l) = \Sigma_{i:Fin\, n}\, l\, i$. Correspondingly, we need a map on positions which reflects the summation structure of finite types:

$$f_{cflatt} : \forall (n, l) : T_{(\mathbb{N} \triangleleft Fin)} \mathbb{N}.\, Fin\, (\sum_{i:Fin\, n} l\, i) \to \Sigma i : Fin\, n.\, Fin\, (l\, i).$$

Again, the 'wrong' direction is easy. We may readily construct the general injection using *finl* and *finr*, as follows:

```
Definition finj (n : nat) (l : Fin n -> nat) (i : Fin n) :
    Fin (l i) -> Fin (sum_n l).
 intros n l i k;   induction i.
 exact (finl (l (fz n))
       (sum_n (fun z : Fin n => l (fs z))) k).
 exact (finr (l (fz n))
       (sum_n (fun z => l (fs z))) (IHi (fun z => l (fs z)) k)).
Defined.
```

From here, we may once again present the direction we need as a view:

```
Inductive FinSumm (n : nat) (l : Fin n -> nat) :
    Fin (sum_n l)-> Set :=
 finPair : forall (i: Fin n) (k : Fin (l i)),
    FinSumm l (finj l i k).
```

```
Definition finSumm (n:nat) (l: Fin n -> nat)
    (x : Fin (sum_n l)) : FinSumm l x.
```

4.3   Reasoning about Reverse

Views also play an important part in our reasoning toolkit. An interesting example is the theorem

$$\forall l : List(List(\tau)). \, rev(flatten(l)) = flatten(map(rev, rev(l))), \tag{8}$$

where *rev* is given by (1) on p.97. This is specified in our container formalisation as

```
Theorem map_flatt_rev: Eqmor
  (m_comp cflatt crev)
  (m_comp (m_comp (ap_mor crev Lst) map_rev) cflatt),
```

where map_rev is the (*map rev*) in (8), and is given as a container morphism

$$(\mathbb{N} \triangleleft Fin) \circ (\mathbb{N} \triangleleft Fin) \rightarrow (\mathbb{N} \triangleleft Fin) \circ (\mathbb{N} \triangleleft Fin)$$

```
Definition map_rev :=
 let pmap :=
  (fun a : Ext Lst nat => fun ps : CPos Lst a  =>
  cpos Lst a (cs ps) (rv (cp ps))) in
   ucmr (cComp Lst Lst)(cComp Lst Lst)(id (Ext Lst nat)) pmap,
```

and (ap_mor crev Lst) is the container morphism which represents the function

$$revList : List(List(\tau)) \rightarrow List(List(\tau))$$

which reverses its input. Following on from the discussion in section (2.1) on p.101; for the map on shapes, we need to show that

$$u_{cflatt}(n, f) = u_{cflatt}(n, (f_{crev} \, n)), \tag{9}$$

and for the map on positions

$$\frac{\begin{array}{c} p_1 : Fin(u_{cflatt}(n, f)) \\ p_2 : Fin(u_{cflatt}(n, (f_{crev} \, n))) \\ H : p_1 =_{jm} p_2 \end{array}}{f_{cflatt}(u_{cflatt}(n, f)) \, p_1 = f_{cflatt}(u_{cflatt}(n, (f_{crev} \, n))) \, p_2}. \tag{10}$$

Proving (9) is trivial. We observe that that f_{crev}, $f_{cappend}$ and f_{cflatt} define different operations on the type Fin . So in order to prove (10), we will need to analyze Fin according to these operations.

Firstly, any element of type $Fin(Sn)$ can be given either as the maximum element $topn$ or for some $i : Finn$, as the embedding $emb \, i$ (c.f. (7) on p.101). This suggests the need for a view on $Fin(Sn)$ so we can analyze it in terms of these constructions. We formalise this as:

```
Inductive FinEmtp (n : nat) : Fin (S n) -> Set :=
  | isTp : FinEmtp (tp n)
  | isEmb : forall (i : Fin n), FinEmtp (emb i).
```

```
Definition finEmtp (n : nat) (i : Fin (S n)) : FinEmtp i.
```

where $finEmtp$ gives the required view.

The need for each of these views is suggested by the position maps of *cappend*, *cflatt* and *crev* respectively: when reasoning about *crev* we may require a view on $Fin\,(S\,n)$ in terms of *top* and *emb*; when reasoning about about *cappend*, we may require the view on $Fin(n+m)$ in terms of $Fin\,n$ and $Fin\,m$ and when reasoning about *cflatt*, we may require the view on $Fin\,(\Sigma_{i:Fin\,n}(l\,i))$. In the case of (10), these views are necessary.

4.4 Simultaneous Rewriting

Completing the proof of (10) requires another piece of machinery. In our construction of equality for container morphisms (Definition 3.2 on p.105), $=_{jm}$ was required to compare objects which are provably equal. Often in our proofs, it necessary to substitute objects of a dependent type that are (heterogeneously) equal, given that we have a proof about the (homogeneous) equality of the objects on which they depend. To do this we may derive an additional substitution rule for $=_{jm}$:

$$
\begin{array}{c}
a\ a' : A \\
B : A \to Type \\
ba : B\,a \quad ba' : B\,a' \\
H : a = a' \quad H_{jm} : ba =_{jm} ba' \\
\Phi : \forall(x:A)\,(bx:B\,x).\,Type \\
\Phi\ a\ ba \\
\hline
\Phi\ a'\ ba'
\end{array}
\tag{11}
$$

For example, consider proving the following:

$$\forall(n\,m\,x : \mathbb{N}), \forall i : Fin\,x.\ finr\,n\,(m+x)\,(finr\,m\,x\,i) =_{jm} finr\,(n+m)\,x\,i.$$

Assuming $+$ is defined by recursion on its first argument, we can proceed by induction on n but get stuck at:[3]

$$\frac{finr\,n\,(m+x)\,(finr\,m\,x\,i) =_{jm} finr\,(n+m)\,x\,i}{fs\,(finr\,n\,(m+x)\,(finr\,m\,x\,i)) =_{jm} fs\,(finr\,(n+m)\,x\,i)}.$$

But this can be unstuck by (11) and a proof of the associativity of $+$, and the proof completed.

5 Discussion

For reasons already discussed, we were only interested in properties of polymorphic functions. However, in their formalisation of the ellipsis technique, Bundy and Richardson in [7] also sought to consider functions which are not polymorphic. For instance, the function *member* : $\tau \times List\,(\tau) \to$ **Bool** was considered as $member(x, \square(n, f)) \leftrightarrow \exists i \leq n.\,x = (f\,i)$. All attempts to prove properties of this function failed. Although, we

---

[3] The elimination rule for $=_{jm}$ resolves the base case (see section 3.1).

can give a representation of *member* via containers, it cannot be expressed as a container morphism. Our current approach is to exploit **Theorem** 3.1 and reason in terms of container morphisms; so functions like *member* could not be considered since it is not polymorphic.

We indicated earlier that the ellipsis technique stumbled while proving properties involving $+\!\!+$. In [7] $+\!\!+$ was represented as:

$$\square(n\,f) +\!\!+ \square(m, g) = \square(n + m, comb(n, f, g))$$

where comb is defined by:

$$comb(n, f, g)(i) = \begin{cases} f\,i & \text{if } i \leq m \\ g\,(i - m) & \text{if } i > m \end{cases}$$

Proving properties involving $+\!\!+$ thus became very difficult, as it involved reasoning about inequalities and performing conditional rewriting. An ellipsis technique was implemented in [14] which addressed these issues, but the limitations mentioned in section 1 still remained.

When the work in [7] was completed, the theory of containers was not yet developed, nor had most of the the techniques we use to represent and reason about container morphisms (*e.g.* views). It therefore seems that the limitations of the ellipsis technique were primarily due to the existing state of the art. We believe that containers represent a fundamental improvement of the ellipsis technique, where the use of dependent types ensures that the representation of lists is unique and, hence, many probems encountered with the latter did not arise. For instance, the use of views makes reasoning about functions like $+\!\!+$ much easier than was the case even in [14].

Our container approach has proved significantly more effective than the ellipsis technique at systematically capturing the inductions underlying properties of list-manipulating functions: below, we show a selection of well-known theorems amenable to the former but not the latter:

$$flatten(a +\!\!+ b) = flatten(a) +\!\!+ flatten(b)$$
$$rev(rev\,a) = a$$
$$rev(a +\!\!+ b) = rev(b) +\!\!+ rev(a)$$
$$rev(flatten(a)) = flatten(map(rev, rev(a)))$$
$$(a +\!\!+ b) +\!\!+ c = a +\!\!+ (b +\!\!+ c).$$

6   Related Work

Despite well known limitations of inductive inference (*cf.* section (1) on p.97), the theorem proving community does not seem to have shown much interest in alternative approaches to reasoning about lists and recursive types in general. The ellipsis technique in [7], thus seem to be an isolated exception.

As far as we are aware, ours is the first attempt at developing a container-based reasoning system. We did suggest, however, that our approach can be adopted as a means of formalising ellipsis, as was the case in [7], as well as a means from which schematic proofs [6] (of properties of polymorphic functions between strictly positive datatypes) can be extracted.

We have detailed the limitations of the ellipsis technique, and addressed them earlier in the discourse. We have also shown that our container approach is successful in cases where the ellipsis technique failed.

7 Conclusion and Future Work

In this paper, we have investigated containers. We have seen how to represent lists as containers and how we can reason about polymorphic functions in terms of container morphisms. We have also seen that this representation of list not only refines the ellipsis technique, but also instructs a robust reasoning system.

The central difficulty which we faced in this work was to convince Coq of essentially unremarkable facts about arithmetic on Fin, arising from the representation of container morphisms over $(\mathbb{N} \triangleleft Fin)$. Neither the libraries nor the tactics of Coq are as well adapted to this presentation of arithmetic problems as they are to ranges expressed via order relations. However, it is clear from the success of tactics like Omega, [15,9] that this difficulty can be overcome. Our container approach directly captures the visual intuition behind these properties of operations on lists, factoring their inductive proofs into a schematic argument with arithmetic details. With suitable technology for the latter, these tasks will finally become as easy as our intuition suggests they should be.

Now that we know how to reason with containers, one consideration is to explore reasoning about other datatypes. However, we would also like to consider our proof method in more general context. Containers have been considered as an alternative approach to generic programming [3,13]; we wish to explore this application, and the associated proof techniques. In particular, a wide variety of common first-order inductive datatypes can be expressed as *small* containers, whose shapes have a decidable equality and whose position sets are finite, making them particularly amenable to the techniques in this paper.

Acknowledgment

We thank Peter Hancock and Nicolas Oury for helpful discussions on the topic. Special thanks to Russell O'Connor for developing a library on finite types, available on the Coq Wiki (http://cocorico.cs.ru.nl/coqwiki), which we found quite useful. Finally, our grateful thanks to those anonymous referees for their useful comments and suggestions for improving this paper.

References

1. Abbott, M.: Categories of Containers. PhD thesis, University of Leicester (2003)
2. Abbott, M., Altenkirch, T., Ghani, N.: Categories of Containers. In: Gordon, A.D. (ed.) FOSSACS 2003. LNCS, vol. 2620, pp. 23–38. Springer, Heidelberg (2003)

3. Altenkirch, T., McBride, C., Morris, P.: Generic Programming with Dependent Types. In: Backhouse, R., Gibbons, J., Hinze, R., Jeuring, J. (eds.) SSDGP 2006. LNCS, vol. 4719, pp. 209–257. Springer, Heidelberg (2007)
4. Bundy, A.: The automation of proof by mathematical induction. In: Robinson, A., Voronkov, A. (eds.) Handbook of Automated Reasoning, vol. I, ch. 13, pp. 845–911. Elsevier, Amsterdam (2001)
5. Bundy, A., Basin, D., Hutter, D., Ireland, A.: Rippling: Meta-level Guidance for Mathematical Reasoning. Cambridge Tracts in Theoretical Computer Science, vol. 56. Cambridge University Press, Cambridge (2005)
6. Bundy, A., Jamnik, M., Fugard, A.: What is a proof? In: Philosophical Transactions of The Royal Society A: Mathematical, Physical and Engineering Sciences, vol. 363, pp. 2377–2392 (2005)
7. Bundy, A., Richardson, J.: Proofs about lists using ellipsis. In: Logic Programming and Automated Reasoning (1999)
8. Ghani, N., Abbott, M., Altenkirch, T.: Containers - constructing strictly positive types. Theoretical Computer Science 341(1), 3–27 (2005)
9. INRIA. The Coq Proof Asistant Reference Manual Version 8.1 (2006), http://coq.inria.fr/V8.1pl3/refman/index.html
10. McBride, C.: Dependently Typed Functional Programs and their Proofs. PhD thesis, University of Edinburgh (1999)
11. McBride, C.: Elimination with a motive. In: Callaghan, P., Luo, Z., McKinna, J., Pollack, R. (eds.) TYPES 2000. LNCS, vol. 2277, pp. 197–216. Springer, Heidelberg (2002)
12. McBride, C., McKinna, J.: The view from the left. Journal of Functional Programming 14(1), 69–111 (2004)
13. Morris, P.: Constructing Universes for Generic Programming. PhD thesis, University of Nottingham (2007)
14. Prince, R.: An extension of the ellipsis technique. Master's thesis, University of Edinburgh (2005)
15. Pugh, W.: The Omega test: A fast and practical integer programming algorithm for dependence analysis. In: Supercomputing 1991: Proceedings of the 1991 ACM/IEEE conference on Supercomputing, pp. 4–13. ACM Press, New York (1991)

Termination of Narrowing
in Left-Linear Constructor Systems*

Germán Vidal

Technical University of Valencia, Spain
gvidal@dsic.upv.es

Abstract. Narrowing extends rewriting with logic capabilities by allowing logic variables in terms and replacing matching with unification. Narrowing has been widely used in different contexts, ranging from theorem proving to language design. Surprisingly, the termination of narrowing has been mostly overlooked. In this paper, we present a new approach for analyzing the termination of narrowing in left-linear constructor systems—a widely accepted class of systems—that allows us to reuse existing methods in the literature on termination of rewriting.

1 Introduction

The narrowing principle [35] generalizes term rewriting by allowing logic variables in terms—as in logic programming—and by replacing pattern matching with unification in order to (non-deterministically) reduce them. Unrestricted narrowing (i.e., not following any particular strategy for selecting reducible expressions) may have a huge—often infinite—search space, mainly because one can freely select any reducible expression *and* applicable rewrite rule at each narrowing step. Narrowing, originally introduced as an *E*-unification mechanism in equational theories, has been mostly used as the operational semantics of so called *functional logic* programming languages [21]. Recent examples of such languages based on narrowing are Curry [15] and Toy [27]. Currently, narrowing is regaining popularity in a number of other areas, like protocol verification [16,28], model checking [17], partial evaluation [1,32], refining methods for proving the termination of rewriting [8], type checking in the language *Ω*mega [34], etc.

Termination is a fundamental problem in term rewriting, as witnessed by the extensive literature on the subject (see, e.g., [13] and references therein). Surprisingly, the termination of narrowing has been mostly overlooked so far. To the best of our knowledge, no software tool for proving the termination of narrowing has ever been developed. Indeed, only a few approaches to this subject can be found in the literature (see a detailed account in Sect. 6).

In this work, we introduce a new approach to analyze the termination of narrowing by reusing existing results and tools for analyzing the termination of rewriting. The key idea is to consider variables as *data generators* in the context of rewriting. This means that one can analyze the termination of narrowing for

---

* This work has been partially supported by the EU (FEDER) and the Spanish MEC under grants TIN2005-09207-C03-02 and *Acción Integrada* HA2006-0008.

J. Garrigue and M. Hermenegildo (Eds.): FLOPS 2008, LNCS 4989, pp. 113–129, 2008.

the term $\mathsf{add}(x, \mathsf{z})$, where add is a defined function, x is a logic variable, and z is a constructor constant, by analyzing the termination of *rewriting* for all terms of the form $\mathsf{add}(t, \mathsf{z})$, where t stands for an arbitrary—possibly infinite—term. Intuitively speaking, we want t to take any possible value that could be computed by narrowing for the logic variable x in any derivation issuing from $\mathsf{add}(x, \mathsf{z})$, even if it goes on infinitely.

This relation between logic variables and (possibly infinite) terms has been recently exploited in order to eliminate logic variables from functional logic computations [6,12]. A similar idea is also used in the termination analysis for logic programs of [33], where logic programs are transformed to rewrite systems and logic variables are then replaced with infinite terms (see Sect. 6).

Since data generators are, by definition, nonterminating, we introduce the use of *argument filterings* in Sect. 4 in order to filter away these data generators in rewrite derivations. Essentially, we consider two alternative approaches:

- The first technique is based on the well-known dependency pair framework [8,20] for proving the termination of rewriting. We will show that only some slight modifications are required in order to be applicable in our setting.
- The second technique is based on the argument filtering transformation of Kusakari *et al.* [26] and, given a TRS $\mathcal{R}$, produces a new rewrite system $\mathcal{R}'$ so that the termination of rewriting in $\mathcal{R}'$ implies the termination of narrowing in $\mathcal{R}$. Therefore, any method or termination tool for rewrite systems can be applied to $\mathcal{R}'$ in order to prove the termination of narrowing in $\mathcal{R}$.

Section 5 presents a technique for inferring appropriate argument filterings and reports on a prototype implementation of a termination tool, TNT, that follows the second approach above. First, the user introduces a rewrite system and an *abstract call* indicating the entry function to the program. The tool computes an argument filtering from the abstract call and, then, transforms the input system using this argument filtering. The termination of the transformed system is currently checked by using the APT**VE** tool [19].

The main contributions of this work can be summarized as follows: i) we introduce a sufficient and necessary condition for the termination of narrowing in left-linear constructor systems, a widely accepted class of systems; ii) we introduce two alternative approaches for analyzing the termination of narrowing w.r.t. a given argument filtering; and iii) we present an automatic tool for proving the termination of narrowing.

Finally, Sect. 6 includes a comparison to related work and Sect. 7 concludes. More details and proofs of all technical results can be found in [36].

2   Preliminaries

We assume familiarity with basic concepts of term rewriting and narrowing. We refer the reader to, e.g., [9] and [21] for further details.

Terms and Substitutions. A *signature* $\mathcal{F}$ is a set of function symbols. We often write $\mathsf{f}/n \in \mathcal{F}$ to denote that the arity of function f is n. Given a set of variables $\mathcal{V}$ with $\mathcal{F} \cap \mathcal{V} = \varnothing$, we denote the domain of *terms* by $\mathcal{T}(\mathcal{F}, \mathcal{V})$. We assume that $\mathcal{F}$ always contains at least one constant $f/0$. We use $f, g, \ldots$ to denote functions and $x, y, \ldots$ to denote variables. A *position* p in a term t is represented by a finite sequence of natural numbers, where ϵ denotes the root position. Positions are used to address the nodes of a term viewed as a tree. The root symbol of a term t is denoted by $\text{root}(t)$. We let $t|_p$ denote the *subterm* of t at position p and $t[s]_p$ the result of *replacing the subterm* $t|_p$ by the term s. $\mathcal{V}ar(t)$ denotes the set of variables appearing in t. A term t is *ground* if $\mathcal{V}ar(t) = \varnothing$. We write $\mathcal{T}(\mathcal{F})$ as a shorthand for the set of ground terms $\mathcal{T}(\mathcal{F}, \varnothing)$.

A *substitution* $\sigma : \mathcal{V} \mapsto \mathcal{T}(\mathcal{F}, \mathcal{V})$ is a mapping from variables to terms such that $\mathcal{D}om(\sigma) = \{x \in \mathcal{V} \mid x \neq \sigma(x)\}$ is its domain. The set of variables introduced by a substitution σ is denoted by $\mathcal{R}an(\sigma) = \cup_{x \in \mathcal{D}om(\sigma)} \mathcal{V}ar(x\sigma)$. Substitutions are extended to morphisms from $\mathcal{T}(\mathcal{F}, \mathcal{V})$ to $\mathcal{T}(\mathcal{F}, \mathcal{V})$ in the natural way. We denote the application of a substitution σ to a term t by $t\sigma$ (rather than $\sigma(t)$). The identity substitution is denoted by id. A *variable renaming* is a substitution that is a bijection on $\mathcal{V}$. A substitution σ is *more general* than a substitution θ, denoted by $\sigma \leqslant \theta$, if there is a substitution δ such that $\delta \circ \sigma = \theta$, where "$\circ$" denotes the composition of substitutions (i.e., $\sigma \circ \theta(x) = x\theta\sigma$). The *restriction* $\theta\!\restriction_V$ of a substitution θ to a set of variables V is defined as follows: $x\theta\!\restriction_V = x\theta$ if $x \in V$ and $x\theta\!\restriction_V = x$ otherwise. We say that $\theta = \sigma \; [V]$ if $\theta\!\restriction_V = \sigma\!\restriction_V$.

A term t_2 is an *instance* of a term t_1 (or, equivalently, t_1 is *more general* than t_2), in symbols $t_1 \leqslant t_2$, if there is a substitution σ with $t_2 = t_1\sigma$. Two terms t_1 and t_2 are *variants* (or equal up to variable renaming) if $t_1 = t_2\rho$ for some variable renaming ρ. A *unifier* of two terms t_1 and t_2 is a substitution σ with $t_1\sigma = t_2\sigma$; furthermore, σ is the *most general unifier* of t_1 and t_2, denoted by $\text{mgu}(t_1, t_2)$ if, for every other unifier θ of t_1 and t_2, we have that $\sigma \leqslant \theta$.

TRSs and Rewriting. A set of rewrite rules $l \to r$ such that l is a nonvariable term and r is a term whose variables appear in l is called a *term rewriting system* (TRS for short); terms l and r are called the left-hand side and the right-hand side of the rule, respectively. We restrict ourselves to finite signatures and TRSs. Given a TRS $\mathcal{R}$ over a signature $\mathcal{F}$, the *defined* symbols $\mathcal{D}$ are the root symbols of the left-hand sides of the rules and the *constructors* are $\mathcal{C} = \mathcal{F} \setminus \mathcal{D}$.

We use the notation $\mathcal{F} = \mathcal{D} \uplus \mathcal{C}$ to point out that $\mathcal{D}$ are the defined function symbols and $\mathcal{C}$ are the constructors of a signature $\mathcal{F}$, with $\mathcal{D} \cap \mathcal{C} = \varnothing$. The domains $\mathcal{T}(\mathcal{C}, \mathcal{V})$ and $\mathcal{T}(\mathcal{C})$ denote the sets of *constructor terms* and *ground constructor terms*, respectively. A substitution σ is (ground) *constructor*, if $x\sigma$ is a (ground) constructor term for all $x \in \mathcal{D}om(\sigma)$.

A TRS $\mathcal{R}$ is a *constructor system* if the left-hand sides of its rules have the form $f(s_1, \ldots, s_n)$ where s_i are constructor terms, i.e., $s_i \in \mathcal{T}(\mathcal{C}, \mathcal{V})$, for all $i = 1, \ldots, n$. A term t is *linear* if every variable of $\mathcal{V}$ occurs at most once in t. A TRS $\mathcal{R}$ is *left-linear* if l is linear for every rule $l \to r \in \mathcal{R}$.

For a TRS $\mathcal{R}$, we define the associated rewrite relation $\to_\mathcal{R}$ as follows: given terms $s, t \in \mathcal{T}(\mathcal{F}, \mathcal{V})$, we have $s \to_\mathcal{R} t$ iff there exists a position p in s, a rewrite rule $l \to r \in \mathcal{R}$ and a substitution σ with $s|_p = l\sigma$ and $t = s[r\sigma]_p$; the rewrite step is often denoted by $s \to_{p,l\to r} t$ to make explicit the position and rule used in this step. The instantiated left-hand side $l\sigma$ is called a *redex*.

A term t is called *irreducible* or in *normal form* in a TRS $\mathcal{R}$ if there is no term s with $t \to_{\mathcal{R}} s$. A *derivation* is a (possibly empty) sequence of rewrite steps. Given a binary relation $\to$, we denote by $\to^+$ the transitive closure of $\to$ and by $\to^*$ its reflexive and transitive closure. Thus $t \to_{\mathcal{R}}^* s$ means that t can be reduced to s in $\mathcal{R}$ in zero or more steps; we also use $t \to_{\mathcal{R}}^n s$ to denote that t can be reduced to s in exactly n rewrite steps.

Narrowing. The *narrowing* principle [35] mainly extends term rewriting by replacing pattern matching with unification, so that terms containing logic variables can also be reduced by non-deterministically instantiating these variables. Formally, given a TRS $\mathcal{R}$ and two terms $s, t \in \mathcal{T}(\mathcal{F}, \mathcal{V})$, we have that $s \rightsquigarrow_{\mathcal{R}} t$ is a *narrowing step* iff there exist[1]

- a nonvariable position p of s,
- a variant $R = (l \to r)$ of a rule in $\mathcal{R}$,
- a substitution $\sigma = \mathsf{mgu}(s|_p, l)$ which is the most general unifier of $s|_p$ and l,

and $t = (s[r]_p)\sigma$. We often write $s \rightsquigarrow_{p,R,\theta} t$ (or simply $s \rightsquigarrow_\theta t$) to make explicit the position, rule, and substitution of the narrowing step, where $\theta = \sigma|_{\mathsf{Var}(s)}$ (i.e., we label the narrowing step only with the bindings for the narrowed term). A *narrowing derivation* $t_0 \rightsquigarrow_\sigma^* t_n$ denotes a sequence of narrowing steps $t_0 \rightsquigarrow_{\sigma_1} \ldots \rightsquigarrow_{\sigma_n} t_n$ with $\sigma = \sigma_n \circ \cdots \circ \sigma_1$ (if $n = 0$ then $\sigma = id$). Given a narrowing derivation $s \rightsquigarrow_\sigma^* t$, we say that σ is a computed *answer* for s.

Example 1. Consider the following TRS $\mathcal{R}$ defining the addition $\mathsf{add}/2$ on natural numbers built from $\mathsf{z}/0$ and $\mathsf{s}/1$:

$$\begin{array}{llll}
\mathsf{add}(\mathsf{z}, y) & \to & y & (R_1) \\
\mathsf{add}(\mathsf{s}(x), y) & \to & \mathsf{s}(\mathsf{add}(x, y)) & (R_2)
\end{array}$$

Given the term $\mathsf{add}(x, \mathsf{s}(\mathsf{z}))$, we have infinitely many narrowing derivations issuing from $\mathsf{add}(x, \mathsf{s}(\mathsf{z}))$, e.g.

$$\mathsf{add}(x, \mathsf{s}(\mathsf{z})) \rightsquigarrow_{\epsilon, R_1, \{x \mapsto \mathsf{z}\}} \mathsf{s}(\mathsf{z})$$
$$\mathsf{add}(x, \mathsf{s}(\mathsf{z})) \rightsquigarrow_{\epsilon, R_2, \{x \mapsto \mathsf{s}(y_1)\}} \mathsf{s}(\mathsf{add}(y_1, \mathsf{s}(\mathsf{z}))) \rightsquigarrow_{1, R_1, \{y_1 \mapsto \mathsf{z}\}} \mathsf{s}(\mathsf{s}(\mathsf{z}))$$
$$\ldots$$

with computed answers $\{x \mapsto \mathsf{z}\}$, $\{x \mapsto \mathsf{s}(\mathsf{z})\}$, etc.

3   Termination of Narrowing Via Termination of Rewriting

We first introduce our notion of termination, which is parameterized by a given binary relation:

---

[1] We consider the so called *most general* narrowing, i.e., the mgu of the selected subterm and the left-hand side of a rule—rather than an ordinary unifier—is computed at each narrowing step.

Definition 1 (termination). *Let T be a set of terms. Given a binary relation $\propto$ on terms, we say that T is $\propto$-terminating iff there is no term $t_1 \in T$ such that there exists an infinite sequence of the form $t_1 \propto t_2 \propto t_3 \propto \ldots$*
We say that a term t is $\propto$-terminating iff the set $\{t\}$ is $\propto$-terminating.

The usual notion of termination can then be formulated as follows: a TRS is *terminating* iff $\mathcal{T}(\mathcal{F})$ is $\rightarrow_{\mathcal{R}}$-terminating. As for narrowing, we say that a TRS $\mathcal{R}$ is terminating *w.r.t. narrowing* iff $\mathcal{T}(\mathcal{F}, \mathcal{V})$ is $\leadsto_{\mathcal{R}}$-terminating.

In general, however, only rather trivial TRSs are terminating w.r.t. narrowing. Consider, for instance, the following TRS $\mathcal{R} = \{f(s(x), y) \rightarrow f(x, y)\}$. Although every term of the form $f(t_1, t_2)$ has a finite rewrite derivation, we can easily find a term, e.g., $f(w, z)$, such that an infinite narrowing derivation exists:

$$f(w, z) \leadsto_{\{w \mapsto s(x_1)\}} f(x_1, z) \leadsto_{\{x_1 \mapsto s(x_2)\}} f(x_2, z) \leadsto_{\{x_2 \mapsto s(x_3)\}} \cdots$$

Therefore, we focus on the termination of narrowing w.r.t. a *given set of terms*, which explains our formulation of termination in Def. 1 above.

The following result provides a first—sufficient but not necessary—condition for the termination of narrowing in terms of the termination of rewriting.

Theorem 1. *Let $\mathcal{R}$ be a TRS and T be a finite set of terms. Let $T^* = \{t\sigma \mid t \in T$ and $t \leadsto_{\sigma}^* s$ in $\mathcal{R}\}$. T is $\leadsto_{\mathcal{R}}$-terminating if T^* is finite (modulo variable renaming) and $\rightarrow_{\mathcal{R}}$-terminating.*

The following example illustrates why the above condition is not necessary:

Example 2. Consider the following TRS: $\mathcal{R} = \{f(a) \rightarrow b, a \rightarrow a\}$. Given the set of terms $T = \{f(x)\}$, we have that T is $\leadsto_{\mathcal{R}}$-terminating since the only narrowing derivation is $f(x) \leadsto_{\{x \mapsto a\}} b$. However, $T^* = \{f(a)\}$ is finite but not $\rightarrow_{\mathcal{R}}$-terminating: $f(a) \rightarrow f(a) \rightarrow \ldots$

Verifying the finiteness and $\rightarrow_{\mathcal{R}}$-termination of T^* is generally, not only undecidable, but also rather difficult to approximate since one should approximate all possible narrowing derivations issuing from the terms in T. Therefore, we now introduce an alternative—easier to check—condition.

Firstly, we restrict ourselves to a narrowing strategy over a class of TRSs in which the terms introduced by instantiation cannot be narrowed (this will avoid, e.g., the situation of Ex. 2). Many useful narrowing strategies fulfill this condition, e.g., basic [23] and innermost basic narrowing [22] over arbitrary TRSs, lazy [29] and needed[2] narrowing [5] over left-linear constructor TRSs, etc. Actually, any narrowing strategy over left-linear constructor systems computes only constructor substitutions (a formal proof can be found in [36]).

Secondly, as mentioned in the introduction, we regard variables in narrowing as *generators* of possibly infinite (constructor) terms from the point of view of

---

[2] Although needed narrowing [5] does not compute mgu's (basically, some bindings are anticipated to ensure that all narrowing steps are *needed*), it computes constructor substitutions (see [3, Lemma 11]) and, thus, our forthcoming results also apply.

rewriting. For this purpose, we introduce a fixed fresh function symbol "gen" which does not appear in the signature of any TRS. The following definition is a simplified version of the original notion of a *generator* in [6]:

Definition 2 (data generator, gen). *Let $\mathcal{R}$ be a TRS over a signature $\mathcal{F} = \mathcal{D} \uplus \mathcal{C}$. We denote by $\mathcal{R}_{gen}$ a TRS over $\mathcal{F} \uplus \{gen\}$ resulting from augmenting $\mathcal{R}$ with the following set of rewrite rules:*

$$\{gen \rightarrow c \mid c/0 \in \mathcal{C}\} \cup \{gen \rightarrow c(\overbrace{gen, \ldots, gen}^{n \ times}) \mid c/n \in \mathcal{C}, \ n > 0\}$$

Example 3. For instance, for the TRS $\mathcal{R}$ of Ex. 1 with $\mathcal{C} = \{z/0, s/1\}$, we have $\mathcal{R}_{gen} = \mathcal{R} \cup \{gen \rightarrow z, \ gen \rightarrow s(gen)\}$.

Trivially, the function gen can be (non-deterministically) reduced to any ground constructor term. Variables are then replaced by generators in the obvious way:

Definition 3 (variable elimination, $\hat{t}$, $\hat{T}$). *Given a term $t \in \mathcal{T}(\mathcal{F}, \mathcal{V})$ over a signature $\mathcal{F}$, we let $\hat{t} = t\sigma$, with $\sigma = \{x \mapsto gen \mid x \in \mathcal{V}ar(t)\}$. Analogously, given a set of terms $T \subseteq \mathcal{T}(\mathcal{F}, \mathcal{V})$, we let $\hat{T} = \{\hat{t} \mid t \in T\} \subseteq \mathcal{T}(\mathcal{F} \uplus \{gen\})$.*

Note that $\hat{t}$ is always ground for any given term t since all variables occurring in t are replaced by function gen.

Now, we state the correctness of the variable elimination, an easy consequence of the results in [6] (a complete proof can be found in [36]). Our first result shows that every narrowing computation can be mimicked by a rewrite derivation if logic variables are replaced with gen in the initial term:

Lemma 1 (completeness). *Let $\mathcal{R}$ be a left-linear constructor TRS over a signature $\mathcal{F} = \mathcal{D} \uplus \mathcal{C}$ and $s \in \mathcal{T}(\mathcal{F}, \mathcal{V})$ be a term. If $s \leadsto_{p,R,\sigma} t$ in $\mathcal{R}$, then $\hat{s} \rightarrow^* \widehat{s\sigma} \rightarrow_{p,R} \hat{t}$ in $\mathcal{R}_{gen}$.*

Unfortunately, variable elimination is not generally sound because repeated variables are bound to the same value in a narrowing computation, while different occurrences of gen, though arising from the replacement of the same variable, can be reduced to different terms:

Example 4. Consider again the TRS $\mathcal{R}$ of Ex. 1 and the term $t = add(x, x)$. Clearly, it can only be narrowed to an even number: z, s(s(z)), ... However, $\hat{t}$ can also be reduced to an odd number, e.g., $\hat{t} = add(gen, gen) \rightarrow add(z, gen) \rightarrow gen \rightarrow s(gen) \rightarrow s(z)$.

To avoid such derivations, the notion of *admissible* derivation [6] is introduced:

Definition 4 (admissible derivation). *Let $\mathcal{R}$ be a TRS over $\mathcal{F}$ and $t \in \mathcal{T}(\mathcal{F}, \mathcal{V})$ be a term. A derivation for $\hat{t}$ in $\mathcal{R}_{gen}$ is called admissible iff all the occurrences of gen originating from the replacement of the same variable are reduced to the same term in this derivation.*

Now, we can already state the soundness of variable elimination:

Lemma 2 (soundness). *Let $\mathcal{R}$ be a left-linear constructor TRS over a signature $\mathcal{F} = \mathcal{D} \uplus \mathcal{C}$ and $s' \in \mathcal{T}(\mathcal{F} \cup \{\mathsf{gen}\}, \mathcal{V})$ be a term. If $s' \rightarrow^* s'' \rightarrow_{p,R} t'$ is an admissible derivation in $\mathcal{R}_{\mathsf{gen}}$ and $R \in \mathcal{R}$, then $s \rightsquigarrow^*_{\mathcal{R}} t$ with $\widehat{s} = s'$ and $\widehat{t\sigma} = t'$ for some constructor substitution σ.*

Obviously, given a TRS $\mathcal{R}$, no set of terms containing occurrences of gen is generally $\rightarrow_{\mathcal{R}_{\mathsf{gen}}}$-terminating because of the definition of function gen. Luckily, we are interested in a weaker property: we may allow infinite derivations in $\mathcal{R}_{\mathsf{gen}}$ as long as the number of functions different from gen reduced in these derivations is kept finite (i.e., gen is only used to produce the values needed to perform the next rewrite step). This idea is formalized by using the notion of *relative termination* [25]:

Definition 5 (relative termination). *Let $\mathcal{R}$ and $\mathcal{Q}$ be rewrite systems. Let T be a set of terms. T is relatively $\rightarrow_{\mathcal{R} \cup \mathcal{Q}}$-terminating to $\mathcal{R}$ if every infinite derivation $t_0 \rightarrow_{\mathcal{R} \cup \mathcal{Q}} t_1 \rightarrow_{\mathcal{R} \cup \mathcal{Q}} \ldots$ contains only finitely many $\rightarrow_{\mathcal{R}}$-steps.*

The following theorem states one of the main results of this paper:

Theorem 2. *Let $\mathcal{R}$ be a left-linear constructor TRS over a signature $\mathcal{F} = \mathcal{D} \uplus \mathcal{C}$ and let $T \subseteq \mathcal{T}(\mathcal{F}, \mathcal{V})$ be a set of terms. Then, T is $\rightsquigarrow_{\mathcal{R}}$-terminating iff $\widehat{T}$ is relatively $\rightarrow_{\mathcal{R}_{\mathsf{gen}}}$-terminating to $\mathcal{R}$.*

The above result lays the ground for analyzing the termination of narrowing by reusing existing techniques for proving the termination of rewriting. The next section presents two such approaches.

4   Automating the Termination Analysis

4.1   From Abstract Terms to Argument Filterings

In general, we are not interested in providing a set of terms T for proving that T is $\rightsquigarrow$-terminating. Rather, it is much more convenient to allow the user to provide a higher-level specification of the function calls in which she is interested in. For this purpose, we introduce the notion of an *abstract term*, which is inspired by the *mode declarations* of logic programming.

Definition 6 (abstract term). *Let $\mathcal{F} = \mathcal{D} \uplus \mathcal{C}$ be a signature. An abstract term over $\mathcal{F}$ has the form $\mathsf{f}(m_1, \ldots, m_n)$, where $\mathsf{f} \in \mathcal{D}$ is a defined function symbol and m_i, $i = 1, \ldots, n$, is either g (definitely **g**round) or v (possibly **v**ariable).*

Any abstract term implicitly induces a (possibly infinite) set of terms:

Definition 7 (concretization, γ). *Let $\mathcal{F}$ be a signature and t^α an abstract term over $\mathcal{F}$. The concretization of t^α, in symbols $\gamma(t^\alpha)$, is obtained as follows:*

$$\gamma(\mathsf{f}(m_1, \ldots, m_n)) = \{\mathsf{f}(t_1, \ldots, t_n) \in \mathcal{T}(\mathcal{F}, \mathcal{V}) \mid t_i \in \mathcal{T}(\mathcal{C}) \text{ if } m_i = g,\ i = 1, \ldots, n\}$$

Given a set of abstract terms T^α, we let $\gamma(T^\alpha) = \{\gamma(t^\alpha) \mid t^\alpha \in T^\alpha\}$.

Consider the TRS of Ex. 1 and the abstract term $\mathsf{add}(g, v)$. Then, $\gamma(\mathsf{add}(g, v)) = \{\mathsf{add}(\mathsf{z}, x), \mathsf{add}(\mathsf{z}, \mathsf{z}), \mathsf{add}(\mathsf{s}(\mathsf{z}), x), \mathsf{add}(\mathsf{s}(\mathsf{z}), \mathsf{z}), \mathsf{add}(\mathsf{s}(\mathsf{z}), \mathsf{s}(x)), \mathsf{add}(\mathsf{s}(\mathsf{z}), \mathsf{s}(\mathsf{z})), \ldots\}$.

Thanks to Theorem 2, given a set of abstract terms T^α, we can prove that $\gamma(T^\alpha)$ is $\leadsto_{\mathcal{R}}$-terminating by proving that $\widehat{\gamma(T^\alpha)}$ is relatively $\to_{\mathcal{R}_{\text{gen}}}$-terminating to $\mathcal{R}$. This approach, however, presents two drawbacks:

- the set $\gamma(T^\alpha)$ is generally infinite and
- checking relative termination require non-standard techniques and tools.

In order to overcome these drawbacks, we introduce the use of (a simplified version of) argument filterings:

Definition 8 (argument filtering, π). *An argument filtering over a signature $\mathcal{F} = \mathcal{D} \uplus \mathcal{C}$ is a function π such that, for every defined function $\mathsf{f}/n \in \mathcal{D}$, we have $\pi(\mathsf{f}) \subseteq \{1, \ldots, n\}$. Argument filterings are extended to terms as follows:*[3]

- $\pi(x) = x$ *for all* $x \in \mathcal{V}$,
- $\pi(\mathsf{c}(t_1, \ldots, t_n)) = \mathsf{c}(\pi(t_1), \ldots, \pi(t_n))$ *for all* $\mathsf{c}/n \in \mathcal{C}$, $n \geq 0$, *and*
- $\pi(\mathsf{f}(t_1, \ldots, t_n)) = \mathsf{f}(\pi(t_{i_1}), \ldots, \pi(t_{i_m}))$ *for all* $\mathsf{f}/n \in \mathcal{F}$, $n \geq 0$,
  where $\pi(\mathsf{f}) = \{i_1, \ldots, i_m\}$ *and* $1 \leq i_1 < \ldots < i_m \leq n$.

Given a TRS $\mathcal{R}$, we let $\pi(\mathcal{R}) = \{\pi(l) \to \pi_{rhs}(r) \mid l \to r \in \mathcal{R}\}$, where the auxiliary function π_{rhs} is defined as follows:

- $\pi_{rhs}(x) = \bot$ *for all* $x \in \mathcal{V}$,
- $\pi_{rhs}(\mathsf{c}(t_1, \ldots, t_n)) = \mathsf{c}(\pi_{rhs}(t_1), \ldots, \pi_{rhs}(t_n))$ *for all* $\mathsf{c}/n \in \mathcal{C}$, $n \geq 0$, *and*
- $\pi_{rhs}(\mathsf{f}(t_1, \ldots, t_n)) = \mathsf{f}(\pi(t_{i_1}), \ldots, \pi(t_{i_m}))$ *for all* $\mathsf{f}/n \in \mathcal{F}$, $n \geq 0$,
  where $\pi(\mathsf{f}) = \{i_1, \ldots, i_m\}$ *and* $1 \leq i_1 < \ldots < i_m \leq n$

where $\bot$ is a fresh constant constructor not appearing in $\mathcal{C}$.

The original notion of *argument filtering* in [8,26] may return a single argument position so that $\pi(\mathsf{f}(t_1, \ldots, t_n)) = \pi(t_i)$ if $\pi(\mathsf{f}) = i$; furthermore, it applies to both constructor and defined function symbols. We consider a simpler definition because our argument filterings will be automatically derived from a set of abstract terms (cf. Sect. 5), where only defined function symbols occur.

On the other hand, our argument filterings replace those variables of the right-hand sides that are not below a defined function symbol by a fresh constant $\bot$. This is done in order to avoid the introduction of *extra* variables (i.e., variables that appear in the right-hand side of a rule but not in its left-hand side). Consider, e.g., the rule $\mathsf{add}(\mathsf{z}, y) \to y$ and the argument filtering $\pi = \{\mathsf{add} \mapsto \{1\}\}$. Then, $(\pi(\mathsf{add}(\mathsf{z}, y)) \to \pi(y)) = (\mathsf{add}(\mathsf{z}) \to y)$ that contains an extra variable y. Our definition above returns instead $(\pi(\mathsf{add}(\mathsf{z}, y)) \to \pi_{rhs}(y)) = (\mathsf{add}(\mathsf{z}) \to \bot)$.

In the following, though, we are not interested in arbitrary argument filterings but only in what we call *safe* argument filterings.

---

[3] By abuse of notation, we keep the same symbol for the original function and the filtered function with a possibly different arity.

Definition 9 (safe argument filtering). *Let $\mathcal{R}$ be a TRS over a signature $\mathcal{F} = \mathcal{D} \uplus \mathcal{C}$ and let T^α be a finite set of abstract terms. We say that an argument filtering π is safe for T^α in $\mathcal{R}$ iff*

- *for all $t^\alpha \in T^\alpha$, if $\pi(t^\alpha) = f(m_1, \ldots, m_n)$, then $m_i = g$ for all $i = 1, \ldots, n$;*
- *for all narrowing step $s_1 \leadsto_\mathcal{R} s_2$, if $\pi(s_1|_p) \in \mathcal{T}(\mathcal{F})$ for all subterm $s_1|_p$ with $\mathsf{root}(s_1|_p) \in \mathcal{D}$, then $\pi(s_2|_q) \in \mathcal{T}(\mathcal{F})$ for all subterm $s_2|_q$ with $\mathsf{root}(s_2|_q) \in \mathcal{D}$.*

Intuitively speaking, an argument filtering π is safe for a set of abstract terms T^α if π filters away all non-ground arguments of the terms in $\gamma(T^\alpha)$ as well as the non-ground arguments of any function call that can be obtained by narrowing.

Example 5. Consider the TRS $\mathcal{R} = \{f(s(x), y) \to f(y, x)\}$ and the set $T^\alpha = \{f(g, v)\}$. Given the argument filtering $\pi = \{f \mapsto \{1\}\}$, although $\pi(f(g, v)) = f(g)$ holds (the first condition in Def. 9), this argument filtering is not safe because there exists a narrowing step $f(s(z), x) \leadsto f(x, z)$ such that $\pi(f(s(z), x)) = f(s(z))$ is ground but $\pi(f(x, z)) = f(x)$ is not.

A useful property is that the filtered form of a TRS does not contain extra variables when the argument filtering is safe (see [36]).

In the following, we consider that the input for the termination analysis is a left-linear TRS together with a safe argument filtering. An algorithm for generating safe argument filterings from abstract terms can be found in Sect. 5.

4.2   A Direct Approach to Termination Analysis

In this section, we present a direct approach for proving the termination of narrowing by extending the well-known *dependency pair* technique [8].

The remainder of this section adapts and extends some of the developments in [8]. Given a TRS $\mathcal{R}$ over a signature $\mathcal{F}$, for each $f/n \in \mathcal{F}$, we let $f^\sharp/n$ be a fresh *tuple symbol* (a constructor); we often write F instead of $f^\sharp$. Given a term $f(t_1, \ldots, t_n)$ with $f \in \mathcal{D}$, we let $t^\sharp$ denote $f^\sharp(t_1, \ldots, t_n)$.

Definition 10 (dependency pair [8]). *Given a TRS $\mathcal{R}$ over a signature $\mathcal{F} = \mathcal{D} \uplus \mathcal{C}$, the associated set of dependency pairs, $DP(\mathcal{R})$, is defined as follows:*[4]

$$DP(\mathcal{R}) = \{l^\sharp \to t^\sharp \mid l \to r \in \mathcal{R}, \ r|_p = t, \ and \ \mathsf{root}(t) \in \mathcal{D}\}$$

Example 6. Consider the following TRS $\mathcal{R}$ defining the functions append and reverse over lists built from nil (the empty list) and cons:

$$
\begin{aligned}
\mathsf{append}(\mathsf{nil}, y) &\to y \\
\mathsf{append}(\mathsf{cons}(x, xs), y) &\to \mathsf{cons}(x, \mathsf{append}(xs, y)) \\
\mathsf{reverse}(\mathsf{nil}) &\to \mathsf{nil} \\
\mathsf{reverse}(\mathsf{cons}(x, xs)) &\to \mathsf{append}(\mathsf{reverse}(xs), \mathsf{cons}(x, \mathsf{nil}))
\end{aligned}
$$

---

[4] Note that if $\mathcal{R}$ is a TRS, so is $DP(\mathcal{R})$.

Here, we have the following dependency pairs $DP(\mathcal{R})$:

$$\mathsf{APPEND}(\mathsf{cons}(x, xs), y) \rightarrow \mathsf{APPEND}(xs, y) \qquad (1)$$
$$\mathsf{REVERSE}(\mathsf{cons}(x, xs)) \rightarrow \mathsf{REVERSE}(xs) \qquad (2)$$
$$\mathsf{REVERSE}(\mathsf{cons}(x, xs)) \rightarrow \mathsf{APPEND}(\mathsf{reverse}(xs), \mathsf{cons}(x, \mathsf{nil})) \qquad (3)$$

In order to prove termination, we should try to prove that there are no infinite chains of dependency pairs. The standard notion of *chain* in [8], however, cannot be used because we are interested in the termination of narrowing (i.e., the relative termination of rewrite sequences in which variables are replaced by gen).

Definition 11 (chain). *Let $\mathcal{R}$ be a TRS over a signature $\mathcal{F}$ and let π be an argument filtering over $\mathcal{F}$ that is extended over tuple symbols so that $\pi(f^\sharp) = \pi(f)$ for all $f \in \mathcal{D}$. A (possibly infinite) sequence of pairs $s_1 \rightarrow t_1$, $s_2 \rightarrow t_2$, ...from $DP(\mathcal{R})$ is a $(DP(\mathcal{R}), \mathcal{R}, \pi)$-chain if the following conditions hold:[5]*

- *there exists a constructor substitution σ such that $\widehat{t_i\sigma} \rightarrow^*_{\mathcal{R}_{gen}} \widehat{s_{i+1}\sigma}$ for every two consecutive pairs in the sequence;*
- *we have $\pi(\widehat{s_i\sigma}), \pi(\widehat{t_i\sigma}) \in \mathcal{T}(\mathcal{F})$ for all $i > 0$ (i.e., π filters away all occurrences of gen).*

Example 7. Consider the TRS $\mathcal{R}$ of Example 6 and its dependency pairs $DP(\mathcal{R})$. Here, $\mathcal{R}_{gen} = \mathcal{R} \cup \{\mathsf{gen} \rightarrow \mathsf{nil}, \mathsf{gen} \rightarrow \mathsf{cons}(\mathsf{gen}, \mathsf{gen}), \mathsf{gen} \rightarrow \mathsf{z}, \mathsf{gen} \mapsto \mathsf{s}(\mathsf{gen})\}$. Then, we have that "$(1), (1), \ldots$" is an infinite $(DP(\mathcal{R}), \mathcal{R}, \pi)$-chain for any argument filtering in which $\pi(\mathsf{APPEND}) = \{2\}$ since there exists a substitution $\sigma = \{y \mapsto \mathsf{nil}\}$ such that (we denote the dependency pair (1) by $l_1 \rightarrow t_1$)

$$\widehat{t_1\sigma} = \mathsf{APPEND}(\mathsf{gen}, \mathsf{nil}) \rightarrow_{\mathcal{R}_{gen}} \mathsf{APPEND}(\mathsf{cons}(\mathsf{gen}, \mathsf{gen}), \mathsf{nil}) = \widehat{l_1\sigma}$$

and $\pi(\mathsf{APPEND}(\mathsf{gen}, \mathsf{nil})) = \pi(\mathsf{APPEND}(\mathsf{cons}(\mathsf{gen}, \mathsf{gen}), \mathsf{nil})) = \mathsf{nil} \in \mathcal{T}(\mathcal{F})$. Note that it would be not a chain in the standard dependency pair method.

The following result states the soundness of our approach:

Theorem 3. *Let $\mathcal{R}$ be a left-linear constructor TRS over a signature $\mathcal{F} = \mathcal{D} \uplus \mathcal{C}$ and let T^α be a finite set of abstract terms. Let π be a safe argument filtering for T^α in $\mathcal{R}$ that is extended over tuple symbols so that $\pi(f^\sharp) = \pi(f)$ for all $f \in \mathcal{D}$. If there is no infinite $(DP(\mathcal{R}), \mathcal{R}, \pi)$-chain, then $\gamma(T^\alpha)$ is $\leadsto_\mathcal{R}$-terminating.*

In order to show the absence of $(DP(\mathcal{R}), \mathcal{R}, \pi)$-chains automatically, we can follow the *DP framework* [20]. In this context, a *DP problem* is a tuple $(\mathcal{P}, \mathcal{R}, \pi)$ where $\mathcal{P}$ and $\mathcal{R}$ are TRSs and π is an argument filtering. If there is no associated infinite $(\mathcal{P}, \mathcal{R}, \pi)$-chain, we say that the DP problem is *finite*. Termination methods are then formulated as *DP processors* that take a DP problem and return a new set of DP problems that should be solved instead.

A DP processor Proc is *sound* if, for all DP problems d, we have that d is finite if all DP problems in Proc(d) are finite. Therefore, a termination proof starts

---

[5] As in [8], we assume fresh variables in every (occurrence of a) dependency pair and that the domain of substitutions may be infinite.

with the initial DP problem $(DP(\mathcal{R}), \mathcal{R}, \pi)$ and applies sound DP processors until an empty set of DP problems is obtained.

We could adapt most of the standard DP processors in order to deal with the use of data generators and argument filterings following similar ideas as those in [33]. For the sake of brevity, we only present one of such DP processors:

Theorem 4 (argument filtering processor). *Given a DP problem* $(\mathcal{P}, \mathcal{R}, \pi)$, *let* Proc *return* $\{(\pi(\mathcal{P}), \pi(\mathcal{R}), id)\}$, *where* $id(\mathsf{f}) = \{1, \ldots, n\}$ *for all defined function symbol* f/n *occurring in* $\pi(\mathcal{R})$. *Then* Proc *is sound.*

The nice property of this DP processor is that, after its application, all existing DP processors of [20] for proving the termination of rewriting can also be used for proving the termination of narrowing.

Example 8. Consider the TRS of Example 6, the set of abstract terms $T^\alpha = \{\mathsf{append}(g, v)\}$, and the argument filtering $\pi = \{\mathsf{append} \mapsto \{1\}, \mathsf{reverse} \mapsto \{1\}\}$ which is safe for T^α. Given this DP problem, the argument filtering processor returns a new DP problem that consists of the following elements:

$$
\textit{Dependency pairs:} \left\{
\begin{array}{l}
\mathsf{APPEND}(\mathsf{cons}(x, xs)) \rightarrow \mathsf{APPEND}(xs) \\
\mathsf{REVERSE}(\mathsf{cons}(x, xs)) \rightarrow \mathsf{REVERSE}(xs) \\
\mathsf{REVERSE}(\mathsf{cons}(x, xs)) \rightarrow \mathsf{APPEND}(\mathsf{reverse}(xs))
\end{array}
\right.
$$

$$
\textit{Rewrite system:} \left\{
\begin{array}{r}
\mathsf{append}(\mathsf{nil}) \rightarrow \bot \\
\mathsf{append}(\mathsf{cons}(x, xs)) \rightarrow \mathsf{cons}(x, \mathsf{append}(xs)) \\
\mathsf{reverse}(\mathsf{nil}) \rightarrow \mathsf{nil} \\
\mathsf{reverse}(\mathsf{cons}(x, xs)) \rightarrow \mathsf{append}(\mathsf{reverse}(xs))
\end{array}
\right.
$$

Argument filtering: $id = \{\mathsf{append} \mapsto \{1\}, \mathsf{reverse} \mapsto \{1\}\}$

The derived DP problem can be proved terminating using standard techniques.

4.3   A Transformational Approach

In this section, we present an alternative approach for proving the termination of narrowing. The basic idea is similar to that in the previous section: using an argument filtering to eliminate those subterms that might be bound to a data generator. Now, however, our aim is to transform the original TRS $\mathcal{R}$ into a new TRS $\mathcal{R}'$ so that narrowing terminates in $\mathcal{R}$ if rewriting terminates in $\mathcal{R}'$. As a consequence, *any* termination technique for rewrite systems can be applied to prove the termination of narrowing.

Our transformation is based on the *argument filtering transformation* of [26], that we simplify because, in our case, an argument filtering never returns a single argument position and, moreover, it is only defined over defined function symbols. Roughly speaking, our program transformation generates, for every rule $l \rightarrow r$ of the original program,

- a filtered rule $\pi(l) \rightarrow \pi_{rhs}(r)$ and
- an additional rule $\pi(l) \rightarrow \pi(t)$, for each subterm t of r that is filtered away in $\pi_{rhs}(r)$ and such that $\pi(t)$ is not a constructor term.

Definition 12 (argument filtering transformation). *Let $\mathcal{R}$ be a TRS over a signature $\mathcal{F} = \mathcal{D} \uplus \mathcal{C}$ and let π be an argument filtering over $\mathcal{F}$. The argument filtering transformation AFT_π is defined as follows:*

$$\mathsf{AFT}_\pi(\mathcal{R}) = \pi(\mathcal{R}) \cup \{\pi(l) \to \pi(r') \mid l \to r \in \mathcal{R}, \ r' \in \mathsf{dec}_\pi(r), \ \pi(r') \notin \mathcal{T}(\mathcal{C}, \mathcal{V})\}$$

where the auxiliary function dec_π is defined inductively as follows:

$$
\begin{array}{ll}
\mathsf{dec}_\pi(x) = \varnothing & (x \in \mathcal{V}) \\
\mathsf{dec}_\pi(c(t_1, \ldots, t_n)) = \bigcup_{i=1}^n \mathsf{dec}_\pi(t_i) & (c \in \mathcal{C}) \\
\mathsf{dec}_\pi(f(t_1, \ldots, t_n)) = \bigcup_{i \notin \pi(f)} \{t_i\} \ \cup \ \bigcup_{i=1}^n \mathsf{dec}_\pi(t_i) & (f \in \mathcal{D})
\end{array}
$$

Example 9. Consider the TRS $\mathcal{R}$ of Ex. 6. If we consider the argument filtering $\pi_1 = \{\mathsf{append} \mapsto \{1\}, \ \mathsf{reverse} \mapsto \{1\}\}$ of Ex. 8, then $\mathsf{AFT}_{\pi_1}(\mathcal{R})$ returns the same filtered rewrite system of Ex. 8.

Consider now the argument filtering $\pi_2 = \{\mathsf{append} \mapsto \{2\}, \ \mathsf{reverse} \mapsto \{1\}\}$. Then, $\mathsf{AFT}_{\pi_2}(\mathcal{R})$ returns the following TRS:

$$
\begin{array}{l}
\mathsf{append}(y) \to y \\
\mathsf{append}(y) \to \mathsf{cons}(\bot, \mathsf{append}(y)) \\
\mathsf{reverse}(\mathsf{nil}) \to \mathsf{nil} \\
\mathsf{reverse}(\mathsf{cons}(x, xs)) \to \mathsf{append}(\mathsf{cons}(x, \mathsf{nil})) \\
\mathsf{reverse}(\mathsf{cons}(x, xs)) \to \mathsf{reverse}(xs)
\end{array}
$$

Note that the last rule is introduced because we have

$$\mathsf{dec}_{\pi_2}(\mathsf{append}(\mathsf{reverse}(xs), \mathsf{cons}(x, \mathsf{nil}))) = \{\mathsf{reverse}(xs)\}$$

The next result is the main contribution of this section:

Theorem 5. *Let $\mathcal{R}$ be a left-linear constructor TRS and T^α be a finite set of abstract terms, with $T = \gamma(T^\alpha)$. Let π be a safe argument filtering for T^α in $\mathcal{R}$. If $\mathsf{AFT}_\pi(\mathcal{R})$ is terminating, then T is $\rightsquigarrow_\mathcal{R}$-terminating.*

The significance of Theorem 5 is that $\mathsf{AFT}_\pi(\mathcal{R})$ can be analyzed using standard techniques and tools for proving the termination of TRSs since no data generator is involved in the derivations of $\mathsf{AFT}_\pi(\mathcal{R})$.

We note that [18] proves that the AFT transformation is subsumed by the DP method regarding simple termination (i.e., termination based on simplification orderings). In our case, the approach of this section is not directly subsumed by that of Sect. 4.2 because we consider termination rather than simple termination. Also, the AFT transformation can be seen as a preprocessing stage so that standard techniques (e.g., the DP method, but not only this method) can be applied to the transformed program, as we will see in the next section.

5   The Termination Tool TNT

In this section, we describe the implementation of a program transformation that follows the approach presented in Sect. 4.3. The tool, called TNT, is publicly available from `http://german.dsic.upv.es/filtering.html`.

The tool is written in Prolog (around 650 lines of code) and includes a parser for TRSs (which accepts the TRS format of the *Termination Problem Data Base*, TPDB, see `http://www.lri.fr/~marche/tpdb/`), a static analysis to infer a safe argument filtering from an abstract term—we consider a single abstract term rather than a set of abstract terms for simplicity—and the AFT_π transformation of Sect. 4.3. The tool is available through a web interface, whose input data are

- a left-linear constructor TRS $\mathcal{R}$ (the user can either write it down or choose it from a selection of TRSs from the TPDB) and
- an initial abstract term t^α that describes a (possibly infinite) set of initial terms $\gamma(t^\alpha)$.

The tool returns a transformed TRS $\mathcal{R}'$ whose termination w.r.t. standard rewriting implies the termination of narrowing for $\gamma(t^\alpha)$ in the original TRS $\mathcal{R}$. The termination of $\mathcal{R}'$ can be analyzed using any tool for proving the termination of rewriting. In particular, the web interface allows the user to check the termination of the transformed TRS using the APROVE tool [19].

For generating a safe argument filtering for a given set of abstract terms, we have adapted a simple *binding-time analysis* [24], which is often used in partial evaluation to propagate static (i.e., ground) and dynamic (i.e., possibly nonground) values through a program. We consider *binding-times* g (ground) and v (possibly variable), rather than the more traditional S (static) and D (dynamic) in the partial evaluation literature (though their meaning is the same). The output of the binding-time analysis is a *division* which includes a mapping $\mathsf{f}/n \mapsto (m_1, \ldots, m_n)$ for every defined function $\mathsf{f}/n \in \mathcal{D}$, where each m_i is a binding-time. A binding-time *environment* is a substitution mapping variables to binding-times. The least upper bound over binding-times is defined as follows:

$$g \sqcup g = g \qquad g \sqcup v = v \qquad v \sqcup g = v \qquad v \sqcup v = v$$

The least upper bound operation can be extended to sequences of binding-times and divisions in the natural way, e.g.,

$$(g, v, g) \sqcup (g, g, v) = (g, v, v)$$
$$\{\mathsf{f} \mapsto (g, v), \ \mathsf{g} \mapsto (g, v)\} \sqcup \{\mathsf{f} \mapsto (g, g), \ \mathsf{g} \mapsto (v, g)\} = \{\mathsf{f} \mapsto (g, v), \ \mathsf{g} \mapsto (v, v)\}$$

Following [24], our binding-time analysis includes two auxiliary functions, B_v and B_e, which are defined in our context as follows:

$$
\begin{aligned}
B_v[[x]] \ \mathsf{g}/n \ \rho &= (\overbrace{g, \ldots, g}^{n \ times}) && (\text{if } x \in \mathcal{V}) \\
B_v[[c(t_1, \ldots, t_n)]] \ \mathsf{g}/n \ \rho &= B_v[[t_1]] \ \mathsf{g}/n \ \rho \sqcup \ldots \sqcup B_v[[t_n]] \ \mathsf{g}/n \ \rho && (\text{if } c \in \mathcal{C}) \\
B_v[[\mathsf{f}(t_1, \ldots, t_n)]] \ \mathsf{g}/n \ \rho &= bt \sqcup (B_e[[t_1]] \ \rho, \ldots, B_e[[t_n]] \ \rho) && (\text{if } \mathsf{f} = \mathsf{g}, \ \mathsf{f} \in \mathcal{D}) \\
&\quad\ bt && (\text{if } \mathsf{f} \neq \mathsf{g}, \ \mathsf{f} \in \mathcal{D}) \\
&\quad\text{where } bt = B_v[[t_1]] \ \mathsf{g}/n \ \rho \sqcup \ldots \sqcup B_v[[t_n]] \ \mathsf{g}/n \ \rho
\end{aligned}
$$

$$
\begin{aligned}
B_e[[x]] \ \rho &= x\rho && (\text{if } x \in \mathcal{V}) \\
B_e[[h(t_1, \ldots, t_n)]] \ \rho &= B_e[[t_1]] \ \rho \sqcup \ldots \sqcup B_e[[t_n]] \ \rho && (\text{if } h \in \mathcal{C} \cup \mathcal{D})
\end{aligned}
$$

Roughly speaking, an expression $(B_v[[t]] \ \mathsf{g}/n \ \rho)$ returns a sequence of n binding-times that denote the (least upper bound of the) binding-times of the arguments of the calls to g/n that occur in t in the context of the binding-time environment ρ. An expression $(B_e[[t]]\ \rho)$ then returns g if t contains no variable which is bound to v in ρ, and v otherwise.

The binding-time analysis is computed as the fixpoint of an iterative process. Assuming that the input abstract term is $f_1(m_1, \ldots, m_{n_1})$, the initial division is

$$div_0 = \{f_1 \mapsto (m_1, \ldots, m_{n_1}),\ f_2 \mapsto (g, \ldots, g),\ \ldots,\ f_k \mapsto (g, \ldots, g)\}$$

where $f_1/n_1, \ldots, f_k/n_k$ are the defined functions of the TRS. Then, given a division $div_i = \{f_1 \mapsto b_1,\ \ldots,\ f_k \mapsto b_k\}$, the next division in the sequence is

$$div_{i+1} = \{\ f_1 \mapsto b_1 \sqcup B_v[[r_1]]\ f_1/n_1\ e(b_1, l_1) \sqcup \ldots \sqcup B_v[[r_j]]\ f_1/n_1\ e(b_j, l_j),$$
$$\ldots,$$
$$f_k \mapsto b_k \sqcup B_v[[r_1]]\ f_k/n_k\ e(b_1, l_1) \sqcup \ldots \sqcup B_v[[r_j]]\ f_k/n_k\ e(b_j, l_j)\ \}$$

where $l_1 \to r_1, \ldots, l_j \to r_j,\ j \geq k$, are the rules of $\mathcal{R}$ and the auxiliary function $e(b, l)$ for computing a binding-time environment from a sequence of binding-times and the left-hand side of a rule is defined as follows:

$$e((m_1, \ldots, m_n), f(t_1, \ldots, t_n)) = \bigcup_{i=1}^{n} \{x \mapsto m_i \mid x \in \mathcal{V}ar(t_i)\}$$

Once we get a fixpoint, i.e., $div_{i+1} = div_i$ for some $i \geq 0$, the corresponding safe argument filtering π is easily obtained by filtering away the positions of nonground arguments. For instance, if the computed division is

$$div = \{f_1 \mapsto (m_1^1, \ldots, m_{n_1}^1), \ldots, f_k \mapsto (m_1^k, \ldots, m_{n_k}^k)\}$$

the corresponding argument filtering is

$$\pi_{div} = \{f_1 \mapsto \{i \mid m_i^1 = g\}, \ldots, f_k \mapsto \{i \mid m_i^k = g\}\}$$

The fact that π_{div} is a safe argument filtering is a trivial consequence of the fact that the computed division div is *congruent* [24], i.e., of the fact that an argument of a function is classified as g only when every call to this function has a ground term in this argument (according to the computed binding-times).

6   Related Work

Despite the relevance of narrowing as a symbolic computation mechanism, we find in the literature only a few works devoted to analyze its termination.

For instance, Dershowitz and Sivakumar [14] defined a narrowing procedure that incorporates pruning of some unsatisfiable goals. Similar approaches have been presented by Chabin and Réty [10], where narrowing is directed by a graph of terms, and by Alpuente *et al.* [2], where the notion of *loop-check* is introduced to detect some unsatisfiable equations. Also, Antoy and Ariola [4] introduced a sort of memoization technique for functional logic languages so that, in some cases, a finite representation of an infinite narrowing space can be achieved.

All these approaches, though, are basically related with *pruning* the narrowing search space rather than analyzing the termination of narrowing.

On the other hand, Christian [11] introduced a characterization of TRSs for which narrowing terminates. Basically, he requires the left-hand sides to be *flat*, i.e., all arguments are either variables or ground terms. Unfortunately, as we discussed at the beginning of Sect. 3, the termination of narrowing for arbitrary terms is quite a strong property that almost no TRS fulfills.

Recent approaches to termination analysis of narrowing include [32,7]. However, they focused on *quasi-termination* (i.e., whether only finitely many different function calls are reachable) and its application to partial evaluation. Moreover, only needed narrowing and inductively sequential TRSs were considered.

Nishida and Miura [30] adapted the dependency graph method for proving the termination of narrowing. The presented dependency pair method (an extension of that introduced in [31]) is, in principle, not comparable with ours (Sect. 4.2), since we do not allow extra variables in TRSs and they do not remove some (unnecessary) extra-variables of right-hand sides as we do with π_{rhs}.

The closest approach is that of Schneider-Kamp *et al.* [33], who presented an automated termination analysis for logic programs. In their approach, logic programs are first translated into TRSs and, then, logic variables are replaced by possibly infinite terms. An extension of the dependency pair framework for dealing with argument filterings is presented, which is similar to our extension in Sect. 4.2. Besides considering a different target (proving termination of SLD resolution *vs* proving termination of narrowing), there are a number of differences between both approaches. First, [33] considers the replacement of logic variables by infinite terms, while we use data generators (so that we could reuse existing results relating narrowing and standard *finitary* rewriting). Also, they consider arbitrary argument filterings but require the *variable condition* (i.e., that the filtered TRS contains no extra variables). In our case, argument filterings must be safe which, in principle, do not always imply that the variable condition holds in filtered TRSs. Actually, we allow extra variables above the defined functions of the right-hand sides of the filtered rules (which are then replaced by $\perp$ in π_{rhs} since they play no role for termination in our context). Furthermore, we introduce a simple binding-time analysis in order to automate the generation of safe argument filterings from higher-level abstract terms. Finally, we also present a transformational approach to proving termination, while [33] focuses on a direct approach based on the dependency pair framework.

7   Conclusions

We have presented in this paper new techniques for proving the termination of narrowing in left-linear constructor systems. Our approach allows one to analyze the termination of narrowing by analyzing the termination of rewriting, so that one can reuse existing methods and tools in the extensive literature on termination of rewriting.

Regarding future work, we find it interesting to investigate the application of our results in order to improve the precision of narrowing-driven partial evaluation [32]. Also, it would be useful to extend our approach in order to accept source Curry programs rather than TRSs.

Acknowledgements. We thank Naoki Nishida and the anonymous referees for their many suggestions for improving this paper. We also thank the developers of the AProVE tool for allowing us to interface the TNT tool with the web interface of AProVE.

References

1. Albert, E., Vidal, G.: The Narrowing-Driven Approach to Functional Logic Program Specialization. New Generation Computing 20(1), 3–26 (2002)
2. Alpuente, M., Falaschi, M., Ramis, M.J., Vidal, G.: Narrowing Approximations as an Optimization for Equational Logic Programs. In: Penjam, J., Bruynooghe, M. (eds.) PLILP 1993. LNCS, vol. 714, pp. 391–409. Springer, Heidelberg (1993)
3. Antoy, S.: Optimal non-deterministic functional logic computations. In: Hanus, M., Heering, J., Meinke, K. (eds.) ALP 1997 and HOA 1997. LNCS, vol. 1298, pp. 16–30. Springer, Heidelberg (1997)
4. Antoy, S., Ariola, Z.: Narrowing the Narrowing Space. In: Hartel, P.H., Kuchen, H. (eds.) PLILP 1997. LNCS, vol. 1292, pp. 1–15. Springer, Heidelberg (1997)
5. Antoy, S., Echahed, R., Hanus, M.: A Needed Narrowing Strategy. Journal of the ACM 47(4), 776–822 (2000)
6. Antoy, S., Hanus, M.: Overlapping Rules and Logic Variables in Functional Logic Programs. In: Etalle, S., Truszczyński, M. (eds.) ICLP 2006. LNCS, vol. 4079, pp. 87–101. Springer, Heidelberg (2006)
7. Arroyo, G., Ramos, J.G., Silva, J., Vidal, G.: Improving Offline Narrowing-Driven Partial Evaluation using Size-Change Graphs. In: Puebla, G. (ed.) LOPSTR 2006. LNCS, vol. 4407, pp. 60–76. Springer, Heidelberg (2007)
8. Arts, T., Giesl, J.: Termination of Term Rewriting Using Dependency Pairs. Theoretical Computer Science 236(1-2), 133–178 (2000)
9. Baader, F., Nipkow, T.: Term Rewriting and All That. Cambridge University Press, Cambridge (1998)
10. Chabin, J., Réty, P.: Narrowing Directed by a Graph of Terms. In: Book, R.V. (ed.) RTA 1991. LNCS, vol. 488, pp. 112–123. Springer, Heidelberg (1991)
11. Christian, J.: Some Termination Criteria for Narrowing and E-narrowing. In: Kapur, D. (ed.) CADE 1992. LNCS, vol. 607, pp. 582–588. Springer, Heidelberg (1992)
12. de Dios-Castro, J., López-Fraguas, F.: Extra Variables Can Be Eliminated from Functional Logic Programs. In: Proc. of the 6th Spanish Conf. on Programming and Languages (PROLE 2006), ENTCS, vol. 188, pp. 3–19. (2007)
13. Dershowitz, N.: Termination of Rewriting. Journal of Symbolic Computation 3(1&2), 69–115 (1987)
14. Dershowitz, N., Sivakumar, G.: Goal-Directed Equation Solving. In: Proc. of 7th National Conf. on Artificial Intelligence, pp. 166–170. Morgan Kaufmann, San Francisco (1988)
15. Hanus, M. (ed.): Curry: An Integrated Functional Logic Language, http://www.informatik.uni-kiel.de/~mh/curry/
16. Escobar, S., Meadows, C., Meseguer, J.: A Rewriting-Based Inference System for the NRL Protocol Analyzer and its Meta-Logical Properties. Theoretical Computer Science 367(1-2), 162–202 (2006)

17. Escobar, S., Meseguer, J.: Symbolic Model Checking of Infinite-State Systems Using Narrowing. In: Baader, F. (ed.) RTA 2007. LNCS, vol. 4533, pp. 153–168. Springer, Heidelberg (2007)
18. Giesl, J., Middeldorp, A.: Eliminating Dummy Elimination. In: McAllester, D. (ed.) CADE 2000. LNCS, vol. 1831, pp. 309–323. Springer, Heidelberg (2000)
19. Giesl, J., Schneider-Kamp, P., Thiemann, R.: AProVE 1. In: Furbach, U., Shankar, N. (eds.) IJCAR 2006. LNCS (LNAI), vol. 4130, pp. 281–286. Springer, Heidelberg (2006)
20. Giesl, J., Thiemann, R., Schneider-Kamp, P., Falke, S.: Mechanizing and Improving Dependency Pairs. Journal of Automated Reasoning 37(3), 155–203 (2006)
21. Hanus, M.: The Integration of Functions into Logic Programming: From Theory to Practice. Journal of Logic Programming 19&20, 583–628 (1994)
22. Hölldobler, S. (ed.): Foundations of Equational Logic Programming. LNCS, vol. 353. Springer, Heidelberg (1989)
23. Hullot, J.M.: Canonical Forms and Unification. In: Bibel, W. (ed.) CADE 1980. LNCS, vol. 87, pp. 318–334. Springer, Heidelberg (1980)
24. Jones, N.D., Gomard, C.K., Sestoft, P.: Partial Evaluation and Automatic Program Generation. Prentice-Hall, Englewood Cliffs (1993)
25. Klop, J.W.: Term Rewriting Systems: A Tutorial. Bulletin of the European Association for Theoretical Computer Science 32, 143–183 (1987)
26. Kusakari, K., Nakamura, M., Toyama, Y.: Argument Filtering Transformation. In: Nadathur, G. (ed.) PPDP 1999. LNCS, vol. 1702, pp. 48–62. Springer, Heidelberg (1999)
27. López-Fraguas, F., Sánchez-Hernández, J.: TOY: A Multiparadigm Declarative System. In: Narendran, P., Rusinowitch, M. (eds.) RTA 1999. LNCS, vol. 1631, pp. 244–247. Springer, Heidelberg (1999)
28. Meseguer, J., Thati, P.: Symbolic Reachability Analysis Using Narrowing and its Application to Verification of Cryptographic Protocols. Electronic Notes in Theoretical Computer Science 117, 153–182 (2005)
29. Moreno-Navarro, J.J., Kuchen, H., Loogen, R., Rodriguez-Artalejo, M.: Lazy Narrowing in a Graph Machine. In: Kirchner, H., Wechler, W. (eds.) ALP 1990. LNCS, vol. 463, pp. 298–317. Springer, Heidelberg (1990)
30. Nishida, N., Miura, K.: Dependency Graph Method for Proving Termination of Narrowing. In: Proc. of WST 2006, pp. 12–16 (2006)
31. Nishida, N., Sakai, M., Sakabe, T.: Narrowing-Based Simulation of Term Rewriting Systems with Extra Variables. ENTCS, 86(3) (2003)
32. Ramos, J.G., Silva, J., Vidal, G.: Fast Narrowing-Driven Partial Evaluation for Inductively Sequential Systems. In: Proc. of the 10th ACM SIGPLAN Int'l Conf. on Functional Programming (ICFP 2005), pp. 228–239. ACM Press, New York (2005)
33. Schneider-Kamp, P., Giesl, J., Serebrenik, A., Thiemann, R.: Automated Termination Analysis for Logic Programs by Term Rewriting. In: Puebla, G. (ed.) LOPSTR 2006. LNCS, vol. 4407, pp. 177–193. Springer, Heidelberg (2007)
34. Sheard, T.: Type-Level Computation Using Narrowing in Ωmega. In: In Proc. of PLPV 2006. ENTCS, vol. 174, pp. 105–128 (2007)
35. Slagle, J.R.: Automated Theorem-Proving for Theories with Simplifiers, Commutativity and Associativity. Journal of the ACM 21(4), 622–642 (1974)
36. Vidal, G.: Termination of Narrowing in Left-Linear Constructor Systems. Technical report, DSIC, Technical University of Valencia (2007),
    http://www.dsic.upv.es/~gvidal/german/papers.html#tnt

Complexity Analysis by Rewriting[*]

Martin Avanzini[1] and Georg Moser[2]

[1] Master Program in Computer Science, University of Innsbruck, Austria
martin.avanzini@student.uibk.ac.at
[2] Institute of Computer Science, University of Innsbruck, Austria
georg.moser@uibk.ac.at

Abstract. In this paper we introduce a restrictive version of the multiset path order, called *polynomial path order*. This recursive path order induces polynomial bounds on the maximal number of innermost rewrite steps. This result opens the way to automatically verify for a given program, written in an eager functional programming language, that the maximal number of evaluation steps starting from any function call is polynomial in the input size. To test the feasibility of our approach we have implemented this technique and compare its applicability to existing methods.

1 Introduction

Term rewriting is a conceptually simple but powerful abstract model of computation that underlies much of declarative programming. In rewriting, proving termination is an important research field. Powerful methods have been introduced to establish termination of a given term rewrite system. One of the most natural ways to proof termination is the use of *interpretations*. Consequentially this technique has been introduced quite early. Moreover, if one is interested in automatically proving termination, *polynomial interpretations* provide a natural starting point, cf. [10]. However, termination proofs via polynomial interpretations are limited as the longest possible rewrite sequences admitted by rewrite systems compatible with a polynomial interpretation are double-exponential (in the size of the initial term), see [13]. Another well-studied (and direct) termination technique is the use of reduction orders—for example simplification orders. Still this technique is limited, which can again be shown by the analysis of the induced derivation length, cf. [12,25,15]. In recent years the emphasis shifted towards transformation techniques like the dependency pair method or semantic labeling. Transformation techniques have significantly increased the possibility to automatically prove termination.

Once we have established termination of a given rewrite system $\mathcal{R}$, it seems natural to direct the attention to the analysis of the *complexity* of $\mathcal{R}$. In rewriting the complexity of a rewrite system $\mathcal{R}$ is measured as the *maximal derivation length* with respect to $\mathcal{R}$. As mentioned above for *direct* termination methods

---

[*] This research is supported by FWF (Austrian Science Fund) project P20133.

J. Garrigue and M. Hermenegildo (Eds.): FLOPS 2008, LNCS 4989, pp. 130–146, 2008.

a significant amount of investigations has been conducted, providing a suitable foundation for further research. Unfortunately, almost nothing is known about the length of derivations induced by state-of-the-art termination techniques like the dependency pair method or semantic labeling. For the dependency pair method no results on the induced derivation length are known. Partial result with respect to semantic labeling are reported in [18].

In this paper we introduce a restriction of the multiset path order, called *polynomial path order* (denoted as $>_{\mathsf{pop}*}$). Our main result states that this recursive path order induces polynomial bounds on the maximal length of *innermost* rewrite steps. As we have successfully implemented this technique, we thus can *automatically* verify for a given term rewrite system $\mathcal{R}$ that $\mathcal{R}$ admits at most polynomial innermost derivation length (on the set of *constructor-based* terms). This opens the way to automatically verify for a given program—written in an eager functional programming language—that its runtime complexity is polynomial (in the input size). The only restrictions in the applicability of the result are that (i) the functional program P is transformable into a term rewrite system $\mathcal{R}$ and (ii) a feasible (i.e., polynomial) derivation length with respect to $\mathcal{R}$ gives rise to a feasible runtime complexity of P. In short the transformation has to be *non-termination* and *complexity preserving*.

The definition of polynomial path orders employs the idea of *tiered recursion* [6]. Syntactically this amount to a separation of arguments into *normal* and *safe* argument. (Below this will be governed by the presences of mappings safe and nrm associating with each function symbol a list of argument positions.) We explain our approach by an example rewrite system that clearly admits at most polynomial derivation length.

Example 1. Consider the following rewrite system $\mathcal{R}_{\mathsf{mult}}$.

$$\mathsf{add}(x, 0) \to x \qquad\qquad \mathsf{mult}(0, y) \to 0$$
$$\mathsf{add}(\mathsf{s}(x), y) \to \mathsf{s}(\mathsf{add}(x, y)) \qquad \mathsf{mult}(\mathsf{s}(x), y) \to \mathsf{add}(y, \mathsf{mult}(x, y))$$

We suppose that all arguments of the successor (s) are safe ($\mathsf{safe}(\mathsf{s}) = \{1\}$), that the second argument of addition (add) is safe ($\mathsf{safe}(\mathsf{add}) = \{2\}$) and that all arguments of multiplication (mult) are normal ($\mathsf{safe}(\mathsf{mult}) = \varnothing$). Furthermore let the (strict) precedence $>$ be defined as $\mathsf{mult} > \mathsf{add} > \mathsf{s}$. Then $\mathcal{R}_{\mathsf{mult}}$ is compatible with $>_{\mathsf{pop}*}$ (see Definition 4) and as a consequence of our main theorem (see Section 3) we conclude that the number of rewrite steps starting from $\mathsf{mult}(\mathsf{s}^n(0), \mathsf{s}^m(0))$ is polynomially bounded in n and m. (Here we write $\mathsf{s}^n(0)$ as abbreviation of $\mathsf{s}(\ldots(\mathsf{s}(0)\ldots))$ with n occurrences of the successor symbol s.)

The polynomial path order is an extension of the *path order for* **FP** introduced by Arai and the second author in [1]. A central motivation of this research is the observation that the direct application of the latter order is only successful on a handful of (very simple) rewrite systems. The path order for **FP** gains only power if additional transformations are performed. Unfortunately, such powerful transformations are difficult to find automatically.

Further note that the polynomial path order is to some extent related to the *light multiset path order* introduced by Marion [17]. Roughly speaking the light multiset path order is a tamed version of the multiset path order, characterising the functions computable in polytime. It seems important to stress that the below stated main theorem fails for the light multiset path order. This can be easily seen from the next example.

Example 2. Consider the following rewrite system $\mathcal{R}_{\mathsf{bin}}$. (This is Example 2.21 about binomial coefficients from [22].)

$$\mathsf{bin}(x,0) \to \mathsf{s}(0) \qquad \mathsf{bin}(\mathsf{s}(x),\mathsf{s}(y)) \to +(\mathsf{bin}(x,\mathsf{s}(y)),\mathsf{bin}(x,y))$$
$$\mathsf{bin}(0,\mathsf{s}(y)) \to 0$$

For a precedence that fulfills $\mathsf{bin} > \mathsf{s}$, $\mathsf{bin} > +$ and separations of arguments $\mathsf{safe}(\mathsf{bin}) = \varnothing$, $\mathsf{safe}(+) = \{1,2\}$, we obtain that $\mathcal{R}_{\mathsf{bin}}$ is compatible with the light multiset path order, cf. [17]. However it is straightforward to verify that the (innermost) derivation height of $\mathsf{bin}(\mathsf{s}^n(0),\mathsf{s}^m(0))$ is exponential in n.

To test the feasibility of our approach we have implemented a small complexity analyser based on the polynomial path order and compare its applicability to existing techniques. To do so, we also have implemented the light multiset path order and a restricted form of polynomial interpretations, so-called *additive polynomial interpretations*, cf. [7]. Note that compatibility with addivite polynomial interpretations induces polynomial derivation length for constructor-based terms, cf. [7].

The research in [7,17] falls into the realm of *implicit complexity theory*. In this context related work to our research is due to Bonfante *et al.* [8] but see also seminal work by Hofmann [14] and Schwichtenberg [20]. While [14,20] are incomparable to our techniques, a comparison to [8] is also not straightforward. Our principal concern is that the *termination* techniques employed allow for an *complexity analysis* of the subjected program. On the other hand the crucial feature of *quasi-interpretations* (the central contribution of [8]) is their weak monotonicity, hence termination can only be shown in conjunction with other termination techniques. For example the class of polytime computable functions can be characterised as the class of functions computable by confluent constructor rewrite systems compatible with the multiset path order *and* that admit only additive quasi-interpretations, cf. [8]. This interesting result renders an insightful implicit characterisation of the polytime computable function, but it is of little help, if one wants to obtain a complexity analysis of a term rewrite system subjected to a modern termination prover. Recently an interesting application of quasi-interpretations has been reported by Lucas and Peña [16]. Here the dependency pair method is used in conjunction with quasi-interpretations to obtain bounds on the *memory consumption* of Safe programs. This method is easily automatable, but new ideas are necessary to yield bounds on the *runtime behaviour* of functional programs.

The remainder of this paper is organised as follows. In the next section we recall basic notions and starting points of this paper. In Section 3 we have collected our main results. In order to prove these results we extend results originally presented in [1]. Our findings in this direction are presented in Section 4. The central argument to prove the main theorem is then given in Section 5. In Section 6 we give the experimental evidence mentioned above. In Section 7 we touch upon an application of our main theorem in recent work (together with Hirokawa and Middeldorp) where we study the termination behaviour of Scheme programs. Finally in Section 8 we conclude and mention possible future work.

2 Preliminaries

We assume familiarity with term rewriting [4,23]. Let $\mathcal{V}$ denote a countably infinite set of variables and $\mathcal{F}$ a signature. The set of terms over $\mathcal{F}$ and $\mathcal{V}$ is denoted by $\mathcal{T}(\mathcal{F}, \mathcal{V})$. We always assume that $\mathcal{F}$ contains at least one constant. The *arity* of a function symbol f is denoted as $\mathsf{ar}(f)$. Let $>$ be a precedence on the signature $\mathcal{F}$. The *rank* of a function symbol is defined inductively as follows: $\mathsf{rk}(f) = 1 + \max\{\mathsf{rk}(g) \mid g \in \mathcal{F} \wedge f > g\}$. (Here we employ the convention that the maximum of an empty set equals 0.) We write $\trianglelefteq$ to denote the subterm relation and $\trianglerighteq$ for its converse. The strict part of $\trianglerighteq$ is denoted by $\vartriangleright$. $\mathsf{Var}(t)$ denotes the set of variables occurring in a term t. The *size* (*depth*) of a term t is denoted as $\mathsf{size}(t)$ ($\mathsf{dp}(t)$). The width of a term t is defined inductively as follows: $\mathsf{wd}(t) = 1$, if t is a variable or a constant, otherwise if $t = f(t_1, \ldots, t_n)$ with $n > 0$, we set $\mathsf{wd}(t) = \max\{n, \mathsf{wd}(t_1), \ldots, \mathsf{wd}(t_n)\}$. The *Buchholz norm* of a term t is defined inductively as follows: $\|t\| = 1$, if t is a variable and for $t = f(t_1, \ldots, t_n)$ we set $\|t\| = 1 + \max\{n, \|t_1\|, \ldots, \|t_n\|\}$. We write $[t_1, \ldots, t_n]$ to denote multisets and $\uplus$ for the summation of multisets.

A *term rewrite system* (*TRS* for short) $\mathcal{R}$ over $\mathcal{T}(\mathcal{F}, \mathcal{V})$ is a set of rewrite rules $l \to r$, such that $l \notin \mathcal{V}$ and $\mathsf{Var}(l) \supseteq \mathsf{Var}(r)$. (If not mentioned otherwise, we assume $\mathcal{R}$ is *finite*.) The root symbols of left-hand sides of rewrite rules are called *defined*, while all other function symbols are called *constructors*. For a given signature $\mathcal{F}$ the defined symbols are denoted as $\mathcal{D}$, while the constructor symbol are collected in $\mathcal{C}$. The smallest rewrite relation that contains $\mathcal{R}$ is denoted by $\to_\mathcal{R}$. We simply write $\to$ for $\to_\mathcal{R}$ if $\mathcal{R}$ is clear from context. Let s and t be terms. If exactly n steps are preformed to contract s to t we write $s \to^n t$. A term $s \in \mathcal{T}(\mathcal{F}, \mathcal{V})$ is called a *normal form* if there is no $t \in \mathcal{T}(\mathcal{F}, \mathcal{V})$ such that $s \to t$. The *innermost rewrite relation* $\xrightarrow{i}_\mathcal{R}$ of a TRS $\mathcal{R}$ is defined on terms as follows: $s \xrightarrow{i}_\mathcal{R} t$ if there exist a rewrite rule $l \to r \in \mathcal{R}$, a context C, and a substitution σ such that $s = C[l\sigma]$, $t = C[r\sigma]$, and all proper subterms of $l\sigma$ are normal forms of $\mathcal{R}$. A TRS is called *confluent* if for all $s, t_1, t_2 \in \mathcal{T}(\mathcal{F}, \mathcal{V})$ with $s \to^* t_1$ and $s \to^* t_2$ there exists a term t_3 such that $t_1 \to^* t_3$ and $t_2 \to^* t_3$. A TRS is *non-overlapping* if it has no critical pairs, cf. [4]. A TRS $\mathcal{R}$ is *left-linear* if for all rules $l \to r \in \mathcal{R}$, all variables in l occur at most once. If $\mathcal{R}$ is additionally non-overlapping, then $\mathcal{R}$ is called *orthogonal*. Note that every orthogonal TRS is confluent. A *constructor* TRS is a TRS whose signature $\mathcal{F}$ can be partitioned into the defined symbols $\mathcal{D}$ and constructor symbols $\mathcal{C}$ in such a way that the left-hand side of each rule has the form $f(s_1, \ldots, s_n)$ with $f \in \mathcal{D}$ and for all i: $s_i \in \mathcal{T}(\mathcal{C}, \mathcal{V})$. A defined function symbol is *completely defined* if it does not occur in any ground term in normal form. A TRS is *completely defined* if each defined symbol is completely defined. An element of $\mathcal{T}(\mathcal{C}, \mathcal{V})$ is called a *value*; we set $\mathsf{Val}(\mathcal{R}) = \mathcal{T}(\mathcal{C}, \mathcal{V})$. We call a TRS *terminating* if no infinite rewrite sequence exists. The *derivation length* of a term t with respect to a terminating TRS $\mathcal{R}$ and rewrite relation $\to_{\mathcal{R}}$ is defined as usual: $\mathsf{Dl}_{(\mathcal{R},\to)}(s) = \max\{n \mid \exists t\ s \to^n t\}$. We call a term $t = f(t_1, \ldots, t_n)$ *constructor-based* if all its arguments t_i are values, i.e., $t_i \in \mathcal{T}(\mathcal{C}, \mathcal{V})$ for all $1 \leqslant i \leqslant n$. The set $\mathcal{T}_b$ collects all constructor-based terms. The *runtime complexity* (with respect to $\mathcal{R}$) is defined as follows: $\mathsf{Rc}_{\mathcal{R}}(m) = \max\{\mathsf{Dl}_{(\mathcal{R},\xrightarrow{i})}(t) \mid t = f(t_1, \ldots, t_n) \in \mathcal{T}_b$ and $\sum_i^n \mathsf{size}(t_i) \leqslant m\}$.

A proper order is a transitive and irreflexive relation. The *reflexive closure* of a proper order $\succ$ is denoted as $\succ^=$. A proper order $\succ$ is *well-founded* if there is no infinite decreasing sequence $t_1 \succ t_2 \succ t_3 \cdots$. A well-founded proper order that is also a rewrite relation is called a *reduction order*. We say a reduction order $\succ$ and a TRS $\mathcal{R}$ are *compatible* if $\mathcal{R} \subseteq \succ$. It is well-known that a TRS is terminating if and only if there exists a compatible reduction order.

3   Main Result

In the sequel $\mathcal{R}$ denotes a constructor TRS over a (possible variadic) signature $\mathcal{F}$. Let $>$ denote a precedence on $\mathcal{F}$ such that for all $f \in \mathcal{D}$ we have for all $c \in \mathcal{C}$: $f > c$. (Recall that $\mathcal{F}$ contains at least one constant.) We assume that $\mathcal{R}$ is completely defined, i.e., ground normal forms and ground values coincide.[1]

For each n-ary function symbol $f \in \mathcal{D}$ of fixed arity, we suppose the existence of a mapping safe that associates with f a (possibly empty) list $\{i_1, \ldots, i_m\}$ with $1 \leqslant i_1 < \cdots < i_m \leqslant n$. For a mapping safe and a term $t = f(t_1, \ldots, t_n)$, $\mathsf{safe}(f)$ denotes the *safe argument positions* of t. The argument positions of t *not* included in $\mathsf{safe}(f)$ are called *normal* and are denoted by $\mathsf{nrm}(f)$. The mapping safe (nrm) is referred to as *safe* (*normal*) mapping. We generalise safe (normal) mappings to constructor symbols and variadic function symbols as follows: For each function symbol $f \in \mathcal{C}$, we fix $\mathsf{safe}(f) = \{1, \ldots, \mathsf{ar}(f)\}$ and for each variadic function symbol $f \in \mathcal{D}$ we assert $\mathsf{safe}(f) = \varnothing$. The *normalised signature* $\mathcal{F}^n$ contains a function symbol f^n for each $f \in \mathcal{F}$. If f is of fixed-arity and $\mathsf{nrm}(f) = \{i_1, \ldots, i_p\}$, then $\mathsf{ar}(f) = p$. The normalised signature $\mathcal{C}^n$ is defined accordingly.

Definition 3. *Let $>$ be a precedence and safe a safe mapping. We define $>_{\mathsf{pop}}$ inductively as follows: $s = f(s_1, \ldots, s_n) >_{\mathsf{pop}} t$ if one of the following alternatives holds:*

1. *f is a constructor and $s_i >_{\mathsf{pop}}^= t$ for some $i \in \{1, \ldots, n\}$,*
2. *$s_i >_{\mathsf{pop}}^= t$ for some $i \in \mathsf{nrm}(f)$, or*
3. *$t = g(t_1, \ldots, t_m)$ with $f \in \mathcal{D}$ and $f > g$ and $s >_{\mathsf{pop}} t_i$ for all $1 \leqslant i \leqslant m$.*

We write $s >_{\mathsf{pop}} t \langle i \rangle$ if $s >_{\mathsf{pop}} t$ follows by application of clause (i) in Definition 3. A similar notation will be used for the orders defined below.

---

[1] The assumption that $\mathcal{R}$ is completely defined arises naturally in the context of implicit characterisation of complexity classes. We follow this convention to some extent, but show that this restriction is not necessary.

Definition 4. *Let $>$ be a precedence and* safe *a safe mapping. We define the polynomial path order $>_{\mathsf{pop}*}$ (POP* for short) inductively as follows: $s = f(s_1, \ldots, s_n) >_{\mathsf{pop}*} t$ if one of the following alternatives holds:*

1. $s >_{\mathsf{pop}} t$,
2. $s_i >_{\mathsf{pop}*}^= t$ *for some* $i \in \{1, \ldots, n\}$,
3. $t = g(t_1, \ldots, t_m)$, *with* $f \in \mathcal{D}$, $f > g$, *and the following properties hold:*
   - $s >_{\mathsf{pop}*} t_{i_0}$ *for some* $i_0 \in \mathsf{safe}(g)$ *and*
   - *either* $s >_{\mathsf{pop}} t_i$ *or* $s \rhd t_i$ *and* $i \in \mathsf{safe}(g)$ *for all* $i \neq i_0$,
4. $t = f(t_1, \ldots, t_m)$ *and for* $\mathsf{nrm}(f) = \{i_1, \ldots, i_p\}$, $\mathsf{safe}(f) = \{j_1, \ldots, j_q\}$ *the following properties hold:*
   - $[s_{i_1}, \ldots, s_{i_p}] \; (>_{\mathsf{pop}*})_{\mathsf{mul}} \; [t_{i_1}, \ldots, t_{i_p}]$,
   - $[s_{j_1}, \ldots, s_{j_q}] \; (>_{\mathsf{pop}*}^=)_{\mathsf{mul}} \; [t_{j_1}, \ldots, t_{j_q}]$.

Here $(>_{\mathsf{pop}*})_{\mathsf{mul}}$ denotes the multiset extension of $>_{\mathsf{pop}*}$ and recall that for variadic function symbols, the set of safe arguments is empty.

Example 5. Consider the following TRS $\mathcal{R}_{\mathsf{insert}}$ (This is a simplification of an example from [17].)

$$\mathsf{if}(\mathsf{true}, x, y) \to x \qquad\qquad x \geqslant 0 \to \mathsf{true}$$
$$\mathsf{if}(\mathsf{false}, x, y) \to y \qquad\qquad 0 \geqslant \mathsf{s}(x) \to \mathsf{false}$$
$$\mathsf{ins}(x, \mathsf{nil}) \to \mathsf{cons}(x, \mathsf{nil}) \qquad\qquad \mathsf{s}(x) \geqslant \mathsf{s}(y) \to x \geqslant y$$
$$\mathsf{ins}(x, \mathsf{cons}(y, ys)) \to \mathsf{if}(y \geqslant x, \mathsf{cons}(x, \mathsf{cons}(y, ys)), \mathsf{cons}(y, \mathsf{ins}(x, ys)))$$

We represent lists with the help of the constructors nil and cons. To show compatibility with POP*, we assume a precedence $\succ$ that fulfills $\mathsf{ins} \succ \mathsf{if}$, $\mathsf{ins} \succ \geqslant$, $\mathsf{ins} \succ \mathsf{cons}$, $0 \succ \mathsf{true}$, and $0 \succ \mathsf{false}$. Further we define a safe mapping safe as follows:

$$\mathsf{safe}(\mathsf{s}) = \{1\} \qquad \mathsf{safe}(\mathsf{if}) = \{1, 2, 3\} \qquad \mathsf{safe}(\mathsf{ins}) = \varnothing$$
$$\mathsf{safe}(\mathsf{cons}) = \{1, 2\} \qquad \mathsf{safe}(\geqslant) = \{2\}$$

It is straightforward to verify that the induced polynomial path order $\succ_{\mathsf{pop}*}$ is compatible with $\mathcal{R}_{\mathsf{insert}}$.

An easy inductive argument shows that if $s \in \mathsf{Val}(\mathcal{R})$ and $s >_{\mathsf{pop}*} t$, then $t \in \mathsf{Val}(\mathcal{R})$. Note that $>_{\mathsf{pop}*}$ is *not* a reduction order. Although $>_{\mathsf{pop}*}$ is a well-founded proper order that is closed under substitutions, the order is not closed under contexts due to the restrictive definition of clause 4 in the above definition. However we still have the following theorem, which follows as the multiset path order extends $>_{\mathsf{pop}*}$.

Theorem 6. *Every TRS $\mathcal{R}$ that is compatible with $>_{\mathsf{pop}*}$ for some well-founded precedence $>$ is terminating.*

As *normal* and *safe* arguments are distinguisable, we strengthen the notion of runtime complexity as follows: $\mathsf{Rc}^n_{\mathcal{R}}(m) = \max\{\mathsf{Dl}_{(\mathcal{R},\xrightarrow{i})}(t) \mid t = f(t_1,\ldots,t_n) \in \mathcal{T}_b$ and $\sum_{i \in \mathsf{nrm}(f)} \mathsf{size}(t_i) \leqslant m\}$. This function is called the *normal* runtime complexity.

Main Theorem. *Let $\mathcal{R}$ be a finite, completely defined constructor TRS. Assume further $\mathcal{R}$ is compatible with $>_{\mathsf{pop}*}$, i.e., $\mathcal{R} \subseteq\ >_{\mathsf{pop}*}$. Then the induced (normal) runtime complexity is polynomial.*

Assume $\mathcal{R}$ is a finite, constructor TRS that is not completely defined; i.e., at least one defined function symbol occurs in a ground normal form. To obtain a completely defined TRS it suffices to add suitable rules, thus we arrive at the following corollary, see [3] for the proof.

Corollary 7. *Let $\mathcal{R}$ be a finite, constructor TRS. Assume further $\mathcal{R}$ is compatible with $>_{\mathsf{pop}*}$, i.e., $\mathcal{R} \subseteq\ >_{\mathsf{pop}*}$. Then the induced (normal) runtime complexity is polynomial.*

Definition 8. *The predicative rewrite relation $s \xrightarrow{p} t$ is defined as follows: $s \xrightarrow{p} t$ if $s \to t$ by contracting safe argument positions first, i.e., if there exist a rewrite rule $l \to r \in \mathcal{R}$, a context C, and a substitution σ such that $s = C[l\sigma]$, $t = C[r\sigma]$ and all safe argument position of $l\sigma$ are in normal form.*

Clearly predicative rewriting is a generalisation of innermost rewriting. Essentially following the pattern of the proof of the theorem, we arrive at the following corollary.

Corollary 9. *Let $\mathcal{R}$ be a finite constructor TRS. Assume further $\mathcal{R}$ is compatible with $>_{\mathsf{pop}*}$, i.e., $\mathcal{R} \subseteq\ >_{\mathsf{pop}*}$. Then for all $f \in \mathcal{F}$ of arity n, with $\mathsf{nrm}(f) = \{i_1,\ldots,i_p\}$ and for all values $s_1,\ldots,s_n$: $\mathsf{Dl}_{(\mathcal{R},\xrightarrow{p})}(f(s_1,\ldots,s_n))$ is bounded by a polynomial in the sum of the sizes of the normal argument terms $s_{i_1},\ldots,s_{i_p}$.*

Remark 10. Beckmann and Weiermann observed in [5] that general rewriting is too powerful to serve as a suitable computation model to characterise the class of polytime computable functions as a TRS. Their notion of a *feasible* rewrite system is reflected adequately in the notion of predicative rewriting.

4   Polynomial Path Order on Sequences

In this section we extend definitions and results originally presented in [1]. The main aim is to define a *polynomial path order* $\blacktriangleright$ on sequences of terms such that $\blacktriangleright$ induces polynomial derivation length with respect to a compatible TRS $\mathcal{R}$.

Let $\odot \notin \mathcal{F}^n$ be a variadic function symbol. We extend the normalised signature $\mathcal{F}^n$ by $\odot$ and define $\mathcal{S}eq(\mathcal{F}^n,\mathcal{V}) = \mathcal{T}(\mathcal{F}^n \cup \{\odot\},\mathcal{V})$. Elements of $\mathcal{S}eq(\mathcal{F}^n,\mathcal{V})$ are sometimes referred to as *sequences*. Instead of $\odot(s_1,\ldots,s_n)$, we usually write $(s_1 \cdots s_n)$ and denote the empty sequence () as $\varnothing$. Let $a = (a_1 \ldots a_n)$

and $b = (b_1 \ldots b_m)$ be elements of $\mathcal{S}eq(\mathcal{F}^n, \mathcal{V})$. For $a \neq \varnothing$ and $b \neq \varnothing$ define $a @ b = (a_1 \ldots a_n \, b_1 \ldots b_m)$. If $a = \varnothing$ $(b = \varnothing)$ we set $a @ b = b$ $(a @ b = a)$.

Let $>$ denote the precedence on $\mathcal{F}^n$ induced by the total precedence $>$ on $\mathcal{F}$. Buchholz [9] was the first to observe that finite term rewrite systems compatible with recursive path orders $\succ$ are even compatible to *finite* approximations of $\succ$. This observation carries over to polynomial path orders. The following definitions generalise the *path order on* **FP** (*POP* for short) as defined in [1]. To keep this exposition short, we only state the definition of *approximations* of the *polynomial path order* $\blacktriangleright$ *on sequences*. The general definitions for $>$ and $\blacktriangleright$ is obtained by dropping the restrictions on depth and width, cf. [3]. Note that $\blacktriangleright$ can be conceived as the *limit* of the finite approximations $\blacktriangleright_k$. We use the convention that $f \in \mathcal{F}^n$, i.e., $s = f(s_1, \ldots, s_n)$ implicitly indicates that $f \neq \odot$.

Definition 11. *Let $k, l \geqslant 1$ and let $>$ be a precedence. We define $>^l_k$ inductively as follows: $s >^l_k t$ for $s = f(s_1, \ldots, s_n)$ or $s = (s_1 \cdots s_n)$ if one of the following alternatives holds:*

1. *$s_i \ (>^=)^l_k \, t$ for some $i \in \{1, \ldots, n\}$,*
2. *$s = f(s_1, \ldots, s_n)$ such that of the following two possibilities holds:*
   - *$t = g(t_1, \ldots, t_m)$ with $f > g$ or*
   - *$t = (t_1 \cdots t_m)$,*
   and $s >^{l-1}_k t_i$ for all $1 \leqslant i \leqslant m$, and $m < k + \mathsf{wd}(s)$, or
3. *$s = (s_1 \cdots s_n)$, $t = (t_1 \cdots t_m)$ and the following properties hold:*
   - *$[t_1, \ldots, t_m] = N_1 \uplus \cdots \uplus N_n$,*
   - *there exists $i \in \{1, \ldots, n\}$ such that $[s_i] \neq N_i$,*
   - *for all $1 \leqslant i \leqslant n$ such that $[s_i] \neq N_i$ we have $s_i >^l_k r$ for all $r \in N_i$,*
   - *$m < k + \mathsf{wd}(s)$.*

We write $>_k$ to abbreviate $>^k_k$.

Definition 12. *Let $k, l \geqslant 1$ and let $>$ be a precedence. We define the* approximation *of the polynomial path order $\blacktriangleright^l_k$ on sequences inductively as follows: $s \blacktriangleright^l_k t$ for $s = f(s_1, \ldots, s_n)$ or $s = (s_1 \cdots s_n)$ if one of the following alternatives holds:*

1. *$s >^l_k t$,*
2. *$s_i \ (\blacktriangleright^=)^l_k \, t$ for some $i \in \{1, \ldots, n\}$,*
3. *$s = f(s_1, \ldots, s_n)$, $t = (t_1 \cdots t_m)$, and the following properties hold:*
   - *$s \blacktriangleright^{l-1}_k t_{i_0}$ for some $i_0 \in \{1, \ldots, n\}$,*
   - *$s >^{l-1}_k t_i$ for all $i \neq i_0$, and*
   - *$m < k + \mathsf{wd}(s)$,*
4. *$s = f(s_1, \ldots, s_n)$, $t = f(t_1, \ldots, t_m)$ with $(s_1 \cdots s_n) \blacktriangleright^l_k (t_1 \cdots t_m)$, or*
5. *$s = (s_1 \cdots s_n)$, $t = (t_1 \cdots t_m)$ and the following properties hold:*
   - *$[t_1, \ldots, t_m] = N_1 \uplus \cdots \uplus N_n$,*
   - *there exists $i \in \{1, \ldots, n\}$ such that $[s_i] \neq N_i$,*
   - *for all $1 \leqslant i \leqslant n$ such that $[s_i] \neq N_i$: $s_i >^l_k r$ for all $r \in N_i$, and*
   - *$m < k + \mathsf{wd}(s)$.*

We write $\blacktriangleright_k$ to abbreviate $\blacktriangleright^k_k$.

Note that $\varnothing$ is the minimal element of $>_k$ and $\blacktriangleright_k$ and that $\blacktriangleright$ is a reduction order. The following lemmas are direct consequences of the definitions.

Lemma 13

1. If $s \blacktriangleright_k t$ and $k < l$, then $s \blacktriangleright_l t$.
2. If $s \blacktriangleright_k t$, then $C[s] \blacktriangleright_k C[t]$, where $C[\square]$ denotes a context over $\mathcal{S}eq(\mathcal{F}^n, \mathcal{V})$.

Lemma 14. If $s \blacktriangleright_k^l t$, then $\mathsf{dp}(t) \leqslant \mathsf{dp}(s) + l$ and $\mathsf{wd}(t) \leqslant k + \mathsf{wd}(s)$. Moreover, if $s \blacktriangleright_k^l t$, then $\|t\| \leqslant \|s\| + k + l$.

By Lemma 14, there exists a (uniform) constant c such that $\|t\| \leqslant \|s\| + c$, whenever $s \blacktriangleright_k t$. And thus if we have a $\blacktriangleright_k$-descending sequence $s = t_0 \blacktriangleright_k t_1 \blacktriangleright_k \cdots \blacktriangleright_k t_\ell$ we conclude that $\|t_i\| \leqslant ci + \|s\|$ for all $i \geqslant 1$.

Definition 15. We define

$$\mathsf{G}_k(s) := \max\{\ell \in \mathbb{N} \mid \exists(t_0, \ldots, t_\ell): s = t_0 \blacktriangleright_k t_1 \blacktriangleright_k \cdots \blacktriangleright_k t_\ell\}$$

$$\mathsf{F}_{k,p}(m) := \max\left\{\mathsf{G}_k(f(t_1, \ldots, t_n)): \mathsf{rk}(f) = p \wedge \sum_i \mathsf{G}_k(t_i) \leqslant m\right\}$$

In the definition of $\mathsf{F}_{k,p}$, we assume $f \in \mathcal{F}^n$.

A direct consequence of Definition 15 is that $\mathsf{G}_k((t_1 \cdots t_n)) = n + \sum_{i=1}^n \mathsf{G}_k(t_i)$ holds. The following lemma is generalisation of a similar lemma in [1] and the proof given in [1] can be easily adapted.

Lemma 16. We define $d_{k,0} := k + 1$ and $d_{k,p+1} := (d_{k,p})^k + 1$. Then for all k, p there exists a constant c (depending only on k and p) such that for all m: $\mathsf{F}_{k,p}(m) \leqslant c(m+2)^{d_{k,p}}$.

As a consequence of Lemma 16 we obtain that $\mathsf{F}_{k,p}(m)$ is asymptotically bounded by $m^{d_{k,p}}$ for large enough m. The following lemma follows by a standard inductive argument.

Lemma 17. For all k, there exists a constant c such that for $s \in \mathcal{T}(\mathcal{C}^n \cup \{\odot\}, \mathcal{V})$: $\mathsf{G}_k(s) \leqslant c \cdot \mathsf{size}(s)^2$.

We arrive at the main theorem of this section.

Theorem 18. For all $f \in \mathcal{F}^n$ of arity n, for all $s_1, \ldots, s_n \in \mathcal{T}(\mathcal{C}^n \cup \{\odot\})$, and for all k: $\mathsf{G}_k(f(s_1, \ldots, s_n))$ is bounded by a polynomial in the sum of the sizes of $s_1, \ldots, s_n$. The polynomial depends only on k and the rank of f.

Proof. Let $f \in \mathcal{F}^n$ and let $s_1, \ldots, s_n \in \mathcal{T}(\mathcal{C}^n \cup \{\odot\})$. By Lemma 16 there exists $c_1 \in \mathbb{N}$ depending on k and $\mathsf{rk}(f)$ such that

$$\mathsf{G}_k(f(s_1, \ldots, s_n)) \leqslant m^{c_1} \tag{1}$$

if $\sum_i \mathsf{G}_k(s_i) \leqslant m$ and m is large enough. By Lemma 17, there exists a constant c_2 (depending on the rank of the function symbols in s_i) such that $\mathsf{G}_k(s_i) \leqslant c_2 \cdot \mathsf{size}(s_i)^2$. Replacing m in (1) by $c_2 \cdot (\sum_i \mathsf{size}(s_i))^2$ and setting $c = c_2^{c_1}$ yields:

$$\mathsf{G}_k(f(s_1, \ldots, s_n)) \leqslant \left[c_2 \cdot \left(\sum_i \mathsf{size}(s_i)\right)^2\right]^{c_1} = c \cdot \left(\sum_i \mathsf{size}(s_i)\right)^{2c_1} \qquad \square$$

5   Predicative Interpretation

The purpose of this section is to prove our main theorem. Let $\mathcal{R}$ denote a completely defined, constructor TRS. We embed the order $>_{\mathsf{pop}*}$ into $\blacktriangleright_k$ such that k depends only on $\mathcal{R}$. This becomes possible if we represent the information on normal and safe arguments underlying the definition of $>_{\mathsf{pop}*}$ explicitly by interpreting the signature $\mathcal{F}$ in the normalised signature $\mathcal{F}^{\mathsf{n}}$.

Definition 19. *The* maximal size *of the safe values of a term t is defined as follows:*

$$\mathsf{sv}(t) = \begin{cases} \|t\| & t \in \mathsf{Val}(\mathcal{R}) \\ \max\{\mathsf{sv}(t_i) \mid i \in \mathsf{safe}(f)\} & t = f(t_1, \ldots, t_n) \text{ and } t \notin \mathsf{Val}(\mathcal{R}) \end{cases}$$

We represent $\mathsf{sv}(t)$ unary. Let s denote a fresh constant that is minimal in the precedence $>$ on $\mathcal{F}^{\mathsf{n}}$. We define $\mathsf{SV}(t) = \mathsf{U}(\mathsf{sv}(t))$, where $\mathsf{U}\colon \mathbb{N} \to \mathcal{T}(\{\mathsf{s}, \odot\})$ denotes the representation of n as a sequence $(\mathsf{s} \; \cdots \; \mathsf{s})$ with n occurrences of the constant s. As a direct consequence of the definition, we have: $s \rhd t$ implies $\mathsf{SV}(s) \blacktriangleright_k \mathsf{SV}(t)$ for any k.

Definition 20. *Let* safe *denote a safe mapping. A* predicative interpretation *(with respect to $\mathcal{T}(\mathcal{F}, \mathcal{V})$) is a pair (S, N) of mappings $\mathsf{S}\colon \mathcal{T}(\mathcal{F}, \mathcal{V}) \to \mathcal{T}(\mathcal{F}^{\mathsf{n}}, \mathcal{V})$ and $\mathsf{N}\colon \mathcal{T}(\mathcal{F}, \mathcal{V}) \to \mathcal{T}(\mathcal{F}^{\mathsf{n}}, \mathcal{V})$, defined as follows:*

$$\mathsf{S}(t) = \begin{cases} \varnothing & \text{if } t \in \mathsf{Val}(\mathcal{R}) \\ (f^{\mathsf{n}}(\mathsf{N}(s_{j_1}), \ldots, \mathsf{N}(s_{j_p})) \; \mathsf{S}(s_{i_1}) \; \ldots \; \mathsf{S}(s_{i_q})) & \text{if } t \notin \mathsf{Val}(\mathcal{R}) \end{cases}$$

$$\mathsf{N}(t) = (\mathsf{S}(t)) \; @ \; \mathsf{SV}(t)$$

In the definition of S, *we assume $t = f(s_1, \ldots, s_n)$, $\mathsf{nrm}(f) = \{j_1, \ldots, j_p\}$ and $\mathsf{safe}(f) = \{i_1, \ldots, i_q\}$. (Recall that $\mathsf{safe}(f) \cup \mathsf{nrm}(f) = \{1, \ldots, n\}$.)*

Note that $\mathsf{N}(s) >_k \mathsf{S}(s)$ (and thus $\mathsf{N}(s) \blacktriangleright_k \mathsf{S}(s)$) holds for any k. We arrive at the two main lemmas of this section.

Lemma 21. *Let $f(l_1, \ldots, l_n) \to r \in \mathcal{R}$, let $\sigma\colon \mathcal{V} \to \mathsf{Val}(\mathcal{R})$ be a substitution and let $k = 2 \cdot \max\{\mathsf{size}(r) \mid l \to r \in \mathcal{R}\}$. If $f(l_1, \ldots, l_n) >_{\mathsf{pop}} r$ then $f^{\mathsf{n}}(\mathsf{N}(l_{i_1}\sigma), \ldots, \mathsf{N}(l_{i_p}\sigma)) >_k \mathsf{Q}(r\sigma)$ for $\mathsf{Q} \in \{\mathsf{S}, \mathsf{N}\}$, where $\mathsf{nrm}(f) = \{i_1, \ldots, i_p\}$.*

Proof. We sketch the proof plan: Instead of showing the lemma directly, one shows the following stronger property for terms $s, t \in \mathcal{T}(\mathcal{F}, \mathcal{V})$ where s is either a value or of form $f(s_1, \ldots, s_n)$ such that $s_i\sigma \in \mathsf{Val}(\mathcal{R})$ for all $1 \leqslant i \leqslant n$.

(†)   Let $\ell = \|t\|$, if $f \in \mathcal{D}$, then $s >_{\mathsf{pop}} t$ implies $\mathsf{Q}(s\sigma) >_{2\ell}$ $f^{\mathsf{n}}(\mathsf{N}(s_1\sigma), \ldots, \mathsf{N}(s_p\sigma)) >_{2\ell} \mathsf{Q}(t\sigma)$; otherwise $\mathsf{N}(s\sigma) >_{2\ell}$ $\mathsf{N}(t\sigma)$ holds.

Here we suppose $\mathsf{safe}(f) = \{p+1, \ldots, n\}$. To show (†) one proceeds by induction on $>_{\mathsf{pop}}$. See [3] for the complete proof. □

Lemma 22. *Let $l \to r \in \mathcal{R}$, let $\sigma \colon \mathcal{V} \to \mathsf{Val}(\mathcal{R})$ be a substitution, and let $k = 2 \cdot \max\{\mathsf{size}(r) \mid l \to r \in \mathcal{R}\}$. If $l >_{\mathsf{pop}*} r$ then $\mathsf{Q}(l\sigma) \blacktriangleright_k \mathsf{Q}(r\sigma)$ for $\mathsf{Q} \in \{\mathsf{S}, \mathsf{N}\}$.*

Proof. Similar to the proof of Lemma 21 one shows the following property for terms $s, t \in \mathcal{T}(\mathcal{F}, \mathcal{V})$ where s is either a value or of form $f(s_1, \ldots, s_n)$ such that $s_i \sigma \in \mathsf{Val}(\mathcal{R})$ for all $1 \leqslant i \leqslant n$.

(‡)   Let $\ell = \|t\|$. If $f \in \mathcal{D}$, then $s = f(s_1, \ldots, s_n) >_{\mathsf{pop}*}$ t implies (i) $f^{\mathsf{n}}(\mathsf{N}(s_1\sigma), \ldots, \mathsf{N}(s_p\sigma)) \blacktriangleright_{2\ell} \mathsf{S}(t\sigma)$ and (ii) $(f^{\mathsf{n}}(\mathsf{N}(s_1\sigma), \ldots, \mathsf{N}(s_p\sigma))) @ \mathsf{SV}(s\sigma) \blacktriangleright_{2\ell} \mathsf{N}(t\sigma)$. Otherwise if $f \in \mathcal{C}$ then $\mathsf{N}(s\sigma) \blacktriangleright_{2\ell} \mathsf{N}(t\sigma)$ holds.

Here we suppose $\mathsf{safe}(f) = \{p+1, \ldots, n\}$. To show (‡) one proceeds by induction on $>_{\mathsf{pop}*}$. See [3] for the complete proof.   □

From Lemmata 21 and 22 the main lemma of this section follows.

Lemma 23. *Let s and t be terms such that $s \xrightarrow{\mathsf{i}} t$ and let $k = 2 \cdot \max\{\mathsf{size}(r) \mid l \to r \in \mathcal{R}\}$. Then $\mathsf{Q}(s) \blacktriangleright_k \mathsf{Q}(t)$ for $\mathsf{Q} \in \{\mathsf{S}, \mathsf{N}\}$.*

Main Theorem. *Let $\mathcal{R}$ be a finite, completely defined constructor TRS. Assume further $\mathcal{R}$ is compatible with $>_{\mathsf{pop}*}$. Then the induced (normal) runtime complexity is polynomial.*

Proof. Let $t = f(t_1, \ldots, t_n)$ be term in $\mathcal{T}_{\mathsf{b}}$ and without loss of generality let $\mathsf{safe}(f) = \{p+1, \ldots, n\}$. We set $k = 2 \cdot \max\{\mathsf{size}(r) \mid l \to r \in \mathcal{R}\}$. By Lemma 23 any innermost rewrite steps $t \xrightarrow{\mathsf{i}} u$ induces $\mathsf{S}(t) \blacktriangleright_k \mathsf{S}(u)$. Thus we obtain:

$$\mathsf{Dl}_{(\mathcal{R}, \xrightarrow{\mathsf{i}})}(f(t_1, \ldots, t_n)) = \max\{\ell \mid \exists u \; t \xrightarrow{\mathsf{i}}^{\ell} u\}$$
$$\leqslant \max\{\ell \mid \exists \; (s'_1, \ldots, s'_\ell) \colon \mathsf{S}(t) \blacktriangleright_k s'_1 \blacktriangleright_k \cdots \blacktriangleright_k s'_\ell\}$$
$$\leqslant \mathsf{G}_k(\mathsf{S}(f(t_1, \ldots, t_n)))$$

Next notice that $\mathsf{S}(f(t_1, \ldots, t_n)) = (f^{\mathsf{n}}(\mathsf{N}(t_1), \ldots, \mathsf{N}(t_p)) \; \varnothing \ldots \varnothing)$. By Theorem 18 and the observation following Definition 15 we see that

$$\mathsf{G}_k((f^{\mathsf{n}}(\mathsf{N}(t_1), \ldots, \mathsf{N}(t_p)) \; \varnothing \ldots \varnothing)) \leqslant n + 1 + \mathsf{G}_k(f^{\mathsf{n}}(\mathsf{N}(t_1), \ldots, \mathsf{N}(t_p)))$$

Employing Lemma 16, we see (for a fixed f) that $n + 1 + \mathsf{G}_k(f^{\mathsf{n}}(\mathsf{N}(t_1), \ldots, \mathsf{N}(t_p)))$ is asymptotically bounded by a polynomial in the sum of the sizes of the arguments $\mathsf{N}(t_1), \ldots, \mathsf{N}(t_p)$. By definition $\mathsf{size}(\mathsf{N}(t_i)) = \|t_i\| \leqslant \mathsf{size}(t_i)$ for all $1 \leqslant i \leqslant p$.

Hence for each term $t \in \mathcal{T}_{\mathsf{b}}$, $\mathsf{Dl}_{(\mathcal{R}, \xrightarrow{\mathsf{i}})}(t)$ is bounded by a polynomial in the sum of the sizes of the normal argument terms of t. In particular, as the signature $\mathcal{F}$ is finite, the normal runtime complexity function is polynomial.   □

Remark 24. In the above theorem we assume a constructor TRS. It is not difficult to see that this restriction is not necessary. (Essentially one replaces the application of Lemmata 21 and 22 by the application of the properties (†) and (‡) respectively.) However, the restriction that the arguments of f are in normal form is necessary. Hence we prefer the given formulation of the theorem.

6   Experimental Data

To prove compatibility of a given TRS $\mathcal{R}$ with recursive path orders we have to find a *precedence* $>$ such that the induced order is compatible with $\mathcal{R}$. When we want to orient $\mathcal{R}$ by a polynomial path order $>_{\mathsf{pop*}}$ we additionally require a suitable *safe mapping*. To automate this search we encode the constraint $s >_{\mathsf{pop*}} t$ into a propositional formula:

$$\tau(s >_{\mathsf{pop*}} t) = \tau_1(s >_{\mathsf{pop*}} t) \vee \tau_2(s >_{\mathsf{pop*}} t) \vee \tau_3(s >_{\mathsf{pop*}} t) \vee \tau_4(s >_{\mathsf{pop*}} t)$$

Here $\tau_i(\cdot)$ is designed to encode clause (i) from Definition 4. Based on such an encoding, compatibility of a TRS with $>_{\mathsf{pop*}}$ becomes expressible as the satisfiability of the formula $\left(\bigwedge_{l \to r \in \mathcal{R}} \tau(l >_{\mathsf{pop*}} r)\right) \wedge P \wedge S$. Here the subformula P is satisfiable if and only if all the variables $>_{f,g}$ (defined below) encode a strict precedence, see [26] for a suitable definition of P. The subformula S is used to cover the additional conditions imposed on safe mappings defined in the beginning of Section 3.

We only describe cases (2)–(4), the encoding for case (1)—the comparison using the weaker order $>_{\mathsf{pop}}$—can be easily derived in a similar fashion. If $s = f(s_1, \ldots, s_n)$ we set $\tau_2(s >_{\mathsf{pop*}} t) = \bigvee_i s_i >_{\mathsf{pop*}}^{=} t$, otherwise $\tau_2(s >_{\mathsf{pop*}} t) = \bot$. For case (3) we introduce for every function symbol f and argument position i of f the (propositional) variables $\beta_{f,i}$, such that $\beta_{f,i} = \mathsf{true}$ represents the assertion $i \in \mathsf{safe}(f)$. Moreover, for all function symbols f, g we introduce variables $>_{f,g}$ such that truth of $>_{f,g}$ expresses that $f > g$ holds. If $s = f(s_1, \ldots, s_n)$ and $t = g(t_1, \ldots, t_m)$ for $f \in \mathcal{D}$ with $f \neq g$, we define $\tau_3(s >_{\mathsf{pop*}} t)$ as:

$$>_{f,g} \wedge \bigvee_{i_0=1}^{m} \left(\tau(s >_{\mathsf{pop*}} t_i) \wedge \beta_{g,i_0} \wedge \bigwedge_{i=1, i \neq i_0}^{m} \left(\tau(s >_{\mathsf{pop}} t_i) \vee (\beta_{g,i} \wedge (s \rhd t_i)) \right) \right)$$

(For s, t of different shape, we set $\tau_3(s >_{\mathsf{pop*}} t) = \bot$.) To deal with case (4) we follow [19]. The main idea is to describe a multiset comparison in terms of *multiset covers*. Formally, a multiset cover is a pair of mappings $\gamma \colon \{1, \ldots, m\} \to \{1, \ldots, n\}$ and $\varepsilon \colon \{1, \ldots, n\} \to \{\mathsf{true}, \mathsf{false}\}$ such that for all i, j ($1 \leqslant i \leqslant n$, $1 \leqslant j \leqslant m$): if $\varepsilon(i) = \mathsf{true}$ then the set $\{j \mid \gamma(j) = i\}$ is a singleton. It is easy to see that $[s_1, \ldots, s_n] \ (\succ^=)_{\mathsf{mul}} \ [t_1, \ldots, t_m]$ if there exists a multiset cover (γ, ε) such that for each j there exists an i with $\gamma(j) = i$ and $\varepsilon(i) = \mathsf{true}$ implies $s_i = t_j$, while $\varepsilon(i) = \mathsf{false}$ implies $s_i \succ t_j$. Similarly we obtain $[s_1, \ldots, s_n] \succ_{\mathsf{mul}} [t_1, \ldots, t_m]$ if $[s_1, \ldots, s_n] \ (\succ^=)_{\mathsf{mul}} \ [t_1, \ldots, t_m]$ and $\varepsilon(i) = \mathsf{false}$ for some $i \in \{1, \ldots, n\}$.

This definition allows an easy encoding of multiset comparisons and based on it, clause (4) of Definition 4 becomes representable (for terms $s = f(s_1, \ldots, s_n)$ and $t = f(t_1, \ldots, t_m)$) as the conjunction of the following two conditions together with the assumption that there exists a suitable multiset cover (γ, ε):

- whenever $\gamma(j) = i$ then the indicated argument positions i and j, are either both normal or both safe,
- at least one cover is strict ($\varepsilon(i) = \mathsf{false}$) for some normal argument position i of f.

We introduce variables $\gamma_{i,j}$ and ε_i, where $\gamma_{i,j} = $ true represents $\gamma(j) = i$ and $\varepsilon_i = $ true denotes $\varepsilon(i) = $ true $(1 \leqslant i \leqslant n, 1 \leqslant j \leqslant m)$. Summing up, we set $\tau_4(s (>_{\mathsf{pop*}})_{\mathsf{mul}} t)$ $(s = f(s_1, \ldots, s_n)$ and $t = f(t_1, \ldots, t_m))$ equal to:

$$\bigwedge_{i=1}^{n} \bigwedge_{j=1}^{m} \Big(\gamma_{i,j} \rightarrow \big(\varepsilon_i \rightarrow \tau(s_i = t_j)\big)\Big) \wedge \big(\neg\varepsilon_i \rightarrow \tau(s_i \succ t_j)\big) \wedge \big(\beta_{f,i} \leftrightarrow \beta_{f,j}\big)\Big)$$

$$\wedge \bigwedge_{j=1}^{m} \mathrm{one}(\gamma_{1,j}, \ldots, \gamma_{n,j}) \wedge \bigwedge_{i=1}^{n} \big(\varepsilon_i \rightarrow \mathrm{one}(\gamma_{i,1}, \ldots, \gamma_{i,m})\big) \wedge \bigvee_{i=1}^{n} \big(\neg\beta_{f,i} \wedge \neg\varepsilon_i\big)$$

Here $\mathrm{one}(\alpha_1, \ldots, \alpha_n)$ is satisfiable if and only if exactly one of the variables $\alpha_1, \ldots, \alpha_n$ is true. And if s, t do not have the assumed form, we set $\tau_4(s (>_{\mathsf{pop*}})_{\mathsf{mul}} t) = \bot$.

We compare the polynomial path order POP* to a restricted class of polynomial interpretations (SMC for short) [7] and to LMPO [17]. SMC refers to simple-mixed polynomial interpretations where constructor symbols are interpreted by a strongly linear (also called *additive*) polynomial [7]. Defined symbols on the other hand are interpreted by simple-mixed polynomials [10]. Since POP* and LMPO are in essence syntactic restrictions of MPO we also provide a comparison to MPO. POP* is implemented using the previously described propositional encoding; while the implementation of SMC rests on a propositional encoding of the techniques described in [10]. To check satisfiability we employ MiniSat.[2] LMPO and MPO are implemented using an extension of the constraint solving technique described in [11], which allows us to compare different implementation techniques at the same time.

As testbed we use those TRSs from the termination problem data base version 4.0 that can be shown terminating with at least one of the tools that participated in the termination competition 2007.[3] We use three different testbeds: **T** collects the 957 terminating TRSs from TPDB, **TC** collects the 449 TRSs from the TPDB that are also constructor systems, and **TCO** collects the 236 TRSs that are terminating, constructor based and orthogonal.[4] The results of our comparisons are given in Table 1. The tests presented below were conducted on a small complexity analyser running single-threaded on a 2.1 GHz Intel Core 2 Duo with 1 GB of memory. For each system we used a timeout of 30 seconds.

Some comments: What is noteworthy is the good performance of POP*as a direct *termination* method in comparison to MPO. It is well-known that MPO implies primitive recursive derivation length, cf. [12]. In contrast to this POP* implies polynomial runtime complexity and is thus a much weaker order. Still more than half of the TRSs compatible with MPO are also compatible with

---

[2] Available online at http://minisat.se

[3] These 957 systems can be found online: http://www.lri.fr/~marche/termination-competition/2007/webform.cgi?command=trs&file=trs-standard.db&timelimit=120

[4] The main reason for this delineation is that in related work [7,17] *confluent* constructor TRS are considered.

Table 1. Experimental results

		POP*	LMPO	SMC	MPO
T	Yes	65	74	156	106
	Maybe	892	812	395	847
	Timeout (30 sec.)	0	71	406	4
TC	Yes	41	54	83	65
	Maybe	408	372	271	381
	Timeout (30 sec.)	0	23	95	3
TCO	Yes	19	25	38	29
	Maybe	217	201	147	207
	Timeout (30 sec.)	0	10	51	0
Average yes time (milliseconds)		15	14	1353	10

POP*. On the other hand the comparison between POP* and LMPO is quite favourable for our approach. Compatibility with LMPO tells us that the given TRS is (in principle) polytime computable, while compatibility with POP* tells additionally that the runtime of a straightforward implementation (using an innermost strategy) is polytime computable. Hence compatibility with POP* provides us with a theoretical stronger result, while the difference on the experimental data appears negligible.

The good performance of SMC in strength is a clear indication that currently (restrictions of) semantic termination techniques (like polynomial interpretations) are of some interest in automatically estimating the runtime complexity of TRSs. This may be surprising, as for additive polynomial interpretations it is (almost) trivial to check that the induced upper bound on the derivation height is polynomial. However, the significant increase in the time necessary to find an additive polynomial interpretation, as indicated in Table 1, clearly shows the limits of semantic methods for large examples.

7   An Application: Complexity of Scheme Programs

In recent work together with Hirokawa and Middeldorp (see [2]) we study the runtime complexity of (a subset of) Scheme programs by a translation into so-called *S-expression rewrite systems* (*SRS* for short). By designing the translation to be complexity preserving, the complexity of the initial Scheme program can be estimated by analysing the complexity of the resulting SRS. Here we indicate how our main theorem is applicable to (a subset of) S-expression rewrite systems, cf. [24].

Definition 25. *Let $\mathcal{K}$ be a set of constants, $\mathcal{V}$ be a set of variables such that $\mathcal{V} \cap \mathcal{K} = \varnothing$, and $\circ \notin \mathcal{K} \cup \mathcal{V}$ a variadic function symbol. We define the set $\mathcal{S}(\mathcal{K}, \mathcal{V})$*

of S-expressions *built from* $\mathcal{K}$ *and* $\mathcal{V}$ *as* $\mathcal{T}(\mathcal{K} \cup \{\circ\}, \mathcal{V})$. *We write* $(s_1 \cdots s_n)$ *instead of* $\circ(s_1, \ldots, s_n)$. *An* S-expression rewrite system *(SRS for short) is a TRS with the property that the left- and right-hand sides of all rewrite rules are S-expressions.*

Let $\mathcal{S}$ be an SRS over $\mathcal{S}(\mathcal{K}, \mathcal{V})$ and let $\mathcal{K} = \mathcal{D} \cup \mathcal{C}$ such that $\mathcal{D} \cap \mathcal{C} = \varnothing$. We call the elements of $\mathcal{C}$ *constructor* constants and the elements of $\mathcal{D}$ *defined* constants. We momentarily redefine the notion of *value* in the context of SRSs. The set of *values* $\mathsf{Val}(\mathcal{S})$ of $\mathcal{S}$ with respect to $\mathcal{C}$ is inductively defined as follows:

1. if $v \in \mathcal{K}$ then $v \in \mathsf{Val}(\mathcal{S})$,
2. if $v_1, \ldots, v_n \in \mathsf{Val}(\mathcal{S})$ and $\mathsf{c} \in \mathcal{C}$ then $(\mathsf{c}\ v_1 \ldots v_n) \in \mathsf{Val}(\mathcal{S})$.

Observe that (defined) constants are values, this reflects that in Scheme procedures are values, cf. [21] and allows for a representation of higher-order programs. Scheme programs are conceivable as SRSs allowing conditional if expressions in conjunction with an eager, i.e., innermost rewrite strategy. Thus we can delineate a class of SRSs that easily accommodate a suitably large subset of Scheme programs.

Definition 26. $\mathcal{S}$ *is called a* constructor *if, for every* $l \to r \in \mathcal{S}$, $l = (l_0 \cdots l_n)$ *with* $l_0 \in \mathcal{D}$ *and* $l_i \in \mathsf{Val}(\mathcal{S})$ *for all* $i \in \{1, \ldots, n\}$. *(Here the set of values* $\mathsf{Val}(\mathcal{S})$ *is defined with respect to* $\mathcal{C}$.)

Corollary 27. *Let* $>$ *denote a precedence on* $\mathcal{K}$ *such that for all* $f \in \mathcal{D}$ *we have for all* $\mathsf{c} \in \mathcal{C}$: $f > \mathsf{c}$ *and let* $>_{\mathsf{pop}*}$ *denote the induced POP*. Let* $\mathcal{S}$ *be a constructor SRS compatible with* $>_{\mathsf{pop}*}$. *Then for all* $f \in \mathcal{D}$ *of arity* n *and for all values* $s_1, \ldots, s_n$: $\mathsf{Dl}_{(\mathcal{S}, \xrightarrow{i})}((f\ s_1\ \ldots\ s_n))$ *is bounded by a polynomial in the sum of the sizes of the arguments* $s_1, \ldots, s_n$.

Proof. It is important to note that the set of S-expressions $\mathcal{S}(\mathcal{K}, \mathcal{V})$ equals $\mathcal{T}(\mathcal{K} \cup \{\circ\}, \mathcal{V})$, i.e., SRSs are *first-order* rewrite systems, whose single defined symbol is the variadic function symbol $\circ$.

  Hence Theorem 27 follows almost immediately from Corollary 7. However the fact that according to the above definition values may contain defined symbol need to be taken into account. For that is suffices to redefine Definitions 19 and 20 in the natural way. It is not difficult to argue that suitable adaption of Lemmata 21 and 22 to SRSs are provable.   □

8   Conclusion

In this paper we have introduced a restriction of the multiset path order, called *polynomial path order* (*POP** for short). Our main result states that POP* induces polynomial runtime complexity. In Section 6 we have provided evidence that our approach performs well in comparison to related methods. In Section 7 the necessary theory to apply our main theorem in the context of (higher-order) functional languages with eager evaluations has been developed. In related work (together with Hirokawa and Middeldorp), studying the termination behaviour and the runtime complexity of (a subclass of higher-order) Scheme programs, this basis has proven quite useful, cf. [2].

In concluding we also want to mention that as an easy corollary to our main theorem we obtain that POP* also characterises the polytime computable functions. To be precise the polytime computable functions are exactly the functions computable by an orthogonal constructor TRS (based on a simple signature) compatible with POP*. (Here *simple* signature means that the size of any constructor term depends linearly on its depth, an equivalent restriction is necessary in [17].) See [3] for details.

In future work we will strengthen the applicability of our method. The experimental evidence presented in Section 6 shows that compatibility of rewrite systems with POP* can be easily and quickly tested. However, the strength of the method seems to be improvable. One possible field of future work is to extend POP* to quasi-precedences. The theoretical changes necessary to accomodate quasi-precedences seem to be manageable. Another natural extension is to combine POP* with the transformation technique of semantic labeling, cf. [27]. It is easy to see that semantic labeling (in the basic form) does not affect the derivation length. Furthermore for *finite* models the main theorem remains directly applicable.

References

1. Arai, T., Moser, G.: Proofs of Termination of Rewrite Systems for Polytime Functions. In: Ramanujam, R., Sen, S. (eds.) FSTTCS 2005. LNCS, vol. 3821, pp. 529–540. Springer, Heidelberg (2005)
2. Avanzini, M., Hirokawa, N., Middeldorp, A., Moser, G.: Towards an automatic runtime complexity analysis of Scheme programs by rewriting. (Submitted December 2007).[5]
3. Avanzini, M., Moser, G.: Complexity analysis by rewriting. Draft, [5] (October 2007)
4. Baader, F., Nipkow, T.: Term Rewriting and All That. Cambridge University Press, Cambridge (1998)
5. Beckmann, A., Weiermann, A.: A term rewriting characterization of the polytime functions and related complexity classes. Archive 36, 11–30 (1996)
6. Bellantoni, S., Cook, S.: A new recursion-theoretic characterization of the polytime functions. Comput. Complexity 2(2), 97–110 (1992)
7. Bonfante, G., Cichon, A., Marion, J.-Y., Touzet, H.: Algorithms with polynomial interpretation termination proof. JFP 11(1), 33–53 (2001)
8. Bonfante, G., Marion, J.-Y., Moyen, J.-Y.: Quasi-intepretations and small space bounds. In: Giesl, J. (ed.) RTA 2005. LNCS, vol. 3467, pp. 150–164. Springer, Heidelberg (2005)
9. Buchholz, W.: Proof-theoretic analysis of termination proofs. APAL 75, 57–65 (1995)
10. Contejean, E., Marché, C., Tomás, A.P., Urbain, X.: Mechanically proving termination using polynomial interpretations. JAR 34(4), 325–363 (2005)

---

[5] Available online at
http://cl-informatik.uibk.ac.at/~georg/list.publications.html.

11. Hirokawa, N., Middeldorp, A.: Tsukuba termination tool. In: Nieuwenhuis, R. (ed.) RTA 2003. LNCS, vol. 2706, pp. 311–332. Springer, Heidelberg (2003)
12. Hofbauer, D.: Termination proofs by multiset path orderings imply primitive recursive derivation lengths. TCS 105(1), 129–140 (1992)
13. Hofbauer, D., Lautemann, C.: Termination proofs and the length of derivations. In: Dershowitz, N. (ed.) RTA 1989. LNCS, vol. 355, pp. 167–177. Springer, Heidelberg (1989)
14. Hofmann, M.: Linear types and non-size increasing polynomial time computations. In: Proc. 14th LICS, pp. 464–473 (1999)
15. Lepper, I.: Derivation lengths and order types of Knuth-Bendix orders. TCS 269, 433–450 (2001)
16. Lucas, S., Peña, R.: Termination and complexity bounds for SAFE programs. In: Proc. 7th PROLE, pp. 233–242 (2007)
17. Marion, J.: Analysing the implicit complexity of programs. IC 183, 2–18 (2003)
18. Moser, G.: Derivational complexity of Knuth Bendix orders revisited. In: Hermann, M., Voronkov, A. (eds.) LPAR 2006. LNCS (LNAI), vol. 4246, pp. 75–89. Springer, Heidelberg (2006)
19. Schneider-Kamp, P., Thiemann, R., Annov, E., Codish, M., Giesl, J.: Proving termination using recursive path orders and SAT solving. In: Konev, B., Wolter, F. (eds.) FroCos 2007. LNCS (LNAI), vol. 4720, pp. 267–282. Springer, Heidelberg (2007)
20. Schwichtenberg, H.: An arithmetic for polynomial-time computation. TCS 357(1), 202–214 (2006)
21. Sperber, M., Dybvig, R.K., Flatt, M., Stratten, A.v., et al.: Revised report on the algorithmic language Scheme (2007), http://www.r6rs.org
22. Steinbach, J., Kühler, U.: Check your ordering - termination proofs and open problems. Technical Report SEKI-Report SR-90-25, University of Kaiserslautern (1990)
23. Terese: Term Rewriting Systems. Cambridge Tracts in Theoretical Computer Science, vol. 55. Cambridge University Press, Cambridge (2003)
24. Toyama, Y.: Termination of S-expression rewriting systems: Lexicographic path ordering for higher-order terms. In: van Oostrom, V. (ed.) RTA 2004. LNCS, vol. 3091, pp. 40–54. Springer, Heidelberg (2004)
25. Weiermann, A.: Termination proofs for term rewriting systems with lexicographic path ordering imply multiply recursive derivation lengths. TCS 139, 355–362 (1995)
26. Zankl, H., Middeldorp, A.: Satisfying KBO constraints. In: Baader, F. (ed.) RTA 2007. LNCS, vol. 4533, pp. 389–403. Springer, Heidelberg (2007)
27. Zantema, H.: Termination of term rewriting by semantic labelling. FI 24, 89–105 (1995)

Rewriting and Call-Time Choice: The HO Case[*]

Francisco Javier López-Fraguas, Juan Rodríguez-Hortalá,
and Jaime Sánchez-Hernández

Departamento de Sistemas Informáticos y Computación
Universidad Complutense de Madrid, Spain
fraguas@sip.ucm.es, jrodrigu@fdi.ucm.es, jaime@sip.ucm.es

Abstract. It is known that the behavior of non-deterministic functions with call-time choice semantics, present in current functional logic languages, is not well described by usual approaches to reduction like ordinary term rewriting systems or λ-calculus. The presence of HO features makes things more difficult, since reasoning principles that are essential in a standard (i.e., deterministic) functional setting, like extensionality, become wrong. In this paper we propose *HOlet*-rewriting, a notion of rewriting with local bindings that turns out to be adequate for programs with HO non-deterministic functions, as it is shown by strong equivalence results with respect to *HOCRWL*, a previously existing semantic framework for such programs. In addition, we give a sound and complete notion of *HO-let*-narrowing, we show by a case study the usefulness of the achieved combination of semantic and reduction notions, and finally we prove within our framework that a standard approach to the implementation of HO features, namely translation to FO, is still valid for HO nondeterministic functions.

1 Introduction

Functional logic programming (FLP, for short; see [12,14] for surveys) integrates features of logic programming and functional programming. Typically FLP adopts mostly a (lazy) functional style, thus making intensive use of higher order (HO) functions. However, most of the work about FLP focuses on first order (FO) aspects of programs, thus limiting the applicability of results.

This is not a satisfactory situation, especially taking into account that the presence of functions that are at the same time HO and non-deterministic leads to somehow surprising behaviors, as shown by the example we sent recently to the Curry mailing list [13]:

Example 1. Consider the following program computing with natural numbers represented by the constructors 0 and $s/1$, and where $+$ is defined as usual.

```
g X -> 0          f -> g          f' X -> f X
h X -> s 0        f -> h

fadd F G X -> (F X) + (G X)       fdouble F -> fadd F F
```

[*] This work has been partially supported by the Spanish projects Merit-Forms-UCM (TIN2005-09207-C03-03) and Promesas-CAM (S-0505/TIC/0407).

J. Garrigue and M. Hermenegildo (Eds.): FLOPS 2008, LNCS 4989, pp. 147–162, 2008.
© Springer-Verlag Berlin Heidelberg 2008

Notice that f and f' are non-deterministic functions that are (by definition of f') extensionally equivalent; from the point of view of standard functional programming they should be seen as 'the same function'. However, consider the expressions *(fdouble f 0)* and *(fdouble f' 0)*. In modern FLP languages like Curry [16] or Toy [21], the possible values for *(fdouble f 0)* are *0, s (s 0)*, while *(fdouble f' 0)* can be in addition reduced to *s 0*.

This behavior corresponds to *call-time choice* [17,11], the semantics for non-determinism adopted by those systems. Operationally call-time choice is very close to the *sharing* mechanism used in functional languages to implement lazy evaluation.

The example was sent[1] to point out that η-expansion and η-reduction are not valid for such systems, because extensionally equivalent functions (e.g., f and f') can be semantically distinguishable when put in the same context (e.g., *double [ ] 0*), a fact that does not happen neither in standard (i.e, deterministic) functional programs[2], nor in FO FLP. We remark also that with *run-time choice* [17,11], f and f' will be indistinguishable (*double f 0* and *double f' 0* would both produce *0, s 0, s (s 0)* as possible results). Therefore, it is the combination *HO + Non-determinism + call-time choice* which makes things different.

That combination was addressed in *HOCRWL* [7,8], an extension to HO of $CRWL^3$ [11], a semantic framework specifically devised for FLP with call-time choice semantics for non-determinism (see [28] for a survey of *CRWL* and its extensions). *HOCRWL* provides logic and model-theoretic semantics, based on an *intensional* view of functions, where different descriptions –in the form of *HO-patterns*– of the same extensional function are distinguished as different data. This allows expressive programs and is simpler than λ-calculus-based HO unification, which is an alternative approach followed in the logic programming setting [23]. Previous work on the intensional view of HO-FLP [10] did not consider non-determinism. Other works covering HO in FLP, [24,15], consider orthogonal or inductively sequential (henceforth deterministic) systems; if extended directly to the non-deterministic case, they would realize run-time choice, as happens also with [4], where a type-based translation to FO in the spirit of [29,9] is proposed. We remark also that [15] is close to the theory of HO rewriting [27], and therefore has η-expansion as a valid procedure, against the expected properties of the languages considered by ours. Finally, [1] copes with call-time choice but their approach to HO is again based on a FO-translation, in contrast to ours.

A weak point of the original *(HO)CRWL*-way to FLP is that it does not come with a clear, simple notion of one-step reduction similar to one-step rewriting. In [19] we proposed *let-rewriting*, a notion of rewriting with local bindings adequate to FO *CRWL* semantics, and at the same time simpler and more abstract than other reduction notions based on term graph rewriting [26,6] or natural operational semantics [1]. *Let*-rewriting was generalized to *let*-narrowing in [18].

---

[1] As far as we know, it was the first time that this behavior was noticed.

[2] Although the addition of primitive functions not definable in the language like *seq* in Haskell [25] can also destroy extensionality.

[3] CRWL stands for *Constructor Based Rewriting Logic*.

Our aim in this work is to extend the notion of *let*-rewriting/narrowing to the HO case. We address various foundational aspects –definition of *HOlet*-rewriting and equivalence wrt the declarative semantics given by *HOCRWL* (Sect. 3), *HOlet*-narrowing and its soundness and completeness wrt *HOlet*-rewriting (Sect. 4)– and also more applied aspects, as are the use of our framework to language development (Sect. 5) or the proof of correctness within our framework of a scheme of translation to FO, the basis of a standard approach [29,9,4] to the implementation of HO stuff in FO settings.

There are still some other important issues –evaluation strategies (including concurrency), types, constraints– that have been left out of the scope of the paper. Finally, we are not inventing HO FLP, but only contributing to some aspects of its foundation. Therefore it is not our aim in this paper convincing of the practical interest of HO FLP: other documents [16,28,7,4] contain enough evidences of that. Omitted proofs can be found in [20].

2   Preliminaries: *HOCRWL*

We present here some basic notions and new results about *HOCRWL* [7].

2.1   Expressions, Patterns and Programs

We consider *function* symbols $f, g, \ldots \in FS$, *constructor* symbols $c, d, \ldots \in CS$, and *variables* $X, Y, \ldots \in \mathcal{V}$; each $h \in FS \cup CS$ has an associated *arity*, $ar(h) \in \mathbb{N}$; FS^n (resp. CS^n) is the set of function (resp. constructor) symbols with arity n. The notation $\bar{o}$ stands for tuples of any kind of syntactic objects o. The set of *applicative expressions* is defined by $Exp \ni e ::= X \mid h \mid (e_1 \ e_2)$. As usual, application is left associative and outer parentheses can be omitted, so that $e_1 \ e_2 \ldots e_n$ stands for $((\ldots (e_1 \ e_2) \ldots) \ e_n)$. The set of variables occurring in e is written by $var(e)$. A distinguished set of expressions is that of *patterns* $t, s \in Pat$, defined by: $t ::= X \mid c \ t_1 \ldots t_n \mid f \ t_1 \ldots t_m$, where $0 \le n \le ar(c), 0 \le m < ar(f)$. Patterns are irreducible expressions playing the role of *values*. *FO-patterns*, defined by $FOPat \ni t ::= X \mid c \ t_1 \ldots t_n \ (n = ar(c))$, correspond to FO constructor terms, representing ordinary non-functional data-values. Partial applications of symbols $h \in FS \cup CS$ to other patterns are HO-patterns and can be seen as truly data-values representing functions from an *intensional* point of view. Examples of patterns with the signature of Ex. 1 are: *0, s X, s, f', fadd f' f'*. The last three are HO-patterns. Notice that *f, fadd f f* are not patterns since f is not a pattern $(ar(f) = 0)$.

Expressions $X \ e_1 \ldots e_m \ (m \ge 0)$ are called *flexible* (*variable application* when $m > 0$). *Rigid* expressions have the form $h \ e_1 \ldots e_m$; moreover, they are *junk* if $h \in CS^n$ and $m > n$, *active* if $h \in FS^n$ and $m \ge n$, and *passive* otherwise.

Contexts are expressions with a hole defined as $Cntxt \ni \mathcal{C} ::= [\ ] \mid \mathcal{C} \ e \mid e \ \mathcal{C}$. Application of $\mathcal{C}$ to e (written $\mathcal{C}[e]$) is defined by $[\ ][e] = e$; $(\mathcal{C} \ e')[e] = \mathcal{C}[e] \ e'$; $(e' \ \mathcal{C})[e] = e' \ \mathcal{C}[e]$. Substitutions $\theta \in Subst$ are finite mappings from variables to expressions; $[X_i/e_i, \ldots, X_n/e_n]$ is the substitution which assigns $e_i \in Exp$ to the corresponding $X_i \in \mathcal{V}$. We will mostly use *pattern-substitutions*

$PSubst = \{\theta \in Subst \mid \theta(X) \in Pat, \forall X \in \mathcal{V}\}$. We write ϵ for the identity substitution, $dom(\theta)$ for the domain of θ, and $vRan(\theta) = \bigcup_{X \in dom(\theta)} var(X\theta)$.

As usual while describing semantics of non-strict languages, we enlarge the signature with a new 0-ary constructor symbol $\bot$, which can be used to build the sets $Expr_\bot, Pat_\bot, PSubst_\bot$ of *partial* expressions, patterns and p-substitutions resp. Partial expressions are ordered by the *approximation* ordering $\sqsubseteq$ defined as the least partial ordering satisfying $\bot \sqsubseteq e$ and $e \sqsubseteq e' \Rightarrow \mathcal{C}[e] \sqsubseteq \mathcal{C}[e']$ for all $e, e' \in Expr_\bot, \mathcal{C} \in Cntxt$. This partial ordering can be extended to substitutions: given $\theta, \sigma \in Subst_\bot$ we say $\theta \sqsubseteq \sigma$ if $X\theta \sqsubseteq X\sigma$ for all $X \in \mathcal{V}$.

A *HOCRWL*-program (or simply a *program*) consists of one or more *program rules* for each $f \in FS^n$, having the form $f\ t_1 \ldots t_n \to r$ where $(t_1, \ldots, t_n)$ is a linear (i.e. variables occur only once) tuple of (maybe HO) patterns and r is any expression. Notice that confluence or termination is not required, and that r may have variables not occurring in $f\ t_1 \ldots t_n$ (we write $vExtra(R)$ for such variables in a rule R). The original *HOCRWL* logic considered also *joinability* conditions in rules to achieve a better treatment of strict equality as built-in, which is a subject orthogonal to the aims of this paper. Therefore, we consider only unconditional rules.

Some related languages, like Curry, do not allow HO-patterns in left-hand sides of function definitions. We remark that all the notions and results in the paper are applicable to programs with this restriction and we stress the fact that Example 1 is one of them.

Given a program $\mathcal{P}$, the set of its rule instances is $[\mathcal{P}] = \{(l \to r)\theta \mid (l \to r) \in \mathcal{P}, \theta \in PSubst\}$. The set $[\mathcal{P}]_\bot$ is defined similarly replacing $PSubst$ by $PSubst_\bot$. To require $\theta \in PSubst_{(\bot)}$ instead of $\theta \in Subst_{(\bot)}$ is essential to achieve call-time choice in the next sections.

2.2 The *HOCRWL* Proof Calculus [7]

The semantics of a program $\mathcal{P}$ is determined in *HOCRWL* by means of a proof calculus able to derive reduction statements of the form $e \twoheadrightarrow t$, with $e \in Expr_\bot$ and $t \in Pat_\bot$, meaning informally that t is (or approximates to) a possible value of e, obtained by evaluation of e using $\mathcal{P}$ under call-time choice. Besides this logical semantics, *HOCRWL* programs come in [7] with a model-theoretic semantics based on applicative algebras, with existence of a least Herbrand model. We will not use this aspect of the semantics here.

The *HOCRWL*-proof calculus is presented in Fig. 1. We write $\mathcal{P} \vdash_{HOCRWL} e \twoheadrightarrow t$ to express that $e \twoheadrightarrow t$ is derivable in that calculus using the program $\mathcal{P}$. The *HOCRWL-denotation* of an expression $e \in Expr_\bot$ is defined as $[\![e]\!]^{\mathcal{P}}_{HOCRWL} = \{t \in Pat_\bot \mid \mathcal{P} \vdash_{HOCRWL} e \twoheadrightarrow t\}$. $\mathcal{P}$ and *HOCRWL* are frequently omitted in those notations.

In Example 1 we have $[\![fdouble\ f\ 0]\!] = \{0, s\ (s\ 0), \bot, s\ \bot, s\ (s\ \bot)\}$ and $[\![fdouble\ f'\ 0]\!] = \{0, s\ 0, s\ (s\ 0), \bot, s\ \bot, s\ (s\ \bot)\}$.

We will use the following (new) result stating an important compositionality property of the semantics of *HOCRWL*-expressions: the semantics of a whole expression depends only on the semantics of its constituents, in a particular form

$$\textbf{(B)} \quad \frac{}{e \rightarrow \bot} \qquad \textbf{(RR)} \quad \frac{}{x \rightarrow x} \qquad x \in \mathcal{V}$$

$$\textbf{(DC)} \quad \frac{e_1 \rightarrow t_1 \ \dots \ e_n \rightarrow t_m}{h \ e_1 \dots e_m \rightarrow h \ t_1 \dots t_m} \qquad h \in \Sigma, \text{ if } h \ t_1 \dots t_m \text{ is a partial pattern, } m \geq 0$$

$$\textbf{(OR)} \quad \frac{e_1 \rightarrow t_1 \dots \ e_n \rightarrow t_n \quad r \ a_1 \dots a_m \rightarrow t}{f \ e_1 \dots e_n \ a_1 \dots a_m \rightarrow t} \qquad \text{if } m \geq 0, (f \ t_1 \dots t_n \rightarrow r) \in [\mathcal{P}]_\bot$$

Fig. 1. (*HOCRWL*-calculus)

reflecting the idea of call-time choice. The second part of the theorem is a technical result, needed in some proofs, concerning the size of the involved derivations.

Theorem 1 (Compositionality of *HOCRWL* semantics)

(i) $[\![\mathcal{C}[e]]\!] = \bigcup_{t \in [\![e]\!]} [\![\mathcal{C}[t]]\!]$, *for any program* $\mathcal{P}$ *and expression* $e \in Exp_\bot$.
In other terms, $\mathcal{C}[e] \rightarrow t \Leftrightarrow \exists s.(e \rightarrow s \wedge \mathcal{C}[s] \rightarrow t)$.
(ii) *In the* ($\Rightarrow$) *part of (i), if* $t \neq \bot, \mathcal{C} \neq [\ ]$ *and the derivation of* $\mathcal{C}[e] \rightarrow t$ *has size* K, *then the derivations of* $e \rightarrow s$ *and* $\mathcal{C}[s] \rightarrow t$ *can be chosen with sizes* $< K$ *and* $\leq K$ *respectively.*

3 Higher Order *let*-rewriting

To express sharing, as is required for call-time choice, we enhance the syntax of expressions (and contexts) with a *let* construct for local bindings, in the spirit of [5,22,19]: $LExp \ni e ::= X \mid h \mid e_1 \ e_2 \mid let \ X = e_1 \ in \ e_2$
$\qquad\qquad Cntxt \ni \mathcal{C} ::= [\ ] \mid \mathcal{C} \ e \mid e \ \mathcal{C} \mid let \ X = \mathcal{C} \ in \ e \mid let \ X = e \ in \ \mathcal{C}$
We consider expressions *let* $X = e_1$ *in* e_2 as passive and rigid. The sets $FV(e)$ and $BV(e)$ of free and bound variables resp. of a *let*-expression e are defined as:

$$FV(X) = \{X\}; \ FV(h \ \bar{e}) = \bigcup_{e_i \in \bar{e}} FV(e_i);$$
$$FV(let \ X = e_1 \ in \ e_2) = FV(e_1) \cup (FV(e_2) \backslash \{X\});$$
$$BV(X) = \emptyset; \ BV(h(\bar{e})) = \bigcup_{e_i \in \bar{e}} BV(e_i);$$
$$BV(let \ X = e_1 \ in \ e_2) = BV(e_1) \cup BV(e_2) \cup \{X\}$$

Notice that with the given definition of $FV(let \ X = e_1 \ in \ e_2)$ recursive *let*-bindings are not allowed since the possible occurrences of X in e_1 are not considered as bound and therefore refer to a 'different' X. We assume appropriate renamings of bound variables ensuring that bound and free variables are kept distinct, and that whenever θ is applied to $e \in LExp$, $BV(e) \cap (dom(\theta) \cup vRan(\theta)) = \emptyset$, so that $(let \ X = e_1 \ in \ e_2)\theta = let \ X = e_1\theta \ in \ e_2\theta$ and $(\mathcal{C}[e])\theta = \mathcal{C}\theta[e\theta]$.

The *shell* of an expression, written as $|e|$, is a pattern containing the 'stable' outer information of e, not to be destroyed by reduction:

$$|X \ e_1 \dots e_m| = \begin{cases} X & \text{if } m = 0 \\ \bot & \text{if } m > 0 \end{cases}$$

$$|h \ e_1 \dots e_m| = \begin{cases} h \ |e_1| \dots |e_m| & \text{if } (h \in CS^n, m \leq n) \text{ or } (h \in FS^n, m < n) \\ \bot & \text{otherwise (junk or active expression)} \end{cases}$$

$$|(let \ X = e_1 \ in \ e_2) \ a_1 \dots a_m| = |(e_2[X/e_1]) \ a_1 \dots a_m|$$

Notice that in FO [19] we defined $|(let \ X = e_1 \ in \ e_2)| = |e_2|[X/|e_1|]$. This would lose information in the HO case: for instance, $|let \ X = s \ in \ X \ 0|$ would be $\bot$, instead of the more accurate $s \ 0$ given by the definition above.

The $HOCRWL_{let}$ proof calculus for proving statements $e \twoheadrightarrow t$ ($e \in LExp_\bot, t \in Pat_\bot$) results from adding to Fig. 1 the rule:

$$\textbf{(Let)} \quad \frac{e_1 \twoheadrightarrow t_1 \quad (e_2[X/t_1]) \ a_1 \dots a_m \twoheadrightarrow t}{(let \ X = e_1 \ in \ e_2) \ a_1 \dots a_m \twoheadrightarrow t} \quad (m \geq 0)$$

It is easy to see that for programs and expressions without *lets* both calculi coincide, giving $[\![e]\!]_{HOCRWL} = [\![e]\!]_{HOCRWL_{let}}$, and then we write simply $[\![e]\!]$.

Theorem 1 does not hold as it is for *let*-expressions (assume, for instance, the program rule $f \ 0 = 1$ and take $e \equiv f \ X$, $\mathcal{C} \equiv let \ X=0 \ in \ [\ ]$). However, a more limited form of compositionality will suffice to our needs:

Theorem 2 (Weak compositionality of $HOCRWL_{let}$ semantics)
For any $\mathcal{P}$ and $e, e' \in LExp_\bot$: $[\![C \ [e]]\!] = \bigcup_{t \in [\![e]\!]} [\![C \ [t]]\!]$, if $BV(C) \cap FV(e) = \emptyset$.

As a consequence,   *(i)* $[\![e \ e']\!] = \bigcup_{t \in [\![e]\!]} [\![t \ e']\!]$ *(ii)* $[\![e \ e']\!] = \bigcup_{t \in [\![e']\!]} [\![e \ t]\!]$

         (iii) $[\![let \ X = e \ in \ e']\!] = \bigcup_{t \in [\![e]\!]} [\![e'[X/t]]\!]$

3.1   Rewriting with Local Bindings

Figure 2 defines the *HOlet*-rewriting relation $\rightarrow^l$. Rule *(Fapp)* uses a program rule to reduce a function application, but only when the arguments are already patterns, otherwise call-time choice would be violated. Non-pattern arguments of applications are moved to local bindings by *(LetIn)*. Local bindings of patterns to variables are applied in *(Bind)*, since in this case copying is harmless. *(Elim)* erases useless bindings. *(Flat)* and *(LetAp)* manage local bindings; they are needed to avoid some reductions to get stuck. Notice that with the variable convention, the condition $Y \notin FV(e_3)$ in *(Flat)* and *(LetAp)* would not be needed; we have written it in order to keep the rules independent of the convention. Finally, any of these rules can be applied to any subexpression by *(Contx)*. It includes an additional technical condition to avoid undesired variable captures when *(Fapp)* was applied inside a surrounding context and the used program rule has extra variables. If, for instance, a program rule is $f \rightarrow Y$, the rule *(Contxt)* avoids the step $let \ X=0 \ in \ f \rightarrow^l let \ X=0 \ in \ X$ and also the step $let \ X=f \ in \ X \rightarrow^l let \ X=X \ in \ X$.

The following derivation corresponds to Example 1:

$fdouble \ f \ 0 \rightarrow^l_{\{LetIn,Cntx\}} (let \ F=f \ in \ fdouble \ F) \ 0$
$\rightarrow^l_{LetAp} let \ F=f \ in \ fdouble \ F \ 0 \rightarrow^l_{\{Fapp,Cntx\}} let \ F=f \ in \ fadd \ F \ F \ 0$
$\rightarrow^l_{\{Fapp,Cntx\}} let \ F=f \ in \ F \ 0 + F \ 0$
$\rightarrow^l_{\{Fapp,Cntx\}} let \ F=g \ in \ F \ 0 + F \ 0 \rightarrow^l_{Bind} g \ 0 + g \ 0 \rightarrow^{l*} 0$

(Fapp) $f\ t_1 \ldots t_n \to^l r$,   if $(f\ t_1 \ldots t_n \to r) \in [\mathcal{P}]$

(LetIn) $e_1\ e_2 \to^l let\ X = e_2\ in\ e_1\ X$ (X fresh), if e_2 is an active expression, variable application, junk or *let* rooted expression.

(Bind) $let\ X = t\ in\ e \to^l e[X/t]$,   if $t \in Pat$

(Elim) $let\ X = e_1\ in\ e_2 \to^l e_2$,   if $X \notin FV(e_2)$

(Flat) $let\ X = (let\ Y = e_1\ in\ e_2)\ in\ e_3 \to^l let\ Y = e_1\ in\ (let\ X = e_2\ in\ e_3)$
if $Y \notin FV(e_3)$

(LetAp) $(let\ X = e_1\ in\ e_2)\ e_3 \to^l let\ X = e_1\ in\ e_2\ e_3$,   if $X \notin FV(e_3)$

(Contx) $\mathcal{C}[e] \to^l \mathcal{C}[e']$, if $\mathcal{C} \neq [\ ]$, $e \to^l e'$ using any of the previous rules, and in case $e \to^l e'$ is a (Fapp) step using $(f\ \overline{p} \to r)\theta \in [\mathcal{P}]$ then $vRan(\theta|_{\setminus var(\overline{p})}) \cap BV(\mathcal{C}) = \emptyset$.

Fig. 2. Higher order *let*-rewriting relation $\to^l$

Notice that the fist step is justified because f is active. In contrast, since f' is a pattern, a derivation for *fdouble f' 0* could proceed as follows:

$$fdouble\ f'\ 0 \to^l fadd\ f'\ f'\ 0 \to^l f'\ 0 + f'\ 0 \to^{l^*} f\ 0 + f\ 0 \to^{l^*} g\ 0 + h\ 0 \to^{l^*} s\ 0$$

The rules of $\to^l$ have been carefully tuned up to ensure that program rules are the only possible source of non-termination, as ensured by the following result.

Proposition 1. *The relation* $\to^l_{\setminus Fapp}$ *defined by the rules of Fig. 2 except* (Fapp) *is terminating.*

This is a natural requirement. However, at some point we will find useful to consider the more liberal relation $\to^L$ obtained replacing *(LetIn)* by:

(LetIn') $e_1\ e_2 \to^L let\ X = e_2\ in\ e_1\ X$ (X fresh)

which is less restrictive (then $\to^l \subseteq \to^L$). However $\to^L_{\setminus Fapp}$ becomes non-terminating, as shown by: $s\ 0 \to^l_{LetIn'} let\ X = 0\ in\ s\ X \to^l_{Bind} s\ 0 \to^l \ldots$

3.2   Adequacy of *HOlet*-rewriting to *HOCRWL*

We compare here $\to^l$ to *HOCRWL*-derivability $\twoheadrightarrow$, proving that essentially $\to^l$ gives no more (*soundness*) and no less (*completeness*) results than $\twoheadrightarrow$.

As in [19], the following notion is useful to establish soundness:

Definition 1 (Hypersemantics)

(i) *The hypersemantics of an expression* $e \in LExp_\perp$, *written as* $[\![e]\!]$, *is a mapping* $[\![e]\!] : PSubst_\perp \longrightarrow \mathcal{P}(Pat_\perp)$ *defined by* $[\![e]\!](\theta) = [e\theta]$.
(ii) *Hypersemantics of expressions are ordered as follows:*

$$[\![e_1]\!] \sqsubseteq [\![e_2]\!] \ iff\ [e_1\theta] \subseteq [e_2\theta], \ \forall\theta \in PSubst_\perp$$

The main reason for introducing hypersemantics is that it enjoys the following nice monotonicity-under-contexts property, while $[\![\_]\!]$ does not:

Lemma 1 (Monotonicity of hypersemantics)
$[\![e]\!] \Subset [\![e']\!]$ *implies* $[\![\mathcal{C}[e]]\!] \Subset [\![\mathcal{C}[e']]\!]$, *for any* $e, e' \in LExp_\bot$, $\mathcal{C} \in Cntxt$.

Monotonicity under contexts is the key for our next result, stating that hypersemantics does not grow under *HOlet*-rewriting steps:

Lemma 2 (One-Step Hyper-Soundness of *HOlet*-rewriting)
$e \rightarrow^l e'$ *implies* $[\![e']\!] \Subset [\![e]\!]$, *for any* $e, e' \in LExp$.

Notice that $\Subset$ cannot be replaced here by $=$, due to non-determinism.

Lemma 2, together with the easy observation that $[\![e_1]\!] \Subset [\![e_2]\!]$ implies $[\![e_1]\!] \subseteq [\![e_2]\!]$ (just take $\theta = \epsilon$) and an obvious induction over derivation lengths, leads to our main correctness result for $\rightarrow^l$:

Theorem 3 (Soundness of *HOlet*-rewriting). *Let $\mathcal{P}$ be a program, $e, e' \in LExp$. Then:* *(i)* $e \rightarrow^{l*} e'$ *implies* $[\![e']\!] \subseteq [\![e]\!]$, *and therefore* $e \twoheadrightarrow |e'|$
(ii) $e \rightarrow^{l*} t$ *implies* $e \twoheadrightarrow t$, *for any* $t \in Pat$.

The proof of this result can be easily extended to the larger relation $\rightarrow^L$ (the one which uses (LetIn') instead of (LetIn)).

Regarding completeness of *let*-rewriting, a key in the FO case was the *peeling lemma* ([19], Lemma 7), a technical result giving a kind of standard form in which the implicit or explicit sharing information contained in $e \in Exp$ can be expressed. It is not obvious how to proceed in the HO case, since straightforward generalizations of the FO peeling lemma turn out to be false. However, we have found that the following weak HO version is enough for our purposes:

Lemma 3 (Weak peeling lemma). *Let $h\ e_1 \ldots e_m \in Exp$ with $h \in \Sigma^n$ (n and m can be different). Then $h\ e_1 \ldots e_m \rightarrow^{l*} let\ \overline{X = a}\ in\ h\ t_1 \ldots t_m$, for some $t_1, \ldots, t_m \in Pat, \overline{a} \subseteq Exp$ such that $|\overline{a}| = \bot, t_i \equiv e_i$ for every $e_i \in Pat$. Besides, in this derivation the rule (Fapp) is not applied.*

With this result and some monotonicity properties of *HOCRWL*-derivability, we can prove a very technical but strong completeness result for $\rightarrow^l$ wrt $\twoheadrightarrow$:

Lemma 4 (Completeness lemma for *HOlet*-rewriting). *For any program $\mathcal{P}$, $e \in Exp$ and $t \in Pat_\bot$ with $t \neq \bot$, the following holds: $\mathcal{P} \vdash_{HOCRWL} e \twoheadrightarrow t$ implies $e \rightarrow^{l*} let\ \overline{X = a}\ in\ t'$, for some $t' \in Pat$ and $\overline{a} \subseteq Exp$ in such a way that $t \sqsubseteq |let\ \overline{X = a}\ in\ t'|$ and $|a_i| = \bot$ for all $a_i \in \overline{a}$. As a consequence, $t \sqsubseteq t'[\overline{X/\bot}]$.*

The condition $t \neq \bot$ is needed, as can be seen just taking $\mathcal{P} = \{f \rightarrow f\}$, $e \equiv f$ and $t \equiv \bot$.

From Lemma 4 we can obtain our main completeness result for $\rightarrow^l$:

Theorem 4 (Completeness of *HOlet*-rewriting). *Let $\mathcal{P}$ be a program, $e \in Exp$, and $t \in Pat_\bot$. Then:*

(i) $\mathcal{P} \vdash_{HOCRWL} e \twoheadrightarrow t$ implies $e \rightarrow^{l*} e'$, for some $e' \in LExp$ such that $t \sqsubseteq |e'|$.
(ii) If in addition $t \in Pat$, then $e \rightarrow^{l*} t$.

Joining together the last parts of Theorems 3 and 4, we obtain a strong equivalence result for $\rightarrow^l$ and $\twoheadrightarrow$:

Theorem 5 (Equivalence of *HOlet*-rewriting and *HOCRWL*)
$\mathcal{P} \vdash_{HOCRWL} e \twoheadrightarrow t$ *iff* $e \rightarrow^{l*} t$, *for any* $\mathcal{P}$, $e \in Exp$, *and* $t \in Pat$.

This justifies our claim that $\rightarrow^l$ is truly the reduction face of *HOCRWL*-semantics.

4   Higher Order *let*-narrowing

For some FLP computations rewriting is not enough, and must be lifted to some kind of *narrowing*; this happens when the expression being reduced contains variables for which different bindings might produce different evaluation results. Narrowing is an old subject in the fields of theorem proving and declarative programming. Since classical rewriting is not correct for call-time choice, classical narrowing cannot be either (because rewriting is a particular case of narrowing). In [18] we proposed a notion of narrowing adequate to FO *let*-rewriting, and now we extend it to HO. As happens in [7,4], *HOlet*-narrowing may bind variables to HO-patterns.

Figure 3 contains the rules for the one-step *HOlet*-narrowing relation $e \leadsto^l_\theta e'$, expressing that e is narrowed to e' producing the substitution $\theta \in PSubst$. In *(X)* we collect those cases of *HOlet*-rewriting corresponding also to narrowing steps with empty substitution. *(Narr)* is the proper rule of narrowing for function application; it may produce HO bindings if the used program rule has HO patterns. Notice that, for the sake of generality, we do not require that θ is a mgu. *(VAct)* and *(VBind)* are rules producing HO bindings for flexible expressions (or subexpressions, in the case of *(VBind)*). We have preferred this pair of rules instead of the rule

$$\textbf{(VNarr)} \quad X \ e \leadsto^L_{[X/t]} t \ (e[X/t]), \text{ for any } t \in Pat$$

which is simpler, but also 'wilder' because it creates a larger search space. Finally, (Contxt) is a contextual rule where, as in [18], it is crucial to protect bound variables from narrowing (condition (i)) and to avoid variable capture (condition (ii), automatically fulfilled if mgu's are used in *(Narr)* and *(VAct)*, and fresh *shallow* patterns –i.e., of the form $h \ X_1 \ldots X_n$– in *(VBind)*).

Taking Example 1, a narrowing derivation for *fdouble F 0* would start with some *(X)* 'rewriting' steps:

$$fdouble \ F \ 0 \leadsto^l_\epsilon fadd \ F \ F \ 0 \leadsto^l_\epsilon F \ 0 + F \ 0 \leadsto^l_\epsilon let \ X{=}F \ 0 \ in \ X + F \ 0$$

At this point, notice first that we cannot narrow on X, because it is a bound variable. Instead, we can apply *(VAct+Contx)*:

$$let \ X{=}F \ 0 \ in \ X + F \ 0 \leadsto^l_{\{F/g\}} let \ X{=}0 \ in \ X + g \ 0 \leadsto^{l*}_\epsilon 0$$

Other similar derivations using *(VAct+Contx)* would bind F to h (with final result $s \ (s \ 0)$), or to f' (with possible results 0, $s \ 0$, $s \ (s \ 0)$). Notice that the binding X/f is not legal, since f is not a pattern.

> **(X)** $e \leadsto^l_\epsilon e'$ if $e \to^l e'$ using $X \in \{Elim, Bind, Flat, LetIn, LetAp\}$ in Figure 2.
>
> **(Narr)** $f \ \bar{t} \leadsto^l_\theta r\theta$, for any fresh variant $(f \ \bar{p} \to r) \in \mathcal{P}$ and $\theta \in PSubst$ such that $f \ \bar{t}\theta \equiv f \ \bar{p}\theta$.
>
> **(VAct)** $X \ t_1 \ldots t_k \leadsto^l_\theta r\theta$, if $k > 0$, for any fresh variant $(f \ \bar{p} \to r) \in \mathcal{P}$ and $\theta \in PSubst$ such that $(X \ t_1 \ldots t_k)\theta \equiv f \ \bar{p}\theta$.
>
> **(VBind)** $let \ X = e_1 \ in \ e_2 \leadsto^l_\theta e_2\theta[X/e_1\theta]$, if $e_1 \notin Pat$, for any $\theta \in PSubst$ that makes $e_1\theta \in Pat$, provided that $X \notin (dom(\theta) \cup vRan(\theta))$.
>
> **(Contx)** $\mathcal{C}[e] \leadsto^l_\theta \mathcal{C}\theta[e']$ for $\mathcal{C} \neq [\ ]$, if $e \leadsto^l_\theta e'$ by any of the previous rules, and the following conditions hold:
>   i) $dom(\theta) \cap BV(\mathcal{C}) = \emptyset$
>   ii) • If the step is *(Narr)* or *(VAct)* using $(f \ \bar{p} \to r) \in \mathcal{P}$, then $vRan(\theta|_{\backslash var(\bar{p})}) \cap BV(\mathcal{C}) = \emptyset$
>   • If the step is *(VBind)* then $vRan(\theta) \cap BV(\mathcal{C}) = \emptyset$

Fig. 3. Higher order *let*-narrowing calculus $\leadsto^l$

Alternatively we could have applied *(VBind)*, obtaining:

$$let \ X{=}F \ 0 \ in \ X \ + \ F \ 0 \leadsto^l_{\{F/s\}} s \ 0 \ + \ s \ 0 \leadsto^{l^*}_\epsilon s \ (s \ 0)$$

We remark that, in our untyped framework, other 'ill-typed' bindings could be tried, like $F/fadd$ 0 or $F/fdouble$. This is a symptom of known problems [4,8] of the interaction with types of the intensional view of HO, that are partially alleviated in [4] by a typed version of a FO translation (see Sect. 6), but in general require (see [8]) bringing types to computations, a problem yet not well solved in practice. All these type-related issues are out of the scope of the paper.

A basic fact about completeness of *let*-narrowing in the FO case was that $e \leadsto^{l^*}_\theta e'$ implied $e\theta \to^{l^*} e'$, $\forall \theta \in CSubst$, which is closely related to the fact that FO *let*-rewriting is closed under c-substitutions. None of both facts hold with HO $\leadsto^l$, $\to^l$ and $\theta \in PSubst$: consider for instance $e \equiv s \ (Y \ 0) \to^l let \ X = Y \ 0 \ in \ s \ X \equiv e'$ and $\theta = [Y/s]$, for which $e\theta \equiv s \ (s \ 0) \not\to^l let \ X = s \ 0 \ in \ s \ X \equiv e'\theta$. Similarly, we have $e \equiv s \ (Y \ 0) \leadsto^L_\epsilon let \ X = Y \ 0 \ in \ s \ X \leadsto^L_{[Y/s]} let \ X = s \ 0 \ in \ s \ X \equiv e'$, but $e\theta \equiv s \ (s \ 0) \not\to^l e'$.

At this point the relation $\to^L$ of Sect. 3 becomes useful, because we have:

Lemma 5 (Closedness of $\to^L$ under *PSubst*). *For every* $e, e' \in LExp, \theta \in PSubst$, $e \to^{L^*} e'$ *implies* $e\theta \to^{L^*} e'\theta$.

Now we can prove soundness of HO *let*-narrowing wrt. $\to^L$:

Theorem 6 (Soundness or $\leadsto^l$ wrt $\to^L$). *For any* $e, e' \in LExp$, $e \leadsto^{l^*}_\theta e'$ *implies* $e\theta \to^{L^*} e'$.

And now, taking into account Th. 3 (which holds also for $\to^L$), we get:

Theorem 7 (Soundness of *let*-narrowing). *For any* $e, e' \in LExp, t \in Pat$:
a) *If* $e \leadsto^{l^*}_\theta e'$ *then* $[\![e']\!] \subseteq [\![e\theta]\!]$ b) *If* $e \leadsto^{l^*}_\theta t$ *then* $e\theta \to^{l^*} t$

Regarding completeness, the following lemma shows how we can lift any $\rightarrow^l$ derivation to a $\rightsquigarrow^l$ derivation. This is surely the most involved result in the paper.

Lemma 6 (Lifting lemma for *HOlet*-rewriting). *Let $e, e' \in LExp$ such that $e\theta \rightarrow^{l*} e'$ for some $\theta \in PSubst$, and let $\mathcal{W}, \mathcal{B} \subseteq \mathcal{V}$ with $dom(\theta) \cup FV(e) \subseteq \mathcal{W}$, $BV(e) \subseteq \mathcal{B}$ and $(dom(\theta) \cup vRan(\theta)) \cap \mathcal{B} = \emptyset$, and for each instance of a program rule $R\gamma \in [\mathcal{P}]$ used in an (Fapp) step of $e\theta \rightarrow^{l*} e'$ then $vRan(\gamma|_{vExtra(R)}) \cap \mathcal{B} = \emptyset$. Then there exist a derivation $e \rightsquigarrow^{l*}_{\sigma} e''$ and $\theta' \in PSubst$ such that:*

(i) $e''\theta' = e'$ (ii) $\sigma\theta' = \theta[\mathcal{W}]$ (iii) $(dom(\theta') \cup vRan(\theta')) \cap \mathcal{B} = \emptyset$

*Besides, the *HOlet*-narrowing derivation can be chosen to use mgu's at each (**Narr**) or (**VAct**) step, and fresh shallow patterns in the range for each (**VBind**) step. Graphically:*

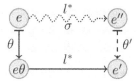

With the aid of this lemma we can reach our completeness result for $\rightsquigarrow^l$:

Theorem 8 (Completeness of *HOlet*-narrowing wrt. *HOlet*-rewriting). *Let $e, e' \in LExp$ and $\theta \in PSubst$. If $e\theta \rightarrow^{l*} e'$, then there exist a HOlet-narrowing derivation $e \rightsquigarrow^{l*}_{\sigma} e''$ and $\theta' \in PSubst$ such that $e''\theta' \equiv e'$ and $\sigma\theta' = \theta[FV(e)]$.*

5   A Case of Study: Correctness of Bubbling

Having equivalent notions of semantics and reduction allows to reason interchangeably at the rewriting and the semantic levels. We demonstrate the power of such technique by a case study where *let*-rewriting provides a good level of abstraction to formulate a new operational rule (*bubbling*), while the semantic point of view is appropriate for proving its correctness.

Bubbling, proposed in [3], is an operational rule devised to improve the efficiency of functional logic computations. Its correctness was formally studied in [2] in the framework of a variant [6] of term graph rewriting.

The idea of bubbling is to concentrate all non-determinism of a system into a *choice* operation ? defined by the rules $X ? Y \rightarrow X$ *and* $X ? Y \rightarrow Y$, and to lift applications of ? out of a surrounding context, as illustrated by the following graph transformation taken from [2]:

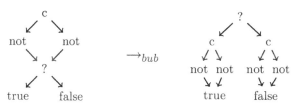

As it is shown in [3], bubbling can be implemented in such a way that many functional logic programs become more efficient, but we will not deal with these issues here.

Due to the technical particularities of term graph rewriting, not only the proof of correctness, but even the definition of bubbling in [3,2] are involved and need subtle care concerning the appropriate contexts over which choices can be bubbled. In contrast, bubbling can be expressed within our framework (moreover, generalized to HO) in a remarkably easy and abstract way as a new rewriting rule: **(Bub)** $\mathcal{C}[e_1?e_2] \to^{bub} \mathcal{C}[e_1]?\mathcal{C}[e_2]$, for $e_1, e_2 \in LExp$

With this rule, the bubbling step corresponding to the graph transformation of the example above is: *let X = true ? false in c (not X) (not X)* $\to^{bub}$ *let X = true in c (not X) (not X) ? let X = false in c (not X) (not X)*

Notice that the effect of this bubbling step is not a shortening of any existing *HOlet*-rewriting derivation; bubbling is indeed a genuine new rule, the correctness of which must be therefore subject of proof. Call-time choice is essential, since bubbling is not correct with respect to run-time choice: in Example 1, *fdouble (g?h) 0* can be reduced with run-time choice to $0, 1$ or 2, while *fdouble g 0 ? fdouble h 0* leads only to 0 and 2.

The fact that bubbling preserves $HOCRWL_{let}$-semantics has a simple formulation:

Theorem 9 (Correctness of bubbling). *If $e \to^{bub} e'$, then $[\![\mathcal{C}[e]]\!] = [\![\mathcal{C}[e']]\!]$. In other terms, $[\![\mathcal{C}[e_1?e_2]]\!] = [\![\mathcal{C}[e_1]?\mathcal{C}[e_2]]\!]$ $(= [\![\mathcal{C}[e_1]]\!] \cup [\![\mathcal{C}[e_2]]\!])$, for any $e_1, e_2 \in LExp$ and context $\mathcal{C}$.*

From this and the equivalence results of Sect. 3 we obtain as immediate corollary the correctness of bubbling in terms of rewriting:

Corollary 1. $e \to_l^* t \Leftrightarrow e (\to_l \cup \to_{bub})^* t$

It is interesting to observe that most of the proof of Th. 9 consists of direct calculations with denotation of expressions, in the form of chains of equalities of denotations, justified by general properties of the semantics like Th. 1. We find this methodology quite appealing and for this reason we include (a part of) the proof.

Proof (For Theorem 9, Correctness of bubbling). The proof uses the following easy (not proved here) lemma about semantics of ?, which justifies also the equation $[\![\mathcal{C}[e_1]?\mathcal{C}[e_2]]\!] = [\![\mathcal{C}[e_1]]\!] \cup [\![\mathcal{C}[e_2]]\!]$ stated in the Theor. 9.

Lemma 7. $[\![e_1?e_2]\!] = [\![e_1]\!] \cup [\![e_2]\!]$, *for any $e_1, e_2 \in LExp_\perp$.*

Now, we reason by induction on the number k of *let*'s occurring in $\mathcal{C}[e_1?e_2]$.

- $k = 0$: Since there is no *let* in $e_1?e_2$, we can apply Theor. 1 to obtain:

$$
\begin{array}{ll}
[\![\mathcal{C}[e_1?e_2]]\!] & = \text{(by Theor. 1)} \\
\bigcup_{t\in[\![e_1?e_2]\!]}[\![\mathcal{C}[t]]\!] & = \text{(by Lemma 7)} \\
\bigcup_{t\in([\![e_1]\!] \cup [\![e_2]\!])}[\![\mathcal{C}[t]]\!] & = \text{(set operations)} \\
\bigcup_{t\in[\![e_1]\!]}[\![\mathcal{C}[t]]\!] \cup \bigcup_{t\in[\![e_2]\!]}[\![\mathcal{C}[t]]\!] & = \text{(by Theor. 1)} \\
[\![\mathcal{C}[e_1]]\!] \cup [\![\mathcal{C}[e_2]]\!] & = \text{(by Lemma 7)} \\
[\![\mathcal{C}[e_1] ? \mathcal{C}[e_2]]\!] &
\end{array}
$$

- $k > 0$: We reason by induction on the structure of $\mathcal{C}$. The most interesting case is that of let bindings:

  - $\mathcal{C} \equiv let\ x = e\ in\ \mathcal{C}'$: then

$$
\begin{aligned}
[\![\mathcal{C}[e_1?e_2]]\!] &= \\
[\![let\ x{=}e\ in\ \mathcal{C}'[e_1?e_2]]\!] &= (by\ Theor.\ 2, \sigma \equiv \{x/t\}) \\
\bigcup_{t\in[\![e]\!]}[\![\mathcal{C}'[e_1?e_2]\sigma]\!] &= \\
\bigcup_{t\in[\![e]\!]}[\![\mathcal{C}'\sigma[e_1\sigma?e_2\sigma]]\!] &= (by\ IH\ on\ k,\ that\ decreases) \\
\bigcup_{t\in[\![e]\!]}[\![\mathcal{C}'\sigma[e_1\sigma]?\mathcal{C}'\sigma[e_2\sigma]]\!] &= (by\ Lemma\ 7) \\
\bigcup_{t\in[\![e]\!]}([\![\mathcal{C}'\sigma[e_1\sigma]]\!]\ \cup\ [\![\mathcal{C}'\sigma[e_2\sigma]]\!]) &= (set\ operations) \\
\bigcup_{t\in[\![e]\!]}[\![\mathcal{C}'\sigma[e_1\sigma]]\!]\ \cup\ \bigcup_{t\in[\![e]\!]}[\![\mathcal{C}'\sigma[e_2\sigma]]\!] &= (by\ Theor.\ 2) \\
[\![let\ x{=}e\ in\ \mathcal{C}'[e_1]]\!]\ \cup\ [\![let\ x{=}e\ in\ \mathcal{C}'[e_2]]\!] &= \\
[\![\mathcal{C}[e_1]]\!] \cup [\![\mathcal{C}[e_2]]\!] &= (by\ Lemma\ 7) \\
[\![\mathcal{C}[e_1]\ ?\ \mathcal{C}[e_2]]\!] &
\end{aligned}
$$

6   Translation to First Order

Since [29], a common technique to implement HO features in FO settings consists in a *HO-to-FO* translation introducing data constructors to represent partial applications and a special function @ (read *apply*) for reducing application of such constructors. This has been used within the context of *FLP* in [9,4]. Here we adapt such a transformation to our context and provide a correctness proof with respect to the semantics of the source and object programs, given by *HOCRWL* and *CRWL* [11,19] respectively.

Definition 2 (First order translation). *Given a HOCRWL-program* $\mathcal{P} = \{f\ \overline{p_1} \to e_1, \ldots, f\ \overline{p_m} \to e_m\}$ *built up over the signature* $\Sigma = FS \cup CS$, *its first order translation* P_{fo} *will be defined over the* **extended signature** $\Sigma_{fo} = FS_{fo} \cup CS_{fo}$ *where:*

$$
FS_{fo} = FS \cup \{@\};\quad CS_{fo} = \bigcup_{c \in CS^n, n \in \mathbb{N}}\{c_0, \ldots, c_n\} \cup \bigcup_{f \in FS^n, n \in \mathbb{N}}\{f_0, \ldots, f_{n-1}\}
$$

being @ *a new function symbol of arity 2 and* $c_0, \ldots, c_n, f_0, \ldots, f_{n-1}$ *new symbols (with arities indicated by the sub-index). The set* $\mathcal{P}_@$ *of* @$-$*rules is defined as:*

$$
\begin{aligned}
@(c_k(X_1, \ldots, X_k), Y) &= c_{k+1}(X_1, \ldots, X_k, Y), for\ each\ c \in DC^n, k < n \\
@(f_k(X_1, \ldots, X_k), Y) &= f_{k+1}(X_1, \ldots, X_k, Y), for\ each\ f \in FS^n, k + 1 < n \\
@(f_{n-1}(X_1, \ldots, X_{n-1}), Y) &= f(X_1, \ldots, X_{n-1}, Y), for\ each\ f \in FS^n
\end{aligned}
$$

The transforming function $fo : Exp_{\Sigma, \perp} \to Exp_{\Sigma_{fo}, \perp}$ *is defined as:*

$$
\begin{aligned}
fo(\perp) &= \perp & fo(X) &= X & fo(h) &= h_0, if\ h \in CS\ or\ h \in FS^n, n > 0 \\
fo(f) &= f, if\ f \in FS^0 & & & fo(e_1\ e_2) &= @(fo(e_1), fo(e_2))
\end{aligned}
$$

The **transformed program** *is defined as* $P_{fo} = \{f(\overline{fo(p_1)\downarrow_@}) \to fo(e_1)\downarrow_@,$ $\ldots, f(\overline{fo(p_m)\downarrow_@}) \to fo(e_m)\downarrow_@\} \cup P_@$, *where* $e\downarrow_@$ *stands for a* **normal form** *for* e *with respect to* @$-$*rules defined above.*

The program rules obtained by the transformation are well defined: it is easy to prove that if p is a pattern then $fo(p)\downarrow_@$ is a FO constructor term.

For the program of Example 1 we have $FS_{fo} = \{+, f, g, h, f', fadd, fdouble, @\}$ and $CS_{fo} = \{0, s_0, s, +_0, +_1, g_0, h_0, f'_0, fadd_0, fadd_1, fadd_2, fdouble_0\}$. The translated rules are:

$$g(X) \rightarrow 0 \qquad f \rightarrow g_0 \qquad f \rightarrow h_0 \qquad f'(X) \rightarrow @(f, X) \qquad h(X) \rightarrow s(0)$$
$$fadd(F, G, X) \rightarrow @(F, X) + @(G, X) \qquad fdouble(F) \rightarrow fadd_2(F, F)$$

And the rules for @ are:

$$@(+_0, X) \rightarrow +_1(X) \qquad @(s_0, X) \rightarrow s(X) \qquad @(h_0, X) \rightarrow h(X)$$
$$@(+_1(X), Y) \rightarrow X + Y \qquad @(g_0, X) \rightarrow g(X) \qquad @(f'_0, X) \rightarrow f'(X)$$
$$@(fadd_0, F) \rightarrow fadd_1(F) \qquad @(fadd_2(F, G), X) \rightarrow fadd(F, G, X)$$
$$@(fadd_1(F), G) \rightarrow fadd_2(F, G) \qquad @(fdouble_0, F) \rightarrow fdouble(F)$$

The translation of the expressions to reduce in that example are:

$$fo(fdouble\ f\ 0)\downarrow_@ = @(fdouble(f), 0) \qquad fo(fdouble\ f'\ 0)\downarrow_@ = @(fdouble(f'_0), 0)$$

In general we cannot expect to prove a statement of the form $fo(e) \twoheadrightarrow fo(t)$ because $fo(t)$ can contain calls to the function @, i.e. $fo(t)$ might not be a FO constructor term. But the same statement makes sense in the form $fo(e) \twoheadrightarrow fo(t)\downarrow_@$ because $fo(t)\downarrow_@$ is a FO constructor term.

Proposition 2. $[\![fo(e)\downarrow_@]\!]^{\mathcal{P}}_{CRWL} = [\![fo(e)]\!]^{\mathcal{P}}_{CRWL}$. *Moreover* $[\![fo(e)]\!] = [\![e']\!]$ *where* e' *is any expression obtained from* e *by reducing some calls of* @.

According to this, when proving a statement $fo(e) \twoheadrightarrow t$ we can use any equivalent expression e' (in the sense of previous lemma) in the left hand side and prove $e' \twoheadrightarrow t$.

The correctness of the transformation can be stated then as follows:

Theorem 10 (Adequacy of HO-to-FO translation). *Let* $\mathcal{P}$ *be a program,* $e \in Exp_\perp$, $t \in Pat_\perp$. *Then:* $\mathcal{P} \vdash_{HOCRWL} e \twoheadrightarrow t \Leftrightarrow \mathcal{P}_{fo} \vdash_{CRWL} fo(e) \twoheadrightarrow fo(t)\downarrow_@$. *Or, in terms of* HOlet-*rewriting:* $e \rightarrow^{l^*} t \Leftrightarrow fo(e) \rightarrow^{l^*} fo(t)\downarrow_@$.

7 Conclusions

Our paper addresses the broad question: *what means 'reduction' for functional logic programming?*, which had no previous satisfactory answer for the combination *HO + non-deterministic functions + call-time choice* supported by current systems in the mainstream of the field (Curry [16], Toy [21]). This leads to subtle behaviors well characterized from the point of view of a declarative semantics [7], but with no corresponding basic notion of one-step reduction. We have made a number of identifiable **contributions** in this sense:

- We propose a notion of rewriting with local bindings (*HOlet-rewriting*) suitable for a large class of HO systems (possibly non-confluent and non-terminating, allowing extra variables in right-hand sides and HO-patterns in left-hand sides).

- We have proved equivalence of *HOlet*-rewriting wrt to *HOCRWL* [7] declarative semantics. Along the way we have extended *HOCRWL* to cope with *let*s, and established new compositional properties of *HOCRWL* semantics.
- We have lifted *HOlet*-rewriting to a notion of *HOlet-narrowing* which is able to bind variables to patterns, even HO ones representing intensional descriptions of functions. We prove soundness and completeness of *HOlet*-narrowing wrt. *HOlet*-rewriting.
- We have recast within our framework the definition and proof of correctness of *bubbling*, an operational rule investigated in [3,2] using term graph rewriting techniques. Apart from extending it to HO, this case study illustrates quite well the power of using indistinctly rewriting and/or semantic-based reasoning.
- To close the panorama, we have formally proved that *translation from HO to FO*, a technique actually used in the implementations of FLP systems, still works properly when *let*-bindings with call-time choice are considered, while previous works [9,4] consider only deterministic functions.

The first three points have been conceived as an extension to HO of our previous work on the FO case [19,18]. However, adapting it has not been routine; on the contrary, some results have been indeed a technical challenge.

Our wish with this work, jointly with [19,18], is to have provided foundational pieces useful to understand how a FLP computation proceeds, serving also as suitable technical basis to address in the call-time choice context other operational issues (rewriting and narrowing strategies, residuation, program optimization, types in computations,. . .), all of which are lines of future work.

References

1. Albert, E., Hanus, M., Huch, F., Oliver, J., Vidal, G.: Operational semantics for declarative multi-paradigm languages. J. of Symb. Comp. 40(1), 795–829 (2005)
2. Antoy, S., Brown, D., Chiang, S.: On the correctness of bubbling. In: Pfenning, F. (ed.) RTA 2006. LNCS, vol. 4098, pp. 35–49. Springer, Heidelberg (2006)
3. Antoy, S., Brown, D., Chiang, S.: Lazy context cloning for non-deterministic graph rewriting. In: Proc. Termgraph 2006. ENTCS, vol. 176(1), pp. 61–70 (2007)
4. Antoy, S., Tolmach, A.P.: Typed higher-order narrowing without higher-order strategies. In: Middeldorp, A. (ed.) FLOPS 1999. LNCS, vol. 1722, pp. 335–353. Springer, Heidelberg (1999)
5. Ariola, Z.M., Felleisen, M., Maraist, J., Odersky, M., Wadler, P.: The call-by-need lambda calculus. In: Proc. POPL 1995, pp. 233–246 (1995)
6. Echahed, R., Janodet, J.-C.: Admissible graph rewriting and narrowing. In: Proc. JICSLP 1998, pp. 325–340. MIT Press, Cambridge (1998)
7. González-Moreno, J., Hortalá-González, M., Rodríguez-Artalejo, M.: A higher order rewriting logic for functional logic programming. In: Proc. ICLP 1997, pp. 153–167. MIT Press, Cambridge (1997)
8. González-Moreno, J., Hortalá-González, T., Rodríguez-Artalejo, M.: Polymorphic types in functional logic programming. J. of Functional and Logic Programming 2001/S01, 1–71 (2001)

9. González-Moreno, J.C.: A correctness proof for warren's ho into fo translation. In: Proc. GULP 1993, pp. 569–584 (1993)
10. González-Moreno, J.C., Hortalá-González, M.T., Rodríguez-Artalejo, M.: On the completeness of narrowing as the operational semantics of functional logic programming. In: Martini, S., Börger, E., Kleine Büning, H., Jäger, G., Richter, M.M. (eds.) CSL 1992. LNCS, vol. 702, pp. 216–230. Springer, Heidelberg (1993)
11. González-Moreno, J.C., Hortalá-González, T., López-Fraguas, F., Rodríguez-Artalejo, M.: An approach to declarative programming based on a rewriting logic. J. of Logic Programming 40(1), 47–87 (1999)
12. Hanus, M.: The integration of functions into logic programming: From theory to practice. J. of Logic Programming 19&20, 583–628 (1994)
13. Hanus, M.: Curry mailing list (March, 2007), http://www.informatik.uni-kiel.de/~curry/listarchive/0497.html
14. Hanus, M.: Multi-paradigm declarative languages. In: Dahl, V., Niemelä, I. (eds.) ICLP 2007. LNCS, vol. 4670, pp. 45–75. Springer, Heidelberg (2007)
15. Hanus, M., Prehofer, C.: Higher-order narrowing with definitional trees. J. of Functional Programming 9(1), 33–75 (1999)
16. Hanus, M. (ed.): Curry: An integrated functional logic language (version 0.8.2) (March, 2006), http://www.informatik.uni-kiel.de/~curry/report.html
17. Hussmann, H.: Non-Determinism in Algebraic Specifications and Algebraic Programs. Birkhäuser, Basel (1993)
18. López-Fraguas, F., Rodríguez-Hortalá, J., Sánchez-Hernández, J.: Narrowing for non-determinism with call-time choice semantics. In: Proc. WLP 2007 (2007)
19. López-Fraguas, F., Rodríguez-Hortalá, J., Sánchez-Hernández, J.: A simple rewrite notion for call-time choice semantics. In: Proc. PPDP 2007, pp. 197–208. ACM Press, New York (2007)
20. López-Fraguas, F., Rodríguez-Hortalá, J., Sánchez-Hernández, J.: Rewriting and call-time choice: the HO case (extended version). Tech. Rep. SIC-3-08 (2008), http://gpd.sip.ucm.es/fraguas/papers/flops08long.pdf
21. López-Fraguas, F., Sánchez-Hernández, J.: $\mathcal{TOY}$: A multiparadigm declarative system. In: Narendran, P., Rusinowitch, M. (eds.) RTA 1999. LNCS, vol. 1631, pp. 244–247. Springer, Heidelberg (1999)
22. Maraist, J., Odersky, M., Wadler, P.: The call-by-need lambda calculus. J. Funct. Program. 8(3), 275–317 (1998)
23. Miller, D.: A logic programming language with lambda-abstraction, function variables, and simple unification. J. Log. Comput. 1(4), 497–536 (1991)
24. Nakahara, K., Middeldorp, A., Ida, T.: A complete narrowing calculus for higher-order functional logic programming. In: Leopold, H., Coulson, G., Danthine, A., Hutchison, D. (eds.) COST-237 1994. LNCS, vol. 882, pp. 97–114. Springer, Heidelberg (1994)
25. Peyton Jones, S.L. (ed.): Haskell 98 Language and Libraries. The Revised Report. Cambridge University Press, Cambridge (2003)
26. Plump, D.: Essentials of term graph rewriting. ENTCS 51 (2001)
27. van Raamsdonk, F.: Higher-order rewriting. In: Term Rewriting Systems, Cambridge University Press, Cambridge (2003)
28. Rodríguez-Artalejo, M.: Functional and constraint logic programming. In: Comon, H., Marché, C., Treinen, R. (eds.) CCL 1999. LNCS, vol. 2002, pp. 202–270. Springer, Heidelberg (2001)
29. Warren, D.H.: Higher-order extensions to prolog: Are they needed? Machine Intelligence 10, 441–454 (1982)

Semantics and Pragmatics of
New Shortcut Fusion Rules

Janis Voigtländer

Institut für Theoretische Informatik
Technische Universität Dresden
01062 Dresden, Germany
voigt@tcs.inf.tu-dresden.de

Abstract. We study various shortcut fusion rules for languages like
Haskell. Following a careful semantic account of a recently proposed rule
for circular program transformation, we propose a new rule that trades
circularity for higher-orderedness, and thus attains better semantic properties. This also leads us to revisit the original foldr/build-rule, as well as
its dual, and to develop variants that do not suffer from detrimental im-
pacts of Haskell's mixed strict/nonstrict semantics. Throughout, we offer
pragmatic insights about our new rules to investigate also their relative
effectiveness, rather than just their semantic correctness.

1 Introduction

These are exciting times for enthusiasts of program transformations akin to
shortcut fusion. After the seminal paper on foldr/build-fusion [4], a number of
transformations derived from free theorems [15] have been developed over the
years, transferring the technique to other types than lists [5,11], or investigat-
ing new transformation schemes of similar flavour [2,10,12]. And recently there
seems to occur another upsurge of successes in this direction. On the one hand,
completely new ideas are developed, such as the circular fusion rule in [3]. On the
other hand, existing techniques are revisited and further developed in a way that
makes them more useful in practice [1]. And with the integration of call-pattern
specialisation into GHC [8], an important building block for successful fusion
(post-processing) is falling into place. With this paper we want to continue and
nurture this trend, by advancing semantic and pragmatic aspects of existing and
new transformations.

We take our start from the pfold/buildp-rule of [3]. It is of particular interest
from a semantic viewpoint as it is, due to its use of a circular local binding,
the first transformation in the shortcut fusion family that is usable exclusively
from a lazy language. This raises questions as to how the rule interacts with the
intricacies of Haskell's semantics surrounding $\bot$, fixpoint recursion, and selective
strictness. The authors of [3] describe their reasoning as "fast and loose" in this
respect. Here we investigate those issues, and prove total and partial correctness
results for the circular pfold/buildp-rule in Haskell.

J. Garrigue and M. Hermenegildo (Eds.): FLOPS 2008, LNCS 4989, pp. 163–179, 2008.
© Springer-Verlag Berlin Heidelberg 2008

Guided by a folklore idea on replacing circularity by higher-orderedness, we then propose a new scheme for pfold/buildp-fusion that not only becomes usable again in a purely strict language, but also plays well with potentially mixed strict/nonstrict evaluation. In fact, we are able to prove total correctness of our new rule without any preconditions on the producer and consumer functions.

The latter is quite remarkable after the completely different experiences made in [6] for the classical foldr/build- and its dual destroy/unfoldr-rule. It leads us to revisit those veteran transformations and to look for potential "repairs" of their semantic deficiencies. And in fact we can transfer some insights and come up with new, and much better behaved, variants of foldr/build- and destroy/unfoldr-fusion.

Throughout, we stay in touch with pragmatic considerations by examining the impact of transformations on concrete examples. This allows us to investigate also the effectiveness, rather than just the correctness, of our new proposals. For example, we carefully weigh the circular and higher-order flavours of pfold/buildp-fusion against each other. And in some cases such pragmatic investigations actually lead to new rule variants.

We deliberately do not focus on a single program transformation. Instead, we report a laboratory-like experience in which working on one rule provides potential insights on another one as well, or indeed sparks a new idea that helps to resolve an issue existing for an at first sight somewhat unrelated fusion problem. This mode of operation has been very fruitful, and we would like to encourage others to push the boundaries of shortcut fusion as well.

2   Circular Shortcut Fusion

In [3] a fusion rule for circular program calculation is proposed. Even though it is originally given for arbitrary algebraic datatypes, we consider only the list case here. For other types the development and results would be similar.

The involved combinators are given as follows:

buildp :: $(forall\ a.\ (b \to a \to a) \to a \to c \to (a,z)) \to c \to ([b],z)$
buildp $g = g\ (:)\ []$

pfold :: $(b \to a \to z \to a) \to (z \to a) \to ([b],z) \to a$
pfold $h_1\ h_2\ (bs,z) =$ foldr $(\lambda b\ a \to h_1\ b\ a\ z)\ (h_2\ z)\ bs$

The idea underlying buildp is that g describes the production of an abstract list (hence the list constructor arguments) over type b, and at the same time delivers an additional result of type z, both guided by an input parameter of type c. A typical application of that scheme is the definition of the following function:

splitWhen :: $(b \to$ BOOL$) \to [b] \to ([b],[b])$
splitWhen $p =$ buildp go
  where go *con nil bs* =
        case *bs* **of**
              $[] \to$ (*nil,bs*)
              b:bs' $\to$ **if** *p b* **then** (*nil,bs*)
                            else let (*xs,ys*) = go *con nil bs'* **in** (*con b xs, ys*)

The idea underlying pfold is that h_1 and h_2 describe the consumption of a list over type b by structural recursion (via the standard function foldr), but can take an additional parameter of type z into account while doing so. A typical application of that scheme is the definition of the following function:

pfilter :: $(b \to z \to$ BOOL$) \to ([b],z) \to [b]$
pfilter p = pfold $(\lambda b\ bs\ z \to$ **if** $p\ b\ z$ **then** $b{:}bs$ **else** $bs) (\lambda\_ \to [])$

This variant of the classical filter-function uses a binary, rather than unary, predicate for selecting list elements, where the second argument of that predicate is fixed throughout and provided as additional input alongside the input list.

The rule from [3] now tells us, in general, to replace as follows:

$$\text{pfold } h_1\ h_2\ (\text{buildp } g\ c) \quad \rightsquigarrow \quad \textbf{let } (a,z) = g\ (\lambda b\ a \to h_1\ b\ a\ z)\ (h_2\ z)\ c\ \textbf{in } a.$$

Note the circularity in the right-hand side, preventing use of the rule in a strict functional language. To see the rule in action, consider the following definition:

repeatedAfter :: EQ $b \Rightarrow (b \to$ BOOL$) \to [b] \to [b]$
repeatedAfter $p\ bs$ = pfilter elem (splitWhen $p\ bs$)

It provides a very natural specification of the following task: from the initial part of an input list before a certain predicate holds for the first time, return those elements that are repeated afterwards. To benefit from the circular pfold/buildp-rule, we inline the definitions of pfilter and splitWhen, apply the rule, and afterwards perform some local optimisations as exemplified and described in more detail in [1]. The result is the following version:

repeatedAfter' $p\ bs$ =
  let
    (a,z) = go' bs
    go' bs = **case** bs **of**
            $[] \to ([],bs)$
            $b{:}bs' \to$ **if** $p\ b$ **then** $([],bs)$ **else**
                     let (xs,ys) = go' bs'
                     in (**if** elem $b\ z$ **then** $b{:}xs$ **else** $xs,\ ys$)
  in a

Note that even though z and go' are mutually defined in terms of each other, there is no "true" circularity, as lazy evaluation can order the computation in an appropriate, terminating way.

However, the selective strictness feature of Haskell can ruin this approach in an unexpected way. As an (admittedly artificial) counterexample, consider $g = (\lambda\_\ nil\ c \to$ seq $nil\ (nil,c))$, $c = 42$, $h_2 = (+1)$, and arbitrary (but appropriately typed) h_1. Then pfold $h_1\ h_2$ (buildp $g\ c$) is 43, while the transformed expression **let** $(a,z) = g\ (\lambda b\ a \to h_1\ b\ a\ z)\ (h_2\ z)\ c\ \textbf{in } a$ does not terminate! To see why, take into account that by inlining g, c, and h_2, it is equivalent to the truly circular **let** (a,z) = seq $(z{+}1)\ (z{+}1,\ 42)\ \textbf{in } a$.

For classical foldr/build-fusion we know from [6] that total correctness even in the presence of seq can be guaranteed by imposing certain restrictions on the arguments to foldr. Trying to transfer those insights to the present setting, we come to investigate whether $h_1 \perp \perp z \neq \perp$ and $h_2 z \neq \perp$ (because the arguments to foldr in the definition of pfold $h_1 h_2$ are $(\lambda b\ a \rightarrow h_1\ b\ a\ z)$ and $h_2 z$). But this raises the question which z to consider here. It seems natural to consider the second element of the pair returned by buildp $g\ c$, as that is exactly what gets passed to pfold $h_1 h_2$ before the circular fusion rule is applied. But tempting as this intuition is, it must be wrong! This is evidenced by the above counterexample, where buildp $g\ c = ([],42)$ and $h_2\ 42 = 43 \neq \perp$ (and h_1 could be chosen arbitrarily, in particular in a way such that $h_1 \perp \perp 42 \neq \perp$ as well), and yet we found that applying the circular fusion rule was not semantics-preserving.

This motivates a more careful study of the latter's semantics than is currently available. To help us in this endeavour, we first establish an auxiliary lemma. By convention, a function f is strict if $f \perp = \perp$; total if $f\ x \neq \perp$ for every $x \neq \perp$.

Lemma 1. *Let* T_1, T_2, *and* T_3 *be types. Let* $c :: T_2$ *and*

$$g :: forall\ a.\ (T_1 \rightarrow a \rightarrow a) \rightarrow a \rightarrow T_2 \rightarrow (a, T_3)\,.$$

Then for every type T', $q :: T_1 \rightarrow T' \rightarrow T'$, *and strict and total* $f :: [T_1] \rightarrow T'$,

$$(q \neq \perp \wedge \forall\ b :: T_1.\ q\ b \neq \perp \wedge \forall\ bs :: [T_1].\ f\ (b{:}bs) = q\ b\ (f\ bs)) \quad (1)$$
$$\Rightarrow g\ q\ (f\ []) \ c = \textbf{case buildp } g\ c \textbf{ of } (bs,z') \rightarrow (f\ bs,\ z')\,.$$

The proof via a free theorem builds on the results from [6] and is given in the appendix. The most important pieces to note here are the preconditions relating to $\perp$ and the strictness and totality restrictions on f. These are exactly the kind of things that one needs to pay close attention to when trying to derive semantic statements that remain valid for Haskell even in the presence of general recursion and selective strictness. Note also that all Haskell types are pointed, so that, for example, the quantification over $b :: T_1$ includes the case $b = \perp$.

Based on Lemma 1, we can now prove the following theorem which provides the desired preconditions for total correctness of circular pfold/buildp-fusion.

Theorem 1. *Let* T_1, T_2, T_3, *and* T_4 *be types. Let* $c :: T_2$, $h_1 :: T_1 \rightarrow T_4 \rightarrow T_3 \rightarrow T_4$, $h_2 :: T_3 \rightarrow T_4$, *and*

$$g :: forall\ a.\ (T_1 \rightarrow a \rightarrow a) \rightarrow a \rightarrow T_2 \rightarrow (a, T_3)\,.$$

If $h_1 \perp \perp \perp \neq \perp$ *and* $h_2 \perp \neq \perp$, *then*

$$\text{pfold } h_1\ h_2\ (\text{buildp } g\ c) \quad = \quad \textbf{let } (a,z) = g\ (\lambda b\ a \rightarrow h_1\ b\ a\ z)\ (h_2\ z)\ c \textbf{ in } a\,.$$

The proof is given in the appendix. In it, the circular binding in the expression after fusion is described by an explicit use of fixpoint recursion. This helps to pin down why it is not enough to require $h_1 \perp \perp z \neq \perp$ and $h_2 z \neq \perp$ for the second element z of the pair returned by buildp $g\ c$: since fixpoint recursion conceptually starts from $\perp$ (as in fix $f = \bigsqcup f^i \perp$; the actual definition used in the proof calculation is fix $f = f$ (fix f)), the circular "hunting" for z in the program after fusion also starts out with $\perp$, which might then interfere with seq. This precisely explains the counterexample we observed earlier, and why it was not sufficient there that h_2 42 $\neq$ $\bot$.

For classical foldr/build-fusion we can avoid preconditions if settling for partial rather than total correctness [6]. Let us see whether the same is possible here. To that end, we need to look at "inequational" versions of the statements we have derived so far. Typically, to any "equational" free theorem correspond two inequational ones. For Lemma 1, one of the two variants is as follows.

Lemma 2. *Let* T_1, T_2, *and* T_3 *be types. Let* $c :: T_2$ *and*

$$g :: \text{forall } a. \ (T_1 \rightarrow a \rightarrow a) \rightarrow a \rightarrow T_2 \rightarrow (a, T_3).$$

Then for every type T', $q :: T_1 \rightarrow T' \rightarrow T'$, *and strict* $f :: [T_1] \rightarrow T'$,

$$(\forall \ b :: T_1, \ bs :: [T_1]. \ f \ (b:bs) \sqsupseteq q \ b \ (f \ bs))$$
$$\Rightarrow g \ q \ (f \ []) \ c \sqsubseteq \textbf{case } \text{buildp } g \ c \textbf{ of } (bs, z') \rightarrow (f \ bs, \ z').$$

Note that the new lemma does not require f to be total. The price to pay for this is that the final statement only provides a semantic approximation. The reading of "$\sqsubseteq$" is that the right-hand side is at least as defined as the left-hand side.

As usual, there is also a second inequational variant. However, we have found that it does not lead to any insight beyond what we already know from the equational setting. That is why we only give Lemma 2 here. Based on it, we can prove (largely by mirroring the proof of Theorem 1) the following theorem which establishes partial correctness of circular pfold/buildp-fusion without preconditions.

Theorem 2. *Let* T_1, T_2, T_3, *and* T_4 *be types. Let* $c :: T_2$, $h_1 :: T_1 \rightarrow T_4 \rightarrow T_3 \rightarrow T_4$, $h_2 :: T_3 \rightarrow T_4$, *and*

$$g :: \text{forall } a. \ (T_1 \rightarrow a \rightarrow a) \rightarrow a \rightarrow T_2 \rightarrow (a, T_3).$$

Then

$$\text{pfold } h_1 \ h_2 \ (\text{buildp } g \ c) \quad \sqsupseteq \quad \textbf{let } (a, z) = g \ (\lambda b \ a \rightarrow h_1 \ b \ a \ z) \ (h_2 \ z) \ c \textbf{ in } a.$$

Note that the counterexample to total correctness given earlier fits into the picture here. There, we observed that 43 got transformed into $\bot$. This certainly agrees with the above statement.

Note also that the partial correctness result does by no means imply that the circular fusion rule decreases definedness *always* when any of the preconditions from Theorem 1 is violated. Indeed, the repeatedAfter-example from earlier in this section does not suffer from any introduction of failure, even though an investigation of the first argument to pfold in that fusion instance shows that the first precondition from Theorem 1 is not fulfilled, given that (**if** elem $\bot$ $\bot$ **then** $\bot$:$\bot$ **else** $\bot$) = $\bot$. However, the problem is that for such consumers we may not *guarantee* total correctness. For example, one can easily come up with a producer whose fusion with pfilter elem does actually lead to a decrease in definedness, so that Theorem 2 is the best one can say. In particular, it does not make sense to try to prove a somehow "better" Theorem 1 that makes do with less strong, and therefore more practical, preconditions. There is no circumventing the fact that there exist g of the given type that make the conditions $h_1 \perp \perp \perp \neq \perp$ and $h_2 \perp \neq \perp$ necessary in their full, combined pessimism. Inventing new rules, however, can make a difference.

3   Higher-Order Shortcut Fusion

It is an old idea to replace circular definitions, such as obtained from the elimination of multiple traversals, by higher-order ones. In the terminology of [7], this is achieved by import and export of information. Thus guided, we would like to develop a variant of pfold/buildp-fusion that is unaffected by selective (or, indeed, full) strict evaluation. In doing so, we clearly want to preserve the advantages of the circular fusion rule such as elimination of the intermediate list and effective handling of the additional result produced by buildp and used by pfold. We know from [13] that a transformation of circularity into higher-orderedness is not always possible. But for the setup we consider here, it turns out that there is a way to achieve it for every fusion instance.

Concretely, we propose to replace as follows:

$$\text{pfold } h_1 \ h_2 \ (\text{buildp } g \ c)$$

$$\rightsquigarrow$$

$$\textbf{case } g \ (\lambda b \ k \ z \rightarrow h_1 \ b \ (k \ z) \ z) \ (\lambda z \rightarrow h_2 \ z) \ c \ \textbf{of } (k,z) \rightarrow k \ z \ .$$

Note that there is no circularity in the right-hand side. Indeed, our new rule is applicable in a strict language just as well as in a lazy or mixed evaluation one. It is higher-order in the sense that it uses a function k where the circular rule used a value a.

To see the new rule in action, consider again the function definition for repeatedAfter. After inlining the definitions of pfilter and splitWhen, applying the higher-order fusion rule, and performing local optimisations as mentioned earlier, the result now is the following version:

```
repeatedAfter'' p bs =
  case
    let go' bs = case bs of
                   [] → (λz → [], bs)
                   b:bs' → if p b then (λz → [], bs)
                           else
                             let (xs,ys) = go' bs'
                             in (λz → if elem b z then b:(xs z) else xs z, ys)
    in go' bs
  of (k,z) → k z
```

Another interesting instance is the counterexample we used earlier to demonstrate the weaknesses of the circular fusion rule: $g = (\lambda\_ \ nil \ c \rightarrow \text{seq } nil \ (nil,c))$, $c = 42$, and $h_2 = (+1)$. For the higher-order fusion rule this poses no problems at all: after fusion, we still get 43 as result.

In order to see whether such positive outcome is obtained for every fusion instance, we investigate total correctness of the new rule. We can reuse Lemma 1 to this purpose. Indeed, based on it, we can prove the following theorem.

Theorem 3. *Let* T_1, T_2, T_3, *and* T_4 *be types. Let* $c :: T_2$, $h_1 :: T_1 \to T_4 \to T_3 \to T_4$, $h_2 :: T_3 \to T_4$, *and*

$$g :: \text{forall } a. (T_1 \to a \to a) \to a \to T_2 \to (a, T_3) .$$

Then

$$\text{pfold } h_1 \ h_2 \ (\text{buildp } g \ c)$$
$$=$$
$$\textbf{case } g \ (\lambda b \ k \ z \to h_1 \ b \ (k \ z) \ z) \ (\lambda z \to h_2 \ z) \ c \ \textbf{of} \ (k, z) \to k \ z .$$

We omit further proof details here. In fact, we will do so also for the remaining theorems in this paper. Suffice it to say that they can all be proved using the general goal-directed approach presented in [14].

Analysing *why* total correctness without preconditions holds in Theorem 3 leads to the realization that **seq** simply cannot do any harm in the presence of the "extra" lambda-abstractions that prevent g from encountering a $\bot$-value when combining its arguments, even though h_1 and/or h_2 might very well contain or produce such values. The need to preserve those protective lambda-abstractions also means that it is not safe to perform eta-reduction of $(\lambda z \to h_2 \ z)$ to h_2. Indeed, eta-reduction is not valid in Haskell with **seq** and should not be performed by any compiler.

That the above theorem establishes total correctness unconditionally is a much more satisfying situation than with circular **pfold**/**buildp**-fusion. However, from a pragmatic, rather than semantic, viewpoint the picture is not quite as clear. Consider, for example, the following function definition:

greaterThanMinAfter :: ORD $b \Rightarrow (b \to$ BOOL$) \to [b] \to [b]$
greaterThanMinAfter p bs = pfilter $(\lambda b \ bs' \to b > \text{minimum } bs')$ (splitWhen p bs)

After inlining the definitions of **pfilter** and **splitWhen**, applying the higher-order fusion rule, and performing the usual local optimisations, we obtain from it a version greaterThanMinAfter′ whose function body differs from that of repeatedAfter″ seen earlier in this section only in that the third-last line looks as follows:

in $(\lambda z \to$ **if** $b > \text{minimum } z$ **then** $b:(xs \ z)$ **else** $xs \ z, ys)$

But precisely this line exposes an issue that we might want to improve on. Namely, we see that minimum z will be computed repeatedly for comparison against all elements of bs until p holds for the first time. There is no apparent way how to avoid this recomputation, even though it is actually the case for given arguments p and bs to greaterThanMinAfter′ that whenever program evaluation reaches this expression, the value of z is the same. But it would simply require too advanced a flow analysis from the compiler to automatically detect this. Similar observations regarding a loss of sharing for shortcut fusion rules were made in [10].

Closer analysis of the above issue reveals that it occurs whenever the consuming pfold would actually be better served with an image, under some function h, of the second element of the pair returned by the producing buildp, rather than with that second element itself. This insight leads us to establish the following slight variation of Theorem 3.

Theorem 4. *Let* T_1, T_2, T_3, T_3', *and* T_4 *be types. Let* $c :: T_2$, $h :: T_3' \to T_3$, $h_1 :: T_1 \to T_4 \to T_3 \to T_4$, $h_2 :: T_3 \to T_4$, *and*

$$g :: \text{forall } a. \, (T_1 \to a \to a) \to a \to T_2 \to (a, T_3') \, .$$

Then

$$\textbf{case } \text{buildp } g \ c \textbf{ of } (bs, z') \to \text{pfold } h_1 \ h_2 \ (bs, h \ z')$$
$$=$$
$$\textbf{case } g \ (\lambda b \ k \ z \to h_1 \ b \ (k \ z) \ z) \ (\lambda z \to h_2 \ z) \ c \textbf{ of } (k, z) \to k \ (h \ z) \, . \qquad (2)$$

Note that this theorem again gives total correctness without any preconditions. Unfortunately, it is not as readily applicable for fusion as our earlier results, because the left-hand side is not a simple combination of a producer- and a consumer-combinator. This is easily remedied, though. We can define variants of the original combinators as follows:

buildp' :: *(forall* $a. \, (b \to a \to a) \to a \to c \to (a, z')) \to c \to (z' \to z) \to ([b], z)$
buildp' $g \ c \ h = \textbf{case } g \ (:) \ [] \ c \textbf{ of } (bs, z') \to (bs, h \ z')$

pfold' :: $(b \to a \to z \to a) \to (z \to a) \to (z' \to z) \to ([b], z') \to a$
pfold' $h_1 \ h_2 \ h \ (bs, z') = \textbf{let } z = h \ z' \textbf{ in } \text{foldr } (\lambda b \ a \to h_1 \ b \ a \ z) \ (h_2 \ z) \ bs$

Then Theorem 4 tells us that we can semantics-preservingly replace either of pfold $h_1 \ h_2$ (buildp' $g \ c \ h$) and pfold' $h_1 \ h_2 \ h$ (buildp $g \ c$) by (2) or, indeed, replace as follows:

$$\text{pfold' } h_1 \ h_2 \ h' \ (\text{buildp' } g \ c \ h)$$
$$\rightsquigarrow$$
$$\textbf{case } g \ (\lambda b \ k \ z \to h_1 \ b \ (k \ z) \ z) \ (\lambda z \to h_2 \ z) \ c \textbf{ of } (k, z) \to k \ (h' \ (h \ z)) \, .$$

The new combinators provide us with the means to define a variant of greaterThanMinAfter that after applying one of the just given semantics-preserving rules leads to a version greaterThanMinAfter'' which avoids repeated computation with minimum by having a function body that differs from the one of repeatedAfter'' only in that the three final lines look as follows:

$$\textbf{in } (\lambda z \to \textbf{if } b > z \textbf{ then } b:(xs \ z) \textbf{ else } xs \ z, \ ys)$$
$$\textbf{in } \text{go' } bs$$
$$\textbf{of } (k, z) \to k \ (\text{minimum } z)$$

Note that all the rules proposed in this section are also applicable in a purely strict language. There, however, they can increase (though never decrease) the definedness of a program. Consider, for example, the rule proposed last. If h_1 is a nonterminating expression, then the left-hand side pfold' $h_1 \ h_2 \ h'$ (buildp' $g \ c \ h$) is nonterminating as well. But the corresponding right-hand side might very well be terminating, for example if g does not use its first argument.

4   Circular Versus Higher-Order Fusion

Having observed that extra effort may be needed to prevent a certain loss of sharing when performing higher-order pfold/buildp-fusion, it should be interesting, by way of comparison, to see whether the same issue exists for the original, circular rule as well. So consider, again, the function definition for greaterThanMinAfter. After inlining the definitions of pfilter and splitWhen, applying the circular fusion rule leads to a version greaterThanMinAfter''' whose function body differs from that of repeatedAfter' seen in Section 2 only in that the next-to-last line looks as follows:

$$\text{in } (\text{if } b > \text{minimum } z \text{ then } b{:}xs \text{ else } xs, \ ys)$$

In contrast to what we had with higher-order fusion, the z is now not locally lambda-bound. In fact, it is not local to the go'-function at all. This means that the full laziness transformation [9], to some extent implemented also in GHC, can effectively avoid recomputations of minimum z by floating that whole expression out. Then, a better degree of sharing is achieved than in higher-order fusion prior to introducing extra combinators and rules. However, recall that for circular fusion one cannot guarantee total correctness unrestrictedly. And indeed, the first argument to pfold in the greaterThanMinAfter-example does not satisfy the first precondition from Theorem 1. So the potential for better sharing here is bought by having to settle for only a partial correctness guarantee, or total correctness under conditions that cannot in general be checked automatically by a compiler.

In case full laziness is not implemented in the compiler, or does not "fire", good sharing can be recovered for circular fusion just as it was for higher-order fusion in the previous section, by giving appropriate rules for the generalised combinators pfold' and buildp'. Note however, that in the absence of full laziness even the original program before any fusion might suffer from a lack of sharing. For example, an expression pfilter $(\lambda b\ bs' \to b > \text{minimum } bs')\ (bs,z)$ is, by the definitions, the same as foldr $(\lambda b\ a \to \text{if } b > \text{minimum } z \text{ then } b{:}a \text{ else } a)\ []\ bs$. Here only full laziness can prevent minimum z from being calculated repeatedly. This reinstates that pragmatics can be as important as semantics when designing and studying program transformations.

5   Variations of Classical Shortcut Fusion

That the higher-order version of pfold/buildp-fusion turned out to be totally correct without any preconditions is rather pleasing, and raises the question whether a similar "repair" is also possible for classical foldr/build-fusion from [4].

Recall that build is defined as follows:

build :: (*forall* a. $(b \to a \to a) \to a \to a) \to [b]$
build $g = g\ ({:})\ []$

and that classical shortcut fusion lets us replace as follows:

$$\text{foldr } h_1\ h_2\ (\text{build } g) \quad \rightsquigarrow \quad g\ h_1\ h_2 .$$

As first observed in [12], this transformation is not totally correct in Haskell (while in [6] we have seen that it is partially correct, and totally correct under the preconditions that $h_1 \perp \perp \neq \perp$ and $h_2 \neq \perp$). As mentioned earlier, the reason that total correctness without preconditions could be proved in Theorem 3 (and 4) is that seq could not do any harm there due to the omnipresent lambda-abstractions. This motivates to consider also, for example, the following rule:

$$\text{foldr } h_1 \; h_2 \; (\text{build } g) \quad \leadsto \quad g \; (\lambda b \; k \; z \rightarrow h_1 \; b \; (k \; z)) \; (\lambda z \rightarrow h_2) \; () \, .$$

Note the use of () :: () as proxy value. Total correctness is established by the following theorem.

Theorem 5. *Let* T_1 *and* T_2 *be types. Let* $h_1 :: T_1 \rightarrow T_2 \rightarrow T_2$, $h_2 :: T_2$, *and*

$$g :: \text{forall } a. \; (T_1 \rightarrow a \rightarrow a) \rightarrow a \rightarrow a \, .$$

Then

$$\text{foldr } h_1 \; h_2 \; (\text{build } g) \quad = \quad g \; (\lambda b \; k \; z \rightarrow h_1 \; b \; (k \; z)) \; (\lambda z \rightarrow h_2) \; () \, .$$

The theorem provides a totally correct foldr/build-rule without preconditions. But what about the pragmatics of transformation? Consider the archetypical example for foldr/build-fusion:

```
upTo :: INT → [INT]
upTo n = build (go 1)
    where go i con nil = if i>n then nil else con i (go (i+1) con nil)

sum :: [INT] → INT
sum = foldr (+) 0

sumTo :: INT → INT
sumTo n = sum (upTo n)
```

Inlining the definitions of sum and upTo into that of sumTo and applying the rule suggested above leads to the following version:

```
sumTo' n = go' 1 () where go' i = if i>n then λz → 0 else λz → i+(go' (i+1) z)
```

It is apparent here that all the z will always be bound to the proxy value (). But there is little hope that the compiler is smart enough to transform this "plumbing" away. Similar issues appear for variations on the theme of employing higher-orderedness to make foldr/build-fusion unconditionally totally correct.

However, there is an alternative. As noted earlier, the essential role of the lambda-abstractions is to protect g from undesired encounters with $\perp$. But the same feat can be achieved without resorting to higher-orderedness. In fact, we propose a variant that is a kind of "defunctionalisation" of the above idea. To this end, we introduce the following datatype (purposefully *not* a **newtype**, in which case we would get $J \perp = \perp$, contrary to what we want):

```
data J a = J {unJ :: a}
```

Then we propose to replace as follows:

$$\text{foldr } h_1 \ h_2 \ (\text{build } g) \quad \rightsquigarrow \quad \text{unJ } (g \ (\lambda b \ a \rightarrow \text{J } (h_1 \ b \ (\text{unJ } a))) \ (\text{J } h_2)) \,.$$

This is justified by the following theorem which establishes unconditional total correctness.

Theorem 6. *Let* T_1 *and* T_2 *be types. Let* $h_1 :: \mathsf{T}_1 \rightarrow \mathsf{T}_2 \rightarrow \mathsf{T}_2$, $h_2 :: \mathsf{T}_2$, *and*

$$g :: \textit{forall } a. \ (\mathsf{T}_1 \rightarrow a \rightarrow a) \rightarrow a \rightarrow a \,.$$

Then

$$\text{foldr } h_1 \ h_2 \ (\text{build } g) \quad = \quad \text{unJ } (g \ (\lambda b \ a \rightarrow \text{J } (h_1 \ b \ (\text{unJ } a))) \ (\text{J } h_2)) \,.$$

If we use this new rule to transform the sumTo-example from above, we get the following version:

sumTo″ n=unJ (go′ 1) **where** go′ i=**if** i>n **then** J 0 **else** J (i+(unJ (go′ (i+1))))

This again uses extra plumbing, now through the J type. However, there exists a very simple idea of eliminating that. In [8], specialisation of functions for constructor-call-patterns is proposed, with an existing implementation in GHC. The paper also discusses an extension to specialisation for function-call-patterns. Assume this were applied above by introducing a new local function unJ′ such that unJ′ i always corresponds to unJ (go′ i). This would give:

sumTo‴ n = unJ′ 1 **where** unJ′ i = unJ (**if** i>n **then** J 0 **else** J (i+(unJ′ (i+1))))

and finally, applying standard optimisations implemented in GHC:

sumTo⁗ n = unJ′ 1 **where** unJ′ i = **if** i>n **then** 0 **else** i+(unJ′ (i+1))

This is the version we ultimately want to see after foldr/build-fusion, and in fact do get to see after standard foldr/build-fusion à la [4] as well, but now it was obtained going only through perfectly safe transformations, rather than relying on the original fusion rule that may or may not be totally correct in a given situation. And the heuristics required for an implementation along the lines of [8] would be very simple: we can always try to specialise unJ for a function call occurring in its argument, assuming that J is a private datatype of the compiler so that unJ is introduced only during shortcut fusion as above.

At least as interesting as the example above is one where the standard foldr/build-rule actually breaks. Consider the following function:

lastEvenOrEmpty :: [INT] → [INT]
lastEvenOrEmpty bs =
    build ($\lambda con \ nil \rightarrow$ foldl′ ($\lambda a \ b \rightarrow$ **if** even b **then** $con \ b \ nil$ **else** a) $nil \ bs$)

It uses the standard Haskell function foldl′ to return, in a singleton list, the last even element from an integer list provided as input. If no even element exists, the empty list is returned. To allow eventual fusion, the output list is abstracted over via build. Consider further the following function, relying on the above to return the last even element without packaging it in a list:

lastEven :: [INT] → INT
lastEven bs = head (lastEvenOrEmpty bs)

Here head is another standard Haskell function, defined via foldr as follows:[1]

head :: [b] → b
head = foldr (λb _ → b) (error "Prelude.head: empty list")

Applying the original foldr/build-rule leads to the following version of lastEven:

lastEven' bs = foldl' (λa b → if even b then b else a) (error "...") bs

Surprisingly, computing lastEven' [1,2] leads to a runtime error, even though lastEven [1,2] = 2. Actually, an occurrence of seq inside the definition of foldl':

foldl' :: (a → b → a) → a → [b] → a
foldl' f = go
  where
    go a bs = **case** bs **of**
                [] → a
                b:bs' → **let** a' = f a b **in** seq a' (go a' bs')

has caused foldr/build-fusion to go wrong, in line with the observation that the rule is in general only partially correct.[2]

How, then, about our new rule that according to Theorem 6 is totally correct? Applying it to lastEven and afterwards inlining the definition of foldl' leads to the following version:

lastEven'' bs = unJ (go (J (error "Prelude.head: empty list")) bs)
  where
    go a bs = **case** bs **of**
                [] → a
                b:bs' → **let** a' = (**if** even b **then** J b **else** a) **in** seq a' (go a' bs')

Here the J-constructors prevent unwarranted encounters of seq with ⊥, so that we still have, for example, lastEven'' [1,2] = 2. Moreover, a clever compiler performing call-pattern specialisation of go for J as implemented in [8], as well as the proposed specialisation of unJ for a fixed function-call-pattern, should be able to transform the above into essentially the following definition without plumbing:

lastEven''' bs = unJ' (error "Prelude.head: empty list") bs
  where
    unJ' a bs = **case** bs **of**
                  [] → a
                  b:bs' → **let** e = even b **in** seq e (unJ' (**if** e **then** b **else** a) bs')

This is safe and effective fusion in the presence of seq!

---

[1] Actually, head is defined by direct pattern matching in the standard Haskell prelude. However, GHC features a specialised head/build-rule whose effect is exactly the same as that of the general foldr/build-rule in combination with the formulation of head in terms of foldr as given here.

[2] Clearly, without that occurrence of seq, and thus with foldl instead of its strictified version foldl', we would have obtained lastEven' [1,2] = 2.

For comparison, if we had sticked with the higher-order approach, Theorem 5 would have led us from lastEven to the following version:

lastEven'''' *bs* = go ($\lambda z \rightarrow$ error "Prelude.head: empty list") *bs* ()
  where
    go *a bs* =
      case *bs* **of**
        [] $\rightarrow$ *a*
        b:*bs'* $\rightarrow$ **let** *a'* = (**if** even *b* **then** $\lambda z \rightarrow b$ **else** *a*) **in** seq *a'* (go *a' bs'*)

This is just as safe as lastEven'' (and lastEven''') above, but seems to offer fewer possibilities for optimising the plumbing away.

6 Variation of the Dual of Classical Shortcut Fusion

Having dealt with classical foldr/build-fusion so successfully, we turn to its dual from [10], trying to tame the impact of seq on that transformation as well. Recall that the relevant combinators are defined as follows:

unfoldr :: $(c \rightarrow$ MAYBE $(b,c)) \rightarrow c \rightarrow [b]$
unfoldr *psi c* = **case** *psi c* **of**
           NOTHING $\rightarrow$ []
           JUST $(b,c') \rightarrow b$:(unfoldr *psi c'*)

destroy :: (*forall c.* $(c \rightarrow$ MAYBE $(b,c)) \rightarrow c \rightarrow a) \rightarrow [b] \rightarrow a$
destroy *g* = *g* ($\lambda bs \rightarrow$ **case** *bs* **of** {[] $\rightarrow$ NOTHING; *b*:*bs'* $\rightarrow$ JUST (b,bs')})

The destroy/unfoldr-rule tells us to replace as follows:

$$\text{destroy } g \text{ (unfoldr } psi \ c) \quad \rightsquigarrow \quad g \ psi \ c \ .$$

But in [6] we found that there are several semantic problems with this rule in Haskell. Even in the absence of seq it is no semantic equivalence, as the right-hand side might be more defined than the left-hand side. And in the presence of seq the even worse situation can occur that there is a decrease of definedness from left to right.

Based on the ideas from the previous section, we can provide a repair now. In fact, the following theorem holds, in the statement of which we use fmap from Haskell's FUNCTOR type class for brevity.

Theorem 7. *Let* T_1, T_2, *and* T_3 *be types. Let* $c :: T_2$, $psi :: T_2 \rightarrow$ MAYBE (T_1,T_2), *and*

$$g :: forall \ c. \ (c \rightarrow \text{MAYBE } (T_1,c)) \rightarrow c \rightarrow T_3 \ .$$

Then

$$\text{destroy } g \text{ (unfoldr } psi \ c) \quad \sqsubseteq \quad g \text{ (fmap (fmap J)} \ . \ psi \ . \ \text{unJ) (J } c) \ .$$

Note that the theorem has no extra preconditions. It thus recovers, for Haskell including seq, the situation that existed for the original destroy/unfoldr-rule in the absence of seq.

To evaluate the new destroy/unfoldr-rule's pragmatic worth, we again consider the sumTo-example, but this time with components expressed as follows:

upTo n = unfoldr psiUT 1 **where** psiUT i = **if** $i>n$ **then** NOTHING **else** JUST $(i, i+1)$

sum = destroy g **where** g psi c = **case** psi c **of**
$\qquad\qquad\qquad\qquad\qquad$ NOTHING $\rightarrow$ 0
$\qquad\qquad\qquad\qquad\qquad$ JUST (b,c') $\rightarrow$ $b+(g\ psi\ c')$

Inlining these two definitions into that of sumTo and applying the rule suggested by Theorem 7 leads to the following version:

sumTo$'$ n = g' (J 1)
$\quad$ **where** g' c = **let** i = unJ c **in if** $i>n$ **then** 0 **else** $i+(g'$ (J $(i+1)))$

To optimise this further, we do not even need an extension of the technique from [8]. Instead, the version of call-pattern specialisation as currently implemented in GHC suffices to give the following version:

sumTo$''$ n = g'' 1 **where** g'' i = **if** $i>n$ **then** 0 **else** $i+(g''$ $(i+1))$

Again, the "safety net" that was introduced during fusion to cope with potentially malicious uses of **seq** could be eliminated completely afterwards.

It would be interesting to see whether one can proceed similarly for stream fusion as recently proposed in [1]. This transformation is essentially derived from destroy/unfoldr-fusion and also suffers from interaction with **seq**. In particular, the authors of [1] remain rather vague on strictness issues as related to semantic correctness. A repair here would immediately benefit the safety of Haskell programs under the stream fusion optimisation scheme.

7 Discussion

During the course of this paper, we have studied various shortcut fusion rules. Our main contributions are a total correctness result for circular pfold/buildp-fusion under appropriate preconditions (Theorem 1), a corresponding partial correctness result without any preconditions (Theorem 2), an unconditionally totally correct higher-order pfold/buildp-fusion rule (Theorem 3), a variation of the latter scheme with improved sharing (Theorem 4), two unconditionally totally correct foldr/build-fusion rules (Theorems 5 and 6), an unconditionally safely approximating destroy/unfoldr-fusion rule (Theorem 7), as well as pragmatic insights about the relative effectiveness of our new rules.

To put the many rules in perspective, a few comparisons seem in place. First of all, the three flavours "parameter-passing fusion", "classical fusion", and "dual of classical fusion" address different kinds of consumer/producer-pairs, so there is no best choice among them. Below that level of distinction, however, some observations can be made.

One lesson we have learnt is that the variants pfold$'$ and buildp$'$ of pfold and buildp, respectively, are more robust with respect to sharing computation on the parameter being passed around. Independently of the correctness issue, the decision whether to prefer circular or higher-order fusion for this setting could be largely influenced by the relative impact of these two strategies on efficiency. Preliminary measurements indicate that both are about on a par, but more systematic experimentation might provide new insights here.

For classical fusion and its dual, we have proposed two alternative strategies to improve semantic properties, in particular to prevent a decrease in program definedness via transformation. Of these, we clearly favour the approach via the datatype J over the approach via extra lambda-abstractions. The reason is that we then see better potential for automatic subsequent removal of the plumbing introduced to prevent undesirable encounters between seq and $\bot$. Even for the J-approach, the situation is not yet fully satisfactory. While for our destroy/unfoldr-example standard constructor-call-pattern specialisation suffices, the kind of post-processing required in the foldr/build-setting was more ad-hoc. Hopefully, a more general solution can be found here. Otherwise, it is unclear how the better behaviour in semantic regards will weigh up against pragmatic efficiency risks. Does correctness really trump performance?

The story of new fusion rules does not end here. One reviewer proposal was to apply the J-approach also to circular pfold/buildp-fusion. In fact, the rule

$$\text{pfold } h_1 \ h_2 \ (\text{buildp } g \ c)$$
$$\rightsquigarrow$$
$$\textbf{let } (a,z) = g \ (\lambda b \ a \rightarrow \text{J} \ (h_1 \ b \ (\text{unJ } a) \ z)) \ (\text{J} \ (h_2 \ z)) \ c \textbf{ in } \text{unJ } a$$

can be shown unconditionally totally correct by a relatively straightforward adaptation of the proof in Appendix A.2, and a variant for pfold$'$ and buildp$'$ is possible as well. However, post-processing becomes even more of a problem here. Already for the repeatedAfter-example from Section 2 the above rule leads to a transformed program for which it is considerably more difficult to conceive of a successful plumbing-removal than for the examples seen in Sections 5 and 6.

Acknowledgements. I thank the anonymous reviewers for their detailed comments and suggestions, most of which I have tried to follow up on.

References

1. Coutts, D., Leshchinskiy, R., Stewart, D.: Stream fusion: From lists to streams to nothing at all. In: International Conference on Functional Programming, Proceedings, pp. 315–326. ACM Press, New York (2007)
2. Domínguez, F., Pardo, A.: Program fusion with paramorphisms. In: Mathematically Structured Functional Programming, Proceedings. Electronic Workshops in Computing, British Computer Society (2006)
3. Fernandes, J.P., Pardo, A., Saraiva, J.: A shortcut fusion rule for circular program calculation. In: Haskell Workshop, Proceedings, pp. 95–106. ACM Press, New York (2007)
4. Gill, A., Launchbury, J., Peyton Jones, S.L.: A short cut to deforestation. In: Functional Programming Languages and Computer Architecture, Proceedings, pp. 223–232. ACM Press, New York (1993)
5. Johann, P.: A generalization of short-cut fusion and its correctness proof. Higher-Order and Symbolic Computation 15(4), 273–300 (2002)

6. Johann, P., Voigtländer, J.: The impact of *seq* on free theorems-based program transformations. Fundamenta Informaticae 69(1–2), 63–102 (2006)
7. Pettorossi, A., Proietti, M.: Importing and exporting information in program development. In: Partial Evaluation and Mixed Computation, Proceedings, pp. 405–425. North-Holland, Amsterdam (1987)
8. Peyton Jones, S.L.: Call-pattern specialisation for Haskell programs. In: International Conference on Functional Programming, Proceedings, pp. 327–337. ACM Press, New York (2007)
9. Peyton Jones, S.L., Lester, D.: A modular fully-lazy lambda lifter in Haskell. Software Practice and Experience 21(5), 479–506 (1991)
10. Svenningsson, J.: Shortcut fusion for accumulating parameters & zip-like functions. In: International Conference on Functional Programming, Proceedings, pp. 124–132. ACM Press, New York (2002)
11. Takano, A., Meijer, E.: Shortcut deforestation in calculational form. In: Functional Programming Languages and Computer Architecture, Proceedings, pp. 306–313. ACM Press, New York (1995)
12. Voigtländer, J.: Concatenate, reverse and map vanish for free. In: International Conference on Functional Programming, Proceedings, pp. 14–25. ACM Press, New York (2002)
13. Voigtländer, J.: Using circular programs to deforest in accumulating parameters. Higher-Order and Symbolic Computation 17(1–2), 129–163 (2004)
14. Voigtländer, J.: Proving correctness via free theorems: The case of the destroy/build-rule. In: Partial Evaluation and Semantics-Based Program Manipulation, Proceedings, pp. 13–20. ACM Press, New York (2008)
15. Wadler, P.: Theorems for free! In: Functional Programming Languages and Computer Architecture, Proceedings, pp. 347–359. ACM Press, New York (1989)

A Proofs Appendix

A.1 Proof of Lemma 1

Proof. The "equational" free theorem derived from the type of g is that for every choice of types T and T', strict and total $f :: T \to T'$, and arbitrary $p :: T_1 \to T \to T$ and $q :: T_1 \to T' \to T'$,

$$((p \neq \bot \Leftrightarrow q \neq \bot)$$
$$\wedge \; \forall \, b :: T_1. \; (p \, b \neq \bot \Leftrightarrow q \, b \neq \bot) \wedge \forall \, bs :: T. \; f \, (p \, b \, bs) = q \, b \, (f \, bs))$$
$$\Rightarrow \forall \, u :: T, \, c :: T_2.$$
$$(g \, p \, u \, c, \, g \, q \, (f \, u) \, c) \in \{(\bot,\bot)\} \cup \{((bs,z),(bs',z')) \mid f \, bs = bs' \wedge z = z'\}$$

We instantiate $T = [T_1]$, $p = (:)$, and $u = []$, observe that then $p \neq \bot$ and $p \, b \neq \bot$ for every $b :: T_1$, and use the definition of buildp. This gives that if the precondition (1) holds, then for every $c :: T_2$,

$$(\text{buildp} \, g \, c, \, g \, q \, (f \, []) \, c) \in \{(\bot,\bot)\} \cup \{((bs,z),(bs',z')) \mid f \, bs = bs' \wedge z = z'\}.$$

The lemma follows easily from this. □

A.2 Proof of Theorem 1

We need the following auxiliary lemma.

Lemma 3. *Let* T_1, T_3, *and* T_4 *be types. Let* $h_1 :: T_1 \to T_4 \to T_3 \to T_4$, $h_2 :: T_3 \to T_4$, $bs :: [T_1]$, *and* $z' :: T_3$. *Then*

$$\text{fst } (\text{fix } (\lambda \,\tilde{}(\_,z) \to (\text{foldr } (\lambda b\ a \to h_1\ b\ a\ z)\ (h_2\ z)\ bs, z')))$$

is equivalent to

$$\text{foldr } (\lambda b\ a \to h_1\ b\ a\ z')\ (h_2\ z')\ bs\,.$$

Proof. Let $\text{exp} = \text{fix } (\lambda \,\tilde{}(\_,z) \to (\text{foldr } (\lambda b\ a \to h_1\ b\ a\ z)\ (h_2\ z)\ bs, z'))$. It is easy to see that exp is equivalent to

$$(\lambda z \to (\text{foldr } (\lambda b\ a \to h_1\ b\ a\ z)\ (h_2\ z)\ bs, z'))\ (\text{snd exp})\,.$$

This implies that fst exp is equivalent to

$$\text{foldr } (\lambda b\ a \to h_1\ b\ a\ (\text{snd exp}))\ (h_2\ (\text{snd exp}))\ bs\,,$$

while snd exp is equivalent to z'. The lemma follows easily from these facts. □

Now we can prove Theorem 1.

Proof. For every $z :: T_3$, Lemma 1 with $T' = T_4$, $q = (\lambda b\ a \to h_1\ b\ a\ z)$, and $f = \text{foldr } (\lambda b\ a \to h_1\ b\ a\ z)\ (h_2\ z)$ gives

$$g\ (\lambda b\ a \to h_1\ b\ a\ z)\ (h_2\ z)\ c$$
$$=$$
$$\textbf{case } \text{buildp } g\ c\ \textbf{of } (bs,z') \to (\text{foldr } (\lambda b\ a \to h_1\ b\ a\ z)\ (h_2\ z)\ bs, z')\,.$$

Note that the assumptions on h_1 and h_2 are equivalent to the requirement that the chosen f is strict and total for every $z :: T_3$.

We express

$$\textbf{let } (a,z) = g\ (\lambda b\ a \to h_1\ b\ a\ z)\ (h_2\ z)\ c\ \textbf{in } a$$

via explicit fixpoint recursion as follows:

$$\text{fst } (\text{fix } (\lambda \,\tilde{}(\_,z) \to g\ (\lambda b\ a \to h_1\ b\ a\ z)\ (h_2\ z)\ c))\,.$$

By the above, this is equivalent to

$$\text{fst } (\text{fix } (\lambda \,\tilde{}(\_,z) \to \textbf{case } \text{buildp } g\ c\ \textbf{of}$$
$$(bs,z') \to (\text{foldr } (\lambda b\ a \to h_1\ b\ a\ z)\ (h_2\ z)\ bs, z')))\,.$$

The subexpression $\text{buildp } g\ c$ is either equivalent to $\bot$ or to (bs,z') for some fixed bs and z'. In both cases, the full expression is equivalent to

$$\textbf{case } \text{buildp } g\ c\ \textbf{of } (bs,z') \to \text{foldr } (\lambda b\ a \to h_1\ b\ a\ z')\ (h_2\ z')\ bs\,.$$

If $\text{buildp } g\ c = \bot$, then this equivalence holds by $\text{fst } (\text{fix } (\lambda\_ \to \bot)) = \bot$. Otherwise, it follows from Lemma 3. By the definition of pfold we finally get equivalence to $\text{pfold } h_1\ h_2\ (\text{buildp } g\ c)$. □

A Generalization of the Folding Rule
for the Clark-Kunen Semantics[*]

Javier Álvez and Paqui Lucio

Basque Country University
{javier.alvez,paqui.lucio}@ehu.es

Abstract. In this paper, we propose more flexible applicability conditions for the folding rule that increase the power of existing unfold/fold systems for normal logic programs. Our generalized folding rule enables new transformation sequences that, in particular, are suitable for recursion introduction and local variable elimination. We provide some illustrative examples and give a detailed proof of correctness w.r.t. the Clark-Kunen semantics.

1 Introduction

Unfold/fold transformation systems were originally adapted by Tamaki and Sato in [29] to logic programming from the well-known Burstall-Darlington method for functional programming (see [7]). Tamaki and Sato's seminal unfold/fold system works on definite logic programs preserving their equivalence in the sense of the least Herbrand model. Since then, unfold/fold transformations of logic programs have been extensively studied and used (see [23] for a survey). In particular, different extensions of the Tamaki and Sato's system for dealing with negation have been proposed. The various semantics of negation in logic programming lead to different requirements in transformation rules depending on which semantics is intended to be preserved. The main motivation of this paper comes from our previous work (see [20,2]) in constructive negation (see [8]), which is sound and complete w.r.t. the Clark-Kunen semantics (see [9,18]). Hence, we are interested in transformation systems that preserve the Clark-Kunen semantics. The choice of the negation semantics is crucial for defining the side conditions of transformation rules. The following example illustrates this point.

Example 1. Given the following two clauses

P_0:   1. $p \leftarrow q, r$ 2. $q \leftarrow q$

by unfolding q in the body of clause 1 with clause 2 we obtain clause 3, which is a copy of the clause 1

P_1:   3. $p \leftarrow q, r$ 2. $q \leftarrow q$.

---

[*] This work has been partially supported by Spanish Project TIN2004-079250-C03-03.

Now, if we allow to fold the body of the clause 3 using clause 1 (which can be seen as either a self-folding or a folding with a deleted clause) then we obtain

P_2:   4. $p \leftarrow p$ 2. $q \leftarrow q$.   □

First, note that the programs in the above example are propositional and positive, which makes more intrinsic the following problem. Let us consider another popular declarative semantics for negation: the well-founded semantics (see [14]). The programs P_0 and P_1 are equivalent w.r.t. both the Clark-Kunen and the well-founded semantics. Besides, P_0 and P_2 are equivalent w.r.t. the well-founded semantics, but they are not equivalent w.r.t. the Clark-Kunen semantics. More precisely, the well-founded model of P_0 and P_2 is ($\emptyset$, $\{p, q, r\}$), where no atom is *true* nor undefined and every atom is assigned to be *false*. However, Clark's completion of P_0 is

$$(p \leftrightarrow (q \wedge r)) \wedge (q \leftrightarrow q) \wedge (r \leftrightarrow false)$$

so that $\neg p$ is a three-valued consequence of it, whereas P_2's completion is

$$(p \leftrightarrow p) \wedge (q \leftrightarrow q) \wedge (r \leftrightarrow false)$$

and $\neg p$ is not a three-valued consequence of P_2's completion. Therefore, we need to provide extra-conditions to the folding rule in order to preserve the Clark-Kunen semantics, but these extra-conditions would be unnecessary if we considered the well-founded semantics.

There are many proposals for extending Tamaki and Sato's system (see [29]) for dealing with different semantic notions of negation. Seki (see [27]) showed that the system in [29] does not preserve finite-failure and introduced a modified folding rule that preserves finite failure and perfect model semantics in stratified normal programs. An extension of this system for general logic programs and for well-founded semantics was presented in [28]. The folding rule of [29] was also generalized in [15] to a simultaneous folding rule. Maher (see [22]) also extended the system to stratified general programs and the perfect model semantics. A more recent work on preserving stable and well-founded model semantics is [24].[1] In fact, as shown in Example 1, all these transformation systems do not preserve, in general, the Clark-Kunen semantics. Regarding the systems designed to preserve some completion-related semantics (see [21,13,5]), they enforce very rigid transformations. Indeed, they disable some useful transformations which do not spoil correctness w.r.t. the Clark-Kunen semantics, as illustrated in the next example.

Example 2. Given the following definition of a predicate q such that $q(x_1, x_2)$ checks whether the list x_1 is not a sublist of x_2

1. $q(x_1, x_2) \leftarrow member(y, x_1), \neg member(y, x_2)$
2. $member(v, [v|_-]) \leftarrow$
3. $member(v_1, [_-|v_2]) \leftarrow member(v_1, v_2)$.

---

[1] It is well known that the well-founded model is one of the stable models, which is minimal in some sense.

First, we unfold $member(y, x_1)$ in clause 1 w.r.t. clauses 2 and 3

4. $q([z_1|_-], z_2) \leftarrow \neg member(z_1, z_2)$
5. $q([_-|z_1], z_2) \leftarrow member(w, z_1), \neg member(w, z_2)$.

Then, we fold clause 5 using clause 1, which has been removed in the previous step. The resulting definition of q is

4. $q([z_1|_-], z_2) \leftarrow \neg member(z_1, z_2)$
6. $q([_-|z_1], z_2) \leftarrow q(z_1, z_2)$.   □

The transformation in Example 2 is forbidden in all the existing systems which consider completion-related semantics, in spite of the fact that it is correct w.r.t. the Clark-Kunen semantics. For example, the so-called *reversible folding* requires the folded and folder clauses to be in the current program. This is the folding used in [21,13]. In the above Example 2, the folder clause is not in the current program, hence the systems in [21,13] cannot be used. In [5], folding is allowed through the use of semantic conditions if the folded clause comes from the folder one, which has to be non-recursive, and all the literals to be folded have been obtained by unfolding. In Example 2, the literal[2] $\neg member(w, z_2)$ is inherited from the original program, thus it is not the result of an unfolding step. Other systems split the predicates into *new/old* predicates, where the old predicates cannot depend on the new predicates and the new predicates are non-recursive. This is case in the previously cited system in [27] where the following two conditions are required:

(1) only the clauses with a new predicate in its head can be used as folder clauses, and
(2) the predicate in the head of the folded clause is an old predicate or all the literals to be folded are the result of a previous unfolding.

In Example 2, the predicate in the head of the folder and folded clause is the same (that is, the predicate q), thus we cannot use the system in [27] since $\neg member(w, z_2)$ is inherited from the original program. The four-step transformation schema proposed in [6] uses the same partition of predicates, and, once again, when the predicate in the head of the folded clause is new, all the literals to be folded have to be the result of an unfolding, therefore this system cannot be used in Example 2. Finally, the folding rule in the system proposed in [25] for first-order general programs, which also uses the new/old partition,[3] requires the same condition.

In this paper, we introduce a transformation system for normal logic programs that preserves the Clark-Kunen semantics and is more flexible than the existing ones with the following two advantages:

1. the folder clause can be taken from any program in the transformation sequence.
2. the folded literals do not necessarily come from unfolding.

---

[2] The negative character of the literal is not relevant for this discussion.
[3] By contrast, the new predicates can be recursive in this proposal.

Outline of the paper. In the next section, Section 2, which is split in three sub-sections, we establish the notations and describe necessary results on semantics of logic programs and unfold/fold systems. Section 3 is devoted to defining new conditions for the folding rule, where we motivate the problem using some examples and we then prove the correctness of the resulting system. In Section 4, we give some concluding remarks and indicate some of the open problems which need to be solved. The interested reader is referred to [1] for an extended version of this paper, where we provide the formal proofs of Lemma 1 and Theorems 3 and 4.

2 Preliminaries

We assume that the reader is familiar with the basic concepts of logic programming. Throughout the paper we use the standard terminology of [19] and [3]. In particular, we will use the standard notions of substitution of variables by terms, unifier and most general unifier (briefly mgu). A *bar* is used to abbreviate tuples of objects. For example, $\overline{x}$ denotes a tuple of variables $x_1, \ldots, x_n$, the tuple of literals $L_1, \ldots, L_n$ is denoted by $\overline{L}$ and the substitution $\sigma = \{x_1 \leftarrow t_1, \ldots, x_n \leftarrow t_n\}$ is abbreviated as $\{\overline{x} \leftarrow \overline{t}\}$. Besides, σ is sometimes interpreted as the conjunction of equations $x_1 \approx t_1 \wedge \ldots \wedge x_n \approx t_n$ (abbreviated as $\overline{x} \approx \overline{t}$), and hence $\neg \sigma$ is interpreted as the disjunction of disequations $x_1 \not\approx t_1 \vee \ldots \vee x_n \not\approx t_n$ (abbreviated as $\overline{x} \not\approx \overline{t}$).

We consider *(normal) logic programs* which are finite sequences (not sets) of normal clauses of the form $A \leftarrow \overline{L}$. Throughout this work, programs are given modulo reordering of the literals in bodies and standardization apart is always assumed.

The *definition of the atom L in a program P*, denoted by $\mathtt{Def}_P[L]$, is the sequence of clauses from P such that its clause head unifies with L. If L is a flat atom on the predicate p, then we also say that $\mathtt{Def}_P[L]$ is the *definition of the predicate p*.

We use the classical notion of resolution as defined in [17]. A goal $(\overline{K}, L, \overline{M})$ *resolves to* $(\overline{K}, \overline{N}, \overline{M})\theta$, denoted by $(\overline{K}, L, \overline{M}) \Longrightarrow (\overline{K}, \overline{N}, \overline{M})\theta$, if there exists a clause $H \leftarrow \overline{N} \in \mathtt{Def}_P[L]$ such that $\theta = \mathtt{mgu}(H, L)$. A *derivation from $\overline{L}^0$ to $\overline{L}^n$*, denoted by $\overline{L}^0 \Longrightarrow^* \overline{L}^n$, is a sequence of n resolution steps $\overline{L}^0 \Longrightarrow \overline{L}_1 \Longrightarrow \ldots \Longrightarrow \overline{L}^{n-1} \Longrightarrow \overline{L}^n$.

An atom L *directly depends on the atom N* in a program P iff there exists a clause $(H \leftarrow \overline{B}) \in \mathtt{Def}_P[L]$ such that $N \in \overline{B}$. Besides, L is also said to *directly depend* on every clause in $\mathtt{Def}_P[L]$. The *dependence* relation on atoms/clauses is given by the reflexive and transitive closure of the directly dependence relation.

2.1 The Clark-Kunen Semantics and Non-failure

In [9], Clark proposed the following to complete the definition of predicates. Supposing that $\mathtt{Def}_P[p(\overline{x})]$ consists of the following m clauses $\langle\, p(\overline{t}^k) \leftarrow \overline{B}^k \mid 1 \leq k \leq m \,\rangle$, the *completion formula of a predicate* $p \in \mathtt{Pred}_{\mathcal{L}}(P)$ is

$$(\, p(\overline{x}) \ \leftrightarrow \ \bigvee_{k=1}^{m} \exists \overline{z}^k \, (\, \overline{x} \approx \overline{t}^k \wedge \overline{B}^k \,) \,)^{\forall} \tag{1}$$

where $\overline{z}^k = \mathtt{Var}(\overline{t}^k \cdot \overline{B}^k)$ for each $1 \leq k \leq m$. If $m = 0$, then it is equivalent to $(\, p(\overline{x}) \ \leftrightarrow \ false \,)^{\forall}$. The *Clark completion of a program* P, denoted by $\mathtt{Comp}(P)$, consists of the conjunction of the completion formulas of each predicate $p \in \mathtt{Pred}_{\mathcal{L}}(P)$ and the axioms of the *free equality theory* $\mathtt{FET}_{\mathcal{L}}$ (see [10]). Whenever the definition of p is free of local variables, the negation of (1)

$$(\, \neg p(\overline{x}) \ \leftrightarrow \ \bigwedge_{k=1}^{m} \forall \overline{z}^k \, (\, \overline{x} \not\approx \overline{t}^k \vee \neg \overline{B}^k \,) \,)^{\forall}$$

can be transformed (see [26,4]) into a logically equivalent formula of the form

$$(\, \neg p(\overline{x}) \ \leftrightarrow \ \bigvee_{h=1}^{n} \exists \overline{w}^h \, (\, \overline{x} \approx \overline{s}^h \wedge \overline{M}^h \,) \,)^{\forall}.$$

From this formula, we obtain a finite sequence of expressions

$$\langle \, \neg p(\overline{s}^h) \leftarrow \overline{M}^h \mid 1 \leq h \leq n \, \rangle$$

which yields $\mathtt{Def}_P[\neg p(\overline{x})]$. Otherwise, if some clause in $\mathtt{Def}_P[p(\overline{x})]$ contains local variables, then we consider that $\mathtt{Def}_P[\neg p(\overline{x})]$ is undefined, i.e. $\neg p(\overline{x})$ has no definition. Once we have a definition for negative literals, the dependence relation is extended to negative literals in the natural way.

Example 3. Let us consider the following definition of the predicate *member*

1. $member(v, [v|\_]) \leftarrow$
2. $member(v_1, [\_|v_2]) \leftarrow member(v_1, v_2) \, .$

The completion formula of member is

$$(\, member(x_1, x_2) \leftrightarrow \exists v, v' \, (\, x_1 \approx v \wedge x_2 \approx [v|v'] \,) \vee$$
$$\exists v_1, v_2, v'' \, (\, x_1 \approx v_1 \wedge x_2 \approx [v''|v_2] \wedge member(v_1, v_2) \,) \,)^{\forall}.$$

From the above formula, we obtain

$$(\, \neg member(x_1, x_2) \leftrightarrow \forall v, v' \, (\, x_1 \not\approx v \vee x_2 \not\approx [v|v'] \,) \wedge$$
$$\forall v_1, v_2, v'' \, (\, x_1 \not\approx v_1 \vee x_2 \not\approx [v''|v_2] \vee \neg member(v_1, v_2) \,).$$

Refining the right-hand subformula, we get

$$(\, \neg member(x_1, x_2) \leftrightarrow [\, \forall v' \, (\, x_2 \not\approx [x_1|v'] \,) \wedge \forall v_2, v'' \, (\, x_2 \not\approx [v''|v_2] \,) \,] \vee$$
$$[\, \forall v' \, (\, x_2 \not\approx [x_1|v'] \,) \wedge$$
$$\exists v_1, v_2, v'' \, (\, x_1 \approx v_1 \wedge x_2 \approx [v''|v_2] \wedge \neg member(v_1, v_2) \,)$$

which is, after simplification, equivalent to

$$(\neg member(x_1, x_2) \leftrightarrow \exists z_1, z_2 \ (\ x_1 \approx z_1 \wedge x_2 \approx z_2 \wedge \forall y_1, y_2 \ (\ z_2 \not\approx [y_1|y_2] \ ) \ ) \vee$$
$$\exists z_1, z_2, z_3 \ (\ x_1 \approx z_1 \wedge x_2 \approx [z_2|z_3] \wedge z_1 \not\approx z_2 \wedge$$
$$\neg member(z_1, z_3) \ ).$$

Since the second argument of $member$ is a list from the last formula we can obtain the following normal[4] clauses that define $\neg member$

3. $\neg member(\_, [\,]) \leftarrow$
4. $\neg member(w_1, [w_2|w_3]) \leftarrow w_1 \not\approx w_2, \ \neg member(w_1, w_3)$. $\square$

In this work, the semantics given to a program is the *Clark-Kunen semantics* as proposed in [18]; that is, the three-valued logical consequence of the Clark completion. Following [23], the *Clark-Kunen semantics of a program P* is defined by

$$\mathtt{COMP}[P, \leftarrow \overline{L}] = \{ \ c \ | \ \mathtt{Comp}(P) \models_3 (\overline{L} \wedge c)^\vee \ \}$$

where $\leftarrow \overline{L}$ is a goal, c is a general equality constraint and $\models_3$ stands for the three-valued logical consequence relation, as defined in [18]. Regarding equivalence of programs, we consider that two programs P_1 and P_2 are *equivalent*, denoted by $P_1 \equiv P_2$, iff the set of logical consequences of $\mathtt{Comp}(P_1)$ and $\mathtt{Comp}(P_2)$ are identical.

Definition 1. *Given two programs P_1 and P_2,*

(i) $P_1 \preceq P_2$ iff $\mathtt{COMP}[P_1, \leftarrow \overline{L}] \subseteq \mathtt{COMP}[P_2, \leftarrow \overline{L}]$ for any goal $\leftarrow \overline{L}$.

(ii) $P_1 \equiv P_2$ iff $P_1 \preceq P_2$ and $P_2 \preceq P_1$. $\square$

A desirable property of a semantic notion is *relevance*, which is defined in [12] and extensively used in [23]. Intuitively, a semantics is relevant iff the semantic value of any goal $\leftarrow \overline{L}$ w.r.t. a program P is exactly given by the clauses on which the literals in $\overline{L}$ depend. In the absence of relevance, some transformation rules, such as *new definition* and *deletion*, are not trivially correct (see [23]). As defined above, the Clark-Kunen semantics is relevant. However, by changing $\models_3$ by the classical bi-valued logical consequence notion (as in [23]), relevance is lost.

Finally, we define the class of goals that do not fail on some variables.

Definition 2. *Let P be a program, $\leftarrow \overline{L}$ a goal and $\overline{x} \subseteq \mathtt{Var}(\overline{L})$. The goal $\leftarrow \overline{L}$ is non-failing on $\overline{x}$ w.r.t. P iff for all substitution σ of domain $\overline{x}$ and any fair literal selection rule there exists a derivation starting from $\leftarrow \overline{L}\sigma$ that does not fail.* $\square$

Next, we illustrate the notion of non-failing goals with two examples.

---

[4] $\ w_1 \not\approx w_2$ is a negative literal since $\approx$ should be defined by the single clause $x \approx x \leftarrow$.

Example 4. Let us consider the following program

1. $add(0, n, n)$
2. $add(s(n_1), n_2, s(n_3)) \leftarrow add(n_1, n_2, n_3)$.

The literal $add(x_1, x_2, x_3)$ is non-failing on the variables $\{x_1, x_2\}$. However, the literal $add(x_1, x_2, x_3)$ is failing on $\{x_2, x_3\}$. □

Example 5. Let us consider the following program

1. $ack(0, n, s(n))$
2. $ack(s(n_1), 0, n_2) \leftarrow ack(n_1, s(0), n_2)$
3. $ack(s(n_1), s(n_2), n_3) \leftarrow ack(s(n_1), n_2, y), \ ack(n_1, y, n_3)$.

The goal $ack(s(x_1), x_2, v), \ ack(x_1, v, x_3)$ is non-failing on $\{x_3\}$. □

The interested reader is referred to [11] for details on algorithms that decide if a goal is non-failing. Roughly speaking, given a goal G and a set $\bar{x}$ of its variables, the algorithm checks whether the set of constraints associated to all the non-failing goals that can be obtained by resolution from G covers all the possible values for $\bar{x}$. According to [11], the covering problem is co-NP-hard.

2.2 Unfold-Fold Transformation Systems

In this section, we recall the classical unfold/fold transformation rules that were introduced in [29], adapting them to our notation. We also provide some well-known correctness results that we will use later.

A sequence of programs $\langle P_0, \ \ldots, \ P_n \rangle$ is a *transformation sequence* if for each $1 \leq i \leq n$, P_i is the result of transforming P_{i-1} using some rule. Besides, $\langle P_0, \ \ldots, \ P_n \rangle$ is *correct* if P_0 and P_i are equivalent for every $1 \leq i \leq n$. By extension, a transformation rule is said to be *correct* if it preserves equivalence.

Program transformation systems usually work with some information related to the transformation process itself. For example, in *à la Tamaki-Sato* systems (see [28,29]), the clauses that are obtained after unfolding are marked *"foldable"*. In [25], literals (instead of clauses) are marked *"foldable"*. In other systems (see [16]), counters of unfolding/folding steps are associated with clauses in order to both formulate folding applicability conditions and to characterize the improvement of execution. In this paper, we associate two natural numbers $\langle L_{\text{unf}}, \ L_{\text{fld}} \rangle$ with each body literal L, called *unfolding* and *folding time-stamps*. A time-stamp $L_{\text{unf}} \ / \ L_{\text{fld}}$ is either zero or the index i of the program P_i in the transformation sequence $\langle P_0, \ \ldots, \ P_n \rangle$ in which L is obtained by unfolding/folding. Hence, in the initial program P_0, all time-stamp are zero and they are appropriately updated at each transformation step.

Before recalling the usual rules in unfold/fold systems, let us fix the following conventions that we will use in the formulation of the transformation rules:

(1) we always refer to a transformation sequence $\langle P_0, \ \ldots, \ P_i \rangle$,
(2) P_{i+1} is the next program obtained by the transformation from P_i, and

(3) if a clause C has not been transformed from P_i to P_{i+1}, then the time-stamps for the literals in C are equal in both programs.

Next, we re-formulate unfold/fold systems incorporating time-stamps issues.

Rule 1. New Definition. If $p \notin \bigcup_{j=0}^{i} \text{Pred}_{\mathcal{L}}(P_j)$ and $S = \langle C_1, \ldots, C_m \rangle$ is a definition of the predicate p such that $\text{Pred}_{\mathcal{L}}(S) \subseteq (\text{Pred}_{\mathcal{L}}(P_i) \cup \{p\})$, then $P_{i+1} = P_i \cup S$. The pair of time-stamps $\langle L_{\text{unf}}, L_{\text{fld}} \rangle$ is $\langle 0, 0 \rangle$ for every literal L occurring in the body of any clause from S.

Rule 2. Unfolding. If $C = H \leftarrow \overline{M}$, L is a clause in P_i (unfolded clause) and $\text{Def}_{P_j}[L] = \langle\, L_k \leftarrow \overline{N}^k \mid 1 \leq k \leq m \,\rangle$ for some $0 \leq j \leq i$, then $P_{i+1} = (P_i \setminus C) \cup \langle\, (H \leftarrow \overline{M}, \overline{N}^k)\theta_k \mid 1 \leq k \leq m \,\rangle$ where $\theta_k = mgu(L, L_k)$ for every $1 \leq k \leq m$. For every clause $(H \leftarrow \overline{M}, \overline{N}^k)\theta_k$ in the program P_{i+1}, the pair of time-stamps $\langle N'_{\text{unf}}, N'_{\text{fld}} \rangle$ is $\langle i+1, L_{\text{fld}} \rangle$ for each literal $N' \in \overline{N}^k \theta_k$ and, besides, the pair $\langle M'_{\text{unf}}, M'_{\text{fld}} \rangle$ is equal to $\langle M_{\text{unf}}, M_{\text{fld}} \rangle$ in P_i for each $M' = M\theta_k \in \overline{M}\theta_k$.

If $P_i = P_j$ and the unfolded clause $(H \leftarrow \overline{M}, L) \in \text{Def}_{P_j}[L]$, then the Unfolding transformation is said to be a *self-unfolding*.

Rule 3. Folding. If $H \leftarrow \overline{M}$, $\overline{N}$ is a clause in P_i (folded clause), $L \leftarrow \overline{N}'$ is a clause in P_j (folder clause) for some $0 \leq j \leq i$ and σ is a substitution such that

(a) $\text{domain}(\sigma) = \text{Var}(L)$,
(b) $H \leftarrow \overline{M}$, $\overline{N}$ and $H \leftarrow \overline{M}$, $\overline{N}'\sigma$ are equal modulo variable renaming,
(c) $L \leftarrow \overline{N}'$ is the only clause in P_j whose head is unifiable with $L\sigma$,

then $P_{i+1} = (\, P_i \setminus (H \leftarrow \overline{M}, \overline{N})\,) \cup (H \leftarrow \overline{M}, L\sigma)$. The pair of time-stamps $\langle L\sigma_{\text{unf}}, L\sigma_{\text{fld}} \rangle$ is $\langle 0, i+1 \rangle$. Besides, the pair $\langle M_{\text{unf}}, M_{\text{fld}} \rangle$ in P_{i+1} is equal to $\langle M_{\text{unf}}, M_{\text{fld}} \rangle$ in P_i for each $M \in \overline{M}$.

Rule 4. Deletion. If S is the definition of the predicate p in P_i, $p \notin \text{Pred}_{\mathcal{L}}(P_0)$ and $p \notin \text{Pred}_{\mathcal{L}}(P_i \setminus S)$, then $P_{i+1} = (P_i \setminus S)$.

Note that the above rules can be used only if the definition of the involved literals exists. The definition of every positive literal always exists, but this is not the case for negative literals.

Using the above set of rules, an unfold/fold transformation system that preserves the Clark-Kunen semantics was introduced in [13].

Theorem 1. *[13]* If $\langle P_0, \ldots, P_n \rangle$ is a transformation sequence that is obtained using the rules New Definition, Unfolding, Folding and Deletion with the following two restrictions for each $0 \leq i \leq n - 1$

- Unfolding is applied at the step $i + 1$ only if it is not self-unfolding and the definition of the unfolded literal is taken from P_i,
- Folding is applied at the step $i + 1$ only if the folder clause is taken from P_i and is different from the folded one,

then P_0 and P_j are equivalent for every $0 \leq j \leq n$.

Proof. A formal proof of this result can be found in [13]. In fact, the authors provide a stronger result there since they prove the preservation of equivalence w.r.t. completion semantics. In particular, the rules New Definition and Deletion are correct since the Clark-Kunen semantics and completion semantics are relevant.   □

In the above unfold/fold transformation system, self-unfolding is not allowed. Next, we show that it is possible to prove the correctness w.r.t. the Clark-Kunen semantics if we allow self-unfolding. However, it is well known that self-unfolding does not preserve completion semantics (see [21]); that is, the logical equivalence between programs' completion.

Lemma 1. *Let* $\langle P_0, \ldots, P_i \rangle$ *be a correct transformation sequence. If the program* P_{i+1} *is obtained by self-unfolding, then* $P_{i+1} \equiv P_j$ *for every* $1 \leq j \leq i$.

The next theorem is a direct consequence of Theorem 1 and Lemma 1.

Theorem 2. *If* $\langle P_0, \ldots, P_n \rangle$ *is a transformation sequence that is obtained using the rules* New Definition, Unfolding, Folding *and* Deletion *with the following two restrictions for each* $0 \leq i \leq n - 1$

- Unfolding *is applied at the step* $i + 1$ *only if the definition of the unfolded literal is taken from* P_i,
- Folding *is applied at the step* $i + 1$ *only if the folder clause is taken from* P_i *and is different from the folded one,*

then P_0 *and* P_j *are equivalent for every* $0 \leq j \leq n$.

However, Example 2 shows a natural way for obtaining a recursive definition that cannot be obtained by the system described in Theorem 2.

3   Generalized Folding

In this section, we introduce less restrictive conditions for the rule Folding than the ones in Theorem 2. Our main aim is twofold. First, we will allow the folder clause to be taken from any program in the transformation sequence $\langle P_0, \ldots, P_i \rangle$. Second, we relax the requirement that every folded literal should come from unfolding. In our proposal, this condition is combined with a non-failure requirement of the literals that do not come from unfolding.

   If the folder clause comes from the actual program P_i, then Theorem 2 only requires the folder and the folded clause to be different, because the so-called self-folding is clearly incorrect. Note that the result of folding a clause $p \leftarrow r$ with itself is $p \leftarrow p$. Besides, when the folder clause could come from a program P_j where $0 \leq j < i$, the self-folding transformation sometimes involves several clauses, which makes difficult to detect it. As a consequence, applicability conditions must be carefully designed to avoid problems related to the self-folding. The following example tries to illustrate this kind of problems.

Example 6. Let us consider the following transformation sequence.

$P_0:$ 1. $p \leftarrow r$ 2. $q \leftarrow r$ 3. $r \leftarrow$

(by folding r in the clause 1 using the clause 2 of P_0)

$P_1:$ 4. $p \leftarrow q$ 2. $q \leftarrow r$ 3. $r \leftarrow$

(by folding r in the clause 2 using the clause 1 of P_0)

$P_2:$ 4. $p \leftarrow q$ 5. $q \leftarrow p$ 3. $r \leftarrow.$

The first two programs are trivially equivalent. However, the goal $\leftarrow p$ loops in P_2, whereas it succeeds in the programs P_0 and P_1.   □

In order to prove that a transformation rule preserves equivalence we have to ensure that $P_{i+1} \preceq P_i$ and $P_i \preceq P_{i+1}$. In Theorem 3, we show that $P_{i+1} \preceq P_i$ holds whenever P_{i+1} is obtained by Folding from P_i.

Theorem 3. *Let* $\langle P_0, \ldots, P_i \rangle$ *be a correct transformation sequence. If the program* P_{i+1} *is obtained by the rule* Folding, *then* $P_{i+1} \preceq P_j$ *for every* $1 \leq j \leq i$.

However, when allowing use of a folder clause from any program in the transformation sequence, additional conditions are necessary in order to accomplish that $P_i \preceq P_{i+1}$. We formulate (in Theorem 4) side conditions for the Folding rule that depend on the literal that is introduced by Folding. To that end, we first introduce the following notion of fold-partitioned goals.

Definition 3. *Let* $\langle P_0, \ldots, P_j, \ldots, P_i \rangle$ *be a transformation sequence and* $(H \leftarrow \overline{M}, \overline{N}) \in P_i$, $(L \leftarrow \overline{N'}) \in P_j$ *be two clauses such that* $\overline{N} = \overline{N'}\sigma$. *The goals* $\leftarrow \overline{N}$ *and* $\leftarrow \overline{N'}$ *are fold-partitioned by* j *into* $\leftarrow \overline{A}, \overline{B}$ *and* $\leftarrow \overline{A'}, \overline{B'}$ *iff*

- $N_{\mathtt{fld}} \leq j$ *for every* $N \in \overline{N}$,
- $B_{\mathtt{unf}} > j$ *for every* $B \in \overline{B}$,
- *no literal in* $\overline{B'}$ *depends on* L *in* P_j.   □

Now, we can formulate the side conditions for Folding in Theorem 4.

Theorem 4. *If* $\langle P_0, \ldots, P_n \rangle$ *is a transformation sequence that is obtained using the rules* New Definition, Unfolding, Folding *and* Deletion *with the following restrictions for each* $0 \leq i \leq n - 1$

- Unfolding *is applied at step* $i + 1$ *only if the definition of the unfolded literal is taken from* P_i.
- Folding *is applied at the step* $i + 1$ *if the folded clause* $(H \leftarrow \overline{M}, \overline{N}) \in P_i$ *and the folder clause* $(L \leftarrow \overline{N'}) \in P_j$ *such that* $0 \leq j \leq i$ *and* $\sigma = \mathtt{mgu}(\overline{N}, \overline{N'})$ *satisfies one of the following conditions:*
  (1) $i = j$ *and the folded clause is different from the folder one.*
  (2) $i > j$ *and the literal* $L\sigma$ *does not depend on* H *in the program* P_i.
  (3) $i > j$, H *and* L *are unifiable,* $\leftarrow \overline{N}$ *is fold-partitioned by* j *into* $\leftarrow \overline{A}, \overline{B}$ *and* $\overline{A}$ *is non-failing on* $\mathtt{Var}(L\sigma)$.

Then, P_0 *and* P_k *are equivalent for every* $0 \leq k \leq n$.

In the above theorem, condition (1) is given by Theorem 2. In condition (2), the literal introduced by Folding does not depend on the head of the folded clause in the program P_i. Condition (2) is illustrated by means of the following example.

Example 7. Given the following program P_1

    1. $add(0, n, n) \leftarrow$
    2. $add(s(n_1), n_2, s(n_3)) \leftarrow add(n_1, n_2, n_3)$
    3. $add3(n_1, n_2, n_3, n_4) \leftarrow add(n_1, n_2, y), \; add(y, n_3, n_4)$.

First, we unfold the literal $add(n_1, n_2, y)$ in clause 3, obtaining

    4. $add3(0, n_2, n_3, n_4) \leftarrow add(n_2, n_3, n_4)$
    5. $add3(s(n_1), n_2, n_3, n_4) \leftarrow add(n_1, n_2, y), \; add(s(y), n_3, n_4)$

and then we unfold the literal $add(s(y), n_3, n_4)$ in clause 5, which yields

    6. $add3(s(n_1), n_2, n_3, s(n_4)) \leftarrow add(n_1, n_2, y), \; add(y, n_3, n_4)$.

Second, we fold the literals $\langle add(n_1, n_2, y), \; add(y, n_3, n_4) \rangle$ in clause 6 using clause 3. Note that this transformation preserves equivalence according to Condition 3, since both literals have been obtained by Unfolding and, hence, $\overline{A}$ denotes the empty tuple. The resulting clause is

    7. $add3(s(n_1), n_2, n_3, s(n_4)) \leftarrow add3(n_1, n_2, n_3, n_4)$

in the program $P_2 = \langle 1, 2, 4, 7 \rangle$. Third, we introduce a new predicate $add4_{/5}$ defined by the single clause

    8. $add4(n_1, n_2, n_3, n_4, n_5) \leftarrow add(n_1, n_2, y_1), \; add(y_1, n_3, y_2),$
                              $add(y_2, n_4, n_5)$

and obtain the program $P_3 = P_2 \cup \{8\}$. By means of Condition (2), the body literals $\langle add(n_1, n_2, y_1), \; add(y_1, n_3, y_2) \rangle$ in clause 8 can be folded using clause 3 in the program P_1 and the resulting literal is $add3(n_1, n_2, n_3, y_2)$, which does not depend on $add4(n_1, n_2, n_3, n_4, n_5)$ in the program P_3. Hence, the final program is

    1. $add(0, n, n) \leftarrow$
    2. $add(s(n_1), n_2, s(n_3)) \leftarrow add(n_1, n_2, n_3)$
    4. $add3(0, n_2, n_3, n_4) \leftarrow add(n_2, n_3, n_4)$
    7. $add3(s(n_1), n_2, n_3, s(n_4)) \leftarrow add3(n_1, n_2, n_3, n_4)$
    9. $add4(n_1, n_2, n_3, n_4, n_5) \leftarrow add3(n_1, n_2, n_3, y_2), \; add(y_2, n_4, n_5)$.   □

It could be argued that there exists a reordering of the above transformation sequence in such a way that the system described in Theorem 2 allows to fold the literals $\langle add(n_1, n_2, y_1), \; add(y_1, n_3, y_2) \rangle$ in the definition of $add4_{/5}$: in this case, it would be enough to introduce $add4_{/5}$ and fold its body literals before transforming the definition of $sum3_{/4}$. However, such a restriction in the order of rule application unnecessarily complicates some transformation sequences, which may involve a large number of clauses.

Regarding condition (3), it is worthwhile to remark that its combination with condition (c) of Folding (that is, the literal introduced by Folding only unifies with the head of the folder clause in the program P_j) ensures that the folded clause has been obtained exclusively by unfolding transformations from the folder clause. Otherwise, if the folded clause is not obtained from the folder one, then the introduced literal would unify with the head of at least two clauses in P_j. Condition (3) corresponds to Examples 2 and 6, where the new literal depends on the clause head in P_i. Note that Example 6 does not satisfy Condition 3 since q and p do not unify. Besides, as we have already mentioned in Example 7, if $\overline{A}$ is an empty tuple (that is, all the literals in the folded clause comes from Unfolding), then the Folding rule using condition (3) is very similar to the one in the proposals [6,25], where the authors also require all the literals to come from an unfolding to allow folding.

Next, we show that the transformation in Example 2 can be performed using the system in Theorem 4.

Example 2 (Contd.). From the initial program $P_0 = \langle 1, 2, 3 \rangle$, we obtain $P_1 = \langle 2, 3, 4, 5 \rangle$ by unfolding $member(y, x_1)$ in clause 1 using the clauses 2 and 3. Then, Theorem 4 allows the folding of the body

$$\langle member(w, z_1), \neg member(w, z_2) \rangle$$

of clause 5 using clause 1 by means of the third condition in Folding . First, the head of the folder and the folded clause, which are taken from different programs (P_1 and P_0 respectively), unify. Second, the literal $member(w, z_1)$ has been obtained by unfolding from P_0. Finally, the literal $\neg member(w, z_2)$, which has not been obtained by unfolding, is non-failing on z_2[5] according to the definition of $\neg member$ in Example 3. That is, there always exists a value for w such that the goal $\leftarrow \neg member(w, z_2)$ does not fail.   □

Note that if the literal $\neg member(w, z_2)$ were failing on z_2, then the goal $\leftarrow q(x_1, x_2)$ would fail in P_0, whereas $q(x_1, x_2)$ could not fail in P_2. That is the case in Example 1, where the literal r is failing and, thus, the goal $\leftarrow p$ fails in the program P_0 and cycles in P_2.

The following example shows a transformation using the system in Theorem 4 that is mentioned in [27] as an example of unfeasible transformation under the system proposed in that paper.

Example 8. Let $\mathcal{F_L} = \{a_{/0}, b_{/0}, c_{/0}\}$ and P_0 be the following program

1. $reach(x, y) \leftarrow arc(x, y)$
2. $reach(x, y) \leftarrow arc(x, w), reach(w, y)$
3. $br(x, y, z) \leftarrow reach(x, z), reach(y, z)$
4. $arc(a, b)$
5. $arc(b, c)$
6. $arc(c, a)$.

---

[5] The variable z_1 from $q(z_1, z_2)$ is omitted since it does not occur in $\neg member(w, z_2)$.

First, we unfold the literal $reach(x, z)$ in the clause 3 using the clauses 1 and 2. The resulting program is $P_1 = \langle 1, 2, 7, 8, 4, 5, 6 \rangle$ where

> 7. $br(x, y, z) \leftarrow arc(x, z), \; reach(y, z)$
> 8. $br(x, y, z) \leftarrow arc(x, w), \; reach(w, z), \; reach(y, z)$.

Then, Theorem 4 allows the folding of literals $\langle reach(w, z), \; reach(y, z) \rangle$ in clause 8 using clause 3 and obtaining the literal $br(w, y, z)$, since $reach(w, z)$ has been obtained by unfolding from clause 3 and $reach(y, z)$, which is inherited from clause 3, is non-failing on $\langle y, z \rangle$. Note that $reach(y, z)$ cannot fail since all the nodes a, b and c are reachable from any node. The resulting program is $P_2 = \langle 1, 2, 7, 9, 4, 5, 6 \rangle$ where

> 9. $br(x, y, z) \leftarrow arc(x, w), \; br(w, y, z)$

which is equivalent to the programs P_0 and P_1.

Now, let us consider the program $P_0' = \langle 1, 2, 3, 4, 5, 6' \rangle$ where

> 6'. $arc(c, b)$.

As before, by unfolding $reach(x, z)$ in the clause 3 using the clauses 1 and 2, we obtain the program $P_1' = \langle 1, 2, 7, 8, 4, 5, 6' \rangle$. However, we cannot fold $\langle reach(w, z), \; reach(y, z) \rangle$ in the clause 8 using the clause 3 since $reach(y, z)$, which is inherited from P_0', is failing on $\langle y, z \rangle$; for example, a is not reachable from b.

It is worth noting that the non-failing condition, which depends on the facts $arc(\_, \_)$, makes the first transformation possible but not the second one. Thus, we allow only the transformations that are correct w.r.t. the graph. However, in [27] any transformation of this kind is forbidden irrespectively of the graph definition. $\square$

4   Conclusions and Future Work

We have introduced syntactic conditions for the rule Folding under which unfold/fold systems perform new kinds of transformations. In particular, the new conditions enable us to obtain recursive definitions and to remove local variables. This is possible because we allow the use of folder clauses from any program in the transformation sequence. The proposed transformation system is applicable to the whole class of normal logic programs and it is worth noting that only the negative literals without definition (due to the presence of local variables in the definition of its positive counterparts) cannot be used by Unfolding and Folding.

The need for providing new applicability conditions for the rule Folding has been motivated by means of some examples that show the risk of allowing transformations which use removed clauses. In this paper, we have concentrated on the rule Folding. However, similar problems arise in other transformation rules, such as Unfolding. For example, if we allowed unfolding by using definitions in previous programs, then the following transformation sequence could be obtained

P_0 : $p \leftarrow q$ $q \leftarrow r$ $r \leftarrow$

(by unfolding q in the 2nd clause using the definition in P_0)

P_1 : $p \leftarrow r$ $q \leftarrow r$ $r \leftarrow$

(by folding h in the 3rd clause using the 2nd clause)

P_2 : $p \leftarrow r$ $q \leftarrow p$ $r \leftarrow$

(by unfolding p in the 3rd clause using the definition in P_0)

P_3 : $p \leftarrow r$ $q \leftarrow q$ $r \leftarrow$

Clearly, the last program is not equivalent to any of the previous ones (even w.r.t. the least Herbrand model), because the goal $\leftarrow q$ loops instead of succeeding. To find syntactic conditions that ensure correctness when using clauses from any program in the transformation sequence in other transformations rules (such as Unfolding, Replacement, etc.) is an interesting open problem.

References

1. Álvez, J., Lucio, P.: A generalization of the folding rule for the clark-kunen semantics. Technical Report UPV-EHU/LSI/TR 01-2008, Dept. of Languages and Information Systems. Basque Country University (January, 2008)
2. Álvez, J., Lucio, P., Orejas, F., Pasarella, E., Pino, E.: Constructive negation by bottom-up computation of literal answers. In: Haddad, H., Omicini, A., Wainwright, R.L., Liebrock, L.M. (eds.) Proceedings of the 2004 ACM Symposium on Applied Computing (SAC), pp. 1468–1475 (2004)
3. Apt, K.R.: Logic programming. In: Handbook of Theoretical Computer Science. Formal Models and Sematics (B), vol. B, pp. 493–574. Elsevier, Amsterdam (1990)
4. Barbuti, R., Mancarella, P., Pedreschi, D., Turini, F.: A transformational approach to negation in logic programming. J. Log. Program. 8(3), 201–228 (1990)
5. Bossi, A., Cocco, N., Etalle, S.: Simultaneous replacement in normal programs. J. Log. Comput. 6(1), 79–120 (1996)
6. Bossi, A., Etalle, S.: More on unfold/fold transformations of normal programs: Preservation of fitting's semantics. In: Fribourg, L., Turini, F. (eds.) LOPSTR 1994 and META 1994. LNCS, vol. 883, pp. 311–331. Springer, Heidelberg (1994)
7. Burstall, R.M., Darlington, J.: A transformation system for developing recursive programs. J. ACM 24(1), 44–67 (1977)
8. Chan, D.: Constructive negation based on the completed database. In: Kowalski, R.A., Bowen, K.A. (eds.) Proceedings of the Fifth International Conference and Symposium on Logic Programming, pp. 111–125. MIT Press, Cambridge (1988)
9. Clark, K.L.: Negation as failure. In: Gallaire, H., Minker, J. (eds.) Logic and Data Bases, pp. 293–322. Plenum Press (1978)
10. Comon, H., Lescanne, P.: Equational problems and disunification. J. Symb. Comput. 7(3/4), 371–425 (1989)
11. Debray, S.K., López-García, P., Hermenegildo, M.V.: Non-failure analysis for logic programs. In: Naish, L. (ed.) Logic Programming. Proceedings of the Fourteenth International Conference on Logic Programming, Leuven, Belgium, July 8-11, 1997, pp. 48–62. MIT Press, Cambridge (1997)
12. Dix, J.: A classification theory of semantics of normal logic programs: II. weak properties. Fundam. Inform. 22(3), 257–288 (1995)

13. Gardner, P.A., Shepherdson, J.C.: Unfold/fold transformations of logic programs. In: Computational Logic - Essays in Honor of Alan Robinson, pp. 565–583 (1991)
14. Van Gelder, A., Ross, K., Schlipf, J.S.: Unfounded sets and well-founded semantics for general logic programs. In: PODS 1988: Proceedings of the seventh ACM SIGACT-SIGMOD-SIGART symposium on Principles of database systems, pp. 221–230. ACM Press, New York, NY, USA (1988)
15. Gergatsoulis, M., Katzouraki, M.: Unfold/fold transformations for definite clause programs. In: Penjam, J. (ed.) PLILP 1994. LNCS, vol. 844, pp. 340–354. Springer, Heidelberg (1994)
16. Kanamori, T., Fujita, H.: Unfold/fold transformation of logic programs with counters. Technical Report TR-179, ICOT Institute for New Generation Computer Technology (1986)
17. Kowalski, R.A.: Predicate logic as programming language. In: IFIP Congress, pp. 569–574 (1974)
18. Kunen, K.: Negation in logic programming. J. Log. Program. 4(4), 289–308 (1987)
19. Lloyd, J.W.: Foundations of Logic Programming, 2nd edn. Springer, Berlin (1987)
20. Lucio, P., Orejas, F., Pino, E.: An algebraic framework for the definition of compositional semantics of normal logic programs. J. Log. Program. 40(1), 89–124 (1999)
21. Maher, M.J.: Correctness of a logic program transformation system. Technical Report RC 13496, IBM T.J. Watson Research Center (1988)
22. Maher, M.J.: A tranformation system for deductive databases modules with perfect model semantics. Theor. Comput. Sci. 110(2), 377–403 (1993)
23. Pettorossi, A., Proietti, M.: Transformation of logic programs. In: Gabbayand, D.M., Hogger, C.J., Robinson, J.A. (eds.) Handbook of Logic in Artificial Intelligence and Logic Programming, vol. 6, pp. 697–787. Oxford University Press, Oxford (1998)
24. Roychoudhury, A., Kumar, K.N., Ramakrishnan, C.R., Ramakrishnan, I.V.: Beyond tamaki-sato style unfold/fold transformations for normal logic programs. Int. J. Found. Comput. Sci. 13(3), 387–403 (2002)
25. Sato, T.: Equivalence-preserving first-order unfold/fold transformation systems. Theor. Comput. Sci. 105(1), 57–84 (1992)
26. Sato, T., Tamaki, H.: Transformational logic program synthesis. In: Proceedings of the International Conference on Fifth Generation Computer Systems, pp. 195–201 (1984)
27. Seki, H.: Unfold/fold transformations of stratified programs. Theor. Comput. Sci. 86(1), 107–139 (1991)
28. Seki, H.: Unfold/fold transformation of general logic programs for the well-founded semantics. J. Log. Program. 16(1), 5–23 (1993)
29. Tamaki, H., Sato, T.: Unfold/fold transformation of logic programs. In: Tärnlund, S.-Å. (ed.) Proceedings of the Second International Logic Programming Conference, Uppsala University, Uppsala, Sweden, pp. 127–138 (1984)

Types for Hereditary Head Normalizing Terms

Makoto Tatsuta

National Institute of Informatics
2-1-2 Hitotsubashi, Tokyo 101-8430, Japan
tatsuta@nii.ac.jp

Abstract. Klop's Problem is finding a type for characterizing hereditary head normalizing terms, that is, lambda-terms whose Böhm trees
do not contain the bottom. This paper proves that this problem does
not have any solution by showing that the set of those terms is not recursively enumerable. This paper also gives a best-possible solution by
providing an intersection type system with a countably infinite set of
types such that typing in all these types characterizes hereditary head
normalizing terms. By using the same technique, this paper also shows
that the set of lambda-terms normalizing by infinite reduction is not
recursively enumerable.

1 Introduction

Klop's Problem [4] is finding a type that characterizes the set of hereditary
head normalizing terms, that is, λ-terms whose Böhm trees do not contain the
bottom. This question expects that there is some type system T with some
type A such that $M : A$ is provable in T if and only if M is hereditary head
normalizing. When we study infinite computation by using λ-calculus, Böhm
trees give computational meaning to non-normalizing λ-terms. Then the bottom
means non-informative computation, and a hereditary head normalizing term
is a nice term that does not contain any meaningless computation. It is an
interesting subject to find a type-theoretic characterization of terms having a
nice property [3,9]. So finding a type-theoretic characterization of hereditary
head normalizing terms is an important subject. Several researchers in European
theoretical computer science community have been trying to answer this question
for several years [4].

We will show that Klop's Problem does not have any solution, and give a
best-possible solution. By using the same technique used to show the first claim,
we will also show that the set of λ-terms normalizing by infinite reduction is not
recursively enumerable.

To show the first claim, we will show that the set of hereditary head normalizing terms is not recursively enumerable. For each unary primitive recursive
function f, we will construct a λ-term whose Böhm-tree computes the values
$f(0), f(1), f(2), \ldots$ so that the term is hereditary head normalizing if and only
if f is positive, that is, $f(x) > 0$ for all x. The set of positive primitive recursive
functions is proved to be not recursively enumerable since it solves the halting
problem.

J. Garrigue and M. Hermenegildo (Eds.): FLOPS 2008, LNCS 4989, pp. 195–209, 2008.

To show the second claim, we will think the set HN_n of λ-terms whose Böhm trees do not contain the bottom at depth less than n, and we will give some type p_n that characterizes HN_n. We use axioms for type constants and type preorder so that our intended model will interpret those constants by the least fixed points of those axioms. We will also need intersection types because of subject expansion [1]. Then we have a characterization of hereditary head normalizing terms by the set of the types p_n because a λ-term is hereditary head normalizing if and only if this term has the type p_n for all n.

A formal system for infinite computation has been studied actively [10]. Infinite λ-calculus [6,2] is an important subject among those formal systems. Infinite λ-calculus gives a theoretical foundation to infinite computation in functional programming languages, as finite λ-calculus did for finite computation in functional programming languages.

The set of λ-terms normalizing by infinite reduction is a fundamental notion in infinite λ-calculus. By applying the tree construction for the first claim to infinite λ-calculus, for each primitive recursive function f, we will construct a λ-term whose reducts compute the values $f(0), f(1), f(2), \ldots$ so that the term has a normal form by infinite reduction if and only if f is positive. By this, we can show that the set of λ-terms normalizing by infinite reduction is not recursively enumerable.

There have been two papers [8] and [7] on Klop's Problem. [8] gave a sufficient condition for hereditary head normalizing terms by using a type system. [7] gave the type system $\Lambda\vee_\star$ and the types a_n that characterize HN_n. We found our system independently from his paper and our system is simpler than his system. Though his system was another best-possible solution, the relationship between his result and the solution of Klop's Problem has not been discussed, because we did not know that there was no solution for Klop's Problem.

Section 2 defines hereditary head normalizing terms, and describes Klop's Problem. Section 3 shows that the set HHN of hereditary head normalizing terms is not recursively enumerable, and there does not exist any solution for Klop's Problem. We will discuss set theoretic properties of HHN in Section 4. Section 5 gives the set of types that characterizes HHN. The soundness is shown in Section 6 and the completeness is proved in Section 7. In Section 8, we discuss infinite λ-calculus and prove that the set of λ-terms normalizing by infinite reduction is not recursively enumerable.

2 Hereditary Head Normalizing Terms

In this section, we will give Klop's Problem as well as basic definitions.

Definition 2.1 (λ-Calculus)
We have variables $x, y, z, \ldots$. λ-terms $M, N, \ldots$ are defined by:

$$M, N, \ldots ::= x | \lambda x.M | MM.$$

$FV(M)$ denotes the set of free variables in M. $M[x := N]$ denotes a standard substitution. $M = N$ denotes the syntactical equality modulo renaming bound variables. Vars is the set of variables and Λ is the set of λ-terms.

One-step β-reduction $M \to_\beta N$ is defined by the compatible closure of

(β) $(\lambda x.M)N \to_\beta M[x := N]$.

β-reduction $M \to_\beta^* N$ is defined as the reflexive transitive closure of the relation $\to_\beta$. β-equality $M =_\beta N$ is defined as the least equivalence relation including $\to_\beta^*$. We say M reduces to N if $M \to_\beta^* N$. A λ-term of the shape $(\lambda x.M)N$ is called a *redex*. A λ-term M is called *normal* if there is not any λ-term N such that $M \to_\beta N$.

One-step head reduction $M \to_h N$ is defined by:

$(head)$ $\lambda x_1 \ldots x_n.(\lambda y.M)NN_1 \ldots N_m \to_h \lambda x_1 \ldots x_n.M[y := N]N_1 \ldots N_m$.

Head reduction $M \to_h^* N$ is defined as the reflexive transitive closure of the relation $\to_h$. We will write $M_0 \to_h^n M_n$ for some n-step head reduction sequence $M_0 \to_h M_1 \to_h \ldots \to_h M_n$. The relation $M \to_i N$ is defined to hold if $M \to_\beta N$ holds and $M \to_h N$ does not hold. Inner reduction $\to_i^*$ is defined as the reflexive transitive closure of the relation $\to_i$. A λ-term M is called *head normal* if there is not any λ-term N such that $M \to_h N$. A λ-term M is called *head normalizing* if there is some head normal term N such that $M \to_\beta^* N$.

Example. $\lambda w.(\lambda x.y)x((\lambda z.z)z) \to_h \lambda w.y((\lambda z.z)z)$ holds, but $\lambda w.(\lambda x.y)$ $x((\lambda z.z)z) \to_h \lambda w.(\lambda x.y)xz$ does not hold. $\lambda w.y((\lambda z.z)z)$ is a head normal form. $\lambda w.(\lambda x.y)xz$ is not a head normal form, but it is head normalizing since it reduces to the head normal form $\lambda w.yz$. $(\lambda x.xx)(\lambda x.xx)$ is not head normalizing.

Remark

(1) $M \to_h N$ implies $M \to_\beta N$.

(2) If M is head normalizing, then there is a head normal form N such that $M \to_h^* N$.

(3) M is a head normal form if and only if M is of the shape $\lambda x_1 \ldots x_n.yN_1 \ldots N_m$.

(4) M is a normal form if and only if M is of the shape $\lambda x_1 \ldots x_n.yN_1 \ldots N_m$ where N_i is a normal form for all i.

Definition 2.2 (Böhm Trees)

We suppose $\bot$ is a constant. A Böhm tree is defined as a (possibly infinite) tree with node labels in $\{\lambda x_1 \ldots x_n.y | x_1, \ldots, x_n, y \in \text{Vars}\} \cup \{\bot\}$. Böhm tree $BT(M)$ of a λ-term M is defined by:

(1) $BT(M) = \bot$ if M is not head normalizing,

(2) $BT(M)$ is

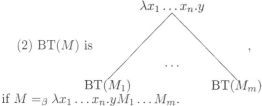

if $M =_\beta \lambda x_1 \ldots x_n.yM_1 \ldots M_m$.

We will sometimes write $[\lambda x_1 \ldots x_n.y, \mathrm{BT}(M_1), \ldots, \mathrm{BT}(M_m)]$ for $\mathrm{BT}(M)$ given in (2), for saving space.

Remark
(1) If $M =_\beta N$, then $\mathrm{BT}(M) = \mathrm{BT}(N)$.
(2) $\mathrm{BT}(M) = \bot$ if and only if M is not head normalizing.

Example. $\mathrm{BT}(\lambda w.(\lambda x.y)x((\lambda z.z)z)w) = \mathrm{BT}(\lambda w.yzw) = [\lambda w.y, z, w]$. $\mathrm{BT}(\lambda w.$ $(\lambda x.xx)(\lambda x.xx)((\lambda z.z)z)w) = \bot$. $\mathrm{BT}(\lambda w.(\lambda x.y)x((\lambda x.xx)(\lambda x.xx))w) = [\lambda w.y,$ $\bot, w]$. $\mathrm{BT}(\lambda w.(\lambda x.y)x((\lambda z.y)((\lambda x.xx)(\lambda x.xx)))) = [\lambda w.y, y]$.

Definition 2.3 (Hereditary Head Normalizing). A λ-term M is called *hereditary head normalizing* if $\mathrm{BT}(M)$ does not contain $\bot$. HHN is defined to be the set of hereditary head normalizing λ-terms.

Klop's Problem [4] is finding a type that characterizes the set of hereditary head normalizing terms. This question expects that there is some type system T with some type A such that $M : A$ is provable in T if and only if M is hereditary head normalizing.

We will answer this question. First, in Section 3 we will show that the set of hereditary head normalizing terms is not recursively enumerable. Hence we will conclude that there does not exist any type that characterizes hereditary head normalizing terms if the system has a recursively enumerable language and a recursively enumerable set of inference rules. Secondly, in Section 5 we will present an intersection type systems with a countably infinite set of types which characterizes hereditary head normalizing terms.

3   Non-existence of a Type for HHN

We will show that there does not exist any type that characterizes the set HHN of hereditary head normalizing terms. First we will show the set PPR of indices of positive primitive recursive functions is not recursively enumerable, by using a diagonal argument. We will define the λ-term T so that $T\bar{e}\bar{0}$ checks if $\{e\}^{pr}(n) > 0$ for each n one by one, and show that $e \in \mathrm{PPR}$ iff $T\bar{e}\bar{0} \in \mathrm{HHN}$. Combining those, we will prove HHN is not recursively enumerable.

Notation. N is the set of natural numbers. We will use a vector notation $\vec{e}$ to denote a sequence $e_1, \ldots, e_n$ $(n \geq 0)$. For example, we will use $\vec{M}$ to denote a sequence of λ-terms $M_1, \ldots, M_n$ $(n \geq 0)$. $M\vec{N}$ denotes $MN_1 \ldots N_n$. $\lambda\vec{x}.M$ denotes $\lambda x_1 \ldots x_n.M$. $f(\vec{x})$ denotes $f(x_1, \ldots, x_n)$ if $\vec{x}$ denotes the sequence $x_1, \ldots, x_n$. We will write $\bar{n}$ for the n-th Church numeral $\lambda fx.f^n x$ where $f^n x$ denotes $f(f(\ldots(fx)\ldots))$ (n times of f).

First, we give several notations for primitive recursive functions.

Definition 3.1. $\langle x, y \rangle$ denotes the standard primitive recursive surjective pairing, and $\pi_0(x)$ and $\pi_1(x)$ are the first and second projections respectively.

We fix some listing of all the unary primitive recursive functions so that the n-th unary primitive recursive function is effectively obtained from n.

For a number n, $\{n\}^{pr}(x)$ is defined as the n-th unary primitive recursive function. The n-th unary partial recursive function $\{n\}(x)$ is defined by $\{\pi_1(n)\}^{pr}(\mu y.(\{\pi_0(n)\}^{pr}(\langle x, y\rangle) = 0))$. We also define $u(x,y) = \{x\}^{pr}(y)$.

Remark. $\pi_0(\langle n, m\rangle) = n$ and $\pi_1(\langle n, m\rangle) = m$ hold. For a total function $g(x)$, $\mu y.(g(y) = 0)$ returns n if $g(y) = 0$ for some y such that $g(n) = 0$ and $g(x) > 0$ for all $x < n$, and is undefined if $g(x) > 0$ for all x. The function u is a universal function for unary primitive recursive functions. u is a total recursive function.

Definition 3.2. For a function $f : N^n \to N$, we say that a λ-term F represents f when $f(m_1, \ldots, m_n) = m$ iff $F\overline{m_1} \ldots \overline{m_n} =_\beta \overline{m}$ for all $m, m_1, \ldots, m_n \in N$.

Theorem 4.15 in Page 53 in [5] showed the following claim.

Theorem 3.3 ([5]). *For every recursive function f, there is some λ-term F such that F represents f.*

Definition 3.4. PPR is defined to be the set $\{n \in N | \forall x(\{n\}^{pr}(x) > 0)\}$.

PPR is the set of indices for positive primitive recursive functions.

Proposition 3.5. *The set PPR is not recursively enumerable.*

Proof. By standard results from recursion theory, we have the primitive recursive function $P : N \to N$ defined by $\{P(n)\}^{pr}(m) = \langle n, m\rangle$, and the primitive recursive function $Q : N^2 \to N$ defined by $\{Q(n,m)\}^{pr}(x) = \{n\}^{pr}(\{m\}^{pr}(x))$.

Assume that PPR is recursively enumerable. We will show contradiction.

Define a partial function $f : N \to N$ by $f(x) = 1$ if $Q(\pi_0(x), P(x))$ is in PPR, and $f(x)$ is undefined otherwise. Then f is partial recursive. There is a number e such that for all x, both $\{e\}(x)$ and $f(x)$ has the same value or both are undefined.

Then we show that $f(x)$ is defined if and only if $\{x\}(x)$ is undefined. It is proved as follows: $f(x)$ is defined iff $Q(\pi_0(x), P(x))$ is in PPR by the definition of f, iff $\forall y(\{\pi_0(x)\}^{pr}(\{P(x)\}^{pr}(y)) > 0)$ by the definition of Q and PPR, iff $\forall y(\{\pi_0(x)\}^{pr}(\langle x, y\rangle) > 0)$ by the definition of P, iff $\{\pi_1(x)\}^{pr}(\mu y.(\{\pi_0(x)\}^{pr}(\langle x, y\rangle) = 0))$ is undefined, iff $\{x\}(x)$ is undefined by the definition of the x-th unary partial recursive function.

If $\{e\}(e)$ is defined, then $f(e)$ is defined by the definition of e, and hence $\{e\}(e)$ is undefined by the above. Hence $\{e\}(e)$ is undefined. However, $f(e)$ is undefined by the definition of e, and hence $\{e\}(e)$ is defined by the above, which leads to contradiction.

Consequently, the set PPR is not recursively enumerable.   □

We define

$$S = \lambda yfx.f(yfx),$$
$$Y_0 = \lambda xy.y(xxy),$$
$$Y = Y_0Y_0,$$
$$\Delta = \lambda x.xx.$$

The term S is the successor for Church numerals. Y is Turing's fixed point operator and we have $YM \to^*_\beta M(YM)$.

We now prove the first main theorem by using PPR.

Theorem 3.6. *The set* HHN *of hereditary head normalizing terms is not recursively enumerable.*

Proof. Assume HHN is recursively enumerable. We will show contradiction. By Theorem 3.3, we have a λ-term U that represents the function u. Fix variables a and w. Define T by

$$T = Y(\lambda txy.Uxy(\lambda w.a)(\Delta\Delta)(tx(\mathsf{S}y))).$$

We show that $T\bar{e}\bar{0}$ is in HHN if and only if e is in PPR. The direction from the right to the left is proved by $\mathrm{BT}(T\bar{e}\bar{0}) = [a, [a, [a, [\ldots]]]]$ when e is in PPR, and hence $T\bar{e}\bar{0}$ is in HHN. In order to show the direction from the left to the right, first we assume e is not in PPR and will show $T\bar{e}\bar{0}$ is not in HHN. From $e \notin$ PPR, we have a number m_0 such that $\{e\}^{pr}(m_0) = 0$ and $\{e\}^{pr}(m) > 0$ for all $m < m_0$. Then $\mathrm{BT}(T\bar{e}\bar{0}) = \overbrace{[a, [a, [\ldots [a, \bot] \ldots]]]}^{m_0}$, and hence $T\bar{e}\bar{0}$ is not in HHN.

If HHN were recursively enumerable, then PPR would be recursively enumerable, which would lead to contradiction. Therefore HHN is not recursively enumerable. □

Non-existence of solutions for Klop's Problem follows immediately from the previous theorem.

Theorem 3.7. *There does not exist any type system T with any type A such that its language and the set of its inference rules are recursively enumerable, and the set of hereditary head normalizing terms is the same as $\{M | \Gamma \vdash M : A$ is provable in T for some $\Gamma\}$.*

Proof. If we had such a type system T, then $\{M | \Gamma \vdash M : A$ is provable in T for some $\Gamma\}$ would be recursively enumerable, and therefore HHN would be recursively enumerable, which would contradict to Theorem 3.6. □

4   Set-Theoretic Properties of HHN

We will discuss some set-theoretic properties of hereditary head normalizing terms. We will define the sets HN_n and Q_n as the set of λ-terms whose Böhm trees do not contain $\bot$ at depth $< n$, and the set of terms in HN_n such that the roots of their Böhm trees do not contain abstractions, respectively. We will show some set-theoretic inequality for those, which will be used in Section 6.

We will write $A^n \to B$ for $A \to \ldots \to A \to B$ (n times of A).

Proposition 4.1. HHN *is the greatest fixed point $X \subseteq \Lambda$ of the equation:*

(1) if $M \in X$, then there exist $N_1, \ldots, N_m \in X$ ($m \geq 0$) such that $M =_\beta \lambda x_1 \ldots x_n.yN_1 \ldots N_m$.

Proof. First, we will show HHN is a solution of (1). Suppose M in HHN. Then M has a head normal form $\lambda\vec{x}.y\vec{N}$ such that M reduces to $\lambda\vec{x}.y\vec{N}$. Then $\mathrm{BT}(N_i)$ does not contain $\bot$. Therefore N_i is in HHN.

Secondly, we will show HHN is the greatest solution of (1). Assume X is a solution. We will show $X \subseteq$ HHN. Assume $M \in X$. We will show that any node at depth $\leq k$ in $\mathrm{BT}(M)$ is not $\bot$ by induction on k.

Case $k = 0$. Since M has a head normal form, the node is not $\bot$.

Case $k + 1$. We have $M =_\beta \lambda\vec{x}.y\vec{N}$, $N_i \in X$. By induction hypothesis, a node at depth $\leq k$ in $\mathrm{BT}(N_i)$ is not $\bot$. Hence a node at depth $\leq k+1$ in $\mathrm{BT}(\lambda\vec{x}.y\vec{N})$ is not $\bot$. Then a node at depth $\leq k+1$ in $\mathrm{BT}(M)$ is not $\bot$.

Therefore a node at depth $\leq k$ in $\mathrm{BT}(M)$ is not $\bot$ for any k. Hence we have $M \in$ HHN.   □

Definition 4.2. HN_0 is the set Λ.
HN_{k+1} is the set $\{M | M \to_\beta^* \lambda\vec{x}.y\vec{N}, N_i \in \mathrm{HN}_k\}$.

Remark

(1) $M \in \mathrm{HN}_k$ iff any node at depth $< k$ in $\mathrm{BT}(M)$ is not $\bot$.
(2) $\mathrm{HN}_{k+1} \subseteq \mathrm{HN}_k$.
(3) HHN $= \cap_{k=0}^\infty \mathrm{HN}_k$.

Definition 4.3. Q_n is defined as $\{M | M \to_\beta^* x\vec{N}, x \in \mathrm{Vars}, N_i \in \mathrm{HN}_{n-1}\}$ for $n \geq 1$.
$X \to Y$ is defined as $\{M | \forall N \in X (MN \in Y)\}$, for $X, Y \subseteq \Lambda$.

Remark. $Q_n \subseteq \mathrm{HN}_n$.

Lemma 4.4

(1) HN_n is closed under $\to_\beta$.
(2) Q_n is closed under $\to_\beta$.
(3) $M \in Q_n$ and $M \to_\beta^* x\vec{N}$ imply $N_i \in \mathrm{HN}_{n-1}$.

Proof.

(1) By induction on n. Case $n + 1$. Suppose $M \in \mathrm{HN}_{n+1}$ and $M \to_\beta N$. We have $M \to_\beta^* \lambda\vec{x}.y\vec{L}$, $L_i \in \mathrm{HN}_n$. By Church-Rosser, we have $N \to_\beta^* \lambda\vec{x}.y\vec{L}'$, $L_i \to_\beta^* L_i'$. By induction hypothesis, $L_i' \in \mathrm{HN}_n$ holds. Then we have $N \in \mathrm{HN}_{n+1}$.
(2) Suppose $M \in Q_n$ and $M \to_\beta N$. We have $M \to_\beta^* x\vec{L}$, $L_i \in \mathrm{HN}_{n-1}$. By Church-Rosser, we have $N \to_\beta^* x\vec{L}'$ and $L_i \to_\beta^* L_i'$. By (1), we have $L_i' \in \mathrm{HN}_{n-1}$. Therefore we have $N \in Q_n$.
(3) By (2), we have $x\vec{N} \in Q_n$. Then we have $x\vec{N} \to_\beta^* x\vec{L}$ and $L_i \in \mathrm{HN}_{n-1}$. Hence $N_i \to_\beta^* L_i$ and $N_i \in \mathrm{HN}_{n-1}$.   □

Proposition 4.5

(1) $Q_{n+1} \subseteq Q_n$ $(n \geq 1)$.
(2) $Q_{n+1} \subseteq \mathrm{HN}_n \to Q_{n+1}$ $(n \geq 0)$.
(3) $\mathrm{HN}_n \supseteq Q_n^m \to Q_n$ $(n \geq 1, m \geq 0)$.

Proof.

(1) From $\mathrm{HN}_n \subseteq \mathrm{HN}_{n-1}$.

(2) Suppose $M \in Q_{n+1}$ and $N \in \mathrm{HN}_n$. We have $M \to_\beta^* x\vec{L}$, $L_i \in \mathrm{HN}_n$. Hence $MN \to_\beta^* x\vec{L}N$. Then we have $MN \in Q_{n+1}$.

(3) Assume $M \in Q_n^m \to Q_n$. By Definition 4.3, we have $x_i \in Q_n$. Then $M\vec{x}^{(m)} \in Q_n$ holds where $\vec{x}^{(m)}$ is $x_1, \ldots, x_m$. Hence M is head normalizing and we have $M \to_\beta^* \lambda \vec{x}^{(l)}.y\vec{N}$. If $m < l$, then we have $M\vec{x}^{(m)} \to_\beta^* \lambda x_{m+1} \ldots x_l.y\vec{N}$ and $M\vec{x}^{(m)} \to_\beta^* z\vec{L}$ does not hold by Church-Rosser, which contradicts to $M\vec{x}^{(m)} \in Q_n$. Hence we get $m \geq l$. Then we have $M\vec{x}^{(m)} \to_\beta^* y\vec{N}x_{l+1} \ldots x_m$. By $M\vec{x}^{(m)} \in Q_n$, from Lemma 4.4 (3), we have $N_i \in \mathrm{HN}_{n-1}$. Hence $M \in \mathrm{HN}_n$. $\square$

5   Types for HHN

This section will present a type system with a countably infinite set of types which characterizes hereditary head normalizing terms.

Definition 5.1.   We define the type system $\mathcal{T}$.

We have type constants p_n, q_m, q, and Ω $(n \geq 0, m \geq 1)$. Types $A, B, \ldots$ are defined by:

$A, B, \ldots ::= p_n | q_m | q | \Omega | A \to A | A \cap A$ $(n \geq 0, m \geq 1)$.

Type preorder $A \leq B$ is defined by:

$$A \leq A \qquad \frac{A \leq B \quad B \leq C}{A \leq C} \qquad A \cap B \leq A \qquad A \cap B \leq B$$

$p_0 = \Omega$

$q_{n+1} \leq p_n \to q_{n+1}$ $(n \geq 0)$

$p_n \geq q_n^m \to q_n$ $(n \geq 1, m \geq 0)$

$q_{n+1} \leq q_n$ $(n \geq 1)$

$q_n \geq q$ $(n \geq 1)$

A type declaration is a finite set of $x : A$ where x is a variable and A is a type. We will write $\Gamma, \Delta, \ldots$ for a type declaration. A judgment is $\Gamma \vdash M : A$. We will also write $x_1 : B_1, \ldots, x_n : B_n \vdash M : A$ for $\{x_1 : B_1, \ldots, x_n : B_n\} \vdash M : A$, and $\Gamma, y : C \vdash M : A$ for $x_1 : B_1, \ldots, x_n : B_n, y : C \vdash M : A$, when Γ is $\{x_1 : B_1, \ldots, x_n : B_n\}$.

Typing rules are given by:

$$\frac{}{\Gamma, x : A \vdash x : A} \; (Ass)$$

$$\frac{\Gamma, x : A \vdash M : B}{\Gamma \vdash \lambda x.M : A \to B} \; (\to I) \qquad \frac{\Gamma \vdash M : A \to B \quad \Gamma \vdash N : A}{\Gamma \vdash MN : B} \; (\to E)$$

$$\frac{\Gamma \vdash M : A \quad \Gamma \vdash M : B}{\Gamma \vdash M : A \cap B} \; (\cap I) \qquad \frac{\Gamma \vdash M : A \quad A \leq B}{\Gamma \vdash M : B} \; (\leq) \qquad \frac{}{\Gamma \vdash M : \Omega} \; (\Omega)$$

Notation. We will write $\{x_1, \ldots, x_n\} : A$ for $\{x_1 : A, \ldots, x_n : A\}$.

This is a standard intersection type system except for constants p_n, q_n, q. Our intended meaning of the constants p_n, q_n, and q are the set HN_n, the set Q_n, and $\cap_n Q_n$ respectively. Our discussion will also go well in the same way when we add other set-theoretically-sound rules for the type preorder such as $A \cap B \leq B \cap A$. Intersection types are necessary since we need the subject expansion property in our proof.

We have a characterization theorem of HHN by this type system with the set of the types p_n.

Theorem 5.2. *M is hereditary head normalizing if and only if* $\mathrm{FV}(M) : q \vdash M : p_n$ *is provable in the type theory* $\mathcal{T}$ *for all n.*

We will finish the proof of this theorem in Section 7. The soundness of this characterization will be proved in Section 6 and its completeness will be shown in Section 7.

[7] gave a similar type system to our system $\mathcal{T}$ so that his type system is an intersection type system with type constants a_n, b_n, c_n and type preorder, each type a_n characterizes HN_n, and the set of the types a_n characterizes HHN. We found our system independently from his work. Our system is simpler because we used only two sets of type constants p_n, q_n with five axioms for $\leq$, while his system used three sets of type constants a_n, b_n, c_n with six axioms for $\leq$ and $\sim$.

6   Soundness

We will prove the soundness part of Theorem 5.2 by using set-theoretic semantics. We will interpret a type by a $=_\beta$-closed set of λ-terms. In particular, p_n is interpreted by HN_n. The soundness of this interpretation will be proved by induction on derivations.

Definition 6.1. The interpretation $[A]$ of a type A is defined by:

$$[p_n] = \mathrm{HN}_n,$$
$$[q_n] = Q_n,$$
$$[q] = \cap_{n=1}^{\infty} Q_n,$$
$$[\Omega] = \Lambda,$$
$$[A{\rightarrow}B] = [A]{\rightarrow}[B],$$
$$[A \cap B] = [A] \cap [B],$$

where $X{\rightarrow}Y = \{M \in \Lambda | \forall N \in X (MN \in Y)\}$ for $X, Y \subseteq \Lambda$.

Proposition 6.2. *$[A]$ is closed under $=_\beta$.*

Proof. By induction on A. If A is either p_n, q_n, or q, the claim holds because their interpretations are closed under β-reduction by Lemma 4.4 (1) and (2), and their interpretations are also closed under β-expansion by their definitions. If A is Ω, the claim holds trivially. If A is $B \cap C$ or $B{\rightarrow}C$, the claim is proved by induction hypothesis. □

Proposition 6.3. *If $A \leq B$ is provable, then $[A] \subseteq [B]$ holds.*

Proof. By induction on the derivation of $A \leq B$. Cases are considered according to the last rule.

The case $q_{n+1} \leq p_n \to q_{n+1}$ is proved by Proposition 4.5 (2). The case $p_n \geq q_n^m \to q_n$ is proved by Proposition 4.5 (3). The case $q_{n+1} \leq q_n$ is proved by Proposition 4.5 (1). □

Definition 6.4. A variable assignment ρ is defined by $\rho : \text{Vars} \to \Lambda$. A variable assignment $\rho[x := M]$ is defined by $(\rho[x := M])(x) = M$ and $(\rho[x := M])(y) = \rho(y)$ if x is not y. The interpretation $[M]\rho$ of a term M with ρ is defined as $M[x_1 := \rho(x_1), \ldots, x_n := \rho(x_n)]$ where $\text{FV}(M) = \{x_1, \ldots, x_n\}$.

Proposition 6.5 (Soundness of Interpretation). *If we have $\overrightarrow{x : B} \vdash M : A$ and $\rho(x_i) \in [B_i]$ $(\forall i)$, then we have $[M]\rho \in [A]$.*

Proof. It is proved by induction on the proof. We consider cases according to the last rule. We will show only interesting cases.

Case $(\to I)$. Assume $N \in [A]$. We will show $[\lambda x.M]\rho N \in [B]$. Let ρ' be $\rho[x := N]$. By induction hypothesis, we have $[M]\rho' \in [B]$. Since we have $[\lambda x.M]\rho N \to_\beta [M]\rho'$, from Proposition 6.2, we get $[\lambda x.M]\rho N \in [B]$. Hence $[\lambda x.M]\rho$ is in $[A \to B]$.

Case $(\leq)$ is proved by Proposition 6.3. □

Proposition 6.6 (Soundness). *M is hereditary head normalizing if $\text{FV}(M) : q \vdash M : p_n$ is provable in the type theory $\mathcal{T}$ for all n.*

Proof. Suppose $\text{FV}(M) : q \vdash M : p_n$. Define ρ by $\rho(x) = x$. We have $x \in [q]$. By Proposition 6.5, we get $[M]\rho \in [p_n]$. Hence M is in HN_n for all n. Consequently M is in HHN. □

7   Completeness

We will show the completeness and finish the proof of the characterization theorem. First we will show the subject expansion property. By using this property, we will show the completeness of the set HN_n for the type p_n.

Lemma 7.1. *If $\Gamma \vdash M[x := N] : A$, then there exists some B such that $\Gamma \vdash N : B$ and $\Gamma, x : B \vdash M : A$.*

Proof. By induction on the proof. Cases are considered according to the last rule. We will show only interesting cases.

Case $x \notin \text{FV}(M)$. Let B be Ω.

Case $(\to E)$ and $M = M_1 M_2$. Then we have

$$\frac{\Gamma \vdash M_1[x := N] : C \to A \quad \Gamma \vdash M_2[x := N] : C}{\Gamma \vdash (M_1 M_2)[x := N] : A}$$

By induction hypothesis, there is B_1 such that $\Gamma \vdash N : B_1$ and $\Gamma, x : B_1 \vdash M_1 : C \to A$. By induction hypothesis, we also have B_2 such that $\Gamma \vdash N : B_2$ and $\Gamma, x : B_2 \vdash M_2 : C$. Let B be $B_1 \cap B_2$. Then we have the claim.

Case $(\cap I)$. This case is proved similarly to Case $(\to E)$ by using an intersection type. $\square$

In order to have this lemma, we need intersection types. The subject expansion property is proved by using this lemma.

Proposition 7.2 (Subject Expansion). *If $M \to_\beta N$ and $\Gamma \vdash N : A$, then we have $\Gamma \vdash M : A$.*

Proof. By induction on the proof. We consider cases according to the last rule. We will discuss only interesting cases.

Case $M = (\lambda x.M_1)M_2$ and $N = M_1[x := M_2]$. By Lemma 7.1, we have B such that $\Gamma \vdash M_2 : B$ and $\Gamma, x : B \vdash M_1 : A$. Then we get $\Gamma \vdash (\lambda x.M_1)M_2 : A$. $\square$

Remark. Subject reduction also holds. However, we do not need subject reduction property for our proof.

Lemma 7.3. *If $M \in \mathrm{HN}_n$, then we have $\mathrm{FV}(M) : q_n \vdash M : p_n$.*

Proof. By induction on n.

Case $n = 0$. The claim holds since $p_0 = \Omega$.

Case $n + 1$. Assume $M \in \mathrm{HN}_{n+1}$. We have $M \to_\beta^* \lambda \vec{x}.y\vec{N}$, $\mathrm{length}(\vec{x}) = m$, $\mathrm{length}(\vec{N}) = l$, and $N_i \in \mathrm{HN}_n$. By induction hypothesis for n, we have $\mathrm{FV}(N_i) : q_n \vdash N_i : p_n$. By $q_{n+1} \leq q_n$, we have $\mathrm{FV}(M), \vec{x} : q_{n+1} \vdash N_i : p_n$. Then we have $y : q_{n+1}$ under the same type declaration. By using $q_{n+1} \leq p_n \to q_{n+1}$ l times, we have $\mathrm{FV}(M), \vec{x} : q_{n+1} \vdash y\vec{N} : q_{n+1}$. Then we get $\mathrm{FV}(M) : q_{n+1} \vdash \lambda \vec{x}.y\vec{N} : q_{n+1}^m \to q_{n+1}$. By $q_{n+1}^m \to q_{n+1} \leq p_{n+1}$, we have $\lambda \vec{x}.y\vec{N} : p_{n+1}$ under the same type declaration. By Proposition 7.2, we have $\mathrm{FV}(M) : q_{n+1} \vdash M : p_{n+1}$. $\square$

By $q_{n+1} \geq q$ and this lemma, we get the next proposition.

Proposition 7.4 (Completeness). *If $M \in \mathrm{HN}_n$, then we have $\mathrm{FV}(M) : q \vdash M : p_n$.*

Remark. We have a similar property:

– If $M \in Q_{n+1}$, then we have $\mathrm{FV}(M) : q \vdash M : q_{n+1}$.

However, we do not need this for our proof.

Now we complete the proof of the characterization theorem.

Proof of Theorem 5.2. The implication from the right-hand side to the left-hand side is proved by Proposition 6.6. The implication from the left-hand side to the right-hand side is proved by Proposition 7.4. $\square$

8   Normalizing Terms in Infinite λ-Calculus

We will discuss infinite λ-calculus [6,2], and show that the set of normalizing λ-terms by infinite reduction is not recursively enumerable. We will define the

λ-term T such that $T\overline{e0}$ checks if $\{e\}^{pr}(n) > 0$ for each n one by one, and show that $e \in$ PPR iff $T\overline{e0}$ is normalizing by infinite reduction. Combining it with non-recursive enumerability of PPR shown in Section 3, we will prove the set of normalizing λ-terms by infinite reduction is not recursively enumerable.

Normalizing terms by infinite reduction are important in infinite λ-calculus since they play a role of values in the same way as normal forms do in usual λ-calculus. When we construct a formal system that describes infinite λ-calculus, we might want to have a system that also characterizes normalizing terms by infinite reduction. The theorem in this section shows that we cannot have such a system.

Definition 8.1. A *position*, denoted by u, is defined to be a finite string of positive integers.

For a λ-term M and a position u, the subterm $M|u$ of M is defined by induction on u by

$$M|\langle\rangle = M,$$
$$(\lambda x.M)|1 \cdot u = M|u,$$
$$(MN)|1 \cdot u = M|u,$$
$$(MN)|2 \cdot u = N|u.$$

The distance $d(M, N)$ for $M, N \in \Lambda$ is defined as 0 if $M = N$, and $\frac{1}{2^l}$ if $M \neq N$ and l is the minimum length of u such that $M|u$ and $N|u$ are both defined, and they are distinct variables, or of different syntactic types.

The set Λ^∞ is defined as $\{(M_0, M_1, M_2, \ldots)|M_i \in \Lambda, \forall \epsilon > 0 \exists n \forall i, j \geq n(d(M_i, M_j) < \epsilon)\}$ where $(M_0, M_1, M_2, \ldots)$ is a countably infinite sequence of λ-terms.

The equality $(M_0, M_1, M_2, \ldots) \equiv_\infty (N_0, N_1, N_2, \ldots)$ on Λ^∞ is defined by $\lim_{n \to \infty} d(M_n, N_n) = 0$.

Remark

(1) d is proved to be actually a distance [6].

(2) The quotient set $\Lambda^\infty / \equiv_\infty$ is the completion of Λ with the distance d.

(3) The tree $T(M)$ of a λ-term M is defined by

$$T(x) = x,$$

$$T(\lambda x.M) = \begin{array}{c} \lambda x \\ | \\ T(M) \end{array},$$

$$T(MN) = \begin{array}{c} @ \\ \diagup \diagdown \\ T(M) \quad T(N) \end{array}.$$

We will identify a λ-term M and its tree $T(M)$. Then the depth of the subterm $M|u$ in M is the length of u. We will extend trees of λ-terms to infinite trees. An infinite λ-term corresponding to an infinite tree T can be described by

$(M_0, M_1, \ldots)$ in Λ^∞ such that for any depth k, if $d(M_i, M_j) < \frac{1}{2^k}$ for all $i, j \geq n$, then $T(M_n)$ and T are the same at depth $\leq k$.

Definition 8.2. For $M \in \Lambda$ and $N \in \Lambda^\infty$, $M \rightarrow^\infty N$ is defined to hold if $N = (M_0, M_1, \ldots)$, $M = M_0 \rightarrow_\beta M_1 \rightarrow_\beta \ldots$, and $\lim_{i \to \infty} d_i = \infty$ where d_i is the depth of the redex for $M_i \rightarrow_\beta M_{i+1}$.

Proposition 8.3. *If we have $M_0 \rightarrow_\beta M_1 \rightarrow_\beta \ldots$ and $\lim_{i \to \infty} d_i = \infty$ where d_i is the depth of the redex for $M_i \rightarrow_\beta M_{i+1}$, then $(M_0, M_1, \ldots)$ is in Λ^∞.*

Proof. For a given ϵ, take k such that $\frac{1}{2^k} < \epsilon$. From $\lim d_i = \infty$, there is n_0 such that $d_i > k$ for all $i \geq n_0$. Then for all $i, j \geq n_0$, we have $d(M_i, M_j) < \frac{1}{2^k} < \epsilon$. $\square$

Our Λ^∞ and $\rightarrow^\infty$ are equivalent to Λ^{111} and the strongly convergent reduction sequence of length ω in [6]. If we add usual finite β-reduction to our infinite reduction, they will become equivalent to the infinite terms and the infinite β-reduction $\rightarrow^\infty$ in [2].

Definition 8.4. We say that $M \in \Lambda^\infty$ has a redex when M is $(M_0, M_1, \ldots)$ and we have u and n such that $M_i|u = (\lambda x.P_i)Q_i$ for all $i \geq n$. $M \in \Lambda^\infty$ is a normal form if M does not have any redex. We say that $M \in \Lambda$ is normalizing by infinite reduction when there is a normal form $N \in \Lambda^\infty$ such that $M \rightarrow^\infty N$. NF_∞ is defined to be the set of normalizing λ-terms by infinite reduction.

Theorem 8.5. *The set NF_∞ of λ-terms normalizing by infinite reduction is not recursively enumerable.*

We will prove this theorem in this section after some preparation.

The next lemma is a standard result in λ-calculus.

Lemma 8.6. *If $M \rightarrow^*_\beta N$ includes n steps of head reduction, then there is L such that $M \rightarrow^*_h L \rightarrow^*_i N$ and $M \rightarrow^*_h L$ has $\geq n$ steps.*

Definition 8.7. We will use $S, Y_0, Y, \overline{n}, u, U$ and Δ defined in Section 3. Fix variables a and w. T is defined by

$$T = Y(\lambda txy.Uxy(\lambda w.tx(Sy)a)(\Delta\Delta)).$$

We will write $M\vec{a}^{(n)}$ for $Ma \ldots a$ (n times of a).

$T\overline{e}\overline{n}$ computes $\{e\}^{pr}(n), \{e\}^{pr}(n+1), \ldots$ and produces extra arguments a's if they are positive, and stops with $\Delta\Delta$ when it encounters some m such that $\{e\}^{pr}(m) = 0$.

Proposition 8.8. *If e is not in PPR, then $T\overline{e}\overline{0}$ is not normalizing by infinite reduction.*

Proof. Assume $T\overline{e}\overline{0}$ is normalizing by infinite reduction. We will show contradiction.

Suppose $T\overline{e}\overline{0} = M_0 \rightarrow_\beta M_1 \rightarrow_\beta M_2 \rightarrow_\beta \ldots$, and M_∞ is $(M_0, M_1, \ldots)$ and normal. Let d_i be the depth of the redex for $M_i \rightarrow_\beta M_{i+1}$.

Since e is not in PPR, there is m_0 such that $\{e\}^{pr}(m_0) = 0$ and $\{e\}^{pr}(m) > 0$ for all $m < m_0$.

Choose a fresh variable z and let T' be $Y(\lambda txy.U xy(\lambda w.tx(Sy)a)z)$. $T'\overline{en} \to^*_\beta$ $T'\overline{en+1}a$ holds when $\{e\}^{pr}(n) > 0$, and $T'\overline{en} \to^*_\beta z$ holds when $\{e\}^{pr}(n) = 0$. Hence $T'\overline{e0} \to^*_\beta z\vec{a}^{(m_0)}$. By Lemma 8.6, we have L such that $T'\overline{e0} \to^*_h L \to^*_i$ $z\vec{a}^{(m_0)}$. Then $L = z\vec{P}$ for some $\vec{P}$. By substituting $\Delta\Delta$ for z, we have $T\overline{e0} \to^*_h$ $\Delta\Delta\vec{P}'$ where $\vec{P}' = \vec{P}[z := \Delta\Delta]$.

Case 1 when $M_0 \to_\beta M_1 \to_\beta \ldots$ includes only finitely many head reduction steps. We have some n such that M_n is a head normal form since M_∞ is normal. Then we have $\Delta\Delta\vec{P}' =_\beta M_n$, which leads to contradiction.

Case 2 when $M_0 \to_\beta M_1 \to_\beta \ldots$ includes infinitely many head reduction steps. Suppose $T\overline{e0} \to^{n_0}_h \Delta\Delta\vec{P}'$ for some n_0. We have some n_1 such that $M_0 \to^*_\beta M_{n_1}$ includes at least n_0 head reduction steps. By Lemma 8.6, we have Q such that $M_0 \to^{n_0 \leq}_h Q \to^*_i M_{n_1}$. Hence $Q = \Delta\Delta\vec{P}'$. Therefore $M_{n_1} = \Delta\Delta\vec{R}$ for some $\vec{R}$, which contradicts to the normality of M_∞. □

Proposition 8.9. *e is in* PPR *if and only if $T\overline{e0} \in \mathrm{NF}_\infty$.*

Proof. From the left-hand side to the right-hand side. We have $T\overline{e0} \to^*_\beta T\overline{e1}a \to^*_\beta$ $T\overline{e2}aa \to^*_\beta T\overline{e3}aaa \to^*_\beta \ldots$. Let this reduction sequence be $M_0 \to_\beta M_1 \to_\beta \ldots$ and M_∞ be the sequence $(M_0, M_1, \ldots)$. Then $T\overline{e0} \to^\infty M_\infty$ holds and M_∞ is a normal form. Hence $T\overline{e0}$ is in NF_∞.

From the right-hand side to the left-hand side. The claim immediately follows from Proposition 8.8. □

Proof of Theorem 8.5. If NF_∞ were recursively enumerable, the set $\{e | T\overline{e0} \in \mathrm{NF}_\infty\}$ would be also recursively enumerable, but this set is the same as PPR from Proposition 8.9, so PPR would be also recursively enumerable, which would contradict to Proposition 3.5. Therefore NF_∞ is not recursively enumerable. □

The same technique will prove that $\mathrm{NF}_\infty \cup \mathrm{NF}_{<\infty}$ is not recursively enumerable, where $\mathrm{NF}_{<\infty}$ is the set of weakly normalizing terms by β-reduction.

9   Concluding Remarks

Future work will be extending our technique developed in this paper to general infinite λ-calculi Λ^{abc} with $\to^\infty$ for $a, b, c = 0, 1$ in [6], in order to (1) prove the set NF^{abc}_∞ of λ-terms having normal forms by $\to^\infty$ in Λ^{abc} is not recursively enumerable and (2) provide an intersection type system with a countably infinite set of types that characterizes the set NF^{abc}_∞.

Acknowledgments

We would like to thank Professor Jan Willem Klop, Professor Mariangiola Dezani-Ciancaglini, and Professor Henk Barendregt for references. We would also like to thank Professor Elio Giovannetti for suggesting Klop's Problem. We would also like to thank Professor Kazushige Terui and Professor Makoto Kanazawa for discussions at NII Logic Seminar. We would also thank the anonymous referees for valuable comments for improving this paper.

References

1. Barendregt, H., Coppo, M., Dezani-Ciancaglini, M.: A Filter Lambda Model and the Completeness of Type Assignment. Journal of Symbolic Logic 48(4), 931–940 (1983)
2. Berarducci, A., Dezani-Ciancaglini, M.: Infinite lambda-calculus and Types. Theoretical Computer Science 212, 29–75 (1999)
3. Dezani-Ciancaglini, M., Honsell, F., Motohama, Y.: Compositional Characterization of λ-terms using Intersection Types. Theoretical Computer Science 340(3), 459–495 (2005)
4. Dezani-Ciancaglini, M.: Private communication (2007)
5. Hindley, J.R., Seldin, J.P.: Introduction to Combinators and λ-Calculus. Cambridge University Press, Cambridge (1986)
6. Kennaway, J.R., Klop, J.W., Sleep, M.R., de Vries, F.J.: Infinitary lambda calculus. Theoretical Computer Science 175(1), 93–125 (1997)
7. Kurata, T.: A Type Theoretical View of Böhm-Trees. In: de Groote, P., Hindley, J.R. (eds.) TLCA 1997. LNCS, vol. 1210, pp. 231–247. Springer, Heidelberg (1997)
8. Raffalli, C.: Data Types, Infinity and Equality in System AF2. In: Meinke, K., Börger, E., Gurevich, Y. (eds.) CSL 1993. LNCS, vol. 832, pp. 280–294. Springer, Heidelberg (1994)
9. Tatsuta, M., Dezani-Ciancaglini, M.: Normalisation is Insensible to lambda-term Identity or Difference. In: Proceedings of Twenty First Annual IEEE Symposium on Logic in Computer Science, pp. 327–336 (2006)
10. Terese (Bezem, M., Klop, J.W., de Vrijer, R. (eds.)), Term Rewriting Systems, Cambridge University Press (2003)

A New Translation for Semi-classical Theories — Backtracking without CPS

Satoshi Kobayashi

Dept. of Computer Science, Kyoto Sangyo University,
Kamigamo Motoyama, Kita-ku, Kyoto, Japan
kbys@cc.kyoto-su.ac.jp

Abstract. Most research of algorithm extraction from classical proofs is based on double negation translation or its variants. From the viewpoint of Curry-Howard isomorphism, double negation translation corresponds to CPS translation. Unfortunately, CPS translation makes resulting programs very complex.

In this paper, we study a new translation for a semi-classical logic which is not based on double negation translation. Though it does not validate full classical logic, it translates Limit Computable Mathematics (LCM) into constructive mathematics.

Our translation is inspired by game semantics with backtracking rules. Using the translation, we can extract an algorithm from a proof of a proposition A in LCM. The extracted algorithm gives a recursive winning strategy for the first mover of the game defined from A, at least when A is implication-free.

1 Introduction

In this paper, we propose a new translational semantics for an arithmetic with a weak version of excluded middle. Most research of algorithm extraction from classical proofs is based on Gödel-Gentzen's double negation translation or its variants such as the Kuroda translation.

Suppose a formula A is proved in classical arithmetic. Let us write $A^{\neg\neg}$ for the result of double negation translation of A. Then $A^{\neg\neg}$ is proved in intuitionistic logic. The proof of A is translated to a proof of $A^{\neg\neg}$. Since the latter proof is constructive, we can extract an algorithm from the proof. From the viewpoint of Curry-Howard isomorphism, the translation of the proof is considered as a kind of CPS translation. (Speaking more exactly, Friedman's A-translation is usually applied after double negation translation.)

There have been many proposals of proof-term calculi for classical logic. CPS is often used in order to investigate various properties of such calculi, for example, strong normalizability.

However, generally speaking, algorithms extracted from classical proofs are complex. It is difficult to understand their meaning by tracing their execution.

Therefore, we take the following approach: We give up full classical logic. Instead, we use only weaker principles as Σ^0_1-excluded middle. Here, Σ^0_1-excluded

J. Garrigue and M. Hermenegildo (Eds.): FLOPS 2008, LNCS 4989, pp. 210–223, 2008.

middle is the excluded middle $A \vee \neg A$ restricted to the case where A is a Σ_1^0 formula. Limit Computable Mathematics (LCM) is mathematics based on such restricted classical logic. It is known that we can develop large part of classical mathematics within LCM[1,14,5]. Roughly speaking, LCM is constructive mathematics extended with Σ_1^0-excluded middle. We give a new translation for LCM not based on double negation translation. Our translation gives a new method of algorithm extraction from LCM proofs. We expect that using the method we can extract more comprehensible algorithms than when we use methods for full classical proofs.

1.1   Limiting Realizability Interpretation

There was already a method of algorithm extraction for LCM: Nakata and Hayashi's "limiting realizability interpretation" [13]. It uses Δ_2^0 functions in place of recursive functions. A Δ_2^0 function f is given as a limit of some recursive function g. The infinite sequence of natural numbers $g(0, \boldsymbol{x}), \ldots, g(n, \boldsymbol{x}), \ldots$ converges to $f(\boldsymbol{x})$ in limit. We can consider f as a "learning algorithm" which converges to "the correct answer" after making finite number of mistakes. We can extract such a learning algorithm from a proof in LCM by using the realizability interpretation. However, generally speaking, the above g becomes quite complex and inefficient. It will be very difficult to understand the computational content of the proof by executing the extracted algorithm.

1.2   Backtracking Game

Therefore, Berardi, Coquand, Hayashi and the author switched to another approach: game semantics with backtracking rules.

The essential idea of the game semantics[7,3] is as follows: Suppose a sentence A is given. Then a two-person game is defined. The two players are called Eloise and Abelard. Eloise is the first mover. Eloise must defend the truth of A. She tries to show evidence for A. Abelard attacks Eloise by trying to find a counter example. A play of the game is a dialogue between these two players. Consider the case where Eloise must defend $B \vee C$. Then she has two choices: she must choose either B or C, and she must defend it. However, she can retract her choice later; she can backtrack. She can go back to this choice point and try another choice. Similarly, consider the case where Eloise must defend $\exists x.P(x)$. Then she has infinitely many choices: she must choose a term t and defend $P(t)$. Also in this case, she can go back to this choice point and try another choice, say, $P(t')$. Only Eloise can backtrack. Abelard is not allowed to backtrack.

Let us consider $\exists x.P(x) \vee \forall x.\bar{P}(x)$, where P is a decidable predicate and $\bar{P}$ is the complement of P. This is an instance of Σ_1^0-excluded middle. Suppose that Eloise must defend this sentence. She can win by the following strategy: She chooses $\forall x.\bar{P}(x)$ for the first time. Then Abelard tries to present a counter example for this formula. He chooses a closed term t and request Eloise to defend $\bar{P}(t)$. If $\bar{P}(t)$ is true (i.e. t is not a counter example), then Eloise wins. Otherwise (i.e. $\bar{P}(t)$ is false and $P(t)$ is true), the previous choice by Eloise was wrong. She goes back to the previous choice point (backtrack). She chooses $\exists x.P(x)$ this time. Then she must show a concrete example for $\exists x.P(x)$. Now she knows that $P(t)$ is true. She answers $P(t)$ and she wins, because she has reached a true atomic sentence $P(t)$. Note that she learned a correct answer from Abelard's attack. We can prove that a proof of A in LCM corresponds to a winning strategy[3]. This result means that we can extract an algorithm from a proof in LCM; an algorithm which gives a winning strategy for Eloise.

Backtracking in this game semantics is *irreversible* in the following sense: Eloise can retract ordinary moves. However, she can not retract previous retractions. That is, she can not undo previous undo's. This restricted version of backtracking is called *1-backtracking*.

Presence of 1-backtracking is essential in this game semantics. Without 1-backtracking, we can not validate Σ_1^0-excluded middle.

Berardi[4] gave a game semantics for intuitionistic logic. 1-Backtracking is not allowed in the games in [4]. Berardi and Yamagada [7] gave a 1-backtracking game semantics for the positive (i.e. implication-free) fragment of LCM. The author [3] gave a 1-backtracking game semantics for full LCM (i.e. with implications).

Note 1. It is known that reversible backtracking (full backtracking) is strictly stronger than 1-backtracking. Coquand[8] gave a game semantics with full backtracking for full classical logic.

1.3   Problems with Game Semantics

However, the author found that the game semantics has some demerits. First, the author feels that game semantics is too operational. Being operational may be a merit when we visualize algorithms. However, it can be troublesome for theoretical analysis. On the other hand, realizability interpretation is much less operational, because it uses purely functional calculus. Secondly, the game semantics given in [7,4,3] is too closely tied to a particular sequent calculus. In contrast, realizability interpretation is independent from proof syntax of logics. It works equally for sequent calculi, natural deduction systems, Hilbert style systems, or any other calculus.

Moreover, it is difficult to understand the meaning of cut rule in game semantics. Consider the simplest form of cut rule:

$$\frac{\vdash A \quad A \vdash B}{\vdash B}$$

The meaning of $\vdash A$ is that the first mover can show A. However, the meaning of $A \vdash B$ is that if the second mover can show A, then the first mover can show B. That is, A has different meanings in $\vdash A$ and $A \vdash B$. Hence, validity of $\vdash B$ is not intuitively clear even if $\vdash A$ and $A \vdash B$ are valid. (This is one of the reasons why the author did not include discussions on cut rule in [3].) Meanwhile, validity of cut rule is trivial in realizability interpretation.

1.4   Realizability Interpretation with Backtracking

For the above reason, the author began to reconsider realizability interpretation for LCM.

We want to find a realizability interpretation so that a realizer of a proposition A corresponds to a winning strategy for the first mover of the game defined from A. The author considered the following two-staged solution:

1. First we define a translation which maps a formula A of LCM to another formula A' in some constructive logic.
2. A realizer of A is defined as a realizer of A'.

Then the most important job is to find a translation which reflects the interpretation of formulas in the game semantics with backtracking.

In the next section, we will give the definition of such a translation.

2   Definition of the Translation

2.1   Fundamental Ideas

First let us have an informal discussion on the key ideas behind our translational semantics. Our translation is defined as a modification of Friedman's A-translation. Recall that Friedman's original A-translation was defined as follows:

– Choose a formula A and fix it.
– For each formula ϕ, we define another formula ϕ^A as follows:
  • If P is atomic, then $P^A \equiv P \vee A$.
  • If $\circ$ is $\wedge$, $\vee$ or $\rightarrow$, then $(B \circ C)^A \equiv B^A \circ C^A$.
  • $(\forall x.B)^A \equiv \forall x.B^A$, $(\exists x.B)^A \equiv \exists x.B^A$.

Let us reconsider the intuitive meaning of B^A. Assume that our main goal is to prove B, and we are trying to show an atomic subformula P as a subgoal. Suppose P is false. Then we are stuck. However, if P is replaced by P^A ($\equiv P \vee A$), then we have a chance of escape. Now we can "escape to A", that is, we may prove A instead of showing P. For example, let A be the top level formula. Then we can go back to the starting position when we are stuck. That looks similar to backtracking of game semantics.

However, this escape mechanism is insufficient for our purpose, because we can go back to the previous position only once. In proving B^A, we can escape to A. However, if A is not of the form B^A, we have no more chance to escape. If we wish to escape twice, we should replace B^A by B^{B^A}; then we can escape to B^A for the first time and can escape to A for the second time. However, twice is not yet sufficient, of course. We must be able to escape as many times as we want. Therefore the right solution is to modify the definition of B^A so that B^A becomes the least fixpoint of the mapping $X \mapsto B^X$. Here it is important that the fixpoint must be the least one, because we should admit only finitely many times of backtracking. That is, we should use inductive definitions to define B^A.

2.2   Formal Definition of the Translation

According to the above idea, we give the formal definition of our translation.

Let IL_2 be intuitionistic predicate logic extended with universal quantification over propositional variables $\forall X.A[X]$ and inductive definition of propositions $\mu X.A[X]$. Here, all ccurrences of the propositional variable X must be positive in $A[X]$. We translate first order formulas into IL_2.

The proposition $\mu X.A[X]$ means the least proposition satisfying $A[\mu X.A[X]]$ $\Leftrightarrow \mu X.A[X]$. We assume that IL_2 has the following two axiom schema for inductive definitions:

1. $A[\mu X.A[X]] \to \mu X.A[X]$
2. $(A[C] \to C) \to \mu X.A[X] \to C$ (Transfinite Induction)

Note 2. It is well-known that we can define $\mu X.A[X]$ using universal quantification over propositions. However, it has an advantage to have both $\forall X.A[X]$ and $\mu X.A[X]$ as primitives; we can define realizability of $\mu X.A[X]$ so that e **r** $\mu X.A[X]$ is equivalent to e **r** $A[\mu X.A[x]]$ by using techniques developed in the author's old work[2]. Though [2] is on inductive definitions of predicates, the technique can be applied to inductive definition of propositions, since propositions are 0-place predicates.

Notation. We often write $A \leq B$ when $A \to B$ holds. We consider $A \leq B$ as an ordering on propositions. We write $A \Leftrightarrow B$ for "$A \leq B$ and $B \leq A$"

Definition 1. *Let A be a first order formula and X be an IL_2 formula. We define another IL_2 formula A^X by induction on the complexity of A as follows:*

- $P^X \equiv P \vee X$ *(P is atomic)*
- $(A \wedge B)^X \equiv A^X \wedge B^X$
- $(A \vee B)^X \equiv \mu P.(A^{P \vee X} \vee B^{P \vee X})$.
- $(A \to B)^X \equiv \forall Y \geq X(A^Y \to B^Y)$. *Without abbreviation, the right hand side is $\forall Y((X \to Y) \to (A^Y \to B^Y))$.*
- $(\forall x.A(x))^X \equiv \forall x.(A(x)^X)$.
- $(\exists x.A(x))^X \equiv \mu P.\exists x.(A(x)^{P \vee X})$.

The intention behind this definition is as follows:

- On disjunction: To prove $A \vee B$, you must choose either A or B and prove it. However, you can go back (backtrack) to this choice point later.
- On existential quantifier: To prove $\exists x.A(x)$, you must choose some t and prove $A(t)$. However, you can go back to this choice point later.

Note that P occurs only positively in A^P (P is a propositional variable). Recall that P must be positive in $A[P]$ when we use inductive definition $\mu P.A[P]$.

We can not "simplify" $(A \to B)^X$ as $A^X \to B^X$. X is not positive in $A^X \to B^X$.

The definition $(A \to B)^X \equiv \forall Y \geq X(A^Y \to B^Y)$ is inspired by the interpretation of implication in intuitionistic Kripke model. If we write P^X as $X \models P$, the definition becomes

$$X \models (A \to B) \Leftrightarrow \forall Y \geq X(Y \models A \to Y \models B).$$

Note 3. It is easy to show that A^X is equivalent to $A \vee X$ in classical logic. In particular, $A^\perp$ is classically equivalent to A. Therefore our translation is just an equivalence from classical viewpoint.

Note 4. $A^\perp$ is not "the dual" of A. It is just A^X with $X = \perp$.

Our backtracking is irreversible. Note that P^X is $P \vee X$ for an atomic P and the disjunction in $P \vee X$ is the ordinary intuitionistic disjunction. When we prove $P \vee X$, we must choose either P or X deterministically. Once we decided to prove X (i.e. to backtrack), we can not retract the decision later. This is the reason why our translation validates only irreversible backtracking.

3 Some Properties and Soundness of the Translation

3.1 Soundness for First-Order Intuitionistic Logic

The following lemma is easy.

Lemma 1

1. $(A^X)[x := t] \equiv (A[x := t])^{X[x:=t]}$, *that is, the translation preserves substitution.*
2. $FV(A^X) = FV(A) \cup FV(X)$, *where $FV(A)$ is the set of free variables in A.*
3. *(Monotonicity) $(X \to Y) \to A^X \to A^Y$.*

Note that, by monotonicity, we have $A^\perp \leftrightarrow \forall X.A^X$.

Lemma 2. $X \leq A^X$.

Note 5. This shows that the $\perp$-elimination rule is valid.

Proof. Induction on the complexity of A:

- For an atomic formula A: $X \leq A \vee X \equiv A^X$.
- If A is $B \wedge C$: By induction hypothesis, we have $B^X \geq X$ and $C^X \geq X$. Therefore, $(B \wedge C)^X \equiv B^X \wedge C^X \geq X \wedge X \Leftrightarrow X$.
- If A is $B \vee C$: Let $P \equiv (B \vee C)^X$. Then, by induction hypothesis, we have $B^{P \vee X} \geq P \vee X$ and $C^{P \vee X} \geq P \vee X$. Hence $P \Leftrightarrow B^{P \vee X} \vee C^{P \vee X} \geq P \vee X \vee P \vee X \geq X$.
- If A is $B \to C$: By induction hypothesis, we have $Y \leq C^Y$. Hence, for each $Y \geq X$, we have $X \leq Y \leq C^Y \leq (B^Y \to C^Y)$. Therefore $X \leq (\forall Y \geq X.(B^Y \to C^Y))$.
- If A is $\forall x.B(x)$: By induction hypothesis, we have $X \leq B(x)^X$. Therefore $X \leq \forall x.(B(x)^X)$.

– If A is $\exists x.B(x)$: Let P be $(\exists x.B(x))^X$. Then $P \Leftrightarrow \exists x.(B(x))^{P \vee X} \geq \exists x.(P \vee X) \geq X$.

Lemma 3

1. Let P be $(A \vee B)^X$, then we have $P \Leftrightarrow A^P \Leftrightarrow B^P$.
2. Let Q be $(\exists x.B(x))^X$, then we have $Q \Leftrightarrow B(t)^Q$ for any term t.

Proof

1. By monotonicity and Lemma 2, $P \leq A^P \leq A^{P \vee X} \leq A^{P \vee X} \vee B^{P \vee X} \Leftrightarrow P$. Therefore $P \Leftrightarrow A^P$. Similarly, $P \Leftrightarrow B^P$.
2. $Q \leq B(t)^Q \leq \exists x.(B(x)^Q) \leq \exists x.(B(x)^{Q \vee X}) \Leftrightarrow Q$.

Note on Lemma 3: Intuitively speaking, $P \Leftrightarrow A^P$ means that the following strategy is safe: To show $A \vee B$, first we try to show A, and when we are "stuck", we backtrack to $A \vee B$. It is similar for $P \Leftrightarrow B^P$.

Similarly, $Q \Leftrightarrow B(t)^Q$ means that the following strategy is safe: To show $\exists x.B(x)$, first we try to show $B(t)$ for an arbitrarily chosen t, and when we are "stuck", we backtrack to $A \vee B$.

Lemma 4. $A^{A^X} \leq A^X$

Proof. Induction on the complexity of A.

– For atomic A: $A^{A^X} \equiv A^{A \vee X} \equiv A \vee A \vee X \equiv A^X$.
– The case $A \equiv B \wedge C$: $(B \wedge C)^{(B \wedge C)^X} \equiv B^{(B \wedge C)^X} \wedge C^{(B \wedge C)^X} \equiv B^{B^X \wedge C^X} \wedge C^{B^X \wedge C^X} \leq B^{B^X} \wedge C^{C^X} \leq B^X \wedge C^X \equiv (B \wedge C)^X$.
– The case $A \equiv B \vee C$: Let $P \equiv (B \vee C)^X$ and $Q \equiv (B \vee C)^P$. Q is the least proposition satisfying $Q \Leftrightarrow B^{Q \vee P} \vee C^{Q \vee P}$. We show $Q \leq P$. By the leastness of Q, it is sufficient to prove $B^{P \vee P} \vee C^{P \vee P} \leq P$. Using Lemma 3, we obtain LHS $\Leftrightarrow B^P \vee C^P \leq P$.
– The case $A \equiv B \rightarrow C$: $(B \rightarrow C)^X$ is $\forall Y \geq X.(B^Y \rightarrow C^Y)$. Let P be this formula, and we show $(B \rightarrow C)^P \leq P$. The LHS is $\forall Y \geq P.(B^Y \rightarrow C^Y)$. Let Q be this formula and we derive P from Q. Take an arbitrary Y with $X \leq Y$ and we derive C^Y from B^Y. By $X \leq Y$, we have $P \leq (B^Y \rightarrow C^Y)$. By B^Y, we have $P \leq C^Y$. From this and Q, we have $B^{C^Y} \rightarrow C^{C^Y}$. On the other hand, from $Y \leq C^Y$ and monotonicity, we have $B^Y \leq B^{C^Y}$. Hence, by the assumption B^Y, we have B^{C^Y}. Therefore C^{C^Y}. By induction hypothesis, we have $C^{C^Y} \leq C^Y$ and hence we can derive C^Y.
– The case $A \equiv \forall x.B(x)$: We have $(\forall x.B(x))^{(\forall x.B(x))^X} \equiv \forall x.B(x)^{\forall x.B(x)^X} \leq \forall x.B(x)^{B(x)^X} \leq \forall x.B(x)^X \leq (\forall x.B(x))^X$.
– The case $A \equiv \exists x.B(x)$: Let $P \equiv \exists x.B(x)^X$ and $Q \equiv \exists x.B(x)^P$. Q is the least proposition satisfying $Q \Leftrightarrow \exists x.(B(x)^{(Q \vee P)})$. We prove $Q \leq P$. By the leastness of Q, it is sufficient to show $\exists x.(B(x)^{(P \vee P)}) \leq P$. By Lemma 3, we have LHS $\Leftrightarrow \exists x.(B(x)^P) \leq P$.

Corollary 1. $A^{A^X} \Leftrightarrow A^X$

Proof. From $X \leq A^X$ and monotonicity, we have $A^X \leq A^{A^X}$. By the above lemma, $A^{A^X} \Leftrightarrow A^X$.

Theorem 1. *(Soundness of the translation) If $\Gamma \vdash A$ in (first order) intuitionistic logic, we have $\Gamma^X \vdash A^X$ in IL_2. Here, Γ^X is defined as $\Gamma^X \equiv A_1{}^X, \ldots, A_n{}^X$ if $\Gamma \equiv A_1, \ldots, A_n$.*

Proof. Induction on the complexity of the derivation of $\Gamma \vdash A$.

- The case of $A_1, \ldots, A_n \vdash A_i$ is trivial.
- $\bot$-elimination: $\bot^X \equiv \bot \vee X \Leftrightarrow X \leq A^X$.
- $\wedge$-introduction: If $\Gamma^X \vdash B^X$ and $\Gamma^X \vdash C^X$, then $\Gamma^X \vdash B^X \wedge C^X$.
- $\wedge$-elimination: $(B \wedge C)^X \equiv B^X \wedge C^X \leq B^X$. Similarly, $(B \wedge C)^X \leq C^X$.
- $\vee$-introduction: Let P be $(B \vee C)^X$. Then $P \Leftrightarrow B^{P \vee X} \vee C^{P \vee X}$. Hence $B^X \leq B^{P \vee X} \leq P$ and $C^X \leq C^{P \vee X} \leq P$.
- $\vee$-elimination: Suppose $\Gamma \vdash A \vee B$ and $\Gamma, A \vdash C$ and $\Gamma, B \vdash C$. By induction hypothesis, for an arbitrary X, we have $\Gamma^X \vdash (A \vee B)^X$ and $\Gamma^X, A^X \vdash C^X$ and $\Gamma^X, B^X \vdash C^X$. We show $\Gamma^X \vdash C^X$. It is sufficient to prove $(A \vee B)^X \leq C^X$. Let $P \equiv (A \vee B)^X$. Then P is the least proposition satisfying $P \Leftrightarrow A^{P \vee X} \vee B^{P \vee X}$. By the leastness of P, it is sufficient to show $\Gamma^X \vdash A^{C^X \vee X} \vee B^{C^X \vee X} \to C^X$. By induction hypothesis and monotonicity, we have $\Gamma^X, A^{C^X \vee X} \vdash C^{C^X \vee X}$ and $\Gamma^X, B^{C^X \vee X} \vdash C^{C^X \vee X}$. On the other hand, by $X \leq C^X$ and Lemma 4, we have $C^{C^X \vee X} \leq C^{C^X} \leq C^X$. Therefore $\Gamma^X \vdash A^{C^X \vee X} \vee B^{C^X \vee X} \to C^X$.
- $\to$-introduction: Suppose $\Gamma, A \vdash B$. We show $\Gamma^X \vdash (A \to B)^X$. By induction hypothesis, for an arbitrary Y, we have $\Gamma^Y, A^Y \vdash B^Y$. By monotonicity, $\Gamma^X, X \to Y, A^Y \vdash B^Y$. Hence we have $\Gamma^X \vdash \forall Y \geq X.(A^Y \to B^Y)$.
- $\to$-elimination: Assume $(A \to B)^X$ and A^X. We derive B^X. By the first assumption, $\forall Y \geq X.(A^Y \to B^Y)$. Taking Y as X, we have $A^X \to B^X$.
- $\forall$-introduction: Assume $\Gamma \vdash A(x)$ and $x \notin FV(\Gamma)$. By induction hypothesis, $\Gamma^X \vdash A(x)^X$. Since $x \notin FV(\Gamma^X)$, we have $\Gamma^X \vdash \forall x.A(x)^X$.
- $\forall$-elimination: Assume $\Gamma \vdash \forall x.A(x)$. By induction hypothesis, $\Gamma^X \vdash \forall x.A(x)^X$. Hence $\Gamma^X \vdash A(t)^X$.
- $\exists$-introduction: Assume $\Gamma \vdash A(t)$. By induction hypothesis, $\Gamma^X \vdash A(t)^X$. Hence $\Gamma^X \vdash \exists x.(A(x)^X)$. Let P be $(\exists x.A(x))^X$, then, by monotonicity, $\Gamma^X \vdash \exists x.(A(x)^{P \vee X})$. Therefore $\Gamma^X \vdash (\exists x.A(x))^X$.
- $\exists$-elimination: Assume $\Gamma \vdash \exists x.A(x)$ and $\Gamma, A(x) \vdash C$. We prove $\Gamma^X \vdash C^X$. By induction hypothesis, $\Gamma^X \vdash (\exists x.A(x))^X$. Let $P \equiv (\exists x.A(x))^X$. Then P is the least proposition satisfying $P \Leftrightarrow \exists x.(A(x))^{P \vee X}$. It is sufficient to prove $\Gamma^X \vdash P \to C^X$. Assume Γ^X. By the leastness of P, it is sufficient to show $A(x)^{C^X \vee X} \to C^X$. By induction hypothesis and monotonicity, $\Gamma^X, A(x)^{C^X \vee X} \vdash C^{C^X \vee X}$. From $X \leq C^X$, we have $C^X \vee X \Leftrightarrow C^X$. Therefore $C^{C^X \vee X} \leq C^{C^X} \leq C^X$.

3.2 Soundness for Arithmetical Axioms

Theorem 2. *If A is an instance of proper axioms of Heyting Arithmetic* **HA**, *then we can prove A^X in Heyting Arithmetic over IL_2.*

Proof

- If A is an atomic axiom such as $0 + x = x$, then $A \to A^X$ is trivial.
- If $A \equiv \neg(0 = 1)$, we have $A^X \Leftrightarrow \forall Y \geq X.(0 = 1 \vee Y \to \bot \vee Y) \Leftrightarrow \forall Y \geq X.(0 = 1 \to Y) \Leftrightarrow 0 = 1 \to X$, and hence $A \to A^X$.
- Consider the case where A is an instance of mathematical induction $B(0) \wedge \forall n.(B(n) \to B(suc(n))) \to \forall n.B(n)$. Then A^X is $\forall Y \geq X.(B(0)^Y \wedge \forall n.\forall Z \geq Y(B(n)^Z \to B(suc(n))^Z) \to \forall n.B(n)^Y$. This is easily derived from an instance of mathematical induction: $B(0)^Y \wedge \forall n.(B(n)^Y \to B(suc(n))^Y) \to \forall n.B(n)^Y$.

3.3 Soundness for Σ_1^0-Excluded Middle

Theorem 3. *Our translation is sound for Σ_1^0-excluded middle. That is, if A is an instance of Σ_1^0-excluded middle, A^X is provable in IL_2.*

Proof. Without loss of generality, we can assume A is of the form $\exists x.B(x) \vee \forall x.\bar{B}(x)$. Here, $B(x)$ and $\bar{B}(x)$ are atomic formulas and $\bar{B}(x)$ is the complement of $B(x)$. We let $P \equiv (\exists x.B(x) \vee \forall x.\bar{B}(x))^\bot$ and show that P is provable in IL_2.

$$P \Leftrightarrow (\exists x.B(x))^{P \vee \bot} \vee (\forall x.\bar{B}(x))^{P \vee \bot}$$
$$\equiv Q \vee \forall x.(\bar{B}(x) \vee P \vee \bot) \tag{1}$$

Here, Q is $(\exists x.B(x))^{P \vee \bot}$ and

$$Q \Leftrightarrow \exists x.(B(x) \vee Q \vee P \vee \bot). \tag{2}$$

Since $B(x)$ and $\bar{B}(x)$ are the complement of each other, we have $B(x) \vee \bar{B}(x)$.

- If $\bar{B}(x)$, we have $\bar{B}(x) \vee P \vee \bot$.
- If $B(x)$, we can derive Q using (2). Therefore, by (1), we have P and hence $\bar{B}(x) \vee P \vee \bot$.

In either case we have $\bar{B}(x) \vee P \vee \bot$. Therefore $\forall x.(\bar{B}(x) \vee P \vee \bot)$. Then, using (1), we can prove P.   □

4   Algorithm Extraction

Using the above results, we can extract an algorithm from a proof in LCM.

4.1 Realizability Interpretation

We show an outline of our realizability interpretation. For an introduction to realizability interpretation, see Troelstra and van Dalen's textbook[15].

First, we define recursive realizability interpretation for IL_2.

Connectives and quantifiers of first order logic is interpreted as usual. For propositional quantifiers, we define $e \, \mathbf{r} \, \forall P.A[P]$ according to the style of Kreisel-Troelstra's realizability:

$$e \, \mathbf{r} \, \forall P.A[P] \quad \text{iff} \quad e \, \mathbf{r} \, A[P] \quad \text{for all valuations to } P$$

For inductive definitions, we define $e \, \mathbf{r} \, \mu P.A[P]$ so that the following equivalence holds:

$$e \, \mathbf{r} \, \mu P.A[P] \quad \text{iff} \quad e \, \mathbf{r} \, A[\mu P.A[P]].$$

The definition is easy if you follow the technique given in [2]. We choose a set variable P^* for each propositional variabvle P. P^* ranges over subsets of the set of natural numbers. We define $e \, \mathbf{r} \, P$ as $e \in P^*$ and define

$$e \, \mathbf{r} \, \mu P.A[P] \quad \text{iff} \quad e \in \mu P^*.\{\, u \mid u \, \mathbf{r} \, A[P] \,\},$$

where $\mu P^*.\{\, u \mid u \, \mathbf{r} \, A[P] \,\}$ is the least fixpoint of the map

$$P^* \mapsto \{\, u \mid u \, \mathbf{r} \, A[P] \,\}.$$

Then we define realizability interpretation of first order arithmetical formula A as follows:

$$e \, \mathbf{r}_X \, A \xrightarrow{def} e \, \mathbf{r} \, A^X.$$
$$e \, \mathbf{r} \, A \xrightarrow{def} e \, \mathbf{r} \, A^\perp.$$

Here X is an arbitrary proposition in IL_2. '$\mathbf{r}_X$' has X as a parameter. Though '$\mathbf{r}_X$' interpretation is sound for any X, the author thinks that '$\mathbf{r}$' (i.e. the special case where X is $\perp$) is sufficient for most applications.

Example — Σ_1^0-Excluded Middle. We gave a proof of $(\exists x.B(x) \vee \forall x.\bar{B}(x))^\perp$ in Section 3.3. From that proof, we can calculate a realizer e of Σ_1^0-Excluded Middle $\exists x.B(x) \vee \forall x.\bar{B}(x)$. We define e as follows:

$$e = \mathrm{inr} \, f$$

where f is defined as

$$f(x) = \begin{cases} \mathrm{inl} * & \text{(if } \bar{B}(x) \text{ is true)} \\ \mathrm{inr}(\mathrm{inl}(\mathrm{inl} \, \langle x, \mathrm{inl} * \rangle)) & \text{(if } B(x) \text{ is true)} \end{cases}$$

Here we assume the following:

- $*$ is a dummy realizer which realizes true atomic formulas. That is, for atomic formula φ, we have $e \, \mathbf{r} \, \varphi \xrightarrow{def} e = * \wedge (\varphi \text{ is true})$
- inl is a realizer of formulas of the form $B \to B \vee C$.
- inr is a realizer of formulas of the form $C \to B \vee C$.

Extracting a Winning Strategy. From the realizer given in the above example, we can extract a recursive winning strategy of the game for Σ_1^0-excluded middle.

We show an outline:

1. Since e is of the form $\mathrm{inr} f$, Eloise first chooses the right disjunct $\forall x.\bar{B}(x)$ and try to defend it.
2. Then Abelard attacks her. He chooses some c and requests Eloise to defend $\bar{B}(c)$. Then we calculate the value of $f(c)$. We have two cases:
   (a) Case where $\bar{B}(c)$ is true: In this case, we have $f(c) = \mathrm{inl} *$ and $* \mathbf{r}\ \bar{B}(c)$. Hence $\bar{B}(c)$ is true. Eloise wins because she has reached a true atomic formula.
   (b) Case where $\bar{B}(c)$ is false: In this case, we have

$$f(c) = \mathrm{inr}(\mathrm{inl}(\mathrm{inl}\ \langle c, \mathrm{inl} * \rangle)).$$

   Since $\mathrm{inl}\ \langle c, \mathrm{inl} * \rangle\ \mathbf{r}\ P$ and P is the translation of the given formula, Eloise retracts the previous choice and backtracks to the start position. Since we have $\langle c, \mathrm{inl} * \rangle\ \mathbf{r}\ (\exists x.B(x))^X$, Eloise chooses the left disjunct $\exists x.B(x)$ this time. Since $* \mathbf{r}\ B(c)$ holds, Eloise chooses c as a concrete example for $\exists x.B(x)$. Because $B(c)$ is true, she wins.

Note that the given formula in this example is implication-free. In general, we can not extract a winning strategy when the given formula includes implication. The reason is that our game semantics[3] does not use functions to interpret implications while we need functions to realize implications.

We have some ideas about this problem. The first one is to transform a realizer to a computation without higher order functions. The transformation may look similar to the procedure which translates natural deduction proofs to sequent calculus proofs. The second idea is to develop a new game which employs functions to interpret implications. However, these ideas are not yet fully investigated by the author.

4.2   Type Theoretical Interpretation

Instead of using realizability interpretation, we may use type theory for algorithm extraction. An outline is given below:

Suppose a type theory $\mathbf{T}$ has polymorphic types $\forall X.A[X]$ and inductive types $\mu X.A[X]$. We also assume $\mathbf{T}$ has products $A \times B$, sums $A + B$, function types $A \Rightarrow B$, dependent products $\Pi x : \sigma.A$, and dependent sums $\Sigma x : \sigma.A$. For each atomic formula P, we assume that a primitive type τ_P which corresponds P is given.

Then $\mathbf{T}$ can interpret IL_2 and therefore we can translate a proof in LCM to a proof term in $\mathbf{T}$.

Let A be a first order formula and X be a type in $\mathbf{T}$. Then we define a type $A|X$ in $\mathbf{T}$ as follows:

- If A is atomic, then $P \mid X = \tau_A + X$.
- $(A \wedge B) \mid X = (A \mid X) \times (B \mid X)$.
- $(A \vee B) \mid X = \mu P.((A \mid (P + X)) + (B \mid (P + X)))$.
- $(A \rightarrow B) \mid X = \forall Y.((X \Rightarrow Y) \Rightarrow (A \mid Y) \Rightarrow (B \mid Y))$
- $(\forall x.A(x)) \mid X = \prod x : \sigma.(A(x) \mid X)$. Here, σ is the type of the variable x. For example, if x is a natural number variable, then σ is the type of natural numbers.
- $(\exists x.A(x)) \mid X = \mu P. \sum x : \sigma.(A(x) \mid P + X)$. Here, σ is the type of the variable of x.

Then we can effectively find a term of type $A \mid X$ when a proof of A in LCM arithmetic is given.

5   Hierarchy of Weak Axioms of Excluded Middle

We write EM_n for Σ_n^0-excluded middle. Since our translation validates EM_1, it is natural to conjecture that the translation reduces the strength of EM_{n+1} to that of EM_n.

In this section, we prove that if A is an instance of EM_{n+1}, then A^X is derived from EM_n in IL_2.

Lemma 5. *Suppose that a formula A is a prenex form $Q_1 x. \cdots .Q_n x.P$ with an atomic formula P, and the sequence of quantifiers $Q_1, \ldots, Q_n$ is alternating. Then,*

1. *If A is a Π_n^0-formula, then $A^X \Leftrightarrow A \vee X$ is derived from EM_n in IL_2.*
2. *If A is a Σ_n^0-formula, then $A^X \Leftrightarrow A \vee X$ is derived from EM_{n-1} in IL_2.*

Here, $n \geq 1$ and EM_0 means $\top$ (true).

Proof. We prove the above 1 and 2 simultaneously by induction on n.

- If $n = 1$:
   - Let A be a Π_1^0-formula $\forall x.B(x)$. Then $A^X = \forall x.(B(x) \vee X)$. Since $B(x)$ is atomic, we have $\forall x.B(x) \vee \exists x.\neg B(x)$ by EM_1. Hence $\forall x.(B(x) \vee X) \Leftrightarrow (\forall x.B(x)) \vee X$. Therefore $A^X \Leftrightarrow A \vee X$.
   - Let A be a Σ_1^0-formula $\exists x.B(x)$ ($B(x)$ is atomic). Let $P \equiv (\exists x.B(x))^X$. Then,

$$P \Leftrightarrow \exists x.(B(x)^{P \vee X})$$
$$\Leftrightarrow \exists x.(B(x) \vee P \vee X)$$
$$\Leftrightarrow P \vee (\exists x.B(x)) \vee X$$

   P is the least proposition satisfying $P \Leftrightarrow P \vee (\exists x.B(x)) \vee X$. However, it is clear that $(\exists x.B(x)) \vee X$ is the least proposition satisfying this equivalence. Therefore, $P \Leftrightarrow (\exists x.B(x)) \vee X$.

– Induction step: We assume the case of $n = k$ and prove the case of $n = k+1$.
  • Let A be a Π^0_{k+1}-formula $\forall x.B(x)$. Then $B(x)$ is a Σ^0_k-formula. By induction hypothesis, we can derive $B(x)^X \Leftrightarrow B(x) \vee X$ from EM_{k-1}. Hence,

$$(\forall x.B(x))^X \Leftrightarrow \forall x.(B(x)^X)$$
$$\Leftrightarrow \forall x.(B(x) \vee X)$$

  Since we have $\forall x.B(x) \vee \exists x.\neg B(x)$ by EM_{k+1}, the right hand side is equivalent to $(\forall x.B(x)) \vee X$.
  • Le A be a Σ^0_{k+1}-formula $\exists x.B(x)$. Then $B(x)$ is a Π^0_k-formula. By induction hypothesis, we can derive $B(x)^X \Leftrightarrow B(x) \vee X$ from EM_k. Let $P \equiv (\exists x.B(x))^X$. Then P is the least proposition satisfying:

$$P \Leftrightarrow \exists x.(B(x)^{P \vee X})$$
$$\Leftrightarrow \exists x.(B(x) \vee P \vee X)$$
$$\Leftrightarrow P \vee (\exists x.B(x)) \vee X.$$

  However, it is clear that $(\exists x.B(x)) \vee X$ is the least proposition satisfying the above equivalence. Therefore we have $P \Leftrightarrow (\exists x.B(x)) \vee X$.   □

Theorem 4. *If* $A \equiv \exists x.B(x) \vee \neg\exists x.B(x)$ *is an instance of* EM_{n+1}, *then* A^X *is derivable from* EM_n *in* IL_2.

Proof. It is sufficient to prove the case where X is $\bot$. We let $P \equiv A^\bot$ and derive P from EM_n. By the above lemma, we can derive $(\exists x.B(x))^X \Leftrightarrow (\exists x.B(x)) \vee X$ from EM_n for arbitrary X. Hence,

$$P \Leftrightarrow (\exists x.B(x))^P \vee \forall Y \geq P.((\exists x.B(x))^Y \to \bot^Y)$$
$$\Leftrightarrow (\exists x.B(x)) \vee P \vee \forall Y \geq P.((\exists x.B(x)) \vee Y \to \bot \vee Y)$$
$$\Leftrightarrow (\exists x.B(x)) \vee P \vee \forall Y \geq P.(\exists x.B(x) \to Y)$$
$$\Leftrightarrow (\exists x.B(x)) \vee P \vee (\exists x.B(x) \to P) \tag{3}$$

Assume $\exists x.B(x)$. Then we can derive P from (3). Therefore $\exists x.B(x) \to P$. By using (3) again, we have P. Thus we have derived P from EM_n.   □

6   Conclusion and Future Work

In this paper, we proposed a new translational semantics for LCM. Unlike most of translations for classical logic, our translation is not based on the idea of double negation translation. By using the translation, we gave a new method of algorithm extraction for LCM.

The author is working in a small project (the leader is Mariko Yasugi) for developing prototype implementation of proof animation system for LCM. The author plans to use our new translation and realizability interpretation to extract algorithms from proofs in LCM. Backtracking games will be used to animate the extracted algorithms.

We are also interested in proof theoretical study of our translation. It may become a new useful tool to analyze sub-classical theories.

References

1. Akama, Y., Berardi, S., Hayashi, S., Kohlenbach, U.: An Arithmetical Hierarchy of the Law of Excluded Middle and Related Principles. In: Proceedings of IEEE Symposium on Logic in Computer Science (LICS), pp. 192–201 (2004)
2. Kobayashi, S., Tatsuta, M.: Realizability Interpretation of Generalized Inductive Definitions. Theoretical Computer Science 131(1), 121–138 (1994)
3. Kobayashi, S.: Kyoukugen Keisan Kanou Suugaku no Geimu Imiron (English title: Game Semantics of Limit Computable Mathematics). In: Proceedings of the 24th JSSST Annual Symposia (2007)
4. Berardi, S.: An Semantic for Intuitionistic Arithmetic based on Tarski Games with retractable moves. In: Della Rocca, S.R. (ed.) TLCA 2007. LNCS, vol. 4583, pp. 23–38. Springer, Heidelberg (2007)
5. Berardi, S.: Some intuitionistic equivalents of classical principles for degree 2 formulas. Ann. Pure Appl. Logic 139(1-3), 185–200 (2006)
6. Berardi, S., Coquand, T., Hayashi, S.: Games with 1-Backtracking. In: Proceedings of Games for Logic and Programming Languages (2005)
7. Berardi, S., Yamagata, Y.: A sequent calculus for 1-backtracking, Technical Report, Turin University, CL&C 2006 (Submitted to the special issue of APAL for the congress) (2006),
   http://www.di.unito.it/~stefano/Yamagata-Berardi-report.pdf
8. Coquand, T.: A Semantics of Evidence for Classical Arithmetic. Journal of Symbolic Logic 60, 325–337 (1995)
9. Friedman, H.: Classically and intuitionistically provably recursive functions. In: Scott, D.S., Muller, G.H. (eds.) Higher Set Theory. Lecture Notes in Mathematics, vol. 699, pp. 21–28. Springer, Heidelberg (1978)
10. Hayashi, S., Nakata, M.: Towards Limit Computable Mathematics, Proceedings of TYPES 2000, Lecture Notes in Computer Science 2277. In: Callaghan, P., Luo, Z., McKinna, J., Pollack, R. (eds.) TYPES 2000. LNCS, vol. 2277, pp. 125–144. Springer, Heidelberg (2002)
11. Hayashi, S.: Mathematics based on incremental learning—Excluded middle and inductive inference. Theoretical Computer Science 350, 125–139 (2006)
12. Hayashi, S.: Can Proofs be animated by games? Fundamenta Informaticae 77, 1–13 (2007)
13. Nakata, M., Hayashi, S.: A Limiting First Order Realizability Interpretation. Scientiae Mathematicae Japonicae 55(3), 567–580 (2002)
14. Toftdal, M.: A Calibration of Ineffective Theorems of Analysis in a Hierarchy of Semi-classical Logical Principles. In: Díaz, J., Karhumäki, J., Lepistö, A., Sannella, D. (eds.) ICALP 2004. LNCS, vol. 3142, pp. 1188–1200. Springer, Heidelberg (2004)
15. Troelstra, A.S., van Dalen, D.: Constructivism in Mathematics, vol. I, II, North-Holland, Amsterdam (1988)

Undoing Dynamic Typing
(Declarative Pearl)

Nick Benton

Microsoft Research
nick@microsoft.com

Abstract. We propose undoable versions of the projection operations used when programs written in higher-order statically-typed languages interoperate with dynamically typed ones, localizing potential runtime errors to the point at which a dynamic value is projected to a static type. The idea is demonstrated by using control operators to implement backtracking projections from an untyped Scheme-like language to ML.

1   Introduction

When working in a statically typed language one often has to deal with data whose types cannot be fully determined, or at least, fully checked, at compile time. Data read at run time from the console or persistent storage and calls to dynamically-linked (local or remote) programs or services must be subject to runtime checks if type safety is to be maintained.

In a typed language, dynamic data is usually given some rather uninformative 'catch all' static type; at a low level this might be `string` or `byte[]`, whilst higher level examples include `Object`, `Dynamic` and `IUnknown`. The interface between the statically checked and unchecked worlds is provided by a collection of *projection, (down)cast, coercion, retraction* or *unmarshalling* operations mapping values of the single dynamic type to various particular static types, and complementary *embedding, (up)cast, section* or *marshalling* operations going the other way. Projection operations in an ML-like language might have signatures along the lines of:

```
val toInt : Dynamic -> int
val toBool : Dynamic -> bool
val toIntToInt : Dynamic -> (int->int)
```

but these operations are naturally partial. `toInt`, for example, will typically raise an exception in the case that its argument turns out to be a `Dynamic` value representing a string or a function. It is good practice to make this possibility more explicit and instead type the projection with an `option`:

```
val toInt : Dynamic -> int option
```

J. Garrigue and M. Hermenegildo (Eds.): FLOPS 2008, LNCS 4989, pp. 224–238, 2008.

The programmer then has to explicitly match on the returned value before using it, making it harder to forget to deal with the case of failure.[1]

There are actually two rather different classes of projection. In the case that values of type `Dynamic` carry an explicit representation of their types (usually called a *tag*, or *runtime type information*) *and* that representation can be trusted, a projection operation can essentially just check the tag and, assuming it matches, proceed to use the underlying value with no further checks. This is the way many proposals for adding dynamic typing to statically typed languages work [1] and is common when one program unmarshalls values that were originally marshalled to persistent storage by a (trusted) program written in the same typed language.

The second case is that in which dynamic values are untagged, incompletely tagged, or the tags are potentially unreliable. Safely projecting values of functional types (or very large values of simple datatypes) cannot then be done all in one go. This is generally the situation when making foreign calls to functions written in an untyped (or differently-typed) language, or when calling a remote function in another address space or over a network. Consider, for example, linking to a remote service that is supposed to compute some function on integers. The service may well have some attached metadata (e.g. WSDL) that we can check at runtime to see that it conforms to the programmer's expectation that there is an operation there that accepts and returns integers. One would expect a projection

```
val toIntToInt : url -> (int->int) option
```

that connects to the service to retrieve and check the metadata, returning `NONE` if it fails to match and `SOME f` it matches, where `f` is an ML wrapper function that sends the service a marshalled version of its argument and returns the unmarshalling of the service's response. But we cannot necessarily trust the metadata we went to all the trouble of checking, so the wrapper usually also incorporates a check that *every* returned value *is* an integer, and raises an exception if that ever fails. Now the programmer has also to deal with the possibility of failure each time he applies the function wrapping the service; we should really have made that possibility explicit by typing the projection as

```
val toIntToInt : url -> (int -> int option) option
```

where the pattern for general higher-order types is that we have to add an `option` in every positive position. A useful point of view is that projection functions wrap untyped values with code that dynamically monitors their adherence to a *contract* associated with the type, in the sense of 'Design by Contract' [14,8].

Higher-order programming in the presence of all these potential runtime errors is, however, painful. The situation is especially bad if one tries to deal with

---

[1] One might choose instead to map inappropriate elements of `Dynamic` either to divergence or to some more defined default value of the target type. Although the first alternative is well-behaved from a denotational perspective, neither has good software engineering properties.

more than one potentially-misbehaving untyped function at the same time (e.g. passing one as an argument to another), in which case impedance matching is a problem and the correct assignment of blame, and hence what error handling is appropriate, can be tricky to ascertain.

What we would really like is to turn the second case into the first, at least from the point of view of the programmer. The initial projection of a dynamic value to a given static type may or may not succeed, but if it does then the programmer should have a typed value in his hand that he can use without further fear of failure. The message of this paper is that we can achieve this goal by making projections undoable: the projection of a dynamic value to a static type may provisionally succeed but subsequently be rolled back to fail retrospectively should runtime type errors (contract violations) occur. We will use control operators to give an implementation of undoable projections from an untyped interpreted language to ML.

2   Background: Embedded Interpreters

In this section, based on an earlier paper [2], we briefly recall how embedding-projection pairs may be used to translate higher type values between typed (ML-like) and untyped (Scheme-like) languages, focussing, for concreteness, on the situation in which the untyped language is the object language of an interpreter written in the typed metalanguage. The underlying semantic idea here is just that of interpreting types as retracts[2] of a suitable universal domain, which goes back to work of Scott [17] in the 1970s, though the realization that this is both implementable and useful in functional programming seems only to have dawned in the mid 1990s [20].

Our starting point is an ML datatype modelling an untyped call-by-value lambda calculus with constants:

```
datatype U = UF of U->U | UP of U*U | UI of int | US of string
             | UUnit | UB of bool
```

An interpreter for an untyped object language, mapping abstract syntax trees to elements of U is then essentially just a denotational semantics. We assume the existence of a parser for a readable object language (typeset in *italic*) and let pi : string -> U be the composition of the parser with the intepretation function.

The idea of embedded interpreters is to define a type-indexed family of pairs of functions that *embed* ML values into the type U and *project* values of type U back into ML values. Here is the relevant part of the signature:

---

[2] Recall that a *section-retraction* pair comprises two morphisms $s : X \to Y$ and $r : Y \to X$ such that $s; r = id_X$. We say X is a *retract* of Y. *Embedding-projection* pairs are a special case: if X and Y are posets, s and r are monotone and additionally $r; s \sqsubseteq id_Y$ then s is an *embedding* and r is a *projection*.

```
signature EMBEDDINGS =
sig
  type 'a EP
  val embed   : 'a EP -> ('a->U)
  val project : 'a EP -> (U->'a)

  val unit   : unit EP
  val bool   : bool EP
  val int    : int EP
  val string : string EP
  val **     : ('a EP)*('b EP) -> ('a*'b) EP
  val -->    : ('a EP)*('b EP) -> ('a->'b) EP
end
```

For an ML type A, an (A EP)-value is a pair of an embedding of type A->U and a projection of type U->A. The interesting part of the definitions of the combinators on embedding/projection pairs is the case for function spaces: given a function from A to B, we turn it into a function from U to U by precomposing with the projection for A and postcomposing with the embedding for B; this is why embeddings and projections are defined simultaneously. The resulting function can then be made into an element of U by applying the UF constructor. Projecting an appropriate element of U to a function type A->B does the reverse: first strip off the UF constructor and then precompose with the embedding for A and postcompose with the projection for B.

Embeddings and projections let one smoothly move values in both directions between the typed and untyped worlds, as demonstrated in the following, rather frivolous, example in which we project an untyped (and untypeable) fixpoint combinator to an ML type and apply it to a function in ML:

```
- let val embY = pi "fn f=>(fn g=> f (fn a=> (g g) a))
                        (fn g=> f (fn a=> (g g) a))"
      val polyY = fn a => fn b=> project
                    (((a-->b)-->a-->b)-->a-->b) embY
      val factorial = polyY int int
        (fn f=>fn n=>if n=0 then 1 else n*(f (n-1)))
  in factorial 5
  end;
val it = 120 : int
```

The above is simple, neat and all works very nicely in the case that untyped values play by the rules and are used correctly. But the code is something of a minefield, being littered with deeply buried non-exhaustive Match and Bind exceptions. Our earlier paper said

> ... these exceptions *should* be caught and gracefully handled, but we will omit all error handling in the interests of space and clarity.

but, in fact, anything other than letting the exceptions propagate up to the top is remarkably tedious and difficult to achieve by hand. Here we will show

how much of that error handling can be built into the embedding infrastructure instead. The SML code that follows relies on `call/cc`, which is supported by both SML/NJ and MLton (though MLton's implementation takes time linear in the current depth of the control stack). There is also a (linear time) `call/cc` library for the OCaml bytecode compiler.

3 Retractable Retractions

There are various ways in which the simple embedded interpreter of our previous work can go wrong. The first is that object programs can contain runtime errors all by themselves, without any attempt being made to cast them to ML types. So, whilst this is OK:

```
- pi "let val x = 4 in x";
val it = UI 4 : U
```

this is not:

```
- pi "let val x = 4 in x 3";
uncaught exception Bind
  [nonexhaustive binding failure]
  raised at: Interpret.sml:37.45-37.63
```

As we are going to be playing fancy games with control flow shortly, it is a good idea to replace these exceptions with something simpler and more explicit. To this end, we add an explicit error constructor `UErr` to our universal type, as is commonly done in denotational semantics [18, p.144][1]. The definition is now

```
datatype U = UF of U->U | UP of U*U | UI of int | US of string
             | UUnit | UB of bool | UErr
```

and we modify the interpreter to yield `UErr` when it would previously have raised an exception, which includes making all the language constructs strict in (i.e. preserve) `UErr`.[3] An extract of the interpreter code is shown in Figure 1; this is entirely standard, though note that we have separated the binding times of variable names and values in environments. We omit the definition of `Builtins`, which uses embedding to add a few pervasives, including arithmetic and comparisons, to the environment.

We now turn to revising the embedding-projection pairs. As one might expect from our initial discussion, we change the signature to reflect the fact that projection will now be partial:

---

[3] One could make the code slightly shorter and more efficient by sticking with implicit exceptions in place of `UErr`, but the choice we have made makes what is going on slightly clearer. In particular, we do not have to worry about interactions between handlers and continuations, as it is now obvious that there are no potentially uncaught exceptions lurking anywhere.

```
signature EMBEDDINGS =
sig
  type 'a EP
  val embed   : 'a EP -> 'a -> U
  val project : 'a EP -> U -> 'a option

  val int    : int EP
  val string : string EP
  val unit   : unit EP
  val bool   : bool EP
  val **     : ('a EP)*('b EP) -> ('a*'b) EP
  val -->    : ('a EP)*('b EP) -> ('a->'b) EP
end
```

The matching structure makes unsurprising definitions of embedding-projection pairs:

```
type 'a EP = ('a->U)*(U->'a option)
fun embed ((e,p) : 'a EP) = e
fun project ((e,p) : 'a EP) = p
```

and the instances at base types are also straightforward:

```
val int    = (UI, fn (UI n) => SOME n | _ => NONE)
val string = (US, fn (US s) => SOME s | _ => NONE)
val unit   = (fn ()=>UUnit, fn UUnit => SOME () | _ => NONE)
val bool   = (UB, fn (UB b) => SOME b | _ => NONE)
```

The embedding-projection for products is only a little more complex:

```
infix **

fun (e,p)**(e',p') =
  (fn (v,v') => UP(e v, e' v'),
   fn uu => case uu
            of UP (u,u') => (case (p u, p' u')
                             of (SOME v, SOME v') => SOME (v,v')
                              | _ => NONE
                            )
             | _ => NONE)
```

To embed a pair of ML values, we simply embed each component and wrap the resulting pair of untyped values in the UP constructor. To project a value of type U to a pair type, we first check that it is indeed a UP and then that we can project each of the components in a pointwise fashion; if so, we return SOME of the paired results, and otherwise we return NONE.

We have now reached the important and tricky part of the paper: dealing with function types. Recall that our intuition is that whenever we have an ML

```
datatype Exp = EI of int                    (* integer constant   *)
             | EId of string                (* identifier         *)
             | EApp of Exp*Exp              (* application        *)
             | EP of Exp*Exp                (* pair               *)
             | ELam of string*Exp           (* lambda abstraction *)
             | EIf of Exp*Exp*Exp           (* conditional *)
             | ... other clauses elided ...

(* interpret : Exp * (string list) -> U list -> U *)
fun interpret (e,static) =
case e of
  EI n => (fn dynamic => (UI n))
| EId s => (case indexof (static,s) of
               SOME n => fn dynamic => List.nth (dynamic,n)
             | NONE => let val lib = Builtins.lookup s
                       in fn dynamic => lib
                       end)
        (* if s not in static env, lookup in pervasives instead *)
| EP (e1,e2) => let val s1 = interpret (e1,static)
                    val s2 = interpret (e2,static)
                in fn dynamic => case s1 dynamic of
                                   UErr => UErr
                                 | v1 => (case s2 dynamic of
                                            UErr => UErr
                                          | v2 => UP(v1, v2))
                end
| EApp (e1,e2) => let val s1 = interpret (e1,static)
                      val s2 = interpret (e2,static)
                  in fn dynamic => case s1 dynamic of
                                     UF(f) => f (s2 dynamic)
                                   | _     => UErr
                  end
| ELam (x,e) => let val s = interpret (e, x::static)
                in fn dynamic => UF(fn v=> case v of UErr => UErr
                                         | _ => s (v::dynamic))
                end
| EIf (e1,e2,e3) => let val s1 = interpret (e1,static)
                        val s2 = interpret (e2,static)
                        val s3 = interpret (e3,static)
                    in fn dynamic => case s1 dynamic of
                                       UB(true) => s2 dynamic
                                     | UB(false) => s3 dynamic
                                     | _ => UErr
                    end
... other clauses elided ...

fun pi s = interpret (read s, []) []
```

Fig. 1. Revised Interpreter (extract)

```
(* Recall:
   type 'a EP = ('a->U)*(U->'a option)
   val --> : ('a EP)*('b EP) -> ('a->'b) EP
*)

infixr -->

fun (e,p)-->(e',p') =
  (fn f => UF (fn u => case p u of SOME a => e' (f a)
                                 | NONE => UErr),
   fn u => case u
           of UF f => callcc (fn k =>
                              SOME (fn a =>
                                   case p' (f (e a))
                                   of SOME b => b
                                    | NONE => throw k NONE))
            | _ => NONE)
```

Fig. 2. Embedding and projection for functions

value of type A in our hand, then we can assume it really will behave itself as an element of type A. In fact, we might have obtained the value by projecting some ill-behaved untyped code, but we will arrange things so that the projected value is 'self-policing' – should it ever violate the contract associated with A then it will backtrack to the point of projection. Hence the violation will never be observable at the actual point of use.

With that idea in mind, the *embedding* component for function types can be fairly straightforward. Just as we made the interpreter 'total', in the sense that dynamic errors are explicitly reified as the UErr value, the embedded version of f : A->B should be a 'total' function from U to U that attempts to project its argument to type A, returning UErr if this fails, and returning the embedding at type B of f applied to the projected value otherwise. In code, assuming p is the projection for A and e' is the embedding for B, the embedding for A->B is

```
fn f => UF (fn u => case p u of SOME a => e' (f a)
                              | NONE => UErr)
```

of type $(A$->$B)$->U. This is simple because nobody is at 'fault' here yet: we can assume the ML function we're embedding will be well-behaved on the given domain and we merely extend it to return UErr on the rest of U.

We now need to define *projection* for a function type A->B, which will be of type U->$((A$->$B)$option). In the case that the argument value is not even a UF, it seems natural to return NONE immediately, though we *could* have chosen to delay even this check until we try to apply the projected function. Otherwise we have a function f of type U->U, which can clearly be turned into one, call it f', of type A->$(B$ option) by precomposition with the (total) embedding for A, e, and postcomposing with the (partial) projection for B, p'. So

$$f' = \mathsf{p'} \circ f \circ \mathsf{e}$$

However, we want something of type $(A\texttt{->}B)$ option, for which we need a control operator. We grab the continuation k that is expecting a value of type $(A\texttt{->}B)$ option and provisionally return SOME g where g : A->B is a wrapper around f' that returns b when f' returns SOME b and throws NONE (of type $(A\texttt{->}B)$ option) to the captured continuation k should f' ever return NONE (of type B option). Putting this together with the embedding component, we arrive at the definition of the --> combinator that is shown in Figure 2.

The code shown in the figure looks rather simple, but the consequences of the way the uses of control are intertwined with the induction on types are perhaps not obvious, so we now present a series of examples to try to understand what we just did.

4   Examples

Our first set of examples are not intended to be representative of actual uses, but merely a set of test cases to demonstrate and check the behaviour of our earlier definitions. Since we want to be able to see *which* coercions fail, we make our test functions return values of the following type:

```
datatype 'a TestResult = Fail of string | Result of 'a
```

We start with an untyped function that behaves like successor on small integers but returns a unit value on larger ones:

```
- val badsucc = pi "fn n => if n < 4 then n+1 else ()";
val badsucc = UF fn : U
```

and define a test function that attempts to project an untyped value down to the ML type int -> int and then maps the result over a list of integers:

```
- fun testIntToInt v l = case (project (int-->int) v)
                           of SOME f => Result (map f l)
                            | NONE => Fail "projection to int->int";
val testIntToInt = fn : U -> int list -> int list TestResult
```

Now, we try our test out on a list of small integers:

```
- val test1 = testIntToInt badsucc [1,2,3];
val test1 = Result [2,3,4] : int list TestResult
```

All the integers in the test list are small and badsucc behaves like a function of type int -> int on all of them, so we don't see any violation. Let's extend the list a little:

```
- val test2 = testIntToInt badsucc [1,2,3,4,5,6,7];
val test2 = Fail "projection to int->int" : int list TestResult
```

This time, `badsucc` behaves itself for the first three calls then violates its contract on the fourth, at which point we backtrack to the original point of projection and make that fail retrospectively. Alternatively, of course, we can project at `int -> unit`, in which case the sets of arguments exhibiting success and failure are swapped:

```
- fun testIntToUnit v l = case (project (int --> unit) v)
                             of SOME f => Result (map f l)
                              | NONE => Fail "projection to int->unit";
val testIntToUnit = fn : U -> int list -> unit list TestResult

- val test3 = testIntToUnit badsucc [7,6,5,4];
val test3 = Result [(),(),(),()] : unit list TestResult

- val test4 = testIntToUnit badsucc [7,6,5,4,3,2,1];
val test4 = Fail "projection to int->unit" : unit list TestResult
```

Note that each call to `project`, even on the same value, yields a new point to which we can backtrack. Let's check that we've stacked things up in the right order to maintain the property that embedding followed by projection is the identity, even on ill-behaved values:

```
- fun testreembed a1 a2 =
    case project (int --> int) badsucc
    of NONE => Fail "first projection"
     | SOME first =>
         let val r1 = first a1
             val reembed = embed (int --> int) first
         in case project (int --> int) reembed
            of NONE => Fail "second projection"
             | SOME second => let val r2 = second a2
                              in Result (r1,r2)
                              end
         end;
val testreembed = fn : int -> int -> (int * int) TestResult

- val test5 = testreembed 2 3;
val test5 = Result (3,4) : (int * int) TestResult

- val test6 = testreembed 2 4;
val test6 = Fail "first projection" : (int * int) TestResult
```

Although the violation is only triggered by the application of the reprojected value `second` to 4, we have correctly unwound all the way to the initial projection.

Now let's try some higher-order examples:

```
- fun testho A x y =
    case project (A-->int) x
```

```
      of NONE => Fail "function projection"
      | SOME f => (case project A y
                      of NONE => Fail "argument projection"
                      | SOME g => Result (f g));
val testho = fn : 'a EP -> U -> U -> int TestResult

- val test7 = testho (int-->int) (pi "fn f => f 1 + f 2")
                                 (pi "fn n => n + 1");
val test7 = Result 5 : int TestResult

- val test8 = testho (int-->int) (pi "fn f => f 1 + f 2")
                                 (pi "fn n => if n = 1 then 7 else ()");
val test8 = Fail "argument projection" : int TestResult

- val test9 = testho (int-->int) (pi "fn f => f 1 + f true")
                                 (pi "fn n => n + 1");
val test9 = Fail "function projection" : int TestResult
```

In these tests, we try to project the first untyped program to (int->int)->int, the second to int->int and then apply one to the other. We can see that in test7, both are well-behaved, in test8 it's the argument that goes wrong whilst in test9 the higher order function is at fault.

What should happen if we try to combine more than one faulty value? We are doing dynamic checking of the contracts: projections are only rolled back in the case that the particular use that is made of them exposes a violation. The checking is eager, in that the context $C[\cdot]$ that tests a projected value v should not have previously violated *its* contract at the point when the v does something wrong; otherwise we should already have rolled back some other projected value in $C[\cdot]$. So when we combine more than one projected value, we roll back the first one which detectably goes wrong in the execution trace:

```
- val test10 = testho (int-->int) (pi "fn f => f 1 + f true")
                                  (pi "fn b => if b then 3 else 4");
val test10 = Fail "argument projection" : int TestResult

- val test11 = testho (int -->int) (pi "fn f => f true + f 1")
                                   (pi "fn b => if b then 3 else 4");
val test11 = Fail "function projection" : int TestResult
```

In test10, the error is signalled in the argument. This is because the first call made by the higher-order function passes an integer, as per the contract, and then the argument tries to use that in a conditional, violating its contract. In test11, we have swapped the order of evaluation in the addition so that the first dynamically occurring violation is the attempt by the higher order function to pass true in place of an integer; in this case the error is detected in the higher-order function. Here's a more complex example:

```
- val test12 = testho ((int-->int)-->(int-->int))
                (pi "fn f => f (f (fn n => n+1)) 5")
                (pi "fn g => if g 2 = 3 then fn n => true
                                    else fn n => n");
val test12 = Fail "argument projection" : int TestResult
```

In this case, the outer call to the function bound to f passes in a function that is not of type int->int, but that function was itself obtained by the inner call to f, which was with a well-behaved argument. Hence blame is correctly assigned to the second of the original terms.

Finally, we present a toy version of a marginally more realistic example. Consider making queries on an external database, modelled as a function that takes a query predicate on strings (of type `string -> bool`) and returns a function of type `int -> string` that enumerates the results. Here are some definitions in the untyped language that construct three different purported databases, using LISP-style lists internally (represented as nested pairs with the unit value for nil):

```
- fun mkdb ds = pi ("let fun query l f n =
                        if isnil l then \"\"
                        else if f (car l)
                              then if n=0 then (car l)
                                    else query (cdr l) f (n-1)
                              else query (cdr l) f n
                    in query " ^ ds)
val mkdb = fn : string -> U
```

```
- val db1 = mkdb "(\"um\",(\"dois\",(\"tres\",(true,()))))"
- val db2 = mkdb "(\"un\",(2,(\"trois\",(\"quatre\",()))))"
- val db3 = mkdb "(\"one\",(\"two\",(\"three\",(\"four\",()))))"
```

Note that the first two contain some non-string values. The following function takes a list of untyped values and returns the first one that projects correctly to our ML type for databases:

```
- fun selectdb [] = (fn f => fn n => "")
    | selectdb (x::xs) =
        case project ((string --> bool) --> (int --> string)) x
        of NONE => selectdb xs
          | SOME db => db
val selectdb = fn : U list -> (string -> bool) -> int -> string
```

Now we can try some queries:

```
- val test15 = let val thedb = selectdb [db1,db2,db3]
                    val results = thedb (fn s => String.size s > 3)
                in [results 0, results 1]
                end
```

```
val test15 = ["dois","tres"] : string list

- val test16 = let val thedb = selectdb [db1,db2,db3]
                   val results = thedb (fn s => String.size s > 3)
               in [results 0, results 1, results 2]
               end
val test16 = ["three","four",""] : string list
```

The first database in the list produces two results without violating the contract, so we get the answers from that database. When we ask for more results, however, the first database tries to apply the filter to a boolean, so gets rolled back; we then try the second database, which also fails because it contains an integer, and finally end up getting all our results from the third one.

5 Discussion

We have shown how continuation-based backtracking combines smoothly with type indexed embedding-projection pairs to yield a convenient form of dynamic contract checking for interoperability between typed and untyped higher-order languages, localizing runtime errors to a single point of failure.

Extensions of statically-typed languages with various forms of dynamic type have been well-studied (see, for example, [1,10]), but undoable projections have not, as far as I'm aware, been proposed before.

The use of embedding-projection pairs to define type-indexed functions in ML-like languages is attributed by Danvy [6] to Filinski and to Yang [20], both of whom used it to implement type-directed partial evaluation [4], which involves type-indexed functions that appear at first sight to call for dependent types. Rose [16] describes an implementation of TDPE in Haskell that uses type classes to pass the pairs representing types implicitly. Kennedy and I have previously used it for writing picklers [12] and interpreters [2], respectively. Similar type-directed constructions have also been used in implementing printf-like string formatting [5] and in generic programming. Ramsey has also applied the technique for embedding an external interpreter for a scripting language (Lua) into OCaml programs [15].

Control operators have, of course, been used to implement various other forms of backtracking before, including that of logic programming languages. Nevertheless, getting the apparently simple code here correct is not entirely trivial (my first couple of attempts were more complex and subtly wrong).

It remains to be seen whether or not the technique presented here is actually useful in practical situations. Even before one worries about the specific technicalities, many reasonable people believe that experience with RPC, distributed objects, persistent programming, and so on, all indicates that trying to hide the differences between operations with widely varying runtime costs, failure models or lifetimes is fundamentally a bad idea – the distinctions should be reflected in the language because programmers need to be aware of them. Holding onto continuations costs space, whilst the possibility of backtracking over expensive computations certainly doesn't make reasoning about time or space behaviour any easier.

There is also the issue of what can be undone. We have been implicitly assuming that the untyped programs that we project, and the typed contexts into which we project them, do not themselves involve side-effects other than potential divergence, as these will not be undone by throwing to the captured continuation. One could certainly extend our technique to effects that are internal to the language, such as uses of state or other uses of control, if one were prepared to modify the compiler, runtime system or bits of the basis library (as in previous work on transactions in ML [9]). But the most exciting examples, namely those that involve external I/O, unfortunately concern side-effects that are rather hard to roll back automatically and generically. If I've sent you some messages and then you start to misbehave, the best general thing I can do is break off further communication with you; I certainly can't unsend the messages. That suffices in the case of pure computations, but in the stateful case a general solution seems to require at least wrapping the underlying messages in a more complex fault-tolerant protocol, and probably introducing explicit transactional commitment points, beyond which rollbacks would no longer be possible. Indeed, explicitly delimiting the the extent of possible rollbacks may be advantageous even in the case of purely internal effects.

The semantics we have chosen to implement here tracks type errors rather strictly along the control flow: any violation will cause the guilty projection to be undone, even if the value that is eventually produced is well-behaved. A small change in the interpreter code to remove strictness in UErr yields a laxer, more data-dependent, semantics, in which 'benign' errors are ignored; this might be useful in some circumstances, but seems harder to reason about and a less natural fit with call-by-value languages.

It would be good to formulate and prove correctness of the code we have presented. The problem here seems not to be one of proof technique, but in coming up with a statement of correctness that covers the correct assignment of blame in the case of multiple ill-behaved untyped programs *and* which is intuitively significantly clearer than the code itself. One starting point might be the operational semantics for interoperability between ML-like and Scheme-like languages recently described by Matthews and Findler [13].

A second, and perhaps more interesting, line of further work is to extend the idea from dynamic checking of the interface between typed and untyped languages to recovery in more general higher-order contract monitoring. Runtime checking of contracts, and the associated issue of blame assignment, have been extensively studied in recent years (see, for example, [8,7,11,3,19]) and the kind of 'transactional' recovery mechanism described here seems eminently applicable in that setting.

Thanks to Josh Berdine, Olivier Danvy, Andrzej Filinski, Norman Ramsey and the referees for many useful comments on earlier drafts of this paper.

References

1. Abadi, M., Cardelli, L., Pierce, B., Plotkin, G.: Dynamic typing in a statically-typed language. ACM Transactions on Programming Languages and Systems (TOPLAS) 13(2) (1991)
2. Benton, N.: Embedded interpreters. Journal of Functional Programming 15(4) (2005)
3. Blume, M., McAllester, D.: Sound and complete models of contracts. Journal of Functional Programming 16(4/5) (2006)
4. Danvy, O.: Type-directed partial evaluation. In: Proceedings of the 23rd ACM Symposium on Principles of Programming Languages (POPL), ACM Press, New York (1996)
5. Danvy, O.: Functional unparsing. Journal of Functional Programming 8(6) (1998)
6. Danvy, O.: A Simple Solution to Type Specialization. In: Larsen, K.G., Skyum, S., Winskel, G. (eds.) ICALP 1998. LNCS, vol. 1443, Springer, Heidelberg (1998)
7. Findler, R.B., Blume, M.: Contracts as Pairs of Projections. In: Hagiya, M., Wadler, P. (eds.) FLOPS 2006. LNCS, vol. 3945, pp. 226–241. Springer, Heidelberg (2006)
8. Findler, R., Felleisen, M.: Contracts for higher-order functions. In: Proceedings of the International Conference on Functional Programming (ICFP) (2002)
9. Haines, N., Kindred, D., Morrisett, J.G., Nettles, S.M., Wing, J.M.: Composing first-class transactions. ACM Transactions on Programming Languages and Systems (TOPLAS) 16(6) (1994)
10. Henglein, F.: Dynamic typing. In: Krieg-Brückner, B. (ed.) ESOP 1992. LNCS, vol. 582, Springer, Heidelberg (1992)
11. Jeuring, J., Hinze, R., Löh, A.: Typed Contracts for Functional Programming. In: Hagiya, M., Wadler, P. (eds.) FLOPS 2006. LNCS, vol. 3945, pp. 208–225. Springer, Heidelberg (2006)
12. Kennedy, A.: Functional pearl: Pickler combinators. Journal of Functional Programming 14(6) (2004)
13. Matthews, J., Findler, R.B.: Operational semantics for multi-language programs. In: Proceedings of the 34th ACM Symposium on Principles of Programming Languages (POPL) (2007)
14. Meyer, B.: Eiffel: The Language. Prentice-Hall, Englewood Cliffs (1992)
15. Ramsey, N.: Embedding an interpreted language using higher-order functions and types. Journal of Functional Programming (to appear, 2008)
16. Rose, K.: Type-directed partial evaluation in Haskell. In: Preliminary Proceedings of the 1998 APPSEM Workshop on Normalization by Evaluation, number NS-98-1 in BRICS Notes (1998)
17. Scott, D.: Data types as lattices. SIAM Journal of Computing 4 (1976)
18. Stoy, J.E.: Denotational Semantics: The Scott-Strachey Approach to Programming Language Theory. MIT Press, Cambridge (1977)
19. Wadler, P., Findler, R.B.: Well-typed programs can't be blamed. In: ACM Workshop on Scheme and Functional Programming (2007)
20. Yang, Z.: Encoding types in ML-like languages. In: Proceedings of the 3rd ACM SIGPLAN International Conference on Functional Programming (ICFP) (September, 1998)

Typed Dynamic Control Operators for Delimited Continuations

Yukiyoshi Kameyama and Takuo Yonezawa

Department of Computer Science, University of Tsukuba
kameyama@acm.org, yone@logic.cs.tsukuba.ac.jp

Abstract. We study the *dynamic* control operators for delimited continuations, control and prompt. Based on recent developments on purely functional CPS translations for them, we introduce a polymorphically typed calculus for these control operators which allows answer-type modification. We show that our calculus enjoys type soundness and is compatible with the CPS translation. We also show that the typed dynamic control operators can macro-express the typed *static* ones (shift and reset), while the converse direction is not possible, which exhibits a sharp contrast with the type-free case.

Keywords: Type System, Delimited Continuation, Dynamic Control Operator, CPS Translation, Polymorphism, Expressivity.

1 Introduction

Delimited continuations represent not the rest of the computation as with traditional continuations [18], but only part of the rest of the computation. As such, delimited continuations have been used to model backtracking in contrast to traditional continuations that are used to model jumps.

In direct style, traditional continuations are accessed with control operators such as call/cc. There is, however, more variety for delimited continuations:

- Felleisen [12] proposed a control delimiter to signify *part* of an evaluation context, or a *delimited* continuation. This lead to the new control operators control and prompt, which are called *dynamic* control operators.
- Danvy and Filinski discovered that delimited continuations are supported by an already existing formalism of 2CPS, the image of iterated CPS translations. They proposed new control operators shift and reset in the direct-style counterpart [9]. They are called *static* control operators.

Since these proposals, the static control operators have been intensively studied while the dynamic ones are relatively less studied. For shift/reset, there are a number of theoretical results [13,14] as well as useful examples in partial evaluation, one-pass CPS translation, and mobile codes, while we do not find many corresponding works for control/prompt in the literature, partly due to the difficulty in reasoning about the dynamic features of control/prompt.

J. Garrigue and M. Hermenegildo (Eds.): FLOPS 2008, LNCS 4989, pp. 239–254, 2008.

Recently, several authors have started to obtain better understanding for dynamic ones, and to connect dynamic and static ones. Shan [7] macro-expressed control and prompt in terms of shift and reset using recursive types. (See also Kiselyov's work [15].) Biernacki, Danvy, and Millikin [6] derived a CPS translation for control and prompt from a definitional abstract machine, and gave another encoding of control/prompt by shift/reset. Dybvig, Peyton Jones, and Sabry [11] gave a uniform monadic framework for delimited continuations including control/prompt. However, no work has studied the direct-style type system for control/prompt in a way comparative to the type system for shift/reset. The proposed encodings were done in either type-free or recursively typed settings,[1] and the proposed CPS translations assumed a restricted direct-style type system in that the control effect of "answer-type modification" was not allowed. We think this effect is indispensable for delimited continuations, for instance, it is needed to type the printf function in direct style [8,1].

In this paper, we propose a direct-style type system for control and prompt, which allows answer-type modification, does not need recursive types, and has ML-like let-polymorphism. We derive the type inference rules from the type structure for the CPS translations for control and prompt recently developed by the above mentioned works. The type system in this paper is a proper extension of that in our previous work [20], which does not allow answer-type modification. We show that our type system enjoys Subject Reduction and Progress properties, and that types are preserved by the CPS translation. The first two properties constitute type soundness, and the third property is necessary for a semantical study.

As an application of our type system, we compare the expressivity of typed control/prompt and that of typed shift/reset. In the type-free setting, they are known to be equally expressive [7,15,4,6]. However, there exists a big asymmetry in the complexity of these encodings, and a question remained whether control/prompt is strictly more expressive than shift/reset under an appropriate typed setting (without recursive types). In this paper we answer this question. Namely, we show:

- typed control/prompt can macro-express typed shift/reset, while
- typed shift/reset cannot macro-express typed control/prompt,

where the type system for shift/reset is the most expressive type system by Asai and Kameyama [2]. This result contrasts with the type-free case.

This paper is organized as follows: in Section 2 we briefly explain the control operators for delimited continuations, and in Section 3 we review the functional CPS translation in the literature. The subsequent three sections are original to this paper: in Section 4 we introduce the type systems for the dynamic control operators, and in Section 5 we give several properties for the type systems. In Section 6, we compare the expressive power of typed control/prompt with typed shift/reset. Section 8 concludes.

---

[1] We distinguish (general) recursive types from inductive types in that the former may contain negative occurrences of the type variable being taken the fixed point, for instance, $\mu X.(X \to \mathtt{int})$ where μ is for the fixed point operator.

2   Informal Explanation of control and prompt

We begin with the examples by Biernacki et al. [6] listed in Figure 1 written in Standard ML syntax.

The functions foo and bar have type int list -> int list, and differ in the names for control operators only: shift and reset for the former and control and prompt for the latter. Both shift and control capture evaluation contexts up to the closest delimiter (reset and prompt, resp.) Given the list [1,2,3], the function foo evaluates as:

```
foo [1,2,3] ⤳ <visit (shift (fn k => 1::(k [2,3])))>
            ⤳ <let k = <visit •> in 1::(k [2,3]) end>
            ⤳ <1::<visit [2,3]>>
            ⤳ <1::<let k = <visit •> in 2::(k [3]) end>>
            ⤳ ...
            ⤳ <1::<2::<3::nil>>>   ⤳ [1,2,3]
```

where < ... > denotes the delimiter inserted by reset, and <visit •> denotes the delimited evaluation context (delimited continuation) captured by shift with • being the hole in it. The expression <v> evaluates to v itself when v is a value, hence the result of this computation is identical to the argument.

The evaluation of bar proceeds as follows (the delimiter is denoted by #):

```
bar [1,2,3] ⤳ #(visit (control (fn k => 1::(k [2,3]))))
            ⤳ #(let k = (visit •) in 1::(k [2,3]) end)
            ⤳ #(1::(visit [2,3]))
            ⤳ #(let k = (1::(visit •)) in 2::(k [3]) end)
            ⤳ #(2::(1::(visit [3])))
            ⤳ ...
            ⤳ #(3::(2::(1::nil)))   ⤳ [3,2,1]
```

```
fun foo xs =
  let fun visit nil = nil
      |   visit (x::xs) = visit (shift (fn k => x::(k xs)))
  in reset (fn () => visit xs) end
```

```
fun bar xs =
  let fun visit nil = nil
      |   visit (x::xs) = visit (control (fn k => x::(k xs)))
  in prompt (fn () => visit xs) end
```

Fig. 1. List-copying and list-reversing functions

The evaluation context captured by `control` is the whole context since there is no other delimiters. Hence, we obtain a a reversed list as the result of computation.

The operational behavior for each set of control operators can be formalized by reduction rules. Let v and P denote a value and a call-by-value evaluation context such that no delimiter encloses the hole, resp. Then we have the reduction rules as follows:

$$\text{(For shift/reset)} \qquad \langle P[\mathcal{S}c.e]\rangle \to \langle \text{let } c = \lambda x.\langle P[x]\rangle \text{ in } e\rangle$$
$$\text{(For control/prompt)} \qquad \#\,(P[\mathcal{F}c.e]) \to \#\,(\text{let } c = \lambda x.P[x] \text{ in } e)$$

Here $\mathcal{S}c.e$ corresponds to (`shift (fn c => e)`), and $\langle e\rangle$ to (`reset (fn () => e)`) in the ML implementation in the previous subsection. Similarly, $\#\ e$ is (`prompt (fn () => e)`), and $\mathcal{F}c.e$ is (`control (fn c => e)`).

Besides the names for control operators, the only difference between them is whether the captured delimited continuation has an extra reset or not: $\lambda x.\langle P[x]\rangle$ for the former, and $\lambda x.P[x]$ for the latter. This small difference in syntax raises a big difference in semantics. Suppose P has other occurrences of `shift` or `control`, and the captured delimited continuation is applied to a value v in a then-current continuation E which may have a delimiter that encloses the hole.

- In the former, we evaluate $E[\langle P[v]\rangle]$ in which other occurrences of `shift` in P will be delimited by this `reset` (unless they are "escaped" in function closures). Namely, the corresponding delimiter for these `shift` is determined when the delimited continuation is captured.
- In the latter, we evaluate $E[P[x]]$ in which other occurrences of `control` ought to be delimited by `prompt` in E. (Note that P does not have any `prompt` which encloses the hole). Consequently, the corresponding delimiter for these `control` is determined not when it is captured, but when the delimited continuation is used.

Hence the former is called static, and the latter is called dynamic by analogy with static and dynamic binding in Scheme and Lisp [5]. The static/dynamic nature of control operators has an impact on their implementation. For `shift/reset`, a delimited continuation can be represented by an ordinary, composable function, which leads to a simple CPS translation [9,10]. For `control/prompt`, we need to keep the captured delimited continuations as they are, until they are actually used, which needs an extra machinery.

3   A CPS Translation for `control/prompt`

We regard a CPS translation as the fundamental analysis tool for control operators. For `control` and `prompt`, three such translations are known: Shan's [7], Dybvig, Peyton-Jones, and Sabry's [11], and Biernacki, Danvy and Millikin's [6]. In this paper we use (a variant of) the last one since it is the simplest. We could use Shan's one as well.

$$v ::= d \mid x \mid \lambda x.e \qquad\qquad\qquad\qquad\qquad \text{value}$$

$$e ::= v \mid e_1 e_2 \mid \mathcal{F}c.e \mid \# \, e \mid \texttt{let } x = e_1 \texttt{ in } e_2$$
$$\mid \texttt{if } e_1 \texttt{ then } e_2 \texttt{ else } e_3 \qquad\qquad \text{expression}$$

$$P ::= [\,] \mid Pe \mid vP$$
$$\mid \texttt{let } x = P \texttt{ in } e \mid \texttt{if } P \texttt{ then } e_1 \texttt{ else } e_2 \qquad \text{pure evaluation context}$$

$$E ::= [\,] \mid Ee \mid vE$$
$$\mid \texttt{let } x = E \texttt{ in } e \mid \texttt{if } E \texttt{ then } e_1 \texttt{ else } e_2 \mid \# \, E \qquad \text{evaluation context}$$

Fig. 2. Syntax of the language with `control/prompt`

$$(\lambda x.e)v \rightsquigarrow e[v/x]$$
$$\texttt{if true then } e_1 \texttt{ else } e_2 \rightsquigarrow e_1$$
$$\texttt{if false then } e_1 \texttt{ else } e_2 \rightsquigarrow e_2$$
$$\texttt{let } x = v \texttt{ in } e \rightsquigarrow e[v/x]$$
$$\# \, (P[\mathcal{F}c.e]) \rightsquigarrow \# \, (\texttt{let } c = \lambda x.P[x] \texttt{ in } e)$$
$$\# \, v \rightsquigarrow v$$

Fig. 3. Reduction rules

Figure 2 gives the syntax of our source language where d is constant and x and c are variables. The expression $\mathcal{F}c.e$ is a construct for `control` in which c is a bound variable. The expression $\# \, e$ is the one for `prompt`. Variables are bound by λ or $\mathcal{F}$, the set of free variables in e is denoted by $\mathrm{FV}(e)$, and we identify α-equivalent expressions. Sequencing $a; \, b$ is an abbreviation of $(\lambda x.b)a$ with $x \notin \mathrm{FV}(b)$. In a pure evaluation context P, no `prompt` may enclose its hole $[\,]$, while a (general) evaluation context E allows such occurrences of `prompt`. Figure 3 gives call-by-value operational semantics to this language where $e[v/x]$ represents the result of capture-avoiding substitution.

Figure 4 defines the CPS translation for this language as a variant of the one given by Biernacki et al. The differences are: (1) they gave a 2CPS translation whch is an iterated translation (its image takes two continuations as its arguments), while we use a more traditional 1CPS translation, and (2) we extend the source language with constant, conditional, and `let`.

The target language of this translation is a call-by-value lambda calculus with constants, conditional, and `let` as well as list-manipulating constructs such as `Nil`, cons (denoted by ::), append (@) and a destructor (`case`). Note that the translation for `let` expression is only meaningful for the typed source language (given in the next section), and we have included it in Figure 4 only to save space. For a type-free source language, we can define it as $[\![\texttt{let } x = e_1 \texttt{ in } e_2]\!] = [\![(\lambda x.e_2)e_1]\!]$.

$$[\_] : \texttt{SourceTerm} \to \texttt{Cont} \to \texttt{Trail} \to \texttt{TargetValue}$$

$$[V] = \lambda k\, t.\, k\, (V)^*\, t$$

$$[e_1 e_2] = \lambda k\, t.\, [e_1](\lambda m_1\, t_1.\, [e_2](\lambda m_2\, t_2.\, m_1\, m_2\, k\, t_2)\, t_1)\, t$$

$$[\texttt{if } e_1 \texttt{ then } e_2 \texttt{ else } e_3] = \lambda k\, t.\, [e_1](\lambda m_1\, t_1.\, \texttt{if } m_1 \texttt{ then } [e_2]\, k\, t_1 \texttt{ else } [e_3]\, k\, t_1)\, t$$

$$[\texttt{let } x = e_1 \texttt{ in } e_2] = \lambda k\, t.\, \texttt{let } x = ([e_1]\, \theta_1\, \texttt{Nil}) \texttt{ in } [e_2]\, k\, t$$

$$[\# e] = \lambda k\, t.\, k([e]\, \theta_1\, \texttt{Nil})\, t$$

$$[\mathcal{F}c.e] = \lambda k\, t.\, \texttt{let } c = \lambda x\, k'\, t'.\, k\, x\, (t\, @\, (k' :: t')) \texttt{ in } [e]\, \theta_1\, \texttt{Nil}$$

$$(\_)^* : \texttt{SourceValue} \to \texttt{TargetValue}$$

$$(d)^* = d \quad \text{for constant}$$

$$(x)^* = x \quad \text{for a variable}$$

$$(\lambda x.e)^* = \lambda x\, k\, t.\, [e]\, k\, t$$

$$\theta_1 = \lambda x\, t.\, \texttt{case } t \texttt{ of}$$
$$\mid \quad \texttt{Nil} \Rightarrow x$$
$$\mid \quad (k_1 :: t_1) \Rightarrow k_1\, x\, t_1$$

Fig. 4. 1CPS translation for the language with `control` and `prompt`

Let us see the types in Figure 4, although these types should be considered informal, and only for explanation. The types `SourceTerm`, `SourceValue`, `Cont`, `TargetValue`, are those for terms and values in the source language, and those for continuations and values in the target language, resp.

The type `Trail` is new to their CPS translation. Recall that, in order to represent the dynamic behavior of `control/prompt`, we need to keep the delimited continuations until they are used. A trail is a list of delimited continuations to store these continuations. Thus, we may informally define `Cont` and `Trail` as follows:

$$\texttt{Cont} = \texttt{TargetValue} \to \texttt{Trail} \to \texttt{TargetValue}$$
$$\texttt{Trail} = \texttt{List(Cont)}$$

This "definition" needs recursive types, which will be examined in the next section.

Next, we look at the term-level translation in Figure 4. For the constructs other than control operators, the translation is the same as the standard (e.g. Plotkin's) translation except that it passes trails without changing them.

The prompt-term $\# e$ initializes its continuation and trail: in its translation $[\# e]$, $[e]$ is applied to θ_1 and the empty trail `Nil`. The continuation θ_1 acts as the identity continuation (the empty evaluation context).

The control-term $\mathcal{F}c.e$ captures a delimited continuation (and initializes the continuation and the trail): it captures the current delimited continuation k for a future use of c. When c is applied to some value, the captured continuation k is "composed" with the then-current continuation k'. Rather than simply composing two delimited continuations, we store (in the trail) the list of all the captured delimited continuations except the current one, namely, we extend the then-current trail t' to a new trail $t \mathbin{@} (k' :: t')$ and use k as the current continuation. Continuations stored in the trail will be used when the current continuation becomes empty (i.e. θ_1).

Note that we can easily extend our source language and the CPS translation with practical language constructs such as the fixed point operator and primitive functions.

Finally, a CPS translation for a complete program e is defined as $[e]\theta_1\mathtt{Nil}$.

4   Type System

We introduce a polymorphic type system for `control/prompt` in this section. Types are an important facility in most programming languages to classify terms and also to ensure a certain kind of safety for computation. We think that, for `control/prompt` to be used by ordinary programmers, a sound type system is definitely needed.

4.1   Design of Type System

Our strategy to construct a type system for `control/prompt` is basically the same as that for `shift/reset` [2]: given a term e, we infer the most general type of its CPS translation $[e]$, and use this type as the type for e. There is, however, two problems in this strategy: (1) the target terms of the CPS translation for `control/prompt` need recursive types if we assign types, and there is no notion of the most general type in a type system with recursive types, and (2) we need arbitrary many type variables to precisely represent types of the CPS translation.

The first problem already appears if we type the identity (delimited) continuation θ_1. Assuming the type of trails is $\mathtt{List}(\tau)$ for some τ, θ_1 must have the type $\alpha \to \mathtt{List}(X) \to \alpha$ for some α, where $X = \alpha \to \mathtt{List}(X) \to \alpha$. Hence we need some sort of recursive types.

The second problem is this: Recall that `Cont` and `Trail` are informally defined as `Cont = TargetValue → Trail → TargetValue` and `Trail = List(Cont)`. When the source language is typed in some way, the type `TargetValue` should be instantiated by more specific types, and in general, a trail has the type:

$$\mathtt{List}(\alpha_1 \to \mathtt{List}(\alpha_2 \to \mathtt{List}(\dots \mathtt{List}(\alpha_n \to \cdots \to \beta_n)\dots) \to \beta_2) \to \beta_1)$$

for different α_i and β_i. Apparently, we cannot represent these types in a finite manner.

We give a simple solution to these problems based on the observation that most (if not all) examples with `control/prompt` in the literature can be typed under the following simple restriction:

– In a trail type, all α_i and β_i is the same type.

This means that any trail must have type $\mu X.\text{List}(\tau \to X \to \tau)$ for some type τ where μ is for recursive types. In the sequel, we adopt this restriction, and write $\text{Trail}(\tau)$ for this type. Note that the restriction does not constrain the type of continuations, that is, a continuation may have type $\alpha \to \text{Trail}(\tau) \to \beta$ for different types α, β, and τ.

We think that this restriction is not too strong, since, most (if not all) examples with control/prompt in the literature follow this restriction (list-reversing function and several variations of search programs [6]). Also we will see later that the typed control/prompt calculus under this restriction can simulate typed shift/reset calculus, which has many interesting examples.

Under this restriction, the target terms of the CPS translation can be typed in the ordinary type system (with let-polymorphism, but without recursive types), in which the most general type always exists (if typable), and, therefore, the first problem is also solved.

Discussion. An anonymous reviewer has suggested us that, we could exclude the circularity in the trail types by introducing an inductive (not recursive) structure. One way to achieve it is: if we change the definition of the trail type from $\text{Trail} = \text{List}(\text{Cont})$ to

$$\text{Trail}(n) = \text{Trail}(0) \mid (\text{Cont} \times \text{Trail}(n-1))$$

where n denotes the length of the list, then we can avoid the circularity (recursiveness) of the trail type. However, the use of dependent types drastically complicates the type structure of the target calculus (and possibly the corresponding source type system). Moreover, it is not our goal to obtain a strongly normalizing calculus for control/prompt by constraining the source type system artificially. Rather, we took Biernacki et al.'s CPS translation as a good starting point, and based on it, we tried to construct a natural type system which is harmonious with their CPS translation.

4.2   Definition of Type System

Now we introduce a type system for control/prompt.

Types and type contexts are defined by:

$$\alpha, \beta \cdots ::= b \mid t \mid \alpha \to (\beta, \gamma, \delta/\tau) \qquad \text{monomorphic types}$$
$$A ::= \alpha \mid \forall t.A \qquad \text{polymorphic types}$$
$$\Gamma ::= [\,] \mid \Gamma, x : A \qquad \text{type contexts}$$

where b is a basic type (including bool), t is a type variable, and $\alpha \to (\beta, \gamma, \delta/\tau)$ is a function type whose meaning will be made clear later. $\text{FTV}(A)$ denotes the set of free type variables in A.

The type system has two forms of judgements, and the first form is:

$$\Gamma \vdash e : \alpha, \beta, \gamma/\tau$$

$$\frac{(x : A \in \Gamma \text{ and } \alpha \leq A)}{\Gamma \vdash_p x : \alpha} \text{ var} \qquad \frac{(d \text{ is constant of type } b)}{\Gamma \vdash_p d : b} \text{ const}$$

$$\frac{\Gamma, x : \alpha \vdash e : \beta, \gamma, \delta/\tau}{\Gamma \vdash_p \lambda x.e : \alpha \to (\beta, \gamma, \delta/\tau)} \text{ fun} \qquad \frac{\Gamma \vdash_p e : \alpha}{\Gamma \vdash e : \alpha, \beta, \beta/\tau} \text{ exp}$$

$$\frac{\Gamma \vdash e_1 : \alpha \to (\beta, \gamma, \delta/\tau), \epsilon, \rho/\tau \quad \Gamma \vdash e_2 : \alpha, \delta, \epsilon/\tau}{\Gamma \vdash e_1 e_2 : \beta, \gamma, \rho/\tau} \text{ app}$$

$$\frac{\Gamma \vdash e_1 : \text{bool}, \delta, \gamma/\tau \quad \Gamma \vdash e_2 : \alpha, \beta, \delta/\tau \quad \Gamma \vdash e_3 : \alpha, \beta, \delta/\tau}{\Gamma \vdash \text{if } e_1 \text{ then } e_2 \text{ else } e_3 : \alpha, \beta, \gamma/\tau} \text{ if}$$

$$\frac{\Gamma \vdash_p e_1 : \rho \quad \Gamma, x : \text{Gen}(\rho; \Gamma) \vdash e_2 : \alpha, \beta, \gamma/\tau}{\Gamma \vdash \text{let } x = e_1 \text{ in } e_2 : \alpha, \beta, \gamma/\tau} \text{ let}$$

$$\frac{\Gamma \vdash e : \tau, \tau, \beta/\tau}{\Gamma \vdash_p \# e : \beta} \text{ prompt} \qquad \frac{\Gamma, c : \alpha \to (\tau, \tau, \beta/\tau) \vdash e : \rho, \rho, \gamma/\rho}{\Gamma \vdash \mathcal{F}c.e : \alpha, \beta, \gamma/\tau} \text{ control}$$

Fig. 5. Type Inference Rules

where Γ is a type context, α, β, γ, and τ are types, and e is an expression. It means that, under the type context Γ, e is an expression of type α, with the answer type modification[2] from β to γ, and the trail type is τ. The roles of the additional types in the judgement can be made clearer by CPS translating it:

$$\Gamma^* \vdash [e] : \text{Cont}(\alpha^*, \beta^*/\tau^*) \to \text{Trail}(\tau^*) \to \gamma^*$$

with

$$\text{Trail}(\tau^*) = \mu X.\text{List}(\tau^* \to X \to \tau^*)$$
$$\text{Cont}(\alpha^*, \beta^*/\tau^*) = \alpha^* \to \text{Trail}(\tau^*) \to \beta^*$$

The second form of judgements is:

$$\Gamma \vdash_p e : \alpha$$

which means e is a pure (effect-free) expression of type α. This form is used to introduce let-polymorphism with control effects in a sound manner[2].

Figure 5 gives the type inference rules where $\alpha \leq A$ in the rule (var) means, if $A \equiv \forall t_1. \cdots \forall t_n.\rho$ for some monomorphic type ρ, then $\tau \equiv \rho[\sigma_1, \cdots, \sigma_n/t_1, \cdots, t_n]$ for some monomorphic types $\sigma_1, \cdots, \sigma_n$. We assume that, a basic type b is associated with each constant d. The type $\text{Gen}(\rho; \Gamma)$ in the rule (let) is defined by $\forall t_1. \cdots \forall t_n.\rho$ where $\{t_1, \cdots, t_n\} = \text{FTV}(\rho) - \text{FTV}(\Gamma)$.

The rule (exp) allows one to switch from the second form to the first form. Since pure expressions are insensitive to continuations and trails, we can introduce arbitrary types for their answer type (β) and the trail type (τ).

---

[2] For the standard CPS translation, we say, the answer type is modified in a computation of e from β to γ, if the CPS transform of e has type $(\alpha \to \beta) \to \gamma$. Without control operators for delimited continuations, the types β and γ are equal. With them, they may be different. See Asai and Kameyama [2] for details.

$$\frac{\Gamma \vdash e : \alpha, \beta, \gamma/t}{\Gamma \vdash e : \alpha, \beta, \gamma/*} \text{ star-intro, if } t \notin \text{FTV}(\Gamma, \alpha, \beta, \gamma) \qquad \frac{\Gamma \vdash e : \alpha, \beta, \gamma/*}{\Gamma \vdash e : \alpha, \beta, \gamma/\tau} \text{ star-elim}$$

$$\frac{\Gamma \vdash e : \alpha \to (\beta, \gamma, \delta/*), \epsilon, \rho/\sigma}{\Gamma \vdash e : \alpha \to (\beta, \gamma, \delta/\tau), \epsilon, \rho/\sigma} \text{ star-fun}$$

Fig. 6. Type Inference Rules for $\lambda_{let}^{c/p+}$

Other rules are naturally derived from the type for the CPS translation. The rule (var) is standard. In the rule (fun), the function type $\alpha \to (\beta, \gamma, \delta/\tau)$ extends the ordinary function type $\alpha \to \beta$ to encapsulate the effect of answer type modification from γ to δ with the trail type τ. The rule (app) reflects this intuition. The rule (let) is for ML-like let-polymorphism. As is well known, we must restrict e_1 in the expression let $x = e_1$ in e_2 to have a sound type system, and we follow Asai and Kameyama's type system [2] which restricts e_1 to be a pure term, i.e., either a value or $\# e$.

For the rule (prompt), look at its CPS translation in Figure 4. It is easy to check θ_1 must have type $\text{Cont}(\tau, \tau/\tau)$ for some τ, and the return type of $[e]$ is the same as that of $[\# e]$. So by letting this return type β, we get the rule (prompt). The rule (control) is more complicated. In the CPS translation of $\mathcal{F}c.e$, a term $\lambda x k' t'. k x (t @ (k' :: t'))$ is substituted for c, which poses constraints that t and t' are of the same list type and k' is of its member type. Since we restricted all trails to be of type $\text{Trail}(\tau)$ for some τ, k' has to have the type $\text{Cont}(\tau, \tau/\tau)$ and t and t' have the type $\text{Trail}(\tau)$. Then we can derive the rule (control).

An example type derivation for a concrete term will be given in a later section. We call the calculus with this type system $\lambda_{let}^{c/p}$.

4.3 Introducing Trail-Polymorphism

The type system of $\lambda_{let}^{c/p}$ can type many useful examples with control/prompt. However, it cannot express a certain kind of polymorphism in trails. We occasionally want to express that a function has type $\alpha \to (\beta, \gamma, \delta/\tau)$ for any τ, i.e., it is insensitive (or polymorphic) to the trail type. To solve this problem with a small cost, i.e., not without introducing impredicative polymorphism, we introduce a limited form of polymorphism, called trail-polymorphism, into $\lambda_{let}^{c/p}$ as follows.

We add a special type constant "$*$" to the definition of types, which can appear in a function type as $\alpha \to (\beta, \gamma, \delta/*)$, or in a judgement as $\Gamma \vdash e : \alpha, \beta, \gamma/*$. Intuitively, $*$ represents a universally quantified type variable.

We add to $\lambda_{let}^{c/p}$ three new type inference rules listed in Figure 6, which reflect the intuitive meaning of $*$. We call the extended calculus $\lambda_{let}^{c/p+}$. Note that the reductions rules are the same as those for $\lambda_{let}^{c/p}$.

We can also introduce impredicative polymorphism in the same manner as that system for shift/reset[2]. Since it is orthogonal to the present type system, we omit the details in this paper.

5 Properties

In this section, we state basic properties of $\lambda_{let}^{c/p}$ and $\lambda_{let}^{c/p+}$. Due to lack of space, we only state proof sketches in this paper.

The first property, subject reduction, is by far the most important property in a typed calculus.

Theorem 1 (Subject Reduction). *If $\Gamma \vdash e_1 : \alpha, \beta, \gamma/\tau$ is derived and $e_1 \rightsquigarrow e_2$, then $\Gamma \vdash e_2 : \alpha, \beta, \gamma/\tau$ can be derived.*

The theorem is proved by the standard induction on the derivation. For the case of the reduction $\# (P[\mathcal{F}c.e]) \rightsquigarrow \# (\text{let } c = \lambda x.P[x] \text{ in } e)$, we decompose it into several smaller reductions as in [3], then the theorem is easy to prove.

The next theorem is the progress property which states the computation of a well typed, closed expression does not get stuck. Here, the word "close" means that the term does not have any free variables and any occurrences of control which are not enclosed by prompt. To ensure the last property, we restrict our attention to an expression in the form $\# e$. A redex is one of the expressions in the lefthand sides of the reduction rules in Figure 3.

Theorem 2 (Progress). *If $\vdash \# e : \alpha, \beta, \gamma/\tau$ is derivable, then $\# e$ is in the form $E[r]$ where E is an evaluation context and r is a redex.*

Note that, if e is a value v, $\# e$ itself is a redex which reduces to v. The progress property is proved by the standard case analysis.

These two theorems together constitute the strong type soundness property.

The next theorem states that our type system is compatible with the CPS translation. For this purpose, we define the type structure of the target calculus depending on the source calculus by:

- for $\lambda_{let}^{c/p}$, the target calculus is (predicatively) polymorphic lambda calculus with conditionals, the trail type $\text{Trail}(\tau)$, and the list type.
- for $\lambda_{let}^{c/p+}$, the target calculus is impredicatively polymorphic lambda calculus (second order lambda calculus) with conditionals, the trail type $\text{Trail}(\tau)$, and the list type.

We define the CPS translation for types and type contexts by:

$$\alpha^* = \alpha \quad \text{for basic type and type variable}$$
$$(\alpha \to (\beta, \gamma, \delta/\tau))^* = \alpha^* \to (\beta^* \to \text{Trail}(\tau^*) \to \gamma^*) \to \text{Trail}(\tau^*) \to \delta^*$$
$$(\alpha \to (\beta, \gamma, \delta/*))^* = \alpha^* \to \forall X.((\beta^* \to \text{Trail}(X) \to \gamma^*) \to \text{Trail}(X) \to \delta^*)$$
$$[\,]^* = [\,]$$
$$(\Gamma, x : \forall t_1 \ldots t_n.\alpha)^* = \Gamma^*, \ x : \forall t_1 \ldots t_n.\alpha^*$$

The third line is for $\lambda_{let}^{c/p+}$ only. We then state type preservation property as a theorem.

Theorem 3 (Type Preservation for CPS Transformation)

- *(For $\lambda_{let}^{c/p}$ and $\lambda_{let}^{c/p+}$) If $\Gamma \vdash e : \alpha, \beta, \gamma/\tau$ is derivable for $\tau \neq *$, then $\Gamma^* \vdash [e] : (\alpha^* \to Trail(\tau^*) \to \beta^*) \to Trail(\tau^*) \to \gamma^*$ is derivable in the target calculus.*
- *(For $\lambda_{let}^{c/p+}$) If $\Gamma \vdash e : \alpha, \beta, \gamma/*$ is derivable, then $\Gamma^* \vdash [e] : (\alpha^* \to Trail(\tau) \to \beta^*) \to Trail(\tau) \to \gamma^*$ is derivable for any τ in the target calculus.*

In this paper, we do not state the property that equality is preserved by CPS translation, since it is independent to our type system, and in order to state the property as a theorem, we need to develop a sophisticated equality theory in the target language. For the latter, we need the following property for an arbitrary pure evaluation context P:

$$\lambda x\ k_1\ t_1.\ [P[x]]\ \theta_1\ (k_1 :: t_1) = \lambda x\ k_1\ t_1.\ [P[x]]\ k_1\ t_1$$

which is about the inductive nature of trails (lists). Since t_1 in this equation is a bound variable, we need to elaborate an inductive theory.

6   Encoding Shift/Reset by Control/Prompt

In type-free setting, shift/reset can be macro-defined by control/prompt [4], and we show in this section that it also holds for the typed setting here. We adopt the calculus $\lambda_{let}^{s/r}$ in [2] for shift/reset, since it is the most liberal type system which allows answer-type modification and let-polymorphism. Its type inference rules are listed in the appendix.

We define a translation from $\lambda_{let}^{s/r}$ to $\lambda_{let}^{c/p+}$ as follows:

Types	$\overline{(\alpha/\gamma \to \beta/\delta)} = \overline{\alpha} \to (\overline{\beta}, \overline{\gamma}, \overline{\delta}/*)$
Expressions	$\overline{\mathcal{S}c.e} = \mathcal{F}c'.\mathtt{let}\ c = \lambda x.\#\ (c'x)\ \mathtt{in}\ \overline{e}$
	$\overline{\langle e \rangle} = \#\ \overline{e}$
Type Contexts	$\overline{\Gamma, x : \forall t_1 \dots t_n.\alpha} = \overline{\Gamma},\ x : \forall t_1 \dots t_n.\overline{\alpha}$

For other constructs, the translation is homomorphic. This translation preserves types and reduction.

Theorem 4

- *If $\Gamma; \beta \vdash e : \alpha;\ \gamma$ is derivable in $\lambda_{let}^{s/r}$, $\overline{\Gamma} \vdash \overline{e} : \overline{\alpha}, \overline{\beta}, \overline{\gamma}/*$ is derivable in $\lambda_{let}^{c/p+}$.*
- *If $\Gamma; \beta \vdash e_1 : \alpha;\ \gamma$ is derivable and $e_1 \leadsto e_2$ in $\lambda_{let}^{s/r}$, $\overline{e_1} \leadsto^* \overline{e_2}$ in $\lambda_{let}^{c/p+}$.*

Proof. We prove this theorem by induction on the derivation of $\Gamma; \beta \vdash e : \alpha; \gamma$. We list two key cases here.

(Reset) Suppose we have a derivation in $\lambda_{let}^{s/r}$:

$$\vdots$$

$$\frac{\Gamma;\ \alpha \vdash e : \alpha;\ \beta}{\Gamma;\ \gamma \vdash \langle e \rangle : \beta;\ \gamma}\ \text{reset}$$

By induction hypothesis, we can derive $\overline{\Gamma} \vdash \overline{e} : \overline{\alpha}, \overline{\alpha}, \overline{\beta}/*$. Then we can derive:

$$\frac{\dfrac{\dfrac{\overline{\Gamma} \vdash \overline{e} : \overline{\alpha}, \overline{\alpha}, \overline{\beta}/*}{\overline{\Gamma} \vdash \overline{e} : \overline{\alpha}, \overline{\alpha}, \overline{\beta}/\overline{\alpha}}}{\overline{\Gamma} \vdash_p \# \,\overline{e} : \overline{\beta}}}{\overline{\Gamma} \vdash \overline{\langle e \rangle} = \# \,\overline{e} : \overline{\beta}, \overline{\gamma}, \overline{\gamma}/*}$$

(Shift) Suppose we have a derivation in $\lambda_{let}^{s/r}$:

$$\vdots$$

$$\frac{\Gamma, c : \forall t.(\beta/t \rightarrow \alpha/t);\ \delta \vdash e : \delta;\ \gamma}{\Gamma;\ \alpha \vdash \mathcal{S}c.e : \beta;\ \gamma}\ \text{shift}$$

Let $\Delta_1 = \overline{\Gamma}, c : \forall t.(\overline{\beta} \rightarrow (\overline{\alpha}, t, t/*))$. By induction hypothesis, we have a derivation for $\Delta_1 \vdash e : \overline{\delta}, \overline{\delta}, \overline{\gamma}/*$ in $\lambda_{let}^{c/p+}$. Let $\Delta_2 = \overline{\Gamma}, c' : \overline{\beta} \rightarrow (s, s, \overline{\alpha}/s)$ where s is a fresh type variable, then we can derive:

$$\frac{\dfrac{\dfrac{\dfrac{\dfrac{\Delta_2, x : \overline{\beta} \vdash c'x : s, s, \overline{\alpha}/s}{\Delta_2, x : \overline{\beta} \vdash_p \# \,(c'x) : \overline{\alpha}}}{\Delta_2, x : \overline{\beta} \vdash \# \,(c'x) : \overline{\alpha}, t, t/*}}{\Delta_2 \vdash_p \lambda x.\# \,(c'x) : \overline{\beta} \rightarrow (\overline{\alpha}, t, t/*)} \quad \Delta_1 \vdash e : \overline{\delta}, \overline{\delta}, \overline{\gamma}/*}{\dfrac{\Delta_2 \vdash_p \lambda x.\# \,(c'x) : \overline{\beta} \rightarrow (\overline{\alpha}, t, t/*) \quad \Delta_1 \vdash e : \overline{\delta}, \overline{\delta}, \overline{\gamma}/\overline{\delta}}{\Delta_2 \vdash \text{let } c = \lambda x.\# \,(c'x) \text{ in } \overline{e} : \overline{\delta}, \overline{\delta}, \overline{\gamma}/\overline{\delta}}}}{\overline{\Gamma} \vdash \mathcal{F}c'.\text{let } c = \lambda x.\# \,(c'x) \text{ in } \overline{e} : \overline{\beta}, \overline{\alpha}, \overline{\gamma}/s}$$

Since $s \notin \text{FTV}(\overline{\Gamma}, \overline{\alpha}, \overline{\beta}, \overline{\gamma})$, we can derive $\overline{\Gamma} \vdash \overline{\mathcal{S}c.e} : \overline{\beta}, \overline{\alpha}, \overline{\gamma}/*$.

We can also show that, if $e \rightsquigarrow e'$ in $\lambda_{let}^{s/r}$, then $\overline{e} \rightsquigarrow^* \overline{e'}$ in $\lambda_{let}^{c/p+}$, whose key case is proved as follows:

$$\overline{\langle P[\mathcal{S}c.e] \rangle} = \# \,(\overline{P}[\mathcal{F}c'.\text{let } c = \lambda x.\# \,c'x \text{ in } \overline{e}])$$

$$\rightsquigarrow \# \,(\text{let } c' = \lambda y.\overline{P}[y] \text{ in } \text{let } c = \lambda x.\# \,c'x \text{ in } \overline{e})$$

$$\rightsquigarrow \# \,(\text{let } c = \lambda y.\# \,(\lambda y.\overline{P}[x])x \text{ in } \overline{e})$$

$$\rightsquigarrow \# \,(\text{let } c = \lambda x.\# \,\overline{P}[x] \text{ in } \overline{e})$$

$$= \overline{\langle \text{let } c = \lambda x.\langle P[x] \rangle \text{ in } e \rangle}$$

We remark that this proof does not work for $\lambda_{let}^{c/p}$.

7 Typed Control/Prompt Is Strictly More Expressive Than Shift/Reset

In the type-free setting, we can encode `control/prompt` in terms of `shift/reset` [7,15,6]. In the typed setting, it is not the case, as we will prove in this section. Since $\lambda_{let}^{s/r}$ is strongly normalizing [2], it is sufficient to construct a typable expression in $\lambda_{let}^{c/p+}$ (or $\lambda_{let}^{c/p}$) whose computation is not terminating.

Let α and $\bullet$, resp. be a type and its inhabitant, resp., for instance, $\alpha = \texttt{bool}$ and $\bullet = \texttt{true}$. Let Γ be the type context $c : \alpha \to (\alpha, \alpha, \alpha/\alpha)$, and recall $e_1; e_2$ is an abbreviation of $(\lambda x.e_2)e_1$ for $x \notin \texttt{FV}(e_2)$. We can type the expression $\#(\mathcal{F}c.(c\bullet;\ c\bullet);\ \mathcal{F}c.(c\bullet;\ c\bullet))$ in $\lambda_{let}^{c/p}$ as follows:

$$\frac{\dfrac{\dfrac{\dfrac{\dfrac{\Gamma \vdash c : \alpha \to (\alpha, \alpha, \alpha/\alpha), \alpha, \alpha/\alpha \quad \Gamma \vdash \bullet : \alpha}{\Gamma \vdash c\ \bullet : \alpha, \alpha, \alpha/\alpha}}{\Gamma \vdash c\ \bullet;\ c\ \bullet : \alpha, \alpha, \alpha/\alpha}}{\vdash_p \mathcal{F}c.(c\ \bullet;\ c\ \bullet) : \alpha}}{\vdash \mathcal{F}c.(c\ \bullet;\ c\ \bullet);\ \mathcal{F}c.(c\ \bullet;\ c\ \bullet) : \alpha, \alpha, \alpha/\alpha}}{\vdash \#(\mathcal{F}c.(c\ \bullet;\ c\ \bullet);\ \mathcal{F}c.(c\ \bullet;\ c\ \bullet)) : \alpha, \beta, \beta/\tau}$$

The computation of this term does not terminate:

$$\begin{aligned}
&\#(\mathcal{F}c.(c\bullet;\ c\bullet);\ \mathcal{F}c.(c\bullet;\ c\bullet)) \\
&\rightsquigarrow \#(\texttt{let } c = \lambda u.(u;\ \mathcal{F}c.(c\bullet;\ c\bullet)) \texttt{ in } (c\bullet;\ c\bullet)) \\
&\rightsquigarrow^* \#(\mathcal{F}c.(c\bullet;\ c\bullet);\ (\lambda u.(u;\ \#\mathcal{F}c.(c\bullet;\ c\bullet)))\bullet) \\
&\rightsquigarrow^* \#(\mathcal{F}c.(c\bullet;\ c\bullet);\ (\lambda u'.(u';\ (\lambda u.(u;\ \#\mathcal{F}c.(c\bullet;\ c\bullet)))\bullet))\bullet) \\
&\rightsquigarrow^* \ldots
\end{aligned}$$

Since this example does not use answer-type modification or polymorphism, it can be typed in a more restricted type system such as our previous one [20].

We can go a step further. After submission of this paper, Kiselyov [16] and the second author (Yonezawa) have independently constructed fixed point combinators in call-by-value:

$$(Kiselyov)\ \ \texttt{Y}_1 = \lambda f.\#(Z_f;\ Z_f) \quad \text{where } Z_f = \mathcal{F}c.\ f\ (\lambda x.\ \#(c\bullet;\ c\bullet)\ x)$$

$$(Yonezawa)\ \ \texttt{Y}_2 = \lambda f.\#(X_f;\ X_f) \quad \text{where } X_f = \mathcal{F}c.\ \lambda x.\ (f\ \#(c\bullet;\ c\bullet))\ x$$

Both $\texttt{Y}_1$ and $\texttt{Y}_2$ are typable in $\lambda_{let}^{c/p}$, and satisfy $\texttt{Y}_1\ f\ x = f\ (\lambda x.\ \texttt{Y}_1\ f\ x)\ x$, and $\texttt{Y}_2\ f\ x = f\ (\lambda x.\ f\ (\texttt{Y}_2\ f)\ x)\ x$. Therefore, they can serve as fixed point combinators. The former satisfies a simpler equation, while $\texttt{Y}_1\ e$ may not terminate for some term e, but $\texttt{Y}_2\ e$ always terminates.

8 Conclusion

We have introduced a polymorphic type system for `control/prompt`, which allows answer type modification and does not need recursive types. We have shown that our calculus enjoys type soundness and is compatible with the CPS translation, and that typed control/prompt is strictly more powerful than typed shift/reset in the absence of recursive types. Although we cannot claim that our type system is *the* only type system for control/prompt, we believe that ours can be a good starting point to study the type structure of these control operators.

Based on this work, Kiselyov and the second author have successfully shown that $\lambda_{let}^{c/p}$ is Turing-complete if we extend the calculus with integers and primitive functions. The situation is similar to the exception mechanism in ML, for which Lillibridge [17] has proved that typed (unchecked) exception can simulate all type-free lambda terms, and therefore can represent all Turing-computable functions. Thielecke also compared the expressive powers of several control operators using a different technique [19].

In this paper we have been concentrating on the foundational aspect of control/prompt in this paper, and the practical aspect of our type systems is unstudied. In particular, more application programs other than those by Biernacki, Danvy, Millikin's are called for, but it is left for future work.

Acknowledgements. We thank Kenichi Asai, Dariusz Biernacki, Olivier Danvy, and Chung-chieh Shan for their insights. Special thanks go to Oleg Kiselyov and anonymous reviewers for valuable comments. This work was partly supported by JSPS Grant-in-Aid for Scientific Research (C) 16500004.

References

1. Asai, K.: On Typing Delimited Continuations: Three New Solutions to the Printf Problem. Technical Report OCHA-IS 07-1, Department of Information Science, Ochanomizu University (September, 2007)
2. Asai, K., Kameyama, Y.: Polymorphic Delimited Continuations. In: Shao, Z. (ed.) APLAS 2007. LNCS, vol. 4807, pp. 239–254. Springer, Heidelberg (2007)
3. Asai, K., Kameyama, Y.: Polymorphic Delimited Continuations. Technical Report CS-TR-07-10, Dept.of Computer Science, University of Tsukuba (September, 2007)
4. Biernacki, D., Danvy, O.: A Simple Proof of a Folklore Theorem about Delimited Control. J. Funct. Program. 16(3), 269–280 (2006)
5. Biernacki, D., Danvy, O., Shan, C.-c.: On the Static and Dynamic Extents of Delimited Continuations. Science of Computer Programming 60(3), 274–297 (2006)
6. Biernacki, D., Danvy, O., Millikin, K.: A Dynamic Continuation-Passing Style for Dynamic Delimited Continuations. TOPLAS (to appear)
7. Shan, C.-c.: Shift to control. In: Proc. Workshop on Scheme and Functional Programming, pp. 99–107 (2004)
8. Danvy, O.: Functional Unparsing. J. Funct. Program. 8(6), 621–625 (1998)
9. Danvy, O., Filinski, A.: Abstracting Control. In: Proc. 1990 ACM Conference on Lisp and Functional Programming, pp. 151–160 (1990)
10. Danvy, O., Filinski, A.: Representing Control: A Study of the CPS Transformation. Mathematical Structures in Computer Science 2(4), 361–391 (1992)
11. Dybvig, R.K., Peyton Jones, S., Sabry, A.: A Monadic Framework for Delimited Continuations. J. Funct. Program (to appear)
12. Felleisen, M.: The Theory and Practice of First-Class Prompts. In: Proc. 15th Symposium on Principles of Programming Languages, pp. 180–190 (1988)

13. Filinski, A.: Representing Monads. In: POPL, pp. 446–457 (1994)
14. Kameyama, Y., Hasegawa, M.: A sound and complete axiomatization for delimited continuations. In: ICFP, pp. 177–188 (2003)
15. Kiselyov, O.: How to remove dynamic prompt: Static and dynamic delimited continuation operators are equally expressive. Technical Report 611, Computer Science Department, Indiana University (March, 2005)
16. Kiselyov, O.: Fixpoint combinator from typed prompt/control (2007), http://okmij.org/ftp/Computation/Continuations.html
17. Lillibridge, M.: Unchecked Exceptions Can Be Strictly More Powerful Than Call/CC. Higher-Order and Symbolic Computation 12(1), 75–104 (1999)
18. Strachey, C., Wadsworth, C.P.: Continuations: A mathematical semantics for handling full jumps. Technical Monograph PRG-11, Oxford Univ. Comput. Lab., Oxford, England, 1974. Reprinted in Higher-Order and Symbolic Computation 13(1/2), pp. 135–152 (2000)
19. Thielecke, H.: On Exceptions Versus Continuations in the Presence of State. In: Smolka, G. (ed.) ESOP 2000. LNCS, vol. 1782, pp. 397–411. Springer, Heidelberg (2000)
20. Yonezawa, T., Kameyama, Y.: A Type System for Dynamic Delimited Continuations. In: IPSJ Transactions on Programming, Information Processing Society of Japan (to appear)

A   Polymorphic Type System for `shift/reset`

We define the type system for $\lambda_{let}^{s/r}$ in [2] except the fixed point operator. Types and type contexts are defined by:

$$\alpha, \beta \cdots ::= b \mid t \mid (\alpha/\beta \rightarrow \gamma/\delta) \qquad \text{monomorphic types}$$
$$A ::= \alpha \mid \forall t.A \qquad \text{polymorphic types}$$
$$\Gamma ::= [\,] \mid \Gamma, x : A \qquad \text{type contexts}$$

where the function type $(\alpha/\beta \rightarrow \gamma/\delta)$ corresponds to $\alpha \rightarrow (\gamma, \beta, \delta/*)$ in $\lambda_{let}^{c/p+}$. Judgements in $\lambda_{let}^{s/r}$ are either $\Gamma; \alpha \vdash e : \beta; \gamma$ or $\Gamma \vdash_p e : \beta$. The former corresponds to $\Gamma \vdash e : \beta, \alpha, \gamma/*$ in $\lambda_{let}^{c/p+}$. Finally, Figure 7 gives several important type inference rules of $\lambda_{let}^{s/r}$.

$$\frac{\Gamma, x : \sigma;\ \alpha \vdash e : \tau;\ \beta}{\Gamma \vdash_p \lambda x.e : (\sigma/\alpha \rightarrow \tau/\beta)} \ \text{fun}$$

$$\frac{\Gamma, k : \forall t.(\tau/t \rightarrow \alpha/t);\ \sigma \vdash e : \sigma;\ \beta}{\Gamma;\ \alpha \vdash \mathcal{S}k.e : \tau;\ \beta} \ \text{shift} \qquad \frac{\Gamma; \sigma \vdash e : \sigma;\ \tau}{\Gamma \vdash_p \langle e \rangle : \tau} \ \text{reset}$$

Fig. 7. Type Inference Rules of $\lambda_{let}^{s/r}$

Strictness Analysis Algorithms Based on an Inequality System for Lazy Types

Hirofumi Yokouchi

Dept. Computer Science, Gunma University
yokouchi@cs.gunma-u.ac.jp

Abstract. This paper deals with type-based analysis of functional programs. In particular we focus on strictness analysis using nonstandard type systems using a special kind of type called lazy type. We propose an inequality system for lazy types, from which two algorithms for strictness analysis are extracted. The key idea is elimination of the transitive law from the inequality system. The algorithms have been implemented. We report experimental results on performance of our algorithms.

1 Introduction

There are two major approaches to static analysis of functional programs — abstract interpretation and type-based analysis. Of them this paper deals with the type-based analysis. Type checking is an indispensable mechanism for programming languages that support strong typing. In the type-based analysis, such type checking or type inference is extended for checking various properties of programs in addition to type consistency. A type expressing a property of programs is called a nonstandard type to distinguish from ordinary types.

One of the earliest works for the type-based approach is Kuo and Mishra's strictness analysis [11]. Jensen [7,8] pointed out that the system proposed by Kuo and Mishra is strictly weaker than the system based on abstract interpretation, and he showed that, if conjunction of nonstandard types is introduced, then the resulting system is equivalent to the system based on abstract interpretation.

In the type-based analysis, most algorithms are designed as variations of Hindley-Milner's unification-based type inference algorithm. For example, see [12,3,9]. However, this paper focuses on lazy type inference proposed by Hankin and Le Métayer [5]. They introduced a new algorithm for strictness analysis. The main idea behind the algorithm is to check strictness on demand rather than deriving systematically the most precise information. They defined a new kind of type $[\Gamma|M]$, called lazy type, where Γ is a nonstandard typing basis and M is a term. The lazy type $[\Gamma|M]$ means the least nonstandard type of M under Γ. Consider how to check whether an application term LN has a nonstandard type ψ under a basis Γ. If we use the unification-based type inference algorithm, then we must compute the principal types for L and N. In the algorithm using lazy type, detailed analysis for N is postponed until it is really needed. It is checked whether L has the nonstandard type $[\Gamma|N] \to \psi$. In [5], the checking algorithm is designed as an abstract machine in the style of [6].

J. Garrigue and M. Hermenegildo (Eds.): FLOPS 2008, LNCS 4989, pp. 255–271, 2008.

In this paper we propose a formal system for lazy types. The main idea is to formalize the lazy type system as an inequality system without the transitive law. The lazy type $[\Gamma|M]$ stands for the least nonstandard type of M under Γ. Therefore, the judgment $\Gamma \vdash M : \psi$ stating that M has the nonstandard type ψ under Γ is expressed as the inequality $[\Gamma|M] \leq \psi$. We can define axioms and rules for inequalities on nonstandard types with lazy types. For the decision procedure for such an inequality system, it is difficult to handle the transitive law directly. The transitive law is the inference rule expressing that $\phi \leq \chi$ and $\chi \leq \psi$ imply $\phi \leq \psi$. In the decision procedure, we must search a suitable χ for checking $\phi \leq \psi$. In general, a heuristic method is needed to find such χ. We hope that the decision procedure becomes much simpler, if the transitive law is eliminated.

Elimination of the transitive law resembles cut-elimination of LK or LJ, Gentzen's sequent calculi [4]. Gentzen's sequent-style formulations are often used for examining properties of various type systems [1,14,18,15]. An inequality like $\phi \leq \phi_1 \to \cdots \to \phi_n \to \psi$ is corresponding to the sequent $\phi, \phi_1, \ldots, \phi_n \longrightarrow \psi$ in LJ. We hope to consult LK and LJ for designing the axioms and rules for inequalities. Furthermore, we can extract the decision procedure on inequalities from the system without the transitive law. This is analogous to the fact that a decision procedure is extracted from LK without the cut rule. In particular, Wang's algorithm [17] is the most remarkable decision procedure extracted from a certain variant of cut-free sequent calculus.

We introduce two algorithms named **ch** and **ev** for strictness analysis based on the inequality system. The algorithm **ch** is a decision procedure that determines whether a given inequality of nonstandard types is derivable. Therefore, we can check that a term M has a nonstandard type ϕ under a context Γ if we check $[\Gamma|M] \leq \phi$ by the algorithm **ch**. The algorithm **ev** computes the nonstandard type for $[\Gamma|M]$ directly. More precisely, **ev** takes a nonstandard type ϕ and a finite list of nonstandard types $\phi_1, \ldots, \phi_n$, and it yields the least nonstandard type ψ such that $\phi \leq \phi_1 \to \cdots \to \phi_n \to \psi$. These two algorithms are almost automatically extracted from the inequality system for lazy types, whose properties can be analyzed formally. In this paper, we show the correctness and termination of the algorithms rigorously.

The algorithm **ch** is essentially the same as the algorithms introduced in [5]. However, the presentation styles are quite different. The algorithm in [5] is defined in the form of an abstract machine like SECD machine, while our algorithm is presented as an ML-like pseudo-code that consists of transformation rules. In contrast, the algorithm **ev** is completely different from **ch** or the algorithm in [5]. The algorithm **ev** computes the nonstandard type for $[\Gamma|M]$, while **ch** checks an inequality like $[\Gamma|M] \leq \psi$. We have implemented the algorithms **ch** and **ev** in OCaml. Our experimental results show that **ev** is much faster than **ch**.

Another related work is chaotic iteration introduced in [2]. The chaotic iteration is a technique for computing an approximation of the fixed point for a given function. In the algorithm **ev** we can replace the part for processing recursion by an algorithm using chaotic iteration. Our experimental results show that, for analysis of higher-order functions, the algorithm **ev** is faster than the modified algorithm with chaotic iteration.

The nonstandard type systems with conjunction are corresponding to intersection type systems for standard types. Type checking or type inference for intersection types is known undecidable. In [10], it has been shown that certain restricted intersection type systems are decidable. In the restricted systems, an intersection type is restricted to a certain shape called a finite-rank intersection type. In particular, the restriction to rank-2 intersection types is often used in designing variou type inference algorithms. A similar restriction can be imposed on the nonstandard type systems. In [9], a type inference algorithm has been proposed for a rank-2 nonstandard type system of strictness analysis. Our algorithms **ch** and **ev**, however, adopt nonstandard types without any restriction.

The rest of the paper organized as follows. In Section 2, we will define the nonstandard type system for strictness analysis. In Section 3 we will introduce inequality system **LS** for nonstandard types. In Section 4 we will introduce inequality system **LT** for lazy nonstandard types by extending **LS**. In Sections 5 and 6, we will define the algorithms **ch** and **ev**, respectively. In Section 7, we will report experimental results on the comparison of the algorithms **ch**, **ev** and the modified algorithm with chaotic iteration.

The full paper with the detailed proofs and the OCaml programs of the algorithms **ch** and **ev** are presented in:

`http://www.keim.cs.gunma-u.ac.jp/~yokouchi/lstrict/index.html`

2   Preliminaries

In this section, following [8], we define the nonstandard type system for strictness analysis. The set of *(standard) types* is defined by the following grammar:

$$\tau \text{ (types)} ::= \iota \mid \tau_1 \to \tau_2$$
$$\iota \text{ (base types)} ::= \mathsf{bool} \mid \mathsf{num} \mid \cdots$$

We use the letters ρ, σ, and τ for types. For each type τ, the set $\mathcal{L}(\tau)$ of *nonstandard types*, shortly *ns-types*, is defined by the following rules:

$$\mathbf{t}^\tau \in \mathcal{L}(\tau) \qquad \mathbf{f}^\tau \in \mathcal{L}(\tau) \qquad \frac{\alpha \in \mathcal{L}(\tau) \qquad \beta \in \mathcal{L}(\tau)}{\alpha \wedge \beta \in \mathcal{L}(\tau)} \qquad \frac{\alpha \in \mathcal{L}(\rho) \qquad \beta \in \mathcal{L}(\sigma)}{\alpha \to \beta \in \mathcal{L}(\rho \to \sigma)}$$

We use the letters α, β and γ for ns-types. Whenever no confusion occurs, the type τ of $\mathbf{t}^\tau$ or $\mathbf{f}^\tau$ is omitted.

An ns-type $\alpha \in \mathcal{L}(\tau)$ informally means a set of values of type τ. In particular, $\mathbf{f}^\tau$ means the singleton set of the undefined value $\bot$, and $\mathbf{t}^\tau$ means the entire set of the values of type τ. The ns-type $\alpha \to \beta$ means the set of functions f such that $f(a)$ is contained in the set expressed by β for every element a in the set expressed by α. Therefore, $\mathbf{t}^{\sigma_1} \to \mathbf{f}^{\sigma_2} \to \mathbf{f}^\iota$ represents the set of binary functions which are strict for the second argument.

We assume that for every type τ infinitely many variables are supplied and that for each variable its type is uniquely determined. The set of *pseudo-terms* is defined by the following grammar:

$$M ::= x \mid c \mid M_1 M_2 \mid \lambda x.M \mid \mu^\xi x.M \mid \text{if } M_1 \text{ then } M_2 \text{ else } M_3$$

The letter ξ stands for a finite sequence of ns-types. The letter c stands for a constant. In a standard way we define the set of *terms*, which are well-typed. We use the letters x, y and z for variables, and we use L, M and N for terms. The term $\mu^\xi x.M$ is an extension of $\mu x.M$. This extension is used for designing the algorithms **ch** and **ev**. In $\mu^\xi x.M$, if the type of M is τ, then every $\phi \in \xi$ and x must be of the type τ, and the type of $\mu^\xi x.M$ is τ. When ξ is empty, we write $\mu x.M$ for $\mu^\xi x.M$.

A *(nonstandard typing) basis* is a finite sequence of the form $x_1 : \alpha_1, \ldots, x_n : \alpha_n$ such that $x_1, \ldots, x_n$ are distinct variables and $\alpha_1, \ldots, \alpha_n$ are ns-types of the same types as of the corresponding variables. We use the letters Γ and Δ for bases. A *(nonstandard typing) judgment* is an expression of the form $\Gamma \vdash M : \beta$ such that the type of M is the same as the type of β. An *(ns-type) inequality* is an expression of the form $\alpha \leq \beta$ such that α and β are ns-types of the same type.

We define the axiomatic systems **NS** for inequalities on ns-types and **NT** for judgments in Figs. 1 and 2. We assume that for each term constant c of type τ at most one ns-type α of type τ is supplied. The set of the pairs $c : \alpha$ is represented by $\mathcal{A}$ in **NT**. The axioms and rules of **NS** and **NT** are standard ones except for the rule of $\mu^\xi x.M$, which is an extension of the rule of $\mu x.M$. Remark that the standard rule for $\mu x.M$ is coincident with the special case of the rule $\mu^\xi x.M$ in which ξ is empty. We say that $\alpha \cong \beta$ is derivable, when $\alpha \leq \beta$ and $\beta \leq \alpha$ are derivable. Similarly, we say that $\alpha \leq \beta \leq \gamma$ is derivable, when $\alpha \leq \beta$ and $\beta \leq \gamma$ are derivable.

$$\alpha \leq \alpha \qquad \frac{\alpha_1 \leq \alpha_2 \quad \alpha_2 \leq \alpha_3}{\alpha_1 \leq \alpha_3} \qquad \frac{\beta_1 \leq \alpha_1 \quad \alpha_2 \leq \beta_2}{\alpha_1 \to \alpha_2 \leq \beta_1 \to \beta_2}$$

$$\frac{\alpha \leq \beta_1 \quad \alpha \leq \beta_2}{\alpha \leq \beta_1 \wedge \beta_2} \qquad \alpha \wedge \beta \leq \alpha \qquad \alpha \wedge \beta \leq \beta$$

$$\alpha \leq \mathbf{t} \qquad \mathbf{f} \leq \beta \qquad \mathbf{t}^{\rho \to \sigma} \leq \mathbf{t}^\rho \to \mathbf{t}^\sigma \qquad \mathbf{t}^\rho \to \mathbf{f}^\sigma \leq \mathbf{f}^{\rho \to \sigma}$$

$$(\alpha \to \beta_1) \wedge (\alpha \to \beta_2) \leq \alpha \to (\beta_1 \wedge \beta_2)$$

Fig. 1. Axioms and rules of **NS**

The most important property of ns-types is finiteness. For each type τ, the set $\mathcal{L}(\tau)$ of ns-types of type τ is infinite. However, if all equivalent ns-types are identified, then $\mathcal{L}(\tau)$ is finite. It is convenient to provide a finite set whose elements represent all ns-types for each type τ.

$$\Gamma \vdash x : \alpha \quad (x : \alpha \in \Gamma) \qquad \Gamma \vdash c : \alpha \quad (c : \alpha \in \mathcal{A})$$

$$\frac{\Gamma \vdash M : \alpha \to \beta \qquad \Gamma \vdash N : \alpha}{\Gamma \vdash MN : \beta} \qquad \frac{\Gamma, x : \alpha \vdash M : \beta}{\Gamma \vdash \lambda x.M : \alpha \to \beta}$$

$$\frac{\Gamma \vdash L : \mathbf{f}}{\Gamma \vdash \text{if } L \text{ then } M \text{ else } N : \mathbf{f}} \qquad \frac{\Gamma \vdash M : \alpha \qquad \Gamma \vdash N : \alpha}{\Gamma \vdash \text{if } L \text{ then } M \text{ else } N : \alpha}$$

$$\frac{\Gamma, x : \alpha_1 \wedge \ldots \wedge \alpha_n \wedge \beta \vdash M : \beta}{\Gamma \vdash \mu^\xi x.M : \alpha_1 \wedge \ldots \wedge \alpha_n \wedge \beta} \quad (\xi \equiv \alpha_1, \ldots, \alpha_n)$$

$$\frac{\Gamma \vdash M : \alpha \qquad \Gamma \vdash M : \beta}{\Gamma \vdash M : \alpha \wedge \beta} \qquad \Gamma \vdash M : \mathbf{t} \qquad \frac{\Gamma \vdash M : \alpha \qquad \alpha \leq \beta}{\Gamma \vdash M : \beta}$$

Fig. 2. Axioms and rules of **NT**

For each type τ we define sets $\mathcal{N}(\tau)$ and $\mathcal{P}(\tau)$ of ns-types simultaneously as follows:

- $\mathcal{N}(\tau) = \{\mathbf{f}^\tau\}$ if τ is a base type,
- $\mathcal{N}(\tau_1 \to \tau_2) = \{\alpha \to \beta \mid \alpha \in \mathcal{P}(\tau_1), \ \beta \in \mathcal{N}(\tau_2)\}$,
- $\mathcal{P}(\tau) \equiv \{\wedge P \mid P \subseteq \mathcal{N}(\tau)\}$.

Here $\wedge P$ is defined as $\alpha_1 \wedge \ldots \wedge \alpha_n$ for $P = \{\alpha_1, \ldots, \alpha_n\}$. When $P = \emptyset$, we define $\wedge P \equiv \mathbf{t}$. For example,

- $\mathcal{N}(\iota \to \iota) = \{\mathbf{t}^\iota \to \mathbf{f}^\iota, \ \mathbf{f}^\iota \to \mathbf{f}^\iota\}$,
- $\mathcal{P}(\iota \to \iota) = \{(\mathbf{t}^\iota \to \mathbf{f}^\iota) \wedge (\mathbf{f}^\iota \to \mathbf{f}^\iota), \ \mathbf{t}^\iota \to \mathbf{f}^\iota, \ \mathbf{f}^\iota \to \mathbf{f}^\iota, \ \mathbf{t}^{\iota \to \iota}\}$,
- $\mathcal{N}((\iota \to \iota) \to \iota) = \{\mathbf{t}^{\iota \to \iota} \to \mathbf{f}^\iota, \ (\mathbf{t}^\iota \to \mathbf{f}^\iota) \to \mathbf{f}^\iota, \ (\mathbf{f}^\iota \to \mathbf{f}^\iota) \to \mathbf{f}^\iota, \ (\mathbf{t}^\iota \to \mathbf{f}^\iota) \wedge (\mathbf{f}^\iota \to \mathbf{f}^\iota) \to \mathbf{f}^\iota\}$,

where ι is a base type.

Lemma 1. *For every ns-types α of type τ there exists $\beta \in \mathcal{P}(\tau)$ such that $\alpha \cong \beta$ is derivable in* **NS**.

3 Another Set of the Rules for Inequalities

In the last section we have defined the axiomatic system **NS** for inequalities on ns-types. We introduce another set of inference rules for inequalities to examine the properties of ns-types. In Fig. 3 we define axiomatic system **LS**, which will be shown equivalent to **NS**.

The axioms and rules in **LS** are defined on the analogy of the rules of LK and LJ, Gentzen's sequent calculi for logic. An inequality $\alpha \leq \beta_1 \to \cdots \to \beta_n \to \gamma$ is regarded as the the sequent $\alpha, \beta_1, \ldots, \beta_n \longrightarrow \gamma$ in LJ. The rule (IntR) is corresponding to the following rule of LJ:

$$\frac{\alpha, \beta_1, \ldots, \beta_n \longrightarrow \gamma_1 \qquad \alpha, \beta_1, \ldots, \beta_n \longrightarrow \gamma_2}{\alpha, \beta_1, \ldots, \beta_n \longrightarrow \gamma_1 \wedge \gamma_2}$$

The point is that **LS** has no rule for transitive law. The transitive law is admissible in **LS**. This fact is corresponding to cut-elimination in LJ.

(Init) $\alpha \leq \alpha$ (IntR) $\dfrac{\alpha \leq \beta_1 \to \cdots \to \beta_n \to \gamma_1 \quad \alpha \leq \beta_1 \to \cdots \to \beta_n \to \gamma_2}{\alpha \leq \beta_1 \to \cdots \to \beta_n \to \gamma_1 \wedge \gamma_2}$

(IntL) $\dfrac{\alpha_1 \leq \beta}{\alpha_1 \wedge \alpha_2 \leq \beta} \quad \dfrac{\alpha_2 \leq \beta}{\alpha_1 \wedge \alpha_2 \leq \beta}$ (Arrow) $\dfrac{\beta_1 \leq \alpha_1 \quad \alpha_2 \leq \beta_2}{\alpha_1 \to \alpha_2 \leq \beta_1 \to \beta_2}$

(t) $\alpha \leq \beta_1 \to \cdots \to \beta_n \to \mathbf{t}$ $(\mathbf{f})_1$ $\mathbf{f} \leq \beta$ $(\mathbf{f})_2$ $\dfrac{\mathbf{t} \leq \alpha_1 \quad \alpha_2 \leq \mathbf{f}}{\alpha_1 \to \alpha_2 \leq \mathbf{f}}$

Fig. 3. Axioms and rules of **LS**

Lemma 2. *In* **LS**, *if* $\alpha \leq \beta$ *and* $\beta \leq \gamma$ *are derivable, then* $\alpha \leq \gamma$ *is derivable.*

Using Lemma 2 we can show that **NS** and **LS** are equivalent.

Lemma 3. *An inequality* $\alpha \leq \beta$ *is derivable in* **NS** *if and only if it is derivable in* **LS**.

The next lemma shows the basic properties of **LS**, which will be used for designing the algorithms.

Lemma 4. *In* **LS** *the following equivalences hold.*

  (i) *The inequality* $\alpha \leq \beta_1 \to \cdots \to \beta_n \to \gamma_1 \wedge \gamma_2$ *is derivable if and only if* $\alpha \leq \beta_1 \to \cdots \to \beta_n \to \gamma_i$ *is derivable for* $i = 1$ *and 2.*
 (ii) *The inequality* $\alpha_1 \wedge \alpha_2 \leq \beta$ *is derivable if* $\alpha_i \leq \beta$ *is derivable for* $i = 1$ *or 2. Furthermore, unless* β *is of the form* $\beta_1 \to \cdots \to \beta_n \to \gamma_1 \wedge \gamma_2$, *the opposite implication also holds.*
(iii) *The inequality* $\alpha_1 \to \alpha_2 \leq \beta_1 \to \beta_2$ *is derivable if and only if either (1)* $\beta_1 \leq \alpha_1$ *and* $\alpha_2 \leq \beta_2$ *are derivable, or (2)* $\mathbf{t} \leq \beta_2$ *is derivable.*
 (iv) *The inequality* $\alpha_1 \to \alpha_2 \leq \mathbf{f}$ *is derivable if and only if* $\mathbf{t} \leq \alpha_1$ *and* $\alpha_2 \leq \mathbf{f}$ *are derivable.*

4 Lazy Nonstandard Types

In this section we introduce lazy ns-types and the axiomatic system **LT** for them. A lazy ns-type is an expression of the form $[\Gamma|M]$, where Γ is a basis and M is a term such that all the free variables in M occur in Γ. Furthermore, it is allowed that another lazy ns-type occurs in Γ or ξ of $\mu^\xi x.L$ in $[\Gamma|M]$. Therefore, ns-types, terms, and bases are defined by mutual recursion. An ns-type that may contain $[\Gamma|M]$ is simply called an ns-type, an ns-type of the form $[\Gamma|M]$ is called a lazy ns-type, and an ns-type in which no lazy ns-type occurs is called a *proper* ns-type. We use the letters ϕ, χ and ψ for ns-types and α, β and γ for proper ns-types.

We define an axiomatic system **LT** as an inequality system on ns-types. For **LT** we use the same set of the axioms and rules of **LS** shown in Fig. 3 together with those in Fig. 4. Note that, when axioms and rules in Fig. 3 are used in **LT**, the ns-types in them may contain lazy types.

$$\text{(Var)} \quad \frac{\phi \leq \psi}{[\Gamma|x] \leq \psi} \quad (x : \phi \in \Gamma) \qquad \text{(Const)} \quad \frac{\phi \leq \psi}{[\Gamma|c] \leq \psi} \quad (c : \phi \in \mathcal{A})$$

$$\text{(Appl)} \quad \frac{[\Gamma|M] \leq [\Gamma|N] \to \psi}{[\Gamma|MN] \leq \psi}$$

$$\text{(Abst)} \quad \frac{[\Gamma, x : \phi|M] \leq \psi}{[\Gamma|\lambda x.M] \leq \phi \to \psi} \qquad \text{(Abst)}_{\mathbf{f}} \quad \frac{[\Gamma, x : \mathbf{t}|M] \leq \mathbf{f}}{[\Gamma|\lambda x.M] \leq \mathbf{f}}$$

$$\text{(if)}_1 \quad \frac{[\Gamma|L] \leq \mathbf{f}}{[\Gamma|\text{if } L \text{ then } M \text{ else } N] \leq \psi} \qquad \text{(if)}_2 \quad \frac{[\Gamma|M] \leq \psi \quad [\Gamma|N] \leq \psi}{[\Gamma|\text{if } L \text{ then } M \text{ else } N] \leq \psi}$$

$$(\mu)_1 \quad \frac{\phi \leq \psi}{[\Gamma|\mu^\xi x.M] \leq \psi} \quad (\phi \in \xi) \qquad (\mu)_2 \quad \frac{[\Gamma, x : [\Gamma|\mu^{\xi,\psi} x.M] \mid M] \leq \psi}{[\Gamma|\mu^\xi x.M] \leq \psi}$$

$$\text{(LazyR)} \quad \frac{\text{for all } \alpha \in \mathcal{N}(\tau) \text{ if } [\Gamma|M] \leq \alpha \text{ then } \phi \leq \psi_1 \to \cdots \to \psi_n \to \alpha}{\phi \leq \psi_1 \to \cdots \to \psi_n \to [\Gamma|M]}$$

$$\text{where } \tau \text{ is the type of } M$$

Fig. 4. Axioms and rules of **LT**

The lazy ns-type $[\Gamma|M]$ means the least ns-type ϕ such that $\Gamma \vdash M : \phi$ is derived. The rules of **LT** in Fig. 4 are designed on the basis of the rules of **NT**. For example, the rule for application terms in **NT** suggests the following rule:

$$\frac{[\Gamma|M] \leq \phi \to \psi \quad [\Gamma|N] \leq \phi}{[\Gamma|MN] \leq \psi}$$

However, the two inequalities in the assumption can be unified into $[\Gamma|M] \leq [\Gamma|N] \to \psi$. The resulting rule is (Appl).

The key to the rules of **LT** is the design of the rules for $\mu x.M$. We explain the role of the rules $(\mu)_1$ and $(\mu)_2$ with the following program presented in [11]:

$$\mu f.\lambda x.\lambda y.\lambda z.\text{if } z = 0 \text{ then } x + y \text{ else } f \, y \, x \, (z - 1)$$

Here $=$, $+$, and $-$ are constants with the ns-type $(\mathbf{f} \to \mathbf{t} \to \mathbf{f}) \wedge (\mathbf{t} \to \mathbf{f} \to \mathbf{f})$. For readability, we use infix notation for these constants. This term has the ns-type $\mathbf{f} \to \mathbf{t} \to \mathbf{t} \to \mathbf{f}$. This fact is proved in **LT** as in Fig. 5, where we use the following symbols:

$$M_0 \equiv \text{if } z = 0 \text{ then } x + y \text{ else } f \, y \, x \, (z - 1)$$
$$M_1 \equiv \lambda x.\lambda y.\lambda z.M_0$$
$$\phi_1 \equiv \mathbf{f} \to \mathbf{t} \to \mathbf{t} \to \mathbf{f}$$
$$\Gamma_1 \equiv f : [|\mu^{\phi_1} f.M_1], x : \mathbf{f}, y : \mathbf{t}, z : \mathbf{t}$$
$$\phi_2 \equiv [\Gamma_1|y] \to [\Gamma_1|x] \to [\Gamma_1|z - 1] \to \mathbf{f}$$
$$\Gamma_2 \equiv f : [|\mu^{\phi_1,\phi_2} f.M_1], x : [\Gamma_1|y], y : [\Gamma_1|x], z : [\Gamma_1|z - 1]$$
$$\phi_3 \equiv [\Gamma_2|y] \to [\Gamma_2|x] \to [\Gamma_2|z - 1] \to \mathbf{f}$$

The point of this example is that the least ns-type of $\mu f.M_1$ is coincident with $\phi_1 \wedge \phi_2$. The components of this ns-type occur at $\mu^{\phi_1,\phi_2} f.M_1$ in the derivation.

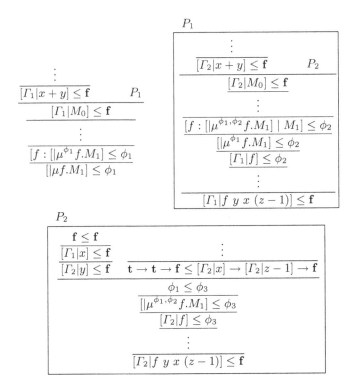

Fig. 5. An example of a derivation in **LT**

In general, ξ of $\mu^\xi x.M$ is used as a candidate or an approximation of the least ns-type of $\mu x.M$. More precisely, the conjunction of the ns-types in ξ is a candidate of $[\Gamma|\mu x.M]$. If we try to design the checking algorithm for inequalities, then the meanings of the rules $(\mu)_1$ and $(\mu)_2$ become clear. For $[\Gamma|\mu x.M] \leq \psi$, we take ψ as a candidate of $[\Gamma|\mu x.M]$ and we continue to check $[\Gamma, x : [\Gamma|\mu^\psi x.M] \mid M] \leq \psi$. This consideration suggests the rule $(\mu)_2$. For $[\Gamma|\mu^\xi x.M] \leq \psi$, we check $\phi \leq \psi$ for each $\phi \in \xi$. The conjunction of the ns-types in ξ is a candidate of $[\Gamma|\mu x.M]$. Therefore, if there is $\phi \in \xi$ such that $\phi \leq \psi$ is valid, then we conclude $[\Gamma|\mu^\xi x.M] \leq \psi$ is valid. From this observation the rule $(\mu)_1$ follows.

In the rest of this section we show a property of **LT**, which will be used in designing the algorithms **ch** and **ev**. We hope to show that the system **LT** is equivalent to **NT**, but it is difficult to prove this fact directly. We will take another method. Intuitively, a lazy ns-type $[\Gamma|M]$ means the least ns-type β such that $\Gamma \vdash M : \beta$. For each type τ the set $\mathcal{L}(\tau)$ of proper ns-types of type τ is finite if all equivalent ns-types are identified. Therefore, we can define the least proper ns-type corresponding to $[\Gamma|M]$. Formally we introduce the following definition.

Definition 1. For an ns-type ϕ and term M we define $\overline{\phi}$ and $\overline{M}$ as follows:

- $\overline{\phi} \equiv \phi$ if ϕ is a proper ns-type.
- $\overline{[\Gamma|M]} \equiv \wedge\{\,\alpha \in \mathcal{N}(\tau) \mid \overline{\Gamma} \vdash \overline{M} : \alpha$ is derivable in **NT** $\}$, where τ is the type of M, and $\overline{\Gamma}$ is the context $x_1 : \overline{\phi_1}, \ldots, x_n : \overline{\phi_n}$ for $\Gamma \equiv x_1 : \phi_1, \ldots, x_n : \phi_n$.
- For each term M, we define $\overline{M}$ as the term obtained from M by replacing each ξ of μ^ξ by $\overline{\xi}$, where $\overline{\xi}$ is the sequence $\overline{\phi_1}, \ldots, \overline{\phi_n}$ for $\xi \equiv \phi_1, \ldots, \phi_n$.

The next lemma shows that $\overline{[\Gamma|M]}$ represents the least proper ns-type β such that $\overline{\Gamma} \vdash \overline{M} : \beta$ is derivable in **NT**.

Lemma 5. *A judgment $\Gamma \vdash M : \beta$ is derivable in **NT** if and only if $\overline{[\Gamma|M]} \leq \beta$ is derivable in **NS**.*

We will show that some rules of **LT** can be applied in the opposite direction. For instance, the following rule corresponding to (Appl) is also admissible:

$$\frac{[\Gamma|MN] \leq \psi}{[\Gamma|M] \leq [\Gamma|N] \to \psi}$$

The next lemma, however, does not directly treat the rules in **LT**, but it shows the equivalence of inequalities obtained by applying the operator $\overline{[\Gamma|M]}$.

For the lemma, we prepare a technical term. An ns-type of the form $\phi_1 \to \cdots \to \phi_n \to \mathbf{t}$ or $\phi_1 \to \cdots \to \phi_n \to \mathbf{f}$ is said to be *non-conjunctive*.

Lemma 6. *In **NS** the following equivalences hold.*

(i) $\overline{[\Gamma|x]} \leq \overline{\psi}$ *is derivable if and only if $\overline{\phi} \leq \overline{\psi}$ is derivable, where $x : \phi \in \Gamma$.*

(ii) $\overline{[\Gamma|c]} \leq \overline{\psi}$ *is derivable if and only if $\overline{\phi} \leq \overline{\psi}$ is derivable, where $c : \phi \in \mathcal{A}$.*

(iii) $\overline{[\Gamma|MN]} \leq \overline{\psi}$ *is derivable if and only if $\overline{[\Gamma|M]} \leq \overline{[\Gamma|N]} \to \psi$ is derivable.*

(iv) $\overline{[\Gamma|\lambda x.M]} \leq \overline{\phi} \to \psi$ *is derivable if and only if $\overline{[\Gamma, x : \phi|M]} \leq \overline{\psi}$ is derivable.*

(v) $\overline{[\Gamma|\lambda x.M]} \leq \mathbf{f}$ *is derivable if and only if $\overline{[\Gamma, x : \mathbf{t}|M]} \leq \mathbf{f}$ is derivable.*

(vi) $\overline{[\Gamma \mid \text{if } L \text{ then } M_1 \text{ else } M_2]} \leq \overline{\psi}$ *is derivable if and only if either (1) $\overline{[\Gamma|L]} \leq \mathbf{f}$ is derivable, or (2) $\overline{[\Gamma|M_i]} \leq \overline{\psi}$ is derivable for $i = 1$ and 2.*

(vii) $\overline{[\Gamma|\mu^\xi x.M]} \leq \overline{\psi}$ *is derivable if either (1) $\overline{\phi} \leq \overline{\psi}$ is derivable for some $\phi \in \xi$, or (2) $\overline{[\Gamma, x : [\mu^{\xi, \psi} x.M] \mid M]} \leq \overline{\psi}$ is derivable. Furthermore, if ψ is non-conjunctive, then the opposite implication also holds.*

(viii) *The following two are equivalent:*
(1) $\overline{\phi} \leq \overline{\psi_1 \to \cdots \to \psi_n \to [\Gamma|M]}$ *is derivable, and*
(2) *for all $\alpha \in \mathcal{N}(\tau)$, if $\overline{[\Gamma|N]} \leq \alpha$ is derivable, then $\overline{\phi} \leq \overline{\psi_1 \to \cdots \to \psi_n \to \alpha}$ is derivable.*

5   The Algorithm ch

The axioms and rules of **LT** together with Lemmas 4 and 6 suggest the type checking algorithm **ch** in Fig. 6. The algorithm **ch** is presented in an ML-like pseudo-code. Taking an inequality $\phi \leq \psi$, it returns **true** if $\overline{\phi} \leq \overline{\psi}$ is derivable,

fun $\mathbf{ch}(\phi \leq \phi) = \mathbf{true}$
   | $\mathbf{ch}(\phi \leq \psi_1 \to \cdots \to \psi_n \to \mathbf{t}) = \mathbf{true}$
   | $\mathbf{ch}(\mathbf{t} \leq \psi_1 \to \cdots \to \psi_n \to \mathbf{f}) = \mathbf{false}$
   | $\mathbf{ch}(\mathbf{f} \leq \psi) = \mathbf{true}$
   | $\mathbf{ch}(\phi_1 \to \phi_2 \leq \mathbf{f}) = \mathbf{ch}(\mathbf{t} \leq \phi_1)$ **and** $\mathbf{ch}(\phi_2 \leq \mathbf{f})$
   | $\mathbf{ch}([\Gamma|x] \leq \psi) = \mathbf{ch}(\phi \leq \psi) \quad (x : \phi \in \Gamma)$
   | $\mathbf{ch}([\Gamma|c] \leq \psi) = \mathbf{ch}(\phi \leq \psi) \quad (c : \phi \in \mathcal{A})$
   | $\mathbf{ch}([\Gamma|MN] \leq \psi) = \mathbf{ch}([\Gamma|M] \leq [\Gamma|N] \to \psi)$
   | $\mathbf{ch}([\Gamma|\lambda x.M] \leq \phi \to \psi) = \mathbf{ch}([\Gamma, x : \phi|M] \leq \psi)$
   | $\mathbf{ch}([\Gamma|\lambda x.M] \leq \mathbf{f}) = \mathbf{ch}([\Gamma, x : \mathbf{t}|M] \leq \mathbf{f})$
   | $\mathbf{ch}([\Gamma|\mathsf{if}\ L\ \mathsf{then}\ M\ \mathsf{else}\ N] \leq \psi)$
     $= \mathbf{ch}([\Gamma|L] \leq \mathbf{f})$ **or** $(\mathbf{ch}([\Gamma|M] \leq \psi)$ **and** $\mathbf{ch}([\Gamma|N] \leq \psi))$
   | $\mathbf{ch}(\phi \leq \phi_1 \to \cdots \to \phi_n \to (\psi_1 \wedge \psi_2))$
     $= \mathbf{ch}(\phi \leq \phi_1 \to \cdots \to \phi_n \to \psi_1)$ **and** $\mathbf{ch}(\phi \leq \phi_1 \to \cdots \to \phi_n \to \psi_2)$
   | $\mathbf{ch}(\phi \leq \psi_1 \to \cdots \to \psi_n \to [\Gamma|M])$
     $= \forall \alpha \in \mathcal{N}(\tau).(\mathbf{not}\ \mathbf{ch}([\Gamma|M] \leq \alpha)$ **or** $\mathbf{ch}(\phi \leq \psi_1 \to \cdots \to \psi_n \to \alpha)$
                             (where τ is the type of M)
   | $\mathbf{ch}(\phi_1 \to \phi_2 \leq \psi_1 \to \psi_2) = \mathbf{ch}(\psi_1 \leq \phi_1)$ **and** $\mathbf{ch}(\phi_2 \leq \psi_2)$
   | $\mathbf{ch}(\phi_1 \wedge \phi_2 \leq \psi) = \mathbf{ch}(\phi_1 \leq \psi)$ **or** $\mathbf{ch}(\phi_2 \leq \psi)$
   | $\mathbf{ch}([\Gamma|\mu^\xi x.M] \leq \psi) = (\exists \phi \in \xi.\mathbf{ch}(\phi \leq \psi))$ **or** $\mathbf{ch}([\Gamma, x : [\Gamma|\mu^{\xi,\psi}x.M]\,|\,M] \leq \psi)$

Fig. 6. Algorithm **ch**

and it returns **false** if $\overline{\phi} \leq \overline{\psi}$ is underivable. The algorithm **ch** performs to simplify the given inequality according to the rules of **LT**. The rules for simplification are obtained from Lemmas 4 and 6.

The order of the transformation rules in **ch** is essential. The pattern matching proceeds sequentially from the top of the rules. Therefore, we should remark that, in the rules for $\mathbf{ch}(\phi_1 \wedge \phi_2 \leq \psi)$ and $\mathbf{ch}([\Gamma|\mu^\xi x.M]) \leq \psi)$ of Fig. 6, ψ is non-conjunctive. Similarly, in the rule for $\mathbf{ch}(\phi_1 \to \phi_2 \leq \psi_1 \to \psi_2)$, the ns-type ψ_2 is of the form $\chi_1 \to \cdots \to \chi_n \to \mathbf{f}$.

Lemma 7. *If the execution of* $\mathbf{ch}(\phi \leq \psi)$ *terminates with* **true** *(***false***), then* $\overline{\phi} \leq \overline{\psi}$ *is derivable (not derivable) in* **NS**.

Lemma 8. *Let* $\Gamma \vdash M : \beta$ *be a judgment in which no lazy ns-type occurs. Then, the execution of* $\mathbf{ch}([\Gamma|M] \leq \beta)$ *terminates.*

Theorem 1. *A judgment* $\Gamma \vdash M : \beta$ *is derivable (not derivable) in* **NT** *if and only if the execution* $\mathbf{ch}([\Gamma|M] \leq \beta)$ *terminates with* **true** *(***false***).*

Using Theorem 1, we can show the equivalence of the systems **NT** and **LT**.

Theorem 2. *A judgment* $\Gamma \vdash M : \beta$ *is derivable in* **NT** *if and only if* $[\Gamma|M] \leq \beta$ *is derivable in* **LT**.

6   The Algorithm ev

The algorithm **ch** is a checking algorithm determining whether $\phi \leq \psi$ is derivable or underivable. In this section, we define another form of algorithm. A lazy

fun ev(t; p**) = t**
  | ev(f; p**) = f**
  | $ev(\phi \rightarrow \psi; \chi, p) =$ **if ch**$(ev(\chi) \leq ev(\phi))$ **then** $ev(\psi; p)$ **else t**
  | $ev(\phi \rightarrow \psi) = ev(\phi) \rightarrow ev(\psi)$
  | $ev(\phi \wedge \psi; p) = \mathbf{min}(ev(\phi; p), ev(\psi; p))$
  | $ev([\Gamma|x]; p) = ev(\phi; p)$ (where $x : \phi \in \Gamma$)
  | $ev([\Gamma|c]; p) = ev(\phi; p)$ (where $c : \phi \in \mathcal{A}$)
  | $ev([\Gamma|MN]; p) = ev([\Gamma|M]; [\Gamma|N], p)$
  | $ev([\Gamma|\lambda x.M]; \phi, p) = ev([\Gamma, x : \phi|M]; p)$
  | $ev([\Gamma|\lambda x.M]) = \wedge\{\alpha \rightarrow ev([\Gamma, x : \alpha|M]) \mid \alpha \in \mathcal{P}(\tau)\}$ (where τ is the type of x)
  | $ev([\Gamma|\text{if } L \text{ then } M \text{ else } N]; p)$
     $=$ **if** $ev([\Gamma|L]) = \mathbf{f}$ **then f else max**$(ev([\Gamma|M]; p), ev([\Gamma|N]; p))$
  | $ev([\Gamma|\mu^{\xi}x.M]; p)$
     $=$ **let val** $\alpha =$ **foldr** (**fn** $\phi\ \beta \Rightarrow$ **min**$(ev(\phi; p), \beta)$ **t** ξ
        fun loop $\gamma =$ **if ch**$(\alpha \leq \gamma)$ **then** α
                    else let val $\gamma' = ev([\Gamma, x : [\Gamma|\mu^{\xi, p \rightarrow \gamma}x.M] \mid M]; p)$
                    in if ch$(\gamma' \leq \gamma)$ **then min**(α, γ') **else loop** γ'
     in loop f

Fig. 7. Evaluation algorithm **ev**

fun min$(\alpha, \beta) =$ **if ch**$(\alpha \leq \beta)$ **then** α **else if ch**$(\beta \leq \alpha)$ **then** β **else** $\alpha \wedge \beta$
fun max$(\alpha_1 \rightarrow \alpha_2, \beta_1 \rightarrow \beta_2) = \mathbf{min}(\alpha_1, \beta_1) \rightarrow \mathbf{max}(\alpha_2, \beta_2)$
  | max(α, β) **when ch**$(\alpha \leq \beta) = \beta$
  | max(α, β) **when ch**$(\beta \leq \alpha) = \alpha$
  | max$(\alpha_1 \wedge \alpha_2, \beta) = \mathbf{max}(\alpha_1, \beta) \wedge \mathbf{max}(\alpha_2, \beta)$
  | max$(\alpha, \beta_1 \wedge \beta_2) = \mathbf{max}(\alpha, \beta_1) \wedge \mathbf{max}(\alpha, \beta_2)$

Fig. 8. Auxiliary functions used in **ev**

ns-type $[\Gamma|M]$ means the proper least ns-type γ such that $\Gamma \vdash M : \gamma$ is derivable. This proper ns-type is represented as $\overline{[\Gamma|M]}$. In Fig 7, we define algorithm **ev** that computes the proper ns-type $\overline{[\Gamma|M]}$ directly. In fact, the algorithm **ev** is defined in a more general form. It takes a pair of an ns-type ϕ and a sequence of ns-types $\phi_1, \ldots, \phi_n$, and it yields the least proper ns-type γ such that $\overline{\phi} \leq \overline{\phi_1} \rightarrow \ldots \rightarrow \overline{\phi_n} \rightarrow \gamma$ is derivable. In Fig. 7, p stands for a sequence of ns-types, and $p \rightarrow \gamma$ represents the ns-type $\phi_1 \rightarrow \cdots \rightarrow \phi_n \rightarrow \gamma$ for $p \equiv \phi_1, \ldots, \phi_n$. If p is empty, then $p \rightarrow \gamma$ is γ.

In the definition of **ev** we use the algorithm **ch** defined in the last section. Note that **ch** is used only to check inequalities on proper ns-types. We also use two auxiliary functions **min** and **max** defined in Fig. 8. The functions **min** and **max** take two proper ns-types and compute the greatest lower bound and the least upper bound, respectively. The greatest lower bound of α and β is equivalent to $\alpha \wedge \beta$. In the definition of **min**, however, a simpler form is returned in case $\alpha \leq \beta$ or $\beta \leq \alpha$.

Lemma 9. *Suppose* $ev(\phi; \phi_1, \ldots, \phi_n)$ *terminates with* α. *Then,* $\overline{\phi} \leq \overline{\phi_1} \rightarrow \cdots \rightarrow \overline{\phi_n} \rightarrow \beta$ *is derivable if and only if* $\alpha \leq \beta$ *is derivable.*

Theorem 3. *Let* $\Gamma \vdash M : \alpha_1 \to \cdots \to \alpha_n \to \beta$ *be a judgment in which no lazy ns-type occurs. Then,* $\mathbf{ev}([\Gamma|M]; \alpha_1, \ldots, \alpha_n)$ *terminates. Moreover,* $\Gamma \vdash M : \alpha_1 \to \cdots \to \alpha_n \to \beta$ *is derivable in* **NT** *if and only if* $\mathbf{ev}([\Gamma|M]; \alpha_1, \ldots, \alpha_n) \leq \beta$.

7   Extension and Experimental Results

The algorithms **ch** and **ev** deal with the most basic strictness analysis, but they are easily extended. For example, we can extend them to treat the 4-point domains introduced in [16]. This extension is also presented in [5]. We have implemented the extended algorithms in OCaml. We report experimental results concerning the comparison with these two algorithms and the algorithm with chaotic iteration mentioned in Section 1.

We first present the extension by the 4-point domains. The 4-point domains are introduced to express abstract properties concerning finite and infinite lists. We introduce a new type constructor list. Namely, if τ is a type, then τ list is also a type. We add new kinds of ns-types ∞ and $\alpha_\in$ defined by the following rules:

$$\infty^\tau \in \mathcal{L}(\tau \text{ list}) \qquad \frac{\alpha \in \mathcal{L}(\tau)}{\alpha_\in \in \mathcal{L}(\tau \text{ list})}$$

For the newly added ns-types we add the following axioms and rules to **NS**:

$$\infty \leq \alpha_\in \qquad \mathbf{t} \leq \mathbf{t}_\in \qquad \frac{\alpha \leq \beta}{\alpha_\in \leq \beta_\in} \qquad \alpha_\in \wedge \beta_\in \leq (\alpha \wedge \beta)_\in$$

Informally ∞^τ stands for the set of the following lists whose elements are of type τ: finite lists ended with undefined value, and infinite lists. The ns-type $\alpha_\in$ of type τ list stands for the set of the following lists: the lists in ∞^τ, and finite lists, at least one element of which is contained in α. For example, $\mathcal{L}(\text{num list list})$ consists of the following six ns-types (and their equivalent ns-types): $\mathbf{f} \leq \infty \leq \mathbf{f}_\in \leq \infty_\in \leq (\mathbf{f}_\in)_\in \leq \mathbf{t}$.

For terms we newly add $\mathsf{cons}(M, N)$ and $\mathsf{case}(L, M, N)$. The term $\mathsf{cons}(M, N)$ stands for the list obtained by adding M to the head of the list N. The term $\mathsf{case}(L, M, N)$ stands for the following term:

if $N = \mathsf{nil}$ then L else M (head N) (tail N)

See [16] for the role of case. The rules for cons and case are defined in Fig. 9. The algorithms **ch** and **ev** are extended by adding the rules defined in Figs. 10 and 11, respectively.

Our algorithms are closely related to chaotic iteration introduced in [2]. It is a method of calculating an approximation of a fixed point of a function defined on a finite domain. A term can be interpreted in the partially ordered sets of ns-types [7,8]. A term $\mu f.\lambda x.M$ of type $\sigma \to \tau$ can be interpreted as the fixed point F of the function corresponding to $\lambda x.M$. Consider the term $(\mu f.\lambda x.M)N$. If we want to have the value of this term, we do not necessarily need to compute the

$$\frac{\Gamma \vdash N : \infty}{\Gamma \vdash \mathsf{cons}(M, N) : \infty} \qquad \frac{\Gamma \vdash M : \beta}{\Gamma \vdash \mathsf{cons}(M, N) : \beta_\in} \qquad \frac{\Gamma \vdash N : \beta_\in}{\Gamma \vdash \mathsf{cons}(M, N) : \beta_\in}$$

$$\frac{\Gamma \vdash N : \mathbf{f}}{\Gamma \vdash \mathsf{case}(L, M, N) : \mathbf{f}} \qquad \frac{\Gamma \vdash M : \mathbf{t} \to \infty \to \beta \quad \Gamma \vdash N : \infty}{\Gamma \vdash \mathsf{case}(L, M, N) : \beta}$$

$$\frac{\Gamma \vdash M : (\mathbf{t} \to \alpha_\in \to \beta) \wedge (\alpha \to \mathbf{t} \to \beta) \quad \Gamma \vdash N : \alpha_\in}{\Gamma \vdash \mathsf{case}(L, M, N) : \beta}$$

$$\frac{\Gamma \vdash L : \beta \quad \Gamma \vdash M : \mathbf{t} \to \mathbf{t} \to \beta}{\Gamma \vdash \mathsf{case}(L, M, N) : \beta}$$

Fig. 9. Rules for cons and case in **NT**

| $\mathbf{ch}([\Gamma|\mathsf{cons}(M, N)] \leq \infty) = \mathbf{ch}([\Gamma|N] \leq \infty)$
| $\mathbf{ch}([\Gamma|\mathsf{cons}(M, N)] \leq \phi_\in) = \mathbf{ch}([\Gamma|M] \leq \phi)$ **or** $\mathbf{ch}([\Gamma|N] \leq \phi_\in)$
| $\mathbf{ch}([\Gamma|\mathsf{cons}(M, N)] \leq \mathbf{f}) = \mathbf{false}$
| $\mathbf{ch}([\Gamma|\mathsf{case}(L, M, N)] \leq \psi) = \mathbf{ch}([\Gamma|N] \leq \mathbf{f})$
     or $(\mathbf{ch}([\Gamma|M] \leq \mathbf{t} \to \infty \to \psi)$ **and** $\mathbf{ch}([\Gamma|N] \leq \infty))$
     or $(\exists \alpha \in \mathcal{N}(\tau).\mathbf{ch}([\Gamma|M] \leq \mathbf{t} \to \alpha_\in \to \psi)$
                   and $\mathbf{ch}([\Gamma|M] \leq \alpha \to \mathbf{t} \to \psi)$ **and** $\mathbf{ch}([\Gamma|N] \leq \alpha_\in))$
     or $(\mathbf{ch}([\Gamma|L] \leq \psi)$ **and** $\mathbf{ch}([\Gamma|M] \leq \mathbf{t} \to \mathbf{t} \to \psi))$

(the type of N is τ list)

Fig. 10. Extension of **ch**

| $\mathbf{ev}([\Gamma|\mathsf{cons}(M, N)]) = \mathbf{case}\ \mathbf{ev}([\Gamma|N])\ \mathbf{of}$
       | $\mathbf{f}\ \to \infty$
       | $\infty \to \infty$
       | $\alpha_\in \to \mathbf{let\ val}\ \beta = \min(\alpha, \mathbf{ev}([\Gamma|M]))\ \mathbf{in}\ \beta_\in$
       | $\mathbf{t}\ \to \mathbf{let\ val}\ \beta = \mathbf{ev}([\Gamma|M])\ \mathbf{in\ if}\ \mathbf{ch}(\mathbf{t} \leq \beta)\ \mathbf{then}\ \mathbf{t}\ \mathbf{else}\ \beta_\in$
| $\mathbf{ev}([\Gamma|\mathsf{case}(L, M, N); p]) = \mathbf{case}\ \mathbf{ev}([\Gamma|N])\ \mathbf{of}$
       | $\mathbf{f}\ \to \mathbf{f}$
       | $\infty \to \mathbf{ev}([\Gamma|M]; \mathbf{t}, \infty, p)$
       | $\alpha_\in \to \max(\mathbf{ev}([\Gamma|M]; \mathbf{t}, \alpha_\in, p), \mathbf{ev}([\Gamma|M]; \alpha, \mathbf{t}, p))$
       | $\mathbf{t}\ \to \max(\mathbf{ev}([\Gamma|L]; p), \mathbf{ev}([\Gamma|M]; \mathbf{t}, \mathbf{t}, p))$

Fig. 11. Extension of **ev**

value $F(b)$ for all arguments b of type σ. In the chaotic iteration, we compute a partial function P approximating F such that P is defined on a set V and $P(b) = F(b)$ for $b \in V$. Moreover, the value of N is contained in V, and the value $P(c)$ for $c \notin V$ is not used in computing the value $P(d)$ for $d \in V$.

We can insert a chaotic iteration algorithm into **ev** by replacing the processing of $\mu x.M$ by the algorithm based on chaotic iteration. The resulting algorithm is named **ci** and shown in Fig. 12. The chaotic iteration algorithm is taken from [13].

```
fun  ci(t; p) = t
  | ...
  | ci([Γ|μx.M]; p) =
    let val P = (ref ∅) val V = (ref ∅) val S = (ref ∅) val T = (ref ∅) in
    begin
      P := ∅;
      repeat
        S := {p};  V := ∅;
        for q ∈ S do
          let val α = ci([Γ, x : ((!P), T) | M]; q) in
          begin
            V := (!V) ∪ {q};
            S := {r ∈ (!S) ∪ (!T) | cieq(r ≅ s) = false for every s ∈ (!V)};
            if (!P) contains r → β such that cieq(q ≅ r) = true then
                remove r → β from (!P);
            P := (!P) ∪ {q → α};
          end
      until (!P) and (!V) are stable;
      Take r → β in (!P) such that cieq(p ≅ r) = true and return β;
    end
  | ci((ξ, T); p)
    = (T := (!T) ∪ {p};
       if ξ contains r → β such that cieq(r ≅ p) = true then β else f)
and  cieq(p ≅ q)
    = (m = n) and
      ∀i (1 ≤ i ≤ n). let val α = ci(φ_i) val β = ci(ψ_i)
                       in ch(α ≤ β) and ch(β ≤ α)
                                    (where p ≡ φ_1, ..., φ_m and q ≡ ψ_1, ..., ψ_n)
```

Fig. 12. Algorithm **ci** with chaotic iteration

We have implemented the algorithms **ch**, **ev** and **ci** in OCaml. We report experimental results on the comparison of these three algorithms. For a test-bet we use the terms defined in Fig. 13. They are list manipulation functions defined in continuation passing style. The terms $test1, \ldots, test4$ are the same as used in [5]. In Fig 13, *Cfoldr*, *Cappend* and *Ccat* occurs several times. They can have different types. Rigorously, these functions with different types should be defined separately in our formulation, but we use the present definition for the sake of brevity. In Table 1, we present the execution time of **ch**, **ev** and **ci**. The execution time of **ch** for each term, say $test1$, is the total sum of the execution time of **ch**($test1 \leq \alpha$) for all $\alpha \in \mathcal{N}(\tau)$, where $\tau \equiv$ (num list list) $\rightarrow$ num is the type of $test1$.

In the implementation, we can adopt a number of optimizations. Of them, 'memoization' is the most effective method in our algorithms. In the memoization, when the computation **ev**($[\Gamma|N]$; p) is completed, the result is registered with the argument p. The registered data is used when **ev**($[\Gamma|N]$; p) is called for the same p. The effectiveness of the memoization is shown in Table 1.

$$Cfoldr \equiv \mu f.\lambda g.\lambda l.\lambda b.\lambda c.\mathsf{case}(c\ b, (\lambda x.\lambda x'.f\ g\ x'\ b\ (\lambda y.g\ x\ y\ c)), l)$$

$$Cappend \equiv \mu a.\lambda l.\lambda l'.\lambda c.\mathsf{case}(c\ l', (\lambda x.\lambda x'.a\ x'\ l'\ (\lambda y.c\ (\mathsf{cons}\ (x, y)))), l)$$

$$Ccat \equiv \lambda l.\lambda c.(Cfoldr\ Cappend\ l\ \mathsf{nil}\ c)$$

$$K \equiv \lambda x.\lambda y.x$$

$$isnil \equiv \lambda l.\mathsf{case}(\mathsf{true}, \lambda x.\lambda x'.\mathsf{false}, l)$$

$$length \equiv \mu f.\lambda l.\mathsf{case}(0, \lambda x.\lambda x'.1 + (f\ x'), l)$$

$$sum \equiv \mu s.\lambda l.\mathsf{case}(0, \lambda x.\lambda x'.x + (s\ x'), l)$$

$$test1 \equiv \lambda l.Ccat\ l\ (K\ 0) \qquad test1' \equiv \lambda l.Ccat\ l\ test1$$

$$test2 \equiv \lambda l.Ccat\ l\ isnil \qquad test2' \equiv \lambda l.Ccat\ l\ test2$$

$$test3 \equiv \lambda l.Ccat\ l\ length \qquad test3' \equiv \lambda l.Ccat\ l\ test3$$

$$test4 \equiv \lambda l.Ccat\ l\ sum \qquad test4' \equiv \lambda l.Ccat\ l\ test4$$

Fig. 13. Sample programs

Table 1. Execution time of the algorithms

	ch		ev		ci		Result
	A	B	A	B	A	B	
$test1$	0.001	0.001	0.000	0.000	0.001	0.020	$\infty_\in \to \mathbf{f}$
$test2$	0.003	0.019	0.001	0.001	0.002	0.165	$\infty_\in \to \mathbf{f}$
$test3$	0.002	0.010	0.000	0.001	0.001	0.085	$\infty_\in \to \mathbf{f}$
$test4$	0.003	0.006	0.000	0.002	0.002	0.084	$(\mathbf{f}_\in)_\in \to \mathbf{f}$
$test1'$	2.536	> 60	0.002	0.205	0.011	> 60	$(\infty_\in)_\in \to \mathbf{f}$
$test2'$	10.475	> 60	0.004	1.028	0.019	> 60	$(\infty_\in)_\in \to \mathbf{f}$
$test3'$	3.961	> 60	0.003	0.622	0.010	> 60	$(\infty_\in)_\in \to \mathbf{f}$
$test4'$	9.746	> 60	0.004	2.131	0.010	> 60	$((\mathbf{f}_\in)_\in)_\in \to \mathbf{f}$

A: with memoization, B : without memoization, Unit: second
CPU: Pentium 4 (3.20 GHz)

Our experimental result shows that **ev** is much faster than **ch**. The reason is twofold. The one is the difference of the ways to process case. The algorithm **ch** contains $\exists \alpha \in \mathcal{N}(\tau).\cdots$, whose execution time depends on the size of $\mathcal{N}(\tau)$. On the other hand, the algorithm **ev** performs in a more direct way. The second reason is in the methods of processing μ-terms. In **ch**, the computation of the rule for $\mathbf{ch}(\cdots \leq \cdots \to [\Delta|N])$ is essentially inefficient since the execution time depends on the size of $\mathcal{N}(\tau)$, where τ is the type of N. This rule is indispensable for processing μ-terms. Consider the computation of $\mathbf{ch}([\Gamma|\mu^{\phi \to \alpha} x.M] \leq \psi \to \beta)$, where $\phi \equiv [\Delta|N]$. In the computation, we must compute $\mathbf{ch}(\psi \leq \phi)$ and thus $\mathbf{ch}(\phi \leq \alpha)$ for all $\alpha \in \mathcal{N}(\tau)$. In **ev**, for computing $\mathbf{ev}([\Gamma|\mu^{\phi \to \alpha} x.M]; \psi)$, the algorithm evaluates $\mathbf{ch}(\mathbf{ev}(\psi) \leq \mathbf{ev}(\phi))$. For the computation of $\mathbf{ev}(\phi)$, we need to compute $\mathbf{ev}([\Delta, y : \beta|L])$ for all $\beta \in \mathcal{P}(\rho)$, if N is $\lambda y.L$ of type $\rho \to \sigma \equiv \tau$. The execution time depends on the size of $\mathcal{P}(\rho)$. However, the size of $\mathcal{P}(\rho)$ is smaller than that of $\mathcal{N}(\tau) = \{\gamma_1 \to \gamma_2 \mid \gamma_1 \in \mathcal{P}(\rho),\ \gamma_2 \in \mathcal{N}(\sigma)\}$, if the size of $\mathcal{N}(\sigma)$ is greater than 1.

The algorithm **ev** is also faster than **ci**. This difference of the performance may be related to computation of $\mathbf{ev}(\phi)$ and $\mathbf{ci}(\phi)$ for a lazy ns-type ϕ of a function type $\tau \equiv \rho \to \sigma$ such that $\phi \equiv [\Delta | \lambda y.L]$, and the size of $\mathcal{P}(\rho)$ is relatively large. In **ev**, this computation occurs in processing μ-terms as shown above. In **ci**, the computation of $\mathbf{ci}(\phi)$ occurs in three places. For $\mathbf{ci}([\Gamma | \mu x.M]; p)$, some ξ is created and $\mathbf{ci}([\Gamma, x : (\xi, T) | M]; p)$ is executed. If $\xi \equiv \phi \to \alpha$ and $p \equiv \psi$, then $\mathbf{ci}(\phi)$ is executed in the computation of $\mathbf{cieq}(\phi \cong \psi)$. In addition, the execution of $\mathbf{ci}(\phi)$ occurs in updating the variables S and P for processing μ-terms. The parts for updating S and P do not occur in **ev**. This is one of the reason why **ev** is faster than **ci**. In case higher-order function is not used, **ev** and **ci** may have similar performance.

8   Conclusion

We have proposed strictness analysis algorithms **ch** and **ev** based on the formal system **LT** for inequalities on ns-types with lazy ns-types. These two algorithms are almost automatically extracted from the system. The key point is that the system is defined without transitive law. The algorithms are defined with pattern matching. This is convenient to implementation in a functional programming language. We have implemented the algorithms in OCaml. We reported experimental results on comparison of the algorithms **ch** and **ev** together with **ci** obtained from **ev** by replacing the algorithm for μ-term by chaotic iteration. Our experimental results show that **ev** is faster than the others.

In our algorithms, conjunction of ns-types is essential. Our method is flexible enough to be applied to various type systems with conjunction in addition to the nonstandard type system for strictness analysis. In particular, it is easy to define an inequality system for intersection type assignment system, and we can extract a (partial) decision procedure for the system. The detailed investigation for application of our method to other type systems is left to the future work.

References

1. Barbanera, F., Dezani-Ciancaglini, M., de'Liguoro, U.: Intersection and union types: Syntax and semantics. Inform. Comp. 119(2), 202–230 (1995)
2. Cousot, P., Cousot, R.: Static determination of dynamic properties of programs. In: Proceedings of the Second International Symposium on Programming, pp. 106–130 (1976)
3. Damiani, F.: Non-standard type inference for functional programs. PhD thesis, Università di Torino (1998)
4. Gentzen, G.: Untersuchungen über das logische Schließen, I, II. Math. Zeitschr. 39, 176–210, 405–431 (1934)
5. Hankin, C., Métayer, D.L.: Lazy type inference and program analysis. Science of Computer Programming 25(2–3), 219–249 (1995)
6. Hannan, J., Miller, D.: From operational semantics for abstract machines. Mathematical Structures in Computer Science 2(4), 415–459 (1992)

7. Jensen, T.P.: Strictness analysis in logical form. In: Hughes, J. (ed.) FPCA 1991. LNCS, vol. 523, pp. 352–366. Springer, Heidelberg (1991)
8. Jensen, T.P.: Abstract Interpretation in Logical Form. PhD thesis, the Imerial College (1992)
9. Jensen, T.P.: Inference of polymorphic and conditional strictness properties. In: POPL 1998: 25th ACM SIGPLAN-SIGACT Symposium on Principles of Programming Languages, pp. 209–221 (1998)
10. Kfoury, A.J., Wells, J.B.: Principality and decidable type inference for finite-rank intersection types. In: POPL 1999: 26th ACM SIGPLAN-SIGACT Symposium on Principles of Programming Languages, pp. 161–174 (1999)
11. Kuo, T.M., Mishra, P.: Strictness analysis: a new perspective based on type inference. In: FPCA 1989: the Fourth International Conference on Functional Programming Languages and Computer Architecture, pp. 260–272 (1989)
12. Nielson, F., Nielson, H., Hankin, C.: Principles of Program Analysis. Springer, Heidelberg (1999)
13. Rosendahl, M.: Higher-order chaotic iteration sequences. In: Penjam, J., Bruynooghe, M. (eds.) PLILP 1993. LNCS, vol. 714, pp. 332–345. Springer, Heidelberg (1993)
14. Seldin, J.P.: A gentzen-style sequent calculus of constructions with expansion rules. Theor. Comput. Sci. 243(1-2), 199–215 (2000)
15. Tiuryn, J.: A sequent calculus for subtyping polymorphism. Inform. Comp. 164(2), 345–369 (2001)
16. Wadler, P.: Strictness analysis on non-flat domains (by abstract interpretation). In: Abramsky, S., Hankin, C. (eds.) Abstract Interpretation of Declarative Languages, pp. 266–275. Ellis-Horwood (1987)
17. Wang, H.: Proving theorems by pattern recognition I. Commun. ACM 3(4), 220–234 (1960)
18. Yokouchi, H.: Completeness of type assignment systems with intersection, union, and type quantifiers. Theor. Comput. Sci. 272(1-2), 341–398 (2002)

Quantitative Logic Programming Revisited[*]

Mario Rodríguez-Artalejo and Carlos A. Romero-Díaz

Departamento de Sistemas Informáticos y Computación
Universidad Complutense de Madrid, Spain
mario@sip.ucm.es, cromdia@fdi.ucm.es

Abstract. Uncertainty in Logic Programming has been investigated since about 25 years, publishing papers dealing with various approaches to semantics and different applications. This paper is intended as a first step towards the investigation of uncertainty in Constraint Functional Logic Programming. We revise an early proposal, namely van Emden's *Quantitative Logic Programming* [22], and we improve it in two ways. Firstly, we generalize van Emden's QLP to a generic scheme $QLP(\mathcal{D})$ parameterized by any given *Qualification Domain* $\mathcal{D}$, which must be a lattice satisfying certain natural axioms. We present several interesting instances for $\mathcal{D}$, one of which corresponds to van Emden's QLP. Secondly, we generalize van Emden's results by providing stronger ones, concerning both semantics and goal solving. We present *Qualified SLD Resolution* over $\mathcal{D}$, a sound and strongly complete goal solving procedure for $QLP(\mathcal{D})$, which is applicable to open goals and can be efficiently implemented using CLP technology over any constraint domain $\mathcal{C}_{\mathcal{D}}$ able to deal with qualification constraints over $\mathcal{D}$. We have developed a prototype implementation for van Emden's QLP as an instance of $QLP(\mathcal{D})$, on top of the $CFLP$ system $\mathcal{TOY}$.

Keywords: Quantitative Logic Programming, Qualification Domains, Qualification Constraints.

1 Introduction

The investigation of uncertainty in logic programming has proceeded along various lines during the last 25 years. A recent recollection by V. S. Subrahmanian [21] highlights some phases in the evolution of the topic from the viewpoint of a committed researcher.

Research on the field has dealt with various approaches to semantics, as well as different applications. One of the earliest approaches was *Quantitative Logic Programming*, QLP for short. This can be traced back to a paper by Shapiro [17], who proposed to use real numbers in the interval $(0, 1]$ as *certainty factors*, as well as *certainty functions* for propagating certainty factors from the bodies to the heads of program clauses. Subsequently, van Emden [22] considered QLP with an *attenuation factor* $f \in (0, 1]$ attached to the implication of each program

---

[*] Research partially supported by projects MERIT-FORMS (TIN2005-09027-C03-03) and PROMESAS-CAM(S-0505/TIC/0407).

J. Garrigue and M. Hermenegildo (Eds.): FLOPS 2008, LNCS 4989, pp. 272–288, 2008.

clause and restricted his attention to the certainty function which propagates to a clause head the certainty factor $f \times b$, where f is the clause's attenuation factor and b is the minimum of the certainty factors known for the body atoms. Van Emden's approach was less general than Shapiro's because of the fixed choice of a particular certainty function, but it allowed to prove more general results on model theoretic and fixpoint semantics, similar to those previously obtained in [23,1] for classical Logic Programming. Moreover, [22] gave a procedure for computing the certainty of atoms in the least Herbrand model of a given program, by applying an alpha-beta heuristic to the atoms' and/or search trees. This procedure worked only for ground atoms having a finite search tree.

Following these beginnings, logic programming with uncertainty developed in various directions. Subrahmanian [19] proposed an alternative to [22], using a different lattice of numeric values (better suited to express the certainty degree of truth an falsity) as well as clauses whose atoms were annotated with values from this lattice. Neither certainty functions nor attenuation factors were used in this approach, which was extended in [20] to provide goal solving procedures enjoying stronger soundness and completeness results. As a brief summary of some significant later contributions let us mention: generalized *annotated logic programs* [10], a quite general framework which will be discussed in more detail in Section 6; semantics based on *bilattices* of generalized truth values with both a 'knowledge' order and a 'truth' order [8]; logic programming with probabilistic semantics and applications to deductive databases [13,14]; quantitative and probabilistic constraint logic programming and applications to natural language processing [15]; *hybrid probabilistic programs* [5]; probabilistic agent programs [7] and their extension to deal with both time and uncertainty [6]; logic programs with similarity based unification and applications to flexible data retrieval [2,11]; and functional logic programming with similarity based unification [12].

We are interested in working out an expressive framework for *Constraint Functional Logic Programming* (briefly *CFLP*) with uncertainty, since functions and constraints seem to have received up to now comparatively few attention in this field. As a first step, we present in this paper a generalization of the early *QLP* proposal by van Emden [22], which is still appealing because of its neat semantics. Syntactically, our proposal is very close to van Emden's *QLP*: we use qualified definite Horn clauses $A \leftarrow d - \overline{B}$ with an attenuation value d attached to the implication and no annotations attached to the atoms. However, we improve [22] in the two ways summarized in the abstract: firstly, we replace numeric certainty values (in particular, those playing the role of attenuation factors in program clauses) by qualification values belonging to a parametrically given *Qualification Domain* $\mathcal{D}$ with a lattice structure, which provides abstract operations generalizing the use of *min* (minimum) and $\times$ (product) in [22]. In this way we get a *generic scheme QLP($\mathcal{D}$)*. Secondly, we present stronger semantic results and a sound and strongly complete goal solving procedure called *Qualified SLD Resolution* over $\mathcal{D}$(in symbols, $SLD(\mathcal{D})$), which extends *SLD* resolution using *annotated atoms* and *qualification constraints* over $\mathcal{D}$. The *QLP($\mathcal{D}$)* scheme enjoys nice semantic properties and has interesting instances that can be efficiently implemented using CLP technology: $QLP(\mathcal{D})$ programs and goals can be easily translated into $CLP(\mathcal{C}_\mathcal{D})$ for any choice of a constraint domain $\mathcal{C}_\mathcal{D}$ able to compute with qualification constraints over $\mathcal{D}$.

After this introduction, the rest of the paper is structured as follows: Section 2 presents the axioms for qualification domains $\mathcal{D}$, showing some basic instances and proving that the class of such domains is closed under cartesian product. Section 3 presents the syntax and declarative semantics of the $QLP(\mathcal{D})$ scheme. Section 4 presents qualified SLD resolution over $\mathcal{D}$ with its soundness and strong completeness properties. Section 5 presents a general implementation technique for $QLP(\mathcal{D})$ and a prototype developed on top of the $CFLP$ system $\mathcal{TOY}$ [3] for the particular instance corresponding to van Emden's QLP. Finally, Section 6 presents our conclusions and plans for future work. Some proofs that have been omitted due to lack of space can be found in [16].

2   Qualification Domains

By definition, a *Qualification Domain* is any structure $\mathcal{D} = \langle D, \sqsubseteq, \bot, \top, \circ \rangle$ such that:

1. $\langle D, \sqsubseteq, \bot, \top \rangle$ is a lattice with extreme points $\bot$ and $\top$ w.r.t. the partial ordering $\sqsubseteq$. For given elements $d, e \in D$, we write $d \sqcap e$ for the *greatest lower bound* (*glb*) of d and e and $d \sqcup e$ for the *least upper bound* (*lub*) of d and e. We also write $d \sqsubset e$ as abbreviation for $d \sqsubseteq e \wedge d \neq e$.
2. $\circ : D \times D \to D$, called *attenuation operation*, verifies the following axioms:
   (a) $\circ$ is associative, commutative and monotonic w.r.t. $\sqsubseteq$.
   (b) $\forall d \in D : d \circ \top = d$.
   (c) $\forall d \in D : d \circ \bot = \bot$.
   (d) $\forall d, e \in D \setminus \{\bot, \top\} : d \circ e \sqsubset e$.
   (e) $\forall d, e_1, e_2 \in D : d \circ (e_1 \sqcap e_2) = d \circ e_1 \sqcap d \circ e_2$.

In the rest of the paper, $\mathcal{D}$ will generally denote an arbitrary qualification domain. For any finite $S = \{e_1, e_2, \ldots, e_n\} \subseteq D$, the *glb* of S (noted as $\bigsqcap S$) exists and can be computed as $e_1 \sqcap e_2 \sqcap \cdots \sqcap e_n$ (which reduces to $\top$ in the case $n = 0$). As an easy consequence of the axioms, one gets the identity $d \circ \bigsqcap S = \bigsqcap \{d \circ e \mid e \in S\}$. We generalize van Emden's QLP to a generic scheme $QLP(\mathcal{D})$ which uses qualification values $d \in D \setminus \{\bot\}$ in place of certainty values $d \in (0, 1]$, the *glb* operator $\bigsqcap$ in place of the minimum operator min, and the attenuation operator $\circ$ in place of the multiplication operator $\times$. Three interesting instances of qualification domains are shown below.

The Domain of Classical Boolean Values: $\mathcal{B} = (\{0, 1\}, \leq, 0, 1, \wedge)$, where 0 and 1 stand for the two classical truth values *false* and *true*, $\leq$ is the usual numerical ordering over $\{0, 1\}$, and $\wedge$ stands for the classical conjunction operation over $\{0, 1\}$. The instance $QLP(\mathcal{B})$ of our $QLP(\mathcal{D})$ scheme behaves as classical Logic Programming.

The Domain of van Emden's Uncertainty Values: $\mathcal{U} = (U, \leq, 0, 1, \times)$, where $U = [0, 1] = \{d \in \mathbb{R} \mid 0 \leq d \leq 1\}$, $\leq$ is the usual numerical ordering, and

$\times$ is the multiplication operation. In this domain, the top element $\top$ is 1 and the greatest lower bound $\sqcap S$ of a finite $S \subseteq U$ is the minimum value $\min(S)$, which is 1 if $S = \emptyset$. For this reason, the instance $QLP(\mathcal{U})$ of our $QLP(\mathcal{D})$ scheme behaves as van Emden's QLP.

The Domain of Weight Values: $\mathcal{W} = (P, \geq, \infty, 0, +)$, where $P = [0, \infty] = \{d \in \mathbb{R} \cup \{\infty\} \mid d \geq 0\}$, $\geq$ is the reverse of the usual numerical ordering (with $\infty \geq d$ for any $d \in P$), and $+$ is the addition operation (with $\infty + d = d + \infty = \infty$ for any $d \in P$). In this domain, the top element $\top$ is 0 and the greatest lower bound $\sqcap S$ of a finite $S \subseteq P$ is the maximum value $\max(S)$, which is 0 if $S = \emptyset$. When working in the instance $QLP(\mathcal{W})$ of our $QLP(\mathcal{D})$ scheme one propagates to a clause head the qualification value $f + b$, where f is the clause's 'attenuation factor' and b is the maximum of the qualification values known for the body atoms. Therefore, qualification values in the instance $QLP(\mathcal{W})$ of our $QLP(\mathcal{D})$ scheme behave as a weighted measure of the depth of proof trees.

It is easily checked that the axioms of qualification domains are satisfied by $\mathcal{B}, \mathcal{U}$ and $\mathcal{W}$. In fact, the axioms have been chosen as a natural generalization of some basic properties satisfied by the ordering $\leq$ and the operation $\times$ in $\mathcal{U}$. In general, the values belonging to a qualification domain are intended to qualify logical assertions in some sense, either as a degree of certainty as in the case of $\mathcal{U}$, or as a measure of complexity as in the case of $\mathcal{W}$, or whatever.

Given two qualification domains $\mathcal{D}_i = \langle D_i, \sqsubseteq_i, \bot_i, \top_i, \circ_i \rangle$ ($i \in \{1, 2\}$), their *cartesian product* $\mathcal{D}_1 \times \mathcal{D}_2$ is defined as $\mathcal{D} =_{\text{def}} \langle D, \sqsubseteq, \bot, \top, \circ \rangle$, where $D =_{\text{def}} D_1 \times D_2$, the partial ordering $\sqsubseteq$ is defined as $(d_1, d_2) \sqsubseteq (e_1, e_2) \Longleftrightarrow_{\text{def}} d_1 \sqsubseteq_1 e_1$ and $d_2 \sqsubseteq_2 e_2$, $\bot =_{\text{def}} (\bot_1, \bot_2)$, $\top =_{\text{def}} (\top_1, \top_2)$, and the attenuation operator $\circ$ is defined as $(d_1, d_2) \circ (e_1, e_2) =_{\text{def}} (d_1 \circ_1 e_1, d_2 \circ_2 e_2)$. The class of the qualification domains is closed under cartesian products, as stated in the following result.

Proposition 1. *The cartesian product $\mathcal{D} = \mathcal{D}_1 \times \mathcal{D}_2$ of two given qualification domains is always another qualification domain.*

Proof. According to the axiomatic definition of qualification domains, one must prove two items:

1. $\mathcal{D}$ is a lattice with extreme points $\bot$ and $\top$ w.r.t. the partial ordering $\sqsubseteq$. This is easily checked using the definition of $\sqsubseteq$ in the product domain. In particular, one gets the equalities $(d_1, d_2) \sqcap (e_1, e_2) = (d_1 \sqcap_1 e_1, d_2 \sqcap_2 e_2)$ and $(d_1, d_2) \sqcup (e_1, e_2) = (d_1 \sqcup_1 e_1, d_2 \sqcup_2 e_2)$.
2. $\circ$ satisfies the five axioms required for attenuation operators, i.e.:
   (a) $\circ$ is associative, commutative and monotonic w.r.t. $\sqsubseteq$.
   (b) $\forall (d_1, d_2) \in D_1 \times D_2 : (d_1, d_2) \circ \top = (d_1, d_2)$.
   (c) $\forall (d_1, d_2) \in D_1 \times D_2 : (d_1, d_2) \circ \bot = \bot$.
   (d) $\forall (d_1, d_2), (e_1, e_2) \in D_1 \times D_2 \setminus \{\bot, \top\} : (d_1, d_2) \circ (e_1, e_2) \sqsubset (e_1, e_2)$.
   (e) $\forall (d_1, d_2), (e_1, e_2), (e_1', e_2') \in D_1 \times D_2 : (d_1, d_2) \circ ((e_1, e_2) \sqcap (e_1', e_2')) = ((d_1, d_2) \circ (e_1, e_2)) \sqcap ((d_1, d_2) \circ (e_1', e_2'))$.

   All these conditions are easily proved, using the hypothesis that both $\mathcal{D}_1$ and $\mathcal{D}_2$ are qualification domains as well as the construction of $\mathcal{D}$ as cartesian product of $\mathcal{D}_1$ and $\mathcal{D}_2$. $\square$

Intuitively, each value (d_1, d_2) belonging to a product domain $\mathcal{D}_1 \times \mathcal{D}_2$ imposes the qualification d_1 *and also* the qualification d_2. In particular, values (c, d) belonging to the product domain $\mathcal{U} \times \mathcal{W}$ impose two qualifications, namely: a certainty value greater or equal than c and a proof tree with depth less or equal than d. This intuition indeed corresponds to the declarative and operational semantics formally defined in Sections 3 and 4.

3   Syntax and Semantics of QLP($\mathcal{D}$)

3.1   Programs, Interpretations and Models

We assume a *signature* Σ providing free function symbols (a.k.a. constructors) and predicate symbols. *Terms* are built from constructors and variables from a countably infinite set $\mathcal{V}ar$, disjoint from Σ. *Atoms* are of the form $p(t_1, \ldots, t_n)$ (abbreviated as $p(\overline{t_n})$) where p is a n-ary predicate symbol and t_i are terms. We write At_Σ for the set of all the atoms, called the *open Herbrand base*. A $QLP(\mathcal{D})$ program $\mathcal{P}$ is a set of *qualified definite Horn clauses* of the form $A \leftarrow d - \overline{B}$ where A is an atom, $\overline{B}$ a finite conjunction of atoms and $d \in D \setminus \{\bot\}$ is the *attenuation value* attached to the clause's implication. In $QLP(\mathcal{B})$ programs, the only choice for d is 1, standing for *true*, and therefore $QLP(\mathcal{B})$ behaves as classical LP. The following example presents two simple programs over the domains $\mathcal{U}$ and $\mathcal{W}$. It is not meant as a realistic application, but just as an illustration.

Example 1

1. The $QLP(\mathcal{U})$ program $\mathcal{P}_\mathcal{U}$ displayed below can be understood as a *knowledge base* given by the facts for the predicates animal, plant, human and eats, along with *knowledge inference rules* corresponding to the clauses with non-empty body. The clauses for the predicate human specify the human beings as the ancestors of adam and eve, with the certainty of being an actual human decreasing as one moves back along the ancestors' chain. Therefore, the certainty of being a cruel human also decreases when moving from descendants to ancestors.

```
cruel(X) <-0.90- human(X), eats(X,Y), animal(Y)
cruel(X) <-0.40- human(X), eats(X,Y), plant(Y)

animal(bird) <-1.0-        human(adam) <-1.0-
animal(cat) <-1.0-         human(eve) <-1.0-
plant(oak) <-1.0-          human(father(X)) <-0.90- human(X)
plant(apple) <-1.0-        human(mother(X)) <-0.90- human(X)

eats(adam, X) <-0.80-
eats(eve,X) <-0.30- animal(X)
eats(eve,X) <-0.60- plant(X)
eats(father(X),Y) <-0.80- eats(X,Y)
eats(mother(X),Y) <-0.70- eats(X,Y)
```

2. The $QLP(\mathcal{W})$ program $\mathcal{P}_\mathcal{W}$ is very similar to $\mathcal{P}_\mathcal{U}$, except that the attenuation value 1 is attached to all the clauses. Therefore, each clause is intended to convey the information that the depth of a proof tree for the head is 1 plus the maximum depth of proof trees for the atoms in the body. As we will see, qualification constraints over $\mathcal{W}$ can be used to impose upper bounds to the depths of proof trees when solving goals w.r.t. $\mathcal{P}_\mathcal{W}$.

Note that the two programs in this example are different qualified versions of the classical LP program $\mathcal{P}$ obtained by dropping all the annotations. Due to the left recursion in the clauses for the predicates human and eats, some goals for $\mathcal{P}$ have an infinite search space where SLD resolution with a leftmost selection strategy would fail to compute some expected answers. For instance, the answer $\{X \mapsto \texttt{mother(eve)}, Y \mapsto \texttt{apple}\}$ would not be computed for the goal eats(X,Y). However, when solving goals for the qualified programs $\mathcal{P}_\mathcal{U}$ and $\mathcal{P}_\mathcal{W}$ using the resolution method presented in Section 4, qualification constraints can be used for imposing bounds to the search space, so that even the leftmost selection strategy leads to successful computations. □

As shown in the example, clauses contain classic atoms in both their head and their body. But for our semantics, we will be interested in not only proving that we can infer an atom for a given program, but proving that we can infer it for at least a given qualification value. For this reason, we introduce $\mathcal{D}$-*annotated atoms* $A \sharp d$, consisting of an atom A with an attached 'annotation' $d \in D \setminus \{\bot\}$. For use in goals to be solved, we consider also *open annotated atoms* of the form $A \sharp W$, where W is a *qualification variable* intended to take values over $D \setminus \{\bot\}$. We postulate a countably infinite set $\mathcal{W}ar$ of qualification variables, disjoint from $\mathcal{V}ar$ and Σ.

The *annotated Herbrand base* over $\mathcal{D}$ is defined as the set $At_\Sigma(\mathcal{D})$ of all $\mathcal{D}$-annotated atoms. The $\mathcal{D}$-*entailment relation* over $At_\Sigma(\mathcal{D})$ is defined as follows: $A \sharp d \succcurlyeq_\mathcal{D} A' \sharp d'$ iff there is some substitution θ such that $A' = A\theta$ and $d' \sqsubseteq d$. Finally, we define an *open Herbrand interpretation* over $\mathcal{D}$ as any subset $\mathcal{I} \subseteq At_\Sigma(\mathcal{D})$ which is closed under $\mathcal{D}$-entailment. That is, an open Herbrand interpretation $\mathcal{I}$ including a given annotated atom $A \sharp d$ is required to include all the 'instances' $A' \sharp d'$ such that $A \sharp d \succcurlyeq_\mathcal{D} A' \sharp d'$, because we intend to formalize a semantics such that all such instances are true whenever $A \sharp d$ is true.

In the sequel we refer to open Herbrand interpretations just as Herbrand interpretations, and we write $Int_\Sigma(\mathcal{D})$ for the family of all Herbrand interpretations over $\mathcal{D}$. The following proposition is easy to prove from the definition of a Herbrand interpretation and the definitions of the union and intersection of a family of sets.

Proposition 2. *The family $Int_\Sigma(\mathcal{D})$ of all Herbrand interpretations over $\mathcal{D}$ is a complete lattice under the inclusion ordering $\subseteq$, whose extreme points are $Int_\Sigma(\mathcal{D})$ as maximum and $\emptyset$ as minimum. Moreover, given any family of interpretations $I \subseteq Int_\Sigma(\mathcal{D})$, its lub and glb are $\bigsqcup I = \bigcup \{\mathcal{I} \in Int_\Sigma(\mathcal{D}) \mid \mathcal{I} \in I\}$ and $\bigsqcap I = \bigcap \{\mathcal{I} \in Int_\Sigma(\mathcal{D}) \mid \mathcal{I} \in I\}$, respectively.* □

Let C be any clause $A \leftarrow d - B_1, \ldots, B_k$ in the program $\mathcal{P}$, and $\mathcal{I} \in \mathrm{Int}_\Sigma(\mathcal{D})$ any interpretation over $\mathcal{D}$. We say that $\mathcal{I}$ is a *model* of C if and only if for any substitution θ and any qualification values $d_1, \ldots, d_k \in D \setminus \{\bot\}$ such that $B_i\theta \sharp d_i \in \mathcal{I}$ for all $1 \leq i \leq k$, one has $A\theta \sharp (d \circ \sqcap\{d_1, \ldots, d_k\}) \in \mathcal{I}$. And we say that $\mathcal{I}$ is a model of the $QLP(\mathcal{D})$ program $\mathcal{P}$ $(\mathcal{I} \models \mathcal{P})$ if and only if $\mathcal{I}$ is a model of each clause in $\mathcal{P}$.

3.2   Declarative Semantics

As in any logic language, we need some technique to infer formulas (in our case, $\mathcal{D}$-annotated atoms) from a given $QLP(\mathcal{D})$ program $\mathcal{P}$. Following traditional ideas, we consider two alternative ways of formalizing an inference step which goes from the body of a clause to its head: an operator $\mathrm{T}_\mathcal{P}$ and a qualified variant of Horn Logic, noted as $QHL(\mathcal{D})$ and called *Qualified Horn Logic*. The operator $\mathrm{T}_\mathcal{P} : \mathrm{Int}_\Sigma(\mathcal{D}) \to \mathrm{Int}_\Sigma(\mathcal{D})$ is defined as:

$$\mathrm{T}_\mathcal{P}(\mathcal{I}) =_{\text{def}} \{A' \sharp d' \mid (A \leftarrow d - B_1, \ldots, B_k) \in \mathcal{P},$$
$$\theta \text{ subst.}, B_i\theta \sharp d_i \in \mathcal{I} \text{ for all } 1 \leq i \leq k, A' = A\theta,$$
$$d' \in D \setminus \{\bot\}, d' \sqsubseteq d \circ \sqcap\{d_1, \ldots, d_k\}\}$$

Intuitively, we can see that for a given interpretation $\mathcal{I}$, $\mathrm{T}_\mathcal{P}(\mathcal{I})$ is the set of those $\mathcal{D}$-annotated atoms obtained by considering $\mathcal{D}$-annotated bodies of clause instances that are included in $\mathcal{I}$ and propagating an annotation to the head via the clause's qualification value.

The logic $QHL(\mathcal{D})$ is defined as a deductive system consisting just of one inference rule $\mathrm{QMP}(\mathcal{D})$, called *Qualitative Modus Ponens* over $\mathcal{D}$. If there are some $(A \leftarrow d - B_1, \ldots, B_k) \in \mathcal{P}$, some substitution θ such that $A' = A\theta$ and $B'_i = B_i\theta$ for all $1 \leq i \leq k$ and $d' \sqsubseteq d \circ \sqcap\{d_1, \ldots, d_k\}$, the following inference step is allowed:

$$\frac{B'_1 \sharp d_1 \quad \cdots \quad B'_k \sharp d_k}{A' \sharp d'} \quad \mathrm{QMP}(\mathcal{D})$$

We will use the notations $\mathcal{P} \vdash_{\mathrm{QHL}(\mathcal{D})} A \sharp d$ (resp. $\mathcal{P} \vdash^n_{\mathrm{QHL}(\mathcal{D})} A \sharp d$) to indicate that $A \sharp d$ can be inferred from the clauses in program $\mathcal{P}$ in finitely many steps (resp. n steps). Note that $QHL(\mathcal{D})$ proofs can be naturally represented as upwards growing *proof trees* with $\mathcal{D}$-annotated atoms at their nodes, each node corresponding to one inference step having the children nodes as premises.

The following proposition collects the main results concerning the declarative semantics of the $QLP(\mathcal{D})$ scheme. We just sketch some key proof ideas. As in [22], full proofs can be developed in analogy to the classical papers [23,1], except that our Herbrand interpretations are open, as first suggested by Clark in [4]. Our use of the $QHL(\mathcal{D})$ calculus has no direct counterpart in the historical papers, but is obviously related to the classical $\mathrm{T}_\mathcal{P}$ operator.

Proposition 3. *The following assertions hold for any $QLP(\mathcal{D})$ program $\mathcal{P}$:*

1. $\mathcal{I} \models \mathcal{P} \iff \mathrm{T}_\mathcal{P}(\mathcal{I}) \subseteq \mathcal{I}$.
2. $\mathrm{T}_\mathcal{P}$ *is monotonic and continuous.*

3. *The least fixpoint $\mu(\mathrm{T}_{\mathcal{P}})$ is the least Herbrand model of $\mathcal{P}$, noted as $\mathcal{M}_{\mathcal{P}}$.*
4. $\mathcal{M}_{\mathcal{P}} = \bigcup_{n \in \mathbb{N}} \mathrm{T}_{\mathcal{P}} \uparrow^n (\emptyset) = \{A \sharp d \mid \mathcal{P} \vdash_{\mathrm{QHL}(\mathcal{D})} A \sharp d\}.$

Proof (Sketch). Item (1) is easy to prove from the definition of $\mathrm{T}_{\mathcal{P}}$. In item (2), monotonicity ($\mathcal{I} \subseteq \mathcal{J} \implies \mathrm{T}_{\mathcal{P}}(\mathcal{I}) \subseteq \mathrm{T}_{\mathcal{P}}(\mathcal{J})$) follows easily from the definition of $\mathrm{T}_{\mathcal{P}}$ and continuity ($\mathrm{T}_{\mathcal{P}}(\bigcup_{n \in \mathbb{N}} \mathcal{I}_n) = \bigcup_{n \in \mathbb{N}} \mathrm{T}_{\mathcal{P}}(\mathcal{I}_n)$ for any chain $\{\mathcal{I}_n \mid n \in \mathbb{N}\} \subseteq \mathrm{Int}_{\Sigma}(\mathcal{D})$ with $\mathcal{I}_n \subseteq \mathcal{I}_{n+1}$ for all $n \in \mathbb{N}$) follows from monotonicity and properties of chains and sets of interpretations. Item (3) follows from (1), (2), Proposition 2 and some known properties about lattices. Finally, item (4) follows from proving the two implications $\mathcal{P} \vdash^n_{\mathrm{QHL}(\mathcal{D})} A \sharp d \implies \exists m\, (A \sharp d \in \mathrm{T}_{\mathcal{P}} \uparrow^m (\emptyset))$ and $A \sharp d \in \mathrm{T}_{\mathcal{P}} \uparrow^n (\emptyset) \implies \exists m\, (\mathcal{P} \vdash^m_{\mathrm{QHL}(\mathcal{D})} A \sharp d)$ by induction on n. $\square$

The next example presents proofs deriving annotated atoms which belong to the least models of the programs $\mathcal{P}_{\mathcal{U}}$ and $\mathcal{P}_{\mathcal{W}}$ from Example 1.

Example 2

1. The proof tree displayed below shows that the $\mathcal{U}$-annotated atom at its root can be deduced from $\mathcal{P}_{\mathcal{U}}$ in $QHL(\mathcal{U})$. Therefore, the atom belongs to $\mathcal{M}_{\mathcal{P}_{\mathcal{U}}}$.

$$
\cfrac{\cfrac{\rule{2cm}{0.4pt}}{\texttt{human(eve)\#1.0}}}{\texttt{human(mother(eve))\#0.90}} \quad \cfrac{\cfrac{\cfrac{\rule{2cm}{0.4pt}}{\texttt{animal(bird)\#1.0}} \quad \texttt{eats(eve,bird)\#0.30}}{\texttt{eats(mother(eve),bird)\#0.21}} \quad \cfrac{\rule{2cm}{0.4pt}}{\texttt{animal(bird)\#1.0}}}{\texttt{cruel(mother(eve))\#0.15}}
$$

It is easy to see which clause was used in each inference step. Note that the atom at the root could have been proved even with the greater certainty value 0.189. However, since $0.15 \leq 0.189$, the displayed inference it is also correct (albeit less informative).

2. A proof tree quite similar to the previous one, but with different annotations, can be easily built to show that `cruel(mother(eve))#4` can be deduced from $\mathcal{P}_{\mathcal{W}}$ in $QHL(\mathcal{W})$. Therefore, this annotated atom belongs to $\mathcal{M}_{\mathcal{P}_{\mathcal{W}}}$. It conveys the information that `cruel(mother(eve))` has a proof tree of depth 4 w.r.t. to the classical LP program $\mathcal{P}$ obtained by dropping $\mathcal{P}_{\mathcal{W}}$'s annotations. $\square$

4   Goal Solving by SLD($\mathcal{D}$) Resolution

4.1   Goals and Solutions

In classical logic programming a goal is presented as a conjunction of atoms. In our setting, proving atoms with arbitrary qualifications may be unsatisfactory, since qualification values too close to $\bot$ may not ensure sufficient information. For this reason, we present goals as conjunctions of open $\mathcal{D}$-annotated atoms and we indicate the minimum qualification value required each of them. Hence initial goals look like: $A_1 \sharp W_1, \ldots, A_n \sharp W_n \,[\![\, W_1 \sqsupseteq \beta_1, \ldots, W_n \sqsupseteq \beta_n$, where $W_i \in \mathcal{W}ar$ and $\beta_i \in D \setminus \{\bot\}$. Observe that we have annotated all atoms in the goal with qualification variables W_i instead of plain values because we are interested in any solution that satisfies the *qualification constraints* $W_i \sqsupseteq \beta_i$, used to impose lower bounds to the atoms' qualifications.

As explained in the next Subsection, goal resolution proceeds from an initial goal through intermediate goals until reaching a final solved goal. The intermediate goals have a more general form, consisting of a composition of three items: a conjunction of $\mathcal{D}$-annotated atoms $\overline{A}$ waiting to be solved, a substitution σ computed in previous steps, and a set of qualification constraints Δ. We consider two kinds of qualification constraints:

1. $\alpha \circ W \sqsupseteq \beta$, where $W \in \mathcal{W}\!ar$ is qualification variable and $\alpha, \beta \in D \setminus \{\bot\}$ are such that $\alpha \sqsupseteq \beta$. This is called a *threshold constraint* for W.
2. $W = d \circ \bigsqcap\{W_1, \ldots, W_k\}$, where $W, W_1, \ldots, W_k \in \mathcal{W}\!ar$ are qualification variables and $d \in D \setminus \{\bot\}$. This is called a *defining constraint* for W.

In order to understand why these two kinds of constraints are needed, think of an annotated atom $A \sharp W$ within an initial goal which includes also an initial threshold constraint $\top \circ W \sqsupseteq \beta$ (i.e. $W \sqsupseteq \beta$) for W. Applying a resolution step with a program clause whose head unifies with A and whose attenuation value is $d \in D \setminus \{\bot\}$ will lead to a new goal including a defining constraint $W = d \circ \bigsqcap\{W_1, \ldots, W_k\}$ for W and a threshold constraint $d \circ \top \circ W_i \sqsupseteq \beta$ for each $1 \leq i \leq k$, where the new qualification variables W_i correspond to the atoms in the clause's body. This explains the need to introduce defining constraints as well as more general threshold constraints $\alpha \circ W \sqsupseteq \beta$. Intuitively, the values α and β within such constraints play the role of an *upper* and a *lower* bound, respectively. As we will see, our goal solving procedure takes advantage of these bounds for pruning useless parts of the computation search space.

Let us now present some notations needed for a formal definition of goals. Given a conjunction of $\mathcal{D}$-annotated atoms $\overline{A}$ and a set of qualification constraints Δ, we define the following sets of variables:

- $\mathrm{var}(\overline{A}) =_{\mathrm{def}} \bigcup \{\mathrm{var}(A) \mid A \sharp W \in \overline{A}\}$.
- $\mathrm{war}(\overline{A}) =_{\mathrm{def}} \bigcup \{W \mid A \sharp W \in \overline{A}\}$.
- $\mathrm{war}(\Delta)$ as the set of qualification variables that appears in any qualification constraint in Δ.
- $\mathrm{dom}(\Delta)$ as the set of qualification variables that appear in the left hand side of any qualification constraint in Δ.

We also say that Δ is *satisfiable* iff there is some $\omega \in \mathrm{Subst}_\Sigma(\mathcal{D})$ –the set of all the substitutions of values in $D\setminus\{\bot\}$ for variables in $\mathcal{W}\!ar$– such that $\omega \in Sol(\Delta)$, what means that ω satisfies every qualification constraint in Δ, i.e. ω is a *solution* of Δ. Moreover, we say that Δ is *admissible* iff it satisfies the following three conditions:

1. Δ is satisfiable,
2. for every $W \in \mathrm{war}(\Delta)$ there exists one and only one constraint for W in Δ (this implies $\mathrm{dom}(\Delta) = \mathrm{war}(\Delta)$), and
3. the relation $>_\Delta$ defined by $W >_\Delta W_i$ iff there is some defining constraint $W = \alpha \circ \bigsqcap\{W_1, \ldots, W_i, \ldots, W_k\}$ in Δ, satisfies that $>_\Delta^*$ is irreflexive.

Finally, we say that Δ is *solved* iff Δ is admissible and only contains defining constraints. Now we are in a position to define *goals* and their *solutions*:

Definition 1 (Goals and its Variables). *Given a conjunction of $\mathcal{D}$-annotated atoms $\overline{A}$, a substitution $\sigma \in \mathrm{Subst}_\Sigma$ –the set of all substitutions of terms for variables in Var– and a set of qualification constraints Δ, we say that $G \equiv \overline{A} \; \| \; \sigma \; \| \; \Delta$ is a goal iff*

  i. $\sigma \in \mathrm{Subst}_\Sigma$ is idempotent and such that $\mathrm{dom}(\sigma) \cap var(\overline{A}) = \emptyset$.
  ii. Δ is admissible.
  iii. For every qualification variable in $\mathrm{war}(\overline{A})$ there is one and only one threshold constraint for W in Δ. And there are no more threshold constraints in Δ.

Furthermore, if $\sigma = \epsilon$ (the identity substitution) then G is called initial, *and if $\overline{A}$ is empty and Δ is solved, then G is called* solved. *For any goal G, we define the set of variables of G as $var(G) =_{\mathrm{def}} var(\overline{A}) \cup \mathrm{dom}(\sigma)$ and the set of qualification variables of G as $\mathrm{war}(G) =_{\mathrm{def}} \mathrm{war}(\overline{A}) \cup \mathrm{dom}(\Delta)$.* $\square$

Definition 2 (Goal Solutions). *A pair of substitutions (θ, ρ) such that $\theta \in \mathrm{Subst}_\Sigma$ and $\rho \in \mathrm{Subst}_\Sigma(\mathcal{D})$ is called a* solution *of a goal $G \equiv \overline{A} \; \| \; \sigma \; \| \; \Delta$ iff:*

  1. $\theta = \sigma\theta$.
  2. $\rho \in Sol(\Delta)$.
  3. $\mathcal{P} \vdash_{\mathrm{QHL}(\mathcal{D})} A\theta \sharp W\rho$ for all $A \sharp W \in \overline{A}$.

  In addition, a solution (σ, μ) for a goal G is said to be more general than another solution (θ, ρ) for the same goal G (one also says in this case that (θ, ρ) is subsumed by (σ, μ)) iff $\sigma \preccurlyeq \theta$ [var(G)] and $\mu \sqsupseteq \rho$ [war(G)], where $\sigma \preccurlyeq \theta$ [var(G)] means that there is some substitution η such that the composition $\sigma\eta$ behaves the same as θ over any variable in the set $var(G)$ and $\mu \sqsupseteq \rho$ [war(G)] means that $\mu(W) \sqsupseteq \rho(W)$ holds for any $W \in \mathrm{war}(G)$. $\square$

Any solved goal $G' \equiv \sigma \; \| \; \Delta$ has the *associated solution* (σ, μ), where $\mu = \omega_\Delta$ is the qualification substitution given by Δ, such that $\omega_\Delta(W)$ is the qualification value determined by the defining constraints in Δ for all $W \in \mathrm{dom}(\Delta)$, and $\omega_\Delta(W) = \bot$ for any $W \in War \setminus \mathrm{dom}(\Delta)$. The solutions associated to solved goals are called *computed answers*.

Example 3

  1. A possible goal for program $\mathcal{P}_\mathcal{U}$ in Example 1 is `eats(father(X),Y)#W1, human(father(X))#W2 | W1>=0.4, W2>=0.6`; and a valid solution for it is $\{X \mapsto \texttt{adam}, Y \mapsto \texttt{apple}\} \; | \; \{\texttt{W1} \mapsto 0.50, \texttt{W2} \mapsto 0.75\}$.
  2. A goal for program $\mathcal{P}_\mathcal{W}$ in Example 1 may be `eats(X,Y)#W | W<=5.0`; and a valid solution is $\{X \mapsto \texttt{father(adam)}, Y \mapsto \texttt{apple}\} \; | \; \{\texttt{W} \mapsto 4.0\}$. $\square$

Note that the goal for $\mathcal{P}_\mathcal{U}$ in the previous example imposes lower bounds to the certainties to be computed, while the goal for $\mathcal{P}_\mathcal{W}$ imposes an upper bound to the proof depth. In general, goal solving in $QLP(\mathcal{W})$ corresponds to depth-bound goal-golving in classical Logic Programming.

4.2 SLD($\mathcal{D}$) Resolution

We propose a sound and strongly complete goal solving procedure called *Qualified SLD Resolution* parameterized over a given qualification domain $\mathcal{D}$, written as $SLD(\mathcal{D})$, which makes use of *annotated atoms* and *qualification constraints* over $\mathcal{D}$. The implementation of this goal solving procedure using CLP technology will be discussed in the next section. Resolution computations are written $G_0 \Vdash_{C_1,\sigma_1} G_1 \Vdash_{C_2,\sigma_2} \cdots \Vdash_{C_n,\sigma_n} G_n$, abbreviated as $G_0 \Vdash_\sigma^* G_n$ with $\sigma = \sigma_1\sigma_2\cdots\sigma_n$. They are finite sequences of resolution steps $G_{i-1} \Vdash_{C_i,\sigma_i} G_i$, starting with an initial goal G_0 and ending up with a solved goal G_n. One single resolution step is formally defined as follows:

Definition 3 (Resolution step). *A resolution step has the form* $\overline{L}, A \sharp W,$ $\overline{R} \ [\!] \ \sigma \ [\!] \ \alpha \circ W \sqsupseteq \beta, \Delta \Vdash_{C_1,\sigma_1} (\overline{L}, B_1 \sharp W_1, \ldots B_k \sharp W_k, \overline{R})\sigma_1 \ [\!] \ \sigma\sigma_1 \ [\!] \ \Delta_1$ *where* $A \sharp W$ *is called the* selected atom, $\Delta_1 = d \circ \alpha \circ W_1 \sqsupseteq \beta, \ldots, d \circ \alpha \circ W_k \sqsupseteq \beta, W = d \circ \bigcap\{W_1, \ldots, W_k\}, \Delta, C_1 \equiv (H \leftarrow d\!-\!B_1, \ldots, B_k) \in_{var} \mathcal{P}$ *is chosen as a variant of a clause in* $\mathcal{P}$ *with fresh variables and such that* $d \circ \alpha \sqsupseteq \beta$, σ_1 *is the m.g.u. between* A *and* H, *and* $W_1, \ldots, W_k \in \mathcal{W}ar$ *are fresh qualification variables.* $\quad\square$

The notation $\alpha \circ W \sqsupseteq \beta, \Delta$ represents a set of qualification constraints including the threshold constraint $\alpha \circ W \sqsupseteq \beta$ plus those in Δ, with no particular ordering assumed. Notice that the condition $d \circ \alpha \sqsupseteq \beta$ is required for the resolution step to be enabled. In this way, threshold constraints $\alpha \circ W \sqsupseteq \beta$ are actively used for pruning parts of the computation search space where no solutions can be found. In the instance of $QLP(\mathcal{B})$ it is easily checked that all the qualification values and constraints become trivial, so that $SLD(\mathcal{B})$ boils down to classical SLD resolution. In the rest of this section we present the main properties of $SLD(\mathcal{D})$ resolution in the general case.

Proposition 4. *If G is a goal and $G_0 \Vdash_{C_1,\sigma_1} G_1$, then G_1 is also a goal.*

Proof (Sketch). Assume a goal G_0 and a $SLD(\mathcal{D})$ resolution step $G_0 \Vdash_{C_1,\sigma_1} G_1$, as in Definition 3. Then G_0 satisfies the conditions required for goals in Definition 1, and we must show that G_1 also satisfies such conditions. This is not difficult to check, using the fact that C_1 has been chosen without variables in common with G_0. In particular, note that the threshold constraint for W in G_0 is absent in G_1, which includes a defining constraint for W and threshold constraints for the new qualification variables W_i. $\quad\square$

The next two theorems are the main theoretical results in the paper. The Soundness Theorem 1 guarantees that every computed answer is correct in the sense that it is a solution of a given goal. The Strong Completeness Theorem 2 ensures that, for any solution of a given goal and any fixed selection strategy, $SLD(\mathcal{D})$ resolution is able to compute an equal, if not better, solution. The proofs, given in [16], use inductive techniques similar to those presented in [18] for classical SLD resolution. Example 4 below illustrates the Completeness Theorem.

Theorem 1 (Soundness). *Assume $G_0 \Vdash^* G$ and $G = \sigma \; [\!] \; \Delta$ solved. Let (σ, μ) be the solution associated to G. Then (σ, μ) –called the computed answer– is a solution of G_0.* ☐

Theorem 2 (Strong Completeness). *Assume a given solution (θ, ρ) for G_0 and any fixed strategy for choosing the selected atom at each resolution step. Then there is some computed answer (σ, μ) for G_0 which subsumes (θ, ρ).* ☐

Example 4

1. The following $SLD(\mathcal{U})$ computation solves the goal for program $\mathcal{P}_{\mathcal{U}}$ presented in Example 3:

```
eats(father(X),Y)#W1,
    human(father(X))#W2 |
    W1 >= 0.4, W2 >= 0.6                    ⊩eats.4,{X↦adam}
eats(adam,Y)#W3,
    human(father(adam))#W2 | {X ↦ adam} |
    W1 = 0.8 * min{W3},
    W2 >= 0.6, 0.8 * W3 >= 0.4              ⊩eats.1,ε
human(father(adam))#W2 | {X ↦ adam} |
    W1 = 0.8 * min{W3},
    W2 >= 0.6, W3 = 0.8                     ⊩human.3,ε
human(adam)#W4 | {X ↦ adam} |
    W1 = 0.8 * min{W3},
    W2 = 0.9 * min{W4},
    W3 = 0.8, 0.90 * W4 >= 0.6              ⊩human.1,ε
| {X ↦ adam} |
    W1 = 0.8 * min{W3},
    W2 = 0.9 * min{W4},
    W3 = 0.8, W4 = 1.0
```

Note that the computed answer $\{X \mapsto \text{adam}\} \; | \; \{\text{W1} \mapsto 0.64, \text{W2} \mapsto 0.90\}$ subsumes the solution for the same goal given in Example 3.

2. Similarly, $SLD(\mathcal{W})$ resolution can solve the goal eats(X,Y)#W | W <= 5.0 for $\mathcal{P}_{\mathcal{W}}$, obtaining a computed answer $\{X \mapsto \text{father(adam)}\} \; | \; \{\text{W} \mapsto 3.0\}$ which subsumes the solution for the same goal given in Example 3. ☐

5 Towards an Implementation

In this section we assume a qualification domain $\mathcal{D}$ and a constraint domain $\mathcal{C}_{\mathcal{D}}$ such that the qualification constraints used in $SLD(\mathcal{D})$ resolution can be expressed as $\mathcal{C}_{\mathcal{D}}$ constraints, and we describe a translation of $QLP(\mathcal{D})$ programs $\mathcal{P}$ and goals G into $CLP(\mathcal{C}_{\mathcal{D}})$ programs $\mathcal{P}^t$ and goals G^t, such that solving G with $SLD(\mathcal{D})$ resolution using $\mathcal{P}$ corresponds to solving G^t with constrained SLD resolution using $\mathcal{P}^t$ and a solver for $\mathcal{C}_{\mathcal{D}}$.

The translation can be used to develop an implementation of $SLD(\mathcal{D})$ resolution for the $QLP(\mathcal{D})$ language on top of any CLP or $CFLP$ system that supports $\mathcal{C}_{\mathcal{D}}$ constraints. In particular, if $\mathcal{D}$ is any of the two qualification domains $\mathcal{U}$ or $\mathcal{W}$, the constraint domain $\mathcal{C}_{\mathcal{D}}$ can be chosen as $\mathcal{R}$, which supports arithmetic constraints over the real numbers [9]. We have developed a prototype implementation for $QLP(\mathcal{U})$ on top of the $CFLP$ system $\mathcal{TOY}$ [3], that supports $\mathcal{R}$ constraints. Note that although the use of a $CLP(\mathcal{R})$ system could lead to a more efficient implementation, we have chosen a $CFLP(\mathcal{R})$ system instead of a $CLP(\mathcal{R})$ one due to our interest in a future extension of the $QLP(\mathcal{D})$ scheme to support qualified functional-logic programming. Some minor modifications of the current prototype would easily lead to an implementation of other interesting instances, such as $QLP(\mathcal{W})$ and $QLP(\mathcal{U} \times \mathcal{W})$.

Our translation of a $QLP(\mathcal{D})$ program works by adding three extra arguments to all predicates and translating each clause independently. Given the $QLP(\mathcal{D})$ clause

$$C \equiv a(\bar{t}) \leftarrow d - b_1(\overline{s_1}), \ldots, b_k(\overline{s_k})$$

its head is translated as $a(\bar{t}, Alpha, W, Beta)$, where the new variables $Alpha$, W and $Beta$ correspond, respectively, to α, W and β in the threshold constraint $\alpha \circ W \sqsupseteq \beta$ related to a $\mathcal{D}$-annotated atom $A \sharp W$ which could be selected for a $SLD(\mathcal{D})$ resolution step using the clause C. The clause's body is translated with the aim of emulating such a resolution step, and the translated clause becomes:

$$
\begin{aligned}
C^t \equiv a(\bar{t}, Alpha, W, Beta) \leftarrow{} & d \circ Alpha \sqsupseteq Beta, \\
& W_1 \sqsupseteq \bot, W_1 \sqsubseteq \top, b_1(\overline{s_1}, d \circ Alpha, W_1, Beta), \\
& \quad \vdots \\
& W_k \sqsupseteq \bot, W_k \sqsubseteq \top, b_k(\overline{s_k}, d \circ Alpha, W_k, Beta), \\
& W = d \circ \textstyle\bigsqcap\{W_1, \ldots, W_k\}
\end{aligned}
$$

The conditions in the body of C^t do indeed correspond to the performance of a $SLD(\mathcal{D})$ resolution step with clause C. In fact, $d \circ Alpha \sqsupseteq Beta$ checks that C is eligible for such a step; the conditions in the next k lines using new variables W_i correspond to placing the annotated atoms from C's body into the new goal; and the last condition introduces the proper defining constraint for W.

The idea for translating goals is similar. Given an initial goal $QLP(\mathcal{D})$ goal G like

$$a_1(\overline{t_1}) \sharp W_1, \ldots, a_m(\overline{t_m}) \sharp W_m \;[\!]\; W_1 \sqsupseteq \beta_1, \ldots, W_m \sqsupseteq \beta_m$$

where $\beta_1, \ldots, \beta_m \in D \setminus \{\bot\}$, the translated goal G^t is

$$a_1(\overline{t_1}, \top, W_1, \beta_1), \ldots, a_m(\overline{t_m}, \top, W_m, \beta_m)$$

where the three additional arguments at each atom are used to encode the initial threshold constraints $W_i \sqsupseteq \beta_i$.

Example 5. As an example of the translation process we present the translation of the program $\mathcal{P}_{\mathcal{U}}$ from Example 1 into a $\mathcal{TOY}$ program which uses $\mathcal{R}$ constraints.

```
min1 [] = 1
min1 [X|Xs] = min2 X (min1 Xs)
min2 W1 W2 = if W1 <= W2 then W1 else W2
data being = adam | eve | bird | cat | oak | apple
            | father being | mother being

cruel(X,F,W,M) :- F*0.9>=M, W1>0, W1<=1.0, human(X,F*0.9,W1,M),
                  W2>0, W2<=1.0, eats(X,Y,F*0.9,W2,M),
                  W3>0, W3<=1.0, animal(Y,F*0.9,W3,M),
                  W == 0.9 * min1 [W1,W2,W3]
cruel(X,F,W,M) :- F*0.4>=M, W1>0, W1<=1.0, human(X,F*0.4,W1,M),
                  W2>0, W2<=1.0, eats(X,Y,F*0.4,W2,M),
                  W3>0, W3<=1.0, plant(Y,F*0.4,W3,M),
                  W == 0.4 * min1 [W1,W2,W3]
animal(bird,F,W,M) :- F*1.0>=M, W == 1.0 * min1 []
animal(cat,F,W,M)  :- F*1.0>=M, W == 1.0 * min1 []
plant(oak,F,W,M)   :- F*1.0>=M, W == 1.0 * min1 []
plant(apple,F,W,M) :- F*1.0>=M, W == 1.0 * min1 []
human(adam,F,W,M)     :- F*1.0>=M, W == 1.0 * min1 []
human(eve,F,W,M)      :- F*1.0>=M, W == 1.0 * min1 []
human(father(X),F,W,M) :- F*0.9>=M, W1>0, W1<=1.0,
        human(X,F*0.9, W1, M), W == 0.9 * min1 [W1]
human(mother(X),F,W,M) :- F*0.8>=M, W1>0, W1<=1.0,
        human(X,F*0.8, W1, M), W == 0.8 * min1 [W1]

eats(adam,X,F,W,M) :- F*0.8>=M, W == 0.8 * min1 []
eats(eve,X,F,W,M) :- F*0.3>=M, W1>0, W1<=1.0,
        animal(X,F*0.3,W1,M), W == 0.3 * min1 [W1]
eats(eve,X,F,W,M) :- F*0.6>=M, W1>0, W1<=1.0,
        plant(X,F*0.6,W1,M), W == 0.6 * min1 [W1]
eats(father(X),Y,F,W,M) :- F*0.8>=M, W1>0, W1<=1.0,
        eats(X,Y,F*0.8,W1,M), W == 0.8 * min1 [W1]
eats(mother(X),Y,F,W,M) :- F*0.7>=M, W1>0, W1<=1.0,
        eats(X,Y,F*0.7,W1,M), W == 0.7 * min1 [W1]
```

To understand this example it is important to notice the following:

1. Since *glbs* in $\mathcal{U}$ are computed as minimums, translated programs must include functions for this task. Here, min1 resp. min2 compute the minimum of a list of numbers resp. two numbers.
2. As $\mathcal{TOY}$ need types for every constructor, we must include suitable datatype declarations in translated programs.
3. The resulting code could be simplified and optimized, but our aim here is to illustrate the literal application of the general translation rules. For this reason, no optimizations have been performed.   □

6   Conclusions and Future Work

We have generalized the early QLP proposal by van Emden [22] to a generic scheme $QLP(\mathcal{D})$ parameterized by a qualification domain $\mathcal{D}$, which must be a lattice with extreme points and equipped with an attenuation operator. The values belonging to a qualification domain are intended to qualify logical assertions, ensuring that they satisfy certain user's expectations. Qualification domains include $\mathcal{B}$ (classical truth values of two-valued logic), $\mathcal{U}$ (van Emden's certainty values) and $\mathcal{W}$ (numeric values representing proof weights), as well as arbitrary cartesian products of given qualification domains. As shown by instances such as $QLP(\mathcal{W})$ and $QLP(\mathcal{U} \times \mathcal{W})$, the $QLP(\mathcal{D})$ scheme can express uncertainty in Logic Programming and more, since the user's expectations qualified by $\mathcal{W}$ do not correspond to uncertain truth values.

The semantic results obtained for $QLP(\mathcal{D})$ are stronger than those in [22]. Each program $\mathcal{P}$ has a least open Herbrand model $\mathcal{M}_\mathcal{P}$ with two equivalent characterizations: as the least fixpoint of the operator $T_\mathcal{P}$, and as the set of qualified atoms deducible from $\mathcal{P}$ in the logic calculus $QHL(\mathcal{D})$. Moreover, the goal solving calculus $SLD(\mathcal{D})$, based on an extension of SLD resolution with qualification constraints, is sound and strongly complete for arbitrary open goals. $SLD(\mathcal{B})$ boils down to classical SLD resolution.

As implementation technique, we have proposed a translation of $QLP(\mathcal{D})$ programs and goals into $CLP(\mathcal{C}_\mathcal{D})$, choosing a constraint domain $\mathcal{C}_\mathcal{D}$ able to compute with qualification constraints over $\mathcal{D}$. If $\mathcal{D}$ is $\mathcal{U}$, $\mathcal{B}$, or $\mathcal{U} \times \mathcal{B}$, the constraint domain $\mathcal{C}_\mathcal{D}$ can be chosen as $\mathcal{R}$, and $QLP(\mathcal{D})$ can be implemented on top of any CLP or $CFLP$ system which supports constraint solving over $\mathcal{R}$. We have implemented a prototype of $QLP(\mathcal{U})$ on top of the $CFLP$ system $\mathcal{TOY}$.

In comparison to the theory of generalized annotated logic programs (GAP for short) presented in [10], our results in this paper also include some interesting contributions. With respect to the syntax and goal solving procedure, the $QLP(\mathcal{D})$ scheme can be made to fit into the GAP framework by viewing our attenuation operators as annotation functions. However, our resolution procedure $SLD(\mathcal{D})$ can be implemented more efficiently than the constrained SLD resolution used in GAP, due to optimized treatments of qualification constraints and, more importantly, because the costly computation of so-called *reductants* between variants of program clauses is needed in GAP resolution but not in $SLD(\mathcal{D})$. The purpose of reductants in GAP is to explicitly compute the *lub*s of several lattice values (qualification values in the case of $QLP(\mathcal{D})$) which would result from finitely many different computations if no reductants were used. In GAP's declarative semantics, interpretations are required to be closed w.r.t. finite *lub*s of lattice values assigned to the same atom, and for this reason reductants are needed for the completeness of goal resolution. In $QLP(\mathcal{D})$ interpretations as defined in Section 3 no closure condition w.r.t. *lub*s is required, and therefore the completeness result stated in Theorem 2 can be proved without reductants. Of course, the $QLP(\mathcal{D})$ approach to semantics means that a user has to observe *several* computed answers for one and the same goal and think of the *lub* of the various $\mathcal{D}$ elements provided by the different computations by himself instead of getting the *lub* computed by one single $SLD(\mathcal{D})$ derivation. In our opinion, this is a reasonable scenario because even in GAP there is no guarantee that the $\mathcal{T}$ value provided by one single computed answer is the best possible one. Moreover, our Theorem 2 is much stronger than the one given in [10], which only ensures the possibility of computing *some* solution for any goal whose solvability holds in the least program model. We conjecture that a stronger completeness theorem could be proved also for GAP by using a proof technique more similar to our's.

As possible lines of future work we consider: to improve and extend the prototype implementation, covering $QLP(\mathcal{U})$, $QLP(\mathcal{W})$ and $QLP(\mathcal{U} \times \mathcal{W})$; to extend the $QLP(\mathcal{D})$ scheme and its implementation to a more expressive scheme which can support qualitative programming with features such as disjunctive goals, negation, lazy functions and parametrically given constraint domains; to explore alternative semantic approaches, considering annotations, bilattices, probabilistic semantics and similarity based unification; and to investigate applications to the computation of qualified answers for web search queries.

Acknowledgements

The authors are thankful to their colleagues Paco López and Rafa Caballero for their valuable hints concerning bibliography and implementation techniques. They also appreciate the constructive comments of the anonymous reviewers, that were helpful for improving the presentation.

References

1. Apt, K.R., van Emden, M.H.: Contributions to the theory of logic programming. Journal of the Association for Computing Machinery (JACM) 29(3), 841–862 (1982)
2. Arcelli, F., Formato, F.: Likelog: a logic programming language for flexible data retrieval. In: Proceedings of the ACM Symposium on Applied computing (SAC 1999), pp. 260–267. ACM Press, New York (1999)
3. Arenas, P., Fernández, A.J., Gil, A., López-Fraguas, F.J., Rodríguez-Artalejo, M., Sáenz-Pérez, F.: $\mathcal{TOY}$, a multiparadigm declarative language. version 2.3.1, R. Caballero and J. Sánchez (Eds.) (2007), http://toy.sourceforge.net
4. Clark, K.L.: Predicate logic as a computational formalism (res. report doc 79/59). Technical report, Imperial College, Dept. of Computing, London (1979)
5. Dekhtyar, A., Subrahmanian, V.S.: Hybrid probabilistic programs. Journal of Logic Programming 43(3), 187–250 (2000)
6. Dix, J., Kraus, S., Subrahmanian, V.S.: Heterogeneous temporal probabilistic agents. ACM Transactions on Computational Logic 7(1), 151–198 (2006)
7. Dix, J., Nanni, M., Subrahmanian, V.S.: Probabilistic agent programs. ACM Transactions on Computational Logic 1(2), 208–246 (2000)
8. Fitting, M.: Bilattices and the semantics of logic programming. Journal of Logic Programming 11, 91–116 (1991)

9. Jaffar, J., Michaylov, S., Stuckey, P.J., Yap, R.H.C.: The CLP(R) language and system. ACM Transactions on Programming Languages and Systems 14(3), 339–395 (1992)

10. Kifer, M., Subrahmanian, V.S.: Theory of generalized annotated logic programs and their applications. Journal of Logic Programming 12(3&4), 335–367 (1992)

11. Loia, V., Senatore, S., Sessa, M.I.: Similarity-based SLD resolution and its role for web knowledge discovery. Fuzzy Sets and Systems 144(1), 151–171 (2004)

12. Moreno, G., Pascual, V.: Programming with fuzzy logic and mathematical functions. In: Bloch, I., Petrosino, A., Tettamanzi, A.G.B. (eds.) WILF 2005. LNCS (LNAI), vol. 3849, pp. 89–98. Springer, Heidelberg (2006)

13. Ng, R.T., Subrahmanian, V.S.: Probabilistic logic programming. Information and Computation 101(2), 150–201 (1992)

14. Ng, R.T., Subrahmanian, V.S.: A semantical framework for supporting subjective and conditional probability in deductive databases. Journal of Automated Reasoning 10(2), 191–235 (1993)

15. Riezler, S.: Probabilistic Constraint Logic Programming. PhD thesis, Neuphilologische Fakultät der Universität Tübingen (1998)

16. Rodríguez-Artalejo, M., Romero-Díaz, C.A.: A generic scheme for qualitative logic programming (Technical Report DSIC 1/08). Technical report, Universidad Complutense, Departamento de Sistemas Informáticos y Computación, Madrid, Spain (2008)

17. Shapiro, E.Y.: Logic programs with uncertainties: A tool for implementing rule-based systems. In: Bundy, A. (ed.) Proceedings of the 8th International Joint Conference on Artificial Intelligence (IJCAI 1983), pp. 529–532. Karlsruhe, Germany, (1983)

18. Stärk, R.F.: A direct proof for the completeness of SLD-resolution. In: Börger, E., Kleine Büning, H., Richter, M.M. (eds.) CSL 1989. LNCS, vol. 440, pp. 382–383. Springer, Heidelberg (1990)

19. Subrahmanian, V.S.: On the semantics of quantitative logic programs. In: Proceedings of the 4th IEEE Symposium on Logic Programming, San Francisco, pp. 173–182 (1987)

20. Subrahmanian, V.S.: Query processing in quantitative logic programming. In: "Rusty" Lusk, E., Overbeek, R. (eds.) CADE 1988. LNCS, vol. 310, pp. 81–100. Springer, Heidelberg (1988)

21. Subrahmanian, V.S.: Uncertainty in logic programming: Some recollections. Association for Logic Programming Newsletter 20(2) (2007)

22. van Emden, M.H.: Quantitative deduction and its fixpoint theory. Journal of Logic Programming 3(1), 37–53 (1986)

23. van Emden, M.H., Kowalski, R.A.: The semantics of predicate logic as a programming language. Journal of the Association for Computing Machinery (JACM) 23(4), 733–742 (1976)

Formalizing a Constraint Deductive Database Language Based on Hereditary Harrop Formulas with Negation

Susana Nieva[1], Jaime Sánchez-Hernández[1], and Fernando Sáenz-Pérez[2,*]

[1] Dept. Sistemas Informáticos y Computación, UCM, Spain
[2] Dept. Ingeniería del Software e Inteligencia Artificial, UCM, Spain
{nieva,jaime,fernan}@sip.ucm.es

Abstract. In this paper, we present an extension of the scheme $HH(\mathcal{C})$ (Hereditary Harrop formulas with Constraints) with a suitable formulation of negation in order to obtain a constraint deductive database query language. In addition to constraints, our proposal includes logical connectives (implication and quantifiers) for defining databases and queries, which altogether are unavailable in current database query languages.

We define a proof theoretic semantic framework based on a sequent calculus, that allows to represent the meaning of a database query by means of a derived constraint answer in the sense of *CLP*. We also introduce an appropriate notion of stratification, which provides a starting point for suitable operational semantics dealing with recursion and negation. We formalize a fixed point semantics for stratifiable databases, whose fixpoint operator is applied stratum by stratum. This semantics is proved to be sound and complete with respect to derivability in the sequent calculus, and it provides the required support for actual implementations, as the prototype we have developed already and introduce in this paper.

1 Introduction

The scheme $HH(\mathcal{C})$ (Hereditary Harrop formulas with Constraints) [10] extends *HH* by adding constraints, in a similar way the extension of *LP* (Logic Programming) with constraints gave rise to the *CLP* (Constraint Logic Programming) scheme [9]. In this scheme, a parametric domain of constraints is assumed, so that it is possible to consider different instances (such as arithmetical constraints over real numbers and finite domain constraints). The extension is completely integrated into the language: Constraints are allowed to occur in goals, bodies of clauses and answers.

For example, considering the instance $HH(\mathcal{R})$, i.e., the domain of arithmetic constraints over real numbers, a circle can be defined by its center and radius, using non-linear constraints (in Prolog-like notation):

```
circle(XC,YC,R,X,Y) :- ((X-XC)**2 + (Y-YC)**2) ≤ R**2.
```

* The authors are partially supported by the Spanish projects 'MERIT-FORMS': TIN2005-09207-C03-03, 'PROMESAS-CAM': S-0505/TIC/0407.

J. Garrigue and M. Hermenegildo (Eds.): FLOPS 2008, LNCS 4989, pp. 289–304, 2008.

We can ask, for instance, if any pair (x, y) such that $x^2 + y^2 = 1$ (the circumference centered in the origin and radius 1) is inside the circle with center $(0, 0)$ and radius 2 by means of the goal:

```
∀ x ∀ y ((x**2 + y**2 ≈ 1) ⇒ circle(0,0,2,x,y)).
```

In this paper, we investigate the use of $HH(\mathcal{C})$ not as a (general purpose) programming language, but as the basis for database systems with constraints. We argue that, in the same way that Datalog [20] and Datalog with constraints [16] arise for modeling database systems inspired in Prolog and CLP respectively, the language $HH(\mathcal{C})$ can offer a suitable starting point for the same purpose.

$HH(\mathcal{C})$ improves the expressivity of traditional deductive database languages because the underlying logic embraces both new connectives and constraints. In particular, implications can be used to write hypothetical queries, universal quantification allows encapsulation, and constraints allow managing infinite data. To the best of our knowledge, former works (e.g., [15,18,17,5]) do not consider all these features altogether.

Let us see an example. Assume an instance in which finite and real constraint domains are combined. We can define the database:

```
flight(mad,par,1.5).    flight(par,ny,10).    flight(lon,ny,9).
travel(X,Y,T) :- flight(X,Y,D), T >= D.
travel(X,Y,T) :- flight(X,Z,T1), travel(Z,Y,T2), T >= T1+T2.
```

The relations `flight` and `travel` represent tuples `<Origin, Destination, FlightTime>` for both direct and linked connections between cities (extensional and intensional database, resp.). The implication

```
flight(mad, lon, T) ⇒ travel(mad, ny,11)
```

(a valid goal in our language) represents the query: Assuming that there is a direct connection between Madrid and London, what duration should it have in order to be able to travel from Madrid to New York in 11 hours at most? The answer to this query will be the constraint $11 \geq T + 9$, which is equivalent to $T \leq 2$ in the constraint system.

Another hypothetical query to the previous database can be whether it is possible to travel from Madrid to some place in any time greater than 1.5. The goal formulation $\forall$ t (t > 1.5 ⇒ ∃ y travel(mad,y,t)) includes also universal quantification, and the corresponding answer is *true*.

However, $HH(\mathcal{C})$ lacks of negation, which is needed to capture set difference in order to be complete with respect to Relational Algebra (RA). As it is well-known, incorporating negation into logic programming languages is a difficult task (see [2] for a survey). Negation in the specific field of deductive database systems has been also widely studied [1,3]. In our language, negation is even more complex due to the presence of implication and universal quantification in goals. Based on an extension of the sequent calculus defined for $HH(\mathcal{C})$ in [10], we provide a proof theoretic meaning of goals (queries) from programs (databases), in such a way that the existence of constraints is exploited to represent answers and to finitely model infinite databases. This is also the case of constraint databases, but as our core logic is very expressive, the resulting language is richer.

Using the database of the previous example, the query $\neg\exists$ t flight(X,Y,t) (or its equivalent $\forall$ t $\neg$ flight(X,Y,t)), which represents the cities in the database that have no direct flights between them, is not available in extended database languages as domain relational calculus or Datalog with constraints. However, in our system —where formulas are interpreted in the context of the constraint domain of the particular instance— $\forall$ t $\neg$ flight(X,Y,t) represents a valid goal, and one of its possible answer constraints is: $(\neg(X \approx mad) \vee \neg(Y \approx par)) \wedge (\neg(X \approx par) \vee \neg(Y \approx ny)) \wedge (\neg(X \approx lon) \vee \neg(Y \approx ny))$, which is equivalent to $X \approx mad \wedge Y \approx ny$ in the domain of the cities registered in the current database.

After formalizing $HH(\mathcal{C})$ with negation in Section 2, by means of the proof theoretical meaning, in Section 3 we focus on the problem that arises when dealing with recursion and negation: Termination. We adapt the usual notions of stratified negation to our context in order to establish syntactic conditions that characterize a limited form of negation, for which an operational semantics could be defined. The main results of this paper appear in Section 4, where a fixed point semantics, based on the previous notion of stratification, is defined and proved to be sound and complete with respect to the proof theoretical one (full proofs can be found in http://gpd.sip.ucm.es/papers/Archivos/nss-tr2008.pdf). As it is shown in Section 5, this semantics provides support for an implementation.

2 $HH(\mathcal{C})$ with Negation

The original formalisms in which $HH(\mathcal{C})$ is founded [10,7] are not enough expressive to represent set difference, so it is incomplete with respect to RA. We will extend the scheme including negation to obtain a complete *Constraint Deductive Database (CDDB)* language w.r.t. RA. Next, we make precise the syntax of the formulas of $HH(\mathcal{C})$ extended with negation, denoted as $HH_\neg(\mathcal{C})$, showing how the usual notions of programs and goals of Logic Programming can be translated into databases and queries, respectively. The evaluation of a query with respect to a deductive database can be seen as the computation of a goal from a set of facts (ground atoms) defining the extensional database, and a set of clauses, defining the intensional database. As it is common in deductive databases, the definition of a predicate, by means of clauses, can be seen in our language as the definition of a view in relational databases.

2.1 Syntax

As usual, formulas will be built up from terms, using predicates and connectives. We consider *defined predicate symbols*, representing the names of database relations, to build atoms, and *non-defined (built-in) predicate symbols*, including at least the equality predicate symbol $\approx$, to build constraints. We will also assume a set of constant and operator symbols in the constraint system, and a set of variables to build terms.

Well formed formulas in $HH_\neg(\mathcal{C})$ can be classified into clauses D (defining database relations) and goals (or queries) G. They are recursively defined by the following rules:

$$D ::= A \mid G \Rightarrow A \mid D_1 \wedge D_2 \mid \forall x D$$
$$G ::= A \mid \neg A \mid C \mid G_1 \wedge G_2 \mid G_1 \vee G_2 \mid D \Rightarrow G \mid C \Rightarrow G \mid \exists x G \mid \forall x G$$

A represents an atom, i.e., a formula of the form $p(t_1, \ldots, t_n)$, where p is a defined predicate symbol of arity n, and t_i are terms; C represents a constraint. The incorporation of negated atoms in goals is the surplus to $HH(\mathcal{C})$.

The constraints we consider belong to a generic system $\mathcal{C} = \langle \mathcal{L_C}, \vdash_\mathcal{C} \rangle$ where $\mathcal{L_C}$ is the constraint language and $\vdash_\mathcal{C}$ is a binary *entailment relation*. $\Gamma \vdash_\mathcal{C} C$ denotes that the constraint C is inferred in the constraint system $\mathcal{C}$ from the set of constraints Γ. Some minimal conditions are imposed to $\mathcal{C}$ to be a constraint system: $\mathcal{L_C}$ contains at least every first-order formula built up using $\top$ (*true*), $\bot$ (*false*), built-in predicate symbols, the connectives $\wedge, \neg$, and the existential quantifier $\exists$. Regarding to $\vdash_\mathcal{C}$, it includes the inference rules related to the considered connectives and quantifiers, valid in intuitionistic logic with equality; in addition, it is compact and generic (see [10] for details). The novelty is that $\mathcal{C}$ is required to deal with negation, because the incorporation of $\neg$ to HH is propagated to the constraint system, which has the responsibility of checking the satisfiability of answers in the constraint domain.

We say that a constraint C is $\mathcal{C}$-satisfiable if $\emptyset \vdash_\mathcal{C} \exists C$, where $\exists C$ stands for the existential closure of C. C and C' are $\mathcal{C}$-equivalent if $C \vdash_\mathcal{C} C'$ and $C' \vdash_\mathcal{C} C$.

For instance, the constraint systems of the examples are assumed to verify the required minimal conditions aforementioned. Moreover, they also include the connective $\vee$, constants to represent numbers and cities, arithmetical operators, and built-in predicates ($\geq, \ldots$).

Programs, denoted by Δ, are sets of clauses and represent databases. Any Δ can always be given as an equivalent set, $elab(\Delta)$, of implicative clauses with atomic heads in the way we precise now. The *elaboration* of a program Δ is the set $elab(\Delta) = \bigcup_{D \in \Delta} elab(D)$, where $elab(D)$ is defined by:

$$elab(A) = \{\top \Rightarrow A\} \qquad elab(D_1 \wedge D_2) = elab(D_1) \cup elab(D_2)$$
$$elab(G \Rightarrow A) = \{G \Rightarrow A\} \qquad elab(\forall x D) = \{\forall x D' \mid D' \in elab(D)\}$$

We will assume that a view defining a predicate is a set of elaborated clauses of the form $\forall x_1 \ldots \forall x_n (G \Rightarrow A)$[1]. In the examples (as before), we will use the common notation $A :\text{-} G$, assuming that capital letters inside A and G represent variables that are implicitly universally quantified, and incorporating the new connectives in goals. A is called the head and G the body of the clause as usual. Negation is not allowed in the head of a clause, but inside its body.

Example 1. Assume a more realistic situation of the flights example in the Introduction, where flight delays may happen:

---

[1] $\forall x_1 \ldots \forall x_n$ will be abbreviated by $\forall \overline{x}$.

```
deltravel(X,Y,T) :- flight(X,Y,T1), delay(X,Y,T2), T ≥ T1+T2.
deltravel(X,Y,T) :- flight(X,Z,T1), delay(X,Z,T2),
                    deltravel(Z,Y,T3), T ≥ T1+T2+T3.
```

Tuples of `delay` may be in the extensional database or may be assumed when the query is formulated. For instance, the goal:

$$(\forall\ x\ \texttt{delay(par,x,1),delay(mad,par,0.5))} \Rightarrow \texttt{deltravel(mad,ny,T)}$$

represents the query: What is the time needed to travel from Madrid to New York assuming that for any destination there is a delay of one hour from Paris, and the flight from Madrid to Paris is half an hour delayed? According to its proof theoretic interpretation, in order to solve the goal `deltravel(mad,ny,T)`, the clauses `delay(par,X,1)` and `delay(mad,par,0.5)` will be added locally to the database, and they will not be considered any more once the goal is solved. Similar queries can be generalized as views (defined by clauses). For instance:

```
needtime(C1,C2,D,T) :- ∀ x delay(C1,x,D) ⇒ deltravel(C1,C2,T).
```

Notice that this clause is neither allowed by Prolog with negation nor Datalog.

Since flights may or may not be delayed, a more general view can be defined in order to know the expected time of a trip:

```
trip(X,Y,T) :- nondeltravel(X,Y,T) ; deltravel(X,Y,T).
nondeltravel(X,Y,T) :- ¬ delayed(X,Y), travel(X,Y,T).
delayed(X,Y) :- ∃ t (delay(X,Y,t), ¬ t ≈ 0).
```

2.2 Sequent Calculus

Several kinds of semantics have been defined for $HH(\mathcal{C})$ without negation, including proof theoretic, operational [10] and fixed point semantics [7], as well as for its higher-order version [11]. The simplest way for explaining the meaning of programs and goals in the present framework is by using a proof theoretic semantics. Queries formulated to a database are interpreted by means of the inference system that governs the underlying logic. This proof system, called $\mathcal{UC}$ (Uniform sequent calculus handling Constraints) [10] is a sequent calculus that combines traditional inference rules with the entailment relation $\vdash_{\mathcal{C}}$ of the generic constraint system $\mathcal{C}$. The rules defining derivability in $\mathcal{UC}$ appear in Figure 1. Sequents have the form $\Delta; \Gamma \vdash C$, where programs and sets of constraints are on the left, and goals on the right.

Next, we explain the rules $(\exists_R)$ and $(Clause)$, the others correspond to widespread intuitionistic rules introducing connectives on the right of the sequent (see, e.g., [13]), except (C_R) which deals with goals that are pure constraints. $(\exists_R)$ captures the fact that the witness in the proof of an existentially quantified formula can be represented by a constraint that can be more general than an equality $x \approx t$ simulating a substitution (e.g., $(x * x \approx 2)$ represents the witness $\sqrt{2}$, which cannot be written as a term). $(Clause)$ represents backchaining and allows to prove an atomic goal $A \equiv p(t_1, \ldots, t_n)$, using a program clause whose head $A' \equiv p(t'_1, \ldots, t'_n)$ is not required to unify with A, but rather solving a new existentially quantified goal that, by applying the $(\exists_R)$ rule, will result in

$$\frac{\Gamma \vdash_C C}{\Delta; \Gamma \vdash C} \ (C_R) \qquad \frac{\Delta; \Gamma \vdash \exists x_1 \ldots \exists x_n ((A' \approx A) \wedge G)}{\Delta; \Gamma \vdash A} \ (Clause) \ (*), \text{where}$$

$$\forall x_1 \ldots \forall x_n (G \Rightarrow A') \text{ is a variant of a formula of } elab(\Delta)$$

$$\frac{\Delta; \Gamma \vdash G_i}{\Delta; \Gamma \vdash G_1 \vee G_2} \ (\vee_R) \ (i = 1, 2) \qquad \frac{\Delta; \Gamma \vdash G_1 \quad \Delta; \Gamma \vdash G_2}{\Delta; \Gamma \vdash G_1 \wedge G_2} \ (\wedge_R)$$

$$\frac{\Delta, D; \Gamma \vdash G}{\Delta; \Gamma \vdash D \Rightarrow G} \ (\Rightarrow_R) \qquad \frac{\Delta; \Gamma, C \vdash G}{\Delta; \Gamma \vdash C \Rightarrow G} \ (\Rightarrow C_R)$$

$$\frac{\Delta; \Gamma, C \vdash G[y/x] \quad \Gamma \vdash_C \exists y C}{\Delta; \Gamma \vdash \exists x G} \ (\exists_R)(**) \qquad \frac{\Delta; \Gamma \vdash G[y/x]}{\Delta; \Gamma \vdash \forall x G} \ (\forall_R)(**)$$

$$(*) \ x_1, \ldots, x_n \text{ fresh for } A$$

$$(**) \ y \text{ fresh for the formulas in the conclusion}$$

Fig. 1. Rules of the Sequent Calculus $\mathcal{UC}$

a search for a constraint that implies the equality $A' \approx A$ (that stands for $t'_1 \approx t_1 \wedge \ldots \wedge t'_n \approx t_n$).

$\mathcal{UC}$ provides only uniform proofs in the sense defined by Miller et al. [13], i.e., goal-oriented proofs. The rules are applied backwards and, at any step, the applied rule is that corresponding to the connective of the goal to be proved.

The Meaning of Negated Atoms. Derivability in $\mathcal{UC}$ provides proof theoretic semantics for $HH(\mathcal{C})$. The incorporation of negation makes necessary to extend the notion of derivability, because there is no rule for this connective in $\mathcal{UC}$. Therefore, we extend $\mathcal{UC}$ with a new rule to incorporate derivability of negated atoms. The idea of interpreting the query $\neg A$ from a database Δ, by means of an answer constraint C, is that whenever C' is a possible answer to the query A from Δ, then $C \vdash_C \neg C'$. This is formalized with the "metarule":

$$\frac{\Gamma \vdash_C \neg C \text{ for every } \Delta; C \vdash A}{\Delta; \Gamma \vdash \neg A} \ (\neg_R)$$

We say that $(\neg_R)$ is a metarule since its premise considers any derivation $\Delta; C \vdash A$ of the atom A. In practice, there is a derivation of $\neg A$ when the set of answer constraints of A from Δ is finite.

We define the inference system $\mathcal{UC}_\neg$ as $\mathcal{UC}$ plus the rule $(\neg_R)$. The notation $\Delta; \Gamma \vdash_{\mathcal{UC}_\neg} G$ means that the sequent $\Delta; \Gamma \vdash G$ has a proof using the rules of $\mathcal{UC}$ and $(\neg_R)$.

Definition 1. *If* $\Delta; C \vdash_{\mathcal{UC}_\neg} G$ *then* C *is called an* answer constraint *to the query* G *in the database* Δ.

Example 2. Consider the program below defining the inside of a rectangle with left-bottom corner (X_1, Y_1) and right-top corner (X_2, Y_2).

$$\Delta = \{ \ \text{rectangle(X1,Y1,X2,Y2,X,Y)} \ \text{:- X} \geq \text{X1, X} \leq \text{X2, Y} \geq \text{Y1, Y} \leq \text{Y2} \ \}$$

It is possible to formulate a query to get the difference between two rectangles (the dashed frame in the next figure) by the goal:

```
rectangle(0,0,4,4,X,Y), ¬ rectangle(1,1,3,3,X,Y)
```

obtaining as an answer constraint:

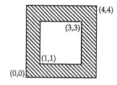

$$C \equiv ((y > 3) \wedge (y \leq 4) \wedge (x \geq 0) \wedge (x \leq 4)) \vee$$
$$((y \geq 0) \wedge (y < 1) \wedge (x \geq 0) \wedge (x \leq 4)) \vee$$
$$((y \geq 0) \wedge (y \leq 4) \wedge (x > 3) \wedge (x \leq 4)) \vee$$
$$((y \geq 0) \wedge (y \leq 4) \wedge (x \geq 0) \wedge (x < 1))$$

by the following deduction:

$$\cfrac{\cfrac{\cfrac{C \vdash_{\mathcal{R}} \exists a_1, a_2, b_1, b_2, x_1, y_1 (a_1 \approx 0 \ldots)}{\Delta; C \vdash \exists a_1, a_2, b_1, b_2, x_1, y_1 (a_1 \approx 0 \wedge x_1 \approx x \wedge x_1 \geq a_1 \wedge \\ a_2 \approx 0 \wedge y_1 \approx y \wedge x_1 \leq b_1 \wedge b_1 \approx 4 \wedge y_1 \geq a_2 \wedge b_2 \approx 4 \wedge y_1 \leq b_2)}}(C_R)}{\Delta; C \vdash rectangle(0, 0, 4, 4, x, y)}(Clause) \quad \mathbf{D}}{\Delta; C \vdash rectangle(0, 0, 4, 4, x, y) \wedge \neg rectangle(1, 1, 3, 3, x, y)}(\wedge_R)$$

where **D** is the deduction:

$$\cfrac{\cfrac{C \vdash_{\mathcal{R}} \neg(x \geq 1 \wedge y \geq 1}{\wedge x \leq 3 \wedge y \leq 3)} \quad \cfrac{\cdots}{\Delta; \begin{array}{c} x \geq 1 \wedge y \geq 1 \\ \wedge x \leq 3 \wedge y \leq 3 \end{array} \vdash rectangle(1, 1, 3, 3, x, y)}}{\Delta; C \vdash \neg rectangle(1, 1, 3, 3, x, y)}(\neg_R)$$

In order to define an operational semantics for $HH_\neg(\mathcal{C})$, some finiteness conditions must be imposed to make viable the metarule $(\neg_R)$. That is, we have to guarantee to get only a finite number of non-equivalent computed answer constraints for any atom that occurs negated in some goal.

In this way, it is possible to impose the following restriction: A predicate q can not occur negated in the definition of a predicate p if "q depends on p". This restriction establishes a limitation on mutually recursive definitions. But, even in the case of adopting this strong syntactic restriction, completeness w.r.t. RA remains, since RA does not include recursion.

In the next section, we formalize the concept of positive and negative dependencies, and the stratifiable database notion is introduced.

3 Dependency Graphs and Stratified Negation

A well-known problem arises in deductive database languages when negation and recursion are considered altogether. Several approaches have been used to deal with this problem. This is the case of *answer set programming* [6] or the use of *stratified negation* [20]. We have found this second approach more suitable to our scheme, because $HH_\neg(\mathcal{C})$ provides constraints as answers, and handles implications, which involves dynamic program increase. Stratification is based on the definition of a *dependency graph* for a program. Given a set of clauses and goals Φ, the corresponding dependency graph DG_Φ is a directed graph whose nodes are the defined predicate symbols in Φ, and the edges are determined by the implication symbols of the formulas.

Here, we adapt those notions as a useful starting point of a fixed point semantics for our language. But now, the construction of dependency graphs must consider the fact that implications may occur not only between the head and the body of a clause, but also inside the goals, and therefore in any clause body. This feature will be taken into account in the following way: An implication of the form $F_1 \Rightarrow F_2$ produces edges (or paths) in the graph from the defined predicate symbols inside F_1 to every defined predicate symbol inside F_2. An edge will be negatively labeled when the corresponding atom occurs negated on the left of the implication. Since constraints do not include defined predicate symbols, they cannot produce dependencies. In [14], we defined an algorithm to compute the dependency graph of any set Φ.

Example 3. Consider a database Δ consisting of the predicates defined in previous examples. The dependency graph for Δ is:

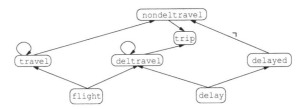

The query $G \equiv \exists\ t\ (\texttt{deltravel(X,Y,t)} \Rightarrow \texttt{delayed(X,Y))}$ would introduce the new edge $\texttt{deltravel} \rightarrow \texttt{delayed}$ into the previous graph.

The dependency graph is used to define stratification in $HH_\neg(\mathcal{C})$.

Definition 2. *Given a set of formulas Φ, its corresponding dependency graph DG_Φ, and two predicates p and q, we say:*

- *q depends on p if there is a path from p to q in DG_Φ.*
- *q negatively depends on p if there is a path from p to q in DG_Φ with at least one negatively labeled edge.*

Definition 3. *Let Φ be a set of formulas and $P = \{p_1, \ldots, p_n\}$ the set of defined predicate symbols of Φ. A stratification of Φ is any mapping $s : P \to \{1, \ldots, n\}$ such that $s(p) \le s(q)$ if q depends on p, and $s(p) < s(q)$ if q negatively depends on p. Φ is stratifiable if there is a stratification for it.*

Example 4. A stratification for the database Δ of Example 3 will collect all the predicates in the stratum 1 except $\texttt{nondeltravel}$ and $\texttt{trip}$, which will be in stratum 2. Intuitively, this means that for evaluating $\texttt{nondeltravel}$, the rest of predicates (except $\texttt{trip}$) should be evaluated before (in particular, $\texttt{delayed}$). Adding the query G in the Example 3, $\Delta \cup \{G\}$ remains stratifiable, but adding $\texttt{trip(mad,lon,T)} \Rightarrow \texttt{delay(mad,ny, T)}$, results in a non-stratifiable set: This adds the dependency $\texttt{trip} \rightarrow \texttt{delay}$, and then, any stratification s must satisfy $s(\texttt{trip}) \le s(\texttt{delay}) < s(\texttt{nondeltravel}) \le s(\texttt{trip})$, that is impossible.

A remarkable point is that we assume, on the follow, the existence of a fixed stratification s for the considered sets $\Delta \cup \{G\}$.

It is useful to have a notion of the stratum of an atom (i.e., the stratum of its predicate symbol), but also to extend this notion to any formula or set of formulas.

Definition 4. *Let F be a goal or a clause. The stratum of a formula F, denoted $str(F)$, is recursively defined as:*

$$str(p(t_1, \ldots, t_n)) = s(p) \qquad str(\neg A) = 1 + str(A) \qquad str(C) = 1$$
$$str(F_1 \square F_2) = max(str(F_1), str(F_2)), \ where \ \square \in \{\wedge, \vee, \Rightarrow\}$$
$$str(QxF) = str(F), \ where \ Q \in \{\exists, \forall\}$$

The stratum of a set of formulas Φ is $str(\Phi) = max\{str(F) \mid F \in \Phi\}$.

4   Fixed Point Semantics

We have extended the semantics presented in [7] in order to interpret full $HH_\neg(\mathcal{C})$. The semantics there defined is based on a *forcing relation* among programs, sets of constraints and goals that states whether an interpretation makes true a goal G in the context $\langle \Delta, \Gamma \rangle$ of a program and a set of constraints. Interpretations were defined as functions able to give meaning to every pair $\langle \Delta, \Gamma \rangle$ as sets of atoms. The interpretation should depend on this context because, when computing implicative goals, Δ or Γ may be augmented.

In order to deal with negation, interpretations and the fixpoint operator will operate over strata. So, contexts will be stratifiable databases (that may augment). An interpretation over a stratum i of a database will be a set of pairs $(A, C) \in At \times \mathcal{SL}_\mathcal{C}$ (atom, $\mathcal{C}$-satisfiable constraint), where $str(A) \leq i$.

4.1   Stratified Interpretations and Forcing Relation

Let $\mathcal{W}$ be the set of stratifiable databases Δ (with respect to the same fixed stratification s), At be the set of open atoms, and $\mathcal{SL}_\mathcal{C}$ be the set of $\mathcal{C}$-satisfiable constraints modulo $\mathcal{C}$-equivalence.

We will consider functions $I : \mathcal{W} \rightarrow \mathcal{P}(At \times \mathcal{SL}_\mathcal{C})$. In order to simplify the notation, we write $(A, C) \in At \times \mathcal{SL}_\mathcal{C}$, assuming that C denotes any constraint $\mathcal{C}$-equivalent to it. The notation $[I(\Delta)]_i$ represents the following subset of $I(\Delta)$,

$$[I(\Delta)]_i = \{(A, C) \in I(\Delta) \mid str(A) = i\}.$$

Notice that if $str(\Delta) = k$, then $\{[I(\Delta)]_i \mid 1 \leq i \leq k\}$ is a partition of $I(\Delta)$.

Interpretations can be classified on strata. An interpretation gives information up to its corresponding stratum.

Definition 5. *Let $i \geq 1$. An interpretation I over the stratum i is a function $I : \mathcal{W} \rightarrow \mathcal{P}(At \times \mathcal{SL}_\mathcal{C})$, such that for any $\Delta \in \mathcal{W}$, and any $j > i$, $[I(\Delta)]_j = \emptyset$. We denote by $\mathcal{I}_i$ the set of interpretations over i.*

For every $i \geq 1$, an order on $\mathcal{I}_i$ can be defined.

Definition 6. *Let $i \geq 1$ and $I_1, I_2 \in \mathcal{I}_i$. I_1 is less or equal than I_2 at stratum i, denoted by $I_1 \sqsubseteq_i I_2$, if for each $\Delta \in \mathcal{W}$ the following conditions are satisfied:*

- *$[I_1(\Delta)]_j = [I_2(\Delta)]_j$, for every $1 \leq j < i$.*
- *$[I_1(\Delta)]_i \subseteq [I_2(\Delta)]_i$.*

It is straightforward to check that for any $i \geq 1$, $(\mathcal{I}_i, \sqsubseteq_i)$ is a poset.

The idea is that when an interpretation over a stratum i increases, the information of the smaller strata remains invariable. In such a way, if $str(\neg A) = i$, since $str(A) = i - 1$, the truth value of $\neg A$ at the stratum i will remain invariable and monotonicity of the truth relation can be guaranteed even for negative atoms, as we will show.

In addition, the following result holds.

Lemma 1. *For any $i \geq 1$, any chain of interpretations of $(\mathcal{I}_i, \sqsubseteq_i)$, $\{I_n\}_{n \geq 0}$, such that $I_0 \sqsubseteq_i I_1 \sqsubseteq_i I_2 \sqsubseteq_i \ldots$, has a least upper bound $\bigsqcup_{n \geq 0} I_n$, which can be defined as: $(\bigsqcup_{n \geq 0} I_n)(\Delta) = \bigcup_{n \geq 0}\{I_n(\Delta)\}$, for any $\Delta \in \mathcal{W}$.*

Proof. Straightforward using the definition of $(\mathcal{I}_i, \sqsubseteq_i)$. □

The following definition formalizes the notion of a query G being "true" for an interpretation I in the context of a database Δ, if the constraint C is satisfied. As already said, we assume that s is not only a stratification for Δ, but also for $\Delta \cup \{G\}$.

Definition 7. *Let $i \geq 1$. The forcing relation $\Vdash$ between pairs I, Δ and pairs (G, C) (where $I \in \mathcal{I}_i$, $str(G) \leq i$, and C is $\mathcal{C}$-satisfiable) is recursively defined by the rules below. When $I, \Delta \Vdash (G, C)$, it is said that (G, C) is forced by I, Δ.*

- *$I, \Delta \Vdash (C', C) \iff C \vdash_{\mathcal{C}} C'$.*
- *$I, \Delta \Vdash (A, C) \iff (A, C) \in I(\Delta)$.*
- *$I, \Delta \Vdash (\neg A, C) \iff$ for every $(A, C') \in I(\Delta)$, $C \vdash_{\mathcal{C}} \neg C'$ holds. If there is no pair of the form (A, C') in $I(\Delta)$, then $C \equiv \top$.*
- *$I, \Delta \Vdash (G_1 \wedge G_2, C) \iff$ for each $i \in \{1, 2\}$, $I, \Delta \Vdash (G_i, C)$.*
- *$I, \Delta \Vdash (G_1 \vee G_2, C) \iff$ for some $i \in \{1, 2\}$ $I, \Delta \Vdash (G_i, C)$.*
- *$I, \Delta \Vdash (D \Rightarrow G, C) \iff I, \Delta \cup \{D\} \Vdash (G, C)$.*
- *$I, \Delta \Vdash (C' \Rightarrow G, C) \iff I, \Delta \Vdash (G, C \wedge C')$.*
- *$I, \Delta \Vdash (\exists x G, C) \iff$ there is C' such that $I, \Delta \Vdash (G[y/x], C')$, where y does not occur free in Δ, $\exists x G$, C, and $C \vdash_{\mathcal{C}} \exists y C'$.*
- *$I, \Delta \Vdash (\forall x G, C) \iff I, \Delta \Vdash (G[y/x], C)$ where y does not occur free in Δ, $\forall x G$, C.*

Those rules are well-defined because if s is a stratification for $\Delta \cup \{G\}$, with $str(G) \leq i$, and G' is a subformula of G, then s is also a stratification for $\Delta \cup \{G'\}$, and $str(G') \leq i$. Notice that, for the particular case $G \equiv D \Rightarrow G'$, s will be also a stratification for $\Delta \cup \{D, G'\}$.

From now on, when we write $I, \Delta \Vdash (G, C)$ we will assume that if $I \in \mathcal{I}_i$, then $str(G) \leq i$ and C is $\mathcal{C}$-satisfiable. The relation $\Vdash$ is not defined otherwise. Formally, $\Vdash$ should be denoted $\Vdash_i$, because there is a forcing relation for each $\mathcal{I}_i$. We avoid the subindex in order to simplify the notation.

The following lemma establishes the monotonicity of the forcing relation.

Lemma 2. *Let $i \geq 1$ and $I_1, I_2 \in \mathcal{I}_i$ such that $I_1 \sqsubseteq_i I_2$. Then, for any $\Delta \in \mathcal{W}$, and $(G, C) \in \mathcal{G} \times \mathcal{SL}_C$, it holds $I_1, \Delta \Vdash (G, C) \implies I_2, \Delta \Vdash (G, C)$.*

Proof. The proof is inductive on the structure of G and it is derived from the definitions of the forcing relation and the order between interpretations. We only show the case of negation.

Assume $I_1, \Delta \Vdash (\neg A, C)$. Then, either $C \vdash_C \neg C'$ for every C' such that $(A, C') \in I_1(\Delta)$, or there is no such C' and $C \equiv \top$. Since $str(\neg A) \leq i$, obviously $str(A) = j$, for some $j < i$. But then $[I_2(\Delta)]_j = [I_1(\Delta)]_j$, because $I_1 \sqsubseteq_i I_2$, and therefore $I_2, \Delta \Vdash (\neg A, C)$. $\qquad\square$

Lemma 3. *Let $i \geq 1$ and let $\{I_n\}_{n \geq 0}$ be a denumerable family of interpretations over the stratum i, such that $I_0 \sqsubseteq_i I_1 \sqsubseteq_i I_2 \sqsubseteq_i \dots$. Then, for any Δ, G and C, $\bigsqcup_{n \geq 0} I_n, \Delta \Vdash (G, C) \iff$ there exists $k \geq 0$ such that $I_k, \Delta \Vdash (G, C)$.*

Proof. The implication to the left is a consequence of Lemma 2, since $I_k \sqsubseteq_i \bigsqcup_{n \geq 0} I_n$ holds for any k. The converse is proved by induction on the structure of G, using the result of Lemma 1. We show one of the cases.

$(\exists x G')$ $\bigsqcup_{n \geq 0} I_n, \Delta \Vdash (\exists x G', C) \iff$ there is a variable y that does not occur free in Δ, $\exists x G'$, and C, such that $\bigsqcup_{n \geq 0} I_n, \Delta \Vdash (G'[y/x], C')$, and $C \vdash_C \exists y C'$. By induction hypothesis, it holds $I_k, \Delta \Vdash (G'[y/x], C')$ for some $k \geq 0$. Therefore, there is a $k \geq 0$ such that $I_k, \Delta, \Vdash (\exists x G', C)$. $\qquad\square$

Next, a continuous operator for every stratum transforming interpretations is defined. Its least fixed point supplies the expected version of truth at each stratum.

Definition 8. *Let $i \geq 1$ represent a stratum. The* operator $T_i : \mathcal{I}_i \longrightarrow \mathcal{I}_i$ *transforms interpretations over i as follows. For any $I \in \mathcal{I}_i$, $\Delta \in \mathcal{W}$, and $(A, C) \in At \times \mathcal{SL}_C$, $(A, C) \in T_i(I)(\Delta)$ when:*

- $(A, C) \in [I(\Delta)]_j$ *for some $j < i$ or*
- $str(A) = i$ *and there is a variant $\forall \overline{x}(G \Rightarrow A')$ of a clause in $elab(\Delta)$, such that the variables $\overline{x}$ do not occur free in A, and $I, \Delta \Vdash (\exists \overline{x}(A \approx A' \wedge G), C)$.*

The crucial aspect of T_i is: For a database Δ, T_i incorporates information obtained exclusively from the clauses of Δ, whose heads are atoms of the stratum i, and the information of smaller strata remains invariable. Notice that if $str(A) = i$, then $str(\exists \overline{x}(A \approx A' \wedge G)) \leq i$ and T_i is well-defined.

In order to establish the existence of a fixed point of T_i, it will be proved to be monotonous and continuous.

Lemma 4 (Monotonicity of T_i). *Let $i \geq 1$ and $I_1, I_2 \in \mathcal{I}_i$ such that $I_1 \sqsubseteq_i I_2$. Then, $T_i(I_1) \sqsubseteq_i T_i(I_2)$.*

Proof. Let us consider any Δ and $(A, C) \in T_i(I_1)(\Delta)$. This implies that $str(A) \leq i$. If $str(A) = j < i$, then $(A, C) \in [I_1(\Delta)]_j = [I_2(\Delta)]_j$, because $I_1 \sqsubseteq_i I_2$ and $j < i$. Hence $(A, C) \in T_i(I_2)(\Delta)$, by definition of T_i. If $str(A) = i$, then there is a variant $\forall \overline{x}(G \Rightarrow A')$ of a clause of Δ, such that the variables $\overline{x}$ do not occur free in A, and $I_1, \Delta \Vdash (\exists \overline{x}(A \approx A' \wedge G), C)$. Using Lemma 2 and the fact that $I_1 \sqsubseteq_i I_2$, we obtain $I_2, \Delta \Vdash (\exists \overline{x}(A \approx A' \wedge G), C)$, which implies $(A, C) \in T_i(I_2)(\Delta)$, by definition of T_i. $\qquad \Box$

Lemma 5 (Continuity of T_i). *Let $i \geq 1$ and $\{I_n\}_{n \geq 0}$ be a denumerable family of interpretations over i, such that $I_0 \sqsubseteq_i I_1 \sqsubseteq_i I_2 \sqsubseteq_i \ldots$. Then $T_i(\bigsqcup_{n \geq 0} I_n) = \bigsqcup_{n \geq 0} T_i(I_n)$.*

Proof. The inclusion $\supseteq$ is a consequence of the monotonicity of T_i. Let us prove the inclusion $\subseteq$. Consider any Δ and $(A, C) \in T_i(\bigsqcup_{n \geq 0} I_n)(\Delta)$. Then $str(A) \leq i$. If $str(A) = j < i$, $(A, C) \in [T_i(\bigsqcup_{n \geq 0} I_n)(\Delta)]_j = [I_0(\Delta)]_j$, then $(A, C) \in T_i(I_0)(\Delta) \subseteq \bigcup_{n \geq 0} T_i(I_n)(\Delta) = (\bigsqcup_{n \geq 0} T_i(I_n))(\Delta)$. If $str(A) = i$, there is a variant $\forall \overline{x}(G \Rightarrow A')$ of a clause of Δ, such that the variables $\overline{x}$ do not occur free in A, and $\bigsqcup_{n \geq 0} I_n, \Delta \Vdash (\exists \overline{x}(A \approx A' \wedge G), C)$. Thanks to Lemma 3, there exists $k \geq 0$, such that $I_k, \Delta \Vdash (\exists \overline{x}(A \approx A' \wedge G), C)$, and therefore $(A, C) \in T_i(I_k)(\Delta)$. As a consequence, also in this case $T_i(\bigsqcup_{n \geq 0} I_n)(\Delta) \subseteq \bigcup_{n \geq 0} T_i(I_n)(\Delta) = (\bigsqcup_{n \geq 0} T_i(I_n))(\Delta)$. $\qquad \Box$

Proposition 1. *The operator T_1 has a least fixed point, which is $\bigsqcup_{n \geq 0} T_1^n(I_\perp)$, where the interpretation $I_\perp$ represents the constant function $\emptyset$.*

Proof. By the Knaster-Tarski fixed point theorem [19], using Lemma 5. $\qquad \Box$

Let fix_1 denote $\bigsqcup_{n \geq 0} T_1^n(I_\perp)$, i.e., the least fixed point at stratum 1.

Consider now the following sequence $\{T_2^n(fix_1)\}_{n \geq 0}$ of interpretations in $(\mathcal{I}_2, \sqsubseteq_2)$. Using the properties of T_i, it is easy to prove by induction on $n \geq 0$ that this sequence is a chain

$$fix_1 \sqsubseteq_2 T_2(fix_1) \sqsubseteq_2 T_2(T_2(fix_1)) \sqsubseteq_2 \ldots, \sqsubseteq_2 T_2^n(fix_1), \ldots$$

As before, in accordance with Lemmas 1 and 5, $\{T_2^n(fix_1)\}_{n \geq 0}$ has a least upper bound, $\bigsqcup_{n \geq 0} T_2^n(fix_1)$, in $(\mathcal{I}_2, \sqsubseteq_2)$ that is a fixed point of T_2, denoted by fix_2. Proceeding successively on the same way, a chain:

$$fix_{i-1} \sqsubseteq_i T_i(fix_{i-1}) \sqsubseteq_i T_i(T_i(fix_{i-1})) \sqsubseteq_i \ldots, \sqsubseteq_i T_i^n(fix_{i-1}), \ldots$$

can be defined for any stratum $i > 1$, and a fixed point of it

$$fix_i = \bigsqcup_{n \geq 0} T_i^n(fix_{i-1})$$

can be found.

In particular, if $str(\Delta) = k$, we simplify fix_k writing fix. Then, $fix(\Delta)$ represents the pairs (A, C) such that A can be deduced from Δ if C is satisfied. Notice that $fix(\Delta)$ is computed by saturating strata sequentially from $fix_1(\Delta)$ up to $fix_k(\Delta)$, using for every i only the clauses of the stratum i.

4.2   Soundness and Completeness

The fixed point semantics defined in [7] for $HH(\mathcal{C})$ was proved to be sound and complete with respect to the calculus $\mathcal{UC}$. Our interest now is to prove soundness and completeness of the new fixed point semantics for $HH_\neg(\mathcal{C})$, with respect to the extended calculus $\mathcal{UC}_\neg$. This means that the forcing relation, considering the least fixed point at the last stratum of a database and a query, coincides with derivability in $\mathcal{UC}_\neg$. More precisely, if $str(G) = i$, (G, C) is forced by fix_i in the context of Δ if and only if C is an answer constraint of G from Δ.

Without negation, any database Δ and query G have a stratification with only one stratum. If this is the case, soundness and completeness are similar to those results for $HH(\mathcal{C})$.

Proposition 2. *For every $\Delta \in W$, and every pair $(G, C) \in \mathcal{G} \times \mathcal{SL}_\mathcal{C}$, if $str(G) = 1$ then: $fix_1, \Delta \Vdash (G, C) \iff \Delta; C \vdash_{\mathcal{UC}_\neg} G$.*

Proof. The proof is an adaptation of those presented in [7] to the definition of the forcing relation defined now for $HH_\neg(\mathcal{C})$. Notice that, since we are assuming that $str(G) = 1$, then the case $G \equiv \neg A$ has not to be considered. $\square$

Now, we consider the general case.

Theorem 1 (Soundness and Completeness). *For every $i \geq 1$, $\Delta \in W$, and every pair $(G, C) \in \mathcal{G} \times \mathcal{SL}_\mathcal{C}$, if $str(G) \leq i$ then:*

$$fix_i, \Delta \Vdash (G, C) \iff \Delta; C \vdash_{\mathcal{UC}_\neg} G.$$

Proof. By induction on i. Proposition 2 is the proof of the case $i = 1$.

For $i > 1$, assume the induction hypothesis: for every Δ, G, C, with $str(G) \leq i - 1$: $fix_{i-1}, \Delta \Vdash (G, C) \iff \Delta; C \vdash_{\mathcal{UC}_\neg} G$.

The proof is analogous to the base case, except for $\neg A$. Let us analyze this case: $fix_i, \Delta \Vdash (\neg A, C) \iff$ for every C' such that $(A, C') \in fix_i(\Delta)$, it holds $C \vdash_\mathcal{C} \neg C'$, or there is no such C' and $C \equiv \top$. Obviously, $str(\neg A) \leq i - 1$, then the previous sentence is equivalent to say that for every C' such that $fix_{i-i}, \Delta \Vdash (A, C')$, it holds $C \vdash_\mathcal{C} \neg C'$, or there is no such C' and $C \equiv \top$. Applying the induction hypothesis, it is equivalent to say that either for every C' such that $\Delta; C' \vdash_{\mathcal{UC}_\neg} A$ and $C \vdash_\mathcal{C} \neg C'$ holds, or there is not such C' and $C \equiv \top$. This is equivalent to $\Delta; C \vdash_{\mathcal{UC}_\neg} \neg A$.

As a consequence of this theorem: $(A, C) \in fix(\Delta) \iff \Delta; C \vdash_{\mathcal{UC}_\neg} A$. This means that the atoms in the fixed point of a database are those that can be derived by the calculus.

The advantage of this fixed point semantics over the proof theoretic one is that it can be considered as the formal basis of particular implementations of database systems based on $HH_\neg(\mathcal{C})$. The prototype presented in the next section is a proof of it. Notice that the previous formalisms are defined for a generic constraint system $\mathcal{C}$ as a black box for which the existence a solver that checks $\mathcal{C}$-satisfiability has been assumed. The complexity of an implementation will depend on the particular instance domain and solver.

5   Implementing an Instance

In this section, we briefly report a Prolog-implemented prototype of $HH_\neg(\mathcal{D})$, where $\mathcal{D}$ is a basic finite domain constraint system with equality and disequality. It has as input a database Δ and, if stratifiable, computes the set $fix(\Delta)$. Δ contains not only the extensional and intensional databases, but also the translation of the user query G into a clause $\texttt{goal}(\overline{X})$:- G, where $\overline{X}$ are the free variables of G. So, if the computed $fix(\Delta)$ contains for instance the pair $(\texttt{goal}(X_1,\dots,X_n),\ X_1 \approx t_1 \wedge \dots \wedge X_n \approx t_n)$, then $X_1 \approx t_1 \wedge \dots \wedge X_n \approx t_n$ is an answer to G.

Computing the outcome corresponding to a set Δ follows some stages: 1) Build the dependency graph, 2) Compute a stratification (if there is any), and, if succeeds, 3) Compute $fix(\Delta)$ as a set of pairs (A, C) for the stratification. For the first stage, the algorithm in [14] has been used. For the second one, the dependency graph is used as an input to an algorithm following Definition 4.

A more elaborated computation is needed for the third stage: $fix(\Delta)$ is computed sequentially, from $fix_1(\Delta)$ up to $fix_k(\Delta)$, where $k = str(\Delta)$. When computing the information of stratum i, only pairs (A, C) such that $str(A) = i$ are calculated, and the information of smaller strata remains invariable. Following Definition 8, the successive iterations of the fixpoint operator T_i deliver new pairs which are obtained by considering the pairs deduced in previous iterations in the context of Δ and every ground instance of the clauses defining predicates of stratum i. As T_i is monotonous (Lemma 4) and we deal with a finite domain constraint system, a terminating loop finds all the pairs for a given $fix_i(\Delta)$. The set $fix_i(\Delta)$ is completely evaluated when no pair (A, C) is added after an iteration of T_i. Therefore, the stratum i is *saturated* and the computation of $fix_{i+1}(\Delta)$ begins, applying T_{i+1} to the just calculated $fix_i(\Delta)$.

The forcing relation is implemented by means of the Prolog predicate $\texttt{force}$ that makes calls to the constraint solver, which solves constraints for the particular finite domain system.

However, care has to be taken when programming $\texttt{force}$ for the case $D \Rightarrow G$. Following Definition 7, G has to be proved in the context of the database augmented with the clause D. This turns out to be more complex to be computed, since the head of the clause added to the current context may belong to stratum j, where $j < i$ and, therefore, $fix_j(\Delta \cup \{D\})$ must be calculated, which we call a subcomputation level (level in short) involving the local clause D. Once G is solved, both D and the deduced pairs are ignored for the rest of the computation.

The pairs proved at each iteration of the fixpoint operator as well as the database clauses are stored as Prolog facts. As there may be facts and clauses belonging to different levels, we identify them with a number for the corresponding level. The main level is identified as 0. For example, when using a clause as $\texttt{p(a):-q(a,b)}$ $\texttt{=> r(b)}$ at level l, the goal $\texttt{q(a,b) => r(b)}$ must be forced, for which the local clause $\texttt{q(a,b)}$ is added at level $l + 1$. Now, the goal $\texttt{r(b)}$ will be tried to be forced at level $l + 1$. When this is done, $\texttt{q(a,b)}$ is removed from the database and the computation returns to level l, where a pair corresponding to $\texttt{p(a)}$ will be added to the current fixed point if $\texttt{r(b)}$ was forced in that augmented context.

As an executable example, let us consider again Example 1, where real constraints have been removed. The query: "Assuming a flight from Paris to London, what cities are reachable from Madrid?" can be represented as $G \equiv$ `flight(par,lon) => trip(mad,X)`. The clause `goal(X):- G` is added to the database for solving G. Executing this example delivers the following meaning:

$$[\ldots, (\text{goal(X)}, X \approx \text{par}), (\text{goal(X)}, X \approx \text{ny}), (\text{goal(X)}, X \approx \text{lon}), \ldots]$$

Therefore, we can conclude that it is possible to travel to Paris, New York and London assuming that flight.

6   Conclusions

We have studied the application of the constraint logic programming scheme $HH(\mathcal{C})$ as a *CDDB* system. With this purpose, this scheme has been extended with a suitable formulation of negation. The result provides a database language more expressive than former ones [15,18,17,5], because $HH_\neg(\mathcal{C})$ owns constraints as well as implication and quantifiers altogether.

Two semantics, based on proof theory and fixed point techniques, have been defined to formalize the system, and proved to be equivalent for stratifiable databases. Both semantics are interesting *per se*. The former allows to represent the meaning of a database query by means of a derived constraint answer. In addition, the uniformity of the sequent calculus that governs $HH_\neg(\mathcal{C})$ is preserved, because only a rule introducing the connective $\neg$ on the right (but not on the left) of the sequent is added. Then, proofs remain guided by the structure of the goal. However, it can not be considered as a practical operational semantics. Some aspects, as finiteness of the set of answers for an atom A when $\neg A$ is computed, are obviated.

The fixed point semantics relies on stratified negation and constitutes a formal basis for practical implementations. Stratification has been defined as a syntactical criterion to determine if a query database can be potentially be computed in a finite number of steps. When $\neg A$ are going to be proved, the stratum of A has been previously saturated and $\neg A$ can be correctly computed.

The prototype introduced at the end of this paper is based in the formal mechanisms that support this semantic approach for a concrete constraint system. In addition, this semantics supplies a framework in which properties of databases can be analyzed. For instance, if Δ_1, Δ_2 are two stratifiable databases (considering the same stratification for simplicity), it can be said that Δ_1 and Δ_2 are equivalent if $fix(\Delta_1) = fix(\Delta_2)$.

Regarding future work: First, investigate the relaxation of the strong requirement about program stratification, as done in answer set programming [6], also extended to include constraints [4,12]. Second, analyze the requirements that should be imposed to $\mathcal{C}$ in order to obtain a safe instance of $HH_\neg(\mathcal{C})$, as done via safety levels in constraint database languages [17]. Finally, develop the current prototype implementation to deal with other particular instances based on useful constraint systems handling combined constraint domains [8].

References

1. Abiteboul, S., Hull, R., Vianu, V.: Foundations of Databases. Addison-Wesley, Reading (1995)
2. Apt, K., Bol, R.: Logic Programming and Negation: A Survey. Journal of Logic Programming 19&20, 9–71 (1994)
3. Benedikt, M., Libkin, L.: Safe constraint queries. In: PODS 1998: Proceedings of the Seventeenth ACM SIGACT-SIGMOD-SIGART Symposium on Principles of Database Systems, pp. 99–108. ACM Press, New York (1998)
4. Bonatti, S.B.P.A., Gelfond, M.: Towards an integration of answer set and constraint solving. In: Gabbrielli, M., Gupta, G. (eds.) ICLP 2005. LNCS, vol. 3668, pp. 52–66. Springer, Heidelberg (2005)
5. Bonner, A.J., McCarty, L.T., Vadaparty, K.: Expressing Database Queries with Intuitionistic Logic. In: Lusk, E.L., Overbeek, R.A. (eds.) Proceedings of the North American Conference on Logic Programming, pp. 831–850 (1989)
6. Ferraris, P., Lifschitz, V.: Mathematical foundations of answer set programming. In: Artëmov, S.N., Barringer, H., d'Avila Garcez, A.S., Lamb, L.C., Woods, J. (eds.) We Will Show Them (1), pp. 615–664. College Publications (2005)
7. García-Díaz, M., Nieva, S.: Providing Declarative Semantics for HH Extended Constraint Logic Programs. In: Proceedings of the 6th ACM SIGPLAN Int. Conf. on PPDP, pp. 55–66 (2004)
8. Hofstedt, P., Pepper, P.: Integration of declarative and constraint programming. Theory Pract. Log. Program. 7(1-2), 93–121 (2007)
9. Jaffar, J., Lassez, J.-L.: Constraint Logic Programming. In: 14th ACM Symp. on Principles of Programming Languages (POPL 1987), Munich, Germany, January 1987, pp. 111–119. ACM Press, New York (1987)
10. Leach, J., Nieva, S., Rodríguez-Artalejo, M.: Constraint Logic Programming with Hereditary Harrop Formulas. TPLP 1(4), 409–445 (2001)
11. Lipton, J., Nieva, S.: Higher-order logic programming languages with constraints: A semantics. In: Della Rocca, S.R. (ed.) TLCA 2007. LNCS, vol. 4583, pp. 272–289. Springer, Heidelberg (2007)
12. Mellarkod, V.S.: Integrating ASP and CLP Systems: Computing Answer Sets from Partially Ground Programs. PhD thesis, Texas Tech University (2007)
13. Miller, D., Nadathur, G., Pfenning, F., Scedrov, A.: Uniform Proofs as a Foundation for Logic Programming. Annals of Pure and Applied Logic 51, 125–157 (1991)
14. Nieva, S., Sáenz-Pérez, F., Sánchez, J.: Towards a constraint deductive database language based on hereditary harrop formulas. In: Lucio, P., Orejas, F. (eds.) Sextas Jornadas de Programación y Lenguajes, PROLE, pp. 171–182 (2006)
15. Pustejovsky, J., Revesz, P.Z. (eds.): Proc. 13th International Symposium on Temporal Representation and Reasoning. IEEE Computer Society Press, Los Alamitos (2006)
16. Revesz, P.Z.: Datalog and Constraints. In: Kuper, G., Libkin, L., Paredaens, J. (eds.) Constraint Databases, ch. 7, pp. 151–174. Springer, Heidelberg (2000)
17. Revesz, P.Z.: Introduction to Constraint Databases. Springer, Heidelberg (2002)
18. Scholl, P.R.M., Voisard, A.: Spatial databases with application to GIS. Morgan Kaufmann Publishers Inc., San Francisco (2002)
19. Tarski, A.: A lattice-theoretical fixpoint theorem and its applications. Pacific Journal of Mathematics 5, 285–309 (1955)
20. Zaniolo, C., Ceri, S., Faloutsos, C., Snodgrass, R.T., Subrahmanian, V.S., Zicari, R.: Advanced Database Systems. Morgan Kaufmann Publishers Inc., San Francisco (1997)

Declarative Diagnosis of Missing Answers in Constraint Functional-Logic Programming

Rafael Caballero, Mario Rodríguez Artalejo,
and Rafael del Vado Vírseda*

Dpto. de Sistemas Informáticos y Computación
Universidad Complutense de Madrid
{rafa,mario,rdelvado}@sip.ucm.es

Abstract. We present a declarative method for diagnosing *missing computed answers* in $CFLP(\mathcal{D})$, a generic scheme for lazy *Constraint Functional-Logic Programming* which can be instantiated by any constraint domain $\mathcal{D}$ given as parameter. As far as we know, declarative diagnosis of missing answers in such an expressive framework has not been tackled before. Our approach combines and extends previous work done separately for constraint logic programming and lazy functional programming languages. Diagnosis can be started whenever a user finds that the set of computed answers for a given goal with finite search space misses some expected solution w.r.t. an *intended interpretation* of the program, that provides a declarative description of its expected behavior. Diagnosis proceeds by exploring a *proof tree*, that provides a declarative view of the *answer-collection* process performed by the computation, and it ends up with the detection of some function definition in the program that is incomplete w.r.t. the intended interpretation. We can prove the *logical correctness* of the diagnosis method under the assumption that the recollection of computed answers performed by the goal solving system can be represented as a proof tree. We argue the plausibility of this assumption, and we describe the prototype of a tool which implements the diagnosis method.

1 Introduction

Debuggers are a practical need for helping programmers to understand why their programs do not work as intended. Declarative programming paradigms involving complex operational details, such as constraint solving and lazy evaluation, do not fit well to traditional debugging techniques relying on the inspection of low-level computation traces. For this reason, the design of usable debugging tools becomes a difficult task. As a solution to this problem, and following a seminal idea by Shapiro [28], *declarative diagnosis* (a.k.a. *declarative debugging* or *algorithmic debugging*) proposes to use *Computation Trees* (shortly, *CT*s) in

---

* The authors have been partially supported by the Spanish National Projects MERIT-FORMS (TIN2005-09027-C03-03) and PROMESAS-CAM (S-0505/TIC/0407).

J. Garrigue and M. Hermenegildo (Eds.): FLOPS 2008, LNCS 4989, pp. 305–321, 2008.

place of traces. CTs are built *a posteriori* to represent the structure of a computation whose top-level outcome is regarded as a symptom of the unexpected behavior by the user, with results attached to their nodes representing the computation of some observable result, and such that the result at any internal node follows from the results at the children nodes, using a program fragment also attached to the node. Declarative diagnosis explores a CT looking for a so-called *buggy node* which computes an unexpected result from children whose results are all expected. Each buggy node points to a program fragment responsible for the unexpected behavior. The search for a buggy node can be implemented with the help of an external *oracle* (usually the user with some semiautomatic support) who has a reliable declarative knowledge of the expected program semantics, the so-called *intended interpretation*.

The generic description of declarative diagnosis in the previous paragraph follows [22]. Declarative diagnosis was first proposed in the field of *Logic Programming (LP)* [28,14,18], and it has been successfully extended to other declarative programming paradigms, including (lazy) *Functional Programming (FP)* [25,24,27,26], *Constraint Logic Programming (CLP)* [1,30,15] and *Functional Logic Programming (FLP)* [23,6,7]. The nature of unexpected results differs according to the programming paradigm. Unexpected results in FP are mainly *incorrect values*, while in CLP and FLP an unexpected result can be either a single computed answer regarded as *incorrect*, or a set of computed answers (for one and the same goal with a finite search space) regarded as *incomplete*. These two possibilities give rise to the declarative diagnosis of *wrong* and *missing* computed answers, respectively. The case of unexpected *finite failure* of a goal is a particular symptom of missing answers with special relevance. However, diagnosis methods must consider the more general case, since finite failure of a goal is often caused by non-failing subgoals that do not compute all the expected answers.

In contrast to alternative approaches to error diagnosis based on *abstract interpretation* techniques [17], declarative diagnosis often involves complex queries to the user. This problem has been tackled by means of various techniques, such as user-given partial specifications of the program's semantics [1,7], safe inference of information from answers previously given by the user [6], or CTs tailored to the needs of a particular debugging problem over a particular computation domain [15]. Another practical problem with declarative diagnosis is that the size of CTs can cause excessive overhead in the case of computations that demand a big amount of computer storage. As a remedy, techniques for piecemeal construction of CTs have been considered; see [26] for a recent proposal in the FP field.

In spite of the above mentioned difficulties, we are confident that declarative diagnosis methods can be useful for detecting programming bugs by observing computations whose demand of computer storage is modest. In this paper, we present a declarative method for diagnosing *missing computed answers* in $CFLP(\mathcal{D})$ [20], a generic scheme for lazy *Constraint Functional-Logic Programming* which can be instantiated by any constraint domain $\mathcal{D}$ given as parameter, and supports a powerful combination of functional and constraint logic programming over $\mathcal{D}$. Sound and complete goal solving procedures for the $CFLP(\mathcal{D})$

scheme have been obtained [19,11,12]. Moreover, useful instances of this scheme have been implemented in the $\mathcal{TOY}$ system [21] and tested in practical applications [13].

The rest of the paper is organized as follows: Section 2 motivates our approach and presents a debugging example, intended to illustrate the main features of our diagnosis method. Section 3 presents the abbreviated proof trees used as CTs in our method, as well as the results ensuring the logical correctness of the diagnosis. Section 4 presents a prototype debugger under development, and Section 5 concludes and gives an overview of planned future work. Full proofs of the main results given in Section 3 are available in [10].

2 Motivation

While methods and tools for the declarative diagnosis of *wrong answers* are known for FLP [23,6,7] and $CFLP$ [4,8] languages, we are not aware of any research concerning the declarative diagnosis of *missing answers* in $CFLP$ languages, except our poster presentation [9]. However, missing answers are a common problem which can arise even in the absence of wrong answers.

We are interested in the declarative diagnosis of missing answers in $CFLP(\mathcal{D})$ [20], a very expressive generic scheme for Functional and Constraint Logic Programming over a constraint domain $\mathcal{D}$ given as parameter. Each constraint domain provides basic values and primitive operations for building domain specific constraints to be used in programs and goals. Useful constraint domains include the Herbrand domain $\mathcal{H}$ for equality (==) and disequality (/=) constraints over constructed data values; the domain $\mathcal{R}$ for arithmetic constraints over real numbers; and the domain $\mathcal{FD}$ for finite domain constraints over integer values.

The $CFLP(\mathcal{D})$ scheme supports programming with lazy functions that may be non-deterministic and/or higher-order. *Programs* $\mathcal{P}$ include *program rules* of the form $f\, t_1 \ldots t_n \to r \Leftarrow \Delta$, abbreviated as $f\, \bar{t}_n \to r \Leftarrow \Delta$, with Δ omitted if empty. Such a rule specifies that f when acting over parameters matching the patterns $\bar{t}_n$ at the left hand side, will return the values resulting from the right hand side expression r, provided that the constraints in Δ can be satisfied. *Goals* G for a given program have the general form $\exists \overline{U}.\,(R \,\square\, S)$, where $\exists \overline{U}$ is an existentially quantified prefix of local variables, $R = (P \,\square\, \Delta)$ is the yet *unsolved part*, including *productions* $e \to s$ in P and *constraints* in Δ, and $S = (\Pi \,\square\, \sigma)$ is the *constraint store*, consisting of *primitive constraints* Π and an *idempotent substitution* σ. Productions $e \to s$ are solved by *lazy narrowing*, a combination of unification and lazy evaluation; the expression e must be narrowed to match the pattern s. *Initial goals* have neither productions nor local variables, and *solved goals* have the form $\exists \overline{U}.\,S$. Solved goals are also called *computed answers* and abbreviated as $\hat{S}$.

In this paper we focus mainly in $CFLP(\mathcal{D})$ programming as implemented in $\mathcal{TOY}$ [21]. The interested reader is referred to [20,19,11] for formal details on the declarative and operational semantics of the $CFLP(\mathcal{D})$ scheme.

The following small $CFLP(\mathcal{H})$-program $\mathcal{P}_{fD}$, written in $\mathcal{TOY}$ syntax, includes program rules for the non-deterministic functions (//) and fDiff, and the deterministic functions gen and even. Note the infix syntax used for (//), as well as the use of the equality symbol = in place of the rewrite arrow --> for the program rules of those functions viewed as deterministic by the user. This is just meant as user given information, not checked by the $\mathcal{TOY}$ system, which treats all the program defined functions as possibly non-deterministic.

```
infixr 40 //                    % non-deterministic choice operator

(//) :: A -> A -> A
X // _ --> X
_ // Y --> Y

fDiff :: [A] -> A
fDiff [X]          --> X
fDiff (X:Y:Zs) --> X // fDiff (Y:Zs) <== X /= Y
fDiff (X:Y:Zs) --> X                 <== X == Y

gen :: A -> A -> [A]         even :: int -> bool
gen X Y = X : Y : gen Y X    even N = true <== (mod N 2) == 0
```

Function fDiff is intended to return any element belonging to the longest prefix Xs of the list given as parameter such that Xs does not include two identical elements in consecutive positions. In general, there will be several such elements, and therefore fDiff is non-deterministic. Function gen is deterministic and returns a potentially infinite list of the form $[d_1, d_2, d_2, d_1, d_1, d_2, ...]$, where the elements d_1 and d_2 are the given parameters. Therefore, the lazy evaluation of (fDiff (gen 1 2)) is expected to yield the two possible results 1 and 2 in alternative computations, and the initial goal G_{fD} : even (fDiff (gen 1 2)) == true for $\mathcal{P}_{fD}$ is expected to succeed, since (fDiff (gen 1 2)) is expected to return the even number 2. However, if the third program rule for function fDiff were missing in program $\mathcal{P}_{fD}$, the expression (fDiff (gen 1 2)) would return only the numeric value 1, and therefore the goal G_{fD} would fail unexpectedly. At this point, a diagnosis for missing answers could take place, looking for a *buggy node* in a suitable CT in order to detect some incomplete function definition (that of function fDiff, in this case) to be blamed for the missing answers.

We propose to use CTs whose nodes have attached so-called *answer collection assertions*, briefly *acas*. The *aca* at the root node has the form $G_0 \Rightarrow \bigvee_{i \in I} \hat{S}_i$, where G_0 is the initial goal and $\bigvee_{i \in I} \hat{S}_i$ (written as the *failure symbol* $\blacklozenge$ if $I = \emptyset$) is the disjunction of computed answers observed by the user. This root *aca* asserts that the computed answers cover all the solutions of the initial goal, and will be regarded as a false statement in case that the user misses computed answers. For example, the root *aca* corresponding to the initial goal G_{fD} for program $\mathcal{P}_{fD}$ is even (fDiff (gen 1 2)) == true $\Rightarrow \blacklozenge$ stating that this goal has (unexpectedly) failed. The *acas* at internal nodes in our CTs have the form $f\bar{t}_n \rightarrow t \square S \Rightarrow \bigvee_{i \in I} \hat{S}_i$, asserting that the disjunction of computed answers

$\bigvee_{i \in I} \hat{S}_i$ covers all the solutions for the intermediate goal $G' : f\bar{t}_n \rightarrow t \square S$. Note that G' asks for the solutions of the production $f\bar{t}_n \rightarrow t$ which satisfy the constraint store S. The *acas* of this form correspond to the intermediate calls to program defined functions f needed for collecting all the answers computed for the initial goal G_0. Due to *lazy evaluation*, the parameters $\bar{t}_n$ and the result t will appear in the most evaluated form demanded by the topmost computation. When these values are functions, they are represented in terms of partial applications of top-level function names. This is satisfactory under the assumption that no local function definitions are allowed in programs, as it happens in $\mathcal{TOY}$.

We build our *CT*s as abbreviated *proof trees* w.r.t. a logically sound inference system for deriving *acas*. For this reason, our *CT*s are such that the validity of the *aca* at each node follows from the validity of the *acas* at their children, under the assumption that the function definition relating the parent node to the children nodes is complete w.r.t. the *intended interpretation* of the program. Any *CT* whose root *aca* is invalid must include at least one *buggy node* labeled with an invalid *aca* and whose children are all labeled with valid *acas*. Each buggy node N is related to some particular function f whose program rules are responsible for the computation of the *aca* at N from the *acas* at N's children. Therefore, the program rules for f can be diagnosed as incomplete. The search for a buggy node can be implemented with the help of an external *oracle* who has a reliable declarative knowledge of the valid *acas* w.r.t. the intended program interpretation. Since the oracle is usually the programmer, she can even experiment with different choices of the intended interpretation in order to obtain different diagnosis of possibly incomplete functions.

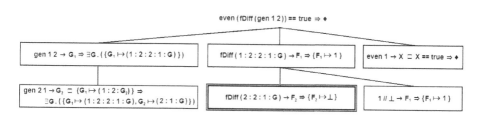

Fig. 1. *CT* for the declarative diagnosis of missing answers

A *CT* corresponding to the goal G_{fD} for program $\mathcal{P}_{fD}$ (with the third program rule for function fDiff omitted) is displayed in Fig. 1. More on its structure and construction will be explained in Section 3. In this case, the programmer will judge the root *aca* as *invalid* because she did not expect finite failure. Moreover, from her knowledge of the intended interpretation, she will decide to consider the *acas* for the functions gen, even and (//) as valid. However, the *aca* fDiff (2:2:1:G) $\rightarrow F_2 \Rightarrow (F_2 \mapsto \perp)$ asserts that the *undefined value* $\perp$ is the only possible result for the function call fDiff (2:2:1:G), while the user expects also the result 2. Therefore, the user will judge this *aca* as invalid. The node where it sits (enclosed within a double box in Fig. 1) has no children and thus becomes buggy, leading to the diagnosis of `fDiff` as incomplete. This particular incompleteness symptom could be mended by placing the third rule for `fDiff` within the program.

3   Declarative Diagnosis of Missing Answers

As explained in the previous sections, the declarative diagnosis method proposed in this paper relies on building CTs as *abbreviated proof trees* w.r.t. a logically sound inference system for deriving *acas*. In this section, we present such an inference system, whose *negative proof trees* represent the deduction of *acas* from the *negative theory* $\mathcal{P}^-$ associated to a given $CFLP(\mathcal{D})$-program $\mathcal{P}$. We also present results ensuring the *logical correctness* of the declarative diagnosis method whose CTs are abbreviated representations of negative proof trees.

3.1   Standardized Programs and Negative Theories

Let $\mathcal{P}$ be a $CFLP(\mathcal{D})$-program. Its associated *Negative Theory* $\mathcal{P}^-$ is obtained in two steps. First, each program rule $f\ \bar{t}_n \to r \Leftarrow \Delta$ is replaced by a *standardized* form $f\ \overline{X}_n \to Y \Leftarrow \hat{R}$, where $\overline{X}_n, Y$ are new variables, $\hat{R} = \exists \overline{U}. R$ with $\overline{U} = var(R) \setminus \{\overline{X}_n, Y\}$, and the condition R is $X_1 \to t_1, \ldots, X_n \to t_n, \Delta, r \to Y$. Next, $\mathcal{P}^-$ is built by taking one *axiom* $(f)_{\overline{\mathcal{P}}}$ of the form $\forall \overline{X}_n, Y.\ (f\ \overline{X}_n \to Y \Rightarrow (\bigvee_{i \in I} \hat{R}_i) \vee (\bot \to Y))$ for each function symbol f whose standardized program rules are $\{f\ \overline{X}_n \to Y \Leftarrow \hat{R}_i\}_{i \in I}$. By convention, we may use the notation D_f for the disjunction $(\bigvee_{i \in I} \hat{R}_i) \vee (\bot \to Y)$, and we may leave the universal quantification of the variables $\overline{X}_n, Y$ implicit. Intuitively, the axiom $(f)_{\overline{\mathcal{P}}}$ says that any result computed for f must be obtained by means of some of the rules for f in the program. The last alternative $(\bot \to Y)$ within D_f says that Y is bound to the undefined result $\bot$ in case that no program rule for f succeeds to compute a more defined result. For example, let $\mathcal{P}_{fD}$ be the $CFLP(\mathcal{H})$-program given in Section 2, with the third program rule for `fDiff` omitted. Then $\mathcal{P}_{fD}^-$ includes (among others) the following axiom for the function symbol *fDiff*:

$$(\textit{fDiff})_{\overline{\mathcal{P}}_{fD}} : \forall L, F.\ (\textit{fDiff } L \to F \Rightarrow$$
$$\exists X.\ (L \to [X] \wedge X \to F) \vee$$
$$\exists X, Y, Zs.\ (L \to (X : Y : Zs) \wedge X \ /= \ Y \wedge X \ // \ \textit{fDiff}\,(Y : Zs) \to F) \vee$$
$$(\bot \to F))$$

Interpretations $\mathcal{I}$ are formally defined in [20]. Each interpretation represents a certain behavior of the program defined functions. We write $\mathcal{I} \Vdash_{\mathcal{D}} f\bar{t}_n \to t$ to indicate that the statement $f\bar{t}_n \to t$ is *valid* in $\mathcal{I}$. Here, f is a program defined function, $\bar{t}_n$ stand for possibly partially evaluated arguments, and t stands for a possibly partially evaluated result. Knowing the valid assertions $\mathcal{I} \Vdash_{\mathcal{D}} f\bar{t}_n \to t$ suffices for defining the *solution set* $Sol_{\mathcal{I}}(G)$ whose elements are all the *valuations* (i.e., substitutions of domain values for variables) that satisfy the goal G w.r.t. $\mathcal{I}$. We will use similar notations for other solution sets in the rest of the paper, writing $Sol_{\mathcal{D}}$ instead of $Sol_{\mathcal{I}}$ whenever the solutions do not depend on the interpretation $\mathcal{I}$ of program defined functions. The following definition helps to understand the semantics of missing answers:

Definition 1 (Interpretation-Dependent Semantics). *Let $\mathcal{P}$ a CFLP($\mathcal{D}$)-program and $\mathcal{I}$ an interpretation over $\mathcal{D}$.*

1. *$\mathcal{I}$ is a* **model** *of $\mathcal{P}^-$ iff every axiom $(f)_{\mathcal{P}}^- : (f\ \overline{X}_n \rightarrow Y \Rightarrow D_f) \in \mathcal{P}^-$ satisfies $Sol_{\mathcal{I}}(f\ \overline{X}_n \rightarrow Y) \subseteq Sol_{\mathcal{I}}(D_f)$. When this inclusion holds, we say that $(f)_{\mathcal{P}}^-$ is* **valid** *in $\mathcal{I}$, or also that f's definition as given in $\mathcal{P}$ is* **complete** *w.r.t. $\mathcal{I}$.*

2. *The aca $G \Rightarrow \bigvee_{i \in I} \hat{S}_i$ is a* **logical consequence** *of $\mathcal{P}^-$ iff $Sol_{\mathcal{I}}(G) \subseteq \bigcup_{i \in I} Sol_{\mathcal{D}}(\hat{S}_i)$ for any model $\mathcal{I}$ of $\mathcal{P}^-$. When this happens, we also say that the disjunction of answers $\bigvee_{i \in I} \hat{S}_i$ is* **complete** *for G w.r.t. $\mathcal{P}$.*

3.2 Negative Proof Trees for Answer Collection Assertions

The declarative debugging of missing answers presupposes an *intended interpretation* of the program, starts with the observation of an *incompleteness symptom* and ends with an *incompleteness diagnosis*. A more precise definition of this *debugging scenario* is as follows:

Definition 2 (Debugging Scenario). *For any given CFLP($\mathcal{D}$)-program $\mathcal{P}$:*

1. *The* **intended interpretation** *is some interpretation $\mathcal{I}_{\mathcal{P}}$ over $\mathcal{D}$ which represents the behavior of the functions defined in $\mathcal{P}$ as expected by the programmer.*

2. *An* **incompleteness symptom** *occurs if the goal solving system computes finitely many solved goals $\{\hat{S}_i\}_{i \in I}$ as answers for an admissible initial goal G, and the programmer judges that $Sol_{\mathcal{I}_{\mathcal{P}}}(G) \not\subseteq \bigcup_{i \in I} Sol_{\mathcal{D}}(\hat{S}_i)$, meaning that the aca $G \Rightarrow \bigvee_{i \in I} \hat{S}_i$ is not valid in the intended interpretation $\mathcal{I}_{\mathcal{P}}$, so that some expected answers are missing.*

3. *An* **incompleteness diagnosis** *is given by pointing to some defined function symbol f such that the axiom $(f)_{\mathcal{P}}^-$ for f in $\mathcal{P}^-$ is not valid in $\mathcal{I}_{\mathcal{P}}$, which means $Sol_{\mathcal{I}_{\mathcal{P}}}(f\ \overline{X}_n \rightarrow Y) \not\subseteq Sol_{\mathcal{I}_{\mathcal{P}}}(D_f)$, showing that f's definition as given in $\mathcal{P}$ is incomplete w.r.t. $\mathcal{I}_{\mathcal{P}}$.*

Some concrete debugging scenarios have been discussed in Section 2 and [9]. Assume now that an incompleteness symptom has been observed by the programmer. Since the goal solving system has computed the disjunction of answers $D = \bigvee_{i \in I} \hat{S}_i$, the *aca* $G \Rightarrow D$ asserting that the computed answers cover all the solutions of G should be derivable from $\mathcal{P}^-$. The <u>C</u>onstraint <u>N</u>egative <u>P</u>roof <u>C</u>alculus $CNPC(\mathcal{D})$ consisting of the inference rules displayed in Fig. 2 has been designed with the aim of enabling logical proofs $\mathcal{P}^- \vdash_{CNPC(\mathcal{D})} G \Rightarrow D$ of *acas*. We use a special operator $\&$ in order to express the result of attaching to a given goal G a solved goal $\hat{S}'$ resulting from a previous computation, so that computation can continue from the new goal $G\ \&\ \hat{S}'$.

SF Solved Form $\dfrac{}{R \,\square\, S \Rightarrow D}$ if $Sol_\mathcal{D}(S) \subseteq Sol_\mathcal{D}(D)$.

CJ Conjunction

$$\frac{R_1 \,\square\, S \Rightarrow \bigvee_{i \in I} \exists \overline{Z}_i.\, S_i \quad \ldots (\hat{R}_2 \,\&\, \hat{S}_i) \Rightarrow \bigvee_{j \in J_i} \exists \overline{Z}_{ij}.\, S_{ij} \ldots (i \in I)}{(R_1 \wedge R_2) \,\square\, S \Rightarrow \bigvee_{i \in I} \bigvee_{j \in J_i} \exists \overline{Z}_i, \overline{Z}_{ij}.\, S_{ij}}$$

if $\overline{Z}_i \notin var((R_1 \wedge R_2) \,\square\, S)$, $\overline{Z}_{ij} \notin var((R_1 \wedge R_2) \,\square\, S) \cup \overline{Z}_i$, for all $i \in I, j \in J_i$.

TS Trivial Statement $\dfrac{}{\varphi : G \Rightarrow D}$

if φ is a trivial *aca* s.t. $Sol(G) \subseteq Sol_\mathcal{D}(D)$.

DC DeComposition $\dfrac{\overline{e_m \to t_m} \,\square\, S \Rightarrow D}{h\overline{e}_m \to h\overline{t}_m \,\square\, S \Rightarrow D}$ if $h\overline{e}_m$ is not a pattern.

IM IMitation $\dfrac{\overline{e_m \to X_m} \,\square\, (S \wedge h\overline{X}_m \to X) \Rightarrow \bigvee_{i \in I} \exists \overline{Z}_i.\, S_i}{h\overline{e}_m \to X \,\square\, S \Rightarrow \bigvee_{i \in I} \exists \overline{X}_m, \overline{Z}_i.\, S_i}$

if $h\overline{e}_m$ is not a pattern, $X \in \mathcal{V}$, and $\overline{X}_m \notin var(h\overline{e}_m \to X \,\square\, S)$.

(AR)$_p$ Argument Reduction for Primitive Functions

$$\frac{\overline{e_n \to X_n} \,\square\, (S \wedge p\overline{X}_n \to^! t) \Rightarrow \bigvee_{i \in I} \exists \overline{Z}_i.\, S_i}{p\overline{e}_n \to^? t \,\square\, S \Rightarrow (S \wedge \bot \to t) \vee (\bigvee_{i \in I} \exists \overline{X}_n, \exists \overline{Z}_i.\, S_i)}$$

if $p \in PF^n$, $\overline{X}_n \notin var(p\overline{e}_n \to^? t \,\square\, S)$, and $\to^? \equiv \to$ (*production*) $\cup \to!$ (*constraint*).
For instance, *equality constraints* $e_1 == e_2$ (resp., *disequality constraints* $e_1 \mathrel{/=} e_2$).
are abbreviations of $e_1 == e_2 \to!$ *true* (resp., $e_1 == e_2 \to!$ *false*).

(AR)$_f$ Argument Reduction for Defined Functions

$$\frac{(\overline{e_n \to X_n} \wedge f\overline{X}_n \to t) \,\square\, S \Rightarrow \bigvee_{i \in I} \exists \overline{Z}_i.\, S_i}{f\overline{e}_n \to t \,\square\, S \Rightarrow \bigvee_{i \in I} \exists \overline{X}_n, \overline{Z}_i.\, S_i}$$

if $f \in DF^n$, and $\overline{X}_n \notin var(f\overline{e}_n \to t \,\square\, S)$.

$$\frac{(\overline{e_n \to X_n} \wedge f\overline{X}_n \to Y \wedge Y\overline{a}_k \to t) \,\square\, S \Rightarrow \bigvee_{i \in I} \exists \overline{Z}_i.\, S_i}{f\overline{e}_n\overline{a}_k \to t \,\square\, S \Rightarrow \bigvee_{i \in I} \exists \overline{X}_n, Y, \overline{Z}_i.\, S_i}$$

if $f \in DF^n$ ($k > 0$), and $\overline{X}_n, Y \notin var(f\overline{e}_n\overline{a}_k \to t \,\square\, S)$.

(DF)$_f$ Defined Function $\dfrac{\ldots R_i[\overline{X}_n \mapsto \overline{t}_n, Y \mapsto t] \,\square\, S \Rightarrow D_i \ldots (i \in I)}{\boxed{f\overline{t}_n \to t \,\square\, S \Rightarrow (S \wedge \bot \to t) \vee (\bigvee_{i \in I} D_i)}}$

if $f \in DF^n$, $\overline{X}_n, Y \notin var(f\overline{t}_n \to t \,\square\, S)$, and $(f\overline{X}_n \to Y \Rightarrow \bigvee_{i \in I} \hat{R}_i) \in \mathcal{P}^-$.

Fig. 2. The Constraint Negative Proof Calculus $CNPC(\mathcal{D})$

Formally, assuming $G = \exists \overline{U}. \ (R \ \square \ (\Pi \ \square \ \sigma))$ and $\hat{S}' = \exists \overline{U}'. \ (\Pi' \ \square \ \sigma')$ a solved goal such that $\overline{U} \setminus dom(\sigma') \subseteq \overline{U}'$, $\sigma\sigma' = \sigma'$ and $Sol_{\mathcal{D}}(\Pi') \subseteq Sol_{\mathcal{D}}(\Pi\sigma')$, the operation $G \ \& \ \hat{S}'$ is defined as $\exists \overline{U}'. \ (R\sigma' \ \square \ (\Pi' \ \square \ \sigma'))$. The inference rule **CJ** infers an *aca* for a goal with composed kernel $(R_1 \wedge R_2) \ \square \ S$ from *acas* for goals with kernels of the form $R_1 \ \square \ S$ and $(\hat{R}_2 \ \& \ \hat{S}_i)$, respectively; while other inferences deal with different kinds of atomic goal kernels.

Any $CNPC(\mathcal{D})$-derivation $\mathcal{P}^- \vdash_{CNPC(\mathcal{D})} G \Rightarrow D$ can be depicted in the form of a <u>N</u>egative <u>P</u>roof <u>T</u>ree over $\mathcal{D}$ (shortly, NPT) with *acas* at its nodes, such that the *aca* at any node is inferred from the *acas* at its children using some $CNPC(\mathcal{D})$ inference rule. We say that a goal solving system for $CFLP(\mathcal{D})$ is *admissible* iff whenever finitely many solved goals $\{\hat{S}_i\}_{i \in I}$ are computed as answers for an admissible initial goal G, one has $\mathcal{P}^- \vdash_{CNPC(\mathcal{D})} G \Rightarrow \bigvee_{i \in I} \hat{S}_i$ with some witnessing NPT. The next theorem is intended to provide some plausibility to the pragmatic assumption that actual $CFLP$ systems such as *Curry* [16] or $\mathcal{TOY}$ [21] are admissible goal solving systems.

Theorem 1 (Existence of Admissible Goal Solving Calculi). *There is an admissible Goal Solving Calculus $GSC(\mathcal{D})$ which formalizes the goal solving methods underlying actual CFLP systems such as Curry or $\mathcal{TOY}$.*

Proof. A more general result can be proved, namely: If $(\widehat{\underline{R} \wedge R'}) \ \& \ \hat{S} \ \Vdash^p_{\mathcal{P}, GSC(\mathcal{D})}$ D (with a partially developed search space of finite size p built using the program $\mathcal{P}$, a *Goal Solving Calculus $GSC(\mathcal{D})$* inspired in [19,11], and a certain selection strategy that only selects atoms descendants of the part R) then $\mathcal{P}^- \vdash_{CNPC(\mathcal{D})}$ $\hat{R} \ \& \ \hat{S} \Rightarrow D$ with some witnessing NPT. The proof proceeds by induction of p, using an auxiliary lemma to deal with compound goals whose kernel is a conjunction. Details are given in [10]. $\qquad \square$

We have also proved in [10] the following theorem, showing that any *aca* which has been derived by means of a NPT is a logical consequence of the negative theory associated to the corresponding program. This result will be used below for proving the correctness of our diagnosis method.

Theorem 2 (Semantic Correctness of the $CNPC(\mathcal{D})$ Calculus). *Let $G \Rightarrow D$ be any aca for a given $CFLP(\mathcal{D})$-program $\mathcal{P}$. If $\mathcal{P}^- \vdash_{CNPC(\mathcal{D})} G \Rightarrow D$ then $G \Rightarrow D$ is a logical consequence of $\mathcal{P}^-$ in the sense of Definition 1.*

3.3 Declarative Diagnosis of Missing Answers Using Negative Proof Trees

We are now prepared to present a declarative diagnosis method for missing answers which is based on $NPTs$ and leads to correct diagnosis for any admissible goal solving system. First, we show that incompleteness symptoms are caused by incomplete program rules. This is guaranteed by the following theorem:

Theorem 3 (Missing Answers are Caused by Incomplete Program Rules). *Assume that an incompleteness symptom has been observed for a given $CFLP(\mathcal{D})$-program $\mathcal{P}$ as explained in Definition 2, with intended interpretation $\mathcal{I}_\mathcal{P}$, admissible initial goal G, and finite disjunction of computed answers $D = \bigvee_{i \in I} \hat{S}_i$. Assume also that the computation has been performed by an admissible goal solving system. Then there exists some defined function symbol f such that the axiom $(f)_\mathcal{P}^-$ for f in $\mathcal{P}^-$ is not valid in $\mathcal{I}_\mathcal{P}$, so that f's definition as given in $\mathcal{P}$ is incomplete w.r.t. $\mathcal{I}_\mathcal{P}$.*

Proof. Because of the admissibility of the goal solving system, we can assume $\mathcal{P}^- \vdash_{CNPC(\mathcal{D})} G \Rightarrow D$. Then the *aca* $G \Rightarrow D$ is a logical consequence of $\mathcal{P}^-$ because of Theorem 2. By Definition 1, we conclude that $Sol_\mathcal{I}(G) \subseteq Sol_\mathcal{D}(D)$ holds for any model $\mathcal{I}$ of $\mathcal{P}^-$. However, we also know that $Sol_{\mathcal{I}_\mathcal{P}}(G) \not\subseteq Sol_\mathcal{D}(D)$, because the disjunction D of computed answers is an incompleteness symptom w.r.t. $\mathcal{I}_\mathcal{P}$. Therefore, we can conclude that $\mathcal{I}_\mathcal{P}$ is not a model of $\mathcal{P}^-$, and therefore the completeness axiom $(f)_\mathcal{P}^-$ of some defined function symbol f must be invalid in $\mathcal{I}_\mathcal{P}$.   □

The previous theorem does not yet provide a practical method for finding an incomplete function definition. As explained in Section 2, a declarative diagnosis method is expected to find the incomplete function definition by inspecting a CT. We propose to use abbreviated NPTs as CTs. Note that $(\mathbf{DF})_f$ is the only inference rule in the $CNPC(\mathcal{D})$ calculus that depends on the program, and all the other inference rules are correct w.r.t. arbitrary interpretations. For this reason, abbreviated proof trees will omit the inference steps related to the $CNPC(\mathcal{D})$ inference rules other than $(\mathbf{DF})_f$. More precisely, given a NPT $\mathcal{T}$ witnessing a $CNPC(\mathcal{D})$ proof $\mathcal{P}^- \vdash_{CNPC(\mathcal{D})} G \Rightarrow D$, its associated <u>A</u>bbreviated <u>N</u>egative <u>P</u>roof <u>T</u>ree (shortly, $ANPT$) $\mathcal{AT}$ is constructed as follows:

(1) The root of $\mathcal{AT}$ is the root of $\mathcal{T}$.
(2) The children of any node N in $\mathcal{AT}$ are the closest descendants of N in $\mathcal{T}$ corresponding to *boxed acas* introduced by $(\mathbf{DF})_f$ inference steps.

As already explained, declarative diagnosis methods search a given CT looking for a *buggy node* whose result is unexpected but whose children's results are all expected. In our present setting, the CTs are $ANPT$s, the "results" attached to nodes are *acas*, and a given node N is *buggy* iff the *aca* at N is *invalid* (i.e., it represents an incomplete recollection of computed answers in the intended interpretation $\mathcal{I}_\mathcal{P}$) while the *aca* at each children node N_i is *valid* (i.e., it represents a complete recollection of computed answers in the intended interpretation $\mathcal{I}_\mathcal{P}$).

As a concrete example, Fig. 3 displays a NPT which can be used for the diagnosis of missing answers in the example presented in Section 2. Buggy nodes are highlighted by encircling the *acas* attached to them within double boxes. The CT shown in Fig. 1 is the $ANPT$ constructed from this NPT.

Our last result is a refinement of Theorem 3. It guarantees that declarative diagnosis with $ANPT$s used as CTs leads to the correct detection of incomplete program functions. A proof can be found in [10].

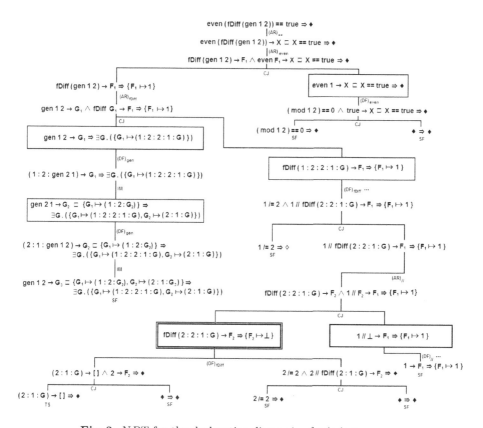

Fig. 3. NPT for the declarative diagnosis of missing answers

Theorem 4 ($ANPT$s Lead to the Diagnosis of Incomplete Functions).
As in Theorem 3, assume that an incompleteness symptom has been observed for a given $CFLP(\mathcal{D})$-program $\mathcal{P}$ as explained in Definition 2, with intended interpretation $\mathcal{I}_\mathcal{P}$, admissible initial goal G, and finite disjunction of answers $D = \bigvee_{i \in I} \hat{S}_i$, computed by an admissible goal solving system. Then $\mathcal{P}^- \vdash_{CNPC(\mathcal{D})} G \Rightarrow D$, and the $ANPT$ constructed from any NPT witnessing this derivation, has some buggy node. Moreover, each such buggy node points to an axiom $(f)^-_\mathcal{P}$ which is incomplete w.r.t. the user's intended interpretation $\mathcal{I}_\mathcal{P}$.

4   Implementation in the *TOY* System

In this section, we discuss the implementation in the $\mathcal{TOY}$ system of a tool based on the debugging method presented in the previous sections. The current prototype only supports the Herbrand constraint domain $\mathcal{H}$, although the same principles can be applied to other constraint domains $\mathcal{D}$.

We summarize first the normal process followed by the $\mathcal{TOY}$ system when compiling a source program $\mathcal{P}.toy$ and solving an initial goal G w.r.t. $\mathcal{P}$. During the compilation process the system translates a source program $\mathcal{P}.toy$ into a Prolog program $\mathcal{P}.pl$ including a predicate for each function in $\mathcal{P}$. For instance the function even of our running example is transformed into a predicate

even(N,R,IC,OC):- ... code for even ... .

where the variable N corresponds to the input parameter of the function, R to the function result, and IC, OC represent, respectively, the input and output constraint store. Moreover, each goal G of $\mathcal{P}$ is also translated into a Prolog goal and solved w.r.t. $\mathcal{P}.pl$ by the underlying Prolog system. The result is a collection of answers which are presented to the user in a certain sequence, as a result of Prolog's backtracking.

If the computation of answers for G finishes after having collected finitely many answers, the user may decide that there are some missing answers (*incompleteness symptom*, in the terminology of Definition 2) and type the command /missing at the system prompt in order to initiate a *debugging session*. The debugger proceeds carrying out the following steps:

1. The object program $\mathcal{P}.pl$ is transformed into a new Prolog program $\mathcal{P}^{\mathcal{T}}.pl$. The debugger can safely assume that $\mathcal{P}.pl$ already exists because the tool is always initiated *after* some missing answer has been detected by the user. The transformed program $\mathcal{P}^{\mathcal{T}}$ behaves almost identically to $\mathcal{P}$, the only difference being that it produces a suitable *trace* of the computation in a text file. For instance here is a fragment of the code for the function even of our running example in the transformed program:

```
1  % this clause wraps the original predicate
2  even(N,R,IC,OC):-
3      % display the input values for even
4      write(' begin('), write(' even,'), writeq(N), write(','),
5      write(R), write(', '), writeq(IC), write(').'), nl,
6      % evenBis corresponds to the original predicate for even
7      evenBis(N,R,IC,OC),
8      % display an output result
9      write(' output('), write(' even,'), writeq(N), write(','),
10     write(R), write(', '), writeq(OC), write(').'), nl.

11 % when all the possible outputs of the function have been produced
12 even(N,R,IC,OC):-
13     nl, write(' end(even).'), nl,
14     !,
15     fail.
16 evenBis(N,R,IC,OC) :- ... original code for even ... .
```

As the example shows, the code for each function now displays information about the values of the arguments and the contents of the constraint store at the moment of using any user defined function (lines 4-5). Then the predicate corresponding to the original function, now renamed with the Bis suffix, is called (line 7). After any successful function call the trace displays again the values of the arguments and result, which may have changed, and the contents of the output constraint store (lines 9, 10). A second clause (lines 12-15) displays the value end when the function has exhausted its possible output. The clause fails in order to ensure that the program flow is not changed. The original code for each function is kept unaltered in the transformed program except for the renaming (evenBis instead of even in the example, line 16). This ensures that the program will behave equivalently to the original program, except for the trace produced as a side-effect.

2. In order to obtain the trace file, the debugger repeats the computation of all the answers for the goal G w.r.t. $\mathcal{P}^{\mathcal{T}}$. After each successful computation the debugger enforces a fail in order to trigger the backtracking mechanism and produce the next solution for the goal. The program output is redirected to a file, where the trace is stored.

3. The trace file is then analyzed by the CT builder module of the tool. The result is the Computation Tree (an $ANPT$), which is displayed by a Java graphical interface.

4. The tree can be navigated by the user either manually, providing information about the validity of the acas contained in the tree, or using any of the automatic strategies included in the tool which try to minimize the number of nodes that the user must examine (see [29] for a description of some strategies and their efficiency). The process ends when a buggy node is found and the tool points to an incomplete function definition, as explained in Section 3, as responsible for the missing answers. The current implementation of the prototype is available at http://toy.sourceforge.net. The generation of trace files works satisfactorily, while the CT builder module and the Java graphical interface do still need more improvements.

Fig. 4 shows how the tool displays the CT corresponding to the debugging scenario discussed in Section 2. The initial goal is not displayed, but the rest of the CT corresponds to Fig. 1, whose construction as $ANPT$ has been explained in Section 3. When displaying an aca $f\bar{t}_n \to t \square S \Rightarrow \bigvee_{i \in I} \hat{S}_i$, the tool uses list notation for representing the disjunction $\bigvee_{i \in I} \hat{S}_i$ and performs some simplifications: useless variable bindings within the stores S and S_i are dropped, as in the aca displayed as gen 2 1 -> A ==> [A = 2:1:_] in Fig. 4; and if t happens to be a variable X, the case $\{X \mapsto \bot\}$ is omitted from the disjunction $\bigvee_{i \in I} \hat{S}_i$, so that the user must interpret the aca as collecting the possible results for X other than the undefined value $\bot$. The tool also displays the underscore symbol _ at some places. Within any aca, the occurrences of _ at the right hand side of the implication $\Rightarrow$ must be understood as different existentially quantified variables, while each occurrence of _ at the left hand side of $\Rightarrow$ must be understood as $\bot$. For instance, 1 // _ -> A ==> [A = 1] is the aca $1 \,//\, \bot \to A \Rightarrow \{A \mapsto 1\}$ as displayed by the tool. Understanding the occurrences of _ at the left hand side of $\Rightarrow$ as different universally quantified variables would be incorrect. For instance, the aca $1 \,//\, \bot \to A \Rightarrow \{A \mapsto 1\}$ is valid w.r.t. the intended interpretation $\mathcal{I}_{\mathcal{P}_{\mathtt{fD}}}$ of $\mathcal{P}_{\mathtt{fD}}$, while the statement $\forall X.\ (1 \,//\, X \to A \Rightarrow \{A \mapsto 1\})$ has a different meaning and is not valid in $\mathcal{I}_{\mathcal{P}_{\mathtt{fD}}}$.

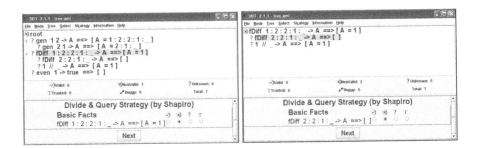

Fig. 4. Snapshots of the prototype

In the debugging session shown in Fig. 4 the user has selected the *Divide &
Query* strategy [29] in order to find a buggy node. The lower part of the left-
hand side snapshot shows the first question asked by the tool after selecting this
strategy, namely the *aca* fDiff 1:2:2:1:_ -> A ==> [A=1]. According to her
knowledge of $\mathcal{I}_{\mathcal{P}_{fD}}$ the user marks this *aca* as invalid. The strategy now prunes
the *CT* keeping only the subtree rooted by the invalid *aca* at the previous step
(every *CT* with an invalid root must contain at least one buggy node). The second question, which can be seen at the right-hand side snapshot, asks about the
validity of the *aca* fDiff 2:2:1:_ -> A ==> [] (which in fact represents fDiff
2:2:1:⊥ → A ⇒ {A ↦ ⊥}, as explained above). Again, her knowledge of $\mathcal{I}_{\mathcal{P}_{fD}}$
leads the user to expect that fDiff 2:2:1:⊥ can return some defined result, and
the *aca* is marked as invalid. After this question the debugger points out at fDiff
as an incomplete function, and the debugging session ends. Regarding the efficiency of this debugging method our preliminary experimental results show that:

1. Producing the transformed $\mathcal{P}^{\mathcal{T}}$. *pl* from $\mathcal{P}$.*pl* is proportional in time to the
   number of functions of the program, and does require an insignificant amount
   of system memory since each predicate is transformed separately.
2. The computation of the goal w.r.t. $\mathcal{P}^{\mathcal{T}}$. *pl* requires almost the same system
   resources as w.r.t. $\mathcal{P}$.*pl* because writing the trace causes no significant overhead in our experiments.
3. Producing the *CT* from the trace is not straightforward and requires several
   traverses of the trace. Although more time-consuming due to the algorithmic
   difficulty, this process only keeps portions of the trace in memory at each
   moment.
4. The most inefficient phase in our current implementation is the graphical
   interface. Although it would be possible to keep in memory only the por-
   tion of the tree displayed at each moment, our graphical interface loads the
   whole *CT* in main memory. We plan to improve this limitation in the future.
   However the current prototype can cope with *CT*s containing thousands of
   nodes, which is enough for medium size computations.
5. As usual in declarative debugging, the efficiency of the tool depends on the
   computation tree size, which in turn usually depends on the size of the data
   structures required and not on the program size.

A different issue is the difficulty of answering the questions by the user. Indeed in complicated programs involving constraints the *acas* can be large and intricate, as it is also the case with other debugging tools for CLP languages. Nevertheless, our prototype works reasonably in cases where the goal's search space is relatively small, and we believe that working with such goals can be useful for detecting many programming bugs in practice. Techniques for simplifying CTs should be worked out in future improvements of the prototype. For instance, asking the user for a concrete missing instance of the initial goal and starting a diagnosis session for the instantiated goal might be helpful.

5 Conclusions and Future Work

We have presented a novel method for the declarative diagnosis of *missing computed answers* in $CFLP(\mathcal{D})$, a declarative programming scheme which combines the expressivity of lazy FP and CLP languages. The method relies on *Computation Trees* (CTs) whose nodes are labeled with *answer collection assertions* (*acas*). As in declarative diagnosis for FP languages, the values displayed at *acas* are shown in the most evaluated form demanded by the topmost computation. On the other hand, and following the CLP tradition, we have shown that our CTs are abbreviated proof trees in a suitable inference system, the so-called *constraint negative proof calculus*. Thanks to this fact, we can prove the correctness of our diagnosis method for any admissible goal solving system whose recollection of computed answers can be represented by means of a proof tree in the constraint negative proof calculus. As far as we know, no comparable result was previously available for such an expressive framework as $CFLP$.

Intuitively, the notion of *aca* bears some loose relationship to programming techniques related to answer recollection, as e.g., *encapsulated search* [2]. However, *acas* in our setting are not a programming technique. Rather, they serve as logical statements whose falsity reveals incompleteness of computed answers w.r.t. expected answers. In principle, one could also think of a kind of logical statements somewhat similar to *acas*, but asserting the *equality* of the observed and expected sets of computed answers for one and the same goal with a finite search space. We have not developed this idea, which could support the declarative diagnosis of a third kind of unexpected results, namely *incorrect answer sets* as done for *Datalog* [5]. In fact, we think that a separate diagnosis of wrong and missing answers is pragmatically more convenient for users of $CFLP$ languages.

On the practical side, our method can be applied to actual $CFLP$ systems such as *Curry* or $\mathcal{TOY}$, leading to correct diagnosis under the pragmatic assumption that they behave as admissible goal solving systems. This assumption is plausible in so far as the systems are based on formal goal solving procedures that can be argued to be admissible. A prototype debugger under development is available, which implements the method in $\mathcal{TOY}$. Although our implementation is based on the ad-hoc trace generated by the transformed program $\mathcal{P}^T$, we think that it could be possible to obtain the CTs from the *redex trail* for functional-logic programming described in [3]. This would allow reasoning about the correctness of the implementation by using the declarative semantics supporting this structure.

Some important pragmatic problems well known for declarative diagnosis tools in FP and CLP languages also arise in our context: both the CTs and the $acas$ at their nodes may be very big in general, causing computation overhead and difficulties for the user in answering the questions posed by the debugging tool. In spite of these difficulties, the prototype works reasonably in cases where the goal's search space is relatively small, and we believe that working with such goals can be useful for detecting many programming bugs in practice. Techniques for simplifying CTs should be worked out in future improvements of the prototype.

Acknowledgments

The authors are grateful to the referees of previous versions of this paper for their constructive comments and suggestions.

References

1. Boye, J., Drabent, W., Maluszynski, J.: Declarative diagnosis of contraint programs: An assertion-based approach. In: Automated and Algorithmic Debugging, pp. 123–140 (1997)
2. Brassel, B., Hanus, M., Huch, F.: Encapsulating non-determinism in functional logic computations. Journal of Functional and Logic Programming (2004)
3. Brassel, B., Hanus, M., Huch, F., Vidal, G.: A semantics for tracing declarative multi-paradigm programs. In: PPDP 2004, pp. 179–190. ACM Press, New York (2004)
4. Caballero, R.: A declarative debugger of incorrect answers for constraint functional-logic programs. In: WCFLP 2005, pp. 8–13. ACM Press, New York (2005)
5. Caballero, R., García-Ruiz, Y., Sáenz-Pérez, F.: A new proposal for debugging datalog programs. In: WFLP 2007 (2007)
6. Caballero, R., Rodríguez-Artalejo, M.: A declarative debugging system for lazy functional logic programs. Electr. Notes Theor. Comput. Sci. 64 (2002)
7. Rodríguez-Artalejo, M., Caballero, R.: $\mathcal{DDT}$: A declarative debugging tool for functional-logic languages. In: Kameyama, Y., Stuckey, P.J. (eds.) FLOPS 2004. LNCS, vol. 2998, pp. 70–84. Springer, Heidelberg (2004)
8. Caballero, R., Rodríguez-Artalejo, M., del Vado-Vírseda, R.: Declarative diagnosis of wrong answers in constraint functional-logic programming. In: Etalle, S., Truszczyński, M. (eds.) ICLP 2006. LNCS, vol. 4079, pp. 421–422. Springer, Heidelberg (2006)
9. Caballero, R., Rodríguez-Artalejo, M., del Vado-Vírseda, R.: Declarative debugging of missing answers in constraint functional-logic programming. In: Dahl, V., Niemelä, I. (eds.) ICLP 2007. LNCS, vol. 4670, pp. 425–427. Springer, Heidelberg (2007)
10. Caballero, R., Rodríguez-Artalejo, M., del Vado-Vírseda, R.: Algorithmic debugging of missing answers in constraint functional-logic programming. Technical Report DSIC 2/08, Universidad Complutense de Madrid (2008),
http://gpd.sip.ucm.es/papers.html

11. del Vado-Vírseda, R.: Declarative constraint programming with definitional trees. In: Gramlich, B. (ed.) FroCos 2005. LNCS (LNAI), vol. 3717, pp. 184–199. Springer, Heidelberg (2005)
12. Estévez, S., del Vado-Vírseda, R.: Designing an efficient computation strategy in $CFLP(\mathcal{FD})$ using definitional trees. In: WCFLP 2005, pp. 23–31. ACM Press, New York (2005)
13. Fernández, A.J., Hortalá-González, M.T., Sáenz-Pérez, F., del Vado-Vírseda, R.: Constraint functional logic programming over finite domains. Theory and Practice of Logic Programming 7(5), 537–582 (2007)
14. Ferrand, G.: Error diagnosis in logic programming, an adaption of E. Y. Shapiro's method. J. Log. Program. 4(3), 177–198 (1987)
15. Ferrand, G., Lesaint, W., Tessier, A.: Towards declarative diagnosis of constraint programs over finite domains. ArXiv Computer Science e-prints (2003)
16. Hanus, M.: Curry: An integrated functional logic language (version 0.8.2 of march 28, 2006) (2006), http://www.informatik.uni-kiel.de/~curry
17. Hermenegildo, M., Puebla, G., Bueno, F., López-García, P.: Abstract verification and debugging of constraint logic programs. In: O'Sullivan, B. (ed.) CologNet 2002. LNCS (LNAI), vol. 2627, pp. 1–14. Springer, Heidelberg (2003)
18. Lloyd, J.W.: Declarative error diagnosis. New Gen. Comput. 5(2), 133–154 (1987)
19. López-Fraguas, F.J., Rodríguez-Artalejo, M., del Vado-Vírseda, R.: A lazy narrowing calculus for declarative constraint programming. In: PPDP 2004, pp. 43–54. ACM Press, New York (2004)
20. López-Fraguas, F.J., Rodríguez-Artalejo, M., Vado-Vírseda, R.d.: A new generic scheme for functional logic programming with constraints. Higher-Order and Symbolic Computation 20(1-2), 73–122 (2007)
21. López-Fraguas, F.J., Sánchez-Hernández, J.: $\mathcal{TOY}$: A multiparadigm declarative system. In: Narendran, P., Rusinowitch, M. (eds.) RTA 1999. LNCS, vol. 1631, pp. 244–247. Springer, Heidelberg (1999)
22. Naish, L.: A declarative debugging scheme. Journal of Functional and Logic Programming 1997(3) (1997)
23. Naish, L., Barbour, T.: A declarative debugger for a logical-functional language. DSTO General Document 5(2), 91–99 (1995)
24. Nilsson, H.: How to look busy while being as lazy as ever: the implementation of a lazy functional debugger. J. Funct. Program. 11(6), 629–671 (2001)
25. Nilsson, H., Sparud, J.: The evaluation dependence tree as a basis for lazy functional debugging. Autom. Softw. Eng. 4(2), 121–150 (1997)
26. B. Pope. A Declarative Debugger for Haskell. PhD thesis, Department of Computer Science and Software Engineering, University of Melbourne (2006)
27. Pope, B., Naish, L.: Practical aspects of declarative debugging in haskell 98. In: PPDP 2003, pp. 230–240. ACM Press, New York (2003)
28. Shapiro, E.Y.: Algorithmic Program Debugging. MIT Press, Cambridge, MA, USA (1983)
29. Silva, J.: A comparative study of algorithmic debugging strategies. In: Puebla, G. (ed.) LOPSTR 2006. LNCS, vol. 4407, pp. 143–159. Springer, Heidelberg (2007)
30. Tessier, A., Ferrand, G.: Declarative diagnosis in the CLP scheme. In: Deransart, P., Małuszyński, J. (eds.) DiSCiPl 1999. LNCS, vol. 1870, pp. 151–174. Springer, Heidelberg (2000)

EasyCheck — Test Data for Free[*]

Jan Christiansen and Sebastian Fischer

Department of Computing Science, University of Kiel, Germany
{jac,sebf}@informatik.uni-kiel.de

Abstract. We present a lightweight, automated tool for specification-based testing of declarative programs written in the functional logic programming language Curry and emphasize the usefulness of logic features in its implementation and use. Free variables, nondeterminism and encapsulated search turn out to be elegant and powerful means to express test-data generation.

Keywords: Testing, Nondeterminism, Encapsulated Search, Curry.

1   Introduction

Automatic test tools have to generate values of a certain type. For example, to test the function `reverse` which reverses a list we have to generate a variety of lists of values of some type.

We present the implementation of an automatic test tool for the functional logic programming language Curry. Functional logic languages like Curry extend the functional programming paradigm with *nondeterministic operations* and *free variables*. In [1] it was shown that a free variable can be seen as a nondeterministic generator that yields all values of its type. We argue that this result is not only of theoretical interest. We present a practical application of this new view on free variables. Instead of defining a test-case generator for lists, we can use a free variable of an appropriate list type. Moreover, the notion of nondeterminism greatly simplifies the implementation of custom generators.

In Curry, nondeterminism is introduced by operations with overlapping left hand sides. For example, the operation `bool` is nondeterministic because its left hand sides trivially overlap – they are identical. It is semantically equivalent to a free variable of type `Bool`.

```
bool = False
bool = True
```

The operation `bool` nondeterministically evaluates to `False` or `True`. The operation `bList` is semantically equivalent to a free variable of type `[Bool]`.

```
bList = []
bList = bool : bList
```

---

[*] Partially supported by the German Research Council (DFG) grant Ha 2457/5-2.

J. Garrigue and M. Hermenegildo (Eds.): FLOPS 2008, LNCS 4989, pp. 322–336, 2008.

It yields an empty list or a list with a boolean head and a `bList` as tail. Therefore, `bList` nondeterministically yields all values of type `[Bool]`.

The above definitions are superfluous, because they evaluate to *every* value of their type and we can replace them by free variables. However, we can apply a similar technique to define custom generators that evaluate only to a subset of all possible values. For example, if we do not want to check `reverse` for empty lists, we can define an operation that nondeterministically yields all nonempty lists of type `[Bool]`.

```
neBList = bool : bList
```

We present an automatic test tool that uses nondeterministic operations for the generation of test data.

– We show that the generation of test data is already included in the concepts of functional logic programming. Therefore, the programmer does not have to learn a new syntax and the syntax for test data generation is very simple.
– We separate the generation of test data and its enumeration. Test data generators are nondeterministic operations. The nondeterminism is encapsulated [2] by an operation that yields a tree which contains all possible values. We present a new traversal strategy for such trees that serves well for the purpose of test data generation (Section 4). In contrast to other approaches, this enables us to ensure that every value is enumerated only once and that every value is eventually enumerated. The separation between generation and enumeration of test data allows a clear and flexible implementation of automatic testing.
– We extend the interface of test tools for functional languages with additional operations to specify properties of nondeterministic operations (Section 3).

2   Curry

Curry is a functional logic programming language whose syntax is similar to the syntax of the functional programming language Haskell [3]. In the following, we assume that the reader is familiar with the syntax of Haskell and only explain Curry specifics in detail. Apart from functional features (algebraic datatypes, higher-order functions, lazy evaluation), Curry provides the essential features of logic programming, viz., nondeterminism and free variables. Because of nondeterminism we use the term *operation* in the context of Curry instead of function. Free variables are introduced by the keyword `free` and nondeterminism by overlapping left hand sides. Curry does not follow a top-down strategy but evaluates every matching rule of an operation. For example, the binary operation `(?) :: a -> a -> a` nondeterministically yields one of its arguments.

```
x ? _ = x
_ ? x = x
```

In Curry you can encapsulate a nondeterministic value and get a deterministic tree that contains all possible values. In the following, we will use the term *search*

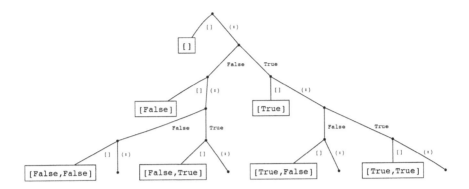

Fig. 1. Search tree for a free variable of type [Bool]

tree when we talk about this tree structure. Note that this is not a search tree in the sense of an AVL or a Red Black tree. A search tree in our sense denotes a value of the following datatype.[1]

```
data SearchTree a = Value a | Or [SearchTree a]
```

The Curry system KiCS [4,5] provides a primitive encapsulating operation `searchTree :: a -> SearchTree a` that takes a possibly nondeterministic value and yields the corresponding search tree. Encapsulating nondeterminism is still a topic of ongoing research. Nevertheless, all Curry implementations provide some kind of encapsulated search. The search tree for a deterministic value is a single `Value` leaf.

```
> searchTree True
Value True
```

Nondeterministic choices are reflected by `Or` nodes in the search tree.

```
> searchTree (False ? True ? False)
Or [Value False,Or [Value True,Value False]]
```

If we apply `searchTree` to `bList` or a free variable of type [Bool], we obtain an infinite search tree because there are infinitely many values of type [Bool]. However, due to lazy evaluation, only those parts of the search tree are generated that are demanded by the surrounding computation. Therefore it is possible to guide the search by user defined traversal operations as the one presented in Section 4. Figure 1 visualizes the first six levels of the search tree that corresponds to a free variable of type [Bool]. Each inner node represents a nondeterministic choice for a constructor and its outgoing edges are labeled with the chosen constructor. The leaves of the tree are labeled with the corresponding lists of booleans.

---

[1] We do not consider *failure* throughout this paper, which could be expressed as `Or []`.

3   Using EasyCheck

The interface of EasyCheck is similar to the interface of QuickCheck [6] or G∀ST [7]. We provide a combinator `property :: Bool -> Property` that is satisfied if its argument deterministically evaluates to `True`. The deterministic equality operator `(-=-) :: a -> a -> Property` is satisfied if its arguments are deterministically evaluated to the same value.

However, EasyCheck is a test tool for a functional *logic* language and has special combinators to deal with nondeterminism. In this section we present the use of additional combinators to specify properties of nondeterministic operations.

We cannot use `(-=-)` to specify properties of nondeterministic operations because `(-=-)` demands its arguments to be deterministic. It would be questionable what a property like `(0?1) -=- 1` should mean and whether it should be equivalent to `1 -=- (0?1)`. We provide different combinators for nondeterministic operations that allow to address multiple values of an expression explicitly: `(~>)`, `(<~)`, `(<~>)` :: `a -> a -> Property`.

- The combinator `(~>)` demands that its left argument evaluates to every value of its right argument. The set of results of the left argument must be a *superset* of the set of results of the right argument.
- The combinator `(<~)` is dual to `(~>)` and demands that the set of results of its left argument is a *subset* of the set of results of the right one.
- Finally, `(<~>)` is satisfied if the sets of results of its arguments are *equal*. Note that `(<~>)` is not equivalent to `(-=-)` because the latter demands that the sets of results of its arguments are singleton sets.

In order to demonstrate nondeterministic testing, we consider an operation that inserts an element at an arbitrary position in a list.

```
insert :: a -> [a] -> [a]
insert x xs     = x : xs
insert x (y:ys) = y : insert x ys
```

The following property states that `insert` should insert the given element (at least) at the first and last position of the given list.

```
insertAsFirstOrLast :: Int -> [Int] -> Property
insertAsFirstOrLast x xs = insert x xs ~> (x:xs ? xs++[x])
```

To check a polymorphic property we have to annotate a type to determine possible test cases. For example `insertAsFirstOrLast` is tested for integers and lists of integers. We can use `easyCheck2` to verify that `insert` satisfies this property for the first 1,000 generated test cases.

```
> easyCheck2 insertAsFirstOrLast
OK, passed 1000 tests.
```

We provide operations `easyCheckn` to test properties of arity n for every reasonable n. As Curry does not support type classes, we cannot provide an operation `easyCheck` that handles properties of arbitrary arities.

We can employ `insert` to define a nondeterministic operation `perm` that computes all permutations of a given list.

```
perm :: [a] -> [a]
perm = foldr insert []
```

In order to test `perm`, we use one of the nondeterministic counterparts of the operation `property`, namely `always`, `eventually :: Bool -> Property`. These operations do not demand their arguments to be deterministic and are satisfied if all and any of the nondeterministic results of the argument are satisfied respectively. Assuming a predicate `sorted :: [Int] -> Bool` we can define a test for `perm` as follows.

```
permIsEventuallySorted :: [Int] -> Property
permIsEventuallySorted xs = eventually (sorted (perm xs))
```

```
> easyCheck1 permIsEventuallySorted
OK, passed 1000 tests.
```

The presented combinators are a relatively straightforward generalization of those found in QuickCheck for nondeterministic operations. We did not present all available combinators in this section. We introduce additional combinators in later sections when we use them.

4   Enumerating Test Cases

The primitive operation `searchTree :: a -> SearchTree a` encapsulates nondeterminism. It takes a possibly nondeterministic expression as argument and deterministically yields a search tree that contains all possible values of this expression. The standard libraries of Curry provide two operations to traverse a search tree and enumerate its values in depth- or breadth-first order. However, for test-case generation, we need a *complete*, *advancing* and *balanced* enumeration.

- We call an enumeration *complete* if every value is eventually enumerated. This property allows us to *prove* properties that only involve datatypes with finitely many values. Moreover, it implies that any node of an infinite search tree is reached in finite time.
- Furthermore, it is desirable to obtain reasonably large test cases early in order to avoid numerous trivial test cases. Therefore we want to visit the first node of the n-th level of a search tree after $p(n)$ other nodes where p is a polynomial. We call an enumeration with this property *advancing*.
- We call an enumeration *balanced* if the enumerated values are independent of the order of child trees in branch nodes. Balance is important in order to obtain diverse test cases.

Neither depth- nor breadth-first search fulfills all properties. Depth-first search is advancing[2] but incomplete and unbalanced. Breadth-first search is complete

---
[2] Not always, however, because it is incomplete.

and almost balanced but not advancing because it generates a lot of small values before larger ones. Therefore, we present a new search tree traversal that is better suited for test-case generation.

4.1 Level Diagonalization

The following operation yields the list of levels of a search forest.

```
levels :: [SearchTree a] -> [[SearchTree a]]
levels ts | null ts   = []
          | otherwise = ts : levels [ u | Or us <- ts, u <- us ]
```

Note that not only values but *all* nodes of the forest are enumerated. If we would only enumerate leaves, we might need to process large sequences of inner nodes without being able to yield a node. As a consequence, large parts of levels would be visited what we aim to avoid due to performance reasons. By yielding also the inner nodes of the tree, we are able to process all levels incrementally. The operation `levelDiag` merges the different levels and extracts the values from the resulting enumeration.

```
levelDiag :: SearchTree a -> [a]
levelDiag t = [ x | Value x <- diagonal (levels [t]) ]
```

We do not simply concatenate the levels like in breadth-first search but use a list diagonalization operation reminiscent to the diagonalizing list comprehensions of Miranda [8]. The operation `diagonal` takes a list of lists and yields a list that contains all elements of the inner lists in a diagonally interleaved order.

```
diagonal :: [[a]] -> [a]
diagonal = concat . foldr diags []
  where diags []     ys  = ys
        diags (x:xs) ys  = [x] : merge xs ys

        merge []        ys       = ys
        merge xs@(_:_)  []       = map (:[]) xs
        merge (x:xs)    (y:ys)   = (x:y) : merge xs ys
```

We can use `diagonal` to merge an infinite list of infinite lists:

```
> take 10 (diagonal [[ (i,j) | j <- [1..]] | i <- [1..]])
[(1,1),(1,2),(2,1),(1,3),(2,2),(3,1),(1,4),(2,3),(3,2),(4,1)]
```

You can think of the list of lists as a matrix. Note that the first element of the nth inner list is returned as $(n(n + 1)/2)$th element of the result (or earlier). This means that `levelDiag` visits the first node of level n after visiting only $O(n^2)$ other nodes (compared to $O(2^n)$ for breadth-first search and $O(n)$ for depth-first search). Figure 2 shows part of the search tree that represents lists of booleans. The first 100 nodes that are visited by `levelDiag` are highlighted. Thanks to lazy evaluation, only a small part of the tree is computed. Observe that all values of lower levels are enumerated and, therefore, boundary cases are covered completely. Moreover, large values are enumerated reasonably early,

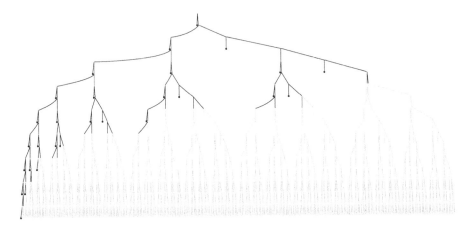

Fig. 2. Level diagonalization for [Bool] values

i.e., levelDiag is advancing. It is also complete since every value is eventually enumerated. However, it is not balanced because it prefers left branches. Also, most of the visited nodes are in the left part of the tree.

4.2   Randomization

We employ shuffle :: Int -> [a] -> [a] in order to choose every branch with equal probability. It takes a random seed and yields a random permutation of its argument. We use this operation to shuffle search trees.

```
shuffleTree :: Int -> SearchTree a -> SearchTree a
shuffleTree _   (Value x) = Value x
shuffleTree rnd (Or ts)   = Or (shuffle r (zipWith shuffleTree rs ts))
  where r:rs = split rnd
```

The function split computes an infinite list of uncorrelated random seeds from a given random seed. We can combine shuffleTree and levelDiag in order to obtain a complete, advancing and balanced search tree traversal. If we start the search with a fixed random seed, we obtain reproducible test cases. This is important because it is difficult to track down a bug if the same property fails in one execution and succeeds in another. Instead of shuffling only the children of nodes we could as well shuffle whole levels. This would give a good distribution but result in unacceptable performance since it causes the evaluation of large parts of the search tree.

Neither left nor right branches are preferred by randomized level diagonalization. But still large parts of the visited nodes are in the same part of the tree. This is desirable from a performance point of view because unvisited parts need not be computed. However, there is also an undesirable consequence: the larger the computed values are the more they resemble each other. QuickCheck does not show this behaviour because its test cases are independent of each other.

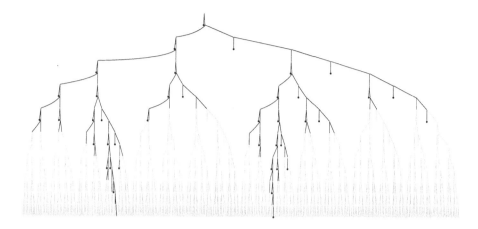

Fig. 3. Combined randomized level diagonalization for [Bool] values

But as a consequence the probability for enumerating a small value twice is very high.

Finding an efficient enumeration scheme that is complete, balanced and generates *sufficiently different* large values *early* deserves future work. In a first attempt, we apply randomized level diagonalization to different subtrees of the initial tree and combine the individual results. Figure 3 visualizes the effect of combining two randomized level diagonalizations.

5 Case Study

In this section we demonstrate how to test a heap implementation with Easy-Check. A heap is a tree that satisfies the *heap property*: the sequence of labels along any path from the root to a leaf must be non-decreasing. We want to evaluate test-case distribution for a complex datatype with multiple recursive components. Therefore, we use a custom datatype for natural numbers in binary notation as heap entries (cf. [9]).

```
data Heap = Empty | Fork Nat [Heap]
data Nat  = One | O Nat | I Nat
```

The heap implementation provides operations `empty :: Heap` to create an empty heap, `insert :: Nat -> Heap -> Heap` to add an element to a heap and `splitMin :: Heap -> (Nat,Heap)` to get the minimum of a nonempty heap and the heap without the minimum. The property `minIsLeqInserted` states that the minimum of a heap after inserting an element is less than or equal to the new entry.

```
minIsLeqInserted :: Nat -> Heap -> Property
minIsLeqInserted v h = property (m<=v)
  where (m,_) = splitMin (insert v h)
```

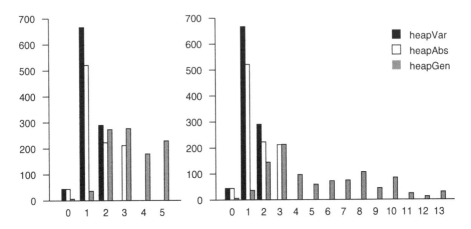

Fig. 4. Depth and size of generated `Heap` values

EasyCheck reports that this property is satisfied for 1000 test cases. The test uses a free variable to generate heaps. Because the test cases are generated by a free variable they do not necessarily satisfy the heap property. To count the number of valid heaps we employ the operation `classify :: Bool -> String -> Property -> Property` and a predicate `valid` on heaps. 505 of the first 1,000 heaps generated by a free variable are valid. We could use the operator `(==>) :: Bool -> Property -> Property` to reject invalid heaps like it is often done in QuickCheck. In this case all test cases – valid and invalid ones – are generated. This is insufficient if the percentage of valid test cases is small.

5.1 Generating Only Valid Heaps

In this subsection we discuss approaches to generate only valid heaps. In Subsection 5.2, we compare the distribution of test data with similar QuickCheck generators.

- We constrain a free variable by the predicate `valid`,
- we employ the abstract heap constructors `empty` and `insert`, and
- we explicitly generate an adequate subset of valid heaps.

For each of these approaches we measure the depth and the size of the generated heaps, i.e., the length of the longest path from the root to a leaf and the number of entries, respectively. The results of these measurements are depicted in Figure 4.

We can define a generator for valid heaps by narrowing a free variable.

```
heapVar | valid h = h where h free
```

This is a very simple and elegant way to generate only valid heaps. The test tool SparseCheck [10] employs the same idea, cf. Section 6 on related work. This definition is more efficient compared to the approach using `(==>)`. Thanks to laziness, invalid heaps are only generated as far as necessary to detect that they are invalid. If we use (==>) all test cases are generated completely and tested afterwards. Narrowing a free variable w.r.t. a predicate only generates valid heaps. Figure 4 shows that the majority of test cases that are generated by `heapVar` are small heaps. The probability that a larger heap that is generated by a free variable is valid is very small. Therefore it is much more effective to directly generate valid heaps. We can directly generate only valid heaps by using the abstract heap constructors `empty` and `insert`.

```
heapAbs = empty
heapAbs = insert unknown heapAbs
```

With `heapAbs` the average depth and size of the generated heaps increase noticably. More than 200 heaps of depth and size 3 are generated in 1,000 trials compared to none with `heapVar`.

Finally, we explicitly generate a subset of valid heaps, in order to further improve test-data distribution.

```
heapGen = Empty
heapGen = fork One

fork n = Fork m (heapList m) where m = n + smallNat

heapList _ = []
heapList n = fork n : heapList n

smallNat = One ? O One ? I One ? O (O One) ? I (O One) ? O (I One)
```

The number that is passed to `fork` defines the minimum size of all entries of the generated heap. That way, we assure that the generated heaps are valid. We also restrict the entries of the generated heaps: the difference of a label at any node and its children is at most 6. In our experiments, `heapGen` generates heaps up to depth 5 with up to 13 entries in the first 1,000 test cases. This is a significant improvement over the previously presented generators.

In order to evaluate the benefits of the presented search tree traversal, we have enumerated 1,000 results of the custom generator `heapGen` in breadth-first order. The largest heap of the first 1,000 results generated by breadth-first search has 5 entries. With combined randomized level diagonalization, the largest heap has 13 entries. The practical results documented in this section show that the new search tree traversal is an improvement over existing ones in the context of test-case generation. We have shown that EasyCheck serves well to generate sufficiently complex test data of non-trivial recursive datatypes like `Heap`. The generation of 1,000 heaps with the presented generators takes about one second on average using KiCS [4,5] on a 2.2 GHz Apple MacBook™.

5.2 Comparison with **QuickCheck**

Due to lack of space, we cannot provide an extensive comparison with all important test tools for declarative languages. Therefore, we restrict ourselves to

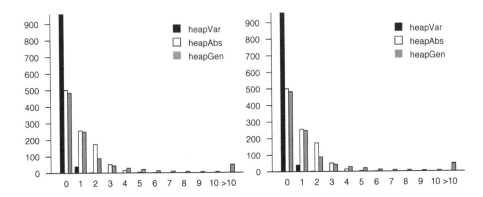

Fig. 5. Depth and size of generated `Heap` values

QuickCheck – the most widely used test tool for Haskell – and only describe data generators that resemble the ones presented before. QuickCheck provides additional combinators that allow to tune the distribution of test input. We want to point out, that the search presented in this paper relieves the programmer from the burden to manually adjust test-case distribution to some extent.

In QuickCheck we define data generators of type `Gen a` instead of nondeterministic values of type `a` by using `oneof :: [Gen a] -> Gen a`. It takes a list of generators and yields a generator where each of its arguments is chosen with equal probability. Figure 5 shows the distribution of the depth and size of the generated heaps for the three adapted generators. We have taken the average of 10 runs of QuickCheck.

The black bars represent the result for a generator that resembles a free variable. We just enumerate the constructors employing `oneof` and use the implication operator (`==>`) to reject invalid heaps. 960 out of 1,000 test cases are empty heaps. At first sight it seems easy to improve this. But if we use (`==>`) to prohibit the generation of empty heaps only around 300 out of the first 10,000 test cases are valid. Another way to improve this generator is by using the `frequency` operator. This operator is similar to `oneof` but each list element is assigned with a probability. Finding good probabilities is nontrivial. For example, we have faced the problem of undesirably large test input leading to a significant slowdown or even stack overflows. If we do not use (`==>`) only about 500 out of 1,000 heaps are valid and about 25 are valid and not empty. This is a well-known deficiency of QuickCheck also tackled by SparseCheck [10] with an approach similar to our restricted free variable. The distribution measured with the QuickCheck generators `heapAbs` and `heapGen` is acceptable. The number of generated heaps decreases with increasing depth and size but, nevertheless, larger heaps are generated.

The generation of test cases with QuickCheck is considerably faster than with EasyCheck. One reason is that a complete search is more time and space consuming than an incomplete random search. Also, the Curry system KiCS is a prototype and not as mature as modern Haskell systems – especially w.r.t. performance. Nevertheless, the run time of EasyCheck is acceptable, viz., a few seconds also for complex test-input.

6   Related Work

There are four implementations of automated test tools in functional languages, namely QuickCheck [6,11], SmallCheck [12] and SparseCheck [10] in Haskell and G∀ST [7] in Clean [13]. Besides these, there are a couple of implementations of QuickCheck in other functional languages.

QuickCheck provides monadic combinators to define random test case generators in an elegant way. In order to test a function, the user has to define an instance of the type class **Arbitrary** for each type used as test input. Functional logic languages like Curry, already provide default generators for all datatypes, viz., free variables. Moreover, custom generators are defined by nondeterministic operations – no type class is necessary. With QuickCheck the user cannot ensure that all values of a datatype are used during a test. Furthermore, the same test data may be generated more than once. In EasyCheck, we employ a complete enumeration scheme for generating test data and ensure that every value is enumerated at most once. Moreover, every value would be eventually enumerated, if we would not abort the generation of test cases. In contrast to EasyCheck, QuickCheck can be used to generate higher order functions as test cases. The extension of EasyCheck to higher order values is future work.

The idea behind SmallCheck is that counter examples often consist of a small number of constructors. Instead of testing randomly generated values, Small-Check tests properties for all finitely many values up to some size. Size denotes the number of constructors of a value. The size of the test cases is increased in the testing process. That is, we get the same results as SmallCheck for Easy-Check by using an iterative deepening or breadth-first traversal for the search trees. This demonstrates the power of the separation of test case generation and enumeration.

The automatic test tool G∀ST uses generic programming to provide test data generators for all types. In contrast to QuickCheck, this relieves the user from defining instances of type classes. If the user wants to define a custom generator he has to employ the generic programming extension of Clean [14]. In our approach, no language extension is necessary from the point of view of a functional logic programmer. Of course, we heavily use logic programming extensions built into functional logic languages. An outstanding characteristics of G∀ST is that properties can be proven if there are only finitely many checks. However, G∀STs enumeration scheme is not complete because left recursive datatypes lead to an infinite loop. In EasyCheck, we can prove properties because of the complete enumeration of test data. Moreover, the algorithm that generates test data is independent from the algorithm that enumerates it. Therefore, we can apply flexible enumeration schemes.

The idea of SparseCheck is based on a work by Fredrik Lindblad [15]. He proposes a system that uses narrowing to generate test cases that fulfil additional requirements. The approach of QuickCheck, SmallCheck and G∀ST is to generate all values and discard the values that do not satisfy these requirements. If only a small percentage of test cases fulfils the requirements this strategy fails. In SparseCheck, values that fulfil the requirements are generated using narrowing implemented in a logic programming library for Haskell [16]. This library provides similar features like Curry but separates functional from logic definitions that use special purpose combinators and operate on values of a special term type.

Recently, an approach to glass-box testing of Curry programs was presented in [17]. Glass-box testing aims at a systematic coverage of tested code w.r.t. a coverage criterion. The main difference between a black-box tool like EasyCheck and a glass-box tool is that EasyCheck generates test input in advance and a glass-box tool narrows test input during the execution of the tested function. An advantage of the glass-box approach is that input that is not processed by the program does not need to be generated. However, a glass-box approach is not lightweight because it requires a program transformation or a modification of the run-time system in order to monitor code coverage. Another disadvantage is that nondeterminism introduced by the tested function cannot be distinguished from the nondeterminism introduced by the test input. For example, a glass-box test tool cannot detect test input that leads to a failure or multiple results of the tested function. EasyCheck has combinators to deal with nondeterminism and, therefore, also with failure. A glass-box tool is usually employed to generate unit tests for deterministic operations.

The Curry implementation PAKCS [18] comes with CurryTest – a unit-test tool for Curry. Unit tests specify test in- and output explicitly, while specification-based tests in QuickCheck, G∀ST and EasyCheck only specify properties and the tool generates test data automatically. Thanks to the simplified form of test-data generation, defining a unit test in EasyCheck is as elegant as in CurryTest.

Checking defined functions against a seperate specification by systematically enumerating the arguments of the function can be seen as (bounded) model checking. See [19] for recent work on this topic. Usually, model checking refers to specifications of concurrent systems in temporal logic. XMC [20] is a model checker based on logic programming.

7   Conclusions and Future Work

We have presented EasyCheck[3] – a lightweight tool for automated, specification-based testing of Curry programs. Compared to similar tools for purely functional languages, we provide additional combinators for testing nondeterministic operations (Section 3).

Functional logic languages already include the concept of test-data generation. Free variables provide default generators for free and the declaration of custom generators is integrated in the programming paradigm via nondeterminism. It

---

[3] Available at http://www-ps.informatik.uni-kiel.de/currywiki/tools/easycheck

does not require additional type classes nor language extensions like generic programming. Logic programming features allow for a simple and elegant declaration of test-data generators. In Section 5 we discussed different approaches to defining custom test-case generators and compared them w.r.t. test-data distribution using a non-trivial datatype representing heap trees.

In EasyCheck, we separate test-case generation and enumeration, i.e., test-data generators can be written without committing to a specific enumeration scheme. Therefore, better enumeration schemes will improve test data distribution for existing generators. We present a new search tree traversal, viz., *combined randomized level diagonalization* (Section 4), and show that it is better suited for generating test cases than other traversals provided by Curry implementations.

Although this traversal turns out to be quite useful already, we plan to investigate new traversals to improve the diversity of large test cases. Another direction for future work is to examine time and space requirements of randomized level diagonalization. Furthermore, we would like to investigate the distribution of values generated by this traversal and to develop traversals with a similar distribution that do not rely on randomization.

References

1. Antoy, S., Hanus, M.: Overlapping rules and logic variables in functional logic programs. In: Etalle, S., Truszczyński, M. (eds.) ICLP 2006. LNCS, vol. 4079, pp. 87–101. Springer, Heidelberg (2006)
2. Braßel, B., Hanus, M., Huch, F.: Encapsulating non-determinism in functional logic computations. In: EAPLS, vol. 6 (2004)
3. Peyton Jones, S.: Haskell 98 Language and Libraries: The Revised Report. Cambridge University Press, Cambridge (2003)
4. Braßel, B., Huch, F.: Translating Curry to Haskell. In: Proc. of the ACM SIGPLAN Workshop on Curry and Functional Logic Programming, pp. 60–65. ACM Press, New York (2005)
5. Braßel, B., Huch, F.: The Kiel Curry System KiCS. In: Seipel, D., Hanus, M., eds.: Preproceedings of the 21st Workshop on (Constraint) Logic Programming, 215–223 Technical Report 434 (2007)
6. Claessen, K., Hughes, J.: QuickCheck: a lightweight tool for random testing of Haskell programs. ACM SIGPLAN Notices 35(9), 268–279 (2000)
7. Koopman, P., Alimarine, A., Tretmans, J., Plasmeijer, R.: Gast: Generic automated software testing. In: Peña, R., Arts, T. (eds.) IFL 2002. LNCS, vol. 2670, pp. 84–100. Springer, Heidelberg (2003)
8. Turner, D.A.: Miranda: a non-strict functional language with polymorphic types. In: Proc. of a conference on Functional programming languages and computer architecture, pp. 1–16. Springer, Heidelberg (1985)
9. Brassel, B., Fischer, S., Huch, F.: Declaring numbers (to be published, 2007)
10. Naylor, M.: A logic programming library for test-data generation (2007), http://www-users.cs.york.ac.uk/~mfn/sparsecheck/
11. Claessen, K., Hughes, J.: Quickcheck: Automatic specification-based testing (2002), http://www.cs.chalmers.se/~rjmh/QuickCheck/
12. Runciman, C.: Smallcheck: another lightweight testing library (2006), http://www.cs.york.ac.uk/fp/darcs/smallcheck/

13. Plasmeijer, R., van Eekelen, M.: Concurrent Clean language report (version 2.0), http://www.cs.ru.nl/~clean
14. Alimarine, A., Plasmeijer, M.J.: A generic programming extension for Clean. In: The 13th International workshop on the Implementation of Functional Languages, Selected Papers. LNCS, pp. 168–185 (2002)
15. Lindblad, F.: Property directed generation of first-order test data. In: Morazan, M.T., Nilsson, H. (eds.) Draft Proceedings of the Eighth Symposium on Trends in Functional Programming (2007)
16. Naylor, M., Axelsson, E., Runciman, C.: A functional-logic library for wired. In: Proceedings of the ACM SIGPLAN workshop on Haskell (2007)
17. Fischer, S., Kuchen, H.: Systematic generation of glass-box test cases for functional logic programs. In: Proc. of the 9th International ACM SIGPLAN Symposium on Principles and Practice of Declarative Programming, ACM Press, New York (2007)
18. Hanus, M.: et al.: PAKCS: The Portland Aachen Kiel Curry System (version 1.8.1) (2007), http://www.informatik.uni-kiel.de/~pakcs/
19. Cheney, J., Momigliano, A.: Mechanized metatheory model-checking. In: PPDP 2007: Proc. of the 9th ACM SIGPLAN International Symposium on Principles and Practice of Declarative Programming, pp. 75–86. ACM Press, New York (2007)
20. Ramakrishnan, C.R., Ramakrishnan, I.V., Smolka, S.A., Dong, Y., Du, X., Roy-choudhury, A., Venkatakrishnan, V.N.: XMC: A logic-programming-based verification toolset. In: Emerson, E.A., Sistla, A.P. (eds.) CAV 2000. LNCS, vol. 1855, pp. 576–580. Springer, Heidelberg (2000)

Author Index

Lecture Notes in Computer Science

Sublibrary 2: Programming and Software Engineering

For information about Vols. 1– 4290
please contact your bookseller or Springer

Vol. 4608: H.W. Schmidt, I. Crnković, G.T. Heineman, J.A. Stafford (Eds.), Component-Based Software Engineering. XII, 283 pages. 2007.

Vol. 4591: J. Davies, J. Gibbons (Eds.), Integrated Formal Methods. IX, 660 pages. 2007.

Vol. 4589: J. Münch, P. Abrahamsson (Eds.), Product-Focused Software Process Improvement. XII, 414 pages. 2007.

Vol. 4574: J. Derrick, J. Vain (Eds.), Formal Techniques for Networked and Distributed Systems – FORTE 2007. XI, 375 pages. 2007.

Vol. 4556: C. Stephanidis (Ed.), Universal Access in Human-Computer Interaction, Part III. XXII, 1020 pages. 2007.

Vol. 4555: C. Stephanidis (Ed.), Universal Access in Human-Computer Interaction, Part II. XXII, 1066 pages. 2007.

Vol. 4554: C. Stephanidis (Ed.), Universal Acess in Human Computer Interaction, Part I. XXII, 1054 pages. 2007.

Vol. 4553: J.A. Jacko (Ed.), Human-Computer Interaction, Part IV. XXIV, 1225 pages. 2007.

Vol. 4552: J.A. Jacko (Ed.), Human-Computer Interaction, Part III. XXI, 1038 pages. 2007.

Vol. 4551: J.A. Jacko (Ed.), Human-Computer Interaction, Part II. XXIII, 1253 pages. 2007.

Vol. 4550: J.A. Jacko (Ed.), Human-Computer Interaction, Part I. XXIII, 1240 pages. 2007.

Vol. 4542: P. Sawyer, B. Paech, P. Heymans (Eds.), Requirements Engineering: Foundation for Software Quality. IX, 384 pages. 2007.

Vol. 4536: G. Concas, E. Damiani, M. Scotto, G. Succi (Eds.), Agile Processes in Software Engineering and Extreme Programming. XV, 276 pages. 2007.

Vol. 4530: D.H. Akehurst, R. Vogel, R.F. Paige (Eds.), Model Driven Architecture - Foundations and Applications. X, 219 pages. 2007.

Vol. 4523: Y.-H. Lee, H.-N. Kim, J. Kim, Y.W. Park, L.T. Yang, S.W. Kim (Eds.), Embedded Software and Systems. XIX, 829 pages. 2007.

Vol. 4498: N. Abdennahder, F. Kordon (Eds.), Reliable Software Technologies - Ada-Europe 2007. XII, 247 pages. 2007.

Vol. 4486: M. Bernardo, J. Hillston (Eds.), Formal Methods for Performance Evaluation. VII, 469 pages. 2007.

Vol. 4470: Q. Wang, D. Pfahl, D.M. Raffo (Eds.), Software Process Dynamics and Agility. XI, 346 pages. 2007.

Vol. 4468: M.M. Bonsangue, E.B. Johnsen (Eds.), Formal Methods for Open Object-Based Distributed Systems. X, 317 pages. 2007.

Vol. 4467: A.L. Murphy, J. Vitek (Eds.), Coordination Models and Languages. X, 325 pages. 2007.

Vol. 4454: Y. Gurevich, B. Meyer (Eds.), Tests and Proofs. IX, 217 pages. 2007.

Vol. 4444: T. Reps, M. Sagiv, J. Bauer (Eds.), Program Analysis and Compilation, Theory and Practice. X, 361 pages. 2007.

Vol. 4440: B. Liblit, Cooperative Bug Isolation. XV, 101 pages. 2007.

Vol. 4408: R. Choren, A. Garcia, H. Giese, H.-f. Leung, C. Lucena, A. Romanovsky (Eds.), Software Engineering for Multi-Agent Systems V. XII, 233 pages. 2007.

Vol. 4406: W. De Meuter (Ed.), Advances in Smalltalk. VII, 157 pages. 2007.

Vol. 4405: L. Padgham, F. Zambonelli (Eds.), Agent-Oriented Software Engineering VII. XII, 225 pages. 2007.

Vol. 4401: N. Guelfi, D. Buchs (Eds.), Rapid Integration of Software Engineering Techniques. IX, 177 pages. 2007.

Vol. 4385: K. Coninx, K. Luyten, K.A. Schneider (Eds.), Task Models and Diagrams for Users Interface Design. XI, 355 pages. 2007.

Vol. 4383: E. Bin, A. Ziv, S. Ur (Eds.), Hardware and Software, Verification and Testing. XII, 235 pages. 2007.

Vol. 4379: M. Südholt, C. Consel (Eds.), Object-Oriented Technology. VIII, 157 pages. 2007.

Vol. 4364: T. Kühne (Ed.), Models in Software Engineering. XI, 332 pages. 2007.

Vol. 4355: J. Julliand, O. Kouchnarenko (Eds.), B 2007: Formal Specification and Development in B. XIII, 293 pages. 2006.

Vol. 4354: M. Hanus (Ed.), Practical Aspects of Declarative Languages. X, 335 pages. 2006.

Vol. 4350: M. Clavel, F. Durán, S. Eker, P. Lincoln, N. Martí-Oliet, J. Meseguer, C. Talcott, All About Maude - A High-Performance Logical Framework. XXII, 797 pages. 2007.

Vol. 4348: S. Tucker Taft, R.A. Duff, R.L. Brukardt, E. Plödereder, P. Leroy, Ada 2005 Reference Manual. XXII, 765 pages. 2006.

Vol. 4346: L. Brim, B.R. Haverkort, M. Leucker, J. van de Pol (Eds.), Formal Methods: Applications and Technology. X, 363 pages. 2007.

Vol. 4344: V. Gruhn, F. Oquendo (Eds.), Software Architecture. X, 245 pages. 2006.

Vol. 4340: R. Prodan, T. Fahringer, Grid Computing. XXIII, 317 pages. 2007.

Vol. 4336: V.R. Basili, H.D. Rombach, K. Schneider, B. Kitchenham, D. Pfahl, R.W. Selby (Eds.), Empirical Software Engineering Issues. XVII, 193 pages. 2007.

Vol. 4326: S. Göbel, R. Malkewitz, I. Iurgel (Eds.), Technologies for Interactive Digital Storytelling and Entertainment. X, 384 pages. 2006.

Vol. 4323: G. Doherty, A. Blandford (Eds.), Interactive Systems. XI, 269 pages. 2007.

Vol. 4322: F. Kordon, J. Sztipanovits (Eds.), Reliable Systems on Unreliable Networked Platforms. XIV, 317 pages. 2007.

Vol. 4309: P. Inverardi, M. Jazayeri (Eds.), Software Engineering Education in the Modern Age. VIII, 207 pages. 2006.

Vol. 4294: A. Dan, W. Lamersdorf (Eds.), Service-Oriented Computing – ICSOC 2006. XIX, 653 pages. 2006.